Taunton Castle

Taunton Castle

By Chris J Webster

with contributions by
John Allan, Jens Andersen, Stuart Blaylock, Kate Brayne, James Brigers, David Dawson, Nicholas Dawson, Lorrain Higbee, David A Higgins, Katie Marsden, Richard Parker, Naomi Payne, Paul Rainbird, Gavyn Rollinson, Mary Siraut, and Susie White

Foreword by Robert Higham

Somerset Archaeological and Natural History Society

Taunton, 2016

Published by
Somerset Archaeological and Natural History Society
Somerset Heritage Centre, Brunel Way, Taunton, TA2 6SF.
www.sanhs.org

First published 2016.

ISBN: 978 0 902152 29 8

The Society is grateful to Taunton Deane Borough Council and to their financial contribution towards this publication.

Front Cover: The Round Tower and West Range of Taunton Castle.
Back Cover: Taunton Castle as it may have appeared *c.*1450 by Richard Parker.

Typeset by the author using LaTeX.
Printed by Short Run Press, Exeter.

Contents

List of Figures

Contributors

John Allan 22 Rivermead Road, Exeter, Devon, EX2 4RL. john.p.allan@btinternet.com

Jens Andersen Camborne School of Mines, Exeter University, Penryn Campus, Penryn, TR10 9EZ. j.c.andersen@exeter.ac.uk

Stuart Blaylock Exeter.

Kate Brayne 2 Green Lane, Codford St Peter, Warminster, Wiltshire, BA12 0NY. rudyard@archaeologist.com

James Brigers Prospect Archaeology, Pebble Cottage, 11 Church Road, Middlezoy, TA7 0PA. james.brigers@btinternet.com

David Dawson Vicky and David Dawson Partnership, 10 Linden Grove, Taunton, TA1 1EF. davidp@dawsonheritage.co.uk

Nicholas Dawson Archaeological Survey West LLP, Flat 5, 13 Frederick Place, Clifton, Bristol, BS8 1AS. nwb_dawson@yahoo.co.uk

Lorrain Higbee Wessex Archaeology, Portway House, Old Sarum Park, Salisbury, Wiltshire SP4 6EB. l.higbee@wessexarch.co.uk

David A Higgins University of Liverpool, 12-14 Abercromby Square, Liverpool, L69 7WZ. david_higgins@talktalk.net

Katie Marsden Cotswold Archaeology, Kemble Enterprise Park, Cirencester, GL7 6BQ. katie.marsden@cotswoldarchaeology.co.uk

Richard Parker Exeter.

Naomi Payne AC Archaeology, 4 Halthaies Workshops, Bradninch, near Exeter, Devon, EX5 4LQ. npayne@acarchaeology.co.uk

Paul Rainbird AC Archaeology, 4 Halthaies Workshops, Bradninch, Near Exeter, Devon, EX5 4LQ. prainbird@acarchaeology.co.uk

Gavyn Rollinson Camborne School of Mines, Exeter University, Penryn Campus, Penryn, TR10 9EZ g.k.rollinson@exeter.ac.uk

Mary Siraut Victoria County History of Somerset, South West Heritage Trust, Taunton, TA2 6SF. mary.siraut@swheritage.org.uk

Chris Webster Somerset Historic Environment Record, South West Heritage Trust, Taunton, TA2 6SF. chris.webster@swheritage.org.uk

Susie White University of Liverpool, 12-14 Abercromby Square, Liverpool, L69 7WZ. susie_white@talktalk.net

Abbreviations

CRAAGS	Committee for Rescue Archaeology in Avon, Gloucestershire and Somerset (defunct).
HRO	Hampshire Record Office, Winchester.
HER	Historic Environment Record.
MOS	The Museum of Somerset.
NCA	New College, Oxford archives.
PRN	Primary Record Number.
SANHS	Somerset Archaeological and Natural History Society.
SCC	Somerset County Council.
SRO	Somerset Record Office, Taunton (now part of Somerset Heritage Centre).
WAT	Western Archaeological Trust (defunct).

Foreword

This volume on Taunton Castle, based on a multi-disciplinary integration of a wide variety of evidence, makes a most significant contribution to castle studies and related fields of scholarship. It explores the origin, form and evolution of a site which – while long-visited on account of its museum – has not been fully appreciated by either the academic world or the general public. It explores more than the medieval castle. It also illuminates the pre-Norman history and topography of Taunton and its minster church, as well as the role of the castle in the evolution of Taunton from rural manor to town. It offers an account of investigations carried out from the nineteenth century onwards and incorporates all the important research of recent years. In exploring the role of Taunton within the estates of the bishops of Winchester, the volume also adds to the on-going discussion of what castles were – or could be – and what they might be used for. The contributors to this publication are to be congratulated on giving its subject the higher profile which it has so long deserved.

Dr Robert Higham
Honorary Fellow
University of Exeter

Acknowledgements

The work reported here had a long gestation and involved many people, who at the time were probably unaware of its final format. The original excavations were undertaken by Somerset County Council's Heritage Service as a community excavation with the aim of clarifying and recording parts of the castle that were to be repaired. Subsequently, further community excavations were undertaken as part of the Museum of Somerset project. I am extremely grateful to all those who took part, both for their hard work and for their questioning attitude to the castle that produced much interesting debate on site. I was assisted in the management and recording of these excavations by James Brigers, and the volunteers were: Penny Alderman, Jan Buchanan, Pat Buck, Liz Caldwell, Eve Cottrell, Nick Dawson, Peter Gooch, Jehane Horwood, John Matthews, Claire Parker, Stephen Parker, Colin Sudlow, Kayleigh Sweet and John Turner. Of those my special thanks must go to Pat, John (Matthews) and Liz who participated in most of the excavations. We were also assisted by various staff from Somerset County Council's Heritage Service who escaped occasionally to do some digging: Talya Bagwell, Carrie Blogg, Rob Browning, Jenny Christoroforou, Bob Croft, Jane de Gruchy, Hannah Firth, Paula Lewis, Marc Cox, Jan Grove and Nic Wall. My apologies to anyone that I have missed.

The Museum of Somerset project's architects, Tim Greensmith and Lee Warr of FCB Studios designed a scheme that affected the historic fabric as little as possible and enabled the archaeological recording and excavation to fit into the construction programme. On site, Jeff Cane of the builders, Henry W Pollard and Sons Ltd, was always willing to consider the archaeological impacts of what was being proposed and allow these to be mitigated. Sheps and Lee of SA Baker, undertook the groundworks and provided interesting company on site. Lee and Peter of Sally Strachey Historic Conservation took a great interest in the castle and reported features that were uncovered during plasterwork repairs and repointing. Andy Stevens and Ian Lewis of SCC Heritage Service repaired Wall C and, with Keith Faxon, paved the courtyard. They were always helpful and interested, as well as providing good company on site.

My greatest debt on site must go to James Brigers who assisted with the recording and excavation during all of the building work with his usual good humour. We were joined by Dick Broomhead and Lorrain Higbee during the unexpected excavation in the Great Hall. I am grateful to both of them for their hard work and good cheer under the rather strange conditions.

During the post-excavation work I am grateful to Teresa Hall for providing copies of two of her papers in advance of publication, and to Roberta Gilchrist and Naomi Sykes who were helpful in providing advice and copies of their work. Naomi Payne generously shared information from her thesis on bishop's palaces and Len Peach obtained for me a copy of his unpublished book on the history of Merdon Castle.

David Bromwich, SANHS' honorary librarian, helped me to navigate the collections of material about the castle acquired by the society over the years and has subsequently assisted with proofreading. Jane Campbell at the University of St Andrews Library swiftly provided information on the Valentine postcards, as did Jennifer Thorp of New College, Oxford on the 17th-century warden's correspondence with the schoolmaster. At the Somerset Heritage Centre, Jane de Gruchy and Esther Hoyle cheerfully assisted with location of records and reading the more awkward handwriting. Tom Mayberry relocated the 1638 agreement and prompted me to reconsider its implications. As well as finding, extracting and translating the relevant bits of the Winchester pipe rolls, which form the basis of Chapter 1, Mary Siraut was unfailingly helpful in providing information on the post-medieval legal system, checking references and translations, and during a visit to the Hampshire Record Office.

Around the castle, the late Hugh Prudden and Dave Soloman gave geological advice on the rocks and stonework and Brian Murless advised on historic bricks. Pauline Rychlewski provided access to the Municipal Buildings. Lisa French provided the information from Linda Witherill identifying the people photographed excavating in 1952. Richard Leese discussed the physical evidence for Civil War damage and alterations to the castle. Andrew Passmore of AC Archaeology coordinated their report on Castle Green.

I am grateful to the authors of the specialist reports: Stuart Blaylock, David Dawson, Nick Dawson, Katie Marsden, David Higgins, Richard Parker and Susie White. In addition to the pottery report, David Dawson discussed the problems of interpreting the castle on many pleasurable occasions and also oversaw the bringing of the report to publication. I am also very grateful to Bob Higham for his foreword, his comments on a draft and, earlier, for discussing the lodgings at Oakhampton Castle.

The work was supported by Somerset County Council, both financially and in the provision of my time, to fulfil its responsibilities as tenant and developer of the castle. This was managed by Russell Lillford and Bob Croft for SCC, and subsequently by Tom Mayberry and Bob Croft for the South West Heritage Trust. I would like to thank them all for their support and also Rob Iles who monitored the work for English Heritage.

The Somerset Archaeological and Natural History Society, as owners of the castle and partners in the Museum of Somerset Project, funded the publication of this volume. The Maltwood Fund of SANHS generously provided a grant to undertake additional radiocarbon dating beyond those required as part of the development work.

Finally, I must thank my wife, Chris, and our daughters, Ellie and Siân, for their support and for their tolerance of the various bits of the castle, its animals and people, that invaded our home.

Chris Webster
Taunton
Michaelmas 2015

Introduction

Chris Webster

Taunton Castle lies at the centre of the modern county town of Somerset, as it has for nearly a thousand years, but most inhabitants, if asked, would probably direct the visitor to the Castle Hotel standing on the East Gate. The castle lies behind the main street frontages and is visible only from the riverbank gardens to the north and the route to the bus station across Castle Green to the south. That the Green itself is the outer bailey of the castle is not easily discerned as there are few ancient walls apparent; the south front of the inner bailey being largely hidden by a tree planted in the 1930s.

The castle is better known as the home of the Somerset County Museum (now the Museum of Somerset) but despite this has attracted little interest from academics, perhaps because the only structures that still stand appear to be of a domestic nature, something that lay outside mainstream castle studies until recently.

The castle is owned by the Somerset Archaeological and Natural History Society (SANHS), who purchased it to preserve it in 1874 and opened it as a museum shortly afterwards. In 1958 they transferred control to Somerset County Council (SCC) who continued to run the Somerset County Museum, leasing and repairing the buildings. Fifty years later, a grant from the Heritage Lottery Fund enabled the establishment of The Museum of Somerset which included substantial repairs to the buildings and required much of the excavation and recording work reported here. In 2014 SCC transferred the management of the museum, together with the Somerset Record Office and historic environment staff to the newly formed South West Heritage Trust.

The Bishops of Winchester

Historically, the castle was a property of the bishops of Winchester and had been from the late Saxon period. Its origins are obscure but it seems to be a Norman conversion of a major site comprising a minster and bishop's residence at the centre of a large estate known as Taunton Deane. The Norman bishops were immensely powerful men, Henry of Blois for example was William the Conqueror's grandson and the brother of King Stephen, but Taunton was far from the axis of their power, which ran from Winchester to their palace at Southwark facing the City of London across the Thames. Taunton seems to have acted more as the centre for the estate rather than a power base, while maintaining the title and appearances of a castle.

The castle appears to have gone out of use by the early 16th century, becoming merely a collection of buildings, with new structures such as bishop Richard Fox's grammar school being built over the walls. It was still defensible during the Civil War but was ordered to be slighted by Charles II following the restoration of the monarchy. Its main function thereafter was as a prison and court, with the assizes and quarter sessions held in the Great Hall. Significant alterations were made in *c*.1790 by Sir Benjamin Hammet to improve the facilities for the judges and prevent a threatened transfer of the courts elsewhere.

Excavations

Antiquarian interest in the castle began at about this time and increased following the establishment of SANHS in 1849. The first excavation was undertaken in 1876 with one of the aims being to raise money to defray the castle purchase. Further excavations took place in the 1920s that appeared to uncover the keep, known from the documentary sources, in the north-east corner of the castle. Further significant, but limited, excavations were undertaken during building work in the 1950s in the Great Hall.

The most recent series of excavations was undertaken by the present author and was initiated by growing concern by the county council about the condition of parts of the structure. It commenced with a small research excavation to

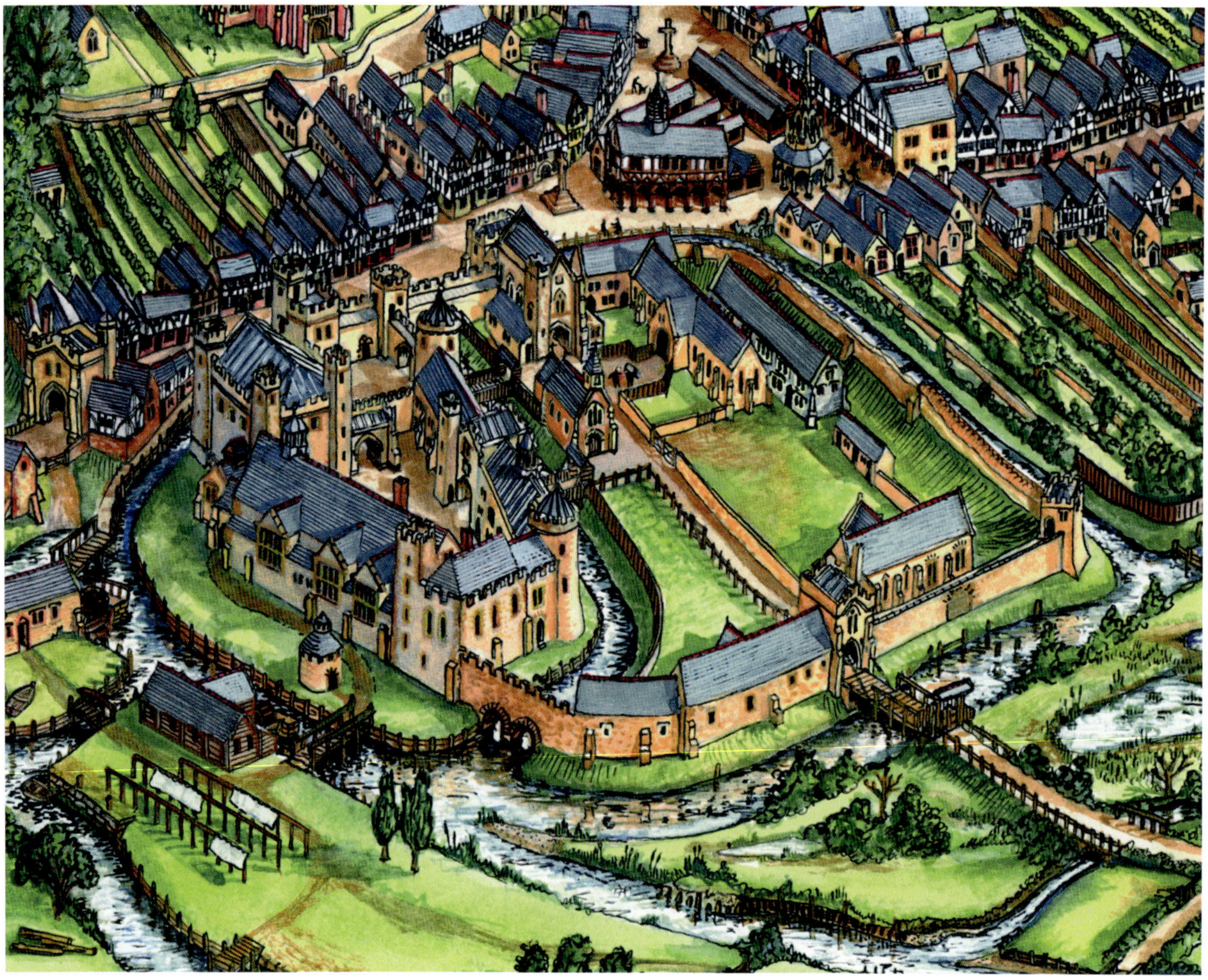

Figure 1: *Reconstruction drawing by Richard Parker of the castle from the north west. An extract from a larger illustration drawn in 2010; some of the details would now be changed but it gives a good idea of the castle within the town in* c.*1450.*

assess the age and structural condition of a wall in the courtyard, followed by repairs to the wall and a further excavation to answer questions posed by the first. At the same time the proposals for The Museum of Somerset were being developed and these led to the evaluation of two areas to the south of the Great Hall that were proposed for new buildings. Once the museum project was confirmed these areas were excavated down to the required level as a community project and only limited monitoring was foreseen for the building works themselves.

As the museum remained open during this time there was a reluctance to allow evaluation through the concrete floor of the Great Hall, a decision that was regretted when construction started. The concrete proved to be much thinner and the archaeological deposits below much more complex than records had suggested. This led to a hastily organised excavation in the Great Hall over three weeks in 2009. Additional work was required by the inflexibility of the structural engineers whose drawings had not fully described the level of disturbance required to emplace their structures. Following the completion of the main building programme, the courtyard was repaved, revealing tantalising glimpses of former structures, and Castle House was refurbished. In parallel with these works, Taunton Deane Borough Council repaved Castle Green and constructed a new access bridge around the west side of the inner ward.

The present book

The recent work began sporadically with small excavations and recording exercises related to repairs to the driveway and courtyard wall and would have been published individually had the Museum of Somerset project not happened. This led to serious research on the castle, which rather surprisingly had not been re-assessed for a

Figure 2: *Aerial view of the castle from the south on 13 May 1947. The outer ward is mostly taken by carparking and beyond the castle are the town mills. Aerofilms A.5341. ©Historic England (Aerofilms Collection).*

hundred years. More areas of the castle became involved in the project and eventually it became clear that a substantial body of evidence, historical, structural and archaeological was being accumulated and would provide the opportunity for synthesis and a re-examination of Taunton castle's role in the town, in the bishopric of Winchester, and in castle studies.

What follows is divided into three parts: a review of the evidence both historical and archaeological, a description of the surviving structures and interpretation of the archaeological evidence, and a discussion of the history and archaeology of the castle in its various contexts.

The Winchester estates retain some of the best documentary records from the medieval period which allows some analysis of building campaigns but it is clear that much of the building work pre-dates the start of the Winchester pipe rolls in 1208. The very size of the records has also been an impediment to their study: only four years have ever been published. The records of SANHS were somewhat scattered but provided exceedingly useful evidence for the castle in the 18th and 19th centuries. As owners of the castle they collected earlier illustrations and used the buildings as subjects for early photography. Examination of these, together with the records of SANHS own works, allows a critical review of research carried out from the mid-Victorian period to the present day.

The castle was not the first human activity on the site and it has proved possible to set the castle in the context of late-Saxon Somerset, as the successor to a minster, and to see how these origins influenced the subsequent development of the castle and town. There is much that remains unclear about the urban form of early Taunton and also much that is unknown about the form of the castle before extensive documentation begins but enough evidence has been recorded to present hypotheses and hopefully guide future research.

Taunton's position as the administrative centre for one of the largest estates of the bishops of Winchester gave it an importance that contrasted with its location, far from the centres of power in which the bishops operated. The castle clearly acted as a collection centre for farm produce for the estate but was also required to be a castle fit to house the bishop and royal guests. Discussion of this provides insights into the role of castles, particularly those in an urban and relatively peaceful place.

Note on nomenclature

Various rooms and buildings in the castle have had names attached in the past, mostly relating to their museum use (Somerset Room, Coin Room etc) and also to memorialise members of the archaeological society (Tite Room, Gray Room etc). Some of these have changed over time and some are now ambiguous. For example, the structure known as the Norman Keep was renamed the Constables Tower by Gray after he discovered the "keep" in the orchard (now garden) to the east of the courtyard. There are also problems with the building given to the society by William Wyndham in 1931. This was called the Wyndham Gallery until Wyndham gave money for another larger building, now known as the Wyndham Galleries. The earlier building became the entrance to the museum and was known as the Entrance Block but has now lost this function. Figure 4 and Figure 5 show the names that will be used to refer to these.

Survey and excavation numbers

All buildings, rooms and features were numbered as part of the survey, as were all excavated contexts. The first excavation was given the site code TCD04 (Taunton Castle Driveway, 2004) and the second TCC05 as it investigated Wall C the following year. When it became apparent that further work would happen it was decided to retain the TCC code and number all future contexts sequentially across TCC06 to TCC11. Features in the building record are also numbered sequentially across TCB08 to TCB13.

James Brigers used the site code TCH for his work at Castle House and TCC16 for monitoring the electricty cable. The code TCG has been applied to the work on Castle Green.

All these prefixes are usually omitted unless this would create ambiguity.

Illustrations

Stone identifications on elevations were done swiftly, and often from distance, so will contain mistakes. Uncredited illustrations are copyright Somerset County Council.

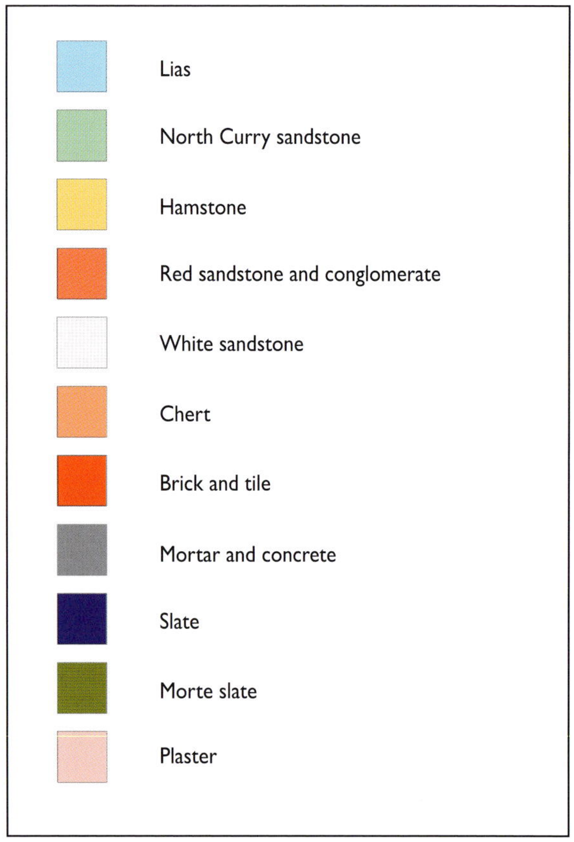

Figure 3: *Key to stone colours used in plans and sections*

Archive

The fieldwork and other archive material generated during the project will be held for SANHS in the Somerset County Museums collections under the following accession numbers: TTNCM 184/2009: Driveway repaving; TTNCM 185/2009: Wall C excavation and recording; TTNCM 186/2009: Excavation of Walls A, C and TCC 105; TTNCM 187/2009: Evaluations in East and West Passages; TTNCM 188/2009: Excavation for the almshouse foundations; TTNCM 189/2009: Excavation for new Welcome Building and cafe foundations; TTNCM 190/2009: Museum of Somerset works and post-excavation archive; TTNCM 191/2009: Burials exposed by Western Power Distribution; TTNCM 192/2009: New electricity cable; TTNCM 12/2010: AC Archaeology's work on Castle Green; TTNCM 50/2010: Excavation for gas main; TTNCM 46/2012: James Brigers' work in Castle House; TTNCM 2/2016: Excavation for electricity cable.

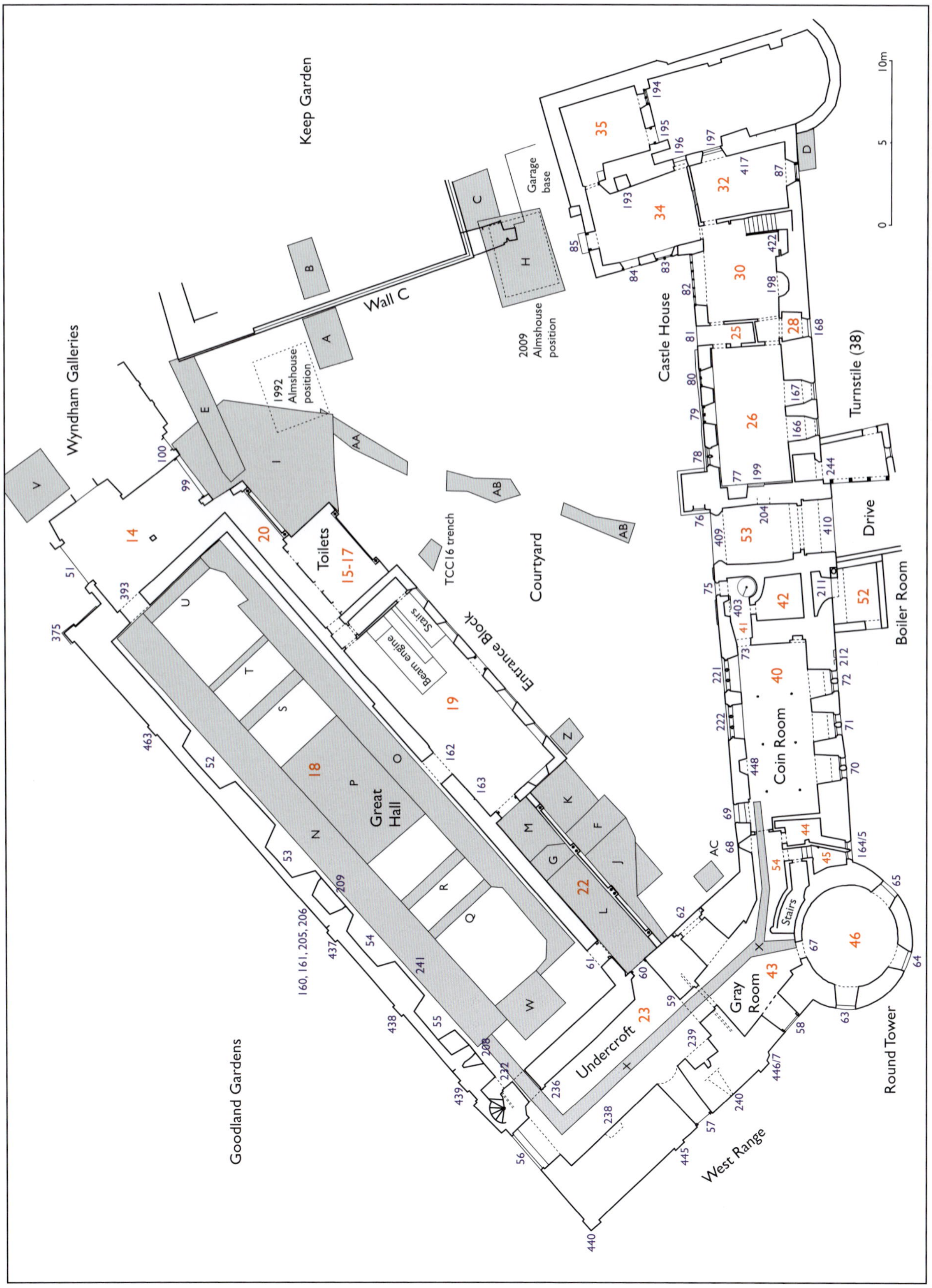

Figure 4: *Ground floor plan of the buildings around the castle courtyard before the alterations to form the Museum of Somerset in 2009. TCB room and feature numbers are indicated in red and blue, some modern ones omitted. TCC trenches are in grey labelled with black letters. The Wyndham Galleries and some recent internal partitions are omitted. For more detailed plans of Castle House see Figure 13.1 on page 220.*

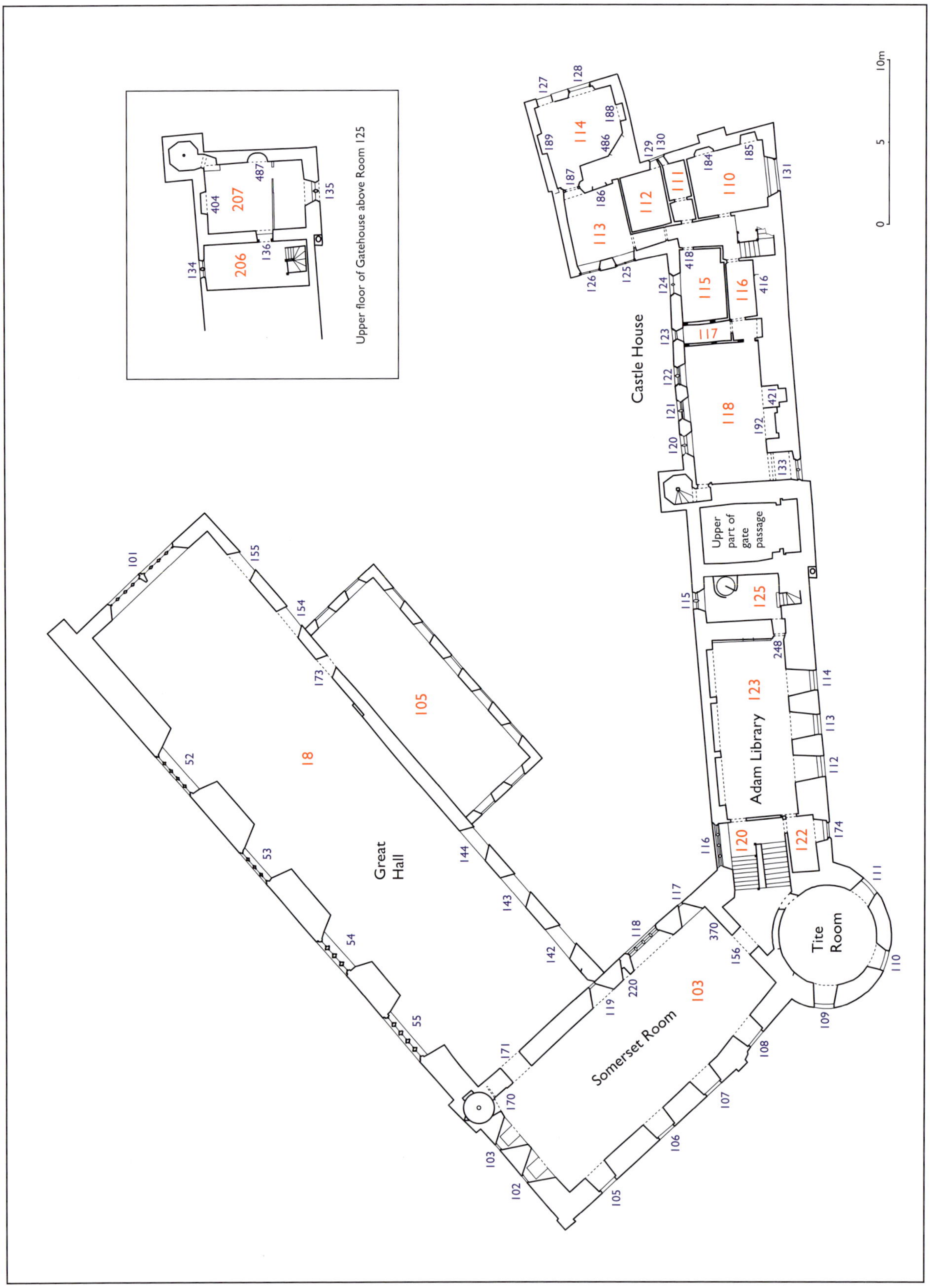

Figure 5: *First and second floor plan of the buildings around the castle courtyard before the alterations to form the Museum of Somerset in 2009. TCB room and feature numbers are indicated in red and blue, some modern ones omitted. The Wyndham Galleries, upper storeys of Castle House and some recent internal partitions are omitted. For more detailed plans of Castle House see Figure 13.2 on page 221.*

Part I

Evidence

Chapter 1

The Bishop of Winchester's Pipe Rolls

Chris Webster and Mary Siraut

The Winchester pipe rolls provide a massive amount of information about the administration of the bishops' vast estate, estimated at over 15,000 separate manorial accounts (Page 2002). Only four of the rolls, which start in 1209, have so far been published (Hall 1903; Barstow 1998; Holt 1964; Page 1996; 1999) but photocopies of the originals, which are now in the Hampshire Record Office (HRO 11M59/B1/1–329), are kept in Somerset (SRO T/PH/win). A contemporary copy of the Taunton part of each roll was also kept in the manorial records at Taunton Castle, as they were used to determine land titles based on the record of entry fines (Page 2002, 12). These are now in the Somerset Record Office (SRO DD/SP/325).

For this report, the photocopies of the Winchester pipe rolls were visually scanned by Mary Siraut and entries relating to castle buildings were extracted and translated from the Latin. The Taunton manorial copies were only examined where years were missing from the pipe rolls but some years are missing from both sets. It is more than likely that information has been missed, especially where it was recorded outside the "Castle" sections. The evidence that these translations provided for castle buildings was collated by Chris Webster and appears below.

It is important to remember that these were financial accounts and that the compilers had little interest in what we would find useful; buildings were only named to provide a label for the expenditure. There will also be omissions: only expenses incurred by the estate will be recorded so payments direct from Winchester will not feature and this might be the largest component of building projects. Similarly, things that could be obtained from within the Taunton estate's own resources will not be listed.

The accounting year ran from Michaelmas to Michaelmas (29 September) and thus covers parts of two calendar years. For clarity, only the closing year of the accounts is used as this would have included most of the summer building season.

There are other documents in the bishops' records, including a valuation survey made in 1566. This is discussed on page 26.

1.1 Measurements

The usual unit of measurement is the perch, usually of 16.5 feet (5m) but other lengths are recorded. Part of the courtyard wall (C1–C8, Figure 4.4 on page 57) was found to be exactly 16.5 feet long, which suggests that a perch of that length was in use when the wall was constructed and this conversion figure will be used below. Perch was also used to mean square perch (25.3m^2).

Sometimes distances are measured in ropes. The rope is described as a Somerset measurement of 20 feet (6m) by Zupko (1985), probably after Billingsley (1794). Rippon (2006, 103) refers to "20 ft lengths, known as ropes" used to measure the drainage clearance obligations of tenants and a rope of 20ft used was used to lay out Wedmore Borough in the 12/13th century (Hudson 1993).

The picture is complicated by the occasional use of both ropes and perches together. In 1347 a distance of "2 ropes 13 perches" is specified twice for two pieces of work on a length of wall and it is possible that this was the same wall as one described as of 16 perches; all seem to be associated with the Janitor's house (or chamber). The 16 perches are close in measurement to 13 perches plus 2 ropes of 20 feet and it may be that the two measurement types were used by different groups of workers when submitting bills.

One other modern calculation has been used, as occasionally the number of crest tiles purchased is mentioned. Archaeological examples of medieval crest tiles seem remarkably consistent at 42cm long, for example at Witney, another residence of the Bishops of Winchester (Allen and Hiller 2002), and medieval Southampton (Platt and Coleman-Smith 1975). It is possible that this length represents a dozen tiles to the perch but it conflicts with a standard laid down in 1477 for 13½inch (34cm) ridge tiles (Salzman 1952, 230–31).

Whatever conversion factors are used it will be seen below that some of the distances indicated at Taunton are clearly impossible, showing that caution must be employed, even when the measurements seem reasonable.

1.2 Building Campaigns

Most of the work recorded in the pipe rolls is repair but it is possible to identify several larger projects. Only the building of the hall, chamber and chapel in 1246–1249 is recorded in any detail and it is possible that other work was accounted in a different way. Table 1.1 on the facing page shows when other substantial changes were made, and also the recorded visits of the bishop. These necessitated work to prepare for the visit and were then followed by improvements and corrections identified during the stay. A lot of activity is recorded in the last decade of the 15th century, when Thomas Langton visited twice and Henry VII once.

1.3 Residential and Elite Buildings

Halls

There appear to have been at least three halls in the castle but their names change through time. The hall built in 1247 (Hunt 1971) is referred to as the "new" hall for several years thereafter and is mentioned alongside the "old" hall, which clearly survived and thus lay elsewhere. The old hall is last mentioned in 1275 in a list together with the bishop's hall. The new hall is last so called in 1330 and three years later another new hall was built, but not referred to subsequently by that name. The constable's hall is first mentioned in 1297 and thus may be the same structure as the old hall. It is last mentioned in 1457.

The third hall is the soldiers' hall in the high tower (1396, 1401) which probably equates to the "Knyghtenhall" in 1432 and the tower hall in 1308 and 1315.

The New Hall of 1247

In the account that follows it is assumed that the built hall in 1247 is that referred to as the bishop's or lord's hall subsequently.

The construction of the hall and associated buildings is one of the best-documented events in the pipe rolls and has been considered in detail by Hunt (1971). Only brief details will be given here. Preparations were made in 1246 when 600 pieces of stone were quarried at Ham Hill and transported to Taunton, by river and using a specially purchased cart (which required "frequent repairs"). The following year more stone was brought from Ham Hill, wood and nails (171,400 of various kinds, including 500 horseshoe nails) were purchased and the ironwork for 10 window shutters made. Carpenters, masons and plumbers were employed, the last to work with 4 loads of lead, which together with 48,000 stone tiles formed the roof. The overall expenses that year, which concentrated on the hall were £75 1s 8¼d.

The hall soon needed repairs, such as re-roofing in 1252; the first of many occasions. In 1271, the hall is referred to as the bishop's (and the lord's) and in 1296 appears to be that referred to as the great hall. A porch was repaired in 1353 and 1400 and one was constructed in 1455 which had stone walls and steps.

Structural problems appear to have affected the hall in 1372 when two masons were employed:

> "breaking great wall in east part of bishop's hall between hall and wall next ditch and below *stillic* [spout?] there and refixing wall to hang one great wallplate the length of said hall and chamber at east end of same hall to carry beams, for 21 days; 2 sawyers sawing board for *stillic*, 2 carpenters for carpentry and for underpinning broken great couple and for *seind* [seating?] beams on studs[?] and fixing wallplate and for mending the said hall 23 days; 5 roofers fixing stone tiles of hall and lathing and roofing hall 5 days; 75 men hired from beadles to assist mason and roofer and clear out stone from hall and carry sand. Iron ring to bind higher part of great couple and board nails to fix *stillic* and beams, 2600 lath nails, cask for carrying water, shovel bought, *marrabisacut* [drill or ram?] bought to break the wall".

The description of the chamber as "at the east end" may be an error, or it may apply to the Constable's Hall (see below on page 12), but it is less easy to explain away the differentiation between the hall and the wall next the ditch; the

Stigand (1047–1070)		
Walkelin (1070–1098)		
William Giffard (1100–1129)		
Henry of Blois (1129–1171)	1158	Visit of bishop (Goodman 1927, 198)
Richard of Ilchester (1173–1188)		
Godfrey de Luci (1189–1204)		
Peter des Roches (1205–1238)	1208	Visit of King John and bishop
	1211	Visit of King John
	1216	Town and castle ditches dug and palisades built, visit of bishop
William Raleigh (1242–1250)	1246–49	Hall, chamber and chapel built
Aymer de Valence (1250–1260)		
John Gervais (1262–1268)	1264	Numerous repairs and putting castle on a war footing
Nicholas of Ely (1268–1280)	1268	Visit of bishop (Bush and Meek 1984, 12)
	1268	Completion of West Gate
John of Pentoise (1282–1304)	1292	New chamber next to old hall
Henry Woodlock (1305–1316)	1317	New building beyond kitchen
John Sandale (1316–1319)		
Rigaud of Assier (1319–1323)	1321	New tower by kitchen
John of Stratford (1323–1333)	1332	New chamber outside gate
	1333	New hall, new house in mill
Adam Orleton (1333–1345)	1337	New dovecot
	1341	Four shops on castle ditch, building next Janitor's chamber
	1342	Constable's kitchen
	1345	Rebuilding Janitor's house, new castle wall to replace palisade
William Edington (1345–1366)	1346	Rebuilding building between hall and kitchen
	1348	Rebuilding clerks' chamber
	1354	Visit of bishop
William Wykeham (1366–1404)	1368	Visit of bishop
	1372	Major repairs to hall roof
	1375	New tower (separately accounted)
	1384	Visit of bishop
Henry Beaufort (1404–1447)	1412	Visit of bishop
	1426–27	Rebuilding Constable's hall
William Waynflete (1447–1486)	1454	New kitchen
	1455	New bridges
	1459	New building in constabulary
	1461	Several months' visit by bishop (Davis 2004)
	1467	New lord's chamber (mostly new roof)
	1469	South and west walls of castle
	1479	Leyhouse built and kitchen improved
	1480	Castle House roof timber felled (dendrochronology)
	×1482	
Peter Courteney (1487–1492)		
Thomas Langton (1493-1501)	1495	Visit of bishop
	1497	Visit of King Henry VII (Batten 1876)
	1498	Visit of bishop
	*c.*1500	Date of chapel roof (architectural style)
Richard Fox (1501–1528)	1508	New bridges
	1519	Demolition of buildings in inner ward
	1522	School built
	1527	Demolition of slaughterhouse

Table 1.1: *Bishops of Winchester 1066–1522 with major building campaigns and visits by bishops and royalty. Some short-lived, contested bishops omitted. From the Winchester Pipe Rolls except where stated.*

current Great Hall's northern wall appearing to form the curtain. Inconsistencies like this are a reminder that there is no certainty in the identification of the present Great Hall with any of the earlier names. The lord's great hall is last recorded in 1536.

The Old and Constable's Halls

A hall is recorded having its gutters repaired in the first pipe roll of 1209 and it was whitewashed in 1225. After the construction of the new hall in 1247, the hall (now the "old hall") was maintained until at least 1275 and the old chamber, associated with it, is last recorded in 1283. In 1297 comes the first mention of the constable's hall, having its roof repaired. This lack of overlap of the two names may suggest that they both refer to the same structure, now passed to the constable. There is no mention of the construction of the constable's hall between 1283 and 1297, a period when the accounts are unbroken except for the three years immediately preceding 1297.

The constable's hall is then mentioned frequently with continuing repairs to the roof, new louvres and fireplaces (1309), whitewashing and colouring (1318) and a new porch (1319). A cellar is mentioned in 1321 and again in 1346. A pentice was constructed "opposite the door" in 1368 and there is also reference to a "tresance to the entrance of the constable's hall" in 1402; it is possible that both of these refer to an elevated corridor leading to the hall. Glass windows are mentioned several times in the late 14th century. The porch (described as being made and as "new") and pentice required further work in 1457 but the constable's hall is not mentioned again.

The constable's hall appears to have run east-west as in 1299 a window was repaired "at the eastern head" of the hall. In 1348 the wall between the constable's hall and the town was repaired and in 1363 the walls of the castle at the east part of the constable's hall were repaired. These indicate that the constable's hall lay adjacent to the east wall of the castle.

The Tower or Soldiers' Hall

This hall is only mentioned five times. The entry for 1401 refers to the "soldiers' hall in the high tower" thus correlating the two names. In the final entry it is called the "Knyghtenhall".

The first entry, in 1308, records "new making the tower hall", although these works were clearly only repairs to the roof. In 1415 a new louvre was constructed and the hall required substantial repairs to the timber and masonry walls below the timber; further tiling of the roof took place in 1401. The final mention is in 1432 when further carpentry was needed. See also the Great Tower on page 17.

Houses

Several "houses" are recorded but it is not always clear what is meant as there is likely to be overlap with terms such as "chamber". The earliest mention is to a "Great House" next to the chapel of St Nicholas (1219); based on later positions this may have been the building that preceded the Great Hall. A house by the West Gate was repaired in 1272, 1274 and 1290. There are several mentions of a Janitor's house, usually unlocated but once recorded by the Middle Gate and once by the Outer Gate. In 1464 it is called the Janitor's "logge" and in 1375 houses called "le logges within the inner gate of the castle courtyard" were repaired, possibly indicating an earlier version of the lodgings that became Castle House. There are single mentions of a carter's house, a house on the dam, a house beyond the oven in the kitchen (see below, page 14), a house outside the East Gate, a house on the castle ditch, a house on the castle wall, a building called "le leyhouse" and two mentions of clerk's house.

Chambers

There are numerous references to chambers throughout the accounts, and although some are clearly identified, there are ambiguities caused by name changes and the erection and demolition of buildings. Most of the payments were for maintenance, particularly re-roofing, and these are not normally discussed below unless they shed extra light on the location of a chamber.

The Bishop's Chamber

The first mention is in 1211 when the pentice of the chamber was repaired and the second in 1245 when lead rainwater spouts were made for it. In the building campaign of 1246–49 a new chamber was constructed as part of the hall complex (Hunt 1971). Thirty trees were purchased for the "bishop's chamber" in 1247 but the main work took place in the following year when the accounts are headed by "expenses incurred in completing the chamber". The work required stone from Hestercombe and smaller quantities from Ham Hill, large numbers of boards and thousands of nails. The expenses for ironwork indicate that there were five windows in the

Figure 1.1: *Watercolour showing the north side of the Great Hall in* c.1800. *SANHS 3506*

chamber and also a fireplace. The building was roofed with lead (7½ cartloads).

The new chamber required mending in 1257 and the lead roof of the bishop's chamber was repaired in 1263 and 1266. Further repairs, perhaps substantial as the chamber is described as being "made", were undertaken in 1272 when its glass windows were also repaired. In 1297 a lock was bought for the "chamber at the head of the great hall". This chamber appears to be called the solar in the following year, when boards were bought to repair it. A new fireplace was constructed in 1299 requiring a "great piece of Hamstone" and there were also payments for "nailing the vaults" of a ruined chamber, which may well refer to the roof of the bishop's chamber which was described as "thrown down" by the wind.

Only maintenance is recorded in the first half of the 14th century but in 1352 work began on a wooden partition, with a door, between the chamber and the chapel. Further work was undertaken in the following two years, involving the construction of a "lattice" with a lock and key, all apparently preparatory to a visit by the bishop. A drain was constructed in 1402 but only repairs are recorded in the first part of the 15th century.

In 1467 a section of the accounts is headed "newly constructing the lord's chamber" and records 4 carpenters working for 16 days "new repairing and making whole of carpentry of the lord's chamber, 1075ft of timber sawn". Leadwork on the roof followed and the roof was daubed and plastered by contract with Thomas Symes. The total cost was 55s 5½d. Despite the heading this would appear to be the replacement of the roof rather than the construction of a new chamber. The new roof needed repairs, including a plumber stopping up holes in 1487, but the bishop's chamber is not otherwise mentioned again before the accounts end.

Subsidiary chambers are occasionally mentioned: the small chamber next to the great chamber (1343), the chamber "east of the lord's hall" (1366) and the "lord's inner chamber" next to the chapel (1391).

The Chamber of the Old Hall

In 1266, the chimney of the "chamber of the old hall" was repaired; this was presumably the bishop's chamber prior to 1248. In 1272 it is distinguished from both the bishop's and constable's chambers. In 1292 a new chamber was constructed next to the Old Hall for £26, about half the cost of the chamber built for the new hall in 1247. A window was made in this new chamber in the following year and a palisade was constructed outside it. It is not further mentioned.

The Constable's Chamber

The constable's chamber is first mentioned in 1272, when it is distinguished from both the bishop's chamber and the chamber of the old hall. A window in the chamber at the "eastern head of the constable's hall" was repaired in 1299. In 1309 hinges and hooks were bought for the door of the chamber next to the constable's hall and four glass windows were new made for the constable's chamber. The chamber was mended in the following year, perhaps associated with the construction of a bakehouse behind it (see page 17). A chimney is mentioned in 1325 and 1400. A drain is mentioned in 1407 when repairs were also made to the stonework. In 1407 "three carpenters [spent] 10½ days making 'le rooles' around the Constable's hall, around great chamber there, within hall and little inner chamber and afterwards removing and reseating them" and a lock and key was bought for the new door between the constable's chamber and a tower. The chamber is not mentioned after 1446.

Several associated chambers are mentioned: the little chamber under the constable's hall and the long chamber there (1345), the lower constable's chamber (1347) which had its window repaired in 1379 and was ceiled in 1412, the constable's inner chamber which had new glass windows in 1382, and the chamber in the constable's ward (1358).

The Janitor's Chamber

The janitor's chamber is first mentioned in 1340 when a partition was made next to it and further expenses were incurred in 1342, 1349, 1350, 1353, 1354, 1357 and 1362. In 1366, a janitor's chamber is described as next to the gate and this may refer to a chamber described as the janitor's servant's in 1347 as next to the great gate. In 1375 the janitor's chamber is located next to the west gate but in 1402 it is at the east. In 1413 the janitor had an inner chamber and in 1427, and again in 1480, the chamber is described as in the Constabulary.

The janitor's chamber is often associated with the clerks' chamber and this is discussed below. It is likely that it is also called the janitor's house (see page 12).

The Clerks' Chamber

In the 1250s there are mentions of repairs to the clerks' chamber and these continue spasmodically. In 1348 the roof of the Janitor's clerk's chamber was repaired as was the wall of the clerks' chamber; these appear to have been different structures. In 1348 the clerk's chamber (presumably that of the Janitor's clerk) is described as next to the outer gate of the castle; it was repaired by a carpenter on new stone "walls 3ft high and 50ft long" which might suggest a building of the order of 5m x 2.5m. Two years later the "chambers of clerks and janitor" were re-roofed, perhaps suggesting that they formed part of one structure.

In 1359, reference to an area between the clerk's chamber and the wall towards the town supports the location of this chamber on the east side of the outer bailey. The chamber had a latrine (roofed in 1365) and in 1367 the roofing of the clerk's and janitor's chambers are mentioned, again together. In 1382, however, the clerks' chamber under the chapel is mentioned, perhaps indicating the location of the lord's clerks' chamber. In 1385 the clerk's chamber had a new door and bridge, and a new window was formed in the wall. References to the clerks' chambers cease shortly after and later references are to the clerks' house.

Chambers about the Kitchen

In 1257 a "small chamber next to the kitchen" is mentioned and a chamber over the kitchen in 1338 and 1346. A chamber on the wall near the kitchen mentioned in 1344 could be either of these. In 1317 a house was made "beyond the oven in the kitchen", which had a chamber and a solar for which hooks and hinges were bought.

Chambers by Gates

Various chambers are mentioned in relationships with gates, such as: the small chamber by the inner gate (1288), the chamber next the gate (1317), the chamber by the east gate (1314), the new chamber by the east gate (1321), the new chamber beyond the postern (1328), the chamber outside the gate of the castle (1332 when "new", 1365, 1369 and 1379 when described as "small"), the east chamber next the gate (1337), the chamber over the postern (1337), the chamber over the east gate (1338, 1339, 1355) and the old chamber between the exchequer and the east gate which was taken down in 1338. In 1382 and 1406, a chamber next to the middle gate is mentioned and in 1399 and 1403, one by the garden gate.

Chambers in Towers

Chambers are mentioned in "the tower" between 1307 and 1355. There is also reference to the chamber of the tower hall, the soldiers' chamber in the (great) tower and the knights' chamber in the (high) tower. In 1432, two chambers in a tower are mentioned, as are two chambers in the Round Tower in 1437.

Chambers associated with Chapels

A chamber under the chapel is mentioned from 1328 until 1412 and a chamber at the end of the chapel in 1372. The former is qualified in 1382 as being the clerks' chamber (see above) and in 1400 as being under the lord's chapel.

Miscellaneous Chambers

A granger's chamber is mentioned twice, in 1306 and 1321, and a Receiver's chamber once in 1362, when they were repaired. In the early 14th century there are three mentions of a chamber beside or above the ditch but with no other information. There is a single mention of a chamber next to the cartshed in 1289.

Other Named Rooms

The bishop's wardrobe is named five times: in 1211 when it was rebuilt, in 1219 when it was enlarged, in 1253 when the door repaired, in 1255 when "the old wardrobe wall [was] remade and reroofed" and in 1273 when the "lord bishop's wardrobe [was] made by carpenter". The Treasury is mentioned nine times between 1306 and 1542, mostly having its door repaired.

Chapels

There are numerous mentions of chapels in the pipe rolls, and during the 13th century these are sometimes distinguished by name: the chapels of St Peter (from 1218 to 1268) and of St Nicholas (1219 to 1273). There is additionally the chapel of St Paul which does not seem to be part of the castle (see page 23). Otherwise the chapel is just referred to in the singular.

The distinction between the chapels of St Peter and St Nicholas is not clear. St Peter is clearly the earlier as it is known from at least *c.*1160 when it appears as "St Peter de Castello" (Bird 1907, 38). It may have been the primary dedication of the minster and may even be the surviving church building. The name is perpetuated in the priory established in 1158, which was dedicated to St Peter and St Paul, but St Peter is clearly the more important as it is sometimes called just by this name (for example in 1324, Haines 2010, 45). Dedications to St Nicholas only became popular after 1086 when his relics were "liberated" from Turkey to Italy and so that chapel is unlikely to have been part of the Anglo-Saxon foundation.

A chapel is recorded as being built as part of the new hall complex in 1249 (believed to be the present Adam Library in the South Range). This may have been the successor to an earlier chapel of St Nicholas. The chapel of St Nicholas may therefore be the castle chapel and the chapel of St Peter may have survived until the church of the new priory was built. If St Peter's chapel then went out of use, it would explain the lack of need to distinguish the chapels by name after 1273. In the absence of any other evidence, the "Old Hall" complex may have been served by the chapel of St Peter prior to 1249.

The chapel built in 1249 required 200 Ham stones and was lit by twelve glazed windows. The chapel of St Peter required strengthening in 1257 and 1265; in the latter year the work was carried out by a carpenter suggesting that the roof may have been the problem. It certainly was in 1268 when the chapel was "unroofed by the great wind". The chapel of St Nicholas had one "great glass window" (1266) but the others appear to have been "glazed" with canvas (1268). If this is the chapel built in 1249 it does not fit with the 12 glazed windows, unless these had broken and were not then replaced with glass. In 1278 one of the chapels is described as "old" when its gutters were repaired.

A further chapel is mentioned in 1321 when 36 hinges were bought for the windows of the "chapel *ultra* the east gate". While this would usually mean beyond the gate, it is probably that "above" is meant in this case as there is archaeological evidence for a chapel in that position (see Section 15.3 on page 244). This is the only mention of a chapel in this location and it may have been short lived; by 1338 the room appears as the chamber over the East Gate.

In fact, from this date there are no mentions of chapels other than the "castle chapel", "lord's chapel" or just the "chapel". This chapel is however constantly needing repairs to windows, walls and, particularly, the lead roof. Not all the windows were glazed as linen was purchased for the windows in 1420. The chapel continued to be repaired until at least 1539.

The later chapel lay next to the bishop's chamber (see page 12) as a partition between them was built in 1352 and it is described as next to the lords inner chamber in 1391. Additional locational information is given as a round tower is located at the end of the chapel in 1412.

The Garden

The garden is mentioned throughout the years recorded in the account rolls although there is a "new garden" mentioned in 1247. Most of the entries relate to repairs to boundaries, doors, gates or bridges but there are occasional mentions of plants, such as the beans in 1247 or the 20 young trees planted in 1288. In 1323 a bakehouse was rebuilt in the garden and a palisade was constructed around the herbarium next to the lord's hall in 1290. Some idea of the size of the garden is given in 1299 when 70 perches (1750m^2) were enclosed. The same entry shows that the garden adjoined the mill pond and the entry for 1339, that it had a pond of its own joined to the river Tone by a sluice. It was also separated from a meadow (called the meadow of Southam in 1359) by a ditch, 34 ropes (*c.*200m) long, that required scouring in 1301.

In 1344 a new hedge in the "south part" of the garden was accounted and in the 1350s there is further evidence that the garden adjoined the mill, when a "hedge was made between the lord's garden and the curtilage of Thomas the tucker" and further work of enclosure "between the mill and garden". Later in the decade there seem to have been problems with erosion as 180 "pots of poplar" were required to mend the riverbank. In 1301 18 perches (90m) of new hedge were laid "on ditch of lord's garden opposite the chapel of St Paul" and in the following year the gate between the kitchen chimney and the garden was repaired, weirs were made in the sluice and the poplars were lopped. The poplars needed lopping again in 1365 and there are also references around this time to problems with thorns and brambles that needed eradicating from the garden.

In 1496 labourers were hired to "mend a breach in the upper part of the lord's garden towards the castle orchard" which may refer to erosion as in 1507 earth was carried for "repairing broken riverbanks in la castell orchard". The orchard is also mentioned in 1537 when timber was bought to repair "the bridge leading from le watergyate to the garden called le castell orchard".

The Curtilage

A "curtilage" is mentioned occasionally throughout the 13th and 14th centuries. It had a door which required maintenance and was sown with an unspecified crop in 1224 at a cost of 6d. In 1226 it was planted with leeks. A "new curtilage" was provided with a gate in 1258, described as "towards St Paul" and in the 1319 the curtilage is described as next to the gate of St Paul suggesting that it lay to the west of the castle. A "long building" lay next to it in 1288. The Constabulary or Constable's curtilage is mentioned in 1355. It is possible that curtilage is used as an alternative name for the garden if the references in 1344 to the curtilage postern and to the north postern are to the same gate.

Dovecot

The dovecot was repaired frequently from its first mention in 1252 until the end of the 15th century. Materials for a new dovecot are recorded in 1337 but this may, of course, be a rebuilding on the same site. It appears to have been surrounded by a hedge and ditch and lay next to the castle ditch (1409) on the west side, joined to the west gate by a wall (1457). It was also joined to the lord's great chamber and the lord's great cellar by palisades built in 1435 and 1457 suggesting that it lay by the West Range.

Constabulary

The constable had his own area known as the Constabulary or Constable's Ward. Individual buildings within this are discussed below but the ward itself is first mentioned in 1331. One of the most frequent entries refers to repairs to the palisade which had a stone wall made under it in 1396. The constabulary also had walls, gutters, doors, a well and "other buildings".

Exchequer

Repairs to the exchequer are recorded from 1338 until 1515. The demolition of a building between the exchequer and the east gate in the first record locates it in the outer ward towards the east but there are no further indications of its location; presumably it was a landmark in itself. Most of the entries relate to the purchase of locks and to re-roofing but there are a few additional details: a room above the exchequer (1414), a new building next to it in 1401 and, in 1510 indications of its use "William Bull carpenter new making one box within exchequer for safekeeping rolls and records".

1.4 Kitchens and Related Buildings

Kitchens

The kitchens follow a similar history to the halls with which they were associated; a single kitchen is mentioned prior to the construction work of 1249 after which work is recorded to either the "old" or "new" kitchen until 1269. The Constable's kitchen is referred to from 1293 onwards. Most of the records are to repairs but in 1343 as well as a carpenter mending the "old constable's kitchen" and two men plastering it for two days, there is a bill for £5 8s ¾d for "foundations, walls, doors, windows and roof for a new kitchen within the castle for the Constable". The work may have been finished the following year when a pentice was constructed between the hall and the constable's kitchen. Further new building is recorded in 1432 when a new building called "sqwylery" (scullery) was built next to the kitchen and in 1454 when a new kitchen was built of timber frames over dwarf walls. Further work the following year (studding, wattling and daubing the lords kitchen) probably refers to the completion of this work. The final mention of new buildings comes in 1479 when a larderhouse and saucery were made.

Associated with the castle kitchen from 1272 was a pantry but only repairs are recorded. The constable's kitchen also had a pantry, first mentioned in 1229.

Bakehouses

Bakehouses are mentioned from 1233 onwards when there were two, one in the castle and one in the garden, that required rebuilding. Repairs to one or other (not distinguished) continued throughout the 13th century: mostly roofing, once with thatch. In 1310 the bakehouse behind the constable's chamber is first noted and a wall around the "constable's bakehouse and stable" was repaired in 1321. The constable's bakehouse itself was repaired throughout the 14th century, including tiling in 1357. In 1382, two bakehouses are again mentioned, the kitchen bakehouse and the constable's, but most work continued to be focused on the constable's until its last mention in 1471. There is a final mention of the bakehouse in "Le Innewarde" in 1519.

Buttery

The buttery is mentioned infrequently from 1272 to 1427, once being re-roofed (1317) and the other eight occasions requiring new locks or keys. The lack of repairs may indicate that it was part of another building and only mentioned when its part of the roof was repaired.

Presshouse

The press or presshouse is mentioned between 1283 and 1317, mostly requiring reroofing but, on one occasion, needing its door repaired. In 1289 more major repairs required a new *vicio* (presumably a screw) and associated tallow and grease.

Salthouses

A salthouse was built as part of the major construction programme of 1246 to 1249 and in 1252 there are references to a chamber (called a solar in one place) above it. In 1266 the "old" salthouse was repaired and in 1312 the salthouse next to the Constable's hall was repaired. In 1427 a salthouse is described as within the kitchen.

Wells

A perhaps surprisingly limited number of repairs to wells is recorded from the first purchase of a rope in 1233. There are a few further purchases of buckets and also repairs to the wells and their superstructures. The wells are variously described as "in the tower" (1233), "in the castle" (1334), "in the constable's ward" (numerous mentions from 1412 to 1427), "in Le Doungeon" (1462) and in "Le Innewarde" (1519). In 1321 comes the first mention of *puteo aquatico/aque* which may have been a rainwater tank as in 1344 stone gutters were purchased for it. A rope was bought for it in 1330 when it was also repaired, perhaps significantly, by a roofer.

1.5 Defensive Structures

Towers and Turrets

Towers and turrets feature commonly in the pipe rolls but, as usual, are often not closely identified. References to simply "tower" are clearly, in some cases, to the Great Tower but, in others, may be indicative of the accountants' lack of interest in exact locations.

The Great Tower

The Great, or High Tower is first mentioned in 1264 when wood was purchased to repair doors and windows in four turrets around it. The turrets, sometimes four, sometimes five, are frequently mentioned in the last decade of the 13th century and the early years of the 14th century when they were reroofed and had windows repaired. In 1347 the turrets were again reroofed as was the knights' chamber. More substantial work is recorded in 1355 when stone was brought from Ham Hill for the chamber in the Great Tower and two loads of stone were brought from Gotton for the walls of the tower.

There were also carpentry works: "stipend of said three carpenters for divers works in the tower namely new bracket for table in turret beyond the prison, new windows in great tower and other turrets and new roof beyond stairway towards said tower and divers others there". Repairs to roofs and woodwork continued but in 1386 there is mention of work to the foundations on the east side and in 1396 a mason was employed to make a step at the entrance. In 1378 is a mention of "taking down one buttress and cleaning the foundations of the said tower" which may refer to the Great Tower as the previous item is to repairs to the knights' chamber.

The final mention of repairs to the high/great tower in the accounts comes in 1439 and after this date references start to "le dongeon" (various spellings) which probably refer to the same structure. As well as the usual repairs to roofs and woodwork, a porch was constructed in 1454 and roofed the following year. The nature of the Great Tower, considering archaeological and documentary evidence, is discussed on page 165.

The Round Tower

There are only ten mentions of a round tower, perhaps surprisingly few for what, today, is a distinctive structure. The tower which survives has been suggested as one of a pair but the accounts give only hints that more than one round tower existed. The first mention is in 1271 when "steps were repaired as far as the round tower", these, or other stairs in the tower were strengthened in 1297 when nails were purchased for the purpose. Most references simply list repairs but in the final mention in 1413 more substantial works were undertaken: "mason making 3 windows, 2 chimneys, 2 latrines in round tower at end of chapel [...] carpenter new making solar in the round [sic] with two partitions there above and below [...], paid William Walter for making ceiling in round tower."

This last entry is one of two which describe the location of the tower, in this case at the end of the chapel. The other entry (1339), however, refers to a wall between the hall and the round tower in the Constabulary. This might suggest the existence of two round towers, one in the Bishop's area and one in the Constable's.

The Constable's Tower

The Constable's Tower is first mentioned in 1375, when the wall between it and the West Gate was (re)made. The only other reference is in 1466 when the wall between it and the East Gate was reroofed. It is unfortunately not clear, whether the tower was close to either the East or West Gates, lay between them, or that either east or west is a mistake. The 1375 account refers to the wall between the tower and the gate twice, once for building and once for roofing, and also to wall building and roofing on the south side of the West Gate. This may strengthen the argument that the West Gate is meant or, conversely, weaken it if the accountant decided that mixed references to both gates should be the same. The presence of the Constable's hall close to the East Gate might support a location there for the tower (see page 12). Vivian-Neal and Gray (1940) refer to the structure at the west end of the Great Hall as the "Constable's Tower" which would fit the location inferred to the north of the West Gate but they state that this is a new name chosen to replace its earlier (but probably only from the period of the Society's occupation) name of the "Norman Keep" following the discoveries in garden area in the 1920s (Vivian-Neal and Gray 1940, 55 n28).

The Kitchen Tower

There are five mentions of a tower by the kitchen between 1252 and 1321. In the first of these, it is described as a turret and in 1289, the tower is described as small. In two cases (1252, 1257) the kitchen is specified as the "old" one. The final reference describes the tower as "newly made".

Other Towers

In 1330 there is mention of mending the foundations of the "lower" tower and in 1368 a "north" tower was underpinned. There was a turret on the East Gate, mentioned in 1338 and the following year. In 1370 both a tower "beyond the East Gate" and a ruinous tower are noted, the latter having its walls covered with reeds – presumably to protect them from the frost. This ruinous tower may have been constructed from cob as later in the accounts for that year is found "1 acre [2.5ha] reed bought to cover earth walls, reaping and gathering same". A "new" tower is listed in 1375 and in 1391 a small tower is mentioned.

Gates

Many entries in the pipe rolls refer to the gates of the castle, which are also closely linked to the bridges that stood outside them (see below). Like the bridges a variety of names is used but there seem to have been three principal gates: the West or Gate of St Paul, the Inner or Middle and the East or Outer gate. All were in existence when the accounts begin but in 1268, stone was bought "for completing the west gate", either a substantial rebuild or perhaps the replacement of a gate further to the south (see page 238).

Another new gate is mentioned in 1284 and 1285 when it was thatched with straw – this is likely to have been temporary thatching to protect the incomplete structure from frost. This would appear to be the East Gate as, in 1291, there is an entry for "roofing the new gate towards the town" which probably dates its completion. Its battlements are referred to in 1338 and a turret in the following year. Later entries to all the major gates refer only to repairs.

There are also mentions of subsidiary gates which include the gate towards the garden (1297, 1345) which is probably the same as the gate next to the kitchen (1351), the Watergate between the castle and garden (1355) and possibly the gate towards the mill (1441). There are also gates connected with the constabulary: the gate next to the door of the constable's hall (1297), the gate opposite the constables kitchen (1328), the gate towards the constable's chamber (1330), the small gate near/of the constables ward (1332, 1413) and the gate to the constable's entrance (1406).

The gate next to the granges of Holway and Staplegrove (1352, 1357, 1358) probably led to the barton there (see page 22) as it seems unlikely that this is an alternative name for the major East Gate. There is also mention of a wicket gate towards a tower in 1355 and a tower gate in 1368.

Posterns are recorded from 1252 onwards but some of these appear to be alternative names for gates. Posterns are associated with the garden, which may refer to the Watergate and this may also be the one associated with a sluice and bridge. It is also likely to have been the postern in the north part of the castle whose drawbridge was repaired in 1338 and probably the curtilage postern repaired in 1344.

There was also a postern with a footbridge between the garden and the meadow of Southam (or Southampmede) in 1347 and, in the same year, payments for a "carpenter making one postern and one drawbridge in a Culverhay towards the field and one wood partition called 'gridel' to keep fish in castle ditch next said postern".

Other posterns are described as "towards the constable's hall", "constable's postern", and "postern between granges"; these are probably the same as the gates described above. Finally there is mention in 1328 of a mason removing and remaking a postern and making a new chamber beyond but these are unlocated.

Bridges

There are over 100 references to bridges, mostly covering repairs but occasionally for the complete rebuilding of the structures. In 1285 wood was prepared for "the four bridges" and these appear to have been the three principal bridges outside the East, West and Inner gates, together with the bridge outside a postern to the north. The bridges are referred to by a variety of names:

- the bridge towards the town, the east gate bridge, the bridge at the outer gate towards the town, the drawbridge outside the castle gate.
- the bridge towards St Paul (but see below), the west gate bridge, the lower gate bridge, the bridge towards Hull.
- the bridge by the inner gate, the middle gate bridge, the bridge towards inner bailey, the bridge towards inner court.
- the bridge towards the garden, the postern bridge in north part of castle, the north gate bridge, the Watergate bridge, the bridge leading from the Watergate to the garden.

There are also mentions of several other bridges. These are either smaller castle structures or lay elsewhere: the footbridge between the garden and the meadow of Southam, the bridge beyond the mill pond, Poulbridge/Powles Brygge/Polewall (at Shuttern), Ellingbrigge and Floddebridge.

The main castle bridges appear to have been constructed of timber with masonry footings and to have had movable sections; drawbridges are mentioned several times, at the East (1297, 1338), Inner (1319, 1339), West (1321) and Postern (1338) gates.

There are also more problematic entries such as those of 1414 "14 workmen hired for 3 days to take down old bridge and raise new one, carpenter making new bridge between two wards of castle, 4 masons making new bay at west end of said bridge", when the bridge between the inner and outer wards runs north to south. The bridge of the Constable's ward, mended in 1417, is unlocated and this is the only indication that the ward was enclosed by a ditch. Similarly the entry in 1448 for "new making south bridge" is the only suggestion of a bridge in that location. It seems most likely that the location is a mistake or refers to either the East or West gate in the southern part of the castle. This appears to be the case in 1455 when new bridges were constructed: "inner and outer bridges towards the south" (both appear to be drawbridges).

Walls and Ditches

The references to walls, ramparts and palisades provide some of the best, and most enigmatic, information about the layout of the castle, particularly as they occasionally refer to the lengths of wall repaired.

The Outer Walls

The descriptions often describe the materials used for the walls or the craftsmen employed, which shows clearly that many of the castle walls were of earth protected by thatch capped by ridge tiles. This appears to apply to the main circuit of the outer ward and would explain why no evidence survives for medieval walling today. The first mention is in 1301 when 33 perches of new earth wall between the outer gate and the town mill were paid for. This equates to a distance of 165m which seems a bit excessive as the distance between the East Gate and the 19th-century location of the town mills is more like 150m. It is certainly farther than the supposed north-east corner of the castle and would also imply that the earth wall ran in front of the stone wall built in 1266 (below) on the east side of the keep area. It is, of course, possible that this was a wall on the outside of the ditch; there certainly was a wall outside some ditches, such as that mended in 1310 "below vineyard and outside ditch outside gate". In 1318, 22 perches (110m) of wall were made running from the castle mill which fits the site better.

Wider maintenance was undertaken in 1325 when the palisade around the castle was repaired, strengthened and underpinned. In 1338 the palisades opposite the bishop's hall and either side of the dovecot were repaired by carpenters, the palisades in the south part were repaired and the rampart walks of the castle walls were enlarged using 47 hurdles made of the bishop's withies. This last entry suggests, again, that the walls were not of masonry and this is made clear in the following year when "new making earth wall opposite said [middle] gate on ditch enclosing castle ward, 14½ perches long [72.5m] and 7ft high [2.1m]" was accounted. This appears to be an appropriate distance for the length of the southern side of the outer bailey.

Other parts of the enclosure appear to have been initially palisaded as in 1345 there is reference to "making 46 perches [230m] of new castle wall around castle in place of old palisade" and the roofing of 43 perches (about 15m less) of wall with slate. This is a significant distance, which would account for most of the rest of the enclosure of the outer bailey, including the part to the north of the East Gate that was built in 1301.

Some parts of the wall were clearly masonry, as shown in 1266 when masons were paid 16s 6d for erecting the "wall next to the tower on the eastern side [and] making battlements and arrow-slits."

In 1400, 65 perches (325m) of wall were apparently made between the West Gate and the middle ditch of the castle, suggesting the wall to the north of the gate, although that can have been at most 70m long if it joined the ditch by the west end of the Great Hall and 80m long if it ran to the mill stream. The north wall of the castle appears to have been damaged by fire in 1449 when it was repaired; curiously no other buildings appear to have been affected.

The outer walls of the castle were clearly not as substantial as might have been hoped; in 1485 they had to be rebuilt after being "broken down by wind" and further repairs were needed in 1487 for "32 ropes [195m] of earth walls prostrated by wind". This reference, though, is to walls built in divers parts around the castle and may be to less-important walls damaged by the same event.

The walls were whitewashed, as shown by an entry for the rebuilding of "part of the wall on the ditch in the middle of the castle at the west end" that was then whitewashed within and without.

The Castle Ditch

It is evident that the castle was encircled by a ditch, not least by the mentions of bridges at the gates. There was also a ditch, that partly survives as the current moat garden, outside the inner ward. The outer ditch was connected to the town mill by a sluice (1272) and was cleaned out in 1290 at a cost of £39 18s, about four times the cost of the better-known reference to "2588 men working for one day using carts and clearing water from flooded castle ditch" in 1326 (£10 12s). This later work also required 64 days of the carpenter to mend the carts, blacksmith's work on ten carts and the purchase of spades and shovels. Twelve carpenter-days were also spent making new flood gates. It seems likely that this event occured in the autumn as the costs continue the following year citing the "flood after Michaelmas" as the cause. Three carters were engaged to carry away the silt and a further 380 men hired for a day each. The problem was presumably excess water and silt as the ditch was clearly water-filled at other times: in 1347 a grid was made to prevent fish escaping from the castle ditch by the dovecot. A hurdle was made in the same year to keep fish in the castle ditch at "La Westgate" and two further ones the following year for unknown locations.

Further significant cleaning of the ditch took place in 1355 and in 1361 men were hired to make an enclosure next to the mill "to stop up water in the castle ditch". In 1377, 87 men were employed to cut down trees around the castle ditch and to scour it and in 1416 the "ditch between two castle wards" was scoured. The "great ditch" was still being scoured in 1494 but by 1543 it appears to have become disused (in the southern part at least) as fines are recorded for several gardens "on the lord's waste on the castle ditch [...] between the watercourse and the wall". This suggests a narrowing of the ditch to a small channel with land reclaimed next to it.

Other walls and ditches

Clearly, not all the walls were the outer enclosing walls of the castle, as references such as "raising one wall in the castle enclosure between the castle and the ditch outside the east part of the castle" (1354) and an "earth wall between the middle gate and the cattleshed" (1360) indicate. The latter wall is referred to several times so it may have been an important division within the castle.

Other references to ditches are concentrated in the area of the vineyard, garden, meadow and dovecot, all of which appear to have been ditched. These may have been hedge banks and ditches, although there is also evidence that they were water-filled and suffered from erosion. In 1347 for instance, 200 "pots of shoots" were purchased for putting on the ditch south of the garden and their purpose is made clear in 1357 when there were expenses for "100 pots of poplar" and "setting them in the garden for saving the earth bank (*t'ra divum*). The erosion continued as more were purchased the following year for "saving the land there".

Watchhouses

A watchhouse is mentioned several times through the 14th century and there is a final reference to two watchhouses in 1453. The reference in 1362 is included with others relating to works in the constabulary.

1.6 Production and Storage

The main storage buildings are referred to in the pipe rolls as "Granges" (*Grangia*), which Barstow (1998, viii) suggests were used to store crops before winnowing as several of the bishops' manors had both a grange and a granary. Both granaries and granges are mentioned at Taunton but it seems likely that they are two names for the same structure, possibly with changing usages through time. The granaries are later identified as those of Hull, Staplegrove and Holway (below) and share features with the granges of those names. It may be significant that the words grange and granary are never mentioned in the same entry. Against this, the granary is often referred to in the singular and never by using the terms wheat, oats and rye as used of the granges.

Granges

The granges are mentioned from the earliest account rolls and are repaired in most years that follow. Until 1326 they are called "wheat", "oats" and "rye" granges although sometimes they are described as "by the west gate" or "by the east gate", or even just "west" and "east". There are also references to the "long grange" in 1226. The oats grange may have been that by the west gate as the entry for 1227 accounts for an allowance to the reeve for "half the grange next to the west gate which had fallen down, reconstructed for £10 2s 8d" and a similar allowance the following year "allowance to reeve for half oat grange newly made for expense £13 1s 5d". The third grange appears to have lain close to one of the others as a gate between two granges (probably wheat and rye near the east gate, see below) is mentioned in 1299; the gate may have led to the barton between the granges mentioned in 1313. In 1224 the dimensions of the hay "remaining at the castle" is given "in the west part from the door, 1 hayrick 70ft long, 30ft wide, 30ft high, below the eaves 8ft and in the east part of the same grange 1 hayrick 40ft long, 30ft wide, 30ft high, below the eaves 8ft". This would give a building, aligned east-west, of at least 35m long and over 10m wide. Unfortunately the accounts do not indicate which grange this was but it seems likely to have been whichever was also called the "long grange".

The granges appear to have been timber framed as most of the work on them was undertaken by carpenters but the roofing is confused as both slates and thatch are mentioned on the granges. The west grange was reroofed with slates in 1300 but all three granges appear with thatch in the following years (wheat and oats in 1301, barley in 1302). The rye and oats granges were reroofed with slates in 1321. A corn grange is mentioned in the same year but from then on the names of the granges change to those of three of the sub-manors: Hull, Holway and Staplegrove. Presumably these were the three whose produce could most easily be brought to the castle, which lay in Bishop's Hull, and the outlying sub-manors had their own storage. Hull grange appears to have been joined to the west gate by a wall, mentioned in 1349 and may therefore be the previous oats grange. The other two appear to have a palisade and gate between them and presumably lay to the east. In 1362 and 1363, there is reference to the old grange of Hull but no mention of any replacement. In the later 14th, and 15th centuries, the annual roofing repairs were let by contract to William (and later Nicholas) Hellier. In 1406, the corn grange of Hull is mentioned and repairs in 1426 included a mason making buttresses under some beams repaired by the carpenter. The structures were clearly still mostly timber as the carpenter made two new ends for the granges of Hull and Staplegrove in 1436 and the repaired walls were wattled in the same year.

In 1401 is the first mention of the Constable's grange, although it is clearly an existing building as it is being tiled that year and underpinned, with a new ground sill the following year. It is possible that it was the previous grange of Staplegrove, as that is not mentioned again, but there are very few references to the granges after that date in any case. After 1497 the references are to a single grange or barn (sometimes the Great Barn). Again this is clearly not a new building as the entries are to ongoing repairs to roofs and underpinning.

The Great Barn is described in a petition of 1627 as leased to the clerk of the castle, George Brown, and having been recently turned into a stable (see page 23 for subsequent history). Brown's complaint was that it had been taken over, turned into a common hostelry and that filth and soil had been laid near the castle gate, to the annoyance of Brown, and to the townspeople trying to access the green. Brown wanted the property back and also some wood to repair the castle gates (SRO DD/SP/18/13). It is not clear if the damage to the gates is related to the misuse of the barn. The Great Barn was clearly close to the gate and this was clearly the East Gate (Castle Bow) if access from the town was being impeded. This will have been the grange behind which the School was built; the loss of rent from the gardens previously there was recorded in 1525.

Granaries

The granary is mentioned from 1212 onwards, usually having its roof or gutters repaired. There are also mentions of stone windows requiring maintenance and replacement in 1299. In 1324 the granary of Holway is first mentioned and its pentice is recorded in 1340. In 1341 the entry reads "carpentry of chamber at east gate, for one granary there made to be granary of Holway" suggesting that the name may have been applied to a new building. Twenty years later a reference to the gate between the granaries of Holway and Staplegrove mirrors the gate between the two granges of the same name. The original granary may be identified by an entry under 1370, "putting stone on roof of old granary next Watergate" but this does not appear to have saved it as the following year records "taking down timber of old granary".

Cattlesheds

As well as cattlesheds such as that mentioned in the Barton (see below) there was also one close to the middle gate of the castle judging by the rebuilding on several occasions of a wall between them. It was also linked to the west gate by a wall and is probably the same as that called "of Hull" in 1363 and the "north cattleshed" in 1435.

Cartsheds

A cartshed is mentioned 15 times from 1201 to 1407. The repairs indicate that it had a wooden superstructure on masonry footings. In 1363 the wall between it and the "cattle shed of Hull" was repaired and in 1368 the wall between it and the Inner Court was similarly repaired. This may suggest that it lay next to the wall of the castle to the north of the West Gate.

Bartons

An unnamed barton, presumably in this context a yard in which animals were kept, is mentioned three times between 1211 when it was cleared of manure and 1354 when the bridge between the castle and barton was repaired and two walls in the same position roofed. In 1226, the cattleshed in the barton outside the castle gate was rebuilt.

A barton of St Paul is also recorded in 1273 and 1315, a hay barton in 1299 and 1321, and a barton "between granges" in 1313. A stable in the barton is recorded in 1349 when a wall was built between it and the wall towards the town. A "stokhous" in the barton was repaired in 1349. It seems clear that these must refer to more than one barton. The barton of St Paul presumably lay outside the west gate (see page 23) and most of the other references could also be to this location. However, the barton with a stable (1349) appears to have lain within the castle (on the east side) as must the barton between granges – these could be well be the same site if the grange locations proposed on the preceding page are accepted.

The Mill

The castle mill is mentioned only three times, a rebuilding in 1219 and the construction of sluices in 1273 and 1293, but it is possible that it was accounted for elsewhere.

The Pound

There were at least two pounds, the earliest mentioned is that at St Paul in 1319; the earliest in the castle is in 1339 when a pound was "made in the castle to serve foreign hundred" (this is believed to be a reference to the more distant sub-manors: the later out-faring). In 1341 the pound is located as next to the grange of Holway and subsequently required frequent repairs to its doors, locks and walls. There is one reference (1403) to the walls being of earth and frequent payments for reroofing the walls support the identification of cob construction. In 1434, 46 perches (230m) of wall around the pound "in the lords castle" were made, suggesting an area some 60m across, if square and not using the castle walls for part of the circuit. This would encompass about half of the area of the outer ward but the pound was of comparable dimensions in 1782 (see page 28). The pound survived into the 19th century and it can be seen in Figure 16.4 on page 253 to the south of the road from Castle Bow.

1.7 Miscellaneous

St Paul

There are several mentions of structures in an area called St Paul, in particular to its chapel, from 1218 when land next to it was taken to enlarge the moat. On the basis of recent names (St Paul's House etc), this is likely to have lain outside the west gate of the castle, which appears to have been called the Gate of St Paul on occasions. The principal castle building here appears to have been a pound, a cattleshed and associated barton/curtilage; the chapel was not part of the castle and is used purely to describe a location.

Prisons

Prisons and prisoners are mentioned from 1218 until 1506 but there are few indication of the location of the rooms involved. The only clear indication occurs in 1555 when there is reference to the turret beyond the prison as part of the works to the Great Tower. There are no mentions of repairs to the prisons, probably indicating that they were part of another structure. Most references are to security apparatus: doors, locks, ropes, staples, shackles and gyves.

Quay

A quay is mentioned only once, in 1227, when it lay in the moat outside the west gate. This would suggest that the moat was navigable from there to the river.

Stables

In an age of horse transport there are, not unexpectedly, large numbers of references to stables in several locations around the castle, often next to gates. Stables are listed, in first date order:

- next to west gate (1265, 1315, 1321, possibly 1482)
- new stable below castle (1265)
- next east gate (1297, 1298, 1311, 1316)
- inner stables (1298)
- constable's stables (1299, 1321, 1331, 1332, 1341, 1342, 1353, 1356, 1360, 1361, 1362, 1364, 1365, 1368, 1369, 1375, 1382, 1383, 1384, 1391, 1399, 1427, 1435, 1457, 1463, 1465, 1467, 1473, 1474)
- stable inside/next the inner gate (1301, 1307, 1312, 1316)
- stable next wheat grange (1306)
- stable near lower gate (1322, 1328)
- great stables (1337)
- long stables (1337, 1338, 1340, 1343, 1345, 1346, 1348)
- janitor's stables (1340, 1361, 1362, 1375, 1376, 1378, 1390, 1406, 1449)
- stables below chapel (1345)
- carthorse stables (1346, 1347)
- small stable (1346)
- stable in outer ward (1349)
- stable next to le stokhouse (1355), affers stable (1357) next to the stockshouse
- stewards stable (1356, 1363 1364, 1365, 1370, 1474)
- clerks stables (1362, 1369, 1375, 1378, 1379)
- cart stable (1367, 1378)
- bishops/lords stable (1372, 1379, 1383, 1387, 1396, 1397, 1400, 1406, 1407, 1413, 1417, 1422, 1423, 1432, 1435, 1457, 1462, 1464, 1480, 1536, 1537, 1542)
- stable next janitors chamber (1382)
- buildings within middle gate where formerly was a stable (1412)
- outer stable (1414)

As mentioned on the facing page, the Great Barn was converted into a stable some time before 1627. This may have been in the previous century as a stable, shared between the porter and the clerk, is recorded in 1566 (SRO DD/SP/71). The stable appears to have survived the Civil War as it is listed in the parliamentary survey for the disposal of the bishops' lands in 1647 (HRO 68M74/E/A2).

Vineyard

There are occasional mentions of a vineyard between 1286 and 1455. They refer to it being surrounded by a palisade (1286) and ditch (1331) and situated in the inner ward (1338) or the Constabulary (1455).

Chapter 2

Post-Medieval Descriptions

Chris Webster

The castle is mentioned by a few topographical writers in the 17th century and appears occasionally in legal documents, most relating to the disturbances of the Civil War. By this time the castle appears to be treated as a collection of buildings and land that were rented out, rather than a coherent whole. Further documents are known from the 18th century and from the 1790s there are antiquarian reports and also illustrations for the first time. These give invaluable information about the castle before the major changes by Benjamin Hammet. The first archaeological observations were reported by members of the archaeological society (SANHS) in the late 19th century during building works.

2.1 Seventeenth Century

Thomas Gerard, 1633

After recounting the story given in the Anglo-Saxon Chronicle (see page 264) Thomas Gerard says that the bishops of Winchester built a castle to replace that destroyed by Ina's queen and continues "This castle has since been severally repaired by several bishops of Winchester, but of latter times it was most beholden to Richard Fox, bishop in the reign of King Henry the seventh who new builded much of it as his arms graven in stone in very many places do testify, which are a pelican in nest wounding her breast for her young. This bishop Fox after in the year 1522 being the very next year after he had finished Corpus Christi College in Oxford of which he was founder, built within the precincts of the castle a fair free school for the training up of youth in good literature and adjoining unto it a house for the schoolmaster [...] Within this castle is the bishops prison for the whole deanery"(Bates 1900, 56–60, spelling modernised).

Lieutenant Hammond, 1635

A slightly later description is given in 1635, when a Lieutenant Hammond described the town as "fortify'd with a defensible castle built by a Saxon king now much ruinated, especially the great Tower, inviron'd with a moted Ditch; within the Court the Judges sit to keep the Assize" (Armitage Robinson 1924; Wickham Legg 1936). The use of the phrase "great tower" appears to be unequivocal evidence for the survival of the keep.

Agreement, 1638

In 1638 Walter Cliffe, who had taken up the combined offices of keeper and bailiff with John Palmer, including the tenancy of the castle, subcontracted the keeping of prisoners to John Jacobb, described as a weaver from Uplowman in Devon. The contract lists the accommodation involved: "Viz the Seller & longe Roome by it, The long Chamber over them both, The Rounde Chamber nexte to it, and the ground Roome under it, the greate Chamber over the Exchequer And the little Chamber within it over the Bride-house, the under roome betweene the Celler and & Exchequer." Robin Bush quotes this (Bush and Meek 1984, 15), referring to "SRO DD/SP box 57, agreement 1638" but it has been recatalogued and is now part of SRO DD/SP/356.

To modern eyes the immediate thought is that the "cellar" is the Undercroft but this assumption does not allow the remainder of the rooms to be identified convincingly. The cellar must be the Gray Room and this can be used to produce the concordance shown in Table 2.1 on the next page. The Gray Room will have appeared much more cellar-like prior to Hammet's alterations, when it may not have had any windows nor any communication eastwards through the wall now replaced by Door 66. Its position at the head of the

the cellar	Gray Room (43)
and long room by it	Undercroft (23)
the long chamber over them both	Somerset Room (103)
the round chamber next to it	Tite Room (121)
and the ground room under it	Office (46)
the great chamber	Adam Library (123)
over the exchequer	Coin Room (40)
and the little chamber within it	Room 125
over the bridehouse	Strong Room (41/42)
the under room between the cellar and the exchequer	Corridor (54)

Table 2.1: *Possible room identities in the 1638 Agreement.*

list is probably because it formed the entrance, as it was to do to the museum in the 19th century. In contrast, the Undercroft may have been very different to its cave-like appearance today (see page 197). The location of the exchequer in the Coin Room (Room 40) is not suggested by any other source but again before Hammet's changes it may have had no windows and been a suitable, secure location. The position of the "bridehouse" may be corroborated by the bars seen in Window 212 (see page 204). The only room missing from the description would be the upper part of Room 54, now the landing but the arrangements there before Hammet are obscure as the floor levels are not known. The description of "under room" suggests that there was something over, perhaps a corridor. The list does seem to provide evidence that there were no further storeys to these ranges in 1638.

Valuation, 1647

Following the parliamentary victory in the Civil War, the bishops' lands were seized and valued for sale. The survey of Winchester Palace, Southwark (1647) contains a detailed description of the buildings of the palace (Seeley *et al.* 2006, 81) and has enabled a plan of the palace to be produced as has also been possible at Witney (Allen and Hiller 2002, 229–30). Other surveys are similarly detailed, for example that at Rose Castle, Carlisle (Weston 2013, 56) but, unfortunately, the court of survey for Taunton (15 December 1647; HRO 68M74/E/A2; with extracts published by Locke 1816), contains few descriptions of the property, merely a list of manorial tenants and officers of the castle. Of the officers, only the Porter has property in the castle: "the mansion house and garden within the same castle" as well as "the castle green and castle ditches, the keeping of the pounds and wards with the fees thereof" and "One stable standing in the castle green for him and the clerk of the castle". The Great Hall is mentioned as housing the manorial court and also "two rooms within the castle commonly called the Exchequer" that held the manorial records. The information is very similar to that given in a valuation of 1566 (HRO 11M59/E2/155649), which may well have been its source.

Roger Hill's deeds

Some details of the sale of the castle following its seizure by parliament are given in a cartulary "Transcribed by Roger Hill with his own hand and by him examined with originalls, 1653" (SRO DD/X/VNL/1), which he described as "Exact and Perfect Coppies of such Deedes and Evidences (of Roger Hill of Poundisforde in the Countie of Somerset Esquier) as were preserved from Plundering by the forces of the Late King Charles in the warres betwixt Him and ye Parliament of England and of such as were afterwards found again."

20 Mar 1647 Sale for £9210 17s ½d by the trustees appointed by parliament for the sale of bishops' lands to Brampton Gurdon and John Hill. "All that the Castle of Taunton [...] and all that the Mannor of Taunton and Taunton Deane [...]. And also the Gatehouse and Porter's Lodge on the south side of the said castle and the house adjoining to the gate of the said castle on the North side thereof. And all other Houses, Outhouses, Edifices, Buildings, Gatehouses, Lodgings, Barns, Stables, Pounds, Curtilages, Yards, Greens, Gardens, Orchards, Backsides and all other appurtenances whatsoever to the said Castle." Except "the Great Barn in the said Castle yard, now converted into a stable."

10 May 1648 Sale for £345 0s 3d by the trustees to Brampton Gurdon and John Hill in trust for Roger Hill. Land at Poundisford and also "All that great Barne with the appurtenances now converted to into a stable situate and being within the Greene of yards of the Castle of Taunton in the County of Somerset near to the Pound there, and all Ponds, Moates and Ditches next or about the walls of the said Castle of Taunton. And also all Bankes and parcells of Land lying or adjoining on each side of the said Pound and moates."

Post-Civil War evidence

Two documents provide some evidence for changes that had been made to the castle during the conflict. The first is a draft brief for an order of ejectment in 1689 (SRO DD/SP/356), which refers to the land in dispute as: "two gardens lying contiguous and adjoining each unto the other under the castle walls of Taunton from the foregate where the draw bridge was in the time of the late wars on the south side of the castle round the wall and west end of the said castle unto the watergate thereof on the north side of the castle". The document states that: "these two gardens were in the time of the late wars between the late King Charles the first and parliament used as moats and ditches and banks thereunto belonging made for the safeguard of the castle. And a great part thereof (to wit) about the one half at least was a moat or ditch time out of mind and lay open to the castle green and used and reputed as part thereof". This description seems to cover the area of the present moat garden round to the east end of the Great Hall, if the "foregate" is the present Inner Gate. As well as indicating the survival of a drawbridge here it also dates the widening of the moat (seen in boreholes; Passmore 2010) to the Civil War, although further work may have been undertaken in the 18th century.

The other document is a letter, also written in 1689, by Edward Allanson, the schoolmaster, which refers to the state of the school (see Chapter 16 on page 249) when he took over (NCA 1635/7). In it he says "when first I came hither I found it a ruinous heap, both the Dwelling-house School and Outlet: ruins of Battlements and fortifications of War of six yards high and above 100 yards length upon the South side of the School and other places; with earth to move away, to dig a Well, build Walls and make the place comfortable cost me [...] £140". This suggests that the school, which appears to have been built on the bank of the outer ward, was partly buried with an earthen rampart added along the south side. Allanson had earlier (1655) petitioned the steward as the boundaries of the school lands had been obliterated by the fortifications (SRO DD/SP/64).

Both of these indicate substantial changes to the outer ward to defend the castle and more information may be found if the documentary evidence is examined more fully.

John Cannon

The Taunton section of John Cannon's autobiographical work (1684–1743) was omitted from the published version (Money 2010) but the origins of the castle are described (probably following Gerard, above). Cannon makes no comment on its contemporary condition or even survival (SRO DD/SAS/C1193/4).

2.2 Eighteenth Century

Little survives from most of the 18th century but several images survive from the final decades, some of which, including the earliest (1773), precede the extensive repairs by Benjamin Hammet. There are limited historical references to these repairs and the events that led to them. Other images show the castle during and after the repairs and there is a description by Toulmin at about the same time.

The Dilapidations Survey, April 1782

This survey was undertaken for the Bishop of Winchester's properties, presumably as one of the first acts of bishop Brownlow North (1781–1820) on taking over the see (HRO W/K1/30). It is not clear how it relates to the work later in the decade by Hammet but it is possible that the (presumed) failure of the bishop to rectify the dilapidations may have prompted the threat to remove the assizes. The estimates are in great detail and, in common with modern practice, appear to cover any items that might conceivably become dilapidated, so protecting the three assessors. They are divided into various areas of the castle estate.

Hall or Court Room, Assembly Room, Round Tower, Grand and Petit Jury Rooms, Porter's Lodge, Gateway etc

If this list is in order around the current courtyard it would suggest that the Assembly Room is the current Somerset Room and that the jury rooms were in the south range as was the Exchequer, which is not listed in the heading. The Grand Jury Room required work to the roof including boarding for lead. This would suggest that it lay on the upper floor of the Gatehouse together with the Exchequer, as it did when described by Toulmin in 1791. The porter's lodge, however, is listed here rather than Toulmin's location at the East Gate. It is clear that the present survey is talking about the Inner Gate as the East Gate is listed separately below. The only repairs listed are to the floor of the porter's room, which may have been in Castle House, perhaps using Door 204 (see page 209). The Great Hall required repairs to the roof as well as new deal shutters on the six windows on the south side and at the east end of the hall.

The House used as a Boarding School

This is likely to be Castle House, described by Toulmin (below) as "for many years a boarding

Figure 2.1: *Drawing of the castle in 1773, before Hammet's alterations. SANHS 3504.*

school" but some details sit awkwardly with this identification. The schoolroom is listed as are a coal shed, garrets, music room, dressing room, kitchen and pantry.

Other buildings

The survey lists several other areas requiring work. Most are clearly in the outer bailey but the exact locations are uncertain.

- Stable building, laundry and wash-house. This may be the "great barn converted to a stable" in the 17th century.
- Garden and fencewalls and stable in the angle. The location is indicated by a mention of the "wall at the east end of the hall" and the stable may be that shown by Carver in the ownership of Mr Abraham (see Figure 12.1 on page 214).
- The archway to Castle Green [East Gate]. The only works suggested were taking down the upper parts and making good.
- The tenement in the possession of [gap] Bluett, milliner. The west front needed to be taken down and rebuilt.
- The tenement in the possession of David White, carpenter.
- The thatched stable. This is another candidate for the stable formerly the Great Barn.
- The Pound. The work suggested comprised the repair and rebuilding of 588 feet (180m) of brick and stone wall and 100 yards (91m) of cob wall. See page 23 for earlier dimensions.
- The Horse and Jockey in the possession of John Stacey.
- The cottages on Castle Green. This entry is in a different format with no itemised entries.

Joshua Toulmin

Toulmin, in his *History of Taunton* (1791), mentions Castle Green ("where the dead in time of war were buried"), the West Gate ("destroyed some years ago") and the East Gate ("called the Porter's Lodge"). He describes the last as partly ruinous but with strong arches and a still-visible portcullis slot. Adjoining was "a dwelling house in the front wall of which is a stone with a coat of arms and a mitre over it. The arms are a cross charged with five roses" (Thomas Langton, bishop 1493–1501) below which was the date 1498. This is probably the "Porter's Mansion" listed in the 1647 parliamentary survey (see page 26)

The moat is described as "25 feet wide and 12 feet deep" (7.6 x 3.6m) and surrounding the castle on the south, west and east sides. Toulmin then describes "the old building" as 195 feet in length (60m – the current south face is 45m plus 9m of round tower) and with a "circular tower at each end: of which only one is now remaining. The other, at the east end has long since been destroyed and a large house built in its room, that has been for many years a boarding school for young ladies." He continues "The west end or wing is the shortest being 66 feet [20m – the current length excluding the tower] in length and was lately standing as it was originally built" and then describes the changes and damage evident from the Civil War (see page 197). He thinks that range was "judged from its appearance to be part of the castle built about the 11th century".

The Great Hall, described as the principal part of the building, is reported to be 119½ feet by 30½ and 20 feet 5 inches high (36.4 x 9.3 x 6.2m – the current internal dimensions) and to be used by the courts. It had a porch with an impaled coat of arms, combining "two keys endorsed and a sword in saltire", the arms of the bishop of Winchester, and "three bugle horns", the arms of Robert Horne (bishop 1560–80), surrounded by a garter with the motto of the Order of the Garter and four cherubs at the corners. Below was the text "Crux et vanitas 1577".

Toulmin then describes the arms of bishop Thomas Langton on both faces of the Inner Gatehouse, those on the outside having additionally a Latin motto and the date 1495. Above this, on the outside, were the arms of Henry VII with the motto "Vive le roi Henri" and to the left of this, the same arms and date as seen on the porch but with the addition of the letters "RH".

Toulmin says that the room above the gate was used for the grand jury "till within these two years" and later refers to Hammet building a new one (below) but not that this resulted in the removal of the porch described above. He then describes the other rooms "a strong room called the Exchequer, in which the records of Taunton-Dean land are reposited", a large room formerly used as an assembly room, a theatre, an armoury for the militia and other purposes (presumably the Somerset Room), a dungeon for prisoners and rooms that have been occupied as tenements. He also reports a tradition of a "subterranaeous passage from the inner court to the powder mills, at present the town mills", which probably refers to a drain. Toulmin connects it with the "lately made" discovery of an "underground arched way" in an adjoining garden, probably that in Ine's garden (Arch 464).

Toulmin also provides information on the works to the castle carried out shortly before the publication of his book. In 1787, the death of the last member of the Lucas family who held the castle from the bishop, led to a threat to remove the assizes from the town which was only averted when Sir Benjamin Hammet MP (to whom Toulmin's book is dedicated) "made a purchase of the castle that the town might have the use of the assize-hall" and "immediately employed architects and masons to put it into a state of sound and decent repair".

This involved the rearrangement of the courts and the construction of a new grand jury room. Hammet then "proceeded to fill up the moat, to lay out the ground around the castle, and to fit up a handsome suit of rooms; rearing again the decayed walls, converting the pile of ruins into a mansion and restoring the castle in a style of magnificence and elegance." Jeffries (1969), however, has shown that Hammet did not in fact buy the castle but only took out a grant of the office of keeper in the names of his sons and nephew. Toulmin's statement appears to have been generally believed, which caused trouble in 1811 when the justices' title to the hall was shown to be invalid (Jeffries 1969).

Paintings and Engravings

The earliest known illustration of the castle is dated 1773 (SANHS 3504, Figure 2.1 on the facing page). This shows the south and west sides from an elevated location in the area of the West Gate. The north part of Castle Green is shown as an open area crossed by paths leading between the three castle gates. The East Gate, consisting only of an arch with a small amount of superstructure, lies in the distance with houses to either side (Figure 15.6 on page 248).

The house on the right, and the south part of the green, appear to be set lower and the two parts of the green are separated by a wall. The house to the north, presumably the one described by Toulmin with the arms of Bishop Langton (which are not shown), also appears to be set lower with an enclosed garden in front surrounded by a wall that joins another along the front of the Inner Moat. This wall is pierced by a formal gateway with large ball-topped gatepiers and by an opening with a wooden gate into the moat.

The Inner Ward is shown with its pre-Hammet fenestration along the south and west sides and with the Round Tower apparently ruined and ivy-covered. A large, gabled roof is visible above the west range but this is probably the Great Hall shown with incorrect perspective.

Toulmin's book includes an engraving dedicated to Coplestone Warre Bampfylde (1720–91), the owner of Hestercombe House and a noted amateur painter (White 1995). The dedication indicates that Bampfylde produced the original drawing for the engraver and this original (Figure 2.2 on the facing page) survives in the SANHS collection (SANHS 3534). It shows Hammet's works partly completed with pointed-arch window openings in the west range and round tower, apparently with different glazing to that which survives. This is likely to be an artistic simplification as the current glazing appears appropriate for a late eighteenth-century date and the glass panes depicted would be larger than usual at that time (Julian Orbach, pers. comm.). The top of the door (57) from the undercroft is shown, with its brick surround but not Door 58 nor the windows in the Adam Library. In the south range three square windows, two possibly blocked, are visible on the first floor; the parapet above the westernmost appears to be damaged, which fits with the archaeological and 1773 picture evidence.

A third drawing, a coloured aquatint, survives in the SANHS collections, one of a series identified by the initials C.C. (Figure 1.1 on page 13). It is not dated but it must post-date Hammet and pre-date the changes to the roof of the Great Hall in 1816 (below). There are some details that seem be incorrect but in general it seems to be an accurate record.

2.3 Nineteenth Century

1816 Roofing Contract

A contract (SRO Q/AC/2), discussed by Jeffries (1969), gives a detailed account of repairs and alterations to the Great Hall in 1816, most particularly the replacement of the roof. The contract comprises a detailed description of the works to be carried out and also plans and drawings of the new roof and associated works. These allow it to be clearly shown that the roof then built is the one that survives today.

The contract is made between Edward Coles, the Deputy Clerk of the Peace for Somerset and William Lewarn, a Taunton builder. A preamble states that a committee had been formed and that this had reported on the need for a new roof and new closets for the justices, accompanied by a plan and specification for the proposed works. The magistrates had agreed to pay £200 towards the works provided that the works were overseen by the county surveyor, Richard Anstice (see Bentley 1987). They were also concerned that, as other repairs had previously been made and paid for, the assizes would continue to use the building once repaired.

The contract then detailed the works that William Lewarn was to undertake for £500: the removal and replacement of the roof and the construction of closets and windows. In detail this involved:

- The roof and ceiling to be taken down.
- Sixty-nine feet of the "back wall" to be taken down (shown on the plan between window 55, included, and window 52, excluded) for at least five feet from the top and rebuilt with the same stone and any additional to match "set in good lyas mortar".
- The tiles or slates covering the slope of the back wall to be replaced with "Hamhill roof pavement stone".
- Arches to be made over the lintels of the three windows in the back wall.
- The roof to be constructed of new wood with the exception of the rafters which may be of sound wood from the old roof. The dimensions of all the timbers are given and the form of the roof shown on a drawing.
- Two hips are indicated, one replacing a gable over the east window (see Figure 1.1 on page 13) which was to be removed.
- The roof to be covered with tile recovered from the old roof and any new to match.
- A new ceiling to be constructed over both courts at the same height as that removed. This appears to have been supported between the beams of the roof rather than to have covered them.
- Two oval ventilators to be provided, in the centre of each court, provided with cords, pulleys and cleats for their operation.
- As the top of the eastern window is above the ceiling height, the ceiling to be stepped from the lintel to the first beam.
- A door, 2 feet 6 inches wide to be made in the eastern end wall with an oak lintel and arch over. Steps to be made to lead from the judges platform to a privy constructed against the outside of the wall.
- The privy to be of nine-inch brickwork, four feet square and seven feet high, roofed with timber from the old roof and tiled - with a "stench funnel from the seat through the roof".
- Details are given of the finishing of the privy and the provision of a door in the new doorway. The "small door of the present water closet" to be hung at the base of the stairs and a drain constructed to join the new to the old privy.

Figure 2.2: *Drawing by Coplestone Warre Bampfylde, dated 1789 and used as the basis for the engraving of the south front in Toulmin (1791). SANHS 3534.*

- Another privy to be constructed "in the old tower with a passage thereto cut out of the western end wall". Similar to the first privy with the exception that ventilation be provided by a window rather than a skylight.
- All "timbers which are now inserted into and projecting from the wall [...] for the support of the building beams" are to be removed and all damage to be made good. The builder to be responsible for the repair of any damage to "galleries, benches, tables, partitions" or other fittings.
- Any reclaimed but unused materials and all rubbish to be removed.

James Savage

Savage (1822) produced a revised and enlarged edition of Toulmin which mentions changes made in the 30 years between the two volumes. He describes works in 1816, when "the two courts underwent several judicious alterations, for the better accommodation of the judges, counsel and jurors and the various officers connected with the proceedings of the assizes and quarter sessions." As this was only six years before publication, it is curious, as Jeffries (1969) noted, that this contains no mention of the roof's replacement. Savage adds the information that Hammet had divided the hall: "the west end being fitted up for the criminal court and the east for that of Nisi Prius". The pillared Grand Jury Room, omitted by Toulmin, is described and the west end of the castle noted as being occupied as a dwelling house by St Albyn Gravenor, Esq, suggesting that it wasn't used as lodging for the judges at that date, unless a similar arrangement to that adopted by the Lodging Company (below) was employed.

Richard Carver

Richard Carver (1792–1862) was the county surveyor from 1830 to 1857 having previously been assistant to Robert Anstice (Bentley 1987). As well as his commissions for public buildings he was a prolific architect in private practice (Lillford 2011). At Taunton Castle, he produced proposals (never executed) for the reconstruction of the courts in 1833, which survive together with a plan of Castle Green showing the ownerships and proposed land acquisitions dated October 1832 (SRO Q/AC/3).

The Judges' Lodgings Company

The minute book for a company formed to provide lodgings for the judges survives (SRO DD/SAS/c795/TN/147). It starts with the formation of the company on 20 November 1838 when it was resolved to buy the property then rented by Mr Abraham of Mr Esdaile for £700, to appoint staff to maintain it, to appoint a committee of the shareholders to manage it and to let the property between court sessions. Mr Abraham's property is shown on Carver's 1832 plan comprising the West and South ranges with the lawn in the castle ditch, a kitchen garden to the north of the Great Hall and stables along the east side of the courtyard.

In 1840 Mr Abraham was replaced by a new tenant, Mr Cox, and the rooms that required furnishing (there may have been others) were listed: two round rooms, four bedrooms on the first floor and one other bedroom for a servant, the large room upstairs and the kitchen. Mr Cox was to have use of the "small room" to store furniture during court sessions. Two other rooms, the cellar "under the Castle House" and the coach house were reserved by the company and let to Mr Hitchcock. This cellar is otherwise unknown but the term Castle House is ambiguous at this date and is more likely to have referred to the West and South Ranges than the modern Castle House, which was a separate property. The coach house is probably that shown by Spencer in 1875, and in the occupation of Miss Prosser by Carver (see Figure 12.1 on page 214). Rooms are listed again in 1846: dwelling room, four best bedrooms, three attics and the kitchen at the east of the long dining room. The later minutes contain less of interest but the shareholders continued until November 1865 (nearly a decade after the courts had moved to Shire Hall).

John Leversedge

A Taunton surveyor, Leversedge produced a plan of the castle (SRO DD/SAS/C1207/2g) in 1853, commissioned by Warre (below) to be engraved for his paper. There are also 8 elevation drawings (SANHS 3515–3517) whose locations are identified on the plan, which provide the earliest detailed information on some castle buildings. He also prepared a plan of a garden beyond the east wall (SANHS 6102).

Francis Warre

The earliest description of the castle which can be described as archaeological is that by the Rev F Warre, published with a plan (see Leversedge above) in 1853. Much of the area of the outer ward had not been built on at that date and Warre describes the stream dividing at the south-west corner. The western defences are described as completely destroyed with the exception of "a mass of masonry" at the south-western corner (Figure 14.1 on page 238) and "another small fragment at the north side of the western gate". On the accompanying plan the mass of masonry is shown as a short linear feature running nearly at right-angles to the stream; it is clearly not part of a curtain wall but could be part of the side of a tower. The remains of the gate are shown attached to the south-west corner of the Winchester Arms, as an L-shaped piece of masonry perhaps suggestive of the base of an arch. Outside the gate Warre recounts that several large wooden beams had been discovered "a few years ago" which he considered to be part of a barbican. It is perhaps more likely that they were the remains of a bridge across the moat. The line of the defences is described as marked by a low bank along the stream.

The line of the moat along the southern and eastern sides of the outer ward is described but "nothing remains until we come to the eastern gate, where, though sadly disfigured by modern additions, stand the very striking remains of a very strong and handsome gatehouse". Warre then relates the discovery "a short time since, the foundations of some strong stone fabric" which he describes as possibly the base for a wall running along the entrance way from outside the moat towards the gate.

Warre describes the Inner Moat as running round the Inner Ward and joining the outer moat at the rear of the Castle Inn. It is not clear how much of the moat actually survived in Warre's time. The plan, unfortunately does not distinguish between surveyed features and inferred ones; all the moats are shown as water-filled, although some are described in the text as infilled.

Warre describes an elevated rectangular platform in the south-east corner of the Inner Ward the sides of which, "in Mr Dyer's garden", were marked by lines of masonry until a few months previously when they were destroyed to plant raspberries. The face towards the moat is described as "undoubted Norman masonry" and had also been destroyed. This platform is clearly that excavated by Gray in the 1920s (see Section 3.4 on page 39) and the southern wall must either be wall B (see page 160) or the remains of a continuation of the present south curtain wall of the Inner Ward. No wall is shown in this location on Leversedge's plan but a wall

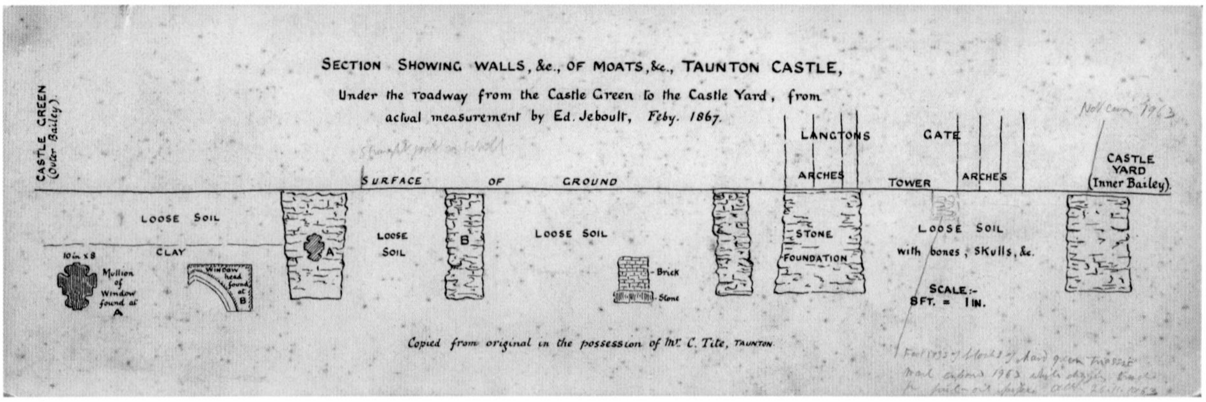

Figure 2.3: Section drawing of pipe trench through Inner Gate in 1867. SANHS 3525. See Figure 4.6 on page 59 for location plan.

is shown running northwards, the southern part of which may be the wall in Dyer's garden. From the platform the plan shows a broad bank running north, bounded by the wall, to the north-east corner where stood "a mount" commanding an outwork and the approach to the town mills. Warre indicates that he thought that this mount was a motte: "one of those [mounts] so often met with in Norman fortifications". He also describes Arch 464, as leading to this outwork, indicating that the outwork is the area now known as Ine's Garden and suggesting that the ground was lower on that side than currently. Very solid masonry is also described along the northern side of the Inner Ward facing the mill stream "but in so mutilated a condition as to defy any attempt at accurate description".

Warre describes a gate to the east of the Great Hall, "flanked by an enormous mass of ruined masonry", with a segmental arch which he dated to "perhaps as early as the latter part of the thirteenth century". His description of the Great Hall and southern ranges adds little to modern knowledge but he does describe round "towers". One is clearly the surviving Round Tower and the other is presumably a half-round tower which is shown on his plan forming part of Castle House. The position of the tower on the plan suggests that the present curved boundary wall follows its inner face. The wall of the tower is shown as the same thickness as the curtain and described in the text as little more than foundations. However, the curtain is described as "little better than rubble work, and decidedly unlike that of the round tower" suggesting that some facing of the tower was visible. Warre also says that the gatehouse is later than the curtain wall to the west.

Warre clearly believed that the Inner Ward, whose topography he could see more clearly than we can today, formed the most defensible location and thus the site of Ine's fortification "as it follows the form of the ground and encloses the highest part of the elevated spot at the confluence of the brook with the Thone [sic]". He believed the platform at the south-east corner was the site of a rectangular Norman keep, a view which probably influenced Gray and others.

Edward Jeboult

Jeboult (1829-93) was a Taunton builder and son of a prominent local businessman and politician (Bush 1983). Two sources describe features he recorded during the digging of a drain across the moat bridge and through the gateway to the Inner Ward: a diagrammatic section in the SANHS collection (Figure 2.3) and a text description. There are several variations of the text but the earliest appears to be in a newspaper cutting in Jeboult's scrapbook of *c.*1866 (SRO L/2205). It appears in Jeboult (1873, 17) and Jeboult (1893, 195), where there is a little additional information on the Great Hall. The text describes the trench as being dug to depths of 12 to 16 feet (3.6–4.9m) during which "the whole of the massive walls which formed portions of the moat and bearings of the drawbridge have been laid open".

Beneath the outer arches of the gatehouse Jeboult recorded a "solid mass of flint masonry foundation, not less than seven to eight feet in thickness (2.1–2.4m) and ten feet in depth, thrown in with liquid lime, and forming a concrete like solid stone." On the section drawing the inner (north) face of this appears to be vertical while the outer side shows a slight batter. This agrees with Spencer's description of the curtain wall to either side (see page 38). Beyond this is a wall described as "of flint and ragstone, 3½ feet [1m] thick and 12 feet [3.6m] in depth which formed the northern side of the moat." This wall is shown with a vertical north face and irregular south face on the section in contrast to what might be expected if this was the side of the moat.

Jeboult reports a similar wall 18 feet (5.5m) to the south forming the southern side of the moat and this is also shown with a vertical north face and a less regular southern face which is what would be expected. Between the two he describes "a pier [which] was erected of flat bricks, which probably formed a centre bearing for the drawbridge." The section drawing shows this pier, not surviving to any great height and standing on a stone plinth. It is not placed centrally between the "moat walls" but further north, some 1.6m from the northern wall. Further south again (over 12m from the gate) was another wall nearly 6 feet (1.8m) thick and over 14 feet (4.3m) deep, "constructed in a most substantial manner". The wall was thickest at the top and contained reused stone, including a Hamstone window mullion; a window head was also found in the southern "moat wall".

The section drawing shows the material between these walls as "loose soil" in the area of the moat which lies above a layer of "clay" to the south of the southernmost wall. This might suggest that this wall was, in fact, the southern revetment of the moat. Below the gatehouse itself the drawing shows "loose soil with bones, skulls &c." and the text describes this deposit ("loose and artificial matter, consisting of old rubbish, stone, sand, earth, &c., with a large quantity of human and other bones, skulls, teeth, &c., and the usual accompaniment of oyster shells, smoking pipes, and broken pieces of ware &c.") as extending for 50 feet (15.3m) to the north of the gatehouse and to a depth of 14 feet (4.3m). No foundations are shown below the inner arch.

About 2m to the north of the gateway Jeboult recorded a wall 12 feet (3.6m) deep and about 5 feet (1.5m) in thickness which is shown on the section with vertical edges. He also reports that "Near this spot tradition says there was formerly a cave, and we have been informed that people now living have actually seen it; but we can find no trace of it." Unfortunately Jeboult gives no indication of the orientation of the wall but it seems likely that it ran parallel to the curtain wall, as the other walls reported are likely to have done, or he might have noted a different alignment. No purpose can be assigned to this wall, which was not seen in 1963 (see page 51) but it appears to be of a thickness that could be defensive. The wall face (F2) seen in the 1978 waterpipe trench (page 53) is also probably this wall.

According to Sloper (1876b), Jeboult was also employed to add a window to the Great Hall and to remove the partition dividing the hall into two courts in 1863. Sloper describes discoveries made at this time and Jeboult (1893, 195) says "several small stone arched doorways, just large enough for one person to pass through, have been discovered. These were, doubtless 'sally ports"'.

Jeboult was also a prolific author, both of books and newspaper articles, and also an early photographer. He produced a scrapbook containing his newspaper articles illustrated with prints that are some of the earliest known of Taunton. Most are not specifically dated but must predate 1866 when the book was produced. See SRO L/2205.

George Clark

The "father of castellology", GT Clark (1809–98) trained as a surgeon but was employed by Brunel as an engineer on the Great Western Railway and later became manager of the Dowlais Iron Company. In addition to this he published over 200 articles on antiquarian subjects. Many of these were on castles and were brought together in *Mediaeval Military Architecture in England* (Clark 1884), launching castle studies as a discrete subject within the field of medieval history (James 2004). His article on Taunton was published by SANHS (Clark 1872) and reprinted with minor alterations in the book (pages 488–92). His description adds little to Warre's but he was clearly of the opinion that the West Range constituted a keep.

Charles Webb

Webb (1874) produced a second revised version of Toulmin but there are fewer changes to the section on the castle than previously. He does say that the western end, having been fitted up for the judges was also used "by the officers of the 1st Somerset militia as a mess-room" and that Castle House had been converted to public baths. He discusses the plans to save the castle by SANHS.

Charles Fox

Fox (1875) adds little to earlier descriptions but does mention the discovery of the foundations of the East Gate bridge "a few years since". The description, however sounds very like Jeboult's findings in the Inner Gate (above). Fox also mentions the eastern Round Tower under Castle House "the basement walls of which still remain".

Chapter 3

Work by the Somerset Archaeological and Natural History Society, 1874–1958

Chris Webster

The destruction of the castle lamented by Warre continued into the later 19th century, when George Clark (1872) suggested that the ruins needed to be taken into sympathetic ownership. This was achieved in 1874 when SANHS purchased the castle property (the Inner Ward, Keep Garden and lands to the north) funded by various activities including charging admission to Edwin Sloper's excavation (below). They then set about converting the buildings to museum use, activities (see, for example, Figure 10.8 on page 195) that would "border on vandalism to modern eyes" (Bush and Meek 1984, 16). Luckily Spencer (1910) recorded many of the changes and others are noted in the society's proceedings and archives. Some of these are reported below but shorter reports are mostly discussed in the sections on individual buildings.

3.1 Edwin Sloper

Edwin Sloper (1840–1905) came to Taunton as a banker and for over 20 years collected information about the town and county. He was influential in the purchase of Taunton Castle by SANHS and continued to research Somerset after moving to London in 1892. He left many of his papers to SANHS on his death (Tite 1905), including his notebook (Sloper 1876b) and his annotated copy (SANHS AR 21-32) of Toulmin. The notebook provides much descriptive evidence of the castle in the years before SANHS's purchase and Sloper also worked with William Bidgood (SANHS's museum curator 1862–1900; Tite 1901) in excavating at the north-east corner (now Ine's Garden). Bidgood produced an ink-washed plan (SANHS 6093) entitled "Plan and Sections of Excavations at north east corner of Taunton Castle" and dated "187-" (see Figure 3.1 on the following page). A different hand in pencil refers to a report in the *County Gazette* for May 16, 1876. A further pencil sketch by Bidgood was discovered in 2011 (see Figure 3.2 on page 37, SRO A/DWX/19). The newspaper report (actually from 13 May 1876) is in the form of a letter from Sloper and together with the drawings gives a comprehensive account of the excavation (Sloper 1876a) – rather better than survives from Gray's work 50 years later.

> By kind permission of Mr Surtees I have recently made some excavations at the north-east angle of the outer wall of Taunton Castle and am glad to say that a very large portion of the old wall has been found in situ. The width varies from seven feet [2.1m] on the east to eight feet six inches [2.6m] on the north face, and the stone used in building was the grey sandstone from Norton, Rumwell or Bradford, the red sandstone from Bishop's Lydeard, and white lias from the neighbourhood of Staple or Curry, with a few flints from Blagdon and one chipping of Ham-hill stone. Apparently the moat did not wash the wall, as appeared evident on laying bare the foundations, the distance from the wall to the inside edge of the moat being about thirteen feet [4m], and the moat itself was twenty-four feet [7.3m] in width. [Discussion of property built in the moat]
>
> [Discussion of legend of secret passage] This tradition is supported by a discovery lately made of an underground archway [...] leading to the ground floor of the inner court, although on the inside it has been covered up by sloping away the earth in later times.
>
> I have now opened this archway, which is four feet two inches [1.3m] deep, and from

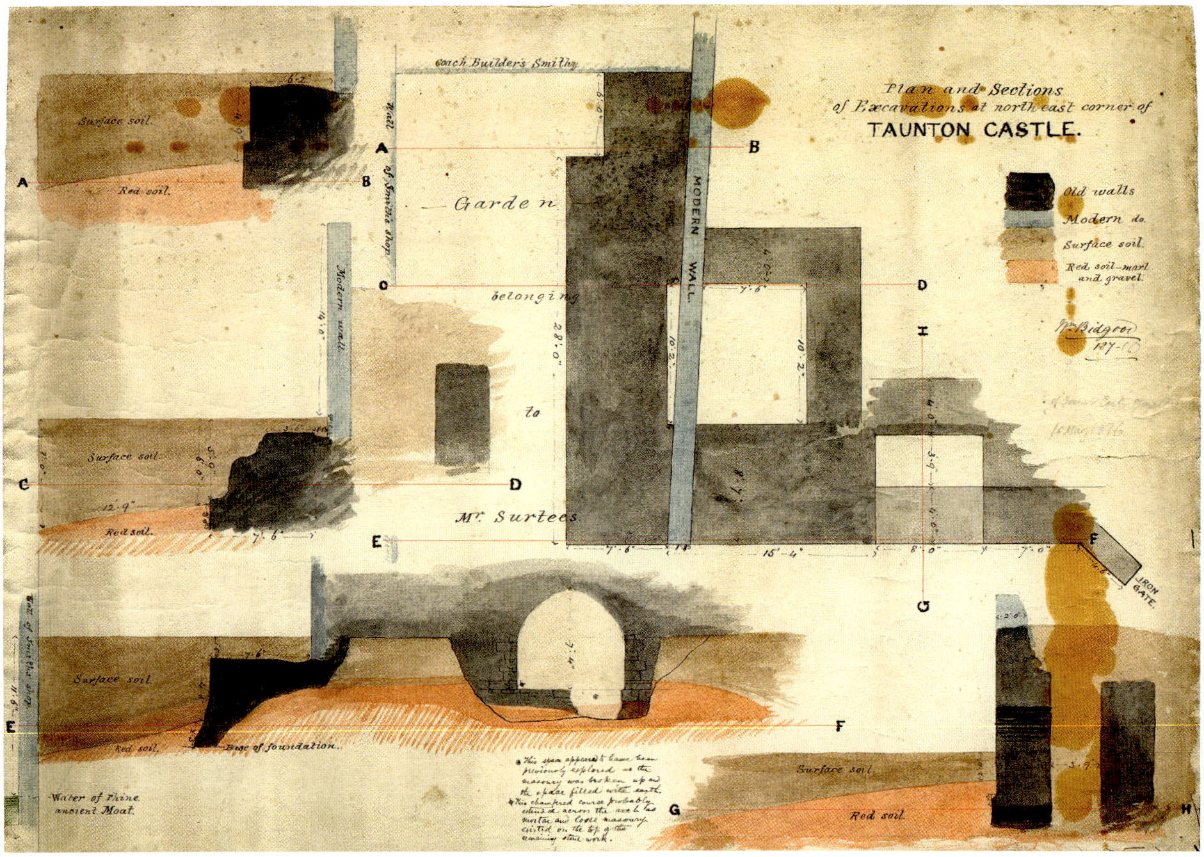

Figure 3.1: Edwin Sloper's excavations in Ine's Garden around Arch 464 as recorded by William Bidgood in 1876. SANHS 6093.

> the spring of the arch the face inside and out is composed of Ham-hill stone, the other materials being of the same construction as the wall with a little slate used for keying. Half the floor has been cut away, and the remaining part is of rough stone covered with a rough mortar. There is apparently an outwork in front of the arch composed of red marl thrown up when the ditches were made, although there is much uncertainty as to its character. I made one cut in the direction of the inner edge of the moat with a view of finding a round tower, and, although there was the skin of some old walling perceptible we could trace no sort of tower or any work joining the wall. [Details that excavation open to public until 20th May in aid of castle purchase fund]
>
> I would mention that we have found some early pottery in a hole close to the archway; in another part two silver pennies of Edward VI and Elizabeth; also a tobacco pipe of the seventeenth century, marked "E. C. in Chard".

Sloper's notebook contains a cutting of the letter which has been annotated "In a further search in beginning of 1877 we proved this to be a garderobe and the inner wall had been driven through to the soil inside to see what was beyond". While not entirely clear this suggests that nothing was found to the south of the arch behind the wall, thus supporting Sloper's identification of the base of a garderobe chute.

The drawings show a wide wall foundation forming the east wall of the castle with a narrower modern wall sitting on, and at a slight angle to, it. The foundations appear to be sitting, at no great depth, on natural red marl suggesting that the platform of Ine's Garden has natural origins. The wall has a small rectangular tower in the corner, which projects slightly to the east but not the north. To the west of this is the archway. The present shape of Ine's Garden (which was there in 1852, SANHS 6102) suggests a Civil War bastion but Sloper describes it (before his excavation) as a "round tower". The finds certainly suggest activity in the 17th century.

Bidgood's drawing of the arch (Figure 3.2 on the facing page) shows the stonework with detailed observations of the nature of the archaeological evidence. He shows the original ground

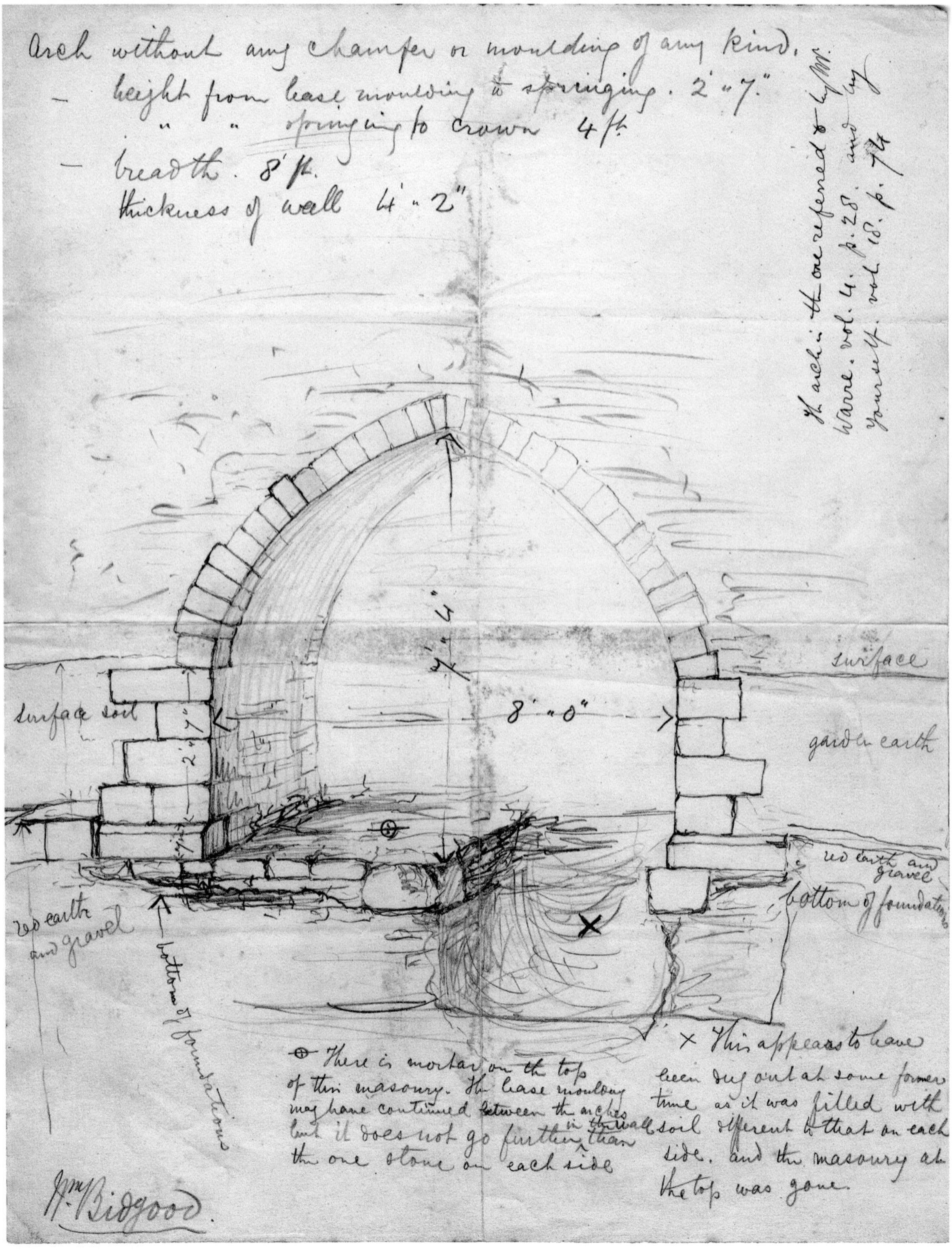

Figure 3.2: *Arch 464 uncovered during Edwin Sloper's excavations at the NE corner as sketched by William Bidgood. The "yourself" at top right was George Clark, noted castellologist and author of a paper on the castle (Clark 1872). SRO A/DWX/19.*

surface, a depth of "garden earth" above "red earth and gravel" upon which the very shallow foundations were set. The left side (east) of the base of the archway is described: "There is mortar on the top of this masonry. The base moulding may have continued between the arches but it does not go further in the wall than the one stone on each side." The reference to the base moulding appears to refer to the lowest stone on either side of the gateway which appears to be set forward and chamfered along the top. There is one course of foundations below this. On the left hand side Bidgood comments "This appears to have been dug out at some former time as it was filled with soil different to that on each side and the masonry at the top was gone." The arch was visible before the excavation, as it is shown on a plan of 1852 (SANHS 6102) and on the plan in Warre (1853).

The notebook (Sloper 1876b) also contains descriptions of the castle, commenting on Warre (1853), and adding much information on the changes to the building immediately before and during the Society's acquisition. These relate particularly to the layout of the Great Hall before and after the removal of the central partition in 1863, the discovery of medieval windows and other features in 1875, the garderobe chute on the inner gate and Castle Bow.

3.2 Joseph Houghton Spencer

Spencer (1844–1914) was a Taunton architect and prominent member of SANHS (Lillford 2011). He produced a set of plans of the castle (SRO DD/SAS/c1207/2b,2c), which were copied and reused for many years. The original plans of 1875 show details of the buildings in the eastern half of the courtyard that were demolished by the society, the locations of some service trenches and, occasionally they and the copies, have had archaeological observations, by Gray and others, annotated on them.

There are other drawings by Spencer, which may include a sketch (SANHS 13158) that appears to show proposals following the purchase of the castle in 1874. Buildings along the south side of the Great Hall are annotated "Buildings erected for convenience of assizes and sessions" with those to the west of the Grand Jury Room marked "Portion removed". In the east part of the courtyard, north of Castle House, dashed lines indicate "Baths and cottage removed", though buildings to the north along the "Old wall" are shown surviving. "Foundations" are shown at the east end of the Great Hall that appear to represent parts of the Watergate.

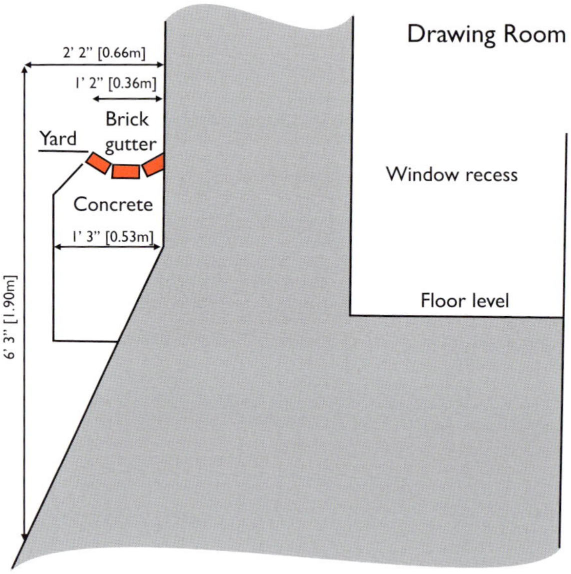

Figure 3.3: *Spencer's section through the curtain wall forming the south side of Castle House in 1912 showing the batter to the wall and drain TCC 103 (redrawn from SANHS 6103).*

The SANHS minutes suggest that these changes were made in 1878.

Spencer's Description, 1910

Following the society's purchase of the castle in 1874, various works were carried out, both immediately and over subsequent years. Many of these are recorded in the annual reports issued as part of the society's *Proceedings* and Spencer was asked to produce a consolidated report of the changes (Spencer 1910). Spencer's account is invaluable as it locates (though not always clearly) and illustrated many of the new windows and doors.

The Moat, 1912

In 1912 Spencer excavated, following concern about the structure of the wall , in the yard to the south of Castle House and reported the results to SANHS by means of a letter (SANHS 6103) with accompanying section drawing (see Figure 3.3). This recorded the brick gutter which runs along the castle wall and lies on a concrete foundation 3 feet (0.9m) deep and 1' 9" (0.5m) wide (seen in 2006, Trench D, page 64). Below this he could see the face of the castle wall battering outwards "in the same way as the wall on the western side of the inner gate shows." The wall to the west is no longer similar to that shown by Spencer, indicating that its current form post-dates 1912.

3.3 The Keep Garden, 1916

Arthur Vivian-Neal, the chairman of SANHS and Harold St George Gray, the curator, briefly note a trial trench in the Keep Garden, dug by Gray's son Lionel, that uncovered the top of a wall. (Vivian-Neal and Gray 1940, 63, n42). Lionel would have been 15 at the time and it is possible that his early death in 1923 (HPP 1923) may have affected his father's later attitude to the site.

3.4 The Keep Garden, 1924–28

From 1924 to 1929 (with the exception of 1926) the area to the east of the courtyard, now the gardens of the Castle Hotel, was excavated by the Society under the direction of Harold St George Gray. No detailed report was ever published, and it is not evident in the Society's archives that many records were ever made. There is a brief description of Gray's interpretation (Vivian-Neal and Gray 1940) with some walls shown on a small plan covering the whole castle area. Gray's excavations were reassessed by Pearson (1984b) after the ruins that Gray had uncovered had been surveyed in detail for the first time in 1977/78 (Rodwell 1978; 1984a). Pearson used two of Gray's notebooks, which he describes as recently discovered in the County Museum, and which he states were then deposited in the Society's library. They can not now be located but, luckily, Pearson took photocopies that are now part of the Western Archaeological Trust's archive (SRO DD/WAT/16).

Pearson refers to a sketch section (now SRO DD/WAT/16/Eiii) but appears to have been unaware of other sources for Gray's excavations: a plan (SANHS 6094) and neatly drawn section (SANHS 6092) of the first season's excavation trenches, as well as several photographs of the beginning of the work (SANHS 12543–12547). There is also a set of photographs (Joel 1–23) taken in the winter of 1932/33 that have been discovered subsequently.

As Pearson noted, the diaries are more concerned with the day-to-day running of the excavation than with the results, but with the benefit of the plan (see Figure 3.4 on the following page), sections and photographs, it is now possible to describe the work more fully.

Gray's Excavation Diary

1924

Gray's excavation began on Monday 24 November 1924 at 11am to allow time for his foreman to arrive by train from Tisbury in Wiltshire. William Young (1890–1971) was an experienced excavator, employed by Gray and others at Avebury, who later became the curator of the Alexander Keiller Museum. Young wrote extensive diaries covering his work but unfortunately those that survive in Devizes Museum only start in April 1930 (Bill Perry, pers. comm.). Three local labourers were also employed and by the end of the next day Cutting I had reached a depth of 5½ feet (1.7m). Work continued principally at the southern end of the cutting, revealing stone walling or footings at a depth of 5 feet (1.5m) and recovering a token (Gray's Find No 3, see page 46). On Friday (28 November), more walling was found at two further points on in the trench, and another wall the following morning. On the Saturday afternoon, the men having worked a half-day, Gray "did some planning, levelling and measuring", presumably starting the plan that survives (SANHS 6094). He also marked out Cutting II, 36 x 10 feet (11m x 3m) and described the work so far:

> This cutting [I] was marked out as 70ft in length and 3ft in width, the western margin being 5ft from the eastern edge of the shed. There was much good soil in the two upper spits. Below that a certain amount of loose stone and mortar was observed, soon after which the red marly earth was reached in which XVII and XVIII century pottery was found; also clay tobacco-pipes, some of the later types sometimes found at greater depth than the earlier ones.
>
> Stone foundation or walling was found at the south end of the cutting at a depth of 5ft (It was not fully uncovered when this was written). Subsequently further walling was found in two other places, and a fourth place to the north on the following day.
>
> These patches of walling were very ruinous, especially the two most northerly portions. Beginning at the south, the depth from the surface of the 4 patches of walling was 5ft, 4.35ft, 5.5ft and 6.4ft respectively. The last named was found to be 7½ins lower than the average courtyard near the SE corner of the Great Hall. The height of the southern (straight) face of the most southerly piece of walling was 1.9ft to rubble mixed with the reddish earth below. Parts of this face were found to be covered with plaster – as if this was the inner face of a "room".

On Monday (1 December), Cutting II was opened across the eastern bank and by the afternoon "a solid red marl profile of the rampart and 'escarpe' was revealed" although no finds "of any

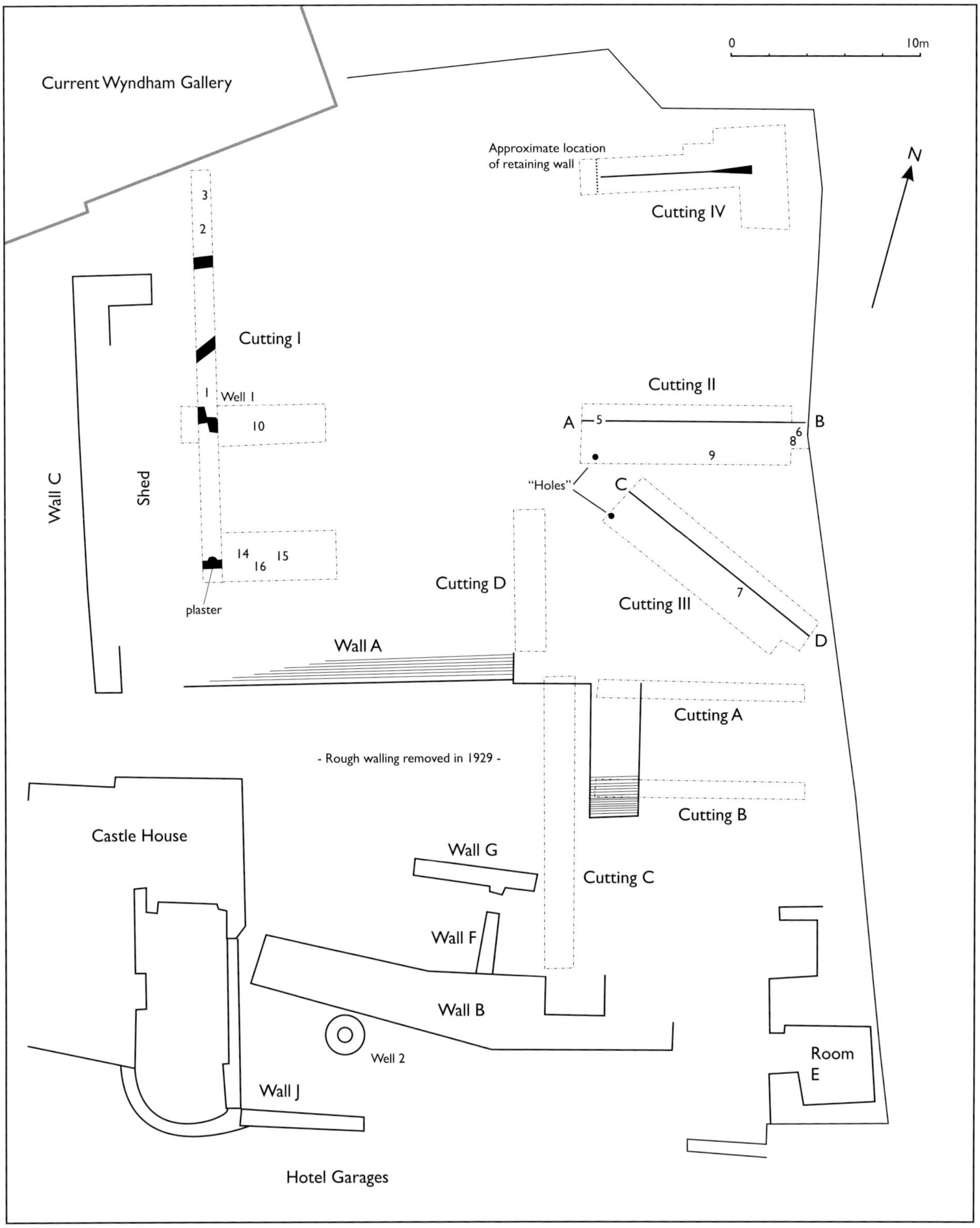

Figure 3.4: *Gray's plan (redrawn from SANHS 6094) of the initial trenches overlaid on the plan of the structures now exposed in the Keep Garden. The small numbers are Gray's finds numbers as shown on his plan (see page 46 for list).*

Figure 3.5: Gray's photograph showing the state of work on Friday 5 December 1924. Cutting II is to the left, exposing the marl bank. The men are working in Cutting III which had been started that morning. SANHS 12544.

consequence" were discovered. On the following days a circular pit was located on the top of the rampart, which contained building waste, including stone, mortar and pieces of slate. By Thursday, Cutting II was nearly complete and the spoil heap was being moved to allow excavation of Cutting III the next morning. On Friday, Cutting II reached a depth of 8ft and a small extension was made to the E from which medieval pottery (Gray's find No 8) was recovered at a depth of 6.3ft; further pottery was recovered on the following Monday (Gray describes this as "the rest of No 6, pottery" but has not mentioned No 6 before). Also on Friday, Gray took a series of 4 photographs showing the work at this point (Figure 3.5).

Work continued on Cuttings II and III through the next week and Gray drew a section on Tuesday (Figure 3.6 on page 44). On Thursday attention returned to Cutting I which was extended eastward to "follow the walling (angle of a room) No. 3". This is the extension to the east of the well. Work concentrated on this trench on Friday extending it 3ft west and 18ft east to a width of 7ft "in the endeavour to trace the E & W wall in this position" but it was shown that the walling did not extend far to the east. A human tibia was recovered but not retained. On the Saturday afternoon, as seems to have been his practice, Gray described the work so far:

> **Cutting III**
>
> Hole. At the N.W. extremity of this cutting, and at a depth of 3.2ft [0.98m] below the surface, an oblong hole 5" x 4" [13 x 10cm] was clearly visible, and from the margin it extended to a depth of 3.8ft [1.16m]. Below the 'oblong', the whole expanded to one of circular section having a diameter of 11". It extended apparently to total depth of 7ft [2.13m] below the surface. Round the hole dark mould outlined in the red marly earth.
>
> **Cutting II**
>
> Hole. Noticed at a depth of 5½ft [1.68m] below the surface as shown in the section, when top was 8" N & S by 7" E & W [20 x 18cm]. It enlarged at

7ft [2.13m] to 13″ N & S by 12″ E & W [33 x 3.66], and the bottom was at a total depth of 8.3ft [2.53m] below the surface.

The descriptions are accompanied by small sketch plans showing the locations of the holes relative to the trench corners. The holes are also shown on the section drawings (see Figure 3.6 on page 44).

On Monday 15 December, work continued extending Cutting I and making a further extension to the east end of Cutting II to recover more of the pottery (Find 6). The next day, the extension to Cutting I is described as "now getting a large excavation owing to the discovery of a stone turret [crossed out] well, square in section with internal sides measuring 3′ 10″ near the top. Depth of the stonework at 4.30pm today was 9 feet [2.74m]. In the filling XVII-XVIII tiles and shards; also 5 or 6 skulls of birds mostly of size of a starling". The following day, the men "excavated the filling of the turret down to water-level, which however did not represent the bottom of the walling. At the lowest part dug the internal sides measured 3′ 9″ [1.15m]. A cross was made on the upper walling which is 5.8ft [1.77m] below the present surface of the ground. From the cross to the surface of the bottom material (so far excavated) was 8.15ft [2.48m], and to water-level, 9.2ft [2.80m]. The filling was more stony as a greater depth was attained and there was a considerable admixture of small pieces of slate. A few small bird skulls were found and pottery at 8.75ft [2.67m] below the 'cross' (No 11). Later in the day followed the walling southward and found at 12 a bronze (?) pin". Little detail is recorded on the next and final day of the excavation season.

1925

Work recommenced on the afternoon of Monday 19 January when Gray drew the section of trench III (Figure 3.6 on page 44) and William Young arrived from Wiltshire. The following days were spent in moving spoil to allow Cutting I to be extended and in clearing out collapses that had occurred over the winter. Some rubble walling was discovered but no interesting finds. On Thursday, the cutting was extended eastwards at its southern end to a width of 8ft (2.44m) and this work continued on Friday when the "walling was traced for a good distance". A bone knife-handle (No 15) and a farthing of Charles I (No 14) were found. On Saturday, further continuations of the "stone walling and rubble walling" were excavated, and a clay pipe marked "ANDREW R[" recovered (No 16).

The following week was very wet but by Wednesday the cutting extension is described as nearly finished with "very little walling beyond the rubble-work". On Thursday, Cutting I was widened south of "the square turret or well" to search for more walling or cobbling. In the afternoon Gray marked out Cutting IV, 32ft by 6ft, in the north-east part of the site across a projecting part of the earthwork where Gray suspected a gun emplacement. This soon exposed a "considerable amount of walling" but no finds earlier than the 19th century were found between the walls. This is the area previously excavated by Sloper (above) and it seems likely that Gray's men were excavating the backfill of his trenches.

On the following Monday morning the men were employed "cleaning up the chert stones (walling and pavement) in Cutting I" but the rest of the week was devoted to Cutting IV. Gray describes finding the "arch in the wall to the N of the Cuttings II & III" and he speculates that it formed the water gate of the castle. On the Monday (9 February), the "water gate" was cleared down to the solid marl bottom; the marl was then followed "down the slope of the main cutting, westwards". Over the next two days the marl earthwork was revealed at the west end of the trench with a retaining wall at its foot. The season ended on Wednesday 11 February.

Further work was undertaken in July with the intention of clearing out the well. The Coles brothers "water experts of Taunton" were employed to extract the water-logged fill. The stonework was found to continue down to the bottom which was formed of red sandstone. Three feet 10 inches (1.17m) above the bottom was an offset below which the sides measured 3ft 6ins (1.07m) square and were of much rougher masonry. Above the offset was 15ft 4ins (4.67m) of walling, formed of 25 courses of diagonally tooled stonework, to the top of the shaft which lay 3ft 10ins (1.17m) below ground level. A carved stone "corbel" (Rodwell 1984b) was found loose in the fill about 1¼ft (0.38m) below the offset. Various pieces of structural timber were recovered together with pieces of wooden buckets, including staves, bases and iron hoops. Also in the lowest 2ft (0.61m) of the shaft were parts of a "Norman or early medieval pottery vessel" and other sherds. Gray took levels on the water in the well and compared them to those in the mill leat, a procedure complicated by changes in the leat level caused by the operation of the mill. He decided that the levels were essentially the same.

1926

No work was undertaken in 1926.

1927

Excavation resumed on 28th February 1927, using only local men, with a new trench 30ft by 3ft (9.14 x 0.91m) "on the extreme east of the castle property in the supposed site of King Ine's fortress". This, Cutting A (Figure 3.4 on page 40), was subsequently extended to 36ft (10.97m) long and a similar trench, Cutting B, laid out parallel and to the south of it. Red marl and some stonework was located in Cutting A. A further trench, Cutting C, was opened later in the week and work continued deepening all three cuttings throughout the following week without "reaching the natural or undisturbed ground" or finds of interest being recorded, apart from some 15th-century pottery from 11 to 11ft 9ins depth (3.35–3.58m).

On Monday, March 14th, Cutting D was begun to the north of Cutting C on the other side of a fence. Gray took levels on the base of Cutting C which was found to be 1.5ft (0.46m) higher than the courtyard of the castle. On Tuesday, the sloping wall (Rodwell's Wall A, see page 53) was found in Cutting D, "apparently resting on red marl". The trench was then extended westwards to follow the wall, although this extension is not marked on the plan.

The work of uncovering this wall, which involved continually extending the cutting west and southwards, took all of the next week and is briefly reported by Gray. On Tuesday March 29th he recorded "A squared block of (?green sand) stone inscribed with a Maltese cross on level of ninth set-off" with no other comment. On the Thursday, 16 "set-offs" had been recorded and also a second set-off on "the small E wall". The latter, which had not been mentioned before, must be the damaged area of differently coursed wall (A2–A3, see Figure 8.3 on page 157).

On Monday, 4th April, one workman "cleaned off the top of the walling and continued uncovering the more modern walling to the W". The other "worked at the other end of the cutting and uncovered the cobble-stones and worked deeper to the N". On Tuesday, one of the men was paid off as there were no more funds but the work continued and Cutting D was again extended, this time northwards to a distance of 33ft (10.06m) from Cutting C and the wall was also followed eastwards. This work continued until the excavation ended on Thursday 14th April and included the back filling of Cutting B. Gray's published photograph (Vivian-Neal and Gray 1940, Plate II) was taken on the 13th and shows the state of the excavation at this point, particularly the narrowness of the trench following Wall A. Gray notes finally that nothing had been found earlier than the later part of the 17th century.

Work resumed on Thursday 28th July as William Young had been engaged to excavate at Kingsdown Camp but was unable to start as the grass crop had not been cut. Gray started a new north-south trench 4.5ft (1.37m) wide "across what might *possibly* prove to be the northern side of a large square keep or other late Norman building of which the southern and western sides were known to exist – the southern having been found in excavating earlier in the year, the western being the ivy-covered wall in the courtyard of the castle". This trench, which was finished on the Monday, does not appear on the plan. Across the middle, at the bottom was found "a very rough piece of broken-down walling, the top 5½ feet [1.67m] below the surface. Mortar adhered to some of the stones of this broken-down walling. The height of it was but slight." At the north end "the flat red marl was reached at a depth of 6.25 ft [1.91m]" while to the south the marl rose up and was mixed with stone. Gray adds a note that this trench was backfilled on 20th August.

On Tuesday, 2 August, Young was working in the southern part of the site where he found a wall running north-south "almost on the line" of the former Cutting C. He continued to expose this wall until he left to work at Kingsdown Camp on 11th August. Again this work was not recorded on the plan and the only wall that would appear to fit is the southern extension of Wall A (A3–7, see Figure 8.3 on page 157) which runs parallel and slightly to the east of Cutting C.

At this point the notebook ends with a list of two photographs, the first taken on December 5th 1924 and showing a general view of Cuttings II and III from the west which was accidentally double exposed. This entry is marked by a number 4 within a square which may indicate that four shots were taken: four survive in the SANHS collection (SANHS 12544–47). The second was taken on 13 April 1927 of Wall C in Cutting D and is that (SANHS 12543) published in Vivian-Neal and Gray (1940, Plate II).

Excavation was resumed on 24 October 1927 with William Young as foreman and recorded in the second notebook. The recording from this point is much less detailed, often with several days recorded together and there is no indication of this work on the plan. Parts appear to have been funded by Mr Spiller of the Castle Hotel who was hoping to purchase part of the garden to expand his buildings. On 31st October he was

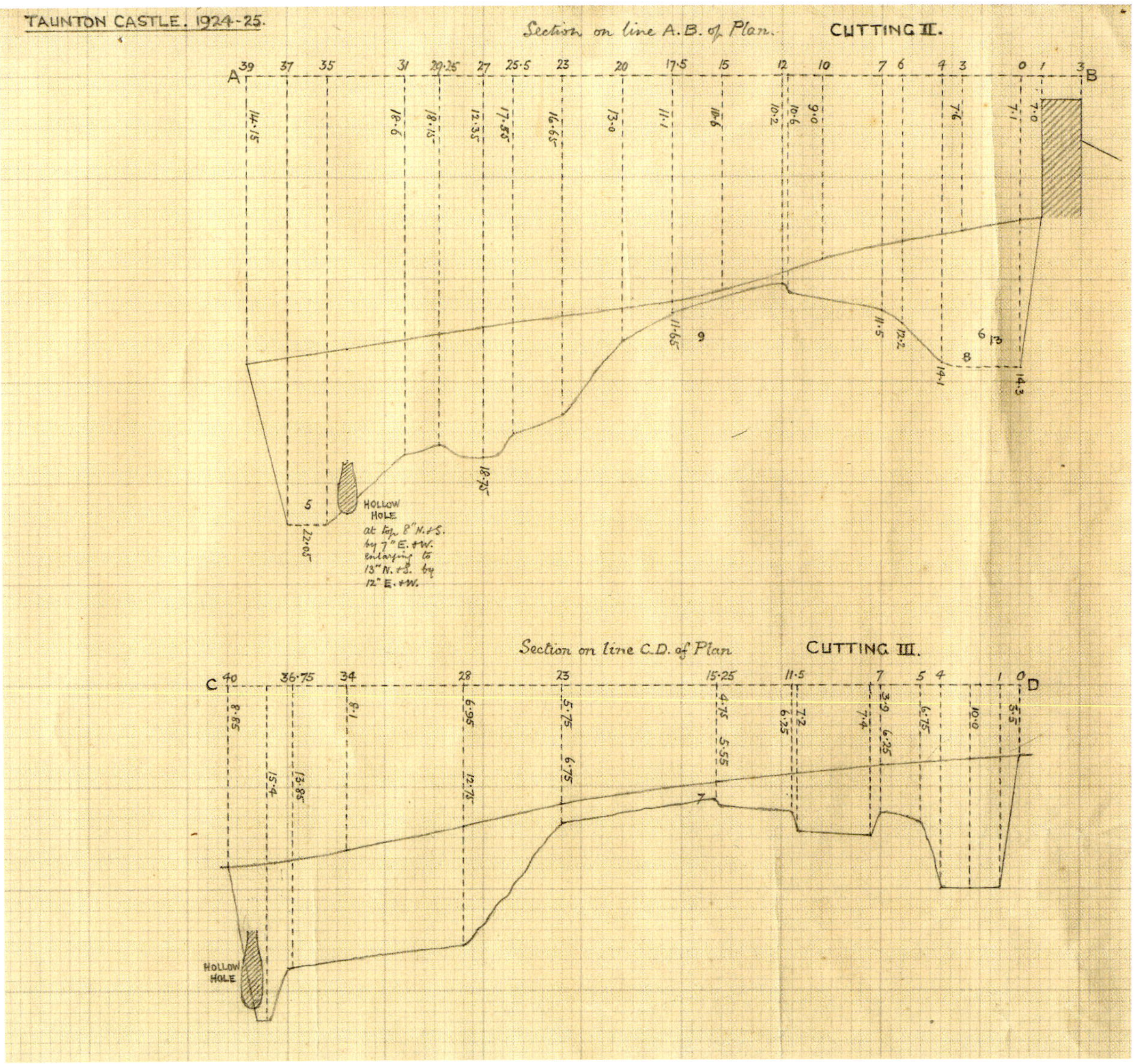

Figure 3.6: *Gray's section drawings (SANHS 6092) along Cuttings II and III (see Figure 3.4 on page 40 for locations). The numbers are finds locations (see page 46). Another less tidy version of section A–B exists in the Western Archaeological Trust copies of Gray's notebook (SRO DD/WAT/16/Ei3). This adds dimensions of the wall at top right and "limit of excavation?" below the lowest point.*

reported to have offered £20 to hire more labour "to determine what walling still remained to be discovered". Spiller's plans were rejected at a meeting on 30 November (SANHS minutes).

A new trench was commenced 5 feet (1.5m) from the "new garage" and 6 feet (1.8m) in width, this was extended over the next few days "towards the garage" and also westwards "towards the 2nd apple tree". "The southern extension was intended for the purpose of tracing the ['rough' added] walling found in the main trench. Walling was found here and the natural red marl was found [deleted and replaced by 'reached'] below: it and the older part of the 'garage' wall [Wall J]. A large northern extension was also begun to trace certain walling northwards." On Friday, 28th, "The northern trench proved very fruitful and at its N end a finely-faced wall was revealed with a considerable slope towards the S [Wall B]. Later this was traced in a westerly direction. The N trench also revealed other walling of a different character, the W side of which was bounded by very hard red marl."

On Saturday morning and throughout Monday the walls were "traced" and the ground cleared for a 7 foot (2.1m) cutting to the east, "near the thorn-tree". On Tuesday, this north-south cutting located Wall B and began to follow it. A further trench was opened in the south-east corner of the area, which located stonework close to the surface and by Friday (November 4th) both these eastern cuttings were being extended. On Monday, a reduced workforce was extending the middle cutting northwards and the following day stone steps were revealed. Four steps were uncovered before William Young had to leave "for Dr Bulleid's excavations at Radstock". It is not clear where these steps were as they are not referred to again.

1928–9

From this point on the diaries become even less useful and only record days worked and wages paid. Gray probably considered this work as more clearance than excavation, as Young was not employed as foreman and the first work is described as "loading and loosening material for cartage". Unfortunately this uncovered most of the remains that are visible today with only a solitary archaeological entry dated November 24 1928.:

> "Note: Rough wall was removed this morning, as it impaired cartage by Small's men. This was to the south of the later Norman wall with off-sets [Wall A], and about 5 yds [4.6m] from the 'near' top of the off-set wall. This rough and shallow walling was only 10in [25cm] wide and was found at an ave. depth of 2ft [0.6m] below the surface, running parallel with the off-set wall. The height of this 'foundation' was only about 15in [0.4m] above the rubble, and must have been of very late construction. The stones were apparently all large lias blocks (*not* in courses)".

The "apparently" is telling of Gray's lack of interest in the excavations but the 1928 work is described in the SANHS *Proceedings*:

> "Bearing upon this matter [the location for a new gallery] is the continuation and completion of certain sections of the excavations on the eastern side of the courtyard, for it is obvious to those who know the site well, that no part of the Society's property in this situation could be built upon before it is ascertained whether any further ancient walls and foundations exist which should be protected, or incorporated in any building scheme which may be projected. This work of excavation and clearing continued during the summer, and the Taunton Town Council will be removing the debris in the autumn to provide foundations for the new market near the railway station." (Gray 1928a, xvi)

and

> "Excavations have been and are still in progress at Taunton Castle for the double object of (1) archaeological discovery, and (2) providing space, not already occupied by ancient walling which will soon become available for Museum extension. It is hoped that the results of these investigations will be reported to the Society at their annual meeting in 1929." (Gray 1928b, liv-lv).

Further reports were published of the following year's work:

> "the walls exposed by further excavation on the site of the ancient Castle have been found to be very extensive and of the greatest interest. The long shed on the E side of the courtyard has been cleared away, and excavations carried out below it have revealed a considerable amount of walling; the digging has also been pressed forward in a southerly direction with excellent results. During the winter the Taunton Town Council hauled away some 2000 tons of excavated material to provide foundations for the new markets near the railway station, and at present we are unable to proceed until another 2000 tons have been removed. Less than a month ago the site was visited by the Mayor and corporation of Taunton, to whom the whole position was explained, and Mr St George Gray's address appeared in most of the local newspapers." (Gray 1929a, xviii)

and

> "The excavations at Taunton Castle were continued during the autumn of 1928 and the spring of 1929, and owing to the extent of Norman and other walling discovered in the area under examination it was decided not to erect any modern buildings in this situation, as was originally intended before it was known that so much remained of the old Castle buried under hundreds of tons of earth, stone and other debris. The Committee's tentative decision had to be entirely revised, and the Society is now left with the additional responsibility of completing the excavations – to

be followed by the protection and repair of the ancient walls." (Gray 1929b, lxiii).

From the payments it can be seen that this work ran from 24 April 1928 to 4 May and then from 7 June to 1 September. A further season ran from 3 October 1928 through to 11 May 1929 with a short break over Christmas and a week when work was suspended due to snow. Saturday 19 January has "well" written beside it; presumably this is Well 2 but it is not clear what work was undertaken as the well is not visible on the Joel photographs of 1932/33 and may not have been cleared until the landscaping work of 1933. The final season ran from 3 June to 8 October 1929.

The newspaper report mentioned above (*Somerset County Gazette*, 22 June 1929) contains a few additional pieces of information about the excavation: no sign of the eastern wall of the "keep" had been found and only "a small portion" of the north. More details are given of the finds, the number of early ("Elizabethan to James I") clay pipes being remarked on; there are said to be 410 pipes with 50 makers represented. Two wells were seen but only the square well (Well 1) has any details: as well as the Norman finds (pottery and "corbel"), an iron helmet of Civil War date from the well had been restored by Mrs Gray (its existence as a "cabasset", but not its findspot, is mentioned by Vivian-Neal and Gray 1940, 65). There was also a trade token of Hugh Graye of Taunton (dating to 1666, see Symonds 1911, 57) but it is not made absolutely clear if this is from the well.

The excavations were said to be finished and covered by tarpaulin lent by the Great Western Railway in 1930. They also were visited by an Inspector of Ancient Monuments, presumably to discuss their future (Gray 1931, xxx). The excavation site was let to the Castle Hotel for a garden in 1933 (Gray 1933, xxiv) and an aerial photograph taken in May of that year (SANHS 13249) shows the landscaping work well underway.

Gray's finds

The notebooks contain a list of 16 finds made during the better-documented parts of the excavation; some are numbered in the text and some are located on the plan (Figure 3.4 on page 40) and section (Figure 3.6 on page 44). These are indicated by T, P, and S appended to Gray's list below.

1. Disc of lead, diam 1½ins. Cutting I, depth 1.5ft. [P]
2. Bowl of clay tobacco-pipe, now black, marked L on heel; XVII century. Cutting I, depth about 2ft. at top or near top of red marl. [P]
3. Nuremberg casting jetton, depth 6.5ft. Cutting I *c.* AD 1660. [TP]
4. Bowl of clay tobacco-pipe, rather small - no mark. Fd. at a depth of 7ft beside the most northerly piece of walling in cutting I.
5. 2 fragments of pottery found on the west side of Cutting II at a depth of 7.5ft. [PS]
6. Pottery (several fragments), apparently medieval – possibly 16th century. Found in Cutting II near the modern walls, depth 5.2ft in mixed red marl, blacka[?] earth and 'rubbish'. [TPS]
7. Pottery similar to 6, found in the red marl of bank near the surface. Cutting III. [PS]
8. Frag of pottery found under no 6 at a depth of 6.3ft below the surface. Cutting II. [TPS]
9. Fragts of medieval (?) pottery. Found 2ft below the surface in the puddled red marl of the rampart. Cutting II. [PS]
10. Greater part of pottery vase of buff colour. Found in E extension of Cutting I, depth 7.75 ft below the surface. [P]
11. Fragments of pottery found in the turret [deleted and replaced by well] debris, depth 14.5ft below the surface of the ground. [T]
12. Pin of brass or bronze, length 2 11/16 (68mm). Found in tracing the northward wall south of the turret [deleted and replaced by well]. Depth about 4.5ft. [T]
13. Handle and part of rim and spout of a glazed jug apparently of Norman or early medieval date. Found in Cutting II near the modern wall, depth 5.4ft in mixed red marl, black a[?] earth and 'rubbish'. [S]
14. Farthing of Charles I [footnote added "struck from AD 1636"] Obv. CAROLV. D.G. MA. BRI. marked with ? roso[?] = Sceptre and crown as on the preceding. Rev. FRA. ET HI. REX marked with crescent = crowned roso. Found in the E extension of the S end of Cutting I, on level of rubble walling, depth below surface 7.8ft. [TP]
15. Bone knife-handle orne? [?] at the butt with crossed double lines forming lozenge-shaped interspaces. Found in the E extension of the S end of Cutting I, depth below surface 4ft. [TP]
16. Clay tobacco-pipe XVII century, marked AND/REWR/??? Found in E extension at the S end of Cutting I. Depth 6ft. [TP]

It is clear that these are not the only finds: several published ones, such as the spoon (Gray 1930b) and "corbel" (Gray 1941; Rodwell 1984b) from the well are not listed and examination of the museum collection has discovered large quantities of medieval pottery body-sherds that probably come from the later clearance work, see page 118.

Landscaping, 1933

The Joel photographs (see Figure 8.7 on page 160) give some additional information on Gray's excavation method and the subsequent landscaping by the Castle Hotel. To the south of Wall A an area had been cleared down to the level of the wall's foundations. This was wider at the east (around the southern projection, A3–A5) and very narrow at the west end of Wall A. There was then a substantial baulk before a further trench exposing Wall B. Wall F can be seen running into the baulk from Wall B and it would appear that Wall G lay within the baulk and had not been found by Gray. There are further, less well-defined trenches to the east into the raised platform which follows the eastern wall and which appears unexcavated to the north. This platform slopes down westwards across the centre of the site until it reaches another area of trenching to the east of Wall C.

Substantial areas of archaeological deposit were removed during the landscaping, primarily from the south and south-east of the site, and these appear to have been used to raise and level the central area.

Gray's Methodology and Results

It is clear that Gray's methodology was to open linear trenches that were excavated in spits (probably of a standard depth, though this is not given). Finds were recorded and some notes taken. The trenches were extended when walls were located and then mostly backfilled. The methodology appears to have changed after the discovery of substantial walls (A and B). After this fewer notes were taken, no plans are known, Young the experienced foreman was not employed and the work appears to have been clearance rather than excavation with large quantities of spoil carted off to raise the ground level in Taunton cattle market.

Further unrecorded ground-level changes were made during the landscaping works of 1933 but it is hard to characterise these last two episodes as not being archaeologically recorded in view of the minimal record of the earlier work.

As Rodwell (1978, 1) noted, "The excavations of 1924–9 were conducted at a much lower standard than might have been expected for the period" and this is in stark contrast to Gray's other excavations (for example, at Avebury) which are recognised as some of the finest of his generation. It would appear that Gray had little interest in medieval archaeology, and thus little knowledge of the structures and deposits that might be encountered. It is specifically likely that Gray would not have recognised the subtle trenches and debris left by wall robbing and therefore would have missed many pieces of ephemeral evidence for structures. He did, however, suggest that he found a robber trench for the north curtain wall (Vivian-Neal and Gray 1940, 65) but this was probably cutting simple deposits. It may also be that Gray's indifference extended to the belief that such recent remains were not worth recording but were merely to be exposed. This may be indicated by his description of the work as being carried out under his "general supervision" (Vivian-Neal and Gray 1940, 63n), seemingly to distance himself from responsibility. It is clear from recent re-excavations (below) that Gray uncovered more than he reported, and that some things that were exposed contradict his interpretations. Gray may have been confused by his findings: the 17th-century finds from the "Norman" well are overlooked, perhaps deliberately, and, appearing not to be very interested in medieval archaeology anyway, he was disinclined to publish.

3.5 The Electricity Showroom, 1937

Gray recorded the excavation for a cellar to the south of Castle Bow in 1937 (see Figure 15.1 on page 244). Much of the hole had been dug by mechanical excavator but Gray was able to record a revetment on the inner side of the moat together with a wall which crossed the moat and the area behind the revetment. The finds were of mixed date from the 14th to the 18th centuries but Gray doesn't indicate from where on the site they came only that they were "mostly in the lower levels" (Vivian-Neal and Gray 1940, 56–8).

3.6 The Moat, 1940

Gray carried out some limited trial excavations during 1940 in an attempt to trace the moat. In October he excavated three holes along the north side of the Great Hall and 20 feet from it. No other indication is given of their location except that they were "at points far apart". The average depth reached was 6.75 feet when water ingress prevented further digging. The upper deposits were "made ground" with silt below that and only modern finds were recovered (Vivian-Neal and Gray 1940, 55n). In November a further pit was excavated at the junction of the inner and outer moats to the west of the Great Hall. Here,

Figure 3.7: Posed press photograph of the excavations of 1952 with Trench II being started by two labourers. Linda Witherill, who worked on the excavation and is measuring the west wall, suggests that the woman in Trench 1 is Mrs Hallam, with Ralegh Radford and AD Hallam studying a plan to the rear right. The brick supports for the former wooden floor can be seen as can wooden scaffolding poles erected along the north wall. On the rear wall the scar of a vault is visible. SANHS 12569

the hole was excavated to 8.5 ft reaching "dark silt and water" (Vivian-Neal and Gray 1940, 55n).

3.7 The Great Hall, 1952

In 1951, grants were obtained from the Carnegie Trust and Museums Association for new cases and displays in the Great Hall and Somerset Room subject to building repairs being carried out beforehand (Seaby 1951, 5). Other grants were obtained for this work and the need for funds may also have been the reason for the sale of land (now Goodland Gardens) to the borough council early in 1952 (Anon 1952, 3, 7). The building work seems to have taken about a year from October 1952 until at least November 1953 when the new floor is reported to have been laid (Anon 1953, 2). The society decided to use the opportunity to excavate under the Great Hall before the area was sealed by the new concrete floor and this was undertaken under the direction of CA Ralegh Radford and AD Hallam. Little provision appears to have been made for any above-ground recording during the works but some notes were made by the excavators and a few photographs survive.

Since Radford's death in 1998, his work at other sites, such as Tintagel and Glastonbury Abbey (Barrowman *et al.* 2007, 3–32; Gilchrist 2013; Gilchrist and Green 2015), has been criticised in the light of modern knowledge while acknowledging that he was working in an era when no set methodologies for excavation or building recording had been established. At Tintagel he appears to have rarely visited the site, relying on workmen to expose ruined walls, while he seems to have taken a more hands-on approach to Glastonbury. It is not clear how much time he spent at Taunton Castle but it may be that Hallam (the keeper of geology at the museum) undertook much of the day-to-day supervision.

What seems most surprising to modern eyes is their digging of trenches into the earth beneath the suspended timber floor as if excavating in a

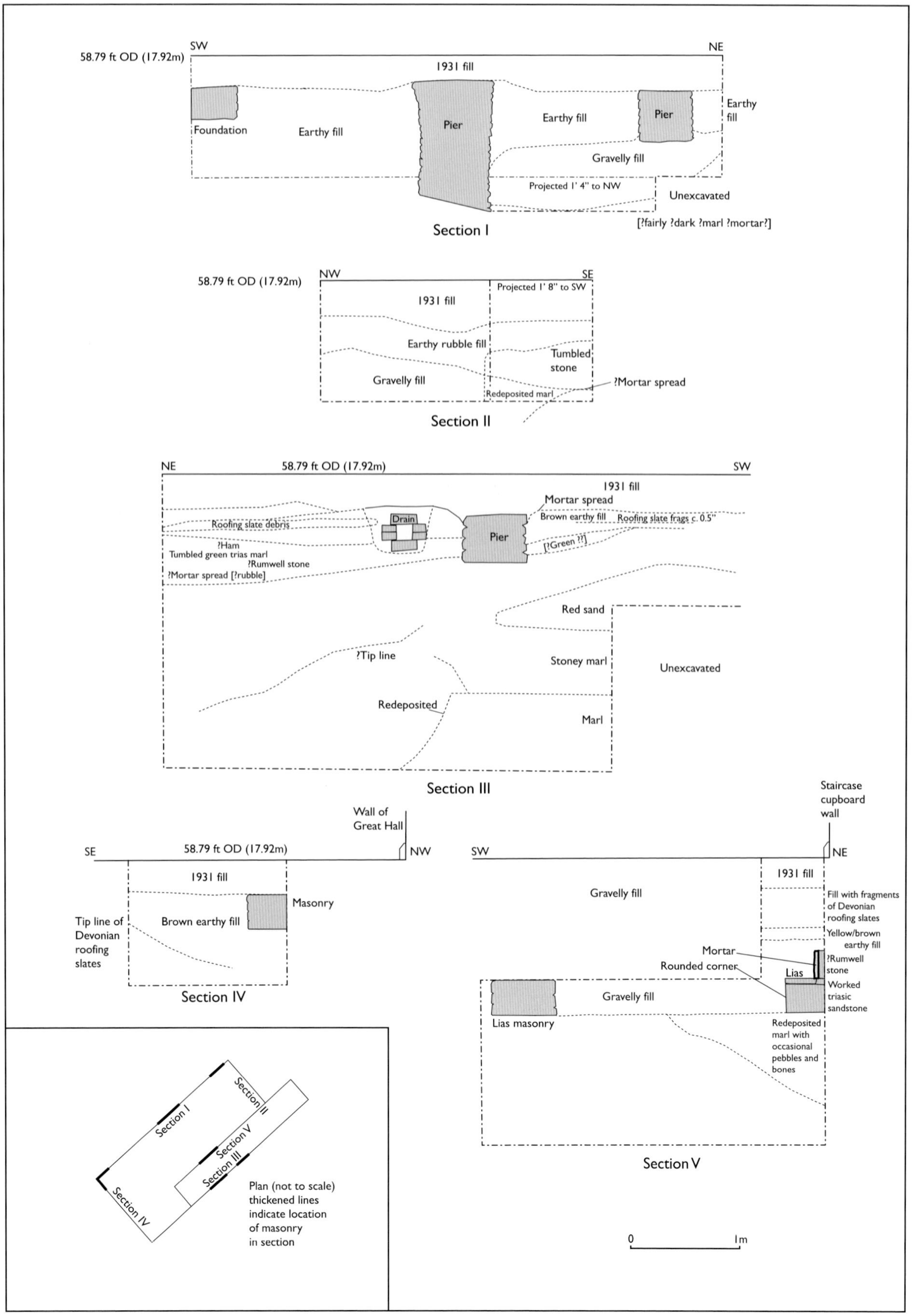

Figure 3.8: *Beam Engine pit, 1956. Sections redrawn from SANHS 6069 (I and II), SANHS 6068 (III), SANHS 6067 (IV and V).*

grassed field. No attempt was made to examine the surface, which when this was done in 2009 revealed great complexity, but it must be remembered that this was 20 years before the full development of open-area excavation. Perhaps the greatest difference, however, is the assumption that there was an "answer" and that men like Radford (and Gray before him) were able to provide it.

The work was published the following year (Radford and Hallam 1953) and this gives a good account of the excavation together with other observations on the castle and its buildings. The site plan made during the work survives in the Society's collections (SANHS 6066) together with some photographs (SANHS 12565–12571, TTNCM 48/2004/7a, see Figure 3.7 on page 48). Most of these appear to be posed press photographs and concentrate on work in progress rather than features discovered. They are also taken from a very limited number of locations leaving some crucial areas unrecorded. The site drawings additionally provide records of some structural features in the Great Hall (not all of which appear in the published report). Some further examination of the building works appears to have taken place (probably by Hallam) as the location of an embrasure has been added to the plan (SANHS 6066) with the date 10/12/52.

It should be noted here that the datum height on the section in the published report (Radford and Hallam 1953, Fig. 2) is clearly wrong; measurements from surviving doorways drawn by Hallam and Radford suggest that it is exactly 3 feet too high and that it should have read 61.09 feet. However re-excavation in 2009 allowed a calculation of 60.63 feet to be made on the basis of the height of the north wall offset.

The photographs show that the excavation proceeded in tandem with the lifting of the wooden floor (Figure 3.7 on page 48). The floor joists can be seen to have been supported on brick dwarf walls, three courses high, resting on the deposits below. Several trenches were excavated by labourers in these deposits, which suggested to Radford and Hallam that most floor layers had been removed by the digging out of the void for the timber floor. Several walls and robbing trenches were recorded however, which showed an earlier structure on the site (Hall I) and successive lengthenings of the present hall (Hall II) to the east.

The evidence for Hall I comprised the robbed foundations of an eastern wall and a central wall which ran between two barrel-vaulted chambers, the shapes of which could be seen as scars in the present west wall (see Figure 3.7 on page 48). The southern wall lay outside the present hall and joined the southern end of the undercroft of the Somerset Room. The hall was replaced by a ground-floor, narrower, longer hall (Hall II), subsequently extended to the east to form the present structure. Radford reconstructed Hall I as a timber-framed structure standing on the stone vaults with a stone Camera (Somerset Room) to the west. Below Hall I a "marl bank" was encountered which was believed to have formed the earliest defences of the castle.

At the east end, it was clear that there was a lot of later disturbance, most of which was assigned to the Civil War. This included the numerous pits that "can be attributed to the bombardment" (Radford and Hallam 1953, 73). A well was discovered that appeared to have been filled with debris from the conflict, including fragments of armour. In addition to the published account there are photographs of the well in the museum collection (PCFILE 1).

3.8 The Beam Engine Pit, 1956

Our only knowledge of the deposits removed by the insertion of a beam engine in a pit in the Wyndham entrance block is a series of drawings (SANHS 6067–6069) showing the sections revealed. It is not clear if the excavation was observed, or just the finished hole. The lack of plans, or indication whether the masonry recorded in section continued across the hole suggests the latter. The lack of publication may indicate that nothing considered significant was found but the drawings show several masonry structures, some described as "piers" that were possibly (but wrongly, see page 180) interpreted as the foundations for the Grand Jury Room.

One of these foundations extended to at least 1.35m below the floor level (ie below 16.57m aOD). The deposits around and below these masonry structures are less easy to interpret from the drawings but stratigraphy was recorded down to 15.3m aOD; it is not clear if all this is anthropogenic but in most areas there appears to be at least 1m of archaeological deposits. Tip lines recorded in the deposits suggest large pits or ditches in this area. The sections further indicate that, contrary to the impression given by photographs taken during the construction of the building, (SANHS 12550–12552) there is about 0.25m of floor make-up (described as "1931 fill") including the concrete floor.

Chapter 4

Investigations for Somerset County Council, 1958–2006

Chris Webster

In the 1950s, SANHS found it increasingly difficult to finance the running of the museum and sought to transfer it to public ownership. Somerset County Council (SCC) was sympathetic and gave grants, but did not have the legal power to run museums. The necessary powers were obtained by act of parliament and SCC were able to take over the running of the museum from SANHS in 1958 when the staff transferred to become the County Museum Service. The castle "(uninhabited parts)" was added to the Schedule of Ancient Monuments in December of that year. The council extended the Wyndham Galleries eastwards, as had originally been planned, in 1959 and converted the ground floor of Castle House to education use with toilets added in the following year. The curator's accommodation became a flat on the upper floors.

With the appointment of Mick Aston as the first archaeologist in the Planning Department in 1974, the council took a more active role in archaeological work in the county including at the castle. The strengthening of Ancient Monuments legislation in 1979 also meant that works should, in future, be carried out in a more controlled way with provisions for archaeological monitoring.

4.1 Fuel Oil Pipe, 1963

The section drawing by Jeboult, (SANHS 3525, described on page 33) additionally records a later pipe trench. Immediately inside the inner (northern) arch of the gatehouse a square area of walling has been added in pencil and annotated "Footings of blocks of hard green Triassic marl exposed 1963 while digging trench for fuel-oil pipe. [initials - probably A D Hallam's] 26.11.1963". The northernmost wall, in the courtyard, is annotated "not seen 1963" and a mark 10.25m from the external (southern) face of the gatehouse is indicated as "straight joint in wall". A drawing (SRO M2-801) shows the route of the pipeline running close to the east side of the entrance passage which may explain the differences as the sewer trench is likely to have been more central.

4.2 The Gray Room, 1964

In a similar manner to that adopted in 1952, building works to turn the former entrance to the museum (Room 43) into the Harold St George Gray Memorial Library were preceded by trenching and recording by AD Hallam (see Figure 5.25 on page 93). The results were published the following year (Hallam 1965) but no other records are known with the exception of slides in the Somerset HER collection (SCCHER 30053–30057, 30104). The work showed that the room had been added to the southern end of the camera block at a slight angle to it, with its west wall now forming part of the curtain wall of the inner ward.

Radford and Hallam (1953) had suggested that this structure was a porch containing a staircase but no trace of internal structures was found. Only the north-west and north-east doors (Doors 59 and 62) were original, the others being products of the late 18th-century renovations. This included the wide arch (Door 66) on the south east side where foundations for the solid wall (TCC 1031) beneath it were found and left partly visible in an inspection pit. Hallam suggested that the tooling on the passage to Door 62 was similar in style to that of the outer arch of the inner gate and thus the building was contemporary with the setting-out of the inner ward, which he dated on documentary evidence to 1210. Later the Camera (Room 103) was extended over the room necessitating the thickening of the east wall to maintain the line of the east wall of the Camera.

4.3 The Western Archaeological Trust

The Western Archaeological Trust (and its predecessor the Committee for Rescue Archaeology in Avon, Gloucestershire and Somerset, CRAAGS) carried out various small pieces of recording in and around the castle, most published in *The Archaeology of Taunton* (Leach 1984a). The volume includes a discussion on the historical information (Bush and Meek 1984), Gray's excavations (Pearson 1984b) and a survey of the surviving remains in the keep garden (Rodwell 1984a), as well as excavation reports.

The Coin Room, 1972

Colin Clements (1984, 26–8) undertook excavations and recording during changes to the Coin Room (Room 40) to form the Local History Library in 1972, locating burials and a well. Draft texts for the publication give some additional information but it has not proved possible to locate the original site records and plans (SRO DD/WAT/16 Fii10 and Fii11).

Landscaping works on Castle Green, 1972–3

Landscaping of Castle Green was monitored, resulting in the recording of the area along the south side of the moat revealing numerous post-medieval pits with some burials recovered from deeper excavations. In the Castle Hotel carpark, work disturbed a section of wall with a doorway (Figure 4.1, for location see Figure 6.1 on page 98). The work was published in summary by Clements (1984, 35–6) but further details and plans are given in an earlier unpublished report (Clements 1973).

In the area along the south side of the moat, where a curved corner was introduced to the wall, human bone was recovered from the new foundation trench. Burials were also recovered from a drainage trap 1.8m deep on the opposite side of the castle drive. Shallow post-medieval pits were recorded from the area of the path to the south of the moat wall (excavated to 0.4m) but no other archaeological features were noted to the south despite excavation to depths of between 0.3m (in the area subsequently grassed) and 0.5m (the pavement to the south).

Figure 4.1: *Wall found in the Castle Hotel carpark in 1973. Somerset HER image 42854.*

In the carpark of the Castle Hotel, deeper excavations than those agreed beforehand uncovered (and removed a large part of) a stone wall (see Figure 4.1 and Figure 6.1 on page 98 for location). The wall, which ran east-west contained a doorway with two large pieces of masonry forming the jambs on the southern side. About three or four courses of wall survived at the west end where the presence of the castle drive wall had prevented its removal. A limited amount of excavation was undertaken around the wall which was found to be 2 feet thick (0.6m) with a stone rubble core that contained reused masonry. The two jamb stones were found to show diagonal tooling characteristic of 12-century work but had clearly been reused. They had been aligned with their best sides to the south and between them, on the line of the south face of the wall, was a line of vertically set slate slabs which appeared to retain a mortar and stone floor. This suggested that the interior of the building lay to the north of the wall. Below the wall and elsewhere was a carefully surfaced mortar floor separated from the wall by a layer of earth. No edge to this floor, which must represent an earlier building, was found.

Wall C, 1975

Clements (nd) recorded observations of Wall C in *c.*1975, which were written up for, but not used in, *The Archaeology of Taunton* (Leach 1984a). The observations were prompted by the discovery of a projecting block of foundation by the museum gardener, shown by an otherwise unexplained "m" on Fig. 4 in Leach (1984a). The foundation was clearly later than the wall and comprised mostly chert with some sandstone and lias and was interpreted as the base of a flight of steps shown on Spencer's 1875 plan. The location is suggested to have been that of a corner turret of the keep with the stair foundation utilising the remains as a firm base. Clements also noted the return of Wall C eastwards at this point (C2), which was not noticed again until 2004 (see page 56).

Courtyard water pipe trench, 1978

A water pipe was laid across the courtyard from Door 75, the strongroom, to an aquarium in the Wyndham block. The lower levels were excavated archaeologically and published (Clements 1984, 32–34, Fig. 9). The finds from the trench have been recovered from the excavator and incorporated in the finds reports in this volume.

The trench recorded three layers of 1930s courtyard surface (also seen in 2007–9), below which was a deposit of rubble which overlay three patches of cobbled surface. The heterogeneous nature of the rubble deposit suggested that it had been dumped to raise the level of the courtyard at some date in the 18th century. Below this, as well as the patches of cobbles, were a wall, parallel to the south range with dressed stone only to the north and suggested to date to the 14th-century on the basis of pottery from the construction trench (this may be the same wall as that seen in 1867, see page 33), another possible wall which stopped half-way across the trench and various drains and steel pipes. The label "steel pipes" may be mistaken as two lie on the line of known ceramic drains, and one appears to be shown with an expanded joint. Several postholes were recorded in the section.

At the north end of the trench, a bank of red-brown silty sand was seen which was identified by AD Hallam as the "marl bank" seen under the Great Hall in 1952. Clements (1984, 34) believed, however, that this was a natural alluvial deposit, which had by that date been observed in other areas around the town. It contained animal bone and other detritus at the top but below, only human bone was found. Clements states that some of the bones were "in groups" aligned on the Great Hall and suggests that this indicates reburial of disturbed bone from the Saxon cemetery. He elsewhere says that part of an intact burial was recorded (Clements 1984, 31).

The Keep Garden, 1977/78

Concerns about the deterioration of the ruins exposed and landscaped after Gray's excavations led to SANHS requesting CRAAGS to prepare a detailed survey of the site, which was done from December 1977 to February 1978 (Rodwell 1978). Some research was done into Gray's records and both reports were subsequently used to form parts of *The Archaeology of Taunton* (Rodwell 1984a; Pearson 1984c).

Benham's Garages, 1978

Benham's Garages (Leach and Pearson 1984) were sited to the west of the castle, between it and the area of St Paul. The area appeared to have been very wet at times in the past but there was evidence of timber buildings built on a layer containing a 10th-century brooch. These were superseded by a metalled road running east-west and appearing to date from the 13th century. This would have lain to the south of the road running west from the West Gate. Leach and Pearson (1984) say that wooden piles were seen on the same alignment when the cinema was constructed in the 1930s and believed these to be the structure of a bridge across the moat. The presence of this road would suggest an otherwise unknown gate in the west wall of the castle (see page 238 for a discussion of this). The road seems to have been overwhelmed by renewed flooding in the 14th century and the area then seems to have remained wet and unoccupied until the 18th century.

It is not clear how the watercourses seen at Benham's garages related to the moat, only a short distance to the east, although it was suggested by Leach and Pearson (1984) that the flooding in the medieval period may have been caused by attempts to divert the stream.

Mill Lane, 1980 and 1990

A small excavation was undertaken outside the north-east corner of the castle (Burrow, I 1984). This showed that the moat appeared to have been widened in the early post-medieval period truncating two medieval features: a pit and a leat, presumably related to the mill. Further work was undertaken over a slightly larger area in 1999, which relocated the leat and provided evidence that the moat had been narrower outside the 1980 excavation, before being infilled in the 17th and 18th centuries (Broomhead 1999).

Figure 4.2: *The collapsed section of Wall C in 1988. See Figure 4.5 on page 58 for location. Note the lack of solid wall core behind the facing stones. Somerset HER image 29721.*

Castle Bow, 1985

The repaving of the area between the East Gate and the Grammar School was monitored by Ian Burrow (Burrow, I and Dennison 1988, 174-76). The area was found to be very disturbed but the remains of the castle bank may have been located at the south end. Three phases of post-medieval steps into the school were identified. The foundations of the buttress on the south side of the East Gate were exposed, revealing two courses of undressed stone foundations above red clay, and a contractors pit immediately to the west of the north side of the gate exposed the head and shoulders of a human burial. Photographs of the work are in the HER collection and parts of the skull were retained in the County Museum (radiocarbon dated in 2013, see Table 7.5 on page 152).

Gazette Offices, Castle Street, 1985

Foundation trenches for a new office block on the site of the former County Gazette offices and printworks were recorded by Ian Burrow (Burrow, I and Dennison 1988, 176–78). The results supported the evidence from the Benham's Garage site (above) on the other side of the road to the south. Very little dating evidence was recovered and it appeared that the area had been very wet until reclaimed in the late post-medieval period.

4.4 The Round Tower, 1988

According to files held by Somerset County Council, and an interim report and photographs by Bob Croft, Scheduled Monument Consent was granted in September 1987 for several works to Taunton Castle, including stone conservation to the coats of arms above the gateway, laying a new path, repairing a collapse in the wall across the courtyard (see Figure 4.2) and various repairs to other buildings.

The repairs included the replacement of the suspended timber floor of the round tower (Room 46) which was carried out in February the following year. Following the removal of the old floor the site was inspected by Croft who noted a layer of sandy mortar below and it was agreed with the contractor that this should form the base for dwarf walls to support the new floor. A week later the contractors were found to have removed the mortar layer and were cutting a slot into exposed masonry along the base of the walls. The work was stopped and the area cleaned archaeologically. Removal of some of the loose material from the sub-floor of the tower showed that the original walls had been considerably thicker and that they had been reduced in thickness by Hammet during his restoration work (Figure 4.3 on the next page).

The present room is 20 feet (6.1m) in diameter and the original room is estimated at c.16 feet (4.8m). The mortar layer seen initially was interpreted as debris from the rebuilding and plastering and examination of a loose area showed that it was over 0.2m thick except where it ran over the base of the wall. The original room was eccentric to the tower to give a wall thickness of over 3m facing the exterior of the castle. The junction of the tower wall with the curtain wall to the east was not visible as a fireplace had been inserted at this point but another wall was seen running east to west below the present doorway into the tower room. This wall was composed of large grey "limestone" blocks and appeared to be that seen Hallam in 1964 (above, page 51). The wall of the tower appeared to butt against it (Croft 1988).

Hallam (1965) believed that the St George Gray Room (Room 43), round tower and curtain wall to the east were part of the documented "new wall" constructed in 1209 but the butt-join seen inside the tower appears to show that there are at least two phases of construction here. Inside the tower, it is clear that Hammet increased the size of the room by cutting back the internal wall and lining the tower, and the inserted window openings, with brick. In its original form the tower appears to have had a flattened back which was probably removed by Hammet and replaced by a thinner curved brick wall. The original wider foundation was seen when the staircase was added in 1910 (Spencer 1910, 39).

Figure 4.3: The lower room of the Round Tower (Room 46) under repair in 1988, looking south-east with Window 65 to the rear. The thicker medieval wall foundations can be seen as well as the late eighteenth-century brick lining to the walls and window reveals with characteristic embedded horizontal beams. Somerset HER image 53542.

4.5 The Gas Pipe Trench, 1988

Later in 1988 Scheduled Monument consent was sought for the replacement of heating oil supply pipes by gas pipes across the courtyard, reusing the original trench. This was granted in October with the condition that the work was archaeologically monitored. The only record of this monitoring appears to be colour slides in the Historic Environment Record and there is confusion as to whether a report was ever written. English Heritage requested one in September 1990 and the letter on file in SCC is endorsed "sent 18/9/90". English Heritage reiterated their request in March 1991 when they were told by Bob Croft that the watching brief on the driveway had been carried out, that the area was "already disturbed" and that therefore no report had been written. This, however, appears to refer to another piece of work when a burst water main had to be repaired. The 1988 work also involved using the gas trench to hold other services and the replaced central heating pipes for the South Range. A further trench was excavated across the north side of Castle House for the heating pipes which is shown in the slides and this must have removed without record part of a substantial wall (1187) seen in 2011 (see page 96).

4.6 Lord Harding's Statue, 1991

In 1991 the foundations for a statue of Lord Harding of Petherton were excavated by SCC staff just to the east of the then museum entrance. The only deposits encountered were the gravel surfaces of the courtyard, which are now known to date from the 1930s.

4.7 The Re-sited Almshouse, Trench I, 1992

In March 1992 foundation trenches for a reconstructed almshouse (that had previously stood in the moat) were excavated by Charles and Nancy Hollinrake, supervised by Peter McCrone of SCC (Hollinrake and Hollinrake 1992a). The whole footprint of the building, next to Wall C in the courtyard, was stripped of turf and topsoil down to a layer of rubble which was considered adequate substrate for the almshouse floor. Foundation trenches were then excavated through this and excavation was halted when medieval stratigraphy was encountered.

The excavators spent time attempting to correlate the deposits found with the supposed walls of buildings shown on Spencer's 1975 plans without success but it is apparent from more recent work (see page 59) that most traces of these structures have been removed from the area. It is also clear from the records that the plans were misaligned in 1992 so that no correlations could be expected.

Below the topsoil was a layer containing much broken slate which was interpreted as demolition of the buildings in the late 1870s and also levelling deposits of redeposited natural clay with building material fragments. Below these were the remains of what appeared to be a Lias stone wall, running north–south, and possibly associated with adjacent spreads of mortar. The wall (TC92:13) was only seen clearly in the southern part of the excavation but a possible continuation or robbing trench was seen on the same alignment in the northern part of the trench. As these were not excavated it was not possible to interpret them further. Excavation to the south in 2005 (see page 59) showed that the "wall" was a dump of stone (TCC05:9) with a straight boundary to the east giving the impression of a wall in plan.

4.8 The Toilet Block, Trench II, 1992

The foundations for a new toilet block, which was to be added along the southern wall of the Great Hall at the eastern end, were monitored by Charles and Nancy Hollinrake in June 1992 (Hollinrake and Hollinrake 1992b). The upper parts of the area were covered by a layer of loose reddish clay containing rubble and finds of 19th- and 20th-century date, over 0.6m deep. A number of recent service trenches had been cut into this deposit. Below this was a well-built drain constructed with stone walls and an arched brick top. Some of the stones in the walls were reused, including a chamfered block like those used in Walls A and C. One small area of intact medieval stratigraphy was seen in the side of the trench for the drain which appeared to comprise the remains of a wall with possible floor layers. The identification as a wall was based on its similarity to the "wall" (TC92:13) seen in the adjacent Trench I for the almshouse (see above) and so may be erroneous.

The foundations of the south wall of the Great Hall were also examined. An offset course was seen projecting between 0.1 and 0.14m out from the wall line. It was constructed from small, faced, stones, which were seen again in 2009.

4.9 The Lift Shaft Evaluation, 1992

Proposals to improve access to the Wyndham Galleries led to a small evaluation to assess the presence of archaeological deposits here; a location where they might have been removed by either Gray in the 1920s or by the construction of the gallery itself. The evaluation was undertaken by AC Archaeology (Hawkes 1992).

The trench was sited on the slope down to the platform on which the Wyndham Gallery had been constructed and revealed the remains of two walls. Wall AC72:4 ran east–west and was composed of "limestone" (probably blue lias) rubble in a mortary, gravelly clay. The northern face had been removed by the scarping and no facing stones were visible along the southern edge. Where the wall was visible in the sides of later features it appeared to have been constructed in a trench which had been partly filled with orange sandy clay containing occasional limestone blocks. A single sherd of 11th/12th-century pottery was recovered from this layer.

The second wall (AC72:7) was identical in composition to AC72:4 but contained larger stones and also appeared to have up to 3 courses (*c.*0.35m) of facing surviving on both its east and west sides. Wall AC72:4 appeared to butt up against the facing stones of Wall AC72:7. To the west of AC72:7 was a large feature (AC72:9), interpreted as one of the backfilled trenches excavated by Gray in the 1920s. The fill was mostly a loamy soil filling the gaps between unworked pieces of limestone (AC72:11) and this extended into a hole (AC72:13) dug into the top of Wall AC72:7. In the base of the hole the underlying deposit could be seen to be a reddish silty or sandy clay (AC72:14). The base of the main 1920s excavation trench (AC72:9) was very sharply defined and formed by a compacted pale orange clay surface becoming paler with depth which also overlay clay AC72:14.

4.10 Courtyard Wall Repairs, 2004–05

In 2004 it was decided that the wall across the courtyard (Wall C) was becoming very eroded and overgrown and Scheduled Monument Consent was obtained to repoint it. The west elevation of the wall was drawn stone-by-stone by the author at a scale of 1:20, together with the north-facing return, in July 2004 (Figure 4.5 on page 58). Further records were made during the works to repair the wall in June 2005, principally the location of the inner faces of the north end (C10–C12), the southern return (C2–C13) and parts of the east face of the wall, once the failed concrete capping had been removed. Locations on the wall have been labelled following the system used by Rodwell (1984a) whose sequence C1–C4 has been extended (shown on Figure 4.4 on the next page). The courses of the wall were lettered from E (foundation) and the stones in each course numbered from the north end.

The major part of the wall (C1–C5) was formed from a battered lower section with, in places, the remains of a vertical wall on top. To the north of this was a vertical section (C1–C8) which returned to the east (C8–C9). At the southern end the wall could be seen to return to the east at C2; beyond this (C2–C5) was a short section of wall that appeared to continue the coursing and beyond that was a mixed, vertical section (C5–C3) which ended at a Hamstone gate pier.

The main section of Wall C was 16.5m long and composed in its lower part of alternate courses of vertical and chamfered blocks. Four courses (K, M, P, R) of chamfered blocks were visible with the lowest (K) partly buried. Excavation (see Section 4.12 on page 59) showed that the wall was vertical below this lowest chamfered course with one vertical course (J) above the foundations. The effect of the chamfers was that the upper vertical wall was 34cm behind the excavated lower vertical face. The lowest two courses of this upper vertical face (S and T) may be coeval with the chamfered section but the courses above (U–X) appeared to be later. The pattern is continued in the southern return (C2–C13) where courses J to R were recorded in 2006.

The northern part of the wall (C1–C8–C9) was L-shaped in plan. The wall was vertical above the lowest chamfered course (K) which could be seen

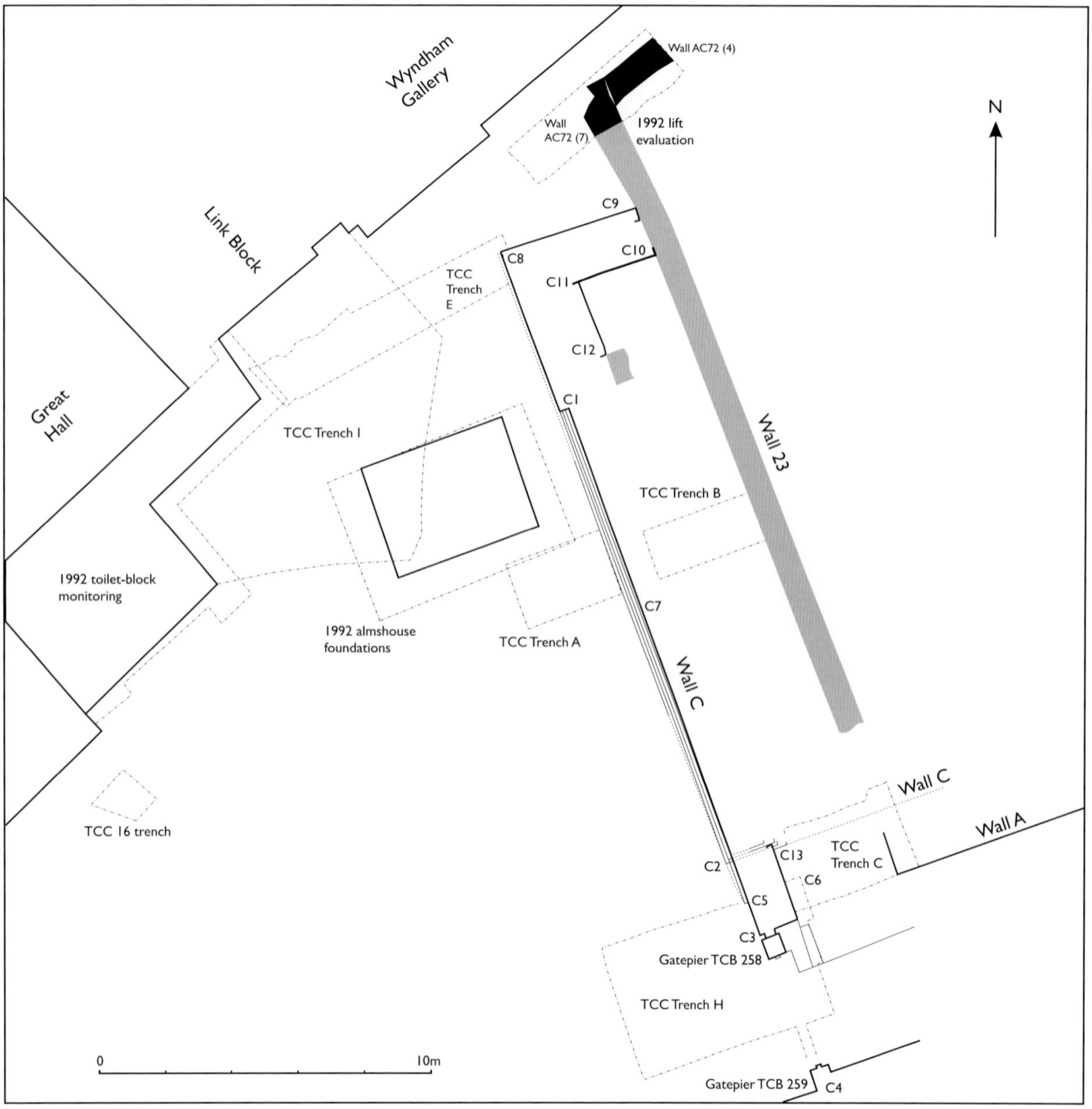

Figure 4.4: *The east part of the courtyard showing the locations of trenches and reference points on Wall C.*

to continue below course L for a short distance to the north of C1 before becoming buried by the rising ground. The rises of the courses (L–R) corresponded to those of the battered main section suggesting that they are contemporary.

During the ground clearance the tops of the rear faces of the wall were exposed (C10–C11–C12). The main wall was 1.9m thick and the northern return varied from 1.6m (at C11) to 1.5m (at C10). At C10 there appeared to be a vertical end to the wall but this could not be seen at C9 as the ground rose up; the wall was also lost to the south of C12 where it was disturbed by tree roots. In the corner (C11) two courses showed that wall C11–12 butted against C10–11.

To the south of the corner at C2, courses M to P were continued to C5 although smaller stones had to be used to achieve the rise of course N. Above this and to the south the wall had clearly been rebuilt in recent times with a hard cement mortar, irregular coursing, and a variety of stone types employed.

This rebuilding also extended to the north of C2 at higher levels. The rear of the wall showed similar rebuilding, mostly in chert, but between C6 and C13 where it butted against the wall return, it was built of squared ashlar blocks, seemingly unmortared. Limited examination below ground level at C13 showed that these had no foundations which may explain the slight

Figure 4.5: *Elevations of Wall C. See Figure 3 on page 4 for key to stone colours.*

irregularity of coursing (further investigated in Trench C, see page 61).

4.11 The Driveway Repaving, 2004

In 2004 it was decided to improve the accessibility of the museum by replacing the surfacing of the castle driveway. Prior to this the majority of the drive comprised chert cobbles with a line of standard concrete paving slabs along the east side, as far as the castle gateway. The cobbling was probably laid in 1937 (SANHS minutes: 6/1/1937) and has now been paved with Pennant sandstone sets. The area was recorded archaeologically after the removal of the chert cobbles in two phases in April and November 2004 (Figure 4.6). No deposits were disturbed below the sand or concrete bed of the driveway and the only features recorded appeared to relate to service trenches, some of recent date.

4.12 Wall C Excavation, 2005 (Trenches A and B)

Two trenches were excavated in the summer of 2005, one each side of Wall C with their southern sides aligned to give a long section through the wall and associated deposits (see Figure 4.4 on page 57). Trench A (to the west of the wall) was intended to investigate deposits seen but not excavated during the work on the almshouse (Hollinrake and Hollinrake 1992a) and to attempt to provide stratigraphic dating for the wall. The area of Trench B was known to have been cleared by Gray in the 1920s but it was hoped that re-excavation would supplement his very meagre records of the rear face of the wall.

Trench A

Natural deposits were encountered at the base of the trench and comprised a buried soil formed on a deposit of mid red-brown silty clay (59). A sondage was excavated through this which showed that the darker grey of the upper deposit gradually became lighter with depth and in places dark lines indicated where roots had carried darker humic material down. Patches of well-sorted gravel were also encountered suggesting an alluvial origin for this deposit. This soil seems identical to others located subsequently in the castle and also to that found under the town bank at Hawke's Yard (Leach 1984b, 67).

Wall C appeared to have been built directly onto this surface with only a very shallow (<5cm)

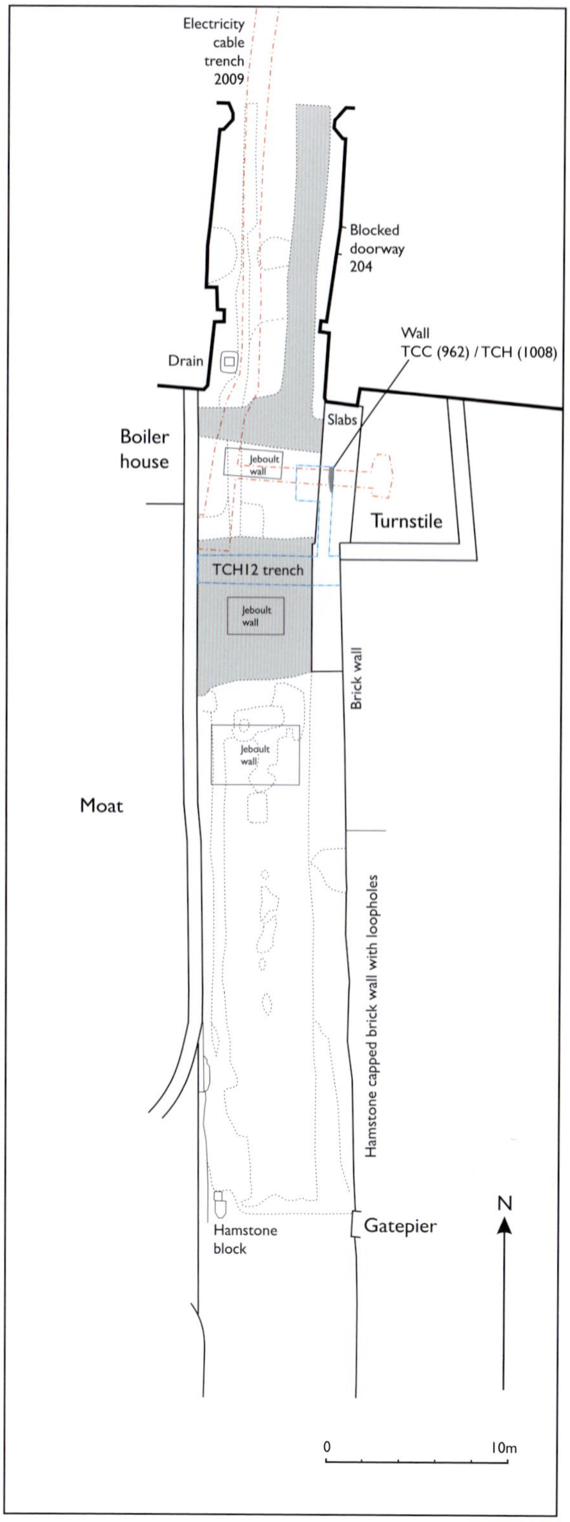

Figure 4.6: Plan showing deposits recorded beneath the cobbles of the driveway with locations of walls seen by Jeboult (Figure 2.3 on page 33) and service trenches dug in 2009 and 2012. Grey areas are earlier service trenches that had been backfilled with concrete.

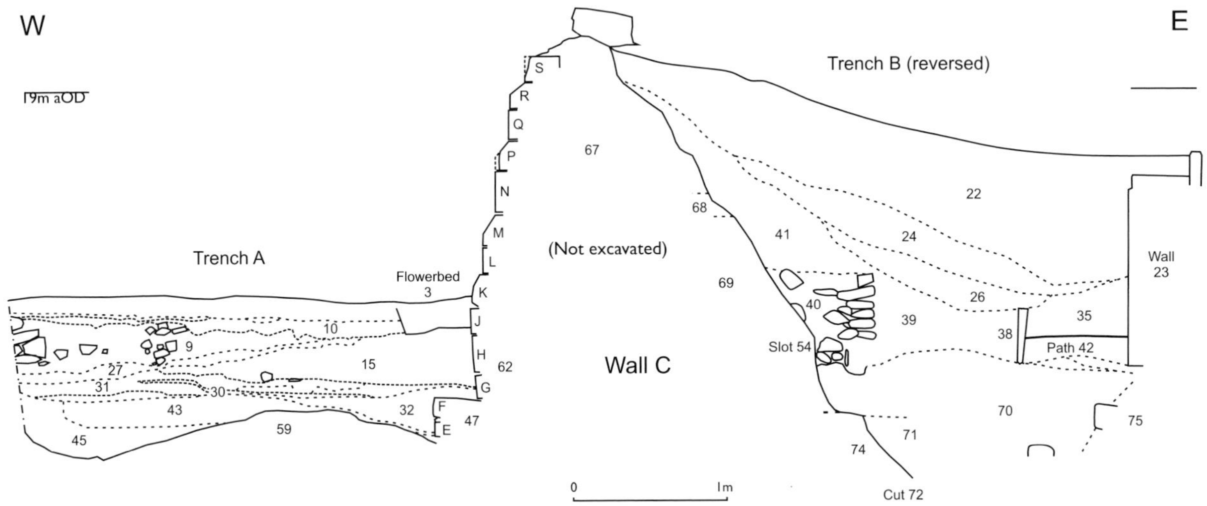

Figure 4.7: *South-facing section through Wall C in Trenches A and B*

construction cut, which suggests that it must be the earliest feature in this area. The foundations comprised two courses bedded in, and bonded with, a red gravelly clay. The wall itself was built off the very rear of the front stones of the foundation, 0.25m back, and its weight appears to have depressed the rear of the foundation stones. In some places the wall did not rest on the front stones and further foundation blocks were visible at these points. The top of the foundation offset retained traces of white mortar spreads which seemed to stop 10cm from the front. The first two courses of the wall proper were clearly also intended not to be seen as they were built with rounded blocks and large quantities of mortar. Above this was a course (J) of squared ashlar similar to those described in the face above (see page 56).

To the west of the wall, the buried soil surface was burnt in places and was overlain by a series of silty clay deposits (redeposited from the soil below), also associated with burning. Some of the deposits were stained dark with charcoal and appeared to fill cuts in the soil, one of which may have been a gully or ditch (63) running across the north-west corner of the trench. It was not possible to determine if these burning events pre- or post-dated the construction of the wall as they faded out before reaching it – although this may suggest in itself that the burning was later.

The burnt deposits were sealed by a layer of mortar (30) mixed with patches of stone fragments, orange gravel and brown clay which continued up to the face of Wall C. These may have been associated with the construction of the wall itself (which would suggest the burning predated the wall) and were covered by a wedge of clean dark red clay (15) which covered the foundations of the wall and thinned to nothing to the west. The clay, and several of the layers beneath it, contained pottery dating to the 11th-century and, as it appears to have been deposited deliberately to cover the foundations, this may indicate the date of the wall's construction.

Above this were further layers (such as 27, Figure 4.7) of construction/demolition waste comprising mortar, stone fragments and patches of gravel that were overlain by a thick layer (9) containing larger stones, 19th-century pottery and brick. This layer appears to be the same as that interpreted as the top of a wall (TC92:13) when seen in plan in 1992 (see page 55) but no wall face or coursing was apparent. Layer 9 was also the first layer to contain pottery later in date than the 11th and 12th centuries, indicating reduction of the ground level perhaps associated with the construction of buildings against Wall C.

The uppermost deposits (such as 10, Figure 4.7) represented the use of the area as a garden, including a flowerbed (3) along the wall which cut various thin soils and deposits interpreted as spoil from the 1992 excavations.

Trench B

Trench B revealed, as expected, that most of the deposits relating to the castle had been removed by Gray's workmen, but the core (67 on Figure 4.7) of Wall C survived sloping steeply down and composed of layers of chert blocks bedded in red clayey gravel identical to that recorded in the footings in Trench A. Various changes (68, 69) were noted in the composition of this core but were not investigated further. A small area of the core was removed at the very top but no other stonework was found indicating that the western face of the wall is only one block thick. A similar situation was found behind a facing block (N55), which was removed and reset during the works.

It was not possible to excavate in detail below the level of the base of the wall core but this appeared to be resting on a similar red-brown silty clay with a burnt upper surface (74) to that in Trench A. It appears that Gray's workmen continued to excavate through this following the sloping line of the wall-core (cut 72), although they may have been following earlier robbing activity that had produced the slope. A stone structure (75) of some kind was partly visible beneath a later wall (23); this may have been the base level of the chert and clay wall core but safety considerations precluded detailed examination.

Following Gray's excavation, the area was landscaped by the construction of Wall 23, parallel to Wall C, built of large blocks of stone (and at least one of concrete) bonded with a hard cement mortar, with a decorative rustic course along the top. At the foot of the wall (1.55m down) a path (42) was discovered 0.65m wide with a line of vertically set stones (38) forming its western edge. The rear of the wall core appeared to have been left exposed and a rough drystone revetment wall (40) had been dug into the back of the core to arrest the erosion of the slope.

Finds from the remainder of the fill of the area suggested a date in the 1960s when the area was levelled to the top of Walls C and 23. It was subsequently discovered that this was undertaken in 1962 with the assistance of the Ministry of Works. The area was surveyed in early February (SCC CB 35/1/5) and the completion of the work is recorded in July (SRO A/CNT/4/1: 6/7/1962). The SCC elevation drawing of the east side of Wall C shows a higher area in the centre and the section drawings to either side of this higher section show the rear of Wall C (described as "rubble and earth") sloping down to a level area that reaches to the base of Wall 23. The top of Wall 23 is indicated as "garden", presumably a flower bed, with a footpath to its east. The central section through the higher area shows a different arrangement: Wall C is shown as 3 ft thick (0.9m) with a vertical eastern face. At the base of this face is a gully 2 ft (0.6m) deep and 1 ft 9 in (0.53m) wide with a rounded base. The gully is shown on the elevation drawing as extending along the whole length of the higher section of the wall. This situation is not shown on the 1932/33 photographs (Joel 15) where the east side of Wall C is shown as an eroding bank along its whole length and this does not appear to have changed after the landscaping in 1933 (SANHS Photos 1934). Finally the 1962 SCC drawing has had a pencilled line added to each section showing the ground profile as encountered in 2005, indicating that these drawings were used when planning the infilling.

No finds earlier than *c.*1600 were discovered in the trench and the post-medieval material was residual in later features, such as imported garden soil and the backfill of Gray's trench. A dump of stone (35) on the 1930s path (42), presumably the beginning of the 1962 infilling, contained exclusively 17th/18th century material and may represent the products of disturbance elsewhere.

Other areas investigated

Removal of the concrete capping of Wall C to the south of the trenches allowed the recording of the rear of the face where it stood above the clay and chert core. This showed areas of plastering and also a line of bricks set into the wall as a horizontal course. These suggested the base of a fireplace but no other evidence for this (such as burning of the wall above) was found.

One further small area was excavated, at the southern end of the wall to accommodate foundations for the new capping. This uncovered the return of the wall towards the east but was otherwise entirely within the backfill of Gray's trench.

4.13 Wall C and Moat Excavation, 2006 (Trenches C and D)

The wall return discovered in 2005 at the southern end of Wall C was further investigated in the following year, in conjunction with proposals to create access ramps in that area of the garden. The opportunity was also taken to excavate a trench in the moat to the south of Castle House to investigate the possibility that a round tower had stood there as described by Warre (see page 33).

Trench C

The trench (3.5m x 2.5m) was opened by hand in the area between the rear of Wall C and the apparent end of Wall A in October 2006 (Figure 4.4 on page 57). The deposits that were removed were very mixed but it became clear that this was due to their all being dumped material, either from the 1933 landscaping or the subsequent infilling of the area behind Wall C in 1962. Once this was established the material was removed without recording down to the base of Gray's, and later construction, trenches.

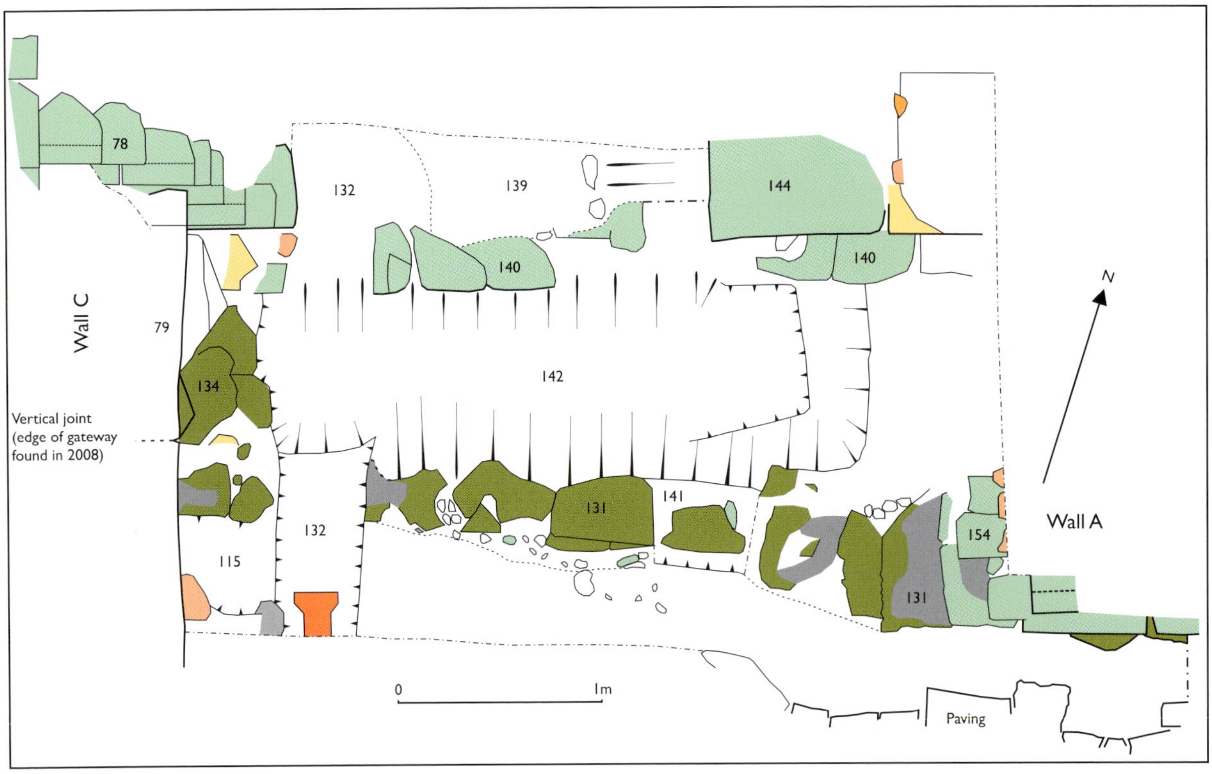

Figure 4.8: Plan of Trench C. For location see Figure 4.4 on page 57. See Figure 3 on page 4 for key to colours.

Figure 4.9: The east end of Trench C showing Wall C turning eastwards (Wall 78) behind the extension (Wall 79). The scale lies on the foundations (140) and in the foreground are the foundations of the predecessor to Wall A (131). Scale 1m.

Figure 4.10: *The west end of Trench C showing the rubble infill of Wall A, whose facing stones are visible to the right. Below these are the foundations (131) and on the left is reconstructed Wall 144. Scales 1m and 30cm.*

Four structural elements were exposed by this work: the southern extension of Wall C (here numbered 79) and its foundations (134), the return of Wall C (78) and its foundations (140), Wall A (154), and the foundations (131) of a wall beneath Wall A and seemingly on a different alignment (Figure 4.8 on the preceding page).

Wall 78 was exposed in the north-west corner of the trench where it consisted of an offset foundation course (140) above which were three vertical courses (G, H, J), a chamfered course (K) and a final vertical course (L). These courses correspond to those recorded on the west face of Wall C. The wall extended about 0.45m east from the rear of Wall C, beyond this it had been robbed. The area to the east of the end of the wall had been disturbed by the construction of a soakaway (132), fed from the south by modern ceramic drain pipes in a trench that had cut through the foundations. The foundations, however, continued beyond the disturbance in the form of a line of three stones (140), with a straight southern edge, retaining a wall-core of compacted gravel and clay (139). This core was similar to that seen at the rear of Wall C and was also visible behind Wall 78, although there were no chert cobbles present at foundation level. Eastwards, again, the foundations had been removed, probably by the construction of a cement-mortared wall (144) whose corner lay in the trench and which had been seen in Trench B (as Wall 23). The southern face of Wall 144 lay, in part, on a continuation of foundations 140 and to the east was unmortared, appearing identical to Wall 78. Taken together this evidence suggests that Wall 78 was originally continuous from the corner with Wall C for an unknown distance eastwards. It would appear unlikely that Gray would not have noticed this wall, although much of it was probably robbed prior to his excavations (but see below). Part of the wall was later incorporated in Wall 23 and the steps up to the garden path.

Wall foundation 131 ran across the trench from east, where it appeared to form the foundations of Wall A, to west where it joined the foundations of Wall 79. It lay at a higher level than the foundations of Wall 78 and seems to have limited the southern side of Gray's trench. It comprised a single line of stones with a straight southern edge and an irregular northern one. The stone appeared to be Morte slate, otherwise uncommon in the Castle, and was in poor condition. The foundations had been laid in a construction trench (141) and packed with sandy mortar containing small packing pieces of sandstone. The northern side of the construction trench had been removed by Gray, although it is possible that his excavation trench followed an earlier disturbance as no construction-trench edge was visible in the section to the east. The foundations appeared to be on a slightly different alignment to that of Wall A, although removal of some of the paving showed that they continued under the wall without emerging from it as might have been expected if the line of their southern face had been projected. In view of this, and the use of a different stone, it seems that these foundations were for an earlier wall and were partly reused when Wall A was built.

Examination of the rear of Wall A showed that it appeared to be a single skin of grey North Curry sandstone blocks backed by a very mixed deposit (151) containing gravel, clay and stone blocks. It is possible, however, that a rear face to Wall A was visible although, if this was not fortuitous in the one section seen, it was extremely loosely constructed and not coursed with the face of the wall. The deposit (151) behind the wall, which was only seen in section, could not be distinguished from material that appeared to form the backfill of robbing trenches for Wall 78 and may be entirely a robbing backfill deposit.

Unfortunately the relationship of foundations 131 with those (134) of Wall 79 was unclear as this area had been removed by the pipe trench (132) leading to the soakaway and also disturbed by a probable planting hole (115). Foundations 134, however, contained Morte slate and may have been part of 131 but they also appeared different in character, being deeper and containing other materials: North Curry sandstone and Hamstone. It is therefore possible that foundations 134 were later and incorporated Morte slate from disturbance of foundation 131. Foundations 134 butted against Wall 78 and were clearly later. The foundations did not seem to be bonded to the wall (79) above them, indeed in places there appeared to be a thin layer of earth between, but without further investigation it was not possible to disentangle the sequence.

The evidence from Trench C showed that Wall C (including Wall 78) is the earliest with Wall A built later. It is possible that Wall 78 was seen by Gray as he refers to Wall A as an "apron-wall" and excludes it from his measurements of the keep (Vivian-Neal and Gray 1940, 63).

Only a very few finds were made, and since none was medieval and all were from modern contexts, none was retained.

Trench D

Warre (1853) stated, that he had seen the foundations of a round tower at the eastern end of Castle House, which would have formed a symmetrical front about the gatehouse. The existence of this tower is further supported by the presence of a curving wall (105) butted against the southern wall of Castle House. Trench D was sited to attempt to locate these foundations and lay in the corner between the curving wall and the southern curtain wall of the inner ward. It was not possible to excavate immediately adjacent to the curtain wall due to the presence of the brick-lined gully (103) on a deep concrete base shown in Houghton Spencer's 1912 drawing (Figure 3.3 on page 38) and still visible in places on the surface.

The trench was excavated to a maximum depth of 1.2m without encountering any deposits earlier than the late 19th century and without reaching the base of either Wall 105 or the concrete foundations of gully 103. Within these deposits, however, was found an earlier yard surface composed of chert blocks (126) which had been cut by various linear features, running north-south, before the gully and its foundations had been inserted.

All the finds were late-19th or 20th century in date and none was retained.

Chapter 5

Investigations for The Museum of Somerset Project, 2007–2011

Chris Webster

Plans to improve the museum crystallised in 2005 with the aim of securing a Heritage Lottery Fund grant for the works, and in 2006 Feilden Clegg Bradley were appointed as architects. They developed a design that was intended to have minimal impact on the historic structure. The main areas of new-build were the construction of an entrance replacing and extending the Link Block and the widening of the West and East Passages to house a cafe and toilets. The timber balcony in the Great Hall would be replaced by a steel-framed walkway providing exhibition space on two floors with views down to the mosaic from High Ham Roman villa that would form the centre-piece of the displays.

It was not possible to evaluate the area of the Great Hall while the museum was still open but the East and West Passage areas were investigated in 2007 to ensure that construction was possible without seriously compromising important deposits. The new entrance required the removal of the reconstructed almshouse that had been sited in the courtyard in 1992 and a new site was chosen adjacent to Castle House. The area for this was archaeologically excavated in 2008.

Detailed plans of the existing buildings were prepared by the author and subsequently by the Greenhatch Group for the architects; the latter work included laser-scanning the exterior to produce elevation drawings. Stonework detail was added to the elevations by the author.

Once funding and permissions for the project were in place, the footprints of the new East and West Passages and the Entrance were excavated down to a level just below the proposed concrete floors and beams. This work was undertaken as a community project, in two two-week seasons using local volunteers during 2008.

Building work on the project started in 2009 with the main contractor being Henry Pollard of Bridgwater, who had built the Wyndham Galleries in the 1930s. All the works were monitored and further building records made when plaster was stripped. A watching brief was maintained on the works in the Great Hall but it soon became apparent that the foundations would be more destructive to the archaeological remains than the plans suggested, and that those remains were more significant than Radford's records implied. It was agreed with English Heritage that the trenches would be excavated archaeologically.

In the courtyard, construction excavations went slightly deeper than originally stated and these were monitored and recorded during the building works in 2009. The limited groundworks for the repaving of the courtyard were monitored during 2010–11.

5.1 The Entrance Building, 2007–08 (Trenches E and I)

Trench E (see Figure 4.4 on page 57 for location) was sited in an area between the previous excavations of 1992 (see page 55). These had shown, on the one hand, undisturbed deposits under the resited almshouse, and on the other, that the area of the toilets had previously been disturbed by numerous service trenches. The evaluation (Trench E) confirmed this picture with service trenches to the west and less disturbance to the east towards Wall C. Since the subsequent excavation (Trench I) was designed only to excavate deposits that would be disturbed by the shallow foundations of the new building, which were to take the form of a ring-beam supported on piles,

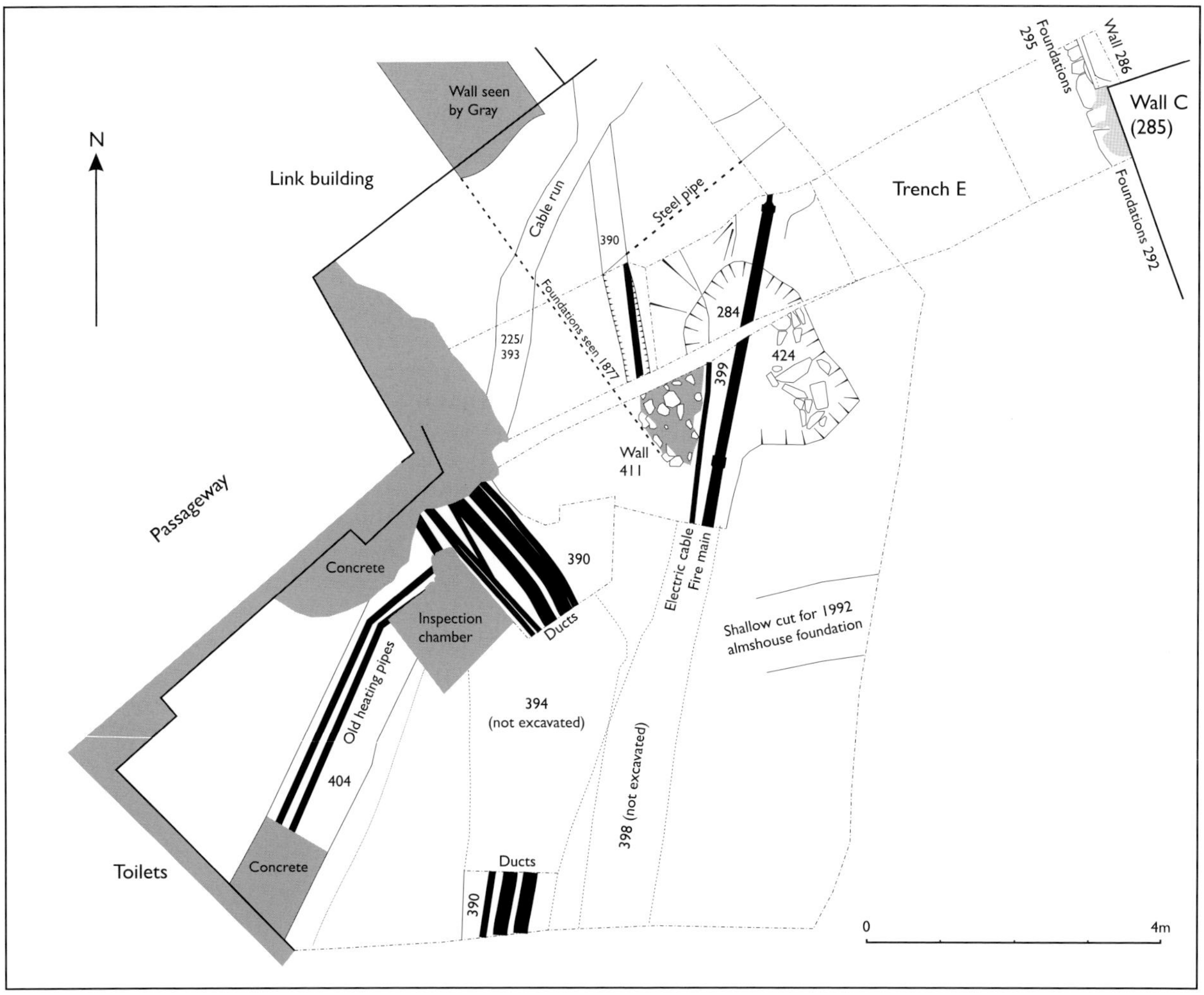

Figure 5.1: *Plan of Trenches E and I. For trench location see Figure 4 on page 5.*

several of the features recorded in the evaluation were not seen again as they lay too deep.

The area of the east passage, where the toilets had been added in 1992 (see pages 55–56) was not available for evaluation or excavation but the results of the 1992 work, together with the foundation design suggested that little further disturbance would be involved. The area was monitored during 2009. In the description that follows, the results of the evaluation are described first followed by any further observations made during the main excavation and monitoring (Figure 5.1).

Only one area of early stratigraphy was located during the evaluation, at the east end of the trench which was deepened to explore a northward continuation of the line of Wall C (here numbered 285) that was known from early photographs (Figure 5.2 on the next page). In the photographs, the coursing of the continuation does not appear to be horizontal or at the same level as the rest of the wall.

This part of Wall C comprised vertical courses, built off a single chamfered course, and formed a corner before heading eastwards. The foundations were similar to those seen in Trench C in 2004, with three foundation courses below the lowest chamfered course; only the top one of these was well laid and dressed. Below these was a wide offset (292) of two courses (it is possible that there were more but this was not confirmed) similar to that seen in 2004, which appeared to turn around the end of the wall to the east (although here slightly narrower). The foundation also continued with a slightly different character (295), to the north. The stone of 295 was more mixed than that of 292, containing chert, lias and sandstone in contrast to the uniform sandstone of 292; the stones were also smaller.

Above both foundations was redeposited red clay (290) which continued to the west into an unexcavated area and contained pottery of 12th-century date. This may be the same as 15 in Trench C (there interpreted as a levelling deposit

Figure 5.2: *Photograph showing Wall C, soon after the demolition of the adjacent buildings (c.1874), scars from which can be seen in the upper parts. The northern extension, 286, is also visible on the left. SANHS 12549*

contemporary with the wall) and the deposits above were also similar; degraded sandstone chips, sand and a layer of mortar, probably from drops when pointing. Above this was a further layer of redeposited clay on which lay the foundations of another wall (286) continuing the line of Wall C but clearly divorced from earlier foundations 295. This wall comprised a rough foundation course on which lay a single chamfered course and then a vertical course. These were not coursed with Wall C but the evidence of the early photographs, which show the wall dipping to the north, suggests that Wall 286 had sunk by about half-a-course at the south end and more to the north. There was no dating evidence that could be associated with this wall.

It appears, therefore, that Wall C originally returned east at this point, with another wall based on foundations 295 continuing the line to the north. There was some evidence (the similarity of the deposits above the foundations) that these walls were contemporary. Wall 295 was subsequently removed down to foundation level but later replaced with ill-founded wall 286, matching the alternate chamfered and vertical coursing seen further to the south. Although the remains of Wall 295 would not have been visible when Wall 286 was constructed, the coincidence of their alignment can be explained as both continued the line of Wall C northwards.

Two other features were located to the west: a pit (284/424) and a wall (411). The pit was initially identified in the evaluation where it contained a complex of rubble deposits; the surfaces of several had been trampled by people standing in the hole. The pit was not completely excavated and was probably quite recent as it cut deposits of 18th-century date. It may well have been dug in connection with the discovery of the wall in the 19th century as shown on Spencer's plans or in the 1930s as recorded by Gray.

Wall 411 had been severely damaged by a trench dug to the Wyndham Galleries containing a cast-iron water main (with the date 1934 cast into the pipes). The backfill (399) of the trench was so full of stone from the wall, in this area, that it initially appeared as a wall itself. The quantity of stone suggests a large part of the wall must have been disturbed by the pipelaying. A very rough face appeared to survive on the west side of what remained, which may have had a corner turning east where it was cut by the pipe trench, although this was not clear. Certainly no evidence of the wall continuing south could be seen, although it could have been completely removed by the pipe trench. The wall was composed of (mostly chert) blocks embedded in much mortar and appeared to represent either foundation or a wall core from which the facings had been robbed. One of Houghton Spencer's plans has a pencilled wall shown (marked "Foundations") running from the east side of the Watergate to the south, which aligns well with the wall fragment recorded here. It is shown continuing in a straight line to the south where it is annotated "Foundations 1877".

A copy of a copy of another of Houghton Spencer's plans (SANHS Gray 1934) has also had a wall added by Gray evidently during the construction of the Wyndham Galleries. The drawing is annotated at the north end "Here the bottom of the ancient wall was 5′ 6″ below the present surface and extended upwards to within 6″ of the surface (Feb 1934)." At the southern end (shown on a line with the south side of the Great Hall) is annotated "December 1933. This anc't wall was found 1.5ft [blank in original] the present surface and its extent downwards was 3.5ft (Bottom of wall 5ft below the surface)". This copy also shows an annotation added to the previous version (SANHS 6017) "Drain traced to this point in 1923. Depth of drain 5ft" with a line running along the east end of the Great Hall. This was not seen during the current excavations as it would have lain too deep but its insertion and subsequent tracing probably accounts for some of the disturbance seen.

Immediately above Wall 411 was a mortar floor (386); the close juxtaposition may indicate that the wall was reduced to this level in order to lay the floor. The floor (then numbered 270) had been seen in the evaluation when its extent was traced eastward and found to run up to Wall C. The mortar contained pottery of mid/late 19th-century date and it is most likely that the floor is associated with the ranges of buildings removed by SANHS in the 1870s.

The rest of the area was disturbed by numerous services, including the major trench (390) containing heating pipes and other service ducts inserted in 1988. There was also an earlier phase of heating pipes wrapped in rubber foam (404). Monitoring of the ground reduction in 1992 had revealed only modern deposits, including the concrete foundations for the East Passage that had preceded the 1992 toilets. These foundations were far more substantial than those seen in the West Passage (below), perhaps because the disturbed nature of the ground here was believed to provide less support.

5.2 The West Passage, 2007–08 (Trenches F, G, J, K, L and M)

The evaluation in 2007 comprised two trenches, Trench F outside and Trench G inside the gallery; an area where no previous excavations have been recorded. The nearest, the courtyard pipeline of 1978 (Clements 1984, 32–34), showed human burials in the so-called marl bank close to the Entrance Block with courtyard surfaces to the south cut by a variety of service trenches. No record appears to have been made when the glazed gallery wall was erected in the 1930s, unless this is when pencilled additions were made to Spencer's plans showing a buttress foundation. The evaluation showed that significant deposits were unlikely to be affected by the construction of a wider passageway on a ring-beam supported on piles and the area for this was then excavated as four trenches, two to either side of the evaluation inside and outside the gallery (Figure 5.3 on the facing page). Further observations were made when the ground level was reduced for the foundations in 2009. For simplicity the site will be described as if the Great Hall lay to the north rather than to the north-west.

A deposit (280, 439, 460, 517, 539, 1106, 1127, 1128, 1129), similar to that interpreted as the natural alluvium, a buff coloured sandy clay, was recorded at several places along the southern edge of the excavation. A soil was not apparent on its surface, in contrast to inside the Great Hall or around Wall C and it appeared to have been disturbed. It did appear similar to the "grave-earth" seen on Castle Green and in view of the presence of burials in the adjacent water pipe trench (Clements 1984) and the recovery of one human finger bone from 1128, it seems likely that this is the same deposit forming the backfilled graveyard. A further fragment of human bone was recorded during post-excavation work from stony-clay 495 in Trench L.

Over most of the area this was obscured by deep pits but in one place the grave-earth was overlain by what is interpreted as the clay foundation for a wooden structure. This was only seen in the side of one of the later pits, and a small section dug across it, but appeared to comprise two phases. The first (458), was an L-shaped linear feature filled with a predominantly brown clay with frequent red flecks (457), which had been mostly cut away by a later feature (443) of similar shape and alignment. The base of 443 was filled with chert cobbles tightly packed in a matrix of mid-brown sandy clay (459) similar to the grave-earth. The chert blocks appeared to have been laid in layers rather than tipped.

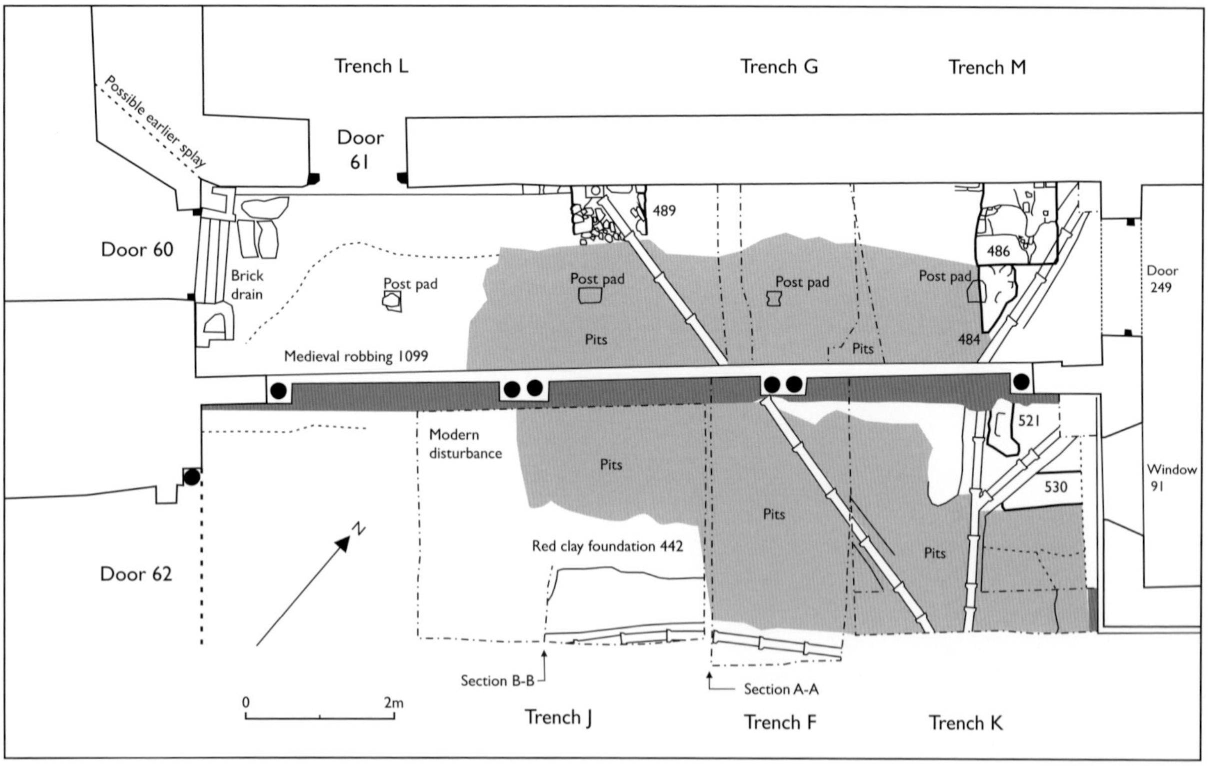

Figure 5.3: Plan of Trenches F, G, J, K, L and M in the West Passage. For trench location see Figure 4 on page 5.

The rest of the vertically-sided cut was filled with a deposit of red clay (442, containing 12th-century pottery) with some more chert cobbles on the surface. Only the south sides of these features were visible, the northern parts of 458 being removed by 443 and the northern part of 443 removed by later pits but both seemed to have an intact internal corner forming the L-shape. Although badly damaged, both these features appear to represent the north-west corner of a structure. layered chert certainly appeared structural and these features may represent successive foundations for a building parallel and to the south of the Great Hall. The chert of 459 may represent one of the times when the foundations of timber buildings were rebuilt as described in the Pipe Rolls.

Most of the area of the southern trenches (J, F and K) was occupied by a group of intercutting pits. The fills of these were similar and appeared to comprise mostly building debris, particularly slate. There was little in the way of domestic debris (although a few animal bones, pottery sherds and glass wine bottles were recovered) and the pits appeared to be fairly contemporaneous and to date from the late 17th to mid 18th centuries. One large dump of stone (265), superficially resembling a wall or other structure, also appeared to have been dumped in a pit, later cut by others. The natural alluvial deposits were reached in the bases of pits 251 and 245 during the evaluation.

Inside the gallery similar deposits were encountered representing the same pit complex. One was excavated during the evaluation (Figure 5.4 on the next page) and found to contain similar amounts of roofing slate, pottery and glass bottles, apparently tipped from the north. At the base the feature appeared to be filled with broken stone which was much wetter than the layers above. It is possible that this was a natural deposit as at this point the north side of the feature appeared to be composed of similar material. It was not, unfortunately, possible to be certain of this in the cramped, dark conditions at the base of the excavation. The pits inside the passage appeared to have a straighter and more vertical edge than those outside.

Considerable difficulty was experienced in determining the relationships between the pits which at the surface appeared fairly clear. It is suggested that, although the pits were dug individually giving a characteristic lobed appearance to their border, they were infilled with deposits that crossed what appeared to be pit boundaries. This would explain the contemporaneity of the fills and the difficulty in establishing edges of what were dumps of very similar materials.

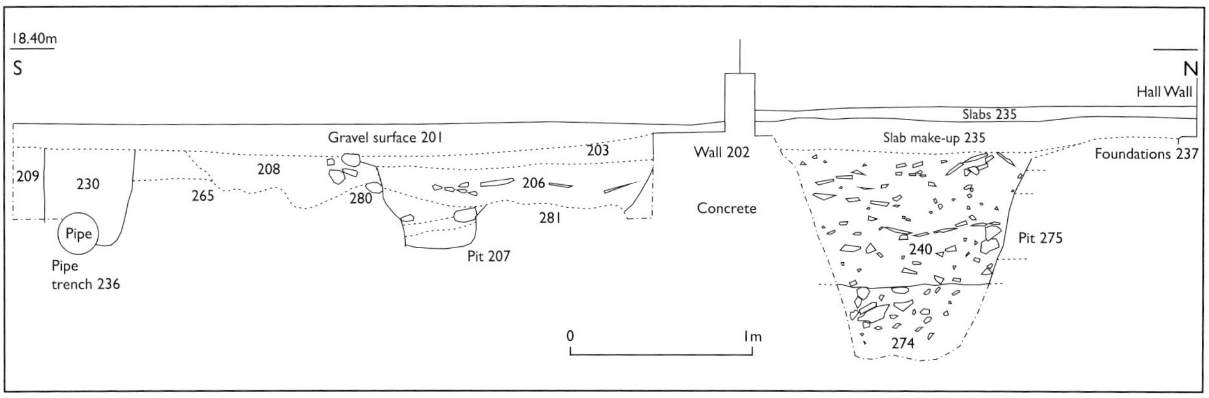

Figure 5.4: *Section A–A of Trenches F and G in the West Passage. For location see Figure 5.3 on the previous page.*

The size and extent of the pit complex (seen particularly clearly during the ground reduction in 2009) suggest that it was dug to rob the south wall of the medieval Phase I hall (see page 183) which would have run along a very similar line to that of the glazed wall of the gallery. The robbing would have been undertaken from the south to avoid undermining the hall wall, which would explain the more regular northern edge of the pit complex. Against this interpretation, there was little of the characteristic debris of stone robbing within the pits, with the possible exception of the stones encountered at the base of Trench G.

The pits appear to have been backfilled with rubbish that had been accumulating for a while: the dates of the wine bottles were spread over a century (see page 131) while the clay pipes suggest a briefer period in the early decades of the 18th century (see page 132). The nature of the finds suggests a non-domestic origin, perhaps from an inn or a club. This could either have been in the town or more immediately local if the judges were accommodated in the castle at this date. The pits extended further to the south at the eastern end which may indicate the presence of robbed walls extending into the courtyard.

The robbing (502, 1100) of the wall of Hall 1 continued to the west of the pit complex, where the fills (491, 1099) were more characteristic of robbing waste and appeared medieval in date; only 11th-century, presumably residual, pottery was recovered from the small area excavated.

Inside the gallery, the footings of the wall of the Great Hall were exposed beneath the make-up for the slab floor. These were not excavated but could be seen to lie in a narrow construction trench. Built into the foundation offset were the remains of the foundations of two buttresses, both unfortunately damaged by the 1930s drainage. The eastern buttress foundation (486) was wider (1.12m) and extended further (1.08m) from the wall than the western one (489, 0.98m by at least 0.76m; the southern edge had been removed by the pit complex). Their construction also differed: 486 comprised very large lias blocks overlying smaller ones (visible in a later post-hole, 449) of more varied geology, while 489 comprised only one large Hamstone block with smaller lias and sandstone blocks in a yellowish mortar.

Leading south from buttress 486, clearly later than it and aligned on its west face, was a wall-foundation (484) which continued (521) outside the gallery in Trench K. The foundation comprised rubble within a large quantity of hard off-white mortar, with charcoal flecks and pieces of tile, that appeared to have been poured to fill a narrow construction trench. It had been badly damaged by the 1930s drainage but in Trench K it appeared to be later than the pit complex, although this could not be proved and if true would preclude the interpretation as a 16th-century porch (below). At its southern end (which had been cut away) it turned eastwards (530) and ran under the standing building. The alignment of the wall on the side of the buttress foundation must indicate that the buttresses were still present when it was constructed (in a similar manner to the buttress preserved within later walling at Castle House). It seems likely that this is the foundation for the porch, dated 1577, mentioned by Toulmin (1791, 48; see page 180).

The only other area of significant deposits lay at the west end of Trench L where a complex series of brick structures was recorded. These appeared to comprise successive phases of rain-water drains, the most recent probably removed in the 1930s when the passageway was built. Below this was a well-mortared brick channel running between two brick boxes for down pipes. From the northern box a similar channel, but

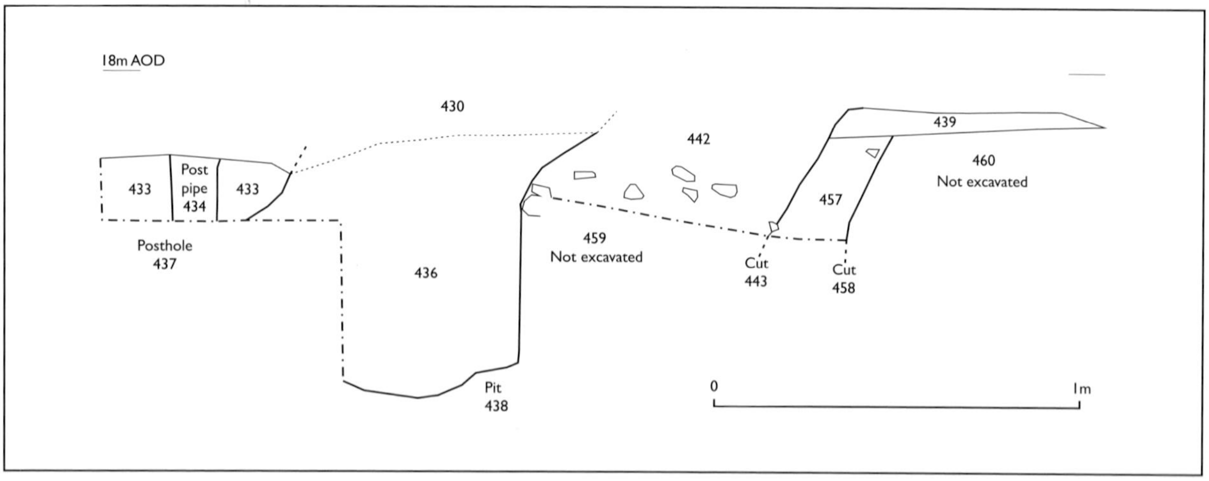

Figure 5.5: *West facing section B–B through clay foundations 442 and 457, pit 438 and posthole 437. For location see Figure 5.3 on page 69*

roofed, ran west under the wall and then under the floor of the undercroft apparently towards Door 57 in the west wall. All these features appeared to overlie a large pit filled with building stone but this was not excavated as it was not to be disturbed.

Four stone post-pads were recorded at a high level along the passageway that corresponded with locations shown on Spencer's plan where posts supported two corridors. See page 182 for a discussion of this building.

The latest features recorded, apart from structures and drainage associated with the construction of the gallery in 1931, were several large (*c.*1m diameter) postholes, often containing circular void postpipes. These are likely to have supported scaffolding poles, such as those seen in photographs of the construction of the Wyndham block in 1931 (SANHS 12551, 12552). None of the posts in the photographs were within the excavated area and the postholes could be of almost any (recent) date.

5.3 The New Almshouse Site, 2008 (Trench H)

Work began here in March 2008 with the removal under archaeological supervision of the southern end of Wall C and the Hamstone gatepier (TCB 258). This part of the wall formed part of the extension (79) to the south of the corner (C2 in Figure 4.4 on page 57) and was itself visibly of two constructions. On the east face a vertical joint was visible (C6) separating walling of large sandstone ashlar at the north from a more mixed stone rubble wall mortared with cement at the south. On the west face this vertical join was not visible but the southern end (C5 to C3) was mortared with cement for a similar distance. The gatepiers were also cement mortared and are known to have been repositioned during the landscaping of 1933 (SANHS minutes: 4/1/1933). It seemed likely therefore that the walling was of a similar date. Following recording, the northern gatepier (258) was carefully demolished with the intention of re-erection. The hardness of the cement and softness of the pieces of Hamstone meant, however, that almost no stones could be recovered unbroken.

The Hamstone was found to be a thin (*c.*100mm) facing on a core of rubble, cement and scrap iron in the form of pipes and bindings. This ironwork continued into the core of the adjacent wall, proving its contemporaneity. One piece of the Hamstone was found to be a reused medieval moulding. The origins of these gatepiers are unknown but they have only three dressed faces, indicating that were intended to stand against buildings rather than at the end of walls. The presence of reused medieval masonry could indicate that they originated at the castle but it is also possible that this piece is part of a repair of 1933 using one piece of the numerous architectural fragments now found in the garden. In view of the impossibility of re-erecting the gatepiers it was decided to leave the southern one (259) in place.

A rectangular area 5.2m x 4.2m covering the area of the new foundations for the almshouse

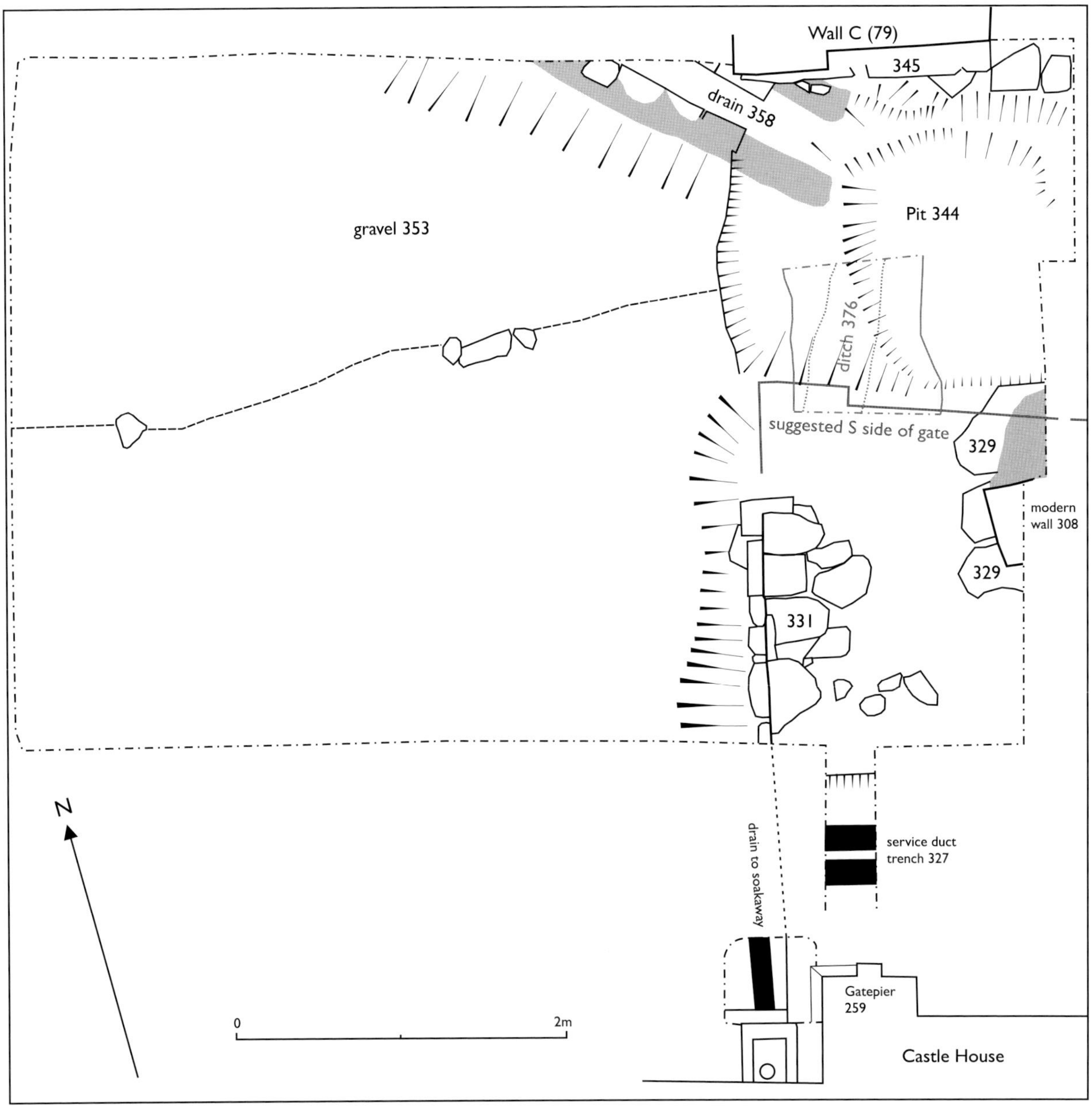

Figure 5.6: *Plan of Trench H at end of excavation. For trench location see Figure 4 on page 5.*

was then opened by hand and excavated down to at least the depth required for the foundations. Excavations were continued in some areas to answer specific problems. The archaeological deposits encountered fell into two distinct areas: to the west of the wall-line they comprised a sequence of surfaces whilst the deposits beneath and to the east of the wall-line were extremely disturbed, specifically by two large pits filled with concrete.

Where exposed the natural geology was a silty clay alluvium similar to that seen in Trench A and elsewhere in the castle. At its surface it was stained dark but lightened with depth; root channels could again be seen carrying the darker material down. The natural was only exposed beneath the line of Wall C and in a deeper part of the excavation along the western edge of the trench where concrete foundations were removed.

The earliest features appeared to be cut from the level of this natural deposit (377) and included a ditch (376) running north-south under, but slightly angled to, the later wall-line. The ditch was filled with a very similar material to that through which it was cut, probably indicating natural silting similar to that which had deposited the "natural". The ditch fill appeared to preserve casts of organic remains but none could be identified when samples were examined (Jones 2008).

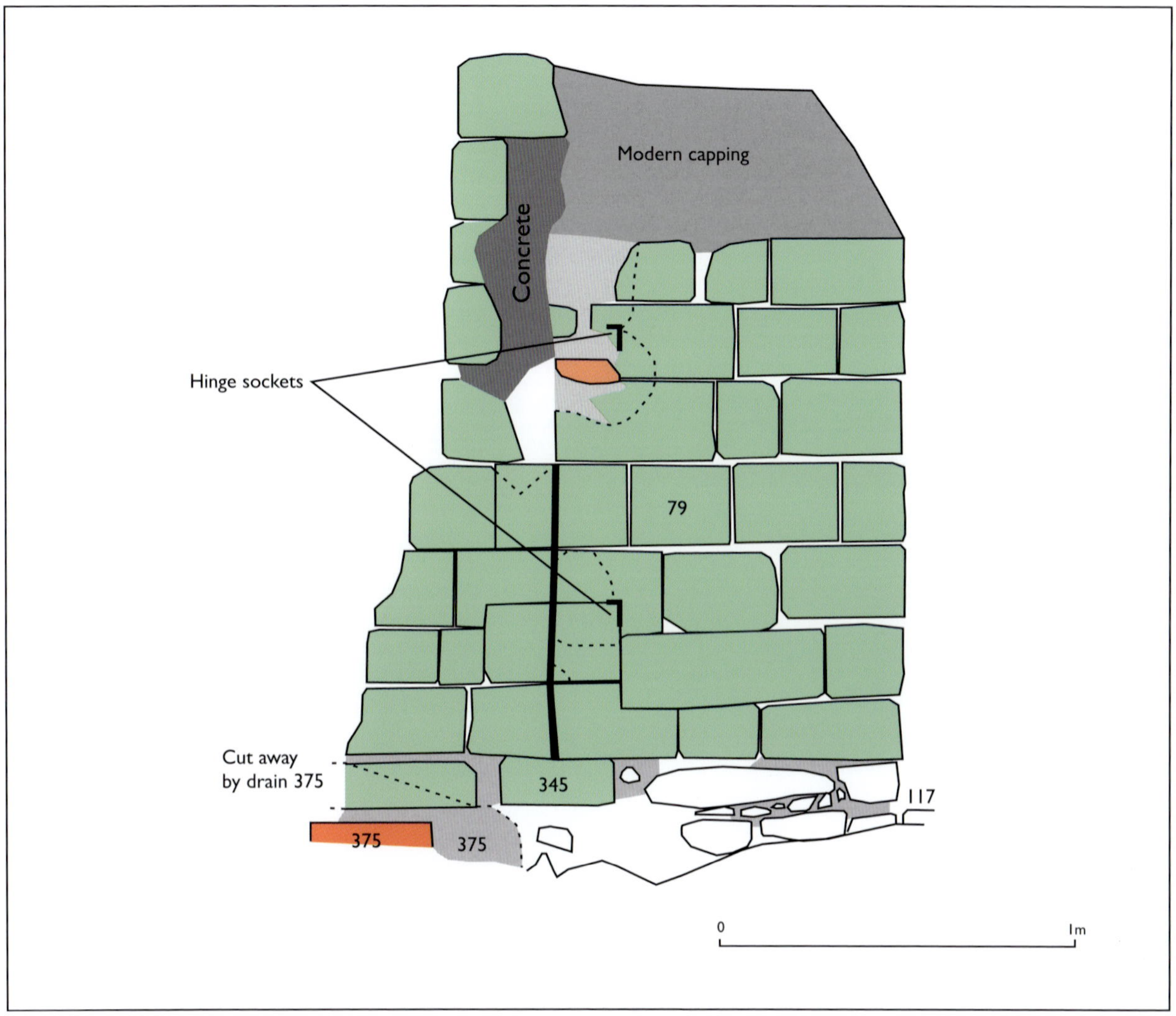

Figure 5.7: Elevation of the north side of Gateway TCB 536 at the southern end of Wall C (excavation context TCC 79) showing the rebate for the gate and the locations of hinges.

Another, shallower feature was seen in the south-west corner of the site but the limited area excavated precluded identification.

Wall C (79) was built on top of this surface, seemingly with no construction trench although this could not be proved as the wall lay outside the excavation. It appeared to have one course of foundation (345), composed of roughly dressed and irregular stones bedded in thick gravelly mortar, sometimes with smaller packing stones. At its east side the foundations appeared to lie on the wall foundation (117) seen in Trench C, although this could not be shown conclusively due to later disturbance. Above the foundations on the east side were seven courses of squared ashlar with a vertical rear face, whilst to the west the face stepped out by 12cm to form a rebate for a gate (TCB 536). The front (west) face of the wall survived four courses high before being replaced by cement-bonded repairs. The lowest three courses were not continuous but contained blocks of different sizes that had been cut to incorporate parts of other blocks.

The rebate was formed alternately at joints and by carved L-shaped blocks and the west face by alternating chamfered and vertical courses to match those of Wall C to the north. Just to the rear of the rebate two large irregular holes were visible which appeared to have been caused by the removal of hinge pintles. In the top right of each, the corner of an original square hole could be seen. The core of the wall was only seen at the top, where it may not have been typical as it had been disturbed, and was composed of gravelly mortar and rubble.

Fragments of the front facing of Wall C (331, Figure 5.8) were found forming the opposite side of the gateway. The wall comprised a maximum

Figure 5.8: *Trench H. Surviving fragments of Wall C (TCC 331) on the south side of Gateway TCB 536, from the west.*

of two courses above a single course of foundation plinth, the top, rear and north all having been cut away by a concrete-filled pit (330). The level of the foundation plinth was the same as that of Wall 79, but the lowest course (K) of Wall 331 was vertical, followed by a chamfered course (L), and thus out of phase with the pattern of Wall 79. The presence of the gateway would have prevented these mismatched courses from meeting and the wall must have been vertical above the battered section or the receding face would have met the rebate for the gate. Wall C suggests that there were two more chamfered courses (P and R) before it became vertical.

The upper courses of Wall 331 were mortared with a fine white mortar and the core may have been composed of rubble and red gravel, although very little survived. A small excavation between the gatepier TCB 259 and a rainwater drain, showed the wall continuing southwards below Castle House and forming the foundations for the gatepier.

To the east of the north end of Wall 331 lay a further area of stones (329) which appeared to form a foundation plinth similar to that of Wall 331. No stones survived above the foundation level but the stones were bedded on red gravel (369) which also appeared to form the bedding for Wall 331. This foundation (329) extended further east than the east face of Wall 79 suggesting that a wall ran east from the gate into the modern garden area. A wall here would have hit the west end of Wall A and therefore they could not have been contemporary.

The width of Gate 536 could not be determined as no facing survived on the southern side but the distance between the foundation plinths 345 and 329 was 1.84m. If the offset was 18cm on the south side, as it was on the north, this would give a width for the gateway of 5 feet (1.5m).

The area of the gate passage itself was occupied by a pit (344) filled with chert cobbles (346, Figure 5.10). At the base the cobbles were randomly dumped in the pit with numerous voids between them. Above this was a levelling course laid flat in mortar and above that the cobbles had been pitched, starting from the north where they leaned onto the foundation course (345). These were covered by a hard compact layer of gravel bonded with sandy clay (343) that formed the base for a wall (318, Figure 5.9), blocking the gateway. The eastern extent of these features had been removed by the pipe trench (132) seen in Trench C. The faces of Wall 318 had been removed by the insertion of the cement-mortared part of Wall 79, except for a small area on the west side where the face appeared to be formed of chert blocks. The core survived higher but had been cut away to the south by a pit (328, the foundations for Gatepier TCB 258) and it was apparent that it had originally extended still higher as traces of the mortar survived on the southern face of Wall 79 and filled the holes left by the removal of the hinges. It is thus likely that the wall filled the entirety of the gateway.

The purpose of the lower parts of these features is not clear. At the time of excavation the chert blocks (346) were seen as forming the founda-

Figure 5.9: *Trench H, walling [318] blocking Gateway TCB 536 from the west.*

Figure 5.10: *Trench H, pitched chert cobbles 346 from the south with the side of Gateway TCB 536 in Wall C (TCC 79) to rear.*

tion for the blocking-wall 318 as there appeared to be no break between them. As a foundation they seem excessive, particularly given the somewhat rough walling built above. It is possible, therefore, that the chert was intended as a solid base for the path through the gateway. No trace of a surface was seen within these deposits but flagstones may have been laid on the compacted gravel (343) which would have been level with the foundation plinth.

Apparently associated with the gateway was a series of courtyard surfaces, the lowest of which appeared to comprise a road (353). This was formed of a compacted deposit of gravel, seemingly with a cambered top, and defined by a shallow gully and a line of stones along the south side (the north side lay outside the excavation). The gravel lay above a layer of clean green sand (356) which lay on the natural sandy clay. It was not clear if this sand was a deliberate levelling layer, or whether it represented stone-working debris that had been protected by the construction of the road. Unfortunately any relationship between the road and the gateway had been destroyed by Drain 358 and cut 344 for the gateway "blocking". It is possible that a relationship might survive to the north but this lay outside the excavated area.

The relationship between the drain and the road was also unclear. The drain itself comprised two lines of re-used dressed stone bedded in mortar which lay directly on the natural clay. There was no sign of a bottom to the drain and the two lines of mortar bedding continued across the base of cut 344 for a short distance. There was also no sign of a cover for the drain. The roadway gravel appeared to have subsided into the drain but it is possible that this was backfill from the robbing of any cover stones. This collapse made it impossible to tell whether the roadway had been laid over the drain or whether the drain had been cut through it and the road relaid over. More gravel had been used to fill the subsidence.

Above the roadway were further layers of courtyard makeup, some extensive and some evidently smaller patches. These mostly comprised gravel but there were also areas of broken stone and mortar and one of sand (342), probably from building works. All these layers contained pottery of 12th-century date with no evidence of the truncation seen elsewhere in the courtyard.

The latest features on the site related to gardening works in 1933 and subsequently. Two pits had been dug and been filled with concrete to act as foundations, one for Gatepier TCB 258 and the other for a platform. This platform had been constructed to support a garage that was removed in 1973 (SRO A/CNT/4/2) when, it is also recorded, the gates from the castle entrance were fixed to block the gap between the gate piers (Clements nd). The retaining walls (308) of the platform were also supported by the medieval foundation 329. An soakaway (341) connected to a downpipe on Castle House probably also dated to the 1930s.

5.4 The Great Hall, Wyndham Galleries and West Range, 2009 (Trenches N–Y) *Chris Webster and James Brigers*

The plans for the Museum of Somerset required the construction of several below-ground structures in the Great Hall (Room 18). These comprised piles and concrete beams to support the steel structure forming the first floor walkway and service ducts to provide heating, electricity and communications around the building. In addition it was intended to excavate two large pits, one for a lift at the west end and one for a sunken display case in the centre of the hall. Another lift pit was to be dug in the basement of the Wyndham Galleries (Room 11). The service ducts also continued through the Undercroft (Room 23) below the Somerset Room (103) and into the south range – these are described on pages 189 and 196.

Examination of the records from the 1952–53 works (see page 48) guided the designs and led to the belief that they would not have a serious impact on buried archaeology (Webster 2007). Scheduled monument consent for the works was obtained on this basis with the proviso that all ground disturbance would be monitored and any disturbance to important deposits would be recorded. Work began with the cutting of the trench through the Undercroft, monitored continuously by the authors. The trench was deeper than had been shown on the plans but in general only disturbed late flooring features and penetrated a single dumped layer (see page 189).

When work started in the Great Hall, however, it became apparent that the situation was different. Three factors were apparent: the concrete floor was less thick than had been determined from boreholes and the 1952–53 records; the archaeological deposits were much more complex than suggested by examination of Radford and Hallam's account and drawings, and additional depths required for construction of the concrete structures had not been shown on the plans.

After discussions with English Heritage, it was decided that the deposits were too complex and too important to be removed by machine

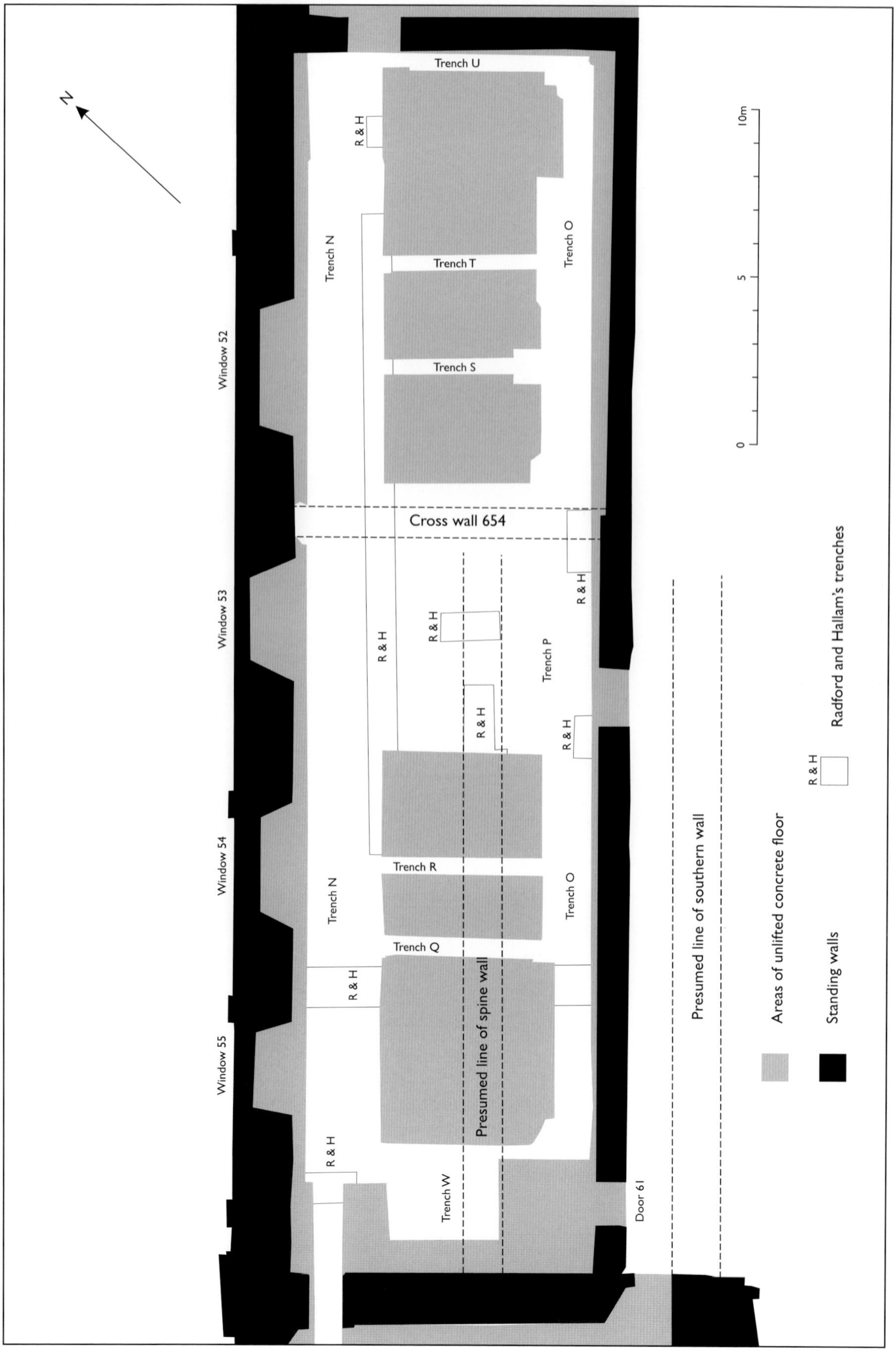

Figure 5.11: Location plan of Trenches N–U and W in the Great Hall, also showing major features used to describe locations in the hall.

Figure 5.12: *Trench N looking west after removal of concrete and initial cleaning. The rubble-filled backfill of Radford and Hallam's Trench I can be seen in the foreground.*

and would have to be archaeologically excavated and recorded in advance of the building work continuing. Consideration was given to the removal of the entire concrete floor, which was felt to be the most effective procedure by both the archaeologists and the builders, but was not deemed possible by the architects. The builders therefore sawed the concrete slab, and broke up and removed the cast concrete and underlying limestone scalpings by machine.

Two main trenches were formed along the north and south walls with a series of cross trenches for services between them. In the central area, where the sunken display case was to be constructed, the whole area of concrete was removed rather than the complex pattern of service trenches shown on the plans. The builders' reason for wishing to remove the entire floor had been the difficulty of moving machinery around the hall once it had been divided by trenches, particularly as each trench had to be revisited and completed after archaeological excavation. Leaving most of the floor in situ led to a complex programme of work (see Figure 5.11 on the previous page).

The lift pit (Trench W) was excavated first followed by the main trench along the N wall (Trench N) from west to east, leaving a short length adjacent to the door for access. Work then started on the southern long trench (O), the cross trenches (Q, R, S, T and U) and the central trench (P). The east end of Trench N was only cleared after the rest of the area had been excavated and then machined to depth. The archaeological work followed the same sequence, with the intention that areas could be handed back to the builders as completed, although in the event, no further building work was undertaken until the excavation was complete.

Although the vast majority of threatened archaeological deposits were excavated by hand, some areas, primarily those identified as extensive dump deposits and the cross trenches, were reduced to the final formation level of 16.30m above Ordnance Datum (aOD) by machine under archaeological supervision. The layout of the

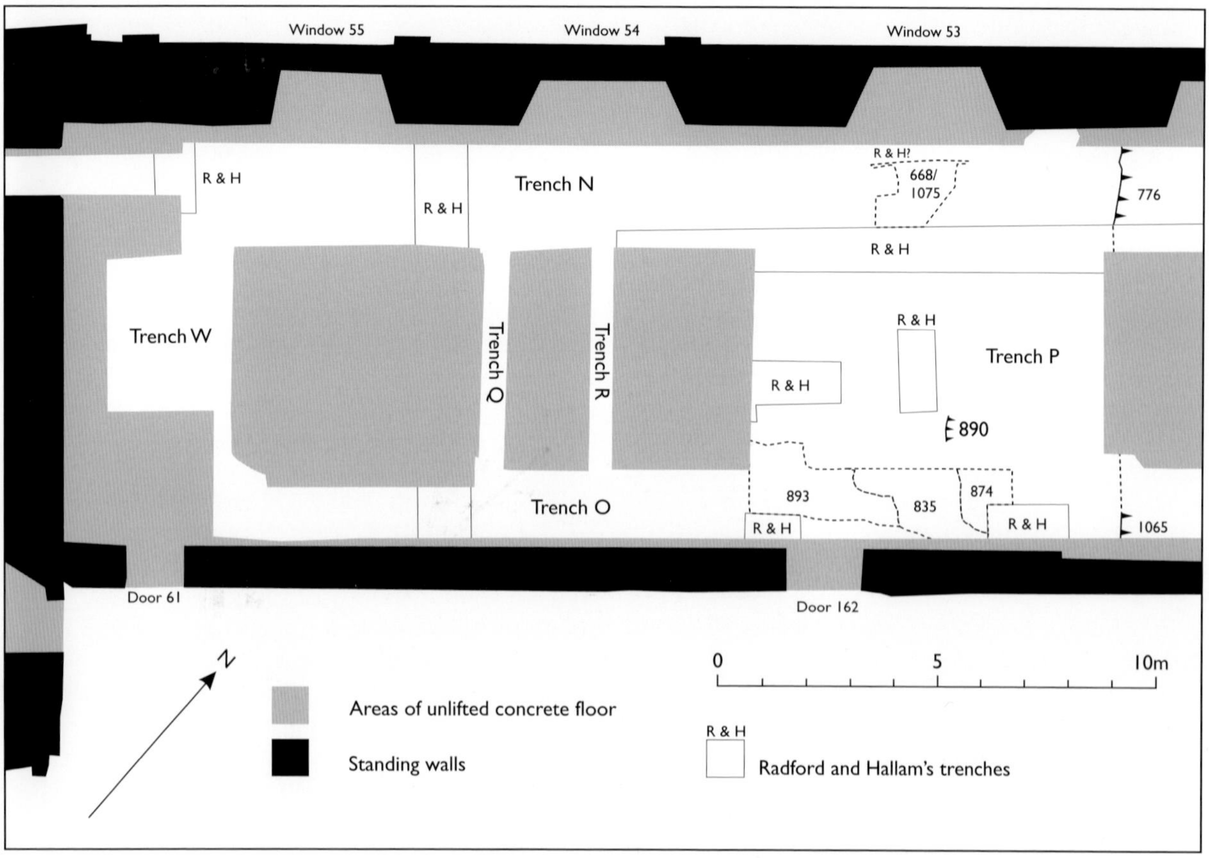

Figure 5.13: *Features in the east end of the Great Hall preceding the first masonry phase.*

trenches and their order of excavation meant that it was not often possible to correlate deposits found in one with those in other areas – the difficulty foreseen when removal of the whole floor was proposed to preclude it.

The excavations within the Great Hall revealed complex archaeological remains appearing to span the whole period of existence of the castle, with some that appear to have pre-dated its construction. Because of the lack of stratigraphic correlation between areas it has not been possible to produce detailed phases and the account that follows is divided into various areas, within which a general phasing is discussed. The precise dating of most features remains problematic due to the general scarcity of artefacts from excavated deposits, and as a result the chronology is largely based on stratigraphic relationships.

For simplicity the Great Hall will be described as if aligned east-west.

Pre-hall features

Several features at the west end of the hall appeared to pre-date the earliest phases of stone buildings, identified by excavation and structural examination. Some of the pottery discovered may be pre-conquest but the features could also relate to early phases of the castle.

Undisturbed solid geology was exposed only in the lift pit excavations, Trench W in the Great Hall and Trench V in the basement of the Wyndham Galleries (Figure 5.15 on page 81), at a highest level of 15.96m aOD. It consisted of hard red marl (571, 778) of the Mercia Mudstone Series overlain by a gravelly-clay with pockets of sand of variable thickness (572, 779). In Trench W the upper, sandy-clay, levels of 571 were found to merge into the base of a horizon of increasingly dark grey clay-sand (570) up to 0.35m in thickness which yielded charcoal, abraded fragments of animal bone and 10th–12th-century pottery, almost exclusively concentrated in the upper, darker, 0.15m of the deposit.

Although not exposed everywhere, this deposit was revealed at a sufficient number of locations throughout the western and central parts of the excavation to indicate that it was originally continuous and consistent. In places the surface of 570 showed evidence of in-situ burning and re-deposited lenses of ash and charcoal along with fragments of iron slag. It seems probable that this material represents a previously cultivated soil forming the local land surface prior to construction work. An identical buried soil has been seen in several other excavations in the castle, such as 59 in Trench A (page 59) and 377 in Trench H (page 72) in the courtyard, and also elsewhere in Taunton, such as beneath the town bank in Hawke's Yard (Leach 1984b, 67).

In the region of Trenches O and P the surface of 570 dipped into a broad, shallow depression in the base of which was cut a deep, steep-sided feature (890, Figure 5.13 on the previous page) which appeared to be a part of a north-south aligned linear, only the west side of which was exposed within a re-excavation (and slight extension) of Radford and Hallam's Trench VI and its full extent to the north was lost due to truncation by a later feature. The lower fill (884) of 890 consisted of highly compacted stony clay which contained a few sherds of 10th-century pottery. Other features were also observed cutting 570 at the north of Trench P: all appeared to be postholes that had been truncated by later features. In the limited area excavated, no pattern could be discerned. To the west of the depression and feature 890 the surface of 570 was sealed by an even layer of small chert rubble (893, Figure 5.13) tightly packed into a matrix of dark red clay. Another deposit of gravel in a dark purple/red clay (668/1075, Figure 5.13) was observed overlying 570 to the north in Trench N and it seems possible that these are two elements of the same extensive deposit, separated by later intrusions.

The nature of these two deposits is strongly suggestive of a deliberately laid surface of chert and they may represent the truncated remains of an external yard or standing, which was clearly cut by all adjacent structural elements of the medieval castle. The depression in natural 570 appears to have been filled by dumps of rubble and mortar, capped with clay, principally consisting of contexts 834, 835 and 874, of which both 834 (comprising red clay with lenses of buried soil) and 835 (mortar with lenses of buried soil) produced pottery exclusively of 10th–12th-century date.

To the east, buried soil 570 had been entirely removed by a substantial north-south cut of which only the western edge was recognised as 776 in Trench N and 1065 in Trench O (Figure 5.13 on the preceding page). Only limited excavation of the edge of this feature was possible within the constraints of the excavation and as such little can be said of its character or the nature of the material it contains, but the absence of any occurrence of 570 further east would seem to indicate that it was at least 10m in width. From this, admittedly limited, evidence it may be speculated that such a feature could have been a large ditch with significant defensive potential or the edge of a cut for a broad terrace, with a platform extending to the east. Stratigraphically, it is possible that 776 could be part of the following phase, but it was certainly infilled by the end of that phase.

The first stone buildings: Hall 1

The earliest structures on the site comprised the existing north and west walls of the Great Hall, together with a spine- and southern wall forming what was described by Radford and Hallam (1953, 60–65) as the "twelfth-century hall" .

The southern edge of the foundation trench (591) for the north wall (589) was observed in the central area of Trench N, cutting through chert and clay spread 668/1075 and buried soil 570, up to 0.3m south of the wall foundation itself. The foundations were predominantly of squared lias blocks bonded by pale grey coarse lime mortar that was offset from the existing superstructure by 0.60m. The precise nature and stratigraphic position of the construction trench was unclear in many places because of later disturbances which took the form of trenching along the wall. Some of these could be attributed to the 1952 excavations (Radford and Hallam 1953, 58) but other lengths appeared to be earlier and may have been pits dug to assess the strength of walls. The line of a continuation (782) of this north wall may be indicated by substantial robber-cut/wall-trench 780 revealed in profile in the lift pit excavation in the basement of the Wyndham Galleries (Trench V, Figure 5.15 on the next page) . Foundation 589 was not seen in the eastern part of the excavation, and appeared to stop 0.6m before the line of later Wall 654, although Radford and Hallam show it towards the east end on their site plan (SANHS 6066).

At the western end of Trench N, in the present opening between the Undercroft (Room 23) and Great Hall, the excavation passed through the foundation (549) of the wall that forms the existing division between the two ranges. The foundation was of similar construction to that of the foundation of the north wall but was not offset from the wall line. Unfortunately the junction between the two walls was not uncovered but the evidence of the barrel vault scars (see page 50) indicates that they must be contemporary.

Evidence for the existence of a second substantial north-south wall was represented by a broad, vertically-sided trench (1053, Figure 5.14 on the facing page) crossing the width of the investigated area, and possibly extending southwards, beyond the existing wall of the hall. Although

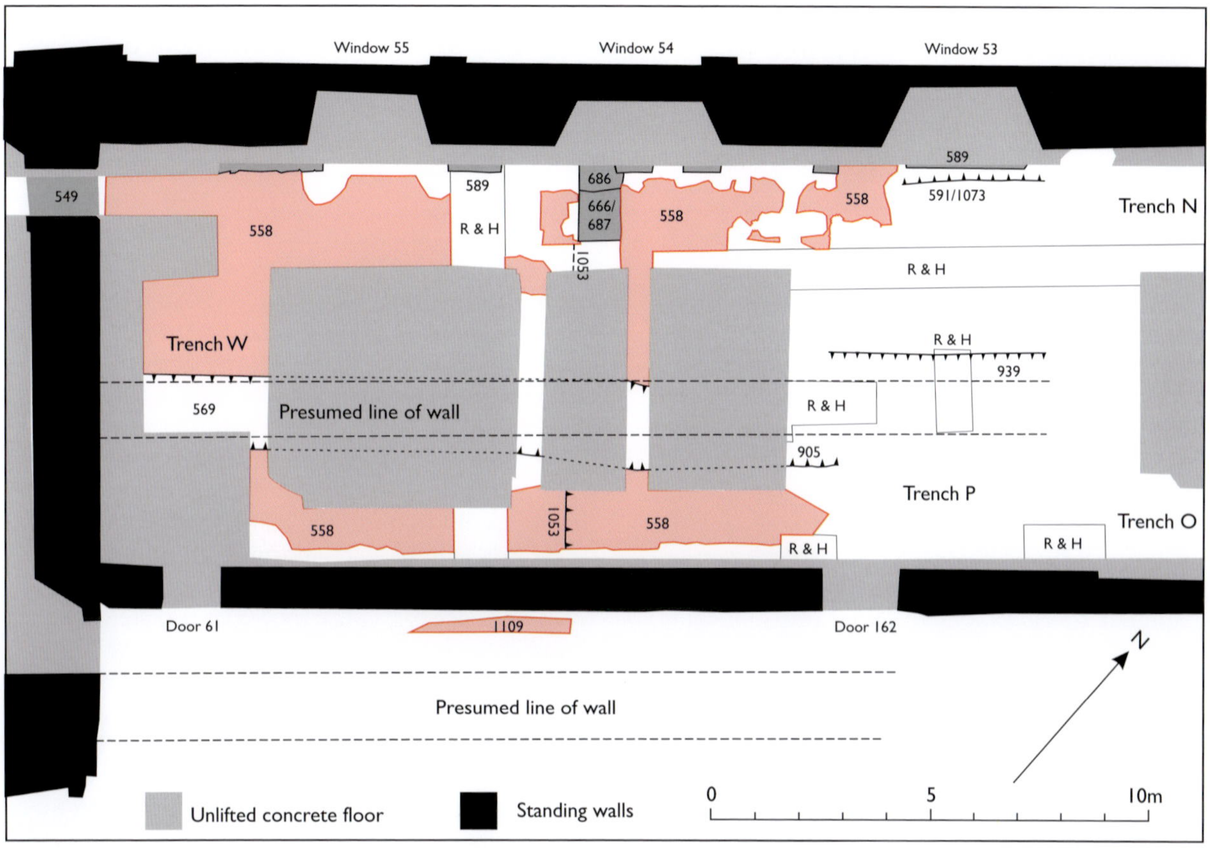

Figure 5.14: *Great Hall, the earliest structural features: Hall 1.*

Figure 5.15: *The east side of the lift pit excavation in the basement of the Wyndham Galleries (Trench V) showing the natural red clay (778) with lenses of dark red gravel (779). To the right, these are cut by the construction/robbing trench (780) for a large wall (782), probably the north curtain wall of the castle.*

only partially excavated, it was possible to trace the position of both edges in Trenches N and O and to establish that 1053 consisted of a foundation trench up to 1.60m in width which appeared to cut buried soil 570 and the foundation trench for the north wall 589. In Trench N a fuller examination of 1053 revealed that later robbing had removed all but the lowest foundation level of chert rubble (666/687) and a short length of mortared lias masonry (686), which may have been left as it was seen as part of the north wall.

In the centre of the site, evidence for the existence of a substantial east-west wall was provided by construction trench 569/905 (Figure 5.14 on the previous page), which was observed intermittently over an 18m length from Trench W in the west to a point where it (here numbered 939) was cut by the construction of later Wall 654 at the eastern edge of Trench P. The trench could not be seen beyond this point but, in view of the limited areas excavated, it is possible that it continued. Examination at three locations revealed that the fills comprised lenses of mortar and other building debris (563 and 565) to the west and compact clay (938) to the east. No in-situ masonry remained and the fills represent the backfill of a robber trench (568/939) apparently coincident with the construction trench.

This feature clearly corresponds with the spine-wall between the two barrel vaults, visible to Radford and Hallam as scars on the west wall. The feature was also located in their Trench I but they appear not to have appreciated the implied sequence of wall construction and robbing as they describe "a foundation trench, 5ft wide [...] The sides were irregular, suggesting that the trench had stood open for a period and started to crumble before being filled with a loose packing of stones gravel and rubbish." (Radford and Hallam 1953, 56–58). Our interpretation would see the irregularity and loose "packing" as indicating a robbing trench. The scar indicated a wall 1.3m wide; the trench appeared to be about 1.6m wide with its north side about on line with the north side of the scar suggesting robbing, and possibly construction, was from the south side.

The western part of the excavated area was covered by a very extensive level dump of clean red clay (558, Figure 5.14 on the preceding page), up to 0.3m in thickness, which appeared to seal the construction levels for the wall contained in 569/905 and the remains of Wall 686. The clay was found not to extend beyond wall 549 into the Undercroft (Room 23). Here, at a corresponding level, a mixed dark grey-brown clay-loam (542) extended throughout the excavated area. This may represent a deliberate dump, but its base matrix was found to be very similar to that of buried soil 570 and it is possible that 542 is a compound of that context and later disturbance. Red clay 1109, similar to 558 and at a similar level ($\approx$17.52m aOD) was seen outside the hall during ground reduction in the area of the former west passage. This had been cut through by the foundation trench for the south wall of the hall (824/1101); its southern extent had been removed by robber trench 1100 (see below).

Although clear relationships could not be determined throughout the excavated area, sufficient evidence was present to suggest that the remains described above were contemporary and are those of Radford and Hallam's (1953) "12th-century hall". At the ground floor level, this comprised the present undercroft (Room 23) together with two further barrel vaults extending eastwards. These were supported by the present north wall, the wall in 569/905 and a further wall, evidence for whose robber trench (1100) was found in the west passage (see page 69). Wall 1100 would have continued the line of the south wall of Room 23. In Radford and Hallam's (1953) interpretation the extensive deposit of red clay (558) was seen as a pre-castle "marl bank", because it appeared to be cut by the "foundation trench" for wall 569/905. This cut is now interpreted as a robber trench and clay 558 as flooring for two of the undercrofts.

The location of the east end of this structure is not clear. Radford and Hallam (1953, 60) identified two pieces of foundation masonry and believed these to form the robbed remains of the east wall. The current excavations, however, showed that these (657 and 895) were not part of a continuous wall and were stratigraphically later. Although neither was completely excavated it was shown that the northern one (657) had never extended further north and that the southern was unlikely to have done so. Radford and Hallam also believed, on the basis of two small trenches dug across the line, that the spine-wall did not extend beyond here. Excavation for the sunken museum case did locate a continuation of the robber trench to the east of masonry 657 and 895 as far as Wall 654; it was not seen to the east of the wall but this is not surprising given the limited area excavated there. The red clay (558), interpreted above as flooring within this building, appears to extend just to the east of masonry 657 but did not quite reach masonry 895 on the south.

This would suggest an end somewhere in the area that Radford and Hallam suggested, and perhaps a little further east. It is unlikely to have been as far east as the line of Wall 654, as if it lay here the south-east corner of the building should have been visible in the hole dug for the beam engine in 1956 (see page 50). Although the records from the beam engine pit are not comprehensive, they do appear to show the absence of a wall or robbing this far east. Against this evidence is the fact that no sign of an end wall was seen in the area between the two pieces of masonry 657 and 895, and Wall 654.

When the line of the wall and its robbing is plotted (Figure 5.14 on page 81) it is noticeable that the robber trench appears to deviate to the south, east of the north-south wall in trench 1053. In Trench R, the edge of the red clay 558 on the north side of the robber trench appears to overlie the projected line of the central wall and this might suggest that the wall in construction trench 1053 formed the end of the pair of barrel vaults. Against this, the red clay floor 558 continues eastwards as described above.

Reconstruction: Hall 2

In the central area of the excavation the spine-wall was demolished and the eastern part of its foundation was removed leaving robber cut 939, which was deliberately backfilled with compact clay 938. To the west it is likely that the northern part of Wall 686 was robbed at or before this time, as an effort was made to reinstate the clay floor in the top of the resulting robber cut (663/948). The backfill (938) of the spine-wall robbing trench (939) was then cut, along with two floor surfaces 707 and 688 by the construction of a large north-south wall (654, Figure 5.16 on the following page) of mortared North Curry stone (up to 1.30m in width), which butted against the face of the existing north hall wall (589). At the southern edge of Trench O the surface of floor 785, and underlying red clay 558/1109, was cut by the construction trench (824 inside and 1101 outside) for east-west wall foundation 789 which forms the base of the south wall of the existing hall with an internal off-set of 0.2m and the buttresses (486, 489) seen outside in 2008 (above, on page 70).

Investigation of the intersection of these two walls suggested that 654 probably bonded into 789 and therefore forms a contemporary return. This was the view of Radford and Hallam (1953, 58) who saw both the junction more clearly and a scar on the south wall of the hall; this was not evident when the wall was recorded in 2007 (see page 178). From the stonework that was visible in 2009 it remains possible that 654 continued to the south with 789 built across it. As noted above (on page 50), no evidence for a wall in this position was noticed on the south side of the south wall in the beam engine pit. The two walls do, however, differ in construction: 789 is made of large blocks of lias rather than the softer North Curry stone used in 654. From the results of this excavation no definite conclusion can be reached regarding this relationship and it therefore remains possible that 654 represents an element of an intermediate modification to the apparently broader Hall 1. Regardless of the precise sequence of events it is clear that the eventual result was a principal stone structure of considerably reduced width defined by 654 to the east and 789 to the south.

Figure 5.17: *Pier base 895 from the north, where cut away diagonally by 926, whose fill (811) can be seen to the left of the scale. 1m scale.*

Figure 5.18: *The north side of pier base 657 completely filling the cut through red gravel 668 (seen in section to right and left) and buried soil 570/708 (seen in the base of the excavation). 30cm scale.*

Apparently contemporary with Wall 654, in that it cut the same floor layers, was an isolated area of mortared masonry (895, Figure 5.17) roughly square in plan with sides of 1.1m extending to a depth of 0.6m. A second area of mortared

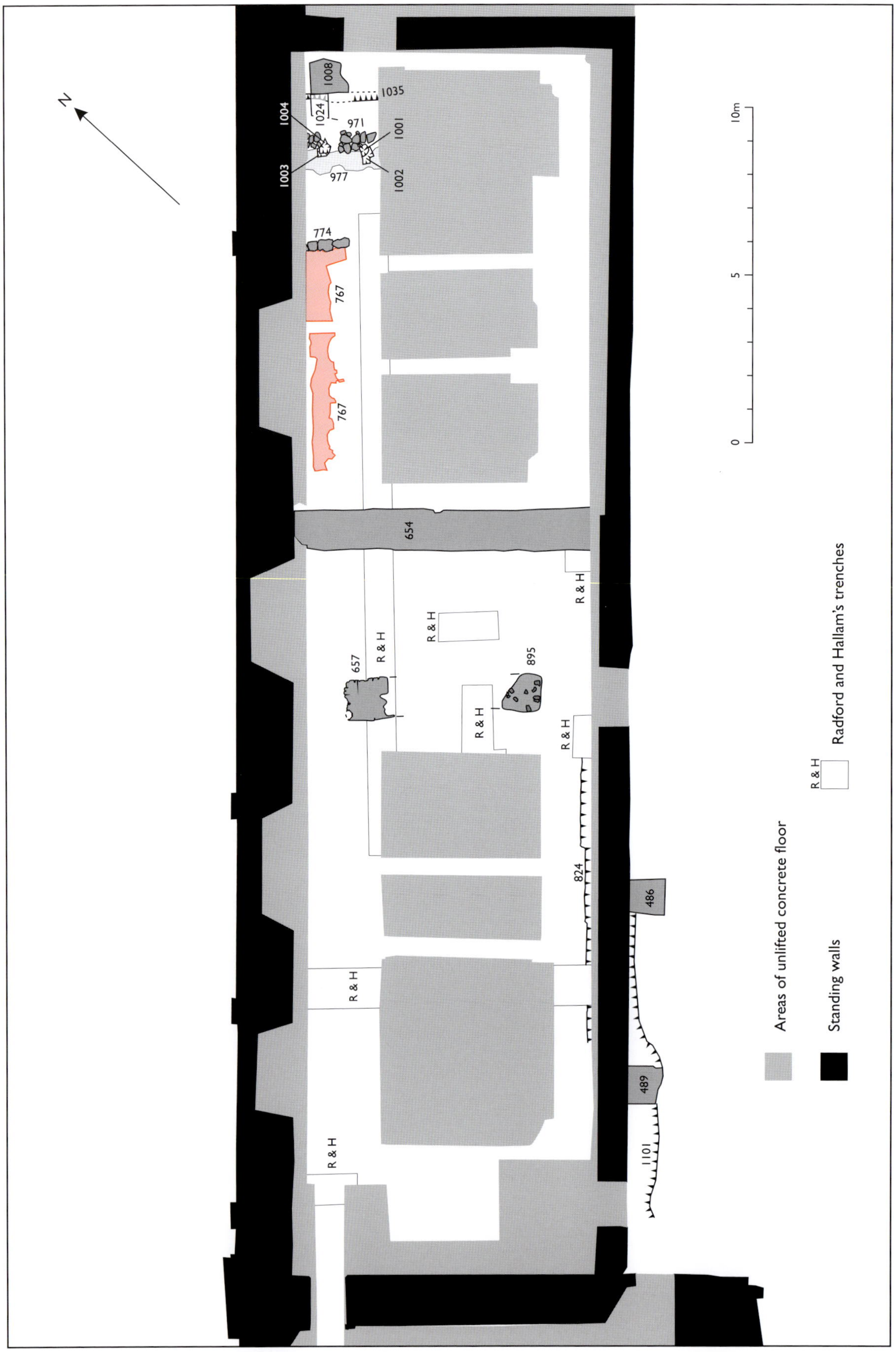

Figure 5.16: *Features associated with Hall 2 together with features to the west of the hall and of possibly earlier dates.*

masonry (657, Figure 5.18 on page 83) of near identical construction and size was encountered in Trench N, 3.4m to the north of 895, the construction of which was cut directly through red clay 558 and gravel 668. The masonry was predominantly North Curry stone with some reused dressed blocks, very similar in style to that of Wall 654.

This similarity of character, stratigraphic location and position on an axis parallel to Wall 654 strongly suggests that these three elements functioned as parts of the same structure. That these two masonry foundations were designed to carry load-bearing vertical supports, either timber or, perhaps more likely, masonry, seems certain. It is unlikely that they formed part of a row of columns along the length of the building as no others were seen, either in the present excavation or by Radford and Hallam. It seems more likely that 657 and 895 formed the foundations for a cross passage with three arched openings into the hall to the west and perhaps a gallery over (see page 184).

Activity to the east of Hall 2

Whereas at the west end of the Great Hall the finished levels required by the builders lay within the red clay (558) and only those features that cut the clay needed to be excavated, at the east end, beyond Hall 2, the deposits that were to be removed were considerably more complex.

Activity possibly associated with Hall 1

The large ditch or terrace (776) appears to have been deliberately infilled with clean red clay (767/1063). No later features reached beneath this clay which must therefore be more than 0.5m thick and it appeared to extend over much of the eastern end of Trench N, although it could not be certain that the isolated areas seen were all of the same deposit. The clay appeared to form the base for a series of compacted, probably internal, floor layers composed of sand, mortar, ground Hamstone and North Curry stone commencing with 775/777/1020. It is possible that these floor deposits extended westwards over the red clay (558) and had been cut by the east wall of Hall 2 (654) but this could not be proved because of the truncation of deposits in this area.

At the east end of Trench N a length of north-south wall (1008), up to 1.3m in width was exposed, comprising a rubble core faced to the west by squared North Curry sandstone; the facing to the east appeared to have been removed by the subsequent construction of the existing east wall of the hall. Full excavation was not possible and robbing of the upper courses of Wall 1008 made understanding of its relationships with surrounding deposits difficult to determine but it appeared to have been constructed at a similar level to the spine-wall contained in 569/905. The robber trench (1035) associated with Wall 1008 was traced the full width of Trench N but its presence in Trench O to the south was not established; it may have remained obscured by an unexcavated later dump (865). Immediately to the west of the remains of Wall 1008 was a shallow flat-bottomed feature (1025). The base of this contained a thin, level deposit of compacted mortar (1024) and it seems probable that the feature was designed to contain a large, flat slab, later removed; this might suggest a threshold slab, which might indicate the exterior side of a door at this point. The wall and putative slab appeared to be later than a red clay (1036, only seen in a robber trench, 1023), which may be the same as 767/1063 (above). If the interpretation of a doorway given here is accepted it would suggest a building to the east with open ground to the west.

Activity probably associated with Hall 2

Wall 1008 was demolished and its foundation partially robbed by cuts 1023, and 1035 (see above) and the holes backfilled. The area was then levelled by a dump of crushed stone and river gravel (1019) to form the base for a mortar floor (974, Figure 5.19 on the next page). The mortar floor ran westwards up to a north-south wall foundation (971) of chert rubble and clay (Figure 5.19) and appeared to be contemporary with it. Three metres to the west of Wall 971, the remains of a second possible narrow north-south wall (774/1032) of clay-bonded slate was identified, the shallow construction cut for which penetrated clay levelling 776/1065 below. This group of contexts appear to be foundations and floor surfaces associated with timber buildings to the east of Hall 2 and serving some form of ancillary function, probably kitchens.

Wall foundation 971 was later cut along its west side by a broad north-south trench (1015), which was filled by a large quantity of hard lime mortar (763/977) into which two square posts of similar dimensions had been pushed before it had fully set, leaving impressions 1002 and 1003. These appear to be the remains of an unusual foundation again supporting a timber structure. The plaster-embedded posts 1002 and 1003 were accompanied by adjacent postholes (1001, 1004) which may indicate the locations of replacement

Figure 5.19: Wall 971 from the south with mortar floor 974 to the right. The white mortar in section to the left is 763/977. 1m scale.

posts, avoiding the hard mortar, or holes dug to extract the posts from the mortar (or both). The fills were indistinguishable when excavated suggesting that both holes were back-filled simultaneously.

Later structures at the east end

Several substantial features at the east end of the hall appeared to form parts of structures lying to the east of Wall 654 and to pre-date the final lengthening of the hall to its present form. Most of these were seen in separate trenches and cannot be certainly connected but similarities of alignment, construction and associated finds suggests that they are contemporary. It is probable that the well excavated by Radford and Hallam in 1952 (not re-investigated during this project) also belongs to this phase of activity.

In Trench O to the south, the position of a north-south wall was indicated by the presence of mortared slate rubble foundation (861) faced with blocks of dressed North Curry stone on the east side. On the west side was a projection (854) of similar, though less substantial, construction with the appearance of a buttress. Limited excavation to the south of 854 suggested that the ground had been raised here, as a deposit of broken mortar and slates (887) was found. The slates lent where they had fallen against both walls and rested on a deposit of red clay (unexcavated), which had been cut to the south, possibly by the construction trench of the south wall of the hall. It would seem likely that these slates had formed the roof of a building of which 861 had been the wall.

To the west of Wall 861 the floor surfaces were sealed by various dumps of clay and crushed stone, principally 844, 845 and 848 of which the last yielded scraps of 12th-century pottery (presumably residual). Over these was laid a coherent, probably external, surface of pitched lias and chert (852/3) which extended to the east to butt against the west face of "buttress" 854. Some of the components of this surface appeared fissured and fractured indicating that it may have been subjected to high temperatures. Its initial appearance suggested a fireplace but its position relative to the wall and Buttress 854 would argue against this. To the east another possible wall (1211) was seen but not investigated during later work by the builders, running north to south about 2m from the present east wall.

To the north in Trench N was a structure of mortared stone and brick (730) measuring over 2.20m from east to west and of uncertain extent to the north and south. The structure had been built in a wide cut (757) and comprised a central drain channel, walled to east and west. The base of the drain was formed of closely-jointed lias slabs and sloped from south to north from a highest point (within the excavated area) of 17.06m down to 16.85m aOD where it left the excavated area in the direction of the north hall wall.

Offset from the west side of the channel was a square brick-walled chamber. This appeared to be the bottom of a chute from a privy; the base was flush with that of the main drain and was also surfaced with lias slabs sloping to form a central gutter. The presence of bricks suggests that this may be of 17th-century date; the size of the bricks (9" x 4¼" x 2¼") is similar to those used in Gray's Almshouses of 1635–40 (Radford and Hallam 1953, 79) and they are likely to be of a similar date. It is possible that they are earlier as, although Gray's Almshouse is the earliest surviving brick building in Somerset, bricks are recorded at Taunton in the Pipe Rolls as early as 1499 (see page 270).

The drain was found filled and covered with similar bricks and stone rubble (743) appearing to have been dumped from the south-west, an area where Radford and Hallam discovered similar bricks in the back-fill of the well. The top metre of the well had been destroyed by a

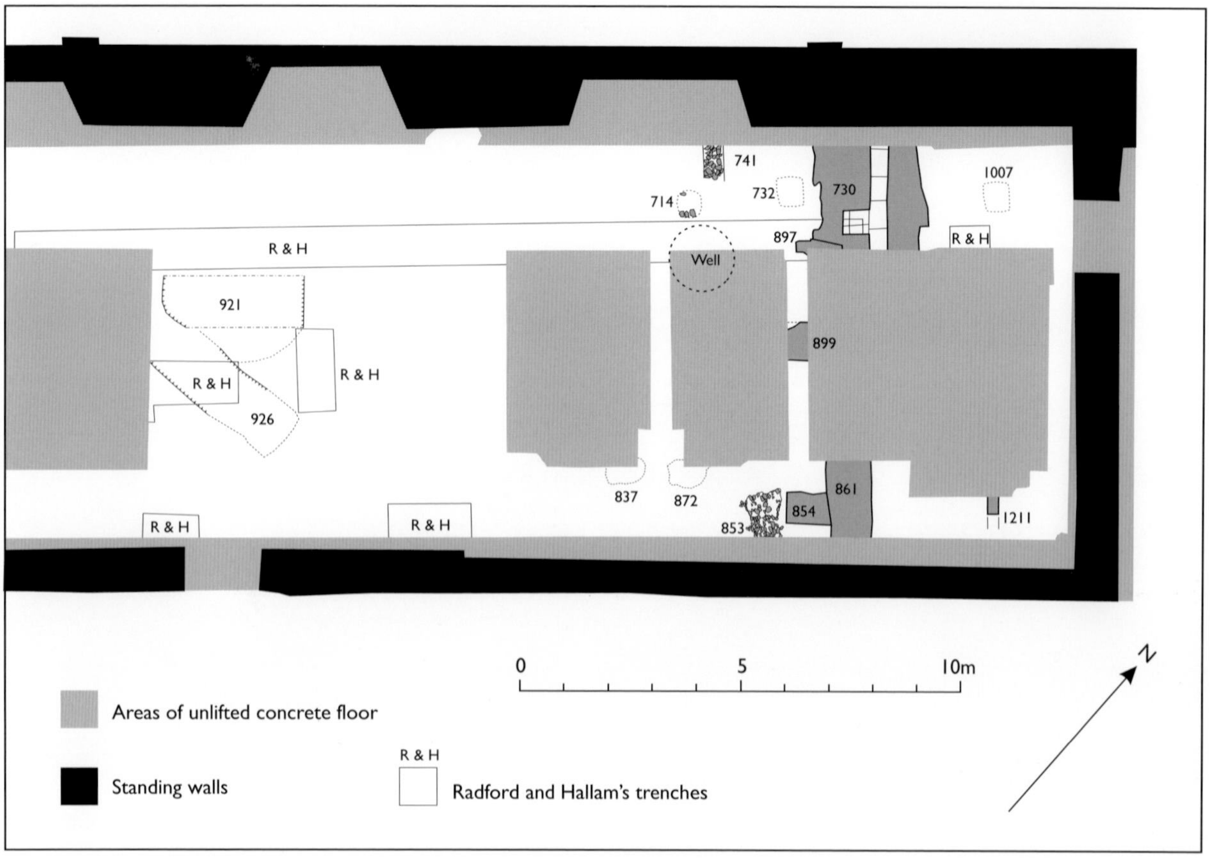

Figure 5.20: *Seventeenth- and eighteenth-century features in the west end of the Great Hall.*

large pit, probably dug to rob the stonework; Radford and Hallam's explanation that it had been destroyed by "bombardment during the Civil War" is unlikely in view of the absence of high-explosive shells at that date. The backfill of the pit and the well below was identical, and appears similar to the backfill (743) of the drain, containing a large number of broken bricks. However, there was more domestic rubbish in the fill of the well and a greater range of building materials (ridge tiles and slates).

It would appear that the in-fills of the well and the drain represent the demolition of the same brick and stone structure at some time after the deposition of clay pipes of *c.*1640–70 (see page 133) in the silt on the base of the drain. Radford and Hallam (1953, 88) suggest that the infilling of the well was part of clearance activities following damage in the Civil War and they date it to 1659 (the date carved on the north-east corner of the Great Hall, see page 168).

In the narrow cross-trench T, further masonry was seen that appeared to be a component of these structures. A Morte slate wall (899) crossed the trench from east to west with an apparent face on the south side. The northern edge was obscured by what appeared to be an area of later disturbance (897) but on the southern edge of Trench N more east-west masonry was evident, possibly a continuation of Wall 899 and certainly bonded into Drain 730. The western extent of this masonry had been removed by the robbing pit for Radford and Hallam's well, or their own excavation and the relationships to the east were unfortunately hidden beneath the concrete.

To the west was a hard packed, lime and crushed stone floor (746) which extended 2m to the west, and beyond the excavated area to the south. It was overlain by a continuous thin layer of finely crushed charcoal (745) throughout its exposed extent (Figure 5.23 on page 90). Towards the western edge of these surfaces a steep-sided, north-south aligned slot (742) was cut which contained stone packing (741) of a character consistent with packing for the supports of a timber structure. The charcoal (745) contained a clay pipe of 1630–50 and appeared to have built up against Wall 899. The date suggests that the charcoal is a product of burning during the Civil War, either a direct result of hostilities or from burnt rubbish during clearance.

Figure 5.21: *Tumbled bricks (743) filling the southern end of drain 730. 2m scale.*

Final Hall extension and associated features

By the commencement of this phase the stone and timber structures described above had been demolished, as was the Hall 2 east wall (654), and the hall was extended westwards to its current extent, although only the construction cut for the present east wall was visible within the excavated areas. Within the area then enclosed, the floor level was raised significantly by substantial clay dumps (735 to the north and 864 to the south). These dumps were only recognised in the eastern part of the excavation but probably originally extended throughout the entire interior of the hall and were subsequently been removed, probably at the time of the insertion of the suspended timber floor. The principal evidence for this is the numerous post holes (discussed below) that appeared to be too shallow to have supported posts and must therefore have been cut from a higher level and then truncated. It seems likely that the western part of the spine-wall foundation was robbed at this time (on the basis of an early 18th-century clay pipe).

Among the large number of post-holes and pits, which are considered below, a few were of a more substantial nature and may have held the supports for internal structures (Figure 5.20 on the previous page). To the eastern end of Trench N pits 732 and 1007 were both of similar size, of square plan and contained dense stone packing; to the west of these, on a different

***Figure 5.22:** Drain 730 fully emptied. The charcoal (745) covering floor 746 is visible to the right. 1m scale.*

line, a third large pit (714) contained a mortared masonry pad (712). To the south, 837 and 872 were of similar size and all these would have been capable of supporting a raised timber structure. Some of these posts may have supported the historically attested gallery in the courts and those that were datable (714, 837 and 1007) appeared to be of the late 17th century.

Three features were of very different character. The first was small pit (631) which was lined with crushed and burnt limestone and filled with reddened sand consistent with the application of intense heat. Although no other residue was present it is possible that this feature was associated with metalworking, perhaps lead during building or demolition work. The second was a large oval pit (921, Figure 5.20 on page 87), over 3.40m in length, which was partly excavated in the centre of the hall, the primary fill of which consisted of a layer hard, pure lime (920). This had clearly been discharged into the pit when wet and allowed to set. The pit may have been used as a bulk store for lime to be kept in readiness prior to mixing with aggregate and use in construction works. This was later cut by the third feature, a very large (3.8 x 1.2m), steep-sided, rectangular pit or trench (926, Figure 5.20) aligned diagonally (true east–west) to the walls of the hall and containing clay pipes suggesting a late 17th- or early 18th-century date; the function of the pit remains uncertain.

In the Undercroft (Room 23), in Trench V, a slate-lined north-south drain (555) and a small portion of a brick-lined feature (552), also probably a drain, were observed cutting the earlier levelling deposit 542. These features may be associated with the extensive renovations by Hammet of the southern range of buildings in *c.*1790.

19th- and 20th-century activity

Evidence for the suspended timber floor that was removed in 1952 survived in a few places as several east-west and north-south aligned sleeper-walls of brick. Another in the Undercroft was traced almost throughout the length of the excavation. Photographs of Radford and Hallam's work (see Figure 3.7 on page 48) show

Figure 5.23: *Mortar floor 746 covered by charcoal deposit 745 and cut by slot 742. Later features include stone-packed posthole 731 (next to the modern pile). In the foreground is the infilled eastern end of Radford and Hallam's Trench II. Scale 2m.*

that these walls were constructed three bricks high with wide ventilation gaps left between each brick. The walls supported wooden joists running north–south covered by floorboards.

Between these walls, in the Great Hall, an intermittent thin spread of compacted grey mortar (609/613 and 966) survived, probably the result of activity associated with the construction of the floor or other contemporary repairs. This was cut by two large, rubble-filled pits (633 and 644, Figure 5.24 on the facing page). The position of these, symmetrically just inside the opening of Window 53 suggests that they may have been involved with its creation, in 1863 according to Sloper's notebook (Sloper 1876b). If this is so, it is likely that the construction of the wooden floor also dates to 1863 when a cross wall dividing the hall into two courts is known to have been removed. No trace of this wall was found during the excavations which suggests that it had shallow foundations that were removed during the construction of the under-floor void.

Undated post holes and pits

Trenches N and O contained many post-holes and pits (Figure 5.24 on the next page), some circular but many rectangular. Most of these were stratigraphically undatable, as their shallow depth suggested that they had been truncated, but most were the latest features across the site. The shallowness may suggest, as argued above, that they pre-date the lowering of the ground to accept the suspended timber flooring. Some certainly cut through the remains of the 17th-century drain 730 and a larger number through clay dumps 735 and 864. It is impossible to be certain what specific function these features performed but it is likely that many were formed to hold scaffolding or small temporary structures associated with construction and alteration works in the Great Hall from the 17th to 20th centuries.

Photographs of Radford and Hallam's work in 1952 shows pairs of timber scaffolding poles along the north wall (some are visible

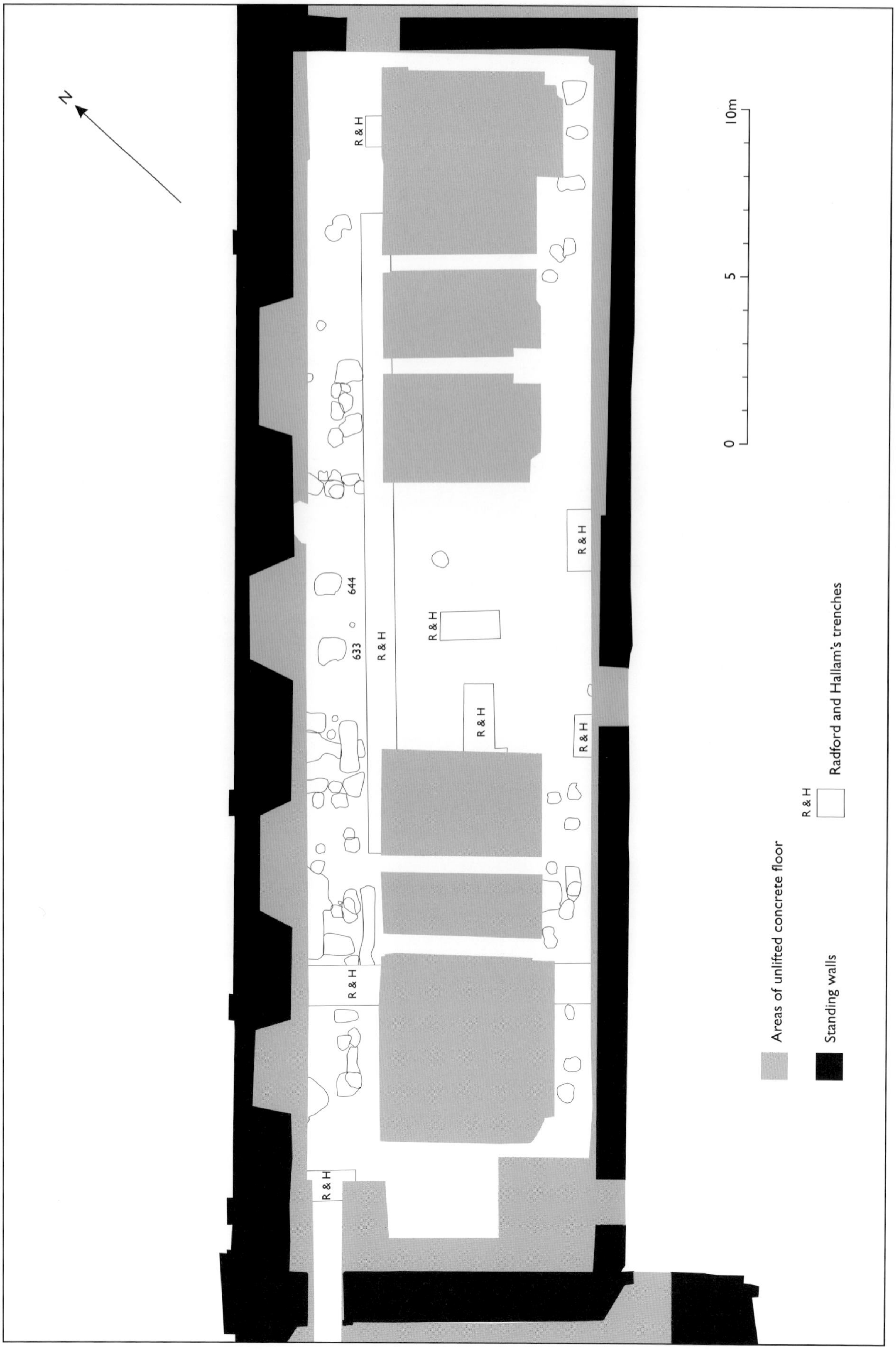

Figure 5.24: *Late pits. Only those mentioned in the text are numbered.*

in Figure 3.7 on page 48) that were presumably earth-fast, although none can be related to excavated features. The post-holes and pits were noticeably absent from the centre of the hall (in Trench P) supporting the suggestion that they relate to structures erected against the north and south walls.

1952 excavations and later

Radford and Hallam's 1952 investigations were clearly recognisable throughout the excavation as rectangular, vertically-sided and generally rubble-filled cuts, the locations of which compared favourably with Radford and Hallam's own plan. However there was some evidence for unrecorded exploration, notably along the edge of Wall 654 and the standing walls of the hall. A long cut (1073), parallel to wall foundation 589, may have been dug at this time but it is also possible that this was the result of some activity associated with the construction of the timber floor. The use of rubble to backfill appears to represent concern about slumping of the fill, as two of the trenches were further capped by concrete slabs before the whole area was sealed by a layer of coarse limestone scalpings, up to 0.30m in thickness, and finally by concrete to form the modern floor of the Great Hall and Undercroft at *c.*16.85m aOD.

The Gray Room (Room 43)

Trench X in the Undercroft (Room 23) was continued across the Gray Room (Room 43, Figure 5.25 on the next page) but, as it was only required to hold service ducts, there was only limited disturbance to deposits below the concrete floor. The foundations (1026) of the south wall of the undercroft were seen crossing Door 59 with a wide (30cm, 1ft) offset on the south side; the north side, within Room 23, was less clear. To the south of the wall was a buried soil (1027), similar to 570 seen in the Great Hall, which covered much of the room.

The wall (1031) forming the original south-east side of Room 43 and discovered in 1964 (Hallam 1965) was seen where the trench bifurcated. It appeared to be mostly North Curry sandstone, faced on both sides, with a rubble core. To its north was a small area of patchy mortar flooring (1030), which may have extended over the stones of the wall foundation (and thus be later than the late 18th century), although this was not certain.

The remainder of the trench, which continued until it reached the void beneath the suspended timber floor in Room 40, was not excavated deep enough to reveal any deposits earlier than the scalpings beneath the concrete floor.

5.5 Cable Trenches on Castle Green, 2009, *James Brigers*

A trench to carry a replacement electricity cable from the south side of Castle Green, across the line of the inner moat and then along the driveway was monitored. For the most part the trench on Castle Green itself was shallow and penetrated only into deposits associated with the construction of the modern road, the 1931 carpark surface and topsoil deposited in 1974 when the area was landscaped. However, an area of deeper excavation next to the moat wall revealed a well-preserved sequence of earlier deposits, the lowest of which sloped towards the moat. Mole-boring beneath the footpath disturbed a burial (1043) that lay beneath the moat wall. A further area of deeper excavation beneath the footpath on the south side of the road across Castle Green penetrated a possible buried soil deposit which lay beneath modern make-up and services and produced an abraded sherd of 12th/13th-century pottery. A French jetton of late medieval date was also recovered from the trench.

Within the courtyard of the castle, the route followed earlier service trenches and revealed little new but in the driveway a spur was taken into the Turnstile (Room 38). Examination here showed that the lower part of the west driveway wall survived, narrower than the upper part (of 1974), and with a 0.2m offset on the east side, 1.05m down. On the east side of the driveway, a stone wall foundation (Wall 962, see Figure 4.6 on page 59) was located below the front of the turnstile (see also page 102 for this wall in 2012/13).

Further human remains (1054) were revealed during coincidental emergency repairs to electricity cables in Castle Way on the west side of Castle Green. The trench had been excavated by contractors to level of approximately 16.83m aOD, 1.80 below the level of the street and at this point pale buff-orange sandy clay was exposed at the southern end. This was generally clean but contained a dense accumulation of human bone to the south including two skulls. Although only limited examination of the human remains was possible it appeared that at least one represented a portion of an intact burial, probably with the head to the west. Some of the bone disturbed by the contractors was retained for future study and dating (see page 151).

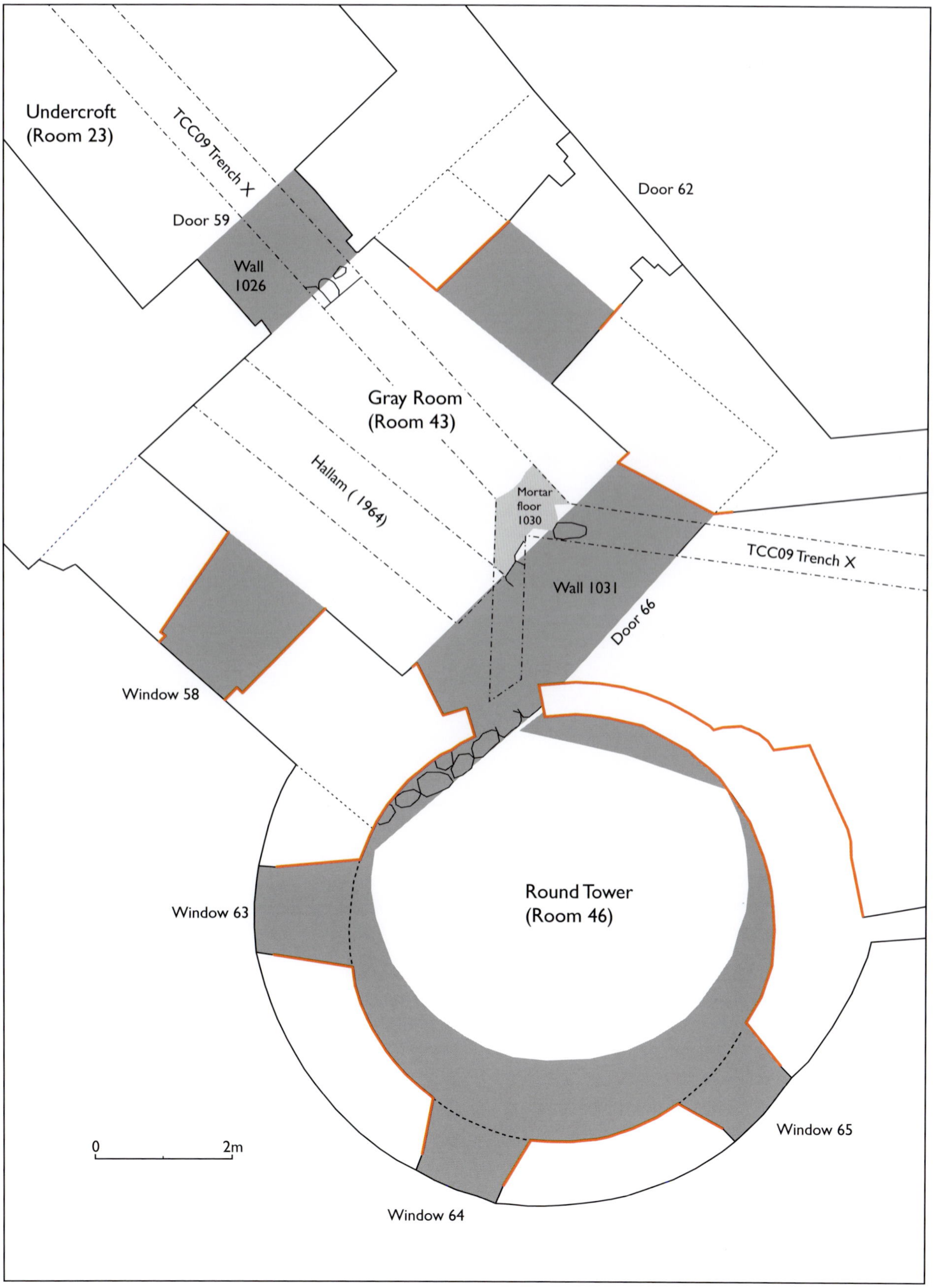

Figure 5.25: *The Gray Room (43) and Round Tower (46) showing earlier walls located in 1964, 1988 and 2009. Walls that have been seen to have been brick-lined are shown in red and 20th-century features are omitted.*

5.6 The Courtyard, 2009–11 (Trenches Z–AD)

Trench Z, 2009

Trench Z was a hole dug by the builders in 2009 for an unplanned inspection chamber and was only recorded after excavation in very wet conditions. It appeared to cut natural deposits, although these were probably the grave-earths recorded close by in Trench K and the 1978 water-pipe trench. Nothing had been seen by the builders, although a brick-built V-drain was visible in the section. A 1971 coin was recovered from the fill of the waterpipe trench.

Trenches AA and AB, 2010

At a late stage in the project it was decided that the gas main laid in 1988 was of inadequate diameter to supply the new boilers. A new supply was therefore proposed which would follow the existing one across the courtyard in the common service trench and then diverge at the northern end as regulations prohibited it from running underneath the concrete slab of the new entrance block. This last section was excavated archaeologically as Trench AA and the excavation by machine of the rest of the trench was monitored and recorded as Trench AB.

Trench AA was 6.5m long by 1m wide, it having been agreed with English Heritage that a narrower trench would not permit adequate recording. Much of the area of the trench contained modern service trenches (1140), specifically those for the fire main also seen in Trench E (page 65) and another steel pipe, probably also a water supply. The remainder of the trench contained medieval features, comprising a large cut feature (1147) with courtyard surfaces and make-up layers. No natural deposits were encountered, the earliest layers (1156 and 1157) were composed of mixed stone debris including chert, North Curry sandstone and Hamstone.

These earliest layers were sealed by a thick deposit (1155) of broken North Curry stone accompanied by broken roof slates and occasional water-worn pebbles. This would appear to be construction waste, rather than representing demolition, as there was no mortar present. Two sherds of 11/12th-century pottery were recovered from this layer as were some of the more uncommon animal bones. These included fish-heads which would suggest that the deposit included kitchen waste and a juvenile cat (Higbee this volume, 145). This is not too surprising as the castle kitchens are believed to lie just to the north.

Above this there was a courtyard surface (1152), of crushed North Curry stone with water-worn gravel pebbles, containing 12th-century pottery. Above this was a layer of green-grey sand (1145/51), derived from North Curry stone, with occasional larger fragments surviving. This may represent stone-dressing waste and was covered by a layer of demolition rubble (1143) and mortar. Large blocks, some dressed but broken were present; the stone was mostly North Curry with some red sandstone.

Layer 1143 may be associated with large cut 1147 which appeared to be a robbing trench for an east–west wall. The lower fills of this comprised broken stone, mostly North Curry but with some Hamstone, including a fragment of moulding, sand and mortar. The upper part of the feature had been filled with a thick deposit (1144) of red clay containing 10th-century pottery. This may be the same as 400, seen in Trench I at a similar level. It appeared that the uppermost deposits had been truncated as both 1143 and 1144 were covered by a thin trampled surface and then by modern building waste. This may date to as late as the 1930s and be associated with the construction of the Wyndham buildings and earthmoving for the laying of the courtyard gravel (1134). The latest feature seen was the construction trench for the siting of the almshouse here in 1992.

To the south, only two areas of early stratigraphy were observed in the side of the machined cut. The northernmost of these appeared to be the remains of a wall (1169) of two courses of mortared North Curry stone seen only in the east side of the trench. This appears to be part of the wall (1175) seen during subsequent landscaping works (see page 96). Further south was a fragment of another wall (1164), this time of mortared lias, which was seen crossing the base of the 1988 common service trench. Beyond this was a stone- and brick-built drain (1160) roofed with a piece of burnt moulded Hamstone, possibly a window mullion.

Courtyard landscaping

Following the departure of the main building contractors, the courtyard was carefully landscaped by Somerset County Council. In most areas this involved only the partial removal of the 1930s gravelled surface; earlier deposits were only exposed in the previously grassed area to the north of Castle House and in small holes excavated for a statue-base and lightning protection.

The new location for the statue of Lord Harding of Petherton required a shallow square trench (AC) to be excavated to the south of Door 62. This

Figure 5.26: *Wall 1187 as exposed in the trench for the heating pipes. The red sandstone face is visible to the left just supporting the north wing of Castle House. 1m scale.*

Figure 5.27: *Wall 1177 with quadrant 1193 and drain pipes 1181. Looking west. 1m scale.*

revealed a brick-lined structure running parallel to the wall. During the ground-reduction for the landscaping this was seen to be part of a French drain (1173) that continued along the south range to the Gateway. A connection to the castle drainage was found at the north end and it is not clear why the system was abandoned, probably in the 1970s, as damp continues to be a problem in the buildings. As part of the current works it was reinstated with permeable plastic pipework. The only other features recorded during the works for the statue base were a brick V-drain and a lead pipe – both marked on Spencer's plan of services (SANHS 6017).

The works to reduce the ground level of the former grassed area discovered two unexpected walls as well as relocating the well (TCB 158). The first wall (1175) was found towards the centre of the courtyard and comprised two lines of red sandstone. Only the surface of these was exposed but they seem to represent two skins of a wall, about 1.2m thick, with a rubble core. A face was clearly visible on the north-east side but the south-west was both less complete and less regular. It is likely that this wall was also seen in the gas main trench (above, page 94) and its alignment suggests a relationship with the Great Hall rather than the South Range. Its construction, but not its alignment, resembled that of the second wall (1187) which was discovered running partly underneath the west wall of the East Wing of Castle House. Wall 1187 also comprised two facings with a rubble core, the east being of red sandstone and the west of more irregular lias. The wing of Castle House appeared to have been built without knowledge of the presence of this wall as it rested only on the easternmost 10cm of the stonework. Wall 1187 continued south and it seems certain that it also pre-dates the main part of Castle House as it does not fit the internal arrangements of that building. Both Wall 1187 and the north wing of Castle House align with Wall C rather than the South Range.

The opportunity was taken to empty the 1988 heating duct trench where it crossed Wall 1187 and this showed that the east face of the wall was made of very finely dressed and fitted red sandstone blocks, some so thin that they almost appeared as a cladding. The wall was also found to turn westward at this point, about 10cm before it would have been found in Trench H, and run along the line of the heating duct trench, which must have removed a large part of it. The wall was traced for about 3m before it became invisible in the trench as they diverged. It is not clear how this wall was not recorded when the trench was dug in 1988 (see page 55). The similarities between these two walls, and the lack of any other wall dressed with red sandstone, suggest that they may have been contemporary and therefore joined. Despite the high level that they were seen, it is likely that they pre-date the construction of the South Range as they are only aligned on the Great Hall or Wall C.

The only other features recorded were late and included another brick V-drain leading to the doorway of Castle House and traces of brick walling to the north and west of the stair turret (Figure 5.27 on the previous page). They comprised a brick wall (1177) running north from the north-east corner of the turret, turning east and then south to meet Castle House. At the south end the wall appeared to curve outwards to form a quadrant (1183) although this may have been a separate feature. Another curving section of brick wall ran parallel perhaps forming a drain. From the northern end of this outer wall, a single line of small diameter tile drains (1181) ran northwards.

Chapter 6

Investigations in Castle Green and Castle House, 2010–2013

6.1 Castle Green, 2010–12 *Paul Rainbird and Chris Webster*

In parallel with The Museum of Somerset project, Taunton Deane Borough Council, through its Project Taunton, landscaped Castle Green (see Figure 6.1 on the following page). This included the construction of a pedestrian bridge giving better access from the riverside to the green and the removal of the carpark, which was replaced by grass and paved areas. Preliminary investigations by means of boreholes and test pits were archaeologically monitored by Exeter Archaeology (Passmore 2010). This provided useful information on the profile of the inner moat (see Section 14.3 on page 239) and showed that the proposals, which mostly involved raising the ground level, would have a limited impact on buried deposits.

Three areas were initially targeted for hand excavation but following changes to the design, the electricity junction box on the northern edge of the current carpark (Area 2) was not excavated, leaving the south bridge abutment for the new bridge over the inner bailey moat (Area 1) and the gully and associated drain runs within the carpark of the Castle Hotel (Area 3).

Other parts of the development were monitored:

- Landscaping within Castle Green grassed area which included the removal of existing street furniture such as kerbs and lampposts.
- New surfaces and planters within Castle Green and the Castle Hotel carpark.
- Ground reduction within the existing carpark and access roads.
- New services within Castle Green and the Castle Hotel carpark, with particular reference to cable access chambers and slotdrains. Although a number of the services and fittings had been designed to be incorporated within new or existing surfaces there were a number of locations in which the excavation for slotdrains and their associated siltboxes had the potential to disturb archaeological deposits.
- The removal of a lime tree and its root plate on Castle Green.
- The creation of the new north entrance to the Museum of Somerset.
- The relocation of the commemorative stones (the Sword in the Stone and the Sarsen Stone).
- The enhancement works adjacent to the moat garden edge and on the approach to the south gate of Taunton Castle.
- Work associated with the construction of the new footbridge.

The fieldwork was managed for AC Archaeology by Tanya James and the reporting by Andrew Passmore. The site work was undertaken by Fiona Pink, Jerry Austin, Chris Caine, Simon Hughes and Kerry Kerr- Peterson. Information on finds from this work can be found in Section 7.6 on page 146 and the report on the human remains in Section 7.7 on page 147.

Excavation: Area 1

The excavation for the southern bridge abutment comprised an area approximately 9.3m long by 2.5m wide and was located immediately to the south of the boundary wall on the south side of the moat garden (see Figure 6.1 on the following page). Approximately 0.4m of modern paving

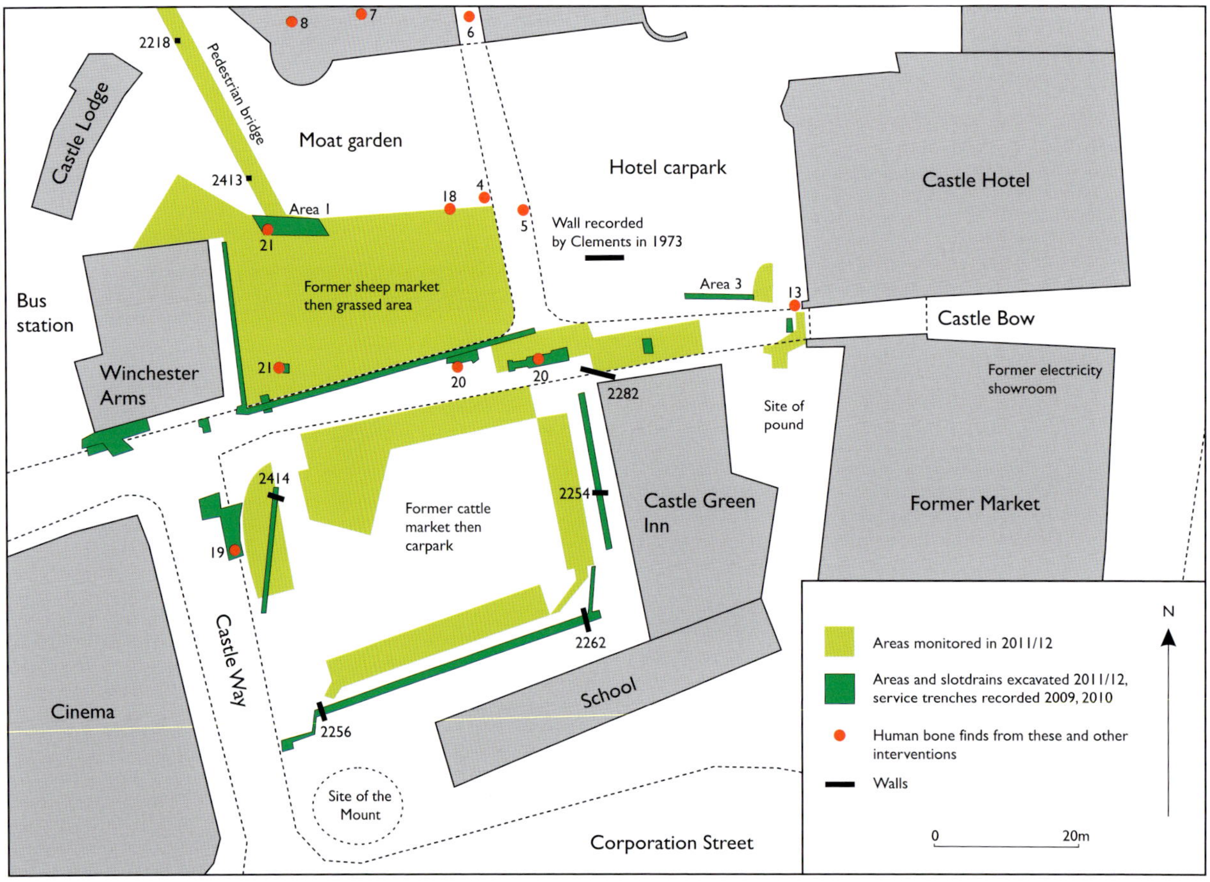

Figure 6.1: *Excavations and monitoring on Castle Green, 2010–2012 with locations of human bone finds (numbers refer to human bone groups listed in Figure 14.2 on page 241). After Rainbird (2015, Fig. 2) with additions.*

slabs and curbing and their associated levelling deposits were removed using a mechanical excavator fitted with a toothless bucket under archaeological control. The post-medieval deposits below were assessed in a smaller area and then the rest of the trench opened by machine down to the level of the cattle market surface (2005).

The earliest deposit encountered was 2115, which contained a burial (2099) but the cut for the grave was difficult to discern. The full extent of the skeleton was not established as the bottom of the excavation had been reached and parts of this skeleton have been left in situ. The skeleton had also been damaged by a post-medieval pit (2049) which cut it on the southern side.

Above this were three layers (2020, 2019 and 2006) of dumping, rich in disarticulated human and animal bone. Deposit 2020 consisted of pale greyish brown sandy clay covering the whole extent of the trench and was similar to 2115, although 2020 contained abundant disarticulated human bone in contrast to the articulated burial in the layer below. The majority of the Saxo-Norman pottery was derived from this layer. This indicates that 2020 was a layer of redeposited Late-Saxon soil, most likely redeposited during the construction of the moat.

Deposit 2019 consisted of redeposited natural also probably derived from the digging of the moat for the inner ward. It was present across the whole trench except where cut by later features and consisted of bright bluish-grey shale. It was most abundant at the west end of the trench where it was 0.15m thick. This bedrock type was not seen elsewhere in the castle but is probably a reduced facies within the Mercia mudstone.

Layer 2006 was exposed over the whole of the Area 1 excavation and contained abundant disarticulated human bone. It was initially thought that it was deposited, like the layers below, during the construction of the castle moat, producing a mixture of redeposited natural clay, early-medieval subsoil and the fill from disturbed graves. However a piece of stem from a clay tobacco pipe and a sherd of 17th-century pottery indicate that this deposit is post-medieval in date and may relate to the refurnishing of the ditch during the Civil War. In general, it was up to 0.43m thick and consisted of bright reddish-orange slightly silty clay.

Figure 6.2: *The well-preserved paving of the 19th-century cattle market. Photo AC Archaeology.*

Deposit 2006 was cut by 24 stake holes ranging in depth from 0.30m to 0.04m and diameter from 0.17m to 0.06m, and six or possibly seven pits. The pits had been filled with material containing disarticulated human and animal bone that was probably the earth dug from them. In the limited area it was not easy to interpret these but there were also four linear features, running south to north, that were probably for drainage of the area into the moat.

Above these were make-up layers for a market surface (2005) formed of tightly-packed sub-angular stones ranging in size from 25mm by 25mm to 75mm by 50mm. This was cut by several large square and circular modern pits.

Excavation: Area 3

An area of approximately 5.8m by 0.6m was excavated in the carpark (see Figure 6.1 on the preceding page) for the purpose of creating a new gully for drainage and the laying of a new drain pipe. The deposits were excavated to a maximum depth of 0.95m and only modern and post-medieval levelling layers were exposed. A deposit (2406) of dark reddish brown clay revealed in patches may represent the remains of material derived from the construction of the moat as it is similar to 2006 in Area 1. It did not, however, contain disarticulated human bones or any other finds.

Monitoring

The ground reduction in the existing Castle Green carpark was monitored in several phases and in all cases this was a shallow operation and did not penetrate below late post-medieval levelling deposits (see Figure 6.1 on the facing page). A large area in front of the Castle Green Inn public house and elsewhere revealed well-preserved brick paving of the former cattle market (Figure 6.2). It was possible to leave much of this in situ with the new surface made up from this level. Elsewhere the paving was removed and the new surface constructed on top of the hardcore present beneath the paving. In the area to the east of the Winchester Arms the deposits had been heavily disturbed by modern services.

The monitoring of the excavation to a depth of 0.5m of a 1m wide drain trench running east-west for a distance of 29.5m on the northern side of the former roadway revealed modern and late post-medieval levelling deposits to a depth of approximately 0.4m below ground surface. At this depth, and where not disturbed by modern services, a greyish brown sandy clay containing common small fragments of slate and occasional crushed oyster shell and charcoal was present across the length of the trench except at the western end where, at a similar depth, a deposit was exposed similar to the redeposited early medieval subsoil (2006) seen in Area 1 containing occasional small fragments of bone.

Another slotdrain ran east-west at the southern edge of the carpark to the north of the School. This also revealed a deposit similar to 2006 at its western end at a depth of 0.55m below ground surface. At the far western end the top of a possible mortared stone wall (2256) was partially revealed, but excavation stopped at this point and it was not possible to characterise the feature, although it is probably of later post-medieval date as it abuts the cattle market surface which did not appear to continue west of this point. At the east end of the drain trench was a north-south aligned stone wall (2262). This was 0.92m wide and survived to a height of 0.60m. It was constructed of blocks of slate bonded by light yellow sandy mortar. It had been constructed within a deposit (2263) of post-medieval date.

A north-south aligned drain trench was excavated running parallel to the east side of the Winchester Arms public house. This trench was excavated to a depth of 0.60m and where not disturbed by modern services a fairly uniform deposit of greyish and reddish brown sandy clay (2411), measuring 0.28m thick, was exposed. At the southern end of the trench a small patch of cobbles (2412) was present below this layer. They were laid into the top of deposit (2006) that contained occasional fragments of bone

This drain was joined to an existing service to the east. The excavation around the pre-existing drain revealed the remains of four discrete skeletons (SK2224, SK2228, SK2231 and SK2234) at a

Figure 6.3: *Skeletons SK2224, SK2228, SK2231 and SK2234 discovered during work to an existing drain. Photo AC Archaeology.*

depth of 0.65m below ground surface (Figure 6.3). Although some articulation was present in all skeletons except SK2224, the remains had been disturbed by the previous drain excavation and probably by other unidentified earlier activities, although they retained an east-west alignment. All the skeletons had been deposited in a matrix of light yellowish grey sandy clay with inclusions of brick and mortar (2238). The cuts for the graves were difficult to discern and the layer (2237) which covered the skeletons, and contained disarticulated human bones, was difficult to distinguish from 2238. However, the collection of bones for juvenile SK2224 was associated with a coffin nail, and it may be that this was a re-interment of a disturbed burial.

A north-east/south-west aligned drain trench was excavated in the north-west corner of the former carpark to a depth of 0.55m. For the majority of this trench only modern hardcore was removed, but this exposed a deposit similar to 2006 at its base. At the north-east end of the trench a late post-medieval north-west to south-east aligned stone wall (2414) was exposed. A trench for a siltbox at the north-east end of the drain trench was dug a further 0.40m into 2006 and occasional small fragments of human bone were recovered.

A cable access pit was excavated on the western side of the carpark adjacent to the bus stops. It measured 1.50m by 1.50m. A deposit (2308) consisting of reddish-brown clay was exposed at a depth of 0.75m and contained animal bone and a sherd of medieval pottery. This appeared to be an undisturbed medieval deposit, although not containing any human bone, that had been heavily disturbed by modern services and the laying of the existing surface.

A north-south aligned drain trench was excavated on the east side of the former carpark. The brick paved surface of the former cattle market was exposed along the full length of the trench and was recorded and then removed. An east-west aligned post-medieval wall (2254) which abutted the cattle market paving was exposed in an area central to the trench.

The stripping of the roadway approaching the Inner Gate exposed only late post-medieval deposits including a short section of north-west/south-east aligned stone wall (2282) measuring 2.1m long and 1m wide. It is difficult to associate this with any other known structures and it may have been a structural support for the former roadway.

Topsoil stripping, the moving of an electricity cable and the piling and pile cap excavations were monitored in the area where the new footbridge crossed the area of the inner moat. Late post-medieval and modern deposits were exposed containing abundant brick and mortar fragments up to a depth of 0.7m below the ground surface in the areas stripped (contexts in this area are numbered 2200–2222). Central to the stripped area a short length of late post-medieval stone wall (2413), 1.75m long and 0.5m wide, was exposed. It was constructed using a greyish yellow lime mortar containing fragments of slate, brick, tile and charcoal.

The pilings, which were 0.45m in diameter, indicated that the depth of post-medieval deposits to the base of the moat ranges from 5.5m to 6.5m matching previous borehole data (Passmore 2010). Piling holes within the central section of the bridge (Piles 1, 3 and 11) indicated that waterlogged deposits are present at the base of the moat. Piles 9 and 12, the southernmost pile cap prior to the south abutment, encountered the natural at approximately 4m indicating the edge of the moat. Piling in the area of the southern abutment (Piles 13–18) showed that the natural was present at 2.50m, above which the early medieval subsoil (2115) survived to a thickness of approximately 0.5m thick.

Excavation for the pile cap above piles 9 and 12 exposed a stone wall (2218) constructed of large sandstone blocks bonded by dark reddish-brown sandy mortar. The wall was constructed within late post-medieval deposits and the top of the wall was approximately 1.50m below the ground surface as existed prior to stripping and digging for the bridge works.

6.2 Castle House, 2012–13 *James Brigers and Chris Webster*

Following the opening of the museum in September 2011, Castle House in the South Range was comprehensively refurbished by the Somerset Building Preservation Trust. Structural details and interpretation of the building can be found in Chapter 13 but a description of earlier structures discovered during groundworks is given here. The monitoring and recording were undertaken by James Brigers (2013a) using site code TCH12 and the description below is based on that report.

Interior

Small holes dug by the builders to assess the ground floor structure and to route services out of the building were recorded without adding much new information but Trench 4, dug to insert a new door threshold, was more informative. This exposed the foundations of the curtain wall below the former Window 87 in Room 32 which could be seen to coincide with the upper part of the wall on the south elevation but to extend northwards further into the room. No dating evidence was recovered but it seems most likely that this was the thicker medieval wall reported by Spencer (Anon 1910). The northern edge of the wall lay outside the trench and another excavation, in former Fireplace 417, did not reach sufficient depth to confirm Spencer's finding.

The Moat

Substantial ground reduction was undertaken in the former courtyard to the south to provide an access route from the Turnstile to the new door replacing Window 87. As Trench D (see page 64) had shown, the upper parts of this area comprised moat infilling and these were removed by machine under supervision, as was the concrete and brick drain (TCC 103, see also Figure 3.3 on page 38). The lowest layer encountered (TCH 907) consisted of stone rubble with occasional brick and tile with pottery and glass dating to the early 19th century, above which was a thick layer of loam (TCH 905) appearing to represent a soil build-up. Both these layers were missing at the eastern end, where they sloped down below the excavation level before reaching the curved wall TCC 105. As seen in Trench D, the wall continued downwards with no sign of a foundation level. It did contain a small brick-lined opening (TCH 825) at the lowest level reached which was used to pass services through from the courtyard to the north-east.

Following the removal of the concrete drain, the batter to the lower part of the curtain wall was seen along the western 10m of the excavation. Here it was predominantly chert-faced with remnants of a brown lime render in places. A hole broken through the wall below Window 168 showed that the wall face was approximately 0.13m thick beyond which was a core of small chert rubble bonded with pale yellow mortar. Three areas of the face had been patched with

Figure 6.4: Wall TCH 12 813 continuing Wall B across the Castle House courtyard. Photo: James Brigers.

18th- or 19th-century brickwork, which was also evident where the batter ended to the east, first becoming a level offset and then merging to the line of the wall face above. This corresponded with the start of the wall of the gable end of the east wing of Castle House and possibly the southern extent of the wall (1187) seen in the courtyard.

The Driveway

Trenches were dug to connect services to those under the driveway, which mostly re-excavated trenches dug in 2009 or earlier (see Section 5.5 on page 92 and Figure 4.6 on page 59). As well as possible drive surfaces, the foundations of a wall (TCH 1008) were recorded that appeared to coincide with those (TCC 962) seen in 2009. It seems likely that these are the foundations for the pre-turnstile building (Section 12.2 on page 216), which Spencer's plans, and early photographs, show running slightly west of the present wall line at this point.

The East Courtyard

Two narrow trenches were excavated across the courtyard for drainage and other services. Much of the area had been disturbed by previous service trenches but small "islands" of medieval stratigraphy remained. The principal discoveries were two stone walls, TCH 810 and TCH 813 (see Figure 8.3 on page 157). The more northerly (813) was 2.6m wide with faces of North Curry sandstone retaining a core of red-brown gravelly clay with North Curry rubble, all bonded by a red-brown lime mortar (Figure 6.4). For the most part, only one course was visible within the trench but a further two possible courses were seen in the sides, which here followed the line of an earlier service trench that had presumably cut through the wall. One stone of the second course survived on the south face, which had been dressed to a batter of about 15° from vertical. The lower course was undressed and clearly formed the foundations. A possibly contemporary surface (TCH 834) was seen to the south and this, the wall and deposits to the north were all buried beneath a substantial dump of material (TCH 818) that appeared to be demolition rubble. This layer appeared to form the base from which the east wall of Castle House had been built.

South of wall TCH 813, and unfortunately divorced from it, was an area containing several deliberately laid surfaces. It is possible that the lowest (TCH 811) was a continuation of surface TCH 834 but this could not be proved. Above these were the make up for a stone slabbed surface, of which one stone remained, and above that a possible brick surface below the present concrete yard.

The second wall (TCH 810) lay to the south and again only small fragments survived. These comprised two courses of red sandstone rubble bonded by a pale yellow sandy lime mortar. A compact dump of red clay to the north may have formed the wall core but its northern edge was obscured by later drain runs.

The curving wall (TCC 105) was uncovered to a depth of 0.4m where the other end of opening TCH 825 was visible. It appeared to continue as a culvert eastwards, built in brickwork with hard grey mortar that contrasted with the soft yellow mortar of the wall suggesting that the opening was cut through the pre-existing wall. It is possible that it formed a drain, exiting into the moat before that was infilled.

At the very north of the courtyard, a hole dug through the foundations of the south wall to connect the services into the building revealed a loose rubble core, from which was recovered a complete wine bottle base of the later 18th or 19th century that appears to provide a *terminus post quem* for the wall's construction.

6.3 Courtyard, 2016 *James Brigers and Chris Webster*

A small hole (see Figure 4.4 on page 57 for location), dug to access an old electricity cable, was monitored by James Brigers (2016) and revealed part of a wall running north–south . It contained red sandstone and appeared to be a continuation of wall 1175 (see page 96).

Chapter 7

Specialist Reports

Most of the reports that follow relate to the work by Somerset County Council. Finds from the work on Castle Green in 2011–13 work are in Section 7.6, and the report on the human remains excavated in that project, in Section 7.7.

7.1 The Pottery *David Dawson with Nicholas Dawson*

This report comprises two component parts. The pottery from the 2005–13 excavations is analysed in the first section. It is accompanied by the fabric type series which has been correlated as far as possible with those of Terry Pearson in *The Archaeology of Taunton* and Cathe Burrow for the excavations at 5–8 Fore Street, Taunton (Pearson 1984c; Burrow, C 1988). The second part is a summary of the pottery found during earlier excavations in and around the castle, notably those by Harold St George Gray. Much, but not all, of this was recorded and analysed by Terry Pearson but was published entirely in microfiche and therefore not widely accessible. His drawings are reproduced here (Figure 7.10 – Figure 7.17). Note that page numbers cited in Pearson (1984c) refer to numbered pages in the microfiche.

A small number of sherds from the fabric type series were subjected to a new technique using QEMSCAN, designed to provide a visual reference, to and quantitative analysis of, the mineralogy of both the matrix and inclusions of individual type sherds (Andersen *et al.* in press). For comparison, samples of waste sherds from seven post-medieval production sites in Somerset were also subjected to the same method of analysis. The results of this are given in Appendix A (from page 285), where four major mineralogical groups, A, B, C and D, with subgroups B1 and B2, are identified and described in detail.

Acknowledgements

The author of this report wishes to acknowledge the many hours of fruitful discussion with Chris Webster. Nicholas Dawson was invaluable in assisting with the sorting, recording and analysis of the sherds from the 2005–10 excavations and in preparing the drawings. Mike Ponsford and John Allan gave valuable advice on aspects of pottery identification. Jens Andersen and Gavyn Rollinson of the Camborne School of Mines, University of Exeter Tremough Campus, enthusiastically ventured into the exciting new realm of mineralogical analysis of sample sherds using QEMSCAN with the fascinating results explained in Appendix A. The Trustees of the Somerset Archaeological and Natural History Society kindly gave permission for the samples to be subjected to analysis. Finally Steve Minnitt, Head of Museums, and his staff, Sam Astill and Bethan Murray, of the Somerset Heritage Service are due thanks for their endless patience and kindness. Any shortcomings in recording and interpretation are the responsibility of the author.

Overall assessment and interpretation

As one would expect, the sequence from the totality of excavation that has been recorded over the past 150 years indicates that the Castle was supplied by its region and beyond. How this pattern changed through time is explored in greater detail below. Further there are four characteristics of the pottery sequence from Taunton Castle that should be noted with the caveat that these conclusions may well be distorted by the limited amount of excavation that has taken place, particularly of primary stratified contexts.

1. 10th/11th century. Pottery of this period is remarkably scarce (3 sherds). There is not the

quantity of material that indicates intensive domestic occupation of the site of the inner bailey. It may be that any such evidence lies under the earthworks of the "keep" and inner ramparts, such as found under the eastern rampart of Bristol Castle (Ponsford 1974) but if so it has yet to be found.

2. 11th/12th century. By far the largest component of the pottery sequence dates to this period – 25% of the sherds from the 2005–10 excavations and over 95% of the material preserved from Gray's excavations of the area of the keep. The overwhelming majority of these are from jars. Despite often being called cooking pots, very few show any signs of being used for this purpose over a fire. Variations in colouration are the flashes one would expect from the processes of oxidation, reduction and reoxidation in open-firing, not the result of subsequent use.

   There seems to be no other deposit of this size recorded from any other excavation of a castle. The sheer quantity seems far beyond the debris one would expect from ordinary domestic occupation. Mike Ponsford has commented to the author that most of the pottery seems to have been made in the mid to late 12th century, while Pearson (1984c) based his dating (see page 117) of this material at Taunton on the probably spurious historical date of 1138 (see page 266). Whilst contexts from which the 2005–13 material was found can be understood in terms of occupation debris, how the large quantities of pottery recovered by Gray came to be associated with the earthworks and structures of the "keep" remains a mystery. Are they containers from 12th-century storehouses that were cast aside for the new works?

3. The Inner Bailey. For the most part the pottery has been disturbed so many times that it reflects the effects of constant rebuilding and repair of the past 800–900 years.

4. The fill of the moats. Although not recorded in detail, pottery from the moat fill is almost invariably from the later 16th century onwards. This both confirms the view that nowhere has the moat and its associated leats been completely excavated in section and that the infilling was occasioned by the peace at the end of the Civil War. Pottery from various investigations survives in the archive in the County Museum but is not well recorded and is not reported on here in detail.

The pottery from the 2005–2013 excavations

The survey and excavations 2005–13 produced the largest assemblage of pottery yet recorded in detail from Taunton Castle of some 1106 sherds. Perhaps, given the undeveloped state of medieval and post-medieval pottery studies when earlier excavations were carried out in and around the castle, it is probable that there were quantities of pottery found but not all were retained for recording. These are revisited in the second part of this report. It has to be acknowledged that most pottery sherds recovered in the recent excavations were unusually small in size. From this and the composition of many contexts one may conclude that apart from a small number of early 11th- to 13th-century contexts much of the material has been mixed and redeposited many times during the complex history of building and alterations to the castle fabric. Yet these deposits do not reflect either a continuum of occupation or the typical range of wares that might be expected from a given period. There are huge gaps in the 13th and 16th centuries and parts of the 19th and 20th centuries. The high end of the spectrum – fine tin-glazed earthenwares, Rhenish stonewares and bone china – are mostly missing from the record. In this respect, the profile of ceramic finds contrasts strangely with the corpus of pottery from excavations in Taunton as whole published by Terry Pearson (1984c).

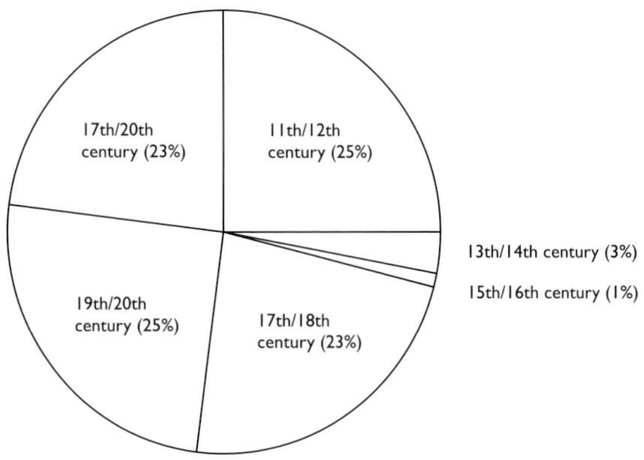

Figure 7.1: Proportion by number of sherds attributed to period from the 2005–13 excavations.

Methodology

An extensive type series was identified from the entire excavation archive. Sherds were sorted by fabric type, finish and forms. Sherds from each context were identified according to type, minimum and maximum vessel numbers were assessed and the sherds of each type were weighed. The extensive types series (prefixed TC) was then correlated with material that was available for comparison: part of the type series from Fore Street, Taunton, as classified by Terry Pearson for Cathe Burrow and the collection of sherds taken for ICP analysis by John Allan and Mike Hughes (Allan *et al.* 2011, 168, 171) from Taunton market place (Weddell 1998). Comparison was also possible with the pottery from Glastonbury Abbey (Allan *et al.* 2015).

Fortunately in March 2012, after the peripetations of the Somerset County Museums reference collections whilst the Museum of Somerset and Somerset Heritage Centre projects were implemented, comparison was possible with a wider range of material including that from excavations at Cheddar Palace (Rahtz 1979), Castle Neroche (Davison 1972), Taunton (Pearson 1984c), Nether Stowey, Donyatt (Coleman-Smith and Pearson 1988), Langford Budville, Wrangway, Wanstrow and Bridgwater (Boore and Pearson 2010), much of which remains unpublished. Correlation with parts of the type series published by Pearson (1984c) was also possible. It should however be noted that the acquisition of much new material since the publication of Pearson's series has tended to increase the complexity and confusion between being able to define and distinguish specific types of ware. More scientific analysis of their mineralogy is essential if further progress is to be made.

A consequence of the unusually small size of most of the sherds from contexts later than the 12th century was that it was difficult to carry out a meaningful identification and analysis of pottery by form and hence come to any significant conclusion about the functions of the pottery assemblage as a whole. A further consequence is that very few of the vessels could be drawn.

Pottery types

Roman

One residual mortarium sherd was identified.

The 11th to 12th centuries

The period roughly equates with the beginning of Pearson's Group 2 from Taunton (see page 117). It should be noted that the classification of forms has little changed since Rahtz (1974). Research into the pottery of this period is summarised by John Allan, and Hughes and Taylor have recently identified three basic types of ware with inclusions characteristic of minerals derived from the Upper Greensand exposures in the south-west corner of Somerset (the Blackdown Hills) and extending into east Devon (Allan *et al.* 2011).

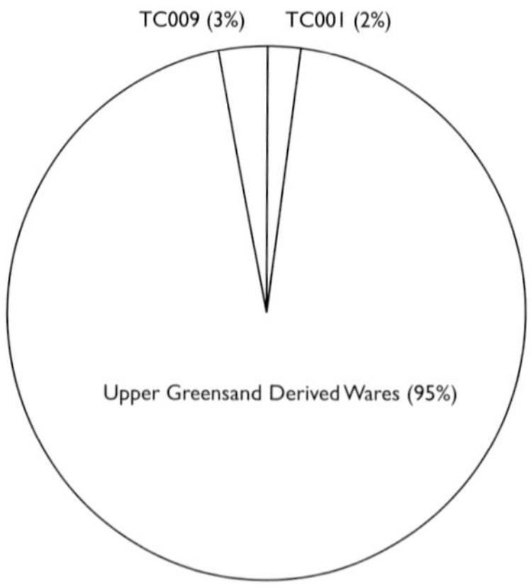

Figure 7.2: *Proportion of fabrics by number of sherds attributed to 11th/12th centuries.*

The types of Saxo-Norman ware identified at Taunton Castle correlate as follows: TC002, 003, 004, 005, 006, 007, 008, 014, 019, 023 and 024 are all variants of fabrics with inclusions of mixed Upper Greensand derived materials. Their mineralogy (see Appendix A) corresponds to Groups B2 (TC003, 007B, 008) and C (TC023). Of the total, 276 sherds attributed to this period, they account for 95% of the whole.

TC009 corresponds to Pearson's Taunton pottery type 50 (Pearson 1984c, 10), which he also dates to this period (Figure 7.12 on page 121). Pearson points out its similarity to Ilchester type B ware (Pearson 1982, 171). Fabric TC001 appears to have no identified analogues.

In summary, all the rim forms correspond to those characterised by Rahtz (1974, 113–19) as his Somerset group 8 (late Saxon) and to Pearson's pre-conquest and late 11th- to early 12th-century types (Pearson 1984c, 7–16). A similar date range is given by Allan when considering the material from Exeter (Allan 1984, 11). Essentially the more recent analysis of Upper Greensand derived fabrics follows the same dating scheme (Allan *et al.* 2011, 173).

The 13th to 14th centuries

There are only 27 sherds attributed to this period. The majority of material is of hand-made jars (cooking pots). Remarkably few pieces of glazed jugs such as Ham Green ware (TC013) were represented. The types of ware identified at Taunton Castle correlate as follows: TC015 tripod pitchers and 021 are all variants of fabrics with inclusions of mixed Upper Greensand derived materials and very similar to ware from Castle

Neroche (Davison 1972), Redcliffe ware from Bristol (TC025) and other Bristol wares (TC010, TC027). The mineralogy of type TC015 is B2. Saintonge (TC017) is represented by two speckled green-glazed sherds. Otherwise there is a marked gap in representative wares of this period.

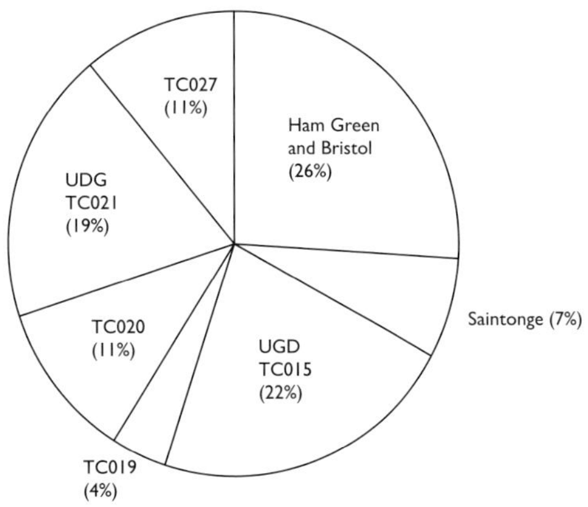

Figure 7.3: Proportion of fabrics by number of sherds attributed to 13th/14th centuries. UGD = Upper Greensand Derived.

The 15th to 16th centuries

Only 13 sherds can be attributed to this period so the proportions given in Figure 7.4 are rather meaningless. Neither TC029 nor TC085 have been identified to a source; TC086 is typical of North Devon ungritted wares and TC073 of South Somerset (Donyatt) wares. TC091 can be identified with some certainty to Bristol.

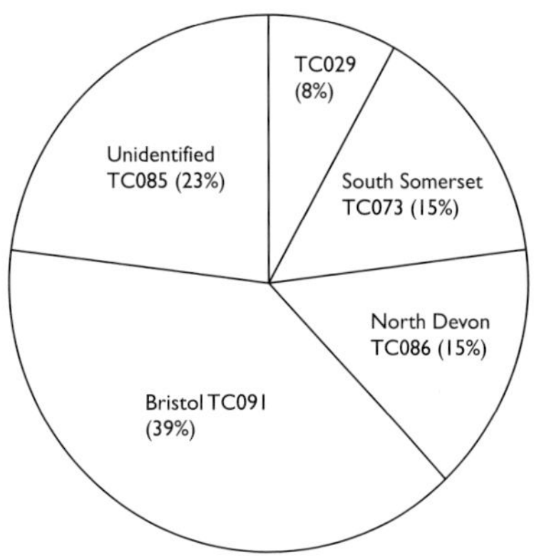

Figure 7.4: Proportion of fabrics by number of sherds attributed to 15th/16th centuries.

The 17th to 18th centuries

A total of 254 sherds are attributed to this period but it should be noted that undifferentiated red earthenwares have been attributed to the wider period of the 17th–20th centuries (Figure 7.7 on page 108). There is a general lack of the late 18th-century finer wares represented, though the relative proportions of local red earthenwares to stonewares and yellow wares is not unusual for urban sites in Somerset.

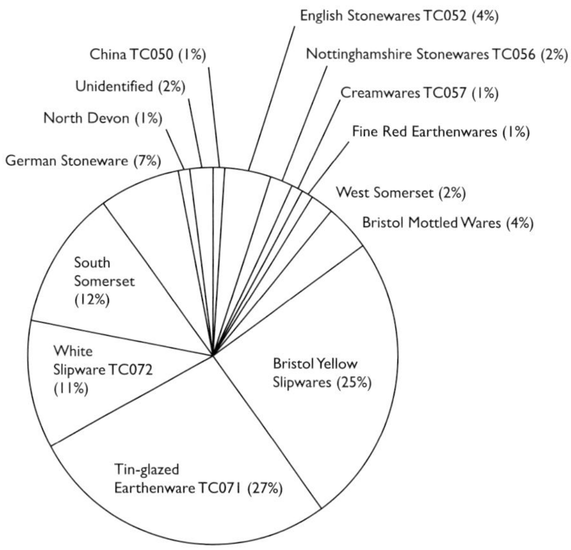

Figure 7.5: Proportion of fabrics by number of sherds attributed to 17th/18th centuries.

It is interesting that just over half the material consists almost equally of tin-glazed earthenwares (TC071) and yellow wares, both thrown hollow wares (TC065) and hump-moulded flatwares (TC064), probably mostly derived from Bristol rather than Staffordshire (Dawson 1979a). Allied to the latter is TC063, the Bristol iron-enriched glazed mottled wares (Dawson 1979b). Stonewares make up a further 24% of the material. The finest earthenware, creamware and Chinese export porcelain are only represented by a total of seven sherds. Red earthenwares make up 17%. There are three components, the largest ranging from the iron-glazed tankards and classic sgraffito decorated wares from South Somerset (Donyatt: Coleman-Smith and Pearson 1988), a smaller component of the simpler slip decorated wares from West Somerset (Nether Stowey: Coleman-Smith and Pearson 1970; Langford Budville and Wrangway: Dawson *et al.* 2001, Pearson *et al.* 2014) and just one sherd of classic North Devon sgraffito (Allan *et al.* 2005).

Tin-glazed earthenwares (TC071) There were two centres of production within and immediately adjacent to Somerset. Production at Bristol started in about 1682 with the establishment by a consortium of Quaker businessmen of a pottery outside the city at St Anne's, Brislington, which was rapidly developed into a major manufacturing activity by a number of potteries within the city during the 18th century. A second but minor centre was established on the outskirts of Wincanton by Nathaniel Ireson in about 1720 but was relatively short-lived (Dunning and Siraut 1999; Dawson and Kent 2008b). Production continued at Bristol into the late 18th century making utilitarian wares such as chamber pots and drug jars (gallypots) when the demand for highly decorated fine wares was superseded by porcelain, and fine cream and white wares from Staffordshire.

Identification of tin-glazed earthenwares is in one sense easy, the distinctive pearl white lead-glaze opacified by a small admixture of tin oxide is readily recognisable. However ascription to production centre is fraught with difficulty and still remains largely based on art historical analysis of the form of decoration applied to the vessel. In a small collection such as this it can be surmised that most of the sample is of English origin but some sherds could easily originate from one of the other major manufacturing centres such as London or Liverpool.

Yellow wares (TC064, TC065) Attempts have been made to differentiate between these distinctive wares made from clay derived from the Coal Measures in Bristol and in Staffordshire. It is perhaps not surprising that their manufacture has proved to be even more extensive with the discovery of a production site at Lazencroft near Leeds. A method of differentiation using chemical analysis was proposed recently but is difficult to transpose into the visual identification of individual sherds (White 2012). The dating of such wares is secured by the stratigraphical sequences in Bristol and elsewhere to between 1670 and 1790 (Barton 1961, 164–68; Dawson 1979a).

Mottled wares (TC063) Mottled wares are very distinctive with their iron-rich glaze over a white-firing body. They are similar in form and appearance to the manganese-glazed wares of Staffordshire and they are clearly imitating each other. However Bristol can be securely identified as the source of this ware where it was produced between about 1710 and 1760 (Dawson 1979b).

17th/18th-century stonewares There are a small number of German stonewares represented but none of the early imports in the 15th and 16th centuries. All seem to be Rhenish wares of the 17th century with some distinctive cobalt-painted later wares from Westerwald (Gaimster 1997). English stonewares range from the fine white stoneware (scratch blue) from Staffordshire to the coarser utilitarian wares, including the distinctively glossy Nottingham-type ware. Some of the coarser wares may have been made in Bristol (Barton 1961, 160–64).

West Somerset red earthenwares These are a group of wares from production sites that have been identified from pottery waste at Wrangway (Dawson *et al.* 2001, 49; Pearson *et al.* 2014), Langford Budville, Crowcombe and Nether Stowey (Coleman-Smith and Pearson 1970, 6–8). Later 19th-century wares from the Chandos glass cone, Bridgwater (Boore and Pearson 2010) also belong to this group of sandy red earthenwares sometimes with specks and larger lumps of limestone. Trailed and wet-slip decoration is common. The rims of utilitarian wares are often strengthened with a thumbed applied strip and the bases of often knife-trimmed. A large 16th-century assemblage of ware, identified to Nether Stowey, was excavated from Narrow Quay, Bristol (Good 1987; Good and Russett 1987, 39–40). Allan summarises the difficulty in identifying any of this type of ware had it occurred in Exeter (Allan 1984, 98). The mineralogical analysis validates the similarity between samples from these production sites and their distinctiveness from products of other centres as all belong to Group A.

South Somerset red earthenwares South Somerset redwares form the largest group of ordinary earthenware represented at the castle though they lose ground to wares from West Somerset in the 19th and 20th centuries. The major centre of production at Horton Cross/Donyatt has been well-researched by Richard Coleman-Smith and Terry Pearson (Coleman-Smith and Pearson 1988; Coleman-Smith 2002) but similar wares have also been found at Chard and Chardstock (Roger Carter and Peter Wood pers. comm.). Allan has shown that petrologically these wares contain material derived from the Upper Greensands of the Blackdown Hills and are allied to the ware from Hemyock. Pottery waste from Lyme Regis is also similar (Draper 1982). Mineralogically the sample from Donyatt Site 13, of perhaps one of the most distinctive South Somerset fabrics, forms its own Group D, though the sample from Donyatt Site 4 has affinities in Group B1 with samples from Wanstrow/Nunney Catch.

They may be products of a ring of potteries following the Upper Greensand outcrop round the Blackdowns. Forms represented at Taunton Castle range from the chert encrusted manganese-glazed cups of the mid-17th century, through classic wet-slip and sgraffito decorated vessels of the 18th and 19th centuries to earthenware jars and pancheons (Coleman-Smith and Pearson 1988, 164–65, 174–217, 231–44). Fabric and forms are very similar to wares from the West Somerset group.

East Somerset red earthenwares This distinctive group is not represented at all. A substantial deposit of wasters was recovered from new road building at Nunney Catch in the early 1980s and evidence for a site of a pottery in the adjoining parish of Wanstrow was published by Vranch (1988). Further waste has since been recorded from other locations in Trudoxhill, Wanstrow and the centre of Nunney. The fabric of "Wanstrow or East Somerset ware" is a fine sandy iron-rich body which characteristically tends to fracture into distinct laminar plates. It generally fires to an oxidised orange to brick-red sometimes with a reduced grey core though occasionally the whole may be reduced. The plain lead glaze is usually very rich and varies from oxidised orange to a distinctive reduced deep olive green. It corresponds with type 96/98 in the Bristol pottery type series. Two samples from Nunney Catch belong to mineralogical Group B1. The distribution of these wares between the 16th and 18th centuries is fairly wide. They have been identified from King Street, Bristol, and significant 18th-century groups from Redcliffe Hill, Bristol and Wells Museum are awaiting publication.

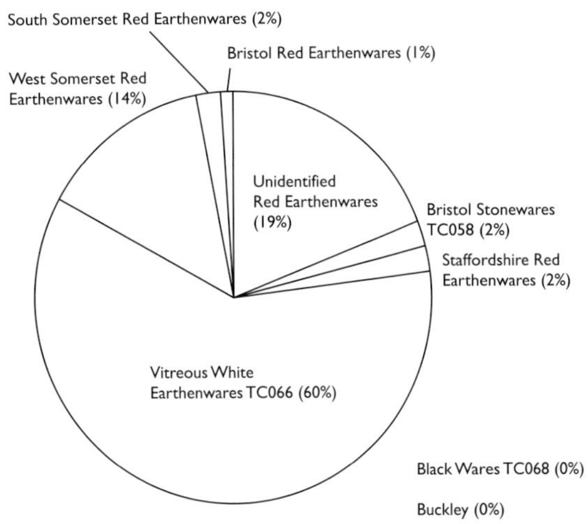

Figure 7.6: *Proportion of fabrics by number of sherds attributed to 19th/20th centuries.*

The 19th to 20th centuries

Slightly more sherds (279) represent this period of use of the castle. Not surprisingly in an age dominated by white vitreous earthenwares, often with transfer-printed decoration (TC066), these represent 66% of the total found. Fine Staffordshire red earthenwares and black earthenwares form a tiny component as does Bristol stoneware. Red earthenwares (17%) derive mostly from West Somerset, characterised by the pottery from the Chandos glass cone, Bridgwater (Boore and Pearson 2010), as opposed to South Somerset. The reason for this may be that at this period many of the West Somerset wares are associated with companies supplying bricks, tiles and other building materials, such as the Somerset Trading Company in Bridgwater and William Thomas and Co at Poole near Wellington. The catalogues of their extensive range of products make it clear that the manufacture of red earthenwares for domestic and horticultural use was an important product of the throwers who were otherwise employed for making chimney pots and similar building goods.

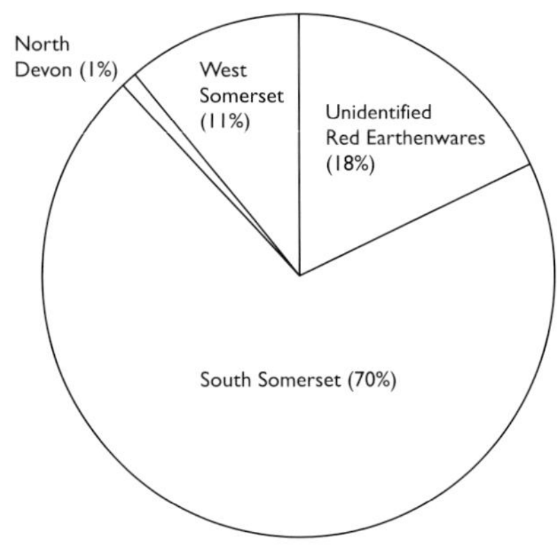

Figure 7.7: *Proportion by number of all red earthenwares from 2005–13 excavations.*

17th to 19th century red earthenwares As so many sherds are very small it was not always possible to attribute a date to them. These have been agglomerated with those already attributed to the period (see above) to draw a comparison (Figure 7.7). South Somerset wares predominate over those from West Somerset. There is a substantial percentage of unclassified material but only a negligible percentage deriving from the North Devon potteries. The distribution of the latter seems to be mainly coastal.

The Pottery Type Series from the 2005–2013 Excavations

Roman

TC022 *Fabric description:* smooth soft-fired brick-red earthenware with crushed quartz impressed into interior. *Forms:* thrown mortarium. *Analogues:* Roman.

Type number	vessel	date range	Fabric and form analogues
TC001 CE	jars	11–12	none
TC002 CE	jars	11–12	UGD mixed; TT 42=FS II.2 (Pearson 1984c, 13–14; Burrow, C 1988, 118)
TC003 CE	jars	11–12	ADR B2 (Figure A.3); UGD mixed; Figure 7.8: D1
TC004 CE	jars	11–12	UGD mixed
TC005 CE	jars	—	none
TC006 CE	jars	—	UGD quartz
TC007 CE	jars	11–12	sample A, ADR C (Figure A.4); sample B, ADR B2 (Figure A.5); UGD mixed; Figure 7.8: D2
TC008 CE	jars	11–12	ADR B2 (Figure A.6); UGD mixed; TT 42=FS II.2 (Pearson 1984c, 13–14; Burrow, C 1988, 118) (=TC026)
TC009 CE	jars	—	TT 50=FS III.3 (Pearson 1984c, 10; Burrow, C 1988, 121); variant of Ilchester B ware
TC010 FGE	jugs	13–14	Bristol Redcliffe ware, BPT 118
TC011 WGE	bowls	18–19	none
TC012 WGE	jars	16–17	South Somerset slipware
TC013 FGE	jugs	12–13	similar to but not Ham Green (Barton 1963); TT 31 (Pearson 1984c, 26–27)
TC014 CE	jars	11–12	ADR B2 (Figure A.7); UGD chert; TT 55=FS II.3 (Pearson 1984c, 9–10; Burrow, C 1988, 118); Ilchester B.
TC015 CE	jars	12–13	Castle Neroche (Davison 1972); ADR B2 (Figure A.8): UGD mixed
TC016 RGE		PM	none
TC017 WGE	jugs	13–14	Saintonge ware (Barton 1963)
TC018 RGE	pans	17–19	South Somerset
TC019 CE	jars	—	UGD mixed
TC020 CE	jars	12–13	TT 42=FS III.2 (Pearson 1984c, 13–14; Burrow, C 1988, [121)
TC021 CGE	jugs	12–13	UGD
TC022 —		2–3	Roman mortarium
TC023 CE	jars	11–12	ADR C (Figure A.9); UGD; TT 222 (Pearson 1984c, 12), Figure 7.8: D4
TC024 CE	jars	11–12	UGD
TC025 FGE	jugs	12–13	Ham Green (Barton 1963); TT 31 (Pearson 1984c, 26–27), BPT 27
TC026			see TC008
TC027 FGE	jugs	13–14	Bristol TT 29=FS IV.1 (Burrow, C 1988, 121)
TC028 RGE		18–19	Slipped red earthenware; FS IV.5 (Burrow, C 1988, 12)
TC029 CGE	jugs	16	none
TC050		18	Qing export porcelain
TC051 VWE		18–20	Staffordshire and elsewhere transfer printed
TC052 SSW		17–19	English salt-glazed stoneware; TT 151 (Pearson 1984c, 56)
TC053 RE		18–20	Flowerpots
TC054 RGE		—	none
TC055 RGE		PM	TT 45; FS V.1 (Burrow, C 1988, 126)
TC056 SSW		18–19	Nottinghamshire-type salt-glazed stoneware TT 150 (Pearson 1984c, 56)
TC057 VWE		18–19	Staffordshire/Bristol creamware
TC058 SW		19–20	Bristol-type stoneware
TC059 RGE		18–19	Possibly Staffordshire red earthenware
			(continued in Table 7.1b on the next page)

***Table 7.1a:** Summary pottery type series. Note: some of Pearson's Taunton types in the reference collection, for example type 58, are not described in* The Archaeology of Taunton *and hence are not referenced here. For abbreviations see Table 7.1c on page 111.*

Pre-conquest wares

No distinctive pre-Conquest fabrics or forms were identified.

11th to 12th century wares

Upper Greensand derived wares form 95% of the pottery found dating from this period. Attributed to this class of ware are:

TC002 *Fabric description:* A hard-fired ware with water-worn quartz and haematite and crushed chert and fragments of limestone inclusions. The surface has fired bright orange-red. *Forms:* hand-built jar. *Analogues:* Upper Greensand derived ware with mixed inclusions; Taunton type 42 = Taunton Fore Street type II.2 (Pearson 1984c, 13–14; Burrow, C 1988, 118).

TC003 *Fabric description:* A hard-fired hand-built ware with water-worn quartz up to 2mm in size and haematite, crushed chert and limestone again up to 2mm in size. The surface has fired bright orange-red (similar to TC 002) to dark buff. Mineralogical type B2 (Figure A.7 on page 301). *Forms:* Jar with flared neck and rolled rim (Figure 7.8: D1). *Analogues:* mixed Upper Greensand derived materials.

Type number	vessel	date range	Fabric and form analogues
			(continued from Table 7.1a on the preceding page)
TC060 RGE		18–19	Staffordshire/Bristol fine red earthenware
TC061 RGE		PM	West Somerset ware
TC062 RGE		PM	ADR D (Figure A.10); South Somerset ware (Figure 7.8: D6–9); TT 7 (Pearson 1984c, 45–46)
TC063 BM		17–18	Bristol mottled ware (Dawson 1979b); TT 214 (Pearson 1984c, 55)
TC064 YSW		17–18	Bristol/Staffordshire press-moulded yellow slipware (Barton 1961; Dawson 1979a); TT 74 (Pearson 1984c, 54)
TC065 YSW		17–18	Bristol/Staffordshire thrown yellow slipware (Barton 1971, Dawson 1979a); TT 74 (Pearson 54)
TC066 VWE		19–20	Staffordshire and other engine-turned slipwares
TC067 RGE		19–20	Buckley ware (Longworth 2004)
TC068 EB		18–19	Staffordshire/Bristol glazed blackware
TC069 RGE		18–19	West Somerset ware (Boore and Pearson 2010); TT 12 and 16 (Pearson 1984c, 47–48)
TC070 AW		18	Staffordshire agate ware; TT 136 (Pearson 1984c, 55)
TC071 TGE		17–18	Tin-glazed earthenwares (Figure 7.8: D10); TT 75 (Pearson 1984c, 54)
TC072 SSW		18	Staffordshire white salt-glazed stoneware
TC073 RGE		16	Possibly South Somerset ware (Figure 7.8: D11)
TC074 RGE		18–19	ADR A (Figure A.11); West Somerset ware; TT 12 and 16 (Pearson 1984c, 47–48)
TC075 RGE		18	South Somerset slipware; DPT 8 (Coleman-Smith and Pearson 1988, 199–201)
TC076 RGE		18	South Somerset slipware; TT 8 (Pearson 1984c, 51–52; Coleman-Smith and Pearson 1988, 199–201)
TC077 SSW		18–19	Westerwald stoneware (Gaimster 1997, 251–53); TT 38 (Pearson 1984c, 56)
TC078 RGE		18–19	West Somerset ware
TC079 RGE		18–19	West Somerset ware
TC080 SSW		16–17	Rhenish salt-glazed stonewares
TC081 RGE		17–18	North Devon slipware (Allan *et al.* 2005, 180-83); TT 25 (Pearson 1984c, 50)
TC082 RGE		18	West Somerset slipware TT 12 and 16 (Pearson 1984c, 47–48)
TC083 RGE		18–19	ADR A (Figure A.12; TT 8 (Pearson 1984c, 51–52) (=TC093)
TC084 RGE		PM	North Devon Gritted ware; TT 24 (Pearson 1984c, 49–50)
TC085 RGE		PM	West Somerset ware
TC086 RGE		PM	North Devon ungritted wares
TC087 RGE		16–17	none
TC088 RGE		PM	none
TC089 RGE		PM	ADR A (Figure A.13); West Somerset ware
TC090 RGE		PM	similar to TC087
TC091 RGE		16	South Somerset ware; TT 6 (Pearson 1984c, 40–41)
TC092 RGE		17	South Somerset encrusted ware (Coleman-Smith and Pearson 1988, 164–65)
TC093			see TC 083
TC094 RGE		PM	Possibly Bristol red earthenware
TC095 RGE		16–17	none
TC096 RGE		17–18	South Somerset ware

Table 7.1b: *Summary pottery type series. Note: some of Pearson's Taunton types in the reference collection, for example type 58, are not described in* The Archaeology of Taunton *and hence are not referenced here. For abbreviations see Table 7.1c on the facing page.*

TC004 *Fabric description:* reduced grey coarse earthenware with buff surface flashes of oxidation; inclusions of crushed quartz and chert up to 1mm in size. *Forms:* hand-built jar. *Analogues:* mixed Upper Greensand derived materials.

TC006 *Fabric description:* sandy hard-fired coarse micaceous earthenware reduced to grey and black with waterworn quartz inclusions. *Forms:* hand-built jar. *Analogues:* no diagnostic forms; Upper Greensand derived polished quartz type.

TC007 *Fabric description:* coarse earthenware with grey reduced core and red flushed with buff exterior; with crushed quartz and limestone inclusions. Sample 7A mineralogical type C (Figure A.4 on page 295); sample 7B mineralogical type B2 (Figure A.5 on page 297). *Forms:* hand-built jar (Figure 7.8: D2). *Analogues:* mixed Upper Greensand derived materials.

TC008=026 *Fabric description:* very coarse reduced grey earthenware with buff oxidised surface with crushed chert, limestone and quartz inclusions (up to 1mm). Mineralogical type B2 (Figure A.6 on page 299). *Forms:* hand-built jar. *Analogues:* Upper Greensand derived wares; Taunton type 42 = Taunton Fore Street type II.2 (Pearson 1984c, 13–14; Burrow, C 1988, 118).

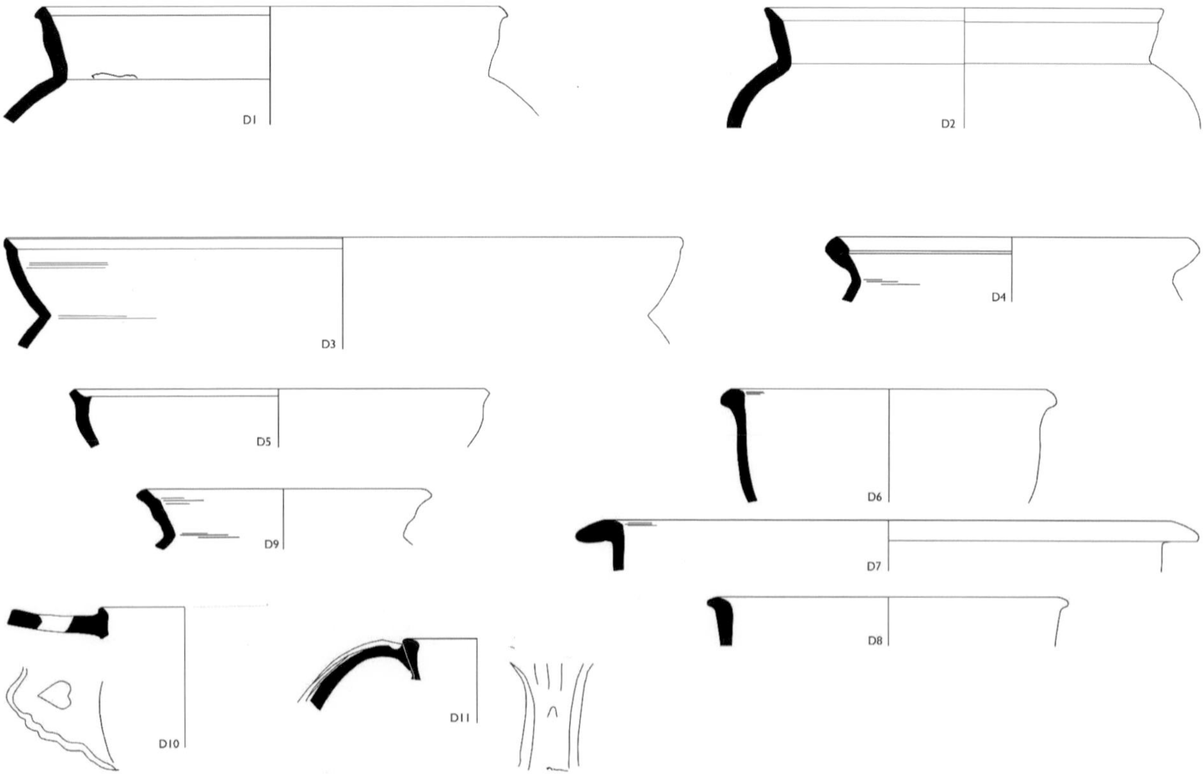

Figure 7.8: *Pottery from 2005-2010 excavations: D1, fabric TC003; D2 TC007; D3 TC014; D4 TC023; D5 TC024; D6-8, TC062; D10 TC071; D11 TC073. Scale 1:4.*

ADR	Andersen, Dawson and Rollinson mineralogical type (see Appendix A, page 285)
AW	agate ware
BM	Bristol mottled ware
BPT	Bristol pottery type
CE	course earthenware
CGE	course glazed earthenware
DPT	Donyatt pottery type
EB	"Egyptian" blackware
FGE	fine glazed earthenware
FS	Taunton Fore Street type (Burrow, C 1988)
PM	Post medieval
TT	Taunton type (Pearson 1984c)
RGE	red glazed earthenware
SSW	salt-glazed stoneware
SW	stoneware
TGE	tin-glazed earthenware
UGD	Upper Greensand Derived ware (Allan *et al.* 2011)
VWE	vitreous white earthenware
WGE	white glazed earthenware
YSW	yellow slipware

Table 7.1c: *Abbreviations used in Table 7.1a and Table 7.1b.*

TC014 *Fabric description:* coarse dark grey reduced earthenware with buff oxidised surface and water-worn quartz inclusions. Mineralogical type B2 (Figure A.7 on page 301). *Forms:* jar (Figure 7.8: D3). *Analogues:* mixed Upper Greensand derived materials, 11th century; Taunton type 55 = Taunton Fore Street type II.3 (Pearson 1984c, 9–10; Burrow, C 1988, 118); Ilchester B.

TC019 *Fabric description:* coarse grey earthenware with quantities of water-worn quartz and haematite; pink oxidised interior, black reduced exterior. *Forms:* hand-built cooking pot. *Analogues:* no diagnostic forms; mixed Upper Greensand derived materials.

TC023 *Fabric description:* coarse reduced grey fabric with red oxidised surface with quantities of crushed chert, quartz, limestone and fossil material. Mineralogical type C (Figure A.9 on page 305). *Forms:* hand-built jar (Figure 7.8: D4). *Analogues:* Upper Greensand derived; Taunton type 222 (Pearson 1984c, 12).

TC024 *Fabric description:* fine sandy orange-grey earthenware with red oxidised surface reducing to dark grey occasional fragments of quartz and lime. *Forms:* hand-built jar

(Figure 7.8: D5). *Analogues:* mixed Upper Greensand derived materials.

Other types which have not been attributed to a source are:

TC001 *Fabric description:* A hard-fired coarse earthenware with inclusions of up to 2mm in size of water worn quartz, fragments of Liassic limestone and fossilised shell in a matrix coloured earth-brown. The surface has fired oxidised orange to more reduced brown. Incised decoration. *Forms:* hand-built. *Analogues:* no diagnostic forms but probably 11th–13th century.

TC005 *Fabric description:* coarse grey reduced earthenware with oxidised red surface; quartz and lime inclusions dissolved out of the surface to produce corky effect. *Forms:* hand-built jar. *Analogues:* no diagnostic forms.

TC009 *Fabric description:* coarse reduced grey earthenware with dark brown surface; heavily gritted with quartz inclusions. *Forms:* hand-built jar. *Analogues:* no diagnostic forms, Taunton type 50 variant of Ilchester B ware = Taunton Fore Street type III.3 (Pearson 1984c, 10; Burrow, C 1988, 121).

TC020 *Fabric description:* fine sandy reduced black earthenware with dark buff flashes of oxidation on surface. *Forms:* hand-built jar. *Analogues:* no diagnostic forms; a finer variant of Taunton type 42 = Taunton Fore Street type III.2 (Pearson 1984c, 13–14; Burrow, C 1988, 121).

12th to 13th century wares

TC013 *Fabric description:* reduced light grey earthenware with quartz, lime and haematite inclusions; reduced green lead-glaze pitted when the glaze has pooled where lime inclusions have been etched out. *Forms:* jugs. *Analogues:* similar but different fabric to Ham Green, 12th–13th century.

TC015 *Fabric description:* reduced dark grey earthenware with red oxidised surface and quantities of water worn quartz and crushed chert; incised lines on handles. Mineralogical type B2 (Figure A.8 on page 303). *Forms:* hand built possible tripod pitchers. *Analogues:* mixed Upper Greensand derived materials; 12th–13th century; Castle Neroche (Davison 1972).

TC021 *Fabric description:* grey reduced coarse earthenware with large (up to 2mm) fragments of crushed quartz, chert and limestone with combed decoration and burnt-off reduced-green lead glaze. *Forms:* hand-built jugs *Analogues:* 12th–13th century; mixed Upper Greensand derived materials.

TC025 *Fabric description:* fine grey reduced earthenware with orange oxidised surface; handles pulled and stabbed with three circular impressions at the top; with speckled green lead-glaze. *Forms:* thrown jugs. *Analogues:* 12th–13th century; Ham Green (Barton 1963); Taunton 31 (Pearson 1984c, 26–27); Bristol type 27.

TC010 *Fabric description:* fine hard-fired reduced grey earthenware with reoxidised buff surface and external highly reduced and partially burnt-off green lead-glaze. *Forms:* thrown jugs and jars. *Analogues:* Bristol Redcliffe ware, 13–14th century, Bristol type 118.

TC017 *Fabric description:* fine pinkish white calcareous earthenware with lead-glaze speckled with copper green. *Forms:* thrown, probably jug or costrel. *Analogues:* Saintonge ware, 13–14th century (Barton 1963).

TC027 *Fabric description:* hard-fired reduced grey earthenware, oxidised orange surface and reduced green lead-glaze. *Forms:* thrown jugs *Analogues:* probably Bristol 13th–14th century; Taunton type 29 = Taunton Fore Street type IV.1 (Burrow, C 1988, 121).

14th to 15th century wares

Post-medieval red earthenwares

TC016 *Fabric description:* gritty red earthenware with reduced black surface and burnt-off glaze. *Forms:* thrown. *Analogues:* post-medieval; no diagnostic forms.

16th century wares

Stonewares

TC080 *Fabric description:* hard-fired reduced buff stoneware with "tiger" iron-wash salt-glaze. *Forms:* tankards. *Analogues:* Rhenish stoneware 16th–17th century.

South Somerset red earthenwares

TC012 *Fabric description:* fine white earthenware with inclusions of lime; white slip decoration under reduced light green lead-glaze with flashes of orange. *Forms:* thrown bowls and jugs. *Analogues:* South Somerset 16th–17th century.

TC073 *Fabric description:* Hard-fired fine granular micaceous body with occasional inclusions of crushed chert; reduced grey core and smooth surface, oxidised dark orange just below surface. *Forms:* Thrown jug with riveted pulled handle slashed at top and with triangular stab marks down centre (Figure 7.8: D11). *Analogues:* Possibly South Somerset 16th century.

TC091 *Fabric description:* hard-fired fine reduced grey earthenware with external and internal dark green reduced lead-glaze with iron specks. *Forms:* thrown tankards or bottles. *Analogues:* Bristol fabrics; South Somerset 16th century; Taunton type 6 (Pearson 1984c, 40–41).

Other red earthenwares

TC029 *Fabric description:* reduced grey coarse earthenware with water-worn quartz grains and fragments; internal and external reduced green lead-glaze. *Forms:* thrown jugs. *Analogues:* 16th century.

TC087 *Fabric description:* Fine red earthenware with copper-splashed lead-glaze over a white slip. *Forms:* thrown jugs with combed sgraffito lines. *Analogues:* Source unidentified; probably 16th–17th century.

TC090 *Fabric description:* Hard fired fine reoxidised red earthenware with specks of haematite; speckled olive-green lead glaze *Forms:* thrown jars. *Analogues:* Similar to TC087.

TC095 *Fabric description:* fine sandy reduced grey earthenware oxidising to orange with occasional crushed quartz inclusions; dark green reduced lead-glaze. *Forms:* thrown jugs. *Analogues:* 16th–17th century.

17th to 18th century wares

Porcelain

TC050 *Fabric description:* fine hard paste body and glaze with painted blue and polychrome decoration; imitation blue mark (Figure 7.9). *Forms:* tea bowl. *Analogues:* Chinese export porcelain; Qing dynasty, 18th century; Taunton type 248 (Pearson 1984c, 51).

Stonewares

TC052 *Fabric description:* fine white to grey stoneware with drab brown salt-glaze. *Forms:* tankards *Analogues:* English stoneware, 18th century; Taunton type 151 (Pearson 1984c, 56).

TC056 *Fabric description:* hard reduced grey fine stoneware with highly glossy brown salt-glaze. *Forms:* thrown bottles. *Analogues:* Nottinghamshire-type stoneware late 18th–19th century; Taunton type 150 (Pearson 1984c, 56).

Figure 7.9: *Mark on base of Chinese export porcelain tea-bowl (TCC09:1098). Photo: John Scaife.*

TC072 *Fabric description:* Dense fine granular white salt-glazed stoneware. *Forms:* Turned tankards with fine foot-ring and dipped iron-rich slip round rim. *Analogues:* Staffordshire white salt-glazed stoneware 1720–1760.

TC077 *Fabric description:* fine grey stoneware with salt-glazed incised decoration emphasised with painted cobalt blue. *Forms:* thrown jars, tankards. *Analogues:* Westerwald-type stoneware (Gaimster 1997, 251–53); Taunton type 38 (Pearson 1984c, 56).

Tin-glazed earthenwares

TC071 *Fabric description:* Fine buff white earthenware with tin-enriched lead glaze; painted with cobalt blue, one example with white slip blobs on all-over cobalt blue. *Forms:* dishes, pedestal cup, porringer (Figure 7.8: D10). *Analogues:* English tin-glazed earthenware 17th–18th century; Taunton type 75 (Pearson 1984c, 54).

Creamwares

TC057 *Fabric description:* fine white earthenware; pearl white to blueish lead-glaze. *Forms:* plates, saucers. *Analogues:* Staffordshire/Bristol creamware, late 18th century.

Fine earthenwares

TC070 *Fabric description:* Fine wedged brown and white clays forming an agate body;

plain lead glaze with some cobalt colouring. *Forms:* cups. *Analogues:* agate ware, probably made in Staffordshire; Taunton type 136 (Pearson 1984c, 55); about 1725–50.

Yellow slipwares

TC064 *Fabric description:* buff earthenware with fragments of grog and haematite; trailed white on brown slip sometimes combed, brown trailed spots under clear lead-glaze. *Forms:* press-moulded plates and dishes often with serrated rims. *Analogues:* Bristol/Staffordshire yellow slipware, late 17th–18th century; Taunton type 74 (Pearson 1984c, 54; Barton 1961; Dawson 1979a).

TC065 *Fabric description:* buff earthenware with fragments of haematite and grog; trailed brown on white slip under clear lead-glaze. *Forms:* thrown cups. *Analogues:* Bristol/Staffordshire yellow slipware, late 17th–18th century; Taunton type 74 (Pearson 1984c, 54; Barton 1961; Dawson 1979a)

Mottled ware

TC063 *Fabric description:* buff earthenware with haematite fragments similar to TC064; iron-rich lead-glaze. *Forms:* thrown tankards, *Analogues:* Bristol mottled ware, late 17th–18th century; Taunton type 214 (Pearson 1984c, 55; Dawson 1979b).

South Somerset red earthenwares

TC062 *Fabric description:* Medium to soft-fired orange buff earthenware with fragments of haematite; thumbed applied strip; thumbing in body under the rim; speckled brown oxidised lead glaze. Mineralogical group D (Figure A.10 on page 307), compare Donyatt Site 13 (Figure A.16 on page 319) *Forms:* thrown bowls, pancheons, jars (Figure 7.8: D6–9). *Analogues:* South Somerset ware, 17th–19th century; similar to Taunton type 7 (Pearson 1984c, 45–46).

TC075 *Fabric description:* Fairly coarse-grained sandy oxidised red earthenware with inclusions of haematite and occasional limestone; white metropolitan style slip decoration and wiped white slip under a clear lead glaze speckled over the body. *Forms:* jars, bowls. *Analogues:* South Somerset, 18th century; Donyatt type 8 (Coleman-Smith and Pearson 1988, 199–201).

TC076 *Fabric description:* hard sandy micaceous red earthenware with fragments of grog and chert; decorated with brown slip trailed and combed on white; clear internal lead-glaze. *Forms:* thrown dishes. *Analogues:* South Somerset, 18th century; Taunton type 8 (Pearson 1984c, 51–52; Coleman-Smith and Pearson 1988, 199–201).

TC083=093 *Fabric description:* sandy red earthenware oxidised red reoxidised buff with fragments of haematite; burnt off white slip bands with combed and incised wave sgraffito decoration and trailed white slip; brown lead-glaze speckled with reduced iron green. Mineralogical type A (Figure A.12 on page 311) compares with samples from West Somerset production sites – an indication of how close the visual appearance of some Somerset redwares can be. *Forms:* thrown jars, bowls. *Analogues:* South Somerset ware; 18th–19th century; Taunton type 8 (Pearson 1984c, 51–52).

TC092 *Fabric description:* sandy red earthenware with reduced core and fragments of chert and haematite; applied swags of crushed chert; plain iron and manganese-rich lead-glaze inside and out. *Forms:* thrown globular cups. *Analogues:* South Somerset; early 17th century (Coleman-Smith and Pearson 1988, 164–65).

TC096 *Fabric description:* fine red earthenware; sgraffito through white slip under clear lead-glaze. *Forms:* thrown bowls. *Analogues:* South Somerset ware; 17th–18th century.

West Somerset red earthenwares

TC069 *Fabric description:* hard-fired red earthenware with reduced grey core; haematite fragments and occasional specks of lime. *Forms:* thrown pancheons, jars. *Analogues:* West Somerset ware, 18th/19th century (Boore and Pearson 2010); Taunton types 12 and 16 (Pearson 1984c, 47–48).

TC074 *Fabric description:* Hard-fired fine granular red earthenware with reduced patches of grey; rich reduced deep olive green/brown lead-glaze. Mineralogical type A (Figure A.11 on page 309) consistent with samples from Crowcombe, Langford Budville, Nether Stowey and Wrangway: all West Somerset wares). *Forms:* thrown jars, bowls with white trailed slip decoration. *Analogues:* West Somerset ware possibly 18th century. Taunton types 12 and 16 (Pearson 1984c, 47–48).

TC078 *Fabric description:* sandy brick-red earthenware with occasional inclusions of limestone and external almost black iron-rich lead-glaze. *Forms:* thrown jars. *Analogues:* West Somerset, 18th–19th century.

TC079 *Fabric description:* sandy red earthenware reduced grey and blackish red oxidised with brown iron finely speckled oxidised lead-glaze, dull green reduced, and splashed with copper over white slip. *Forms:* uncertain. *Analogues:* West Somerset 17th–18th century.

TC082 *Fabric description:* red earthenware with sgraffito decoration under brown lead-glaze splashed with copper. *Forms:* thrown dish. *Analogues:* West Somerset ware, 18th century; Taunton types 12 and 16 (Pearson 1984c, 47–48).

TC085 *Fabric description:* Red earthenware with occasional fine quartz grains; reduced green lead-glaze over a white slip. *Forms:* thrown jugs. *Analogues:* West Somerset ware.

TC089 *Fabric description:* Red earthenware with occasional fragments of grog; brown oxidised lead-glaze. Mineralogical type A (Figure A.13 on page 313) compares with samples from Crowcombe, Langford Budville, Nether Stowey and Wrangway: all West Somerset wares. *Forms:* thrown jars and bowls with sgraffito white slip decoration. *Analogues:* West Somerset ware, 18th century.

North Devon wares

TC081 *Fabric description:* smooth fine reduced grey oxidised red earthenware; sgraffito through white slip under clear lead-glaze. *Forms:* thrown dishes. *Analogues:* North Devon slipware, 17th–18th century (Allan *et al.* 2005, 180–83); Taunton type 25 (Pearson 1984c, 50).

TC084 *Fabric description:* Fine matrix with large inclusions of crushed quartz with reduced grey core and reoxidised red; reduced olive green lead-glaze. *Forms:* thrown pancheons *Analogues:* North Devon Gritted Ware 1600–1940; Taunton type 24 (Pearson 1984c, 49–50).

TC086 *Fabric description:* Fine earthenware reduced grey; reduced olive green lead-glaze. *Forms:* thrown jug with broad handle slashed at base. *Analogues:* North Devon ungritted wares, 17th–18th century.

Unascribed red earthenwares

TC011 *Fabric description:* fine hard-fired white earthenware with reduced light grey core occasional fragments of haematite. *Forms:* thrown bowls. *Analogues:* 18th–19th century.

TC088 *Fabric description:* Red earthenware with clear oxidised brown lead-glaze. *Forms:* thrown bowls. *Analogues:* West Somerset ware or South Somerset ware.

19th to 20th century wares

White earthenwares

TC051 *Fabric description:* fine white vitreous earthenware including transfer-printed wares. *Forms:* various. *Analogues:* English, most probably Staffordshire.

TC066 *Fabric description:* White vitreous earthenware with plain lead glaze; engine-turned bands and chequered brown slip decoration. *Forms:* tankard. *Analogues:* Staffordshire/Bristol and other whitewares (see Marochan 1962 for evidence of Bristol production at Crews Hole).

Stonewares

TC058 *Fabric description:* course grey stoneware with haematite fragments; Bristol-type stoneware glaze. *Forms:* thrown bottles. *Analogues:* "Bristol" stoneware, 19th to mid-20th century.

Fine red earthenwares

TC059 *Fabric description:* hard-fired buff earthenware with fragments of haematite; iron-rich lead–glaze exterior reduced to metallic finish. *Forms:* turned bowls. *Analogues:* Possibly modern Staffordshire earthenware.

TC060 *Fabric description:* very fine red earthenware with fine iron-rich lead-glaze. *Forms:* turned bowls. *Analogues:* fine earthenware probably Staffordshire, 18th–19th century.

Fine black earthenwares

TC068 *Fabric description:* fine-grained hard-fired reduced earthenware with rouletted decoration; plain lead glaze *Forms:* tea pots, bowls. *Analogues:* black ware (not true Egyptian Black), probably Staffordshire but also possibly Bristol, 18th to early-19th century.

Buckley red earthenware

TC067 *Fabric description:* hard-fired fine-grained buff earthenware with brown slip bands under a plain yellow with black specks lead glaze. *Forms:* bowls. *Analogues:* Buckley ware (Longworth 2004), late-19th to early-20th century,

South Somerset red earthenwares

TC018 *Fabric description:* soft fired oxidised red earthenware reduced to off-white with haematite inclusions; yellow with green patches to reduced dark green lead-glaze. *Forms:* thrown pancheons, jars. *Analogues:* 18th–19th century.

West Somerset red earthenwares

TC061 *Fabric description:* hard-fired oxidised red earthenware; reduced dark green lead-glaze. *Forms:* thrown jars. *Analogues:* West Somerset ware, 19th century.

Other post-medieval red earthenwares

TC053 *Fabric description:* fine brick-red earthenware. *Forms:* possibly jollied. *Analogues:* flower pots, 19th-20th century.

TC054 *Fabric description:* soft-fired red earthenware with internal speckled brown lead-glaze. *Forms:* thrown.

TC055 *Fabric description:* soft-fired red earthenware with internal brown lead-glaze. *Forms:* thrown.

TC094 *Fabric description:* fairly coarse reduced grey earthenware with rich green glaze; trailed slip decoration on dishes. *Forms:* thrown jars and dishes. *Analogues:* possibly Bristol red earthenware.

Pottery from earlier excavations at Taunton Castle

Harold St George Gray excavated large quantities of pottery in the Keep Garden area. Unfortunately not all the pottery from these earlier excavations can be found in the collections of what is now the Somerset Heritage Service (the former SANHS and then County Museums Service collections) but from the body and base sherds that are preserved, it is clear that the material derives from primary contexts as the sherds are so large (up to 100mm across) and the breaks unabraded. There are still 41.7kg of sherds of early medieval open jars extant. It is estimated that this represents just over 3000 sherds.

Some of the pottery had been assigned reference numbers, either A.3249 or sub-numbers of it. These are quasi-accession numbers related to a catalogue (*Catalogue of Medieval Antiquities from 1050 to 1450 AD*. 2/2 part 1 of 4) compiled as secondary documentation to the museum accession registers:

> **A.3249** Excavations on east side of courtyard 1924–9 and 1933- All finds including pottery, bone, and antler tools, objects of iron, schist hone, wooden buckets, etc. see P.S.A.[N.H.] S. passim – For base silver spoon found 1928 see Antiquaries Journal X, 156–8.

Later finds were also recorded in the catalogue:

> **A.3277** Same site [as previous entry: fill of one of the wells on electricity showrooms site, see page 47] and donor [the Corporation of Taunton 1937]. Rim of a large jug in grey ware with applied strip decoration with patches of greenish-yellow lead glaze. Three fragments of large glazed jar with applied decoration. ?14th cent.

> **A.3335** Same site and donor. 67 sherds of medieval pottery mainly green-glazed and 3 fragments of roofing tile [annotated in pencil] NB Sherds of Crock Street [ie Donyatt] type marked 'C'.

Gray's response to all the pottery evidence recovered was in contrast to the interest he showed in that from the prehistoric sites in whose excavation he was involved. He does not seems to have enlisted the help of anyone who might have given another view of what he was finding at Taunton Castle. The only pottery he illustrated and published (Gray 1941, 68) were two sherds of early roulette-decorated ware which he noted were similar to pottery found in his fieldwork at Castle Neroche (Gray 1903).

Pearson's corpus with the benefit of that author's extensive knowledge and experience of post-Roman pottery in Somerset and awareness of the excavated sequences in Bristol, Exeter and elsewhere is then the best starting point to assess what was found and is used as the basis for the following catalogue. Unfortunately the decision was made when publishing *The Archaeology of Taunton* in 1984 to commit the corpus in its entirety to microfiche and in the transition Pearson's numeration system was changed so that the reference numbers associated with individual sherds in the collection do not match those in the microfiche catalogue (Pearson's microfiche numbers have been followed here, those prefixed DD have been given to distinctive sherds that were not numbered by Pearson).

Pearson included as much of the pottery from Gray's excavations as he could find when compiling the corpus of pottery for *The Archaeology of Taunton* (Pearson 1984c). In particular numbers A.3249.5 (Taunton type 133), A.3249.6 (Taunton type 83), A.3249.8 (Taunton type 39), A.3249.10 (DD 16, see below), A.3249.11 (Taunton type 558 and DD 24) and A.3249.13 (Taunton type 553) relate to pottery recorded in Gray's list of finds (see page 46). Also included were all the wares then recently excavated under the auspices of the Committee for Rescue Archaeology in Avon, Gloucestershire and Somerset together with some earlier finds.

Catalogue of the pottery from Gray's excavations and other provenanced Castle material

Pearson's chronological and typological framework has been followed. The references indicate the pottery catalogue number in Pearson (1984c). To facilitate access to the data these illustrations have been extracted from the microfiche and are reproduced here, retaining their published reference numbers (Figure 7.10 – Figure 7.17). Those catalogued by the present author from A.3249 and A.3335 but missed by Pearson are prefixed "DD". Sherds described by Pearson and identified by the present author in the existing reference collections are marked with an asterisk: those without an asterisk could not be located and Pearson's description stands unamended. TC refers to the Taunton Castle type series, BPT to that of Bristol.

Pearson divides the early pottery from the 1924–1929 excavations into four chronological groups. The later groups, 5 to 9, also follow Pearson's chronology but derive from a wider range of locations within the castle.

1. Pre-Conquest

   Type 224/239 Figure 7.16: 134, (Pearson 1984c, 8, 67). The only example of this type of limestone-rich fabric found by Pearson and the only pottery sherd from the Castle which he considered to be firmly pre-Conquest.

   Pearson 134, Gray A.3089
   One sherd, illustrated and described. Part of a hand-made vessel with wavy combed decoration.

   Type unrecorded (assigned TC030 for future reference)

   DD 12, Gray A.3249
   Context: not recorded. *Fabric:* coarse grainy reduced body with worn quartz and angular calcite inclusions. *Description:* a body sherd of an open jar decorated on the exterior with shallow incised crossed lines.

2. Late 11th to early 12th century.

   Type 50 Figure 7.12, (Pearson 1984c, 10). Hard-fired reduced hand-built ware with rounded and angular quartz inclusions with some limestone lumps; red to buff reoxidised outer surfaces. Pearson draws similarities in the forms with Ilchester B ware variant type 55 (Pearson 1982, 171). The type is represented by *Pearson 48–66*, nineteen sherds illustrated and described (Pearson 1984c, 62–63). All are hand-made jars with vertical or slightly everted and hollowed rims except for 48 and 49 which are large unglazed pitchers with wavy combed decoration on the shoulder and an applied thumbed cordon (61 only).

   **Pearson 48*
   Context: unknown. *Description:* large heavy unglazed pitcher with applied cordon at the base of the neck and part of an applied ?horseshoe-shaped strip on the shoulder and wavy combed decoration round the shoulder.

   **Pearson 49*
   Context: not recorded. *Description:* two body sherds; the first with part of a single band of wavy combed decoration; the second with parts of three bands of wavy combed decoration.

   **Pearson 61*
   Context: unknown. *Description:* bodysherd with part of a vertical thumbed applied cordon.

   Type 55 Figure 7.16: 132, Pearson (1984c, 9, 66) A form and fabric which Pearson equates with Ilchester B ware (Pearson 1982, 171). The type is represented by *Pearson 132*. One sherd of a hand-made jar with everted rim is illustrated and described.

3. Early 12th century.

   Type 222 Figure 7.10, Figure 7.11 Pearson (1984c, 12). A hard-fired reduced hand-built ware with both rounded and angular quartz inclusions: reduced grey core and occasional red reoxidised surfaces typical of, as Gray (1941, 68) noted, the fabric and decoration of wares found at Castle Neroche, and to those described by Allan *et al.* (2011) as Upper Greensand Derived ware. Equivalent to TC023. The type is represented by *Pearson 3–28*, 26 sherds illustrated and described (Pearson 1984c, 59–61). Hand-made jars and pitchers, some with rouletted bands and some incised decoration. Pearson notes the significance of the fact that one sherd (3) was published by Gray and that most of this type of ware was found in the Keep Garden castle well (Gray 1941; Vivian-Neal and Gray 1940) although a further two sherds were "found at level of foundation of Norman Wall [Wall A] having 18 off-sets" (Pearson 1984c, 12).

However, Pearson and consequently others rely over-confidently on Gray's asserted association between this pottery, the bottom of the "Norman" well and the footings of the "keep" (Gray 1941, 68). Closer study of Gray's notes, sketch plans and sections clearly show that other pottery as late as the

Civil War is similarly associated with these features. Further it must be inappropriate to argue through this perceived association that the date 1138 derived from documentary sources can be applied to these structures, as discussed on page 266, and thereby to this type of ware. However rouletted decoration of this kind is not common and is datable to the 11th to 12th century when used on other wares such as that from Ham Green (Barton 1963, 101, 109; Ponsford 1991) and stratified coarse wares, some, possibly northern French in origin, in Exeter (Allan 1984, 40–43). As an aside, Normandy gritted-ware displays rouletted bands of a similar pattern. This feature appears in the imitations of this type of pottery found at Castle Neroche by Gray (1903, 36, plate III: 8 and 9) but not by Davison (1972). Type 222 is a similar fabric to these imitations but the forms are definitely local. The form of *Pearson 6* is particularly singular.

The seven sherds listed below were and still are kept as exemplars of Type 222 in the CRAAGS (latterly the WAT) fabric type series organised by Pearson but strangely they were not included in Pearson's catalogue.

DD 13, Gray A.3249
Context: marked "bottom of Norman well." One of two sherds drawn and published by Gray (1941, 68). He describes, "some fragments of Norman pottery (probably of one vessel) having a typical ornament consisting of impressions of diamonds or lozenge shapes (others being oblong or almost square). One of the larger fragments is here illustrated." *Description:* body sherd of a jar with parts of two bands of rouletting with networks of lozenges. Thickening for what may be a boss below the second band.

DD 14, Gray A.3249
Context: marked "Taunton Castle" but bagged with DD 13 and probably a sherd of the pottery referred to by Gray. *Description:* body sherd with part of one band of similar rouletting.

DD 15, Gray A.3249
Context: marked "Taunton Castle" but bagged with DD 13 and probably a sherd of the pottery referred to by Gray. *Description:* body sherd with part of two bands of similar rouletting.

DD 16, Gray A.3249
Context: marked "Taunton Castle Norman Well" but bagged with DD 13 and almost certainly a sherd of the pottery referred to by Gray. *Description:* sherd of the basal angle with part of one band of similar rouletting.

DD 17, Gray A.3249
Context: not marked but bagged with DD 13 and probably a sherd of the pottery referred to by Gray. *Description:* sherd of the basal angle with part of one band of similar rouletting. The band is more widely spaced from the base than DD 16 and is a slightly different form raising the possibility of the five sherds representing two similar vessels not just the one suggested by Gray.

DD 18, Gray A.3249
Context: marked "Taunton Castle found at level of foundation of Norman wall having 18 off-sets." *Description:* two joining sherds of an undecorated heavily built jar. The fabric is obscured by mortar and lime but seems to be different from and fired greyer than 222.

**Pearson 3, Gray A.3249*
Context: one of two sherds drawn and published by Gray (1941, 68). Tantalisingly this sherd, published for comparison, and clearly Pearson 3, "was also found in the excavations at Taunton Castle, but not in the square well." *Description:* sherd of an upright rim decorated on both sides with a roulette of a network of lozenges.

**Pearson 4, Gray A.3249*
Context; not recorded. *Description:* rim sherd with a groove in the flat top decorated right up to the rim with a rouletted band of irregular lozenges and hexagons.

**Pearson 5*
Context: marked later in ink, "Taunton Castle C3 Keep." *Description:* rim sherd with grooved top and decorated right up to the rim with a rouletted band of irregular shapes – triangles, lozenges and hexagons.

**Pearson 6, Gray A.3249*
Context: not recorded. *Description:* a substantial part of a bowl, single surviving handle decorated with three incised lines, a rouletted band of a network of lozenges, very similar to Pearson 3, under the rim and a nail-groove round the top. More of the rim survives than indicated by Pearson's drawing.

**Pearson 8*
Context: not recorded. *Description:* body sherd from a rouletted band of a network of hexagons.

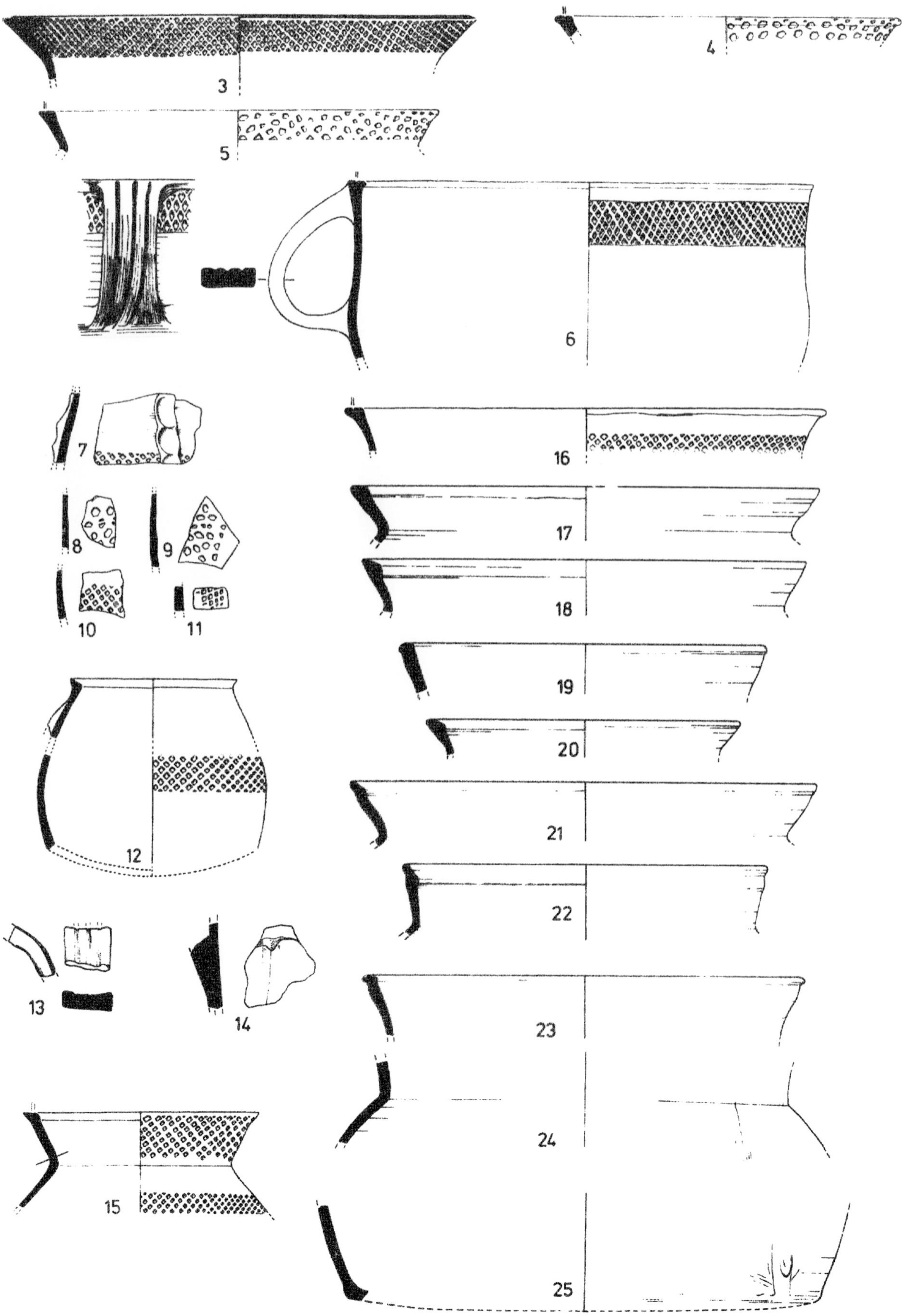

Figure 7.10: *Pearson (1984c) type 222 pottery. Reproduced from microfiche in Leach (1984a). Scale 1:4.*

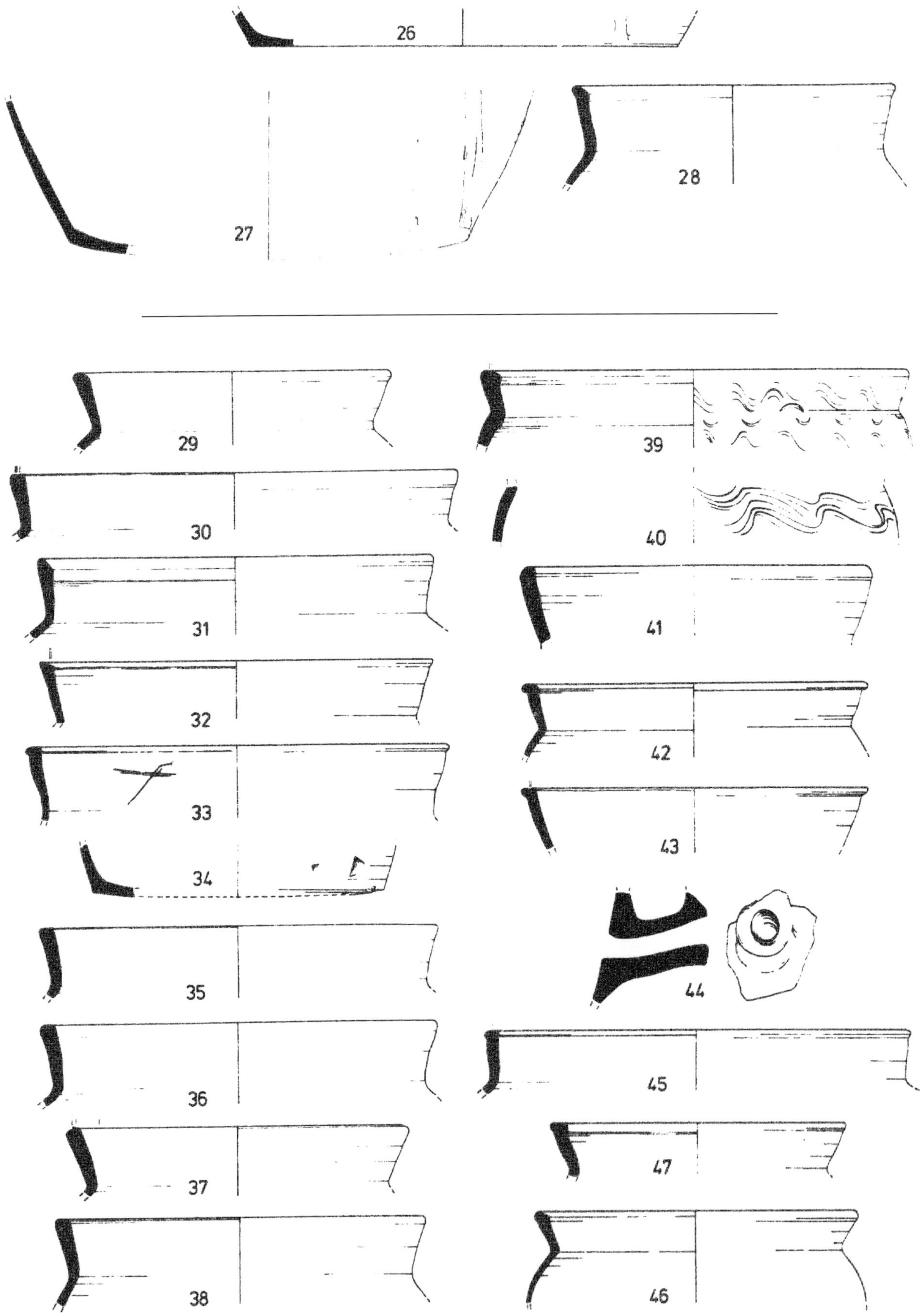

Figure 7.11: *Pearson (1984c) types 222 (26–28) and 224 (29–47) pottery. Reproduced from microfiche in Leach (1984a). Scale 1:4.*

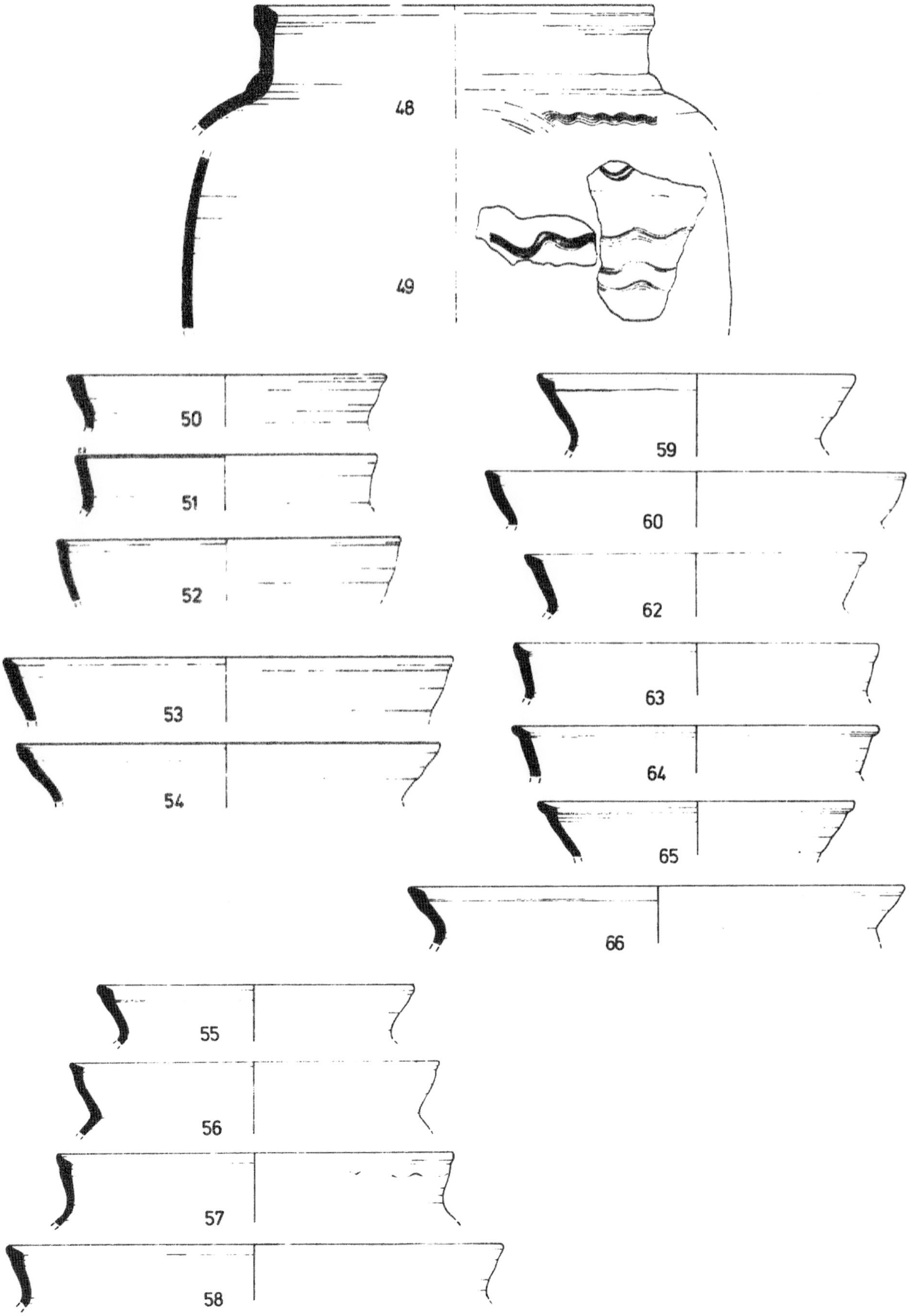

Figure 7.12: *Pearson (1984c) type 50 pottery. Reproduced from microfiche in Leach (1984a). Scale 1:4.*

**Pearson 9*
Context: marked later in ink, "Taunton Castle Keep C3." *Description:* body sherd from a rouletted band of a network of hexagons.

**Pearson 12*
Context: marked later in ink, "Taunton Castle Keep C1." *Description:* Two discreet sherds of a jar. a) rim with applied ridged boss; b) body sherd with basal angle and rouletted band of lozenges lined with triangles.

**Pearson 13, Gray A.3249*
Context: not recorded. *Description:* part of a handle decorated with three incised lines.

**Pearson 14*
Context: not recorded. *Description:* drawn-out tail of a substantial applied vertical cordon.

**Pearson 15*
Context: not recorded. *Description:* rim sherd with grooved top and decorated up to the rim with a rouletted band of lozenges.

**Pearson 16*
Context: not recorded. *Description:* rim sherd with grooved top and rouletted band of lozenges round the neck.

**Pearson 24*
Context: not recorded. *Description:* shoulder of a bellied jar with start of flattened thumbed applied vertical cordon.

**Pearson 25*
Context: not recorded. *Description:* base of an open jar with vertical applied cordon meeting the pronounced squared foot ring.

**Pearson 26*
Context: not recorded. *Description:* similar to 25 but with shallower foot ring.

**Pearson 27*
Context: not recorded. *Description:* similar to 26.

Type 224 Figure 7.11, Pearson (1984c, 12–13) A hard-fired reduced hand-built ware with red reoxidised surface rather corky where limestone inclusions have leached out, also quartz and chert inclusions – a variant of Upper Greensand derived wares. Pearson cites similar style of vessels from Bristol and Exeter to support his dating. The type is represented by *Pearson 29-47*, 19 sherds illustrated and described (Pearson 1984c, 61–62). Hand-made jars and pitchers, some with wavy combed decoration. One sherd (44) is a tubular spout.

**Pearson 39, Gray A.3249.8*
Context: Gray's 1924–25 excavation "found under no 6 at a depth of 6.3ft below the surface. Cutting II" (see pages 41 and 46, No 8). *Description:* rim of an open jar form, probably a tripod pitcher, with two bands of wavy combed decoration either side of interlocked () marks.

**Pearson 44*
Context: not recorded. *Description:* tubular spout with attachment for a short strap handle joining the top end of the spout to the body.

Type 42 Figure 7.13, Pearson (1984c, 13–14) A hard-fired reduced fabric slight reoxidised buff on outer surface. The type is represented by *Pearson 67–88*, 17 sherds illustrated and described (Pearson 1984c, 63–64). Hand-made jars with slightly everted rims, 82 and 83 with thumb-impressed decoration round the rim.

**Pearson probably 82, Gray A.3249.6*
Context: marked on the section and plan of Gray's 1924–25 "Cutting II near modern walls, depth 5.2ft in mixed red marl, black earth and 'rubbish'" (see pages 41 and 46, No 6). *Description:* one sherd of the everted rim of a jar form decorated with diagonal grooves. The only sherd located from Gray's "several fragments" marked 6.

Type 43 Figure 7.14, Pearson (1984c, 14) A fairly hard-fired reduced hand-built ware with quartz and few limestone inclusions. The type is represented by *Pearson 89-103*, 20 sherds illustrated and described (Pearson 1984c, 64–65). All hand-made jars but note one sherd (96) is a handle with incised decoration. Pearson says that these forms equate to 12th/13th-century types in Ilchester and Long Ashton.

DD 19, Gray A.3249
Context: Gray's 1924-25 excavations but precise context not recorded. *Description:* one rim sherd, hollowed with flat rim, of an open jar marked as type 43 but not matching any of the drawings.

**Pearson 96*
Context: not recorded. *Description:* handle probably from a tripod pitcher with three incised lines tapering towards the base.

Type 43/237 Figure 7.15, Pearson (1984c, 14–45) A hard-fired reduced fabric similar to type 43 but also with occasional large chert inclusions. The type is represented by *Pearson 104–114*, 11 sherds illustrated and described (Pearson 1984c, 65–66). All hand-made jars with slightly everted rims.

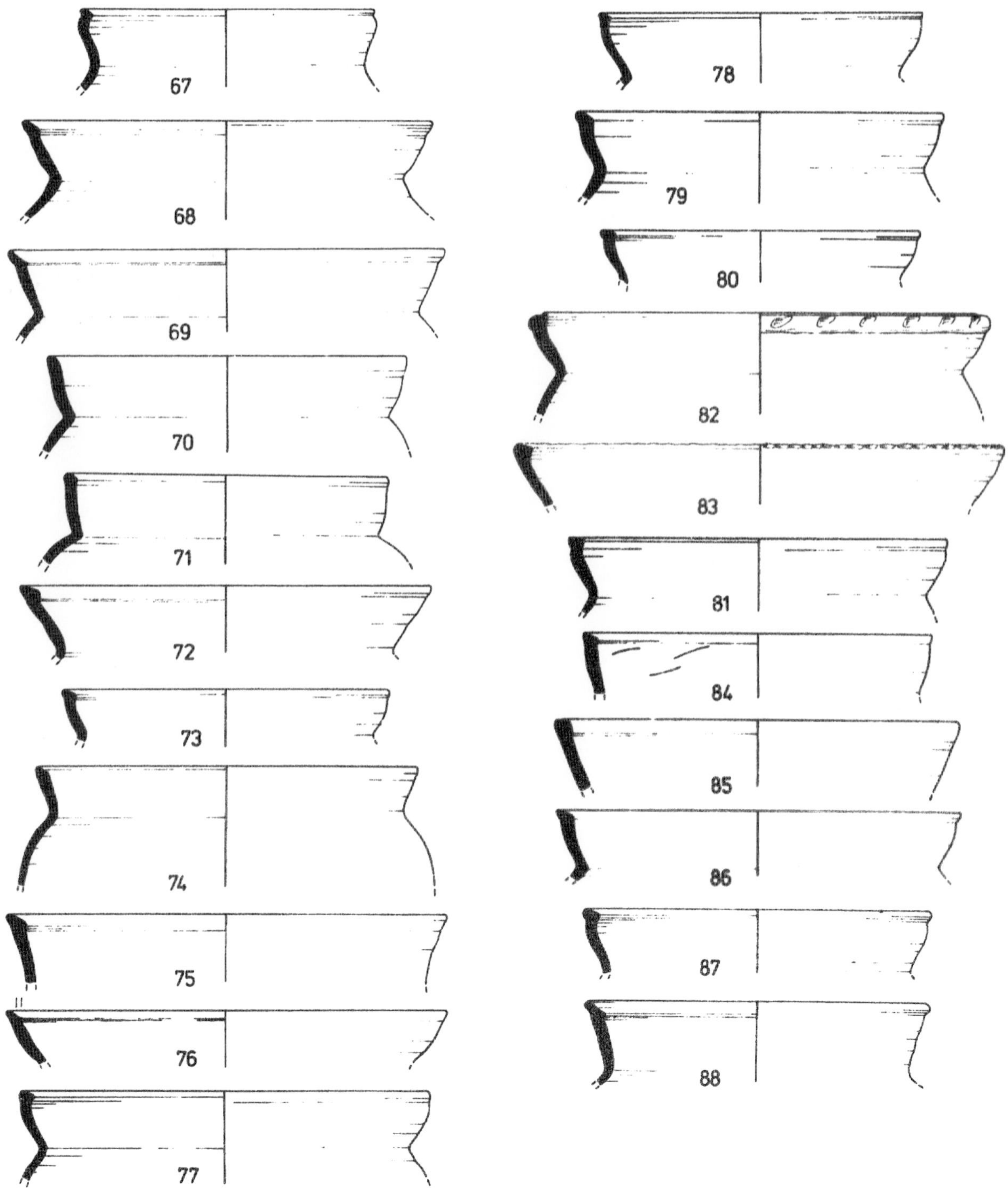

Figure 7.13: *Pearson (1984c) type 42 pottery. Reproduced from microfiche in Leach (1984a). Scale 1:4.*

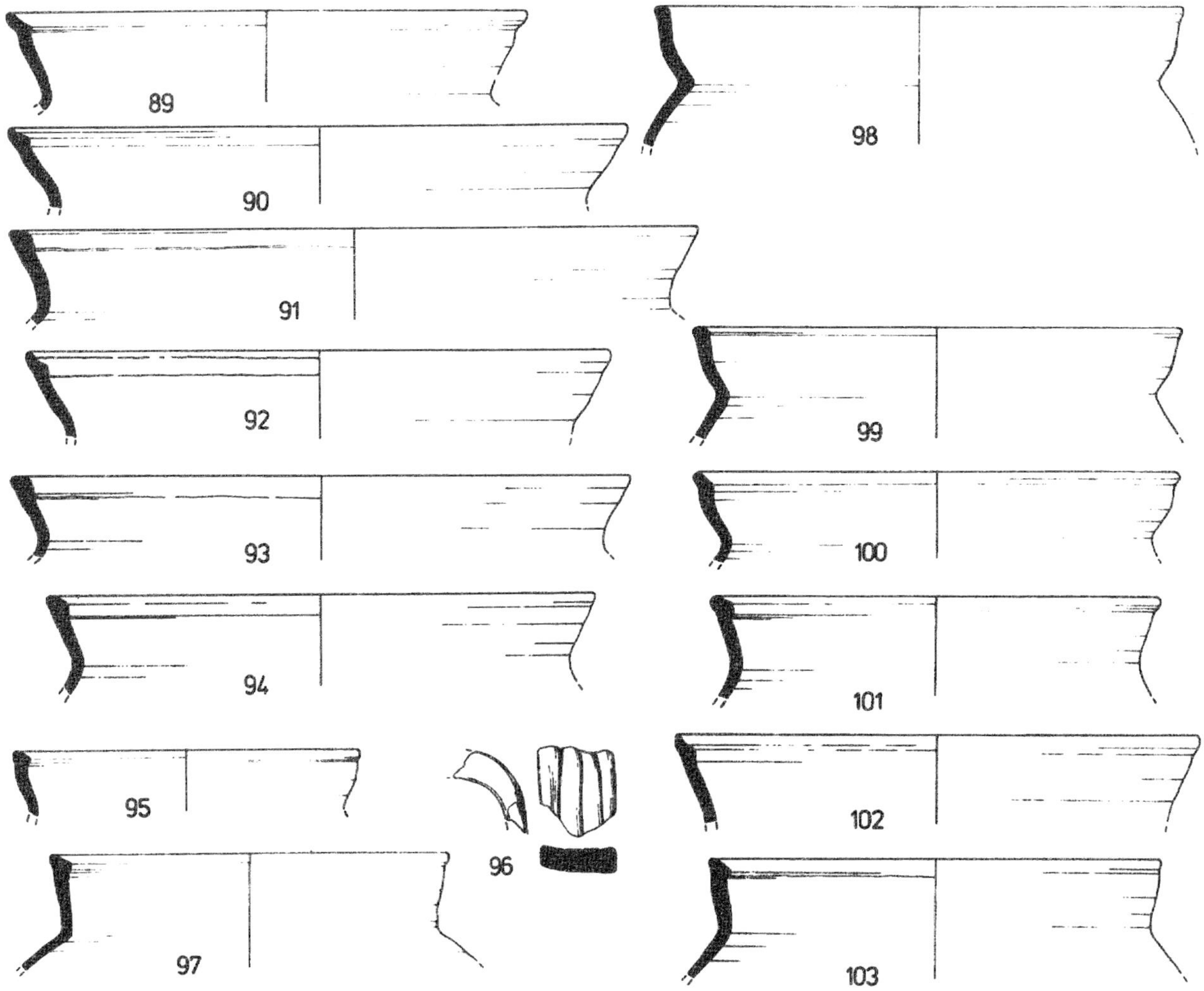

Figure 7.14: *Pearson (1984c) type 43 pottery. Reproduced from microfiche in Leach (1984a). Scale 1:4.*

**Pearson 114*
Context: not recorded. *Description:* shoulder of an open jar, belly impressed with shallow triangular shapes.

Type 235 Figure 7.16, Pearson (1984c, 15) Another variant of a hard-fired reduced hand-built ware with reoxidised red outer surfaces with quartz inclusions – Upper Greensand derived ware. The type is represented by *Pearson 115-124,* 10 sherds illustrated and described (Pearson 1984c, 66). All hand-made jars with vertical or slightly everted rims.

**Pearson 117, Gray A.3335*
Context: Outer Moat electric light showrooms 1937. *Description:* rimsherd of an open jar.

Type 236 Figure 7.16, Pearson (1984c, 15–16). Another hard-fired reduced hand-built ware with reoxidised red outer surfaces and quartz inclusions. The type is represented by *Pearson 125-130,* six sherds illustrated and described (Pearson 1984, 66). All hand-made jars which Pearson notes represent at most six vessels with similarity in fabric to Wiltshire scratch-marked ware.

Type 225 Figure 7.16, Pearson (1984c, 16) A hard-fired reduced ware with reoxidised red outer surfaces and quartz, limestone and occasional chert inclusions. The type is represented by *Pearson 131,* one sherd illustrated and described (Pearson 1984c, 66). A hand-made jar with everted rim.

4. Late 12th to early 13th century.

Type 44 Figure 7.16, A hard-fired reduced ware with reoxidised outer surface with quartz and occasional limestone inclusions Pearson (1984c, 21–22).

**Pearson 133, Gray A.3249.5*
Context: "One of two fragments of pottery found on the west side of Cutting II at a

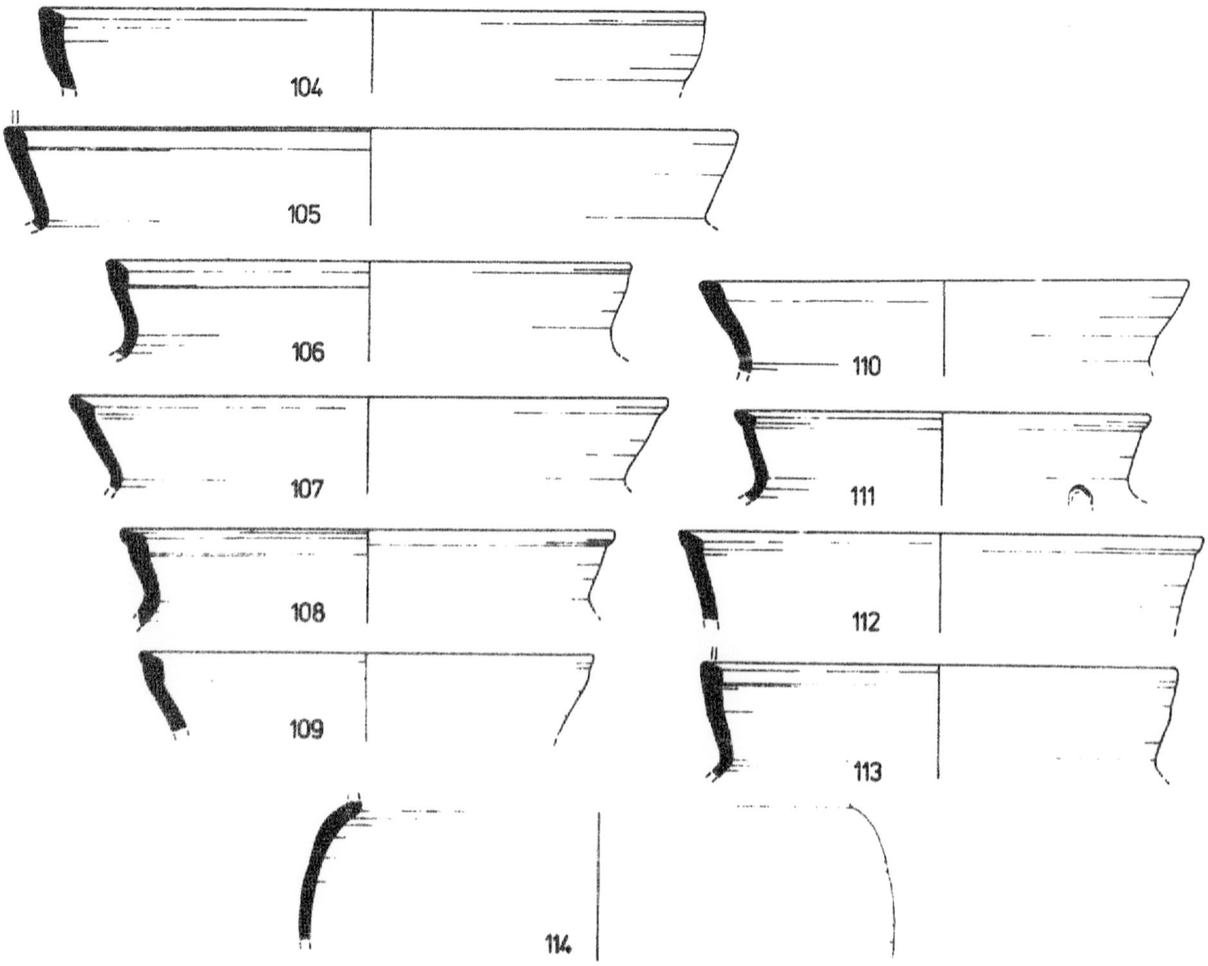

Figure 7.15: Pearson (1984c) type 43/237 pottery. Reproduced from microfiche in Leach (1984a). Scale 1:4.

depth of 7.5ft." (see page 46, No 5). *Description:* one sherd illustrated and described (Pearson 1984c, 67). A hand-made jar with tall everted rim.

Later medieval and later pottery 12th to 18th century.

In common with the 2005-2010 excavation there seems to have been remarkably little later Medieval pottery recovered. Pearson published 16 sherds from Taunton Castle though again these are all large fragments presumably recovered from primary though in most cases unrecorded contexts. Four of the sherds listed here (553, 558, DD 27 and DD 28) are marked from Gray's excavations; five others are marked as from the Outer Moat by the East Gate (555, 556, DD 22, 562 and DD 29). Of these five the first four are later medieval in date indicating that whatever was disturbed here was not post Civil War filling but may have been associated with works in the late medieval period.

5. Late 12th to 13th century.

   Type unrecorded = TC031

   DD 20, Gray A.3249
   Fabric: fabric type TC031, a hard-fired reduced hand-built ware with small black inclusions and reduced green glaze. Source remains unidentified as though the fabric is similar it does not match Ham Green waste. *Context:* not recorded. *Description:* two joining sherds of the frilled base of a jug characteristic of Ham Green A ware; 158mm in diameter.

6. 14th to 15th century.

   Type 208 Figure 7.17, Pearson (1984c, 32) A hard-fired reduced wheel-thrown ware with reoxidised interior and sparse quartz inclusions. Very smooth fine grained feel to the interior.

   **Pearson 553, Gray A.3249.13*
   Context: Gray's 1924-25 excavation "Found in Cutting II near the modern wall, depth

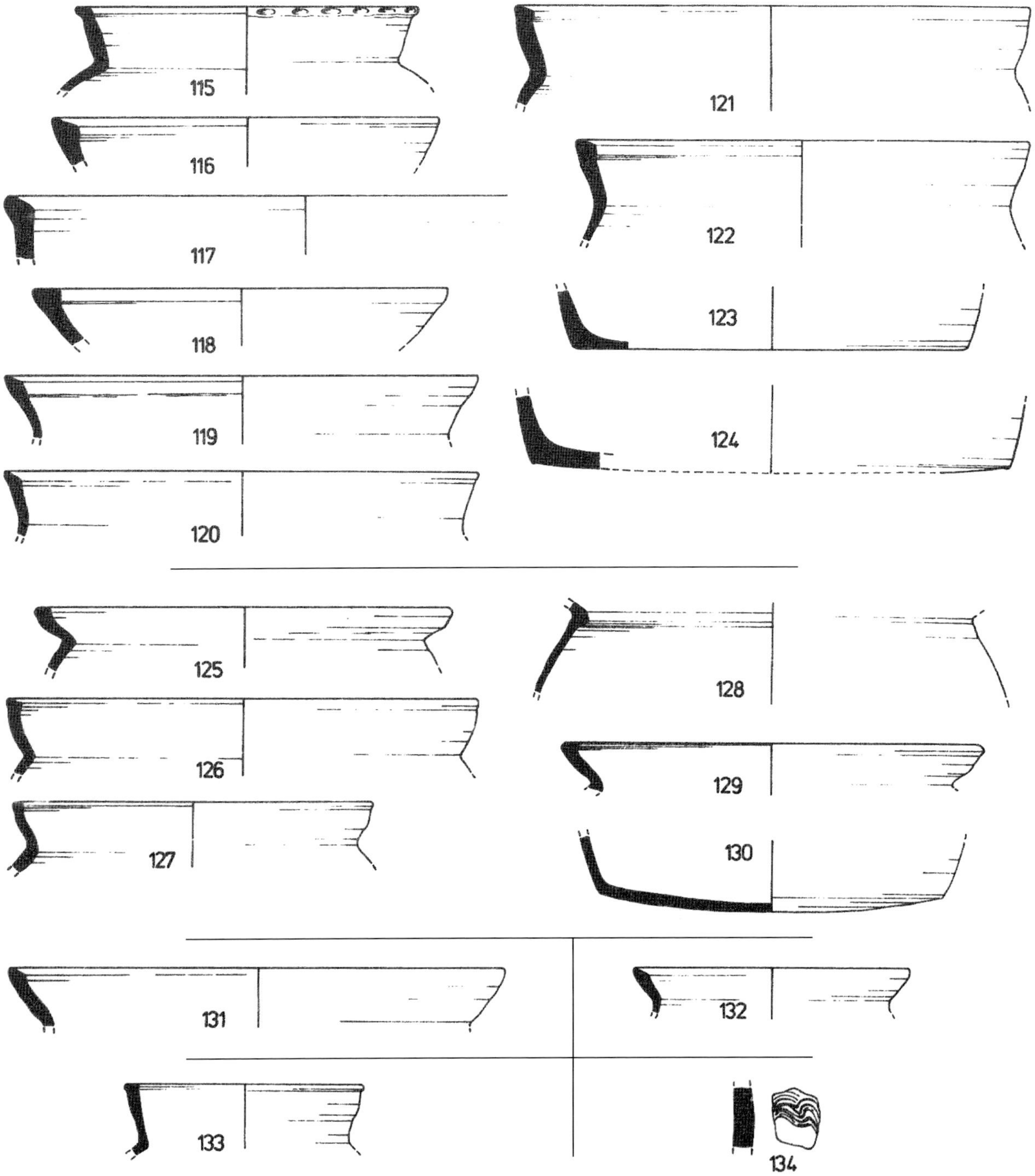

__Figure 7.16:__ Pearson (1984c) types 235 (115–24), 236 (125–30), 225 (131), 55 (132), 44 (133) and 224/239 (134) pottery. Reproduced from microfiche in Leach (1984a). Scale 1:4.

5.4ft in mixed red marl, black earth and 'rubbish"' (see page 46, No 13). *Description:* three sherds illustrated and described (Pearson 1984c, 93). Gray's "handle and part of rim and spout of a glazed jug apparently of Norman or early medieval date." A wheel-thrown baluster jug with a collar thrown in round the base of the neck and with parrot-beak spout, the body is decorated with applied iron-rich pads apparently arranged in inverted chevrons under a reduced lead glaze. A white slip stripe has been added to the left of the spout. The strap handle is attached by being pushed through the body and decorated with stabbing and thumbing.

Type 211 Figure 7.17, fabric type not described by Pearson but represented by one sherd illustrated and described (Pearson 1984c, 93).

Pearson 554.
Context: not recorded. *Description:* A glazed base sherd, with thumbing, of what Pearson identifies as a tripod pitcher form.

Type 212 Figure 7.17, Pearson (1984c, 34) A hard-fired reduced sandy wheel-thrown fabric with reoxidised interior. Type represented by *Pearson 555, 556, 558, 560, 565 and 568*, six sherds illustrated and described (Pearson 1984c, 93–4). All ascribed to Donyatt and of 14th-century date.

**Pearson 555, Gray A.3335*
Context: found in the Outer Moat 1937. *Description:* glazed rim of a jug with parrot-beak spout without the bar, applied thumbed strip round the rim, white slip and sgraffito decoration.

**Pearson 556, Gray A.3335*
Context: found in the Outer Moat close to the East Gate, 1937. *Description:* the lower half of a baluster jug with white slip under a reduced lead glaze and a thumbed foot.

**Pearson 558, Gray A.3249.11*
Context: "Found in the well debris, depth 14.5ft below the surface of the ground." *Description:* the lower part of a baluster jug with thumbed down foot and dark green reduced lead-glaze.

**Pearson 560*
Context: not recorded. *Description:* the lower part of a baluster jug with thumbed foot and dark green reduced lead-glaze with oxidised orange patches.

**Pearson 565*
Context: not recorded. *Description:* the neck of a jug with thrown protruding band and a rich green reduced lead-glaze.

**Pearson 568, Gray A.3249*
Context: not recorded. *Description:* an elaborately decorated jug with no spout, applied and stamped iron-rich pads arranged round a two horizontal white slip bands and a third painted as a band of chevrons under an oxidised lead glaze and with a plain bar handle. *Interpretation:* Coleman-Smith notes that the vessel imitates the form and decoration of products of the potteries at Rouen (Pearson 1984c, 65–66; Barton 1966).

DD 22, Gray A.3335 C
Context: marked "Outer Moat, Taunton Castle, close to E. Outer Gate, 1937". *Description:* a large bodysherd of a cistern with spigot hole and reduced lead-glaze over much of the exterior.

DD 23, Gray A.3249
Context: not recorded. *Description:* bodysherd, possibly of a jug, with external white slip under rather burnt-off dark green lead-glaze.

DD 24 and 25, Gray A.3249
Context: not recorded. *Description:* spigot holes from two cisterns with external dark green reduced lead-glaze.

Type 132 Figure 7.17, Pearson (1984c, 32–33) A hard-fired reduced wheel-thrown fabric with reoxidised interior, similar to Type 208. Type represented by one sherd illustrated and described (Pearson 1984c, 94).

**Pearson 557, Gray A.3249*
Context: not recorded. *Description:* the rim and handle of a baluster jug with vertical white slip stripe on the body and plain strap handle attached by pushing through the body and finished at the base with a pair of thumbed ears. Patchy reduced green lead-glaze.

Type 131 Figure 7.17, fabric type not described by Pearson. A hard-fired wheel-thrown dark-grey reduced rather coarse fabric. The type is represented by one sherd illustrated and described (Pearson 1984c, 94).
**Pearson 559*
Context: not recorded. *Description:* A small body sherd with white slip and applied iron-rich strips possibly part of a letter M.

Type 207 Figure 7.17, Pearson (1984c, 32). A hard-fired fabric with "well distributed white opaque grits (less than 5mm) and larger shale(?) inclusions. Laminated and

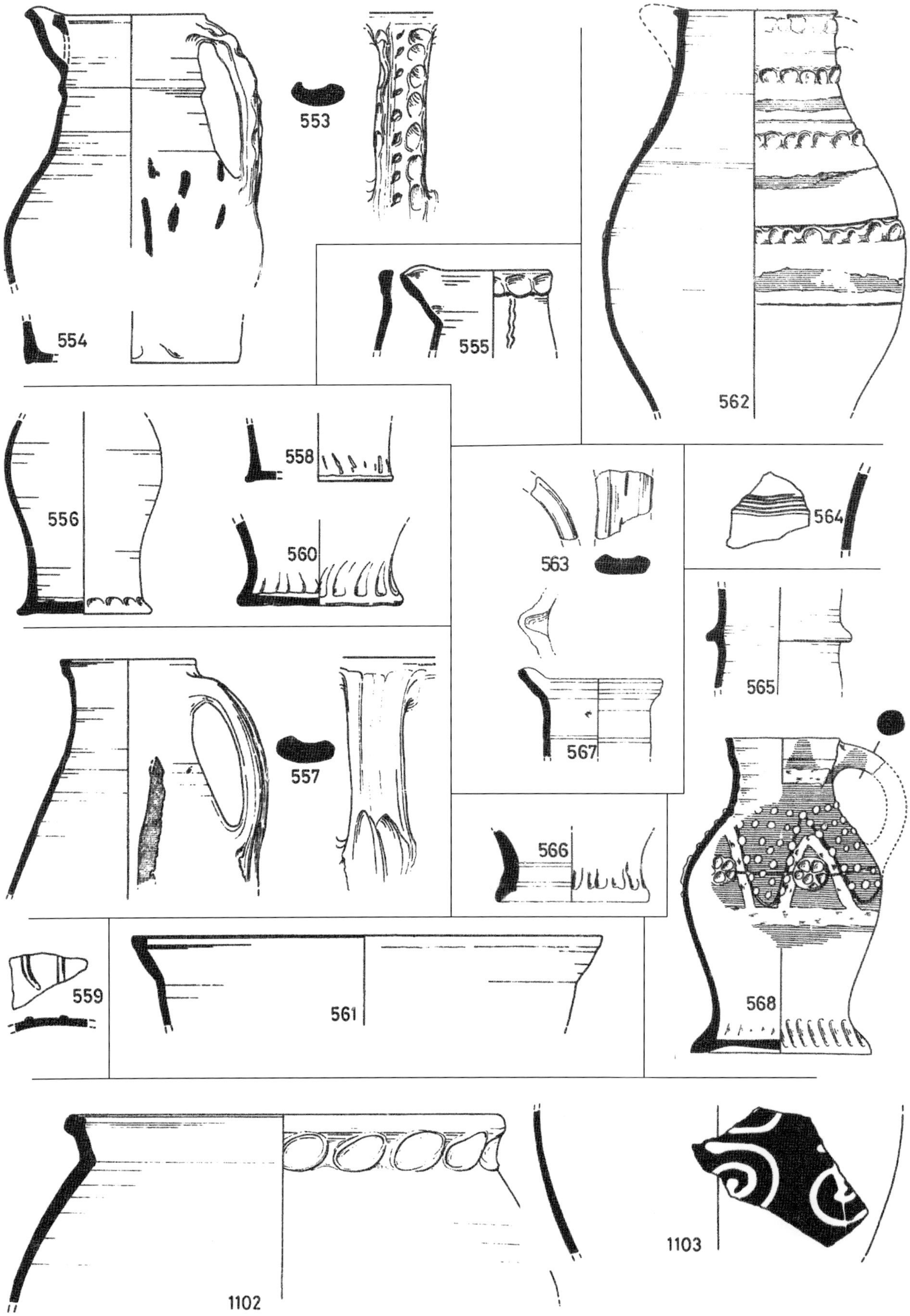

Figure 7.17: *Pearson (1984c) types 208 (553), 211 (554), 212 (555, 556, 558, 560, 565, 568), 182 (557), 131 (559), 4 (561), 207 (562), 5 (563, 567), 210 (654) and 261 (566). Reproduced from microfiche in Leach (1984a). Scale 1:4.*

grainy texture. Reduced black fabric and internal surface with oxidised orange-brown external surface." Represented by one sherd illustrated and described (Pearson 1984c, 94).

Pearson 562, Gray A.3277
Context: Found in the Outer Moat close to the East Gate in 1937 (given by Taunton Corporation). *Description:* . A wheel-thrown baluster jug with parrot-beak spout, horizontal white slip bands alternating with thumbed applied iron-rich strips under a reduced lead glaze; handle missing.

Type 5 Figure 7.17, Pearson (1984c, 35). A hard-fired reduced rather coarse fabric (563 has a reddish reoxidised unglazed surface as well as a large lump of calcite <3mm) with reduced external green glaze; identified as 14th/15th-century Donyatt products. The type is represented by *Pearson 563 and 567*, two sherds illustrated and described (Pearson 1984c, 94).

**Pearson 563*
Context: not recorded. *Description:* part of a slashed strap handle.

**Pearson 567*
Context: not recorded. *Description:* the rim of a jug with an applied and pulled spout.

Type 209 Not illustrated, (Pearson 1984c, 34). Fine sandy fabric with isolated quartz inclusions. In the opinion of the present author these sherds probably date from the 15th to 16th century. DD 27 is the type exemplar and is very well made, finely potted hard-fired with a glossy dark olive-green glaze. The type is represented by three sherds, not catalogued by Pearson.

DD 26, Gray A.3249
Context: Not recorded. *Description:* Green glaze over a white slipped sherd of a jug ascribed to late 13th/early 14th century.

DD 27, Gray A.3249.11
Context: "Fragments of pottery found in the turret well. Depth about 14.5ft." (see page 46, No. 11). *Description:* two sherds, not illustrated, one the pulled spout of a jug, the other a body sherd, both with splashed white slip.

Type 210 Figure 7.17, fabric type not described by Pearson. Represented by one sherd illustrated and described (Pearson 1984c, 94).

Pearson 564, Gray A.3249
Context: Not recorded. *Description:* A glazed body-sherd of a tripod pitcher with wavy combed decoration.

Type 261 Figure 7.17, Pearson (1984c, 31–32). Hard-fired dense fabric with few visible inclusions, occasional quartz. Represented by one sherd illustrated and described (Pearson 1984c, 94).

**Pearson 566, Gray A.3249*
Context: Not recorded. *Description:* The base of a wheel-thrown baluster jug with thumbed foot and reduced lead glaze.

7. 16th century.

Type 4 Figure 7.17, Pearson (1984c, 38–39) A fabric similar to waste from Donyatt Site 4 (16th-century). Represented by one sherd illustrated and described (Pearson 1984c, 94).

Pearson 561
Context: Not recorded. *Description:* glazed rim of a thrown jar.

8. 17th century

Type unrecorded

DD 28, Gray A.3249.10
Fabric: a reduced buff version of the standard Donyatt wheel-thrown fabric of this period. *Context:* "Found in E, extension of Cutting I, depth 7.75 ft below the surface" (see page 46, No 10). *Description:* small wheel-thrown jug or drinking vessel imitating a Rhenish form, neck, rim and handle missing, completely unglazed.

DD 29, Gray A.3335
Fabric: hard-fired reduced red earthenware body, almost a stoneware. *Context:* outer moat close to the east gate, 1937. *Description:* body sherd of a jug imitating a Rhenish bellied krug with upright neck; broad-brush lattice in thick white slip under an olive green to red reduced lead-glaze with reduced iron mottling.

9. 18th century

Type 8 Figure 7.17, Pearson (1984c, 51–52), a fairly hard-fired reduced and reoxidised sandy fabric equivalent to TC083; identified by Pearson and Coleman-Smith as a Donyatt pottery type. Two sherds illustrated and described (Pearson 1984c, 137–38).

**Pearson 1102, Gray A.3249 C*
Context: not recorded. *Description:* rim and body of a typical South Somerset type ware jar with applied thumbed strip under the rim, painted white slip band round shoulder and internal reduced lead-glaze with orange blushes and iron-rich particles bled and run into the glaze.

Pearson 1103, Gray A.3249 C
Context: not recorded. *Description:* bodysherd of an open bowl decorated externally with a metropolitan-style trailed white slip with an oxidised lead-glaze speckled with particles of iron bled into it.

Other pottery from Taunton Castle

There are several collections of sherds that are essentially disassociated from their original context. There is however a group of 36 vessels and six clay-pipes all drawn with accompanying descriptions, apparently prepared for publication by AD Hallam, which appear to be the group recovered in the extension to the printing works of Messrs Goodman & Son on the west side of North Street in 1926 (Vivian-Neal and Gray 1940, 58). They are numbered with the prefix EM and are marked "Outer Moat 1926" and in two, cases "Outer Moat Goodman's". Four of these vessels are registered in the museum collections as from the west side of North Street which suggests that EM might be an abbreviation for Eastern Moat. All the vessels are 17th-century South Somerset ware types (including sgraffito decoration, imitation Rhenish forms and one example of quartz encrusted ware), save for one tin-glazed earthenware drug jar with blue-painted decoration typical of Bristol in the latter half of the 17th-century.

Another much smaller collection from the moat on the site of the "Bus Park 1957" contains Rhenish stoneware and also dates to the 17th century. Together they support the suggestion that the moat was progressively filled with domestic rubbish and perhaps debris from the siege of the town and castle in the years following the end of the Civil War.

A further group of late 17th/early 18th-century Somerset earthenwares some marked, "Taunton Castle Excavations 1933", and possibly a bag of sherds of Rhenish stoneware bottles of similar date, probably result from the landscaping of the hotel gardens in that year but no context was recorded for them.

7.2 The Glass *Katie Marsden*

Glass was present in many contexts and 877 sherds were examined. Due, however, to the fragmentary nature of the assemblage minimum and maximum vessel quantities have been difficult to ascertain. No medieval glass was identified, the vast majority being 18th century or later. Much of the work on this material has taken place in former British colonies where it has been shown that curation and reuse of vessels such as wine bottles was common (Boow 1991, 21). Busch (1987, 78) has identified historical sources suggesting that that this was common practice in Europe as well, which will have implications for the analysis of excavated materials. Bottle typologies and dating schemes have been taken from Noël Hume (1961) where possible with an awareness of the potential for reuse (Busch 1987, 77).

The majority of fragments, 70%, are of post-medieval date and, excluding the window glass, generally belonging to the English dark green, or "olive" glass tradition, developed in the early 17th century with the banning of wood fuel for glassworking (Jones 2011, 22–23) and the subsequent switch to coal. Within this category, the majority of the identifiable fragments are wine bottle. It is interesting that, whilst other types of glass are present, the proportion of these is very low and comprises aqua, blue and amber only. Most notable are six fragments of possible Bristol blue glass, a local industry developed between the late 1700s and 1851.

There are also taphonomic processes at work as the number of necks and bases differs, suggesting that the bottles were not complete when finally dumped. The majority of post-medieval glass fragments are suffering from deterioration and have developed an iridescent patination, more common in vessels of high soda, low lime composition (Lindsey 2012). Some sherds of window glass have also developed a patination rendering dating difficult.

The largest collections of glass came from the pits (particularly context 435, 168 sherds) in the West Passage. The fragments are mainly base and lower side fragments and the neck and rim section of wine bottles. A large group of base fragments, representing the majority if not all of the basal kick from a number of vessels, have not been assigned a date range. It is the interaction between basal kick and vessel wall that provides us with a secure dating option and not enough of the vessel body survives on most of these pieces. However, 30 fragments were identified by date, producing a clear range from c.1652 to 1800. Within these ranges however, only two types have start dates prior to 1675, both in context 436, given by Hume as "before 1652". Similarly, only one fragment can be dated post 1765, from context 435 dated 1770–1800. Context 435 also produced the only bottle seals from the entire site. One complete seal, one fragment and one body sherd with a seal edge, were found (below).

In contrast the largest series of excavations, within the Great Hall, yielded only seven frag-

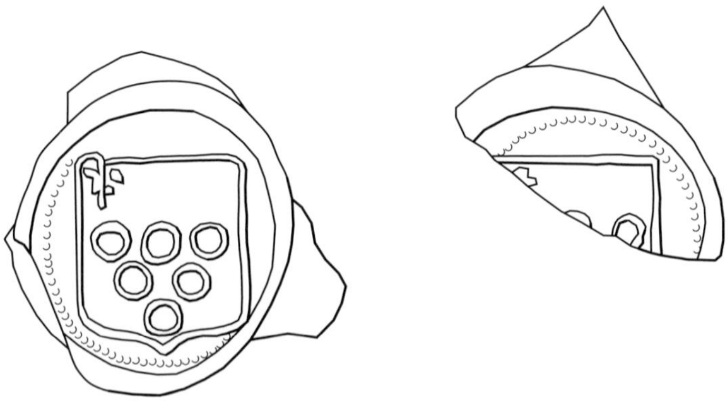

Figure 7.18: *Wine bottle seals from 435. Scale 1:1*

ments and monitoring in 2010 recovered only three sherds of an early 20th-century Bovril jar.

The window glass fragments indicate breakage and replacement, spanning the post-medieval and modern periods. Post-Medieval window glass has a variety of colours from green and pale blue to colourless, made with synthetic soda, all of which are represented in the assemblage. As with the wine bottles, the fragments of window glass are too few to represent whole windows and it is likely that most glass was recovered for resmelting leaving only floor sweepings to enter the archaeological record.

The bottle seals

It is surprising that only two seals were found at Taunton Castle, considering the quantities of appropriate wine bottles recovered. Seals, formed of glass attached to the neck or shoulders of the bottle and stamped with an identifying mark, began to develop in the 17th century, the earliest known dates from 1640 and they continued in use until the early 20th century (Lindsey 2012). They were originally made for gentlemen and taverns before being used by other members of society and to identify contents (Noël Hume 1970, 61).

The complete seal bears a blazon, six annulets, three two and one with fleur-de-lys a canton. The incomplete seal appears to be the same design, with a square-topped shield featuring annulets but there are differences that show it was produced from a different mould. The blazon appears to match that of the Musgrave family, whose branches are known from the parishes of North Petherton, West Monkton, Gotten, Old Cleeve and Nettlecombe in Somerset (Burke 1853, 14). As the fleur-de-lys canton is usually a mark of a sixth son it should be possible to identify the individual but this has not so-far been possible. Sir Benjamin Hammet was the brother-in-law of an Elizabeth Musgrave (Burke 1853, 15), which may provide a link to the Musgraves.

Discussion

Willmott (2002, 31) highlights a difference in urban and elite site deposition patterns. He suggests that urban sites show deposition of large quantities over a short time span or in a single action in pits and infilled cellars, whereas at elite sites the glass appears more fragmentary, from less specific contexts and associated with other general waste. This suggests that at elite sites glass was viewed as a restricted luxury item in which the value was lost with breakage, whereas at urban sites, the glass was seen as a statement of disposable wealth and collections were dumped to reflect changing fashions (Willmott 2002, 32).

By the post-medieval period, much of Taunton Castle had ceased to have a domestic function and the glass recovered reflects this; little evidence for glass vessels other than wine bottles was found. Two fragments from context 435 could indicate a glass plate or pedestal-based glass and the other fragments of possibly post-medieval vessel, those made in aqua glass, only number 13 fragments across all contexts. This, together with the disproportionate ratio between vessel parts, the high volume of body sherds and the fragmentary nature of the assemblage fit better Willmott's elite pattern.

However, this may be explained by the pattern of deposition. The bottles in context 435 range in date over a hundred years. This would seem an excessive span to be accounted for by bottle reuse and it would seem probable that context 435 represents the burying of material that had been dumped elsewhere (possibly outside the castle) over a long period. The latest dated bottle could suggest that the context for this tidying could be the work under Hammet in the late 18th century with material being brought in to infill stone robbing pits.

Later vessels record the return of domestic activity on site until at least 1920s, indicated by a poison bottle and jar of Bovril.

7.3 The Clay Tobacco Pipes *Susie White and David A Higgins*

The clay tobacco pipe fragments were individually examined and recorded using the pipe recording system that has been developed at the University of Liverpool (Higgins and Davey 2004). Impressions have been made of all the marked fragments and details of them have been recorded for the National Clay Tobacco Pipe Stamp Catalogue, which is currently housed in the Department of Archaeology at the University of Liverpool. Where more than one bowl fragment was present in a context and the fragments needed to be differentiated, they were allocated reference letters (A, B, C, etc.) to provide a unique identification. These have been pencilled onto the fragments and are used in this report.

All of the pipes were recorded and dated before any context descriptions were examined. This methodology avoids any pre-conceptions being formed as to the possible date or nature of the various groups while they are being catalogued.

Description of the Pipes

A total of 412 clay pipe fragments were recovered from the excavations comprising 71 bowl fragments (27 of which are marked), 335 stems (three of which have milled decoration on them), and six mouthpiece fragments. These finds came from a total of 68 stratified contexts and two unstratified deposits. The pipes recovered range in date from the 17th century through to the 19th century, although the majority date from the late 17th or early 18th centuries.

A detailed catalogue of all the bowl and marked stem fragments has been prepared for the site archive. The plain stems have been examined and taken into consideration when compiling the context summary, but they have not been individually catalogued. Plain stems are difficult to date accurately and so the dates that have been allocated to them are broad date ranges within which the fragments are likely to have been produced. Stem bore dating requires a sample of several hundred fragments from a single deposit and, in any case, is fraught with problems and often proves unreliable. It has not been used in this study.

The Pipes in Context

Clay tobacco pipes are probably the most useful dating tool for archaeological deposits of Post-Medieval date. They are found almost everywhere, were short-lived and were subject to rapid change in both size and shape. They can often be tied to a specific production site or, at the very least, to a regional centre. Subtle differences in style and quality enable them to be used as indicators of social status as well as a means by which trade patterns can be studied.

Of the 68 pipe-bearing context groups recovered from the excavations, 57 contained ten or fewer fragments of pipe, the majority of which are plain stems, making the dating of these individual deposits difficult. Many of the remaining contexts produced pipe fragments of mixed date, although most were pre 19th century. Three of the contexts, however, (231, 430 and 755) produced larger groups and these are discussed in more detail below. In each case the number of bowls, stems and mouthpieces are given, together with the total in the following format – bowls/stems/mouthpieces = total – therefore (1/2/3=6) would denote one bowl, two stems and three mouthpieces giving a total of 6 fragments.

Context 231 (5/40/1=46) A layer from the pit complex in the west passage (see page 69). Of the five bowl fragments that came from this context only one is marked: Bowl A, dating from c.1690–1730, and stamped EC/TAVN/TON on the heel (Figure 7.19: 6 and 7 for similar examples). This particular bowl, together with a contemporary looking milled rim fragment, is likely to be the earliest of the bowls from this group. The only other heel bowl from this group is of a slightly later date, *c*.1710–1740, with a more slender up-right form (Figure 7.20: 12). This context group also produced two 18th-century spur forms the most complete of which (Figure 7.20: 13) is likely to date to *c*.1720–1750. All of the stems from this context, and the single mouthpiece, are plain and all fall within a broad date range of *c*.1690–1750.

Based on the range of bowl forms present a deposition date of *c*.1710–1740 is suggested for this particular context.

Context 430 (10/30/1=41) A fill from the pit complex in the west passage (see page 69). Of the ten bowls recovered from this context only three are marked. Two (Bowls A and B) have a stamped mark reading

IB/TAVN/TON (Figure 7.19: 9), which is likely to be the mark of James Babb who was working in Taunton from *c*.1707–1722 (Lewcun 1988). These two bowls are interesting in that they were produced in the same mould as other examples from contexts 429 and 1098. The third marked bowl from context 430 bears the mark WV/TAVN/TON, which has been attributed to William Vickery who was working *c*.1660–1700 (Lewcun 1988). The remaining seven bowls from this context group are either plain or fragmentary. Six of them appear to be late 17th- or early 18th-century forms and would fall within an overall date range of 1690–1730. There is one bowl, however, a spur form that appears to be slightly later, *c*.1730–1790, which could be intrusive (Figure 7.20: 14). All of the stems, and the single mouthpiece fragment, are plain and all fall within a broad date range of *c*.1680–1800.

This is a good early 18th-century group. Based on the range of bowl forms present a deposition date of *c*.1700–1730 is suggested, but possibly with some later 18th-century intrusive material.

Context 755 (5/7/0=12) These were found in the silt of the drain in the Great Hall (see page 86). Of the five bowls recovered from this context four are marked, three with GE/ORGE/WEB heel stamps from Chard (Figure 7.19: 2), and one with a IEF/FREY H/VNT mark from Norton St Philip (Figure 7.19: 3). There is also a plain bowl in the same style as the marked bowls (Figure 7.19: 4). All five bowls date to *c*.1640–1670. The stems that were recovered from this group would appear to be contemporary. None of the bowls or the stems are burnished but a number of them have nice glossy surfaces and clearly come from well produced pipes.

This is a good mid 17th-century group with the most likely deposition date being *c*.1640–1670.

The Clay Tobacco Pipes Themselves

Having considered the clay tobacco pipes in context, the following sections go on to look at the pipes themselves. The clay tobacco pipes recovered from the excavations at Taunton Castle represent material from the second quarter of the 17th century right through to the end of the 19th century. All of the bowl forms that are represented are of typical south-west styles, a range of which have been illustrated (Figure 7.19 on page 137 and Figure 7.20 on page 139).

The actual form of the pipe bowl is the one thing that changed rapidly over time and is a feature that is often regionally distinct. In the earlier part of the 17th century, London tended to set the fashions and for most of England at that date the bowl forms are all fairly standard. By the mid 17th century regionally diverse forms start to appear. This may partly be due to the fact that pipe manufacturing was becoming more widespread, and had had time to develop local styles, but the English Civil War may well have also been a catalyst for change. This is certainly true of pipes from Yorkshire, where the Civil War marked a turning point in the development of the bowl form, and this may well have been the case elsewhere in England (White 2004, 158).

By the mid 17th century the pronounced forward leaning "chinned" bowl that became characteristic of the West Country and Somerset had emerged (see Figure 7.19: 3 and 4) and this underlying form continues, albeit in a slightly less pronounced way, into the mid 18th century.

The Taunton Castle pipe assemblage is dominated by 17th- and early 18th-century heel forms and, of the 38 examples, 27 (71%) have a maker's mark stamped on them. These marks are discussed in more detail below.

As a general rule the majority of pipes did not travel further than 10 to 20 miles from their place of manufacture (White 2004, 13). This is certainly the case with the pipes from Taunton Castle as most of them appear to have been produced in Taunton itself. There are, however, three other production centres whose pipes found their way to Taunton – Chard, Norton St Philip and Exeter.

At least five of the pipes in the Taunton Castle assemblage were produced in Chard, which is approximately 17 miles south-east of Taunton. These pipes are the four pipes marked by George Webb (bowls C, D and E from context 755 and one unstratified bowl). The fifth Chard product is marked EC IN CHARD (residual in topsoil). It is possible that this particular maker was Edward Collins (Lewcun 1988). Collins is documented as working in Chard *c*.1663–1673, and then from *c*.1675–84 in Taunton. Given that the Taunton Castle excavations yielded both EC IN CHARD and EC TAVNTON marks Collins would appear to be the most likely candidate for these pipes, although some of the bowl forms do look rather later than the documented dates for this maker.

Two of the pipes from Taunton have come from Norton St Philip, which is approximately 47miles north-east of Taunton. These comprise the bowls marked IEFFRY HVNT (one each from context 431 and 755), which can be attributed to Jeffry Hunt. The Hunt family are interesting in that they managed to develop a market area that was far bigger than was considered "normal" for a pipe manufacturer. The Hunt distribution area took in a very wide area across the whole of central southern England and the West Country, with the marks of Jeffry being particularly widely distributed.

There is also at least one pipe from the Taunton Castle assemblage that may have come from Exeter, approximately 30 miles south-west of Taunton. This is a plain bowl from context 223 (Figure 7.20: 11). The problem with identification is that Exeter pipes are not normally marked but their bowl forms are quite distinctive, often being quite constricted just above the heel and with relatively gentle curves to the front profile of the bowl (for example Oswald 1984, Fig. 160). The Taunton pipes tend to be much thicker above the heel and with a more sharply curved front profile (see Figure 7.19: 6–8). Having said that, the plain bowl form also bears a resemblance to the IB pipes, which were certainly made in Taunton (Figure 7.19: 9). The plain bowl certainly stands out as being rather different from the others recovered from the excavation and it would not be surprising for trade to pass between Exeter and Taunton.

Stamped Pipes

There were a total of 27 stamped marks from the castle, which are discussed in alphabetical order below. A selection of these marks has been illustrated where a good example of the associated the bowl form survives, and twice life size details of the stamps prepared. The other marks can all be matched with examples illustrated in Pearson (1984a), the individual references for which are given in the following descriptions.

IB A single heel bowl of *c.*1630–1650 with an IB mark was recovered from context 745 (Figure 7.19: 1). This distinctive mark has a cross above and below the initials and there are forked serifs to the B. This is the only stamped mark from the site where the lettering is in relief, rather than being incuse. There are at least five other examples of this particular mark in the museum collections: another from Taunton Castle; one from Hawke's Yard (Leach 1984b) and three from Canon Street (Hinchliffe 1984). There are also two examples of an almost identical mark, but with the design incuse, from Canon Street. All eight of these examples occur on bowl forms dating from *c.*1630–60, which is much earlier than the previously suggested date of *c.*1680 for this mark (Pearson 1984a, Nos 2 and 4). These marks must all have been made by the same maker, perhaps John Burrow, whose full name mark occurs on pipes of *c.*1660–90, examples of which have also been found in Taunton (Pearson 1984a, No 6) and whose pipes are distributed from Taunton and Bridgwater to the west to Wells in the east (Lewcun 2007, 675).

There are, however, also at least three other types of incuse IB mark that occur at Taunton on slightly later pipes, ranging from *c.*1670–1730 in date, which could equally have been made by Burrow. These comprise the initials IB within a plain border, the initials IB within a dotted border, and marks reading IB/TAVN/TON within a milled border (see below). The attribution of the IB marks is confused still further by the fact that there was a pipe maker named James Babb recorded at Taunton from at least 1707–22 (Lewcun 1988), who is a strong contender for these later forms. The overall date range of the IB marks (*c.*1630–1730) is far too long for a single maker and so it seems that at least two individuals with the initials IB must have been based at Taunton, one of whom may have been John Burrow, while another was certainly James Babb. It was also common for different generations to share the same name during this period and so these marks could also represent a pipe making family or families operating over a long period of time in the town.

IB TAVNTON Five examples of a heel mark reading IB/TAVN/TON in three lines dating from *c.*1690–1730 were recovered, one example each from contexts 436, 429, and 1098, and two examples from context 430 (Figure 7.19: 9). All of these examples have a very distinctive mould flaw on the right hand side of the heel, which shows that they were all produced in the same mould. All of the marks are poorly impressed and appear to have been hastily applied given that the orientation on the heel varies in every case (there are at least another five examples in the museum collections, two of which have been placed upside down on the heel). These pipes may well have been made by James Babb, who is recorded working in Taunton from 1707–1722 (but see also IB above).

E+C IN CHARD A single heel fragment from a large bowl with thin walls and a heel stamp reading E+C/IN CH/ARD (as Pearson 1984a, No 10) was recovered from topsoil. Lewcun (1988) lists an Edward Collins who is known to have been working in Chard *c.*1663–1673 but this seems rather early for this fragment, which appears to be more likely to date from *c.*1690–1730. There are at least two different versions of the Chard mark that can be attributed to this maker, one (as this example) with a plain border and the other with a milled border (see Pearson 1984a, Nos 9 and 10). These marks are quite common, with at least another 18 examples being present in the museum collections, which suggests that they were produced in a well-established and prolific workshop. Edward Collins appears to have left Chard and turns up in Taunton where he is recorded working from *c.*1675 until his death in 1684 (see the EC TAVNTON pipes below).

EC TAVNTON Five pipes with a heel stamp reading EC/TAVN/TON were recovered, one from context 231, two from context 472, one from context 725 and one unstratified. All five of these bowls can be dated typologically to *c.*1690–1730 – and possibly as early as 1680 (Figure 7.19: 6 and 7). A possible candidate for these pipes is Edward Collins who is known to have been working in Taunton from *c.*1675 until his death in 1684 (Lewcun 1988). He had previously been recorded in Chard *c.*1663–1673 and may well have been responsible for the pipe marked EC IN CHARD given that the style of that mark is almost identical to the Taunton examples (see above). The problem is that the Taunton bowl forms look rather late for a maker who died in 1684. One possible solution is that the Edward, son of Edward and Mary Collins, who was baptised at Chard on 25 June 1672 (IGI 2012), was the son of the pipe maker and went on to work in his own right in Taunton after his father's death.

IEFFRY HVNT Two pipes attributed to Jeffry Hunt were recovered, one each from contexts 431 and 755. The more complete bowl (Figure 7.19: 3) dates from *c.*1640–1670 with the other fragment, a heel only (not illustrated), dates from *c.*1650–1690. In his list of Somerset pipemakers, Lewcun (1988) gives details of two pipe makers with the name Jeffry Hunt. The first (Jeffry Hunt I) was working in Woolverton *c.*1623 before moving to Norton St Philip, where he was working from *c.*1624 until his death in 1690. The second (Jeffry Hunt II) appears to have been working in the Taunton area *c.*1690–1700, but this is too late for the excavated pipes.

The first Jeffry Hunt from Norton St Philip had at least five sons, Jeffry, Flower, John, William and Thomas, all of whom went on to become pipemakers. Jeffry (II) and William appear to have moved away to work in the Taunton area (see WH marks below); Flower and John moved to Bristol to take up the pipe making trade there, becoming founder members of the Bristol Pipemakers' Guild in 1652 (Lewcun 1985, 17), and Thomas appears to have moved to Marlborough in Wiltshire. Pipes with Jeffry Hunt's mark have an unusually wide distribution and appear to have been so well known in their day that contemporary forgeries were produced (Lewcun 2007, 675).

WH Two heel fragments bearing the mark WH were recovered, from contexts 515 and 860, both dating from *c.*1670–1710 (the mark is as shown by Pearson 1984a, No 21). These pipes can probably be attributed to William Hunt who was the son of Jeffry Hunt (I), born 25 August 1633 in Norton St Philip (Lewcun 1985, 16). William is recorded as working in Taunton from at least *c.*1661–1671 (Lewcun 1988).

RP TAVNTON A single example of a heel bowl of *c.*1690–1710 with a stamp reading RP/TAVN/TON was recovered from context 405 (the mark is as shown by Pearson 1984a, Nos 34–35). In his list of Somerset pipe makers Lewcun (1988) lists a Roger Pound whom he records as working in Taunton from *c.*1685–1694 and who may have died in 1732. Pearson (1984a, 150) notes that Roger Pound took on an apprentice called William Pyne on 1st August 1692.

WV TAVNTON A single marked pipe with the lettering WV/TAVN/TON on the heel, dating from *c.*1700–1730 (the mark as shown by Pearson 1984a, No 47) was recovered from context 430. At least three different die types used by this maker have been recorded locally, one reading WV TAVNTON, another reading WV IN TAVNTON and a third reading WV TAVNTON but with a border comprising alternate flowers and dots. According to Lewcun (1988) this WV mark is likely to be the product of

William Vickery, *c.*1660–1700 (although Vickery's actual occupation is not recorded in the contemporary documents).

RW TAVNTON A single pipe with an RW TAVNTON mark was recovered from Context 811 (TCC09) and is dated *c.*1690–1720 (Figure 7.19: 8). The maker of this particular pipe is yet to be identified in the documentary records. Pipes with both this mark and one that reads RW IN TAVNTON have been recorded from a range of sites in Taunton.

GEORGE WEB Three pipes with a GEORGE WEB mark, all context 755 and dating from *c.*1640–1670 (for an example see Figure 7.19: 2). Not only are all three bowl forms very similar, but so are the marks themselves and it is highly likely that all three pipes were produced in the same mould, and marked with the same die. These pipes come from the well-known workshop of George Webb in Chard (see also below).

GEO WEBB IN CHARD A single pipe with the lettering GEO/WEBB/IN/CHARD was recovered unstratified (the mark is as shown by Pearson 1984a, No 43). Lewcun (1988) gives working dates of *c.*1649–1685 for George Webb in Chard. There appear to have been two men by the name George Webb in Chard in the 1650s, one married to Ann and one married to Elizabeth. Both couples baptised sons, also called George, in 1654 and 1656 respectively (IGI 2012). The date 1685 in Lewcun's list relates to the burial of a George Webb, but it is not known which of the two individuals this burial relates to – nor whether one of the sons called George could have carried on the business after 1685, which the bowl forms might suggest was the case. What is clear is that there was a George Webb, pipemaker, working in Chard in the mid to late 17th century. Hundreds of his full-name marks are known and these occur in four main types: GE/ORGE/WEB (as shown in Figure 7.19: 2), GE=/ORGE/WEB, GE=/ORGE/WEB (but with a retrograde R) and GEO/WEBB/IN/CHARD. There are also examples of an incuse initial mark GW surrounded by dots in Chard Museum.

The actual dies that were used to produce the maker's marks are extremely rare and only a handful of examples have survived. One such die has been recovered from George Webb's kiln site and is now in Chard Museum. This is made of pipe clay and appears to have been made from an extruded or rolled rod of clay that has been squashed at one end to produce a "handle" in order that the die could be held between the thumb and forefinger and orientated easily to mark the pipe. The other end is flat and has the relief lettering GEO WEBB IN CHARD in four lines that would have produced an incuse mark when applied. The head of the die is only 16mm across, but the lettering is very finely executed. It is interesting to note that most of the marks from Taunton Castle are incuse. It is generally thought that these clay dies would have been produced from one incuse master, most likely made of metal (White 2004, 83). This master could then be used to produce any number of working clay dies that would, once pressed into the pipe, result in an incuse mark. Although making individual dies in this way may seem like a time consuming activity, it would mean that the pipemaker could produce stamps of the same type whenever he required them and without running the risk of causing wear or damage to his original metal master. It also meant that he could have a number of workers stamping his pipes at any one time and that it was only necessary to pay once for having the finely engraved metal master made (as opposed to a number of individual metal dies for each worker).

Unidentified/Partial Marks Four partial marks were recovered, none of which have been illustrated. Three of these, one each from contexts 232, 461 and 856, are so fragmentary that it is impossible to identify what the original mark would have looked like. The fourth mark, however, from context 240, has the remains of a mark ending in TON, which is almost certainly "Taunton". Although it has not been possible to match it to one of the other marks from the site, it is clearly a local product.

Milled/Decorated Stems

The application of milling on stems usually seems to occur for one of two reasons; either as a means of disguising damage caused to the stem during the production process, or as a purely decorative element.

The excavations produced just three small stem fragments with milling, all of which have relatively small stem bores and so appear likely to date from the early 18th century. The first two

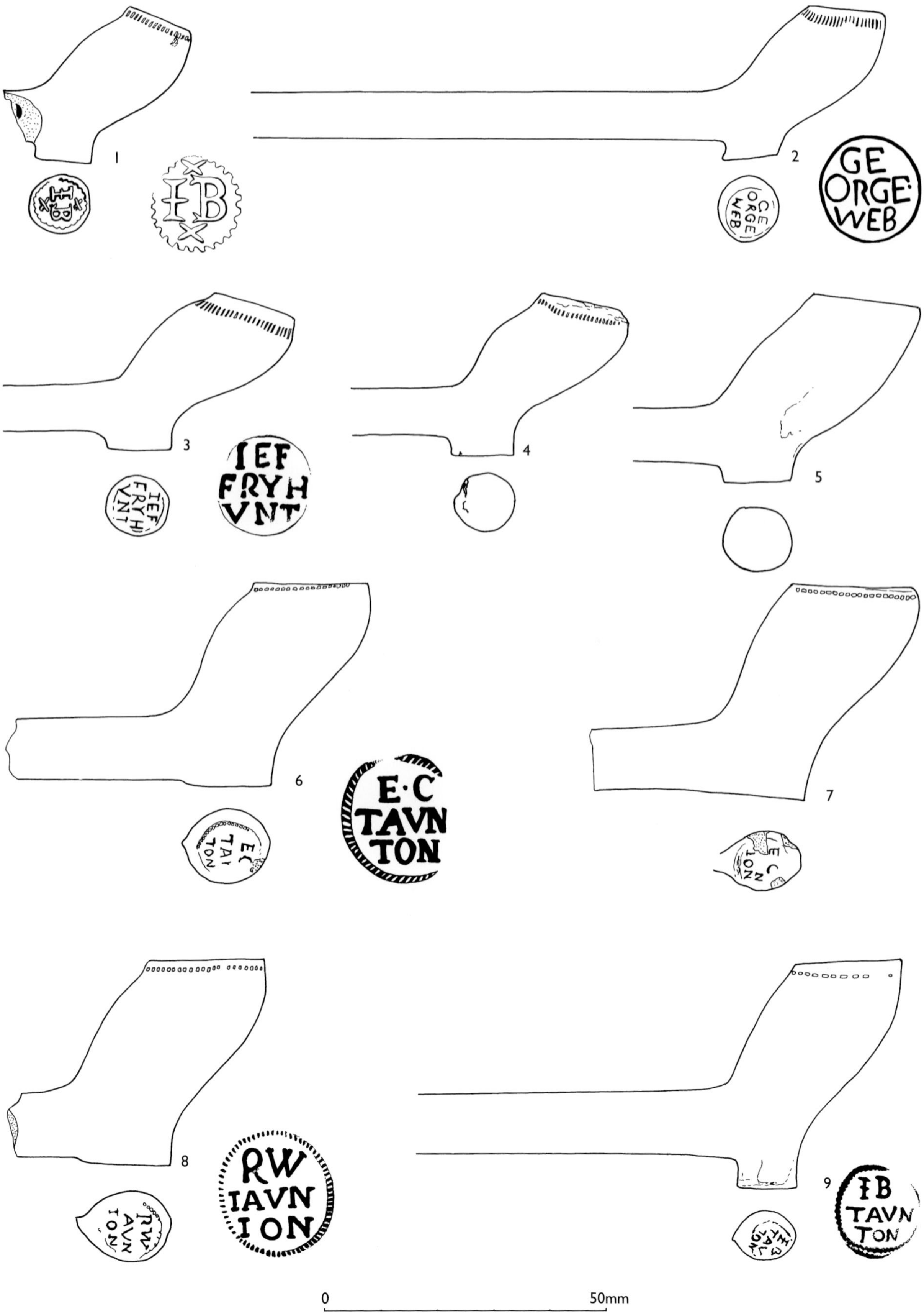

Figure 7.19: *Clay tobacco pipes at 1:1, drawn by SD White, with stamp details at 2:1 drawn by DA Higgins.*

examples (Figure 7.20: 15, from context 210 and Figure 7.20: 16, from context 240) would appear to be of a type that is purely decorative. In both instances there are either one or two bands of milling running all the way round the stem. There are then additional bands of milling arranged at a 45° angle to create a spiral effect. The third and final stem is slightly different in that the decoration is not actually normal milling, but rather a zig-zag or toothed edge that has been impressed at a slight angle into the clay as a long single spiral. This example (Figure 7.20: 17) was recovered from context 302 and the decoration has been applied over a distorted or bulging area on the stem in an attempt to disguise damage caused to the stem prior to firing.

The Hair Curlers

In addition to the clay tobacco pipes, there are fragments from two hair curlers, which are also made from white pipe clay (one each from contexts 232 and 431 (Figure 7.20: 18 and 19 respectively).

The use of wigs, and therefore hair curlers, became popular from the time of the Restoration (*c.*1660) and they remained in fashion until the end of the 18th century. The early examples of hair curlers tend to be hand-rolled without any apparent former so that the end products have slightly irregular forms. These examples are of this slightly irregular type and they were probably both hand-rolled. They are also distinctive in that both have rather conical ends with a coarse surface texture, as if the clay has been rolled in some sort of fabric. Both hair curler fragments have been burnished in the central section, which is interesting given that none of the pipes recovered from the site were burnished. Given the similarities between the two examples, they are almost certainly contemporary and from the same workshop. They are hard to date accurately, but must date from somewhere between *c.*1660 and *c.*1800.

Summary and Conclusions

The pipes from Taunton Castle provide useful dating evidence for the contexts from which they were recovered as well as shedding light on the trading connections of the town. The majority of the pipes appear to have been made locally in Taunton itself but with other examples coming from Chard, possibly Exeter and a few from as far away as Norton St Philip. Deposition of pipes started on the site during the second quarter of the 17th century and there was a marked peak of deposition from around 1690–1740. The numbers of pipes finding their way into the archaeological record remained at a low level during the second half of the 18th century and fell to a very low level throughout the 19th century. This does not mean to say that pipes were no longer in use, merely that there do not appear to have been archaeological deposits containing everyday waste that were being laid down during this period.

One important point to note is that it proved quite difficult to arrive at a good consensus for the dating of the local bowl forms. The extensive series published by Pearson (1984a) are often quite loosely dated, with many examples being simply given as *c.*1700. In other instances his dating seems poor, for example with the very small IB forms (similar to Figure 7.19: 1 of *c.*1630–60 here) being given as *c.*1680. Finally, the bowl form dates suggested by Pearson often do not match the documentary dates for the known makers listed by Lewcun (1988). Pearson, quite reasonably, suggests a date of *c.*1690–1730 for the very large and rather thin-walled bowls with the rim cut parallel with the stem that are marked either EC IN CHARD or EC IN TAUNTON. If these pipes were made by the Edward Collins who is listed by Lewcun (1988) at Chard from 1663–73 and later at Taunton until his death in 1684, then were being produced *c.*1660–80, which seems far too early, particularly when similar forms marked AH TAVNTON can be attributed to one of the Aaaron Hutchings, recorded working from 1716–41. It seems that the problem is a compound one in that the makers' lists are incomplete and need further research, while at the same time there is a lack of good published pit groups or independently dated archaeological sequences that can be used to establish a robust typology of local bowl forms. These two issues clearly form priorities for future research.

Catalogue of illustrated pieces

The cast references given relate to the mark impressions made for the National Clay Tobacco Pipe Stamp Catalogue.

Figure 7.19 on the previous page

1. Heel bowl *c.*1630–1650. Not burnished; no internal bowl cross; rim bottered and fully milled; stem bore 7/64″. Marked with a stamp on the heel reading IB (Cast ref: 685.25). Similar examples published by (Pearson 1984a, Nos 2 and 4). Context 745.
2. Heel bowl *c.*1640–1670. Not burnished; no internal bowl cross; rim bottered and fully

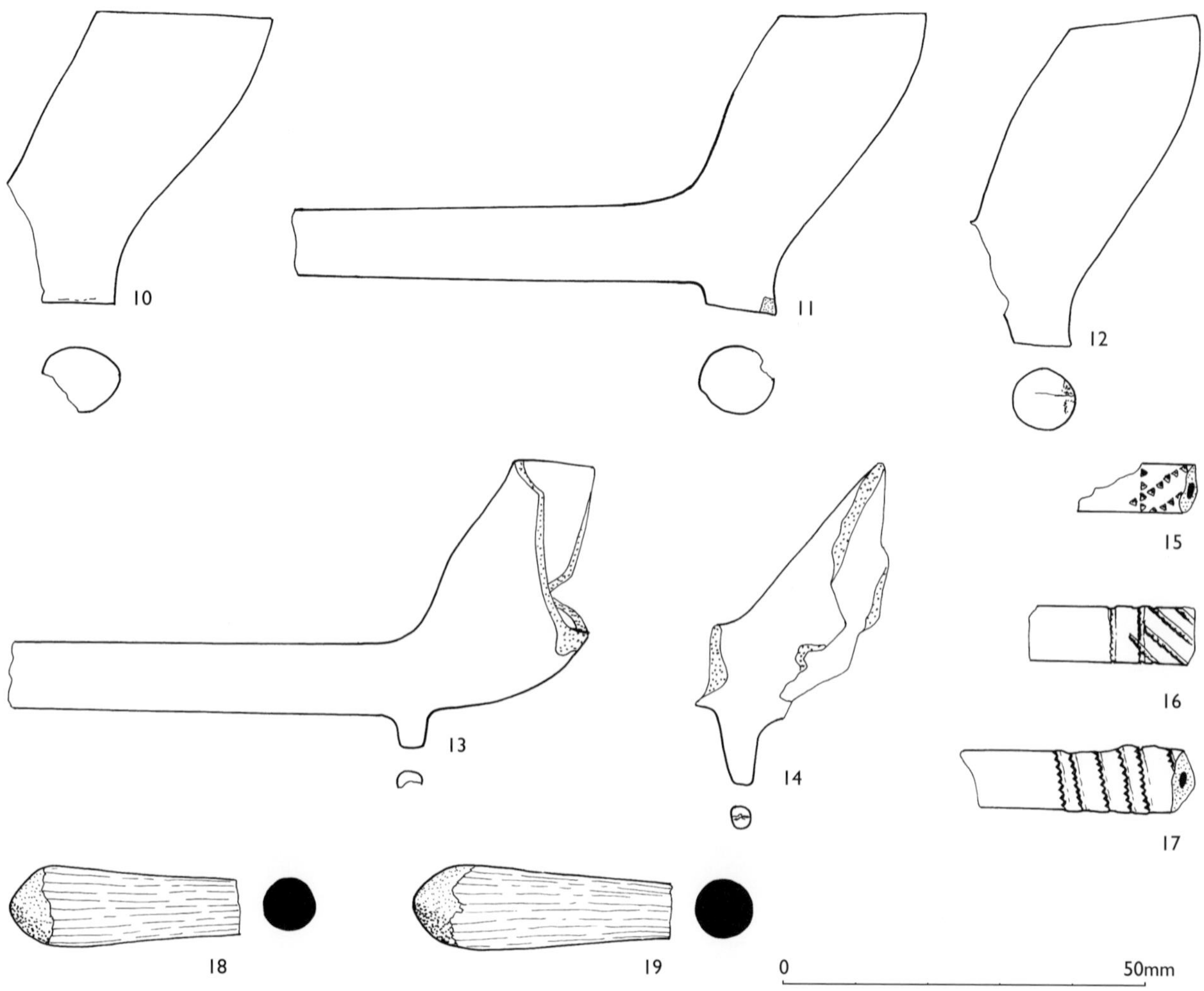

Figure 7.20: Clay tobacco pipes and hair curlers at 1:1, drawn by SD White.

milled; stem bore 8/64″. Marked with a stamp on the heel reading GE/ORGE/WEB (Cast ref: 686.19). Made by George Webb who was working in Chard *c.*1649–1685 (Lewcun 1988). Context 755, Bowl D.

3. Heel bowl *c.*1640–1670. Not burnished; no internal bowl cross; rim bottered and fully milled; stem bore 6/64″. Marked with a stamp on the heel reading IEF/FRY H/VNT (Cast ref: 686.13). Made by Jeffry Hunt (I) who was working in Norton St Philip *c.*1624–1690 (Lewcun 1988). Context 755, Bowl B.
4. Heel bowl *c.*1640–1670. Not burnished; no internal bowl cross; rim bottered and fully milled; stem bore 7/64″. Context 755, Bowl A.
5. Heel bowl *c.*1680–1710. Not burnished; no internal bowl cross; rim cut but not milled; stem bore 7/64″. Plain and very crudely finished bowl. Context 919, Bowl A.
6. Heel bowl *c.*1690–1720. Not burnished; no internal bowl cross; rim cut and three-quarters milled; stem bore 8/64″. Marked with a stamp on the heel reading EC/TAVN/TON (Cast ref: 686.10). Possibly Edward Collins working in Taunton from *c.*1675-84 (Lewcun 1988). Similar example published by Pearson (1984a, No 8). Context 472, Bowl A.
7. Heel bowl *c.*1690–1720. Not burnished; no internal bowl cross; rim cut and fully milled; stem bore 8/64″. Marked with a stamp on the heel reading EC/TAVN/TON (Cast ref: 686.08). Possibly Edward Collins working in Taunton from *c.*1675-84 (Lewcun 1988). Similar example published by Pearson (1984a, No 8). Context 472, Bowl B.
8. Heel bowl *c.*1690–1720. Not burnished; no internal bowl cross; rim bottered and fully milled; stem bore 8/64″. Marked with a stamp on the heel reading RW/TAVN/TON (Cast ref: 686.23). Similar example published by Pearson (1984a, No 46). Context 811.
9. Composite drawing of a heel bowl *c.*1690–

1730. Not burnished; no internal bowl cross; rim bottered and three-quarters milled; stem bore 6/64". Marked with a stamp on the heel reading IB/TAVN/TON (Cast ref: 685.31). The site produced four bowls made in the same mould, all with a very distinctive mould flaw – a bowl from context 429, Bowls A and B from context 430 and a bowl from context 1098. Possibly a product of James Babb who was working in Taunton 1707–1722 (Lewcun 1988). This composite drawing is made up of Bowl A, context 430 and a heel fragment from context 429.

Figure 7.20 on the preceding page

10. Heel bowl *c.*1690–1720. Not burnished; no internal bowl cross; rim cut but not milled; stem bore 7/64". Context 436, Bowl C.
11. Heel bowl *c.*1690–1730. Not burnished; no internal bowl cross; rim cut but not milled; the stem bore is unmeasurable. Plain bowl that is similar to types found in Exeter, and possibly an "import" from there. Context 223.
12. Heel bowl *c.*1710–1740. Not burnished; no internal bowl cross; rim cut but not milled; the stem bore is unmeasurable. Context 231, Bowl B.
13. Spur bowl *c.*1720–1750. Not burnished; no internal bowl cross; rim cut but not milled; stem bore 5/64". Context 231, Bowl C.
14. Spur bowl *c.*1730–1790. Not burnished; no internal bowl cross; no surviving rim; stem bore 4/64". Context 430, Bowl F.
15. Stem fragment with milled bands *c.*1690–1740. Not burnished; stem bore 6/64". Cast ref: 686.25. Context 240.
16. Stem fragment with milled bands *c.*1690–1740. Not burnished; stem bore 6/64". Cast ref: 686.25. Context 302.
17. Stem fragment with a spiral band of zig-zag or saw-tooth decoration applied over an apparent repair, *c.*1690–1740. Not burnished; stem bore 5/64". Cast ref: 686.26. Context 210.
18. Part of a hair curler dating from *c.*1660–1800. The surviving end is of a distinctive conical form with what looks like material impressions on it. The central section has been burnished. The maximum diameter of the thickened end is 11.3mm and the thinnest part of the curler 7.3mm. Context 232.
19. Part of a hair curler dating from *c.*1660–1800. The surviving end is of a distinctive conical form with what looks like material impressions on it. The central section has been burnished. The maximum diameter of the thickened end is 11.9mm and the thinnest part of the curler 7.9mm. Context 431.

7.4 The Chapel Roof *Stuart Blaylock*

Scope and methodology of the work

The roof was examined over two days using the drawings from 1960 (SANHS 6071) as a base for further notes and recording. Only the two westernmost bays of the roof were accessible via the dismantled ceiling of Room 122. The remainder of the roof could be glimpsed through the apex above the collar, looking east, but there is now no routine access to the roof void above the Adam Library. Additional information was recorded on the drawings of the roof trusses with a view to bringing them up to a modern standard: this meant recording the positions of peg holes, the blocks left out of chamfers at the intersection of arch braces and purlins, and other similar details. Details of mouldings were also drawn where they were not previously recorded. This exercise was readily done for the main truss, although the equivalent for the common rafter trusses was more difficult as most were partially obscured by the plastered ceiling of bays 1 and 2, and the only truss both complete and accessible was in turn partially obscured by later applied timbers.

Description

The roof consists of 36 trusses, with every fourth truss ornamented with moulded arch braces giving a roof of nine "bays" (but see page 206). There is some evidence for the roof having had one further truss to the west, ie an end truss (or "main truss 1"): the collar purlin extends some 250mm to the west of the last common rafter truss, and is decayed, implying that it once reached as far as the missing main truss.

Although the bays and trusses provide a useful navigational and terminological tool, in fact close inspection of the carpentry suggests that it is a misnomer to call these ornamented trusses "main trusses", since structurally they are identical in scantling and construction to the intervening "common rafter trusses", and are not essentially any larger or more complex in their construction. The roof is therefore technically a "common rafter truss roof", sometimes called a "wagon roof", an observation of fundamental significance to its interpretation.

The main trusses consist of paired common rafters, joined at the apex and fixed by a peg, and strengthened by a high collar. There is no ridge

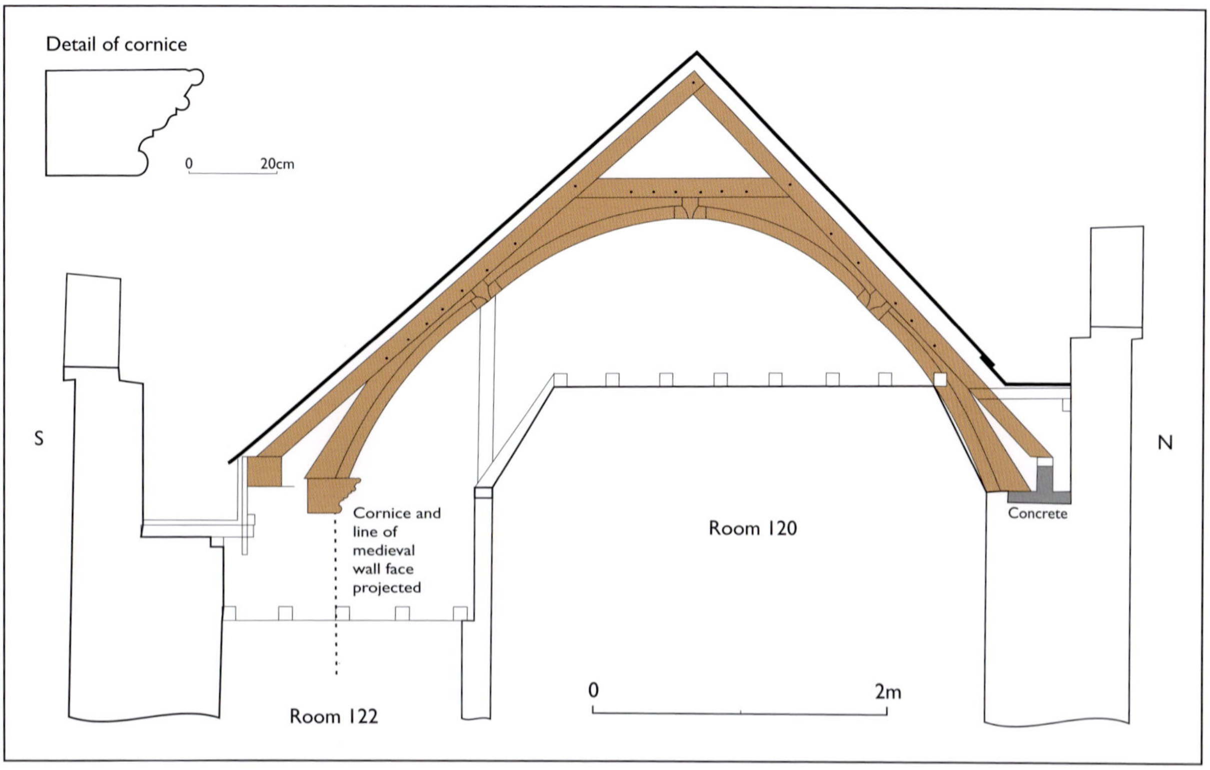

Figure 7.21: *Elevation of roof truss over Rooms 120 and 122. Based on 1960 architect's plan (SANHS 6071) with added details. Note that the lower part of the north side was not accessible in 2009.*

(a feature usually absent in most high-status, as opposed to vernacular, medieval roofs). At the wall top is an outer wall plate receiving the ends of the common rafters and an inner wall plate (or, more strictly, cornice) receiving the ends of the lower arch braces. Four arch-braces are fixed to the rafters and collar by long mortise and tenon joints and secured by pegs. There is one side purlin per side and one central (collar) purlin on the central axis of the roof. The purlins and arch braces all bear the same moulding: a hollow order and an ogee moulding separated by a fillet. Additionally they bear slots cut for a boarded ceiling that has vanished (or which may never have been completed).

The mouldings of the arch braces are interrupted for 100mm or so on each side of each purlin, where solid (ie unmoulded) blocks of timber have been left, presumably to support bosses. Whether the roof actually had bosses it is not possible to say on the evidence now visible: no signs of the iron nails or spikes that are usually used to fix bosses were visible and the pegs visible in the blocks demonstrably relate to the tenons of the purlins (both side and collar), which are staggered at their ends, or "face halved", to maximise the strength of the joint, a technique resulting in the staggered peg positions.

The common rafter trusses repeat the same basic pattern of the main trusses: principal rafters, collar, four arch braces secured by long mortice and tenon joints, although in these trusses the arch braces are unmoulded. This means that the soffits of the arch braces lay flush with the line of the putative boarded ceiling.

Some of the pegs are notable. There are long pointed pegs left projecting from the faces of timbers in places. Where this occurs the pegs confirm the direction of construction and assembly of the roof. Most are inserted from the west, showing that the western side of the timbers was the "face" or assembly side. But there are occasional examples of pegs inserted from the east, especially on "main truss" 2 at collar level. The reason for this remains obscure, as no consistent picture emerges from plotting the incidence of this feature.

Bays 1 and 2 of the roof have a plastered ceiling surviving in places, running against (or even over) the mouldings in places. This can be seen to have terminated against a partition to the east, now gone, but with evidence for nailed laths against the east side of "main truss" 2. There are several reasons for thinking that this ceiling pre-dates the late 18th century alterations to this range that saw the insertion of the Adam library, and relates to an earlier partitioning of the two western bays of the roof. The line of the eastern partition does not coincide with the west wall of the Adam Library, but lies slightly further to the west; projected northwards this line conflicts with the position of a *c.*1790 window (116) in the north wall.

Extensive modifications took place in the roof in the *c.*1790 alterations, when the south wall was thinned to create more space, necessitating a new timber structure at wall top level to support the older roof (structural relationships show that this is of integral construction with the ceilings and partitions of the stair well, Room 120). Other alterations of this period were concerned with the creation of a stair well and landing, and the timber-framed partitions and other finishes presumably also date to this time (although themselves modified with the addition of the new stair in 1910). Certainly the east-west partition at first floor level and rising into the roof space on the south side (separating Room 122 from the stair landing), belongs to this phase of work (and contains a blocked doorway), as does the ceiling of the stair hall/landing itself, above which the upper part of the roof is now accessible.

Some timbers are missing, most notably the wall-top assembly of the south side in bays 1 and 2 (replaced with a series of new supporting timbers in *c.*1790), and the collar purlin in bay 2 (this is likely to be the provenance of the detached fragment now in the museum collection (below). The wall top on the north side is not accessible, being all-but obscured by the later (probably 1910) finishes in this area but is also likely to have been replaced (if only because decay in the past has evidently been concentrated in the area of the parapet gutters).

There is a section of moulded purlin in the museum collection (accession number TTNCM 93/2008/6). This is marked in white ink "Piece of the Oak Roof about A.D. 1500, Removed from under the present ceiling in New Library, Taunton Castle, 1910." The same moulding is applied to the arch braces and the purlins, but since this is a straight timber it must be a section of purlin. In the portion of the roof now accessible the collar purlin is missing in bay 2, so this bay is a possible candidate for the provenance of the loose timber; however this does not quite seem to fit with the description on the timber, which suggests that it came from the ceiling above the library, namely in the bays to the east. It may therefore be that it was recovered during repairs when a larger area of the roof was accessible than now. The timber was assessed for tree-ring dating but insufficient (about 20) rings were present.

Interpretation

The observation that the roof of the south range is a wagon, or common rafter, roof provides the key aspect of its interpretation. Wagon roofs are utterly characteristic of churches in Devon, Cornwall and West Somerset and are very rarely associated with buildings without an ecclesiastical function. Secular buildings invariably possess roofs deriving from other carpentry traditions (mainly the principal rafter truss and common-rafter infill type). Even in cases where there is a superficial resemblance in ornament or arrangement of timbers (the case of the refectory at Cleeve Abbey might be one example to name), close inspection will generally reveal the fundamental difference: principal rafters and formal bay divisions define a secular roof; common rafters throughout define ecclesiastical roofs.

The reasons for this are not clear. It is inconceivable that the differentiation of domestic and church roofs reflects different carpentry workshops; the same craftsmen surely worked on both types of roof. So it is probable that the difference was a matter of convention, that there were types of roof thought appropriate to houses and types appropriate to churches, and by-and-large the two simply did not mix. The question has been briefly discussed by the present author (Blaylock 2004, 188), and there are general descriptions of the wagon roof by Bridget Cherry in the introduction section of the Devon *Pevsner* (Cherry and Pevsner 1989, 46), by JM Slader (1968, 57–59), and recently by John Thorp (2013, 39–44), although no one has been able to offer a better explanation of the differences between secular and ecclesiastical roofs than one of custom. What is clear is that the few examples of common rafter roofs in domestic contexts usually turn out to possess an ecclesiastical connection of some sort, such as roofing a former chapel. Two possible exceptions, neither wholly convincing, are at Fishleigh Barton, Tawstock, and Elmside, Coldridge, both in Devon (Alcock 1968, Fig. 1; Thorp 1998, 79–81).

We can state with some confidence, therefore, that the room at Taunton, roofed by this structure was a chapel; an observation backed up by the documentary evidence, which provides numerous references to a chapel, some specifically to the South Range, from the late 12th century onwards (see pages 15 and 211).

The supporting assembly at wall top level on the south side was necessitated by alterations to the south wall as a part of the *c.*1790 alterations. The very thick medieval wall of the south range was cut into beneath Truss 3 and narrowed at this time, presumably to create a little extra space. The beams for the new ceiling (going with the narrowed wall) support new timbers inserted to support the south ends of the medieval roof trusses, which were otherwise unsupported. Even if these timbers are later than *c*.1790 a similar arrangement would have been necessary on the narrowing of the wall: thus the simplest interpretation is to see them as all of a piece with the *c*.1790 alterations. That the inserted timberwork belongs to this phase is also suggested by evidence of the north partition of Room 122: this is timber framed, with brick infill and forms the southern wall of the stair hall, also generally accepted to have been formed at the same time. The lath and plaster ceiling in this area thus also belongs to the same phase (and incidentally demonstrates that the plastered panels of the first two bays of the medieval roof have to be earlier, as suggested above, although this feature is still probably of post-medieval date).

One further matter deserves a brief consideration: was the medieval roof completed? Evidence for possible bosses has been described above, as has that for close boarding of the intrados of the roof, in the shape of slots cut in the sides of the moulded timbers. From what can be seen today there is no evidence that either bosses or boards were ever present, and certainly there are no traces of paint or limewash finishes. It is therefore possible that these features never existed, and that the roof, although originally intended to have such features did not, in the end, receive them.

7.5 The Bones *Lorrain Higbee*

The hand-collected assemblage comprised 1443 fragments of animal bone (*c*.31% of which is identifiable to species), 48 fragments of shellfish and 19 fragments of human bone. Animal bone and shell was recovered from most of the excavation areas, while human bone was only recovered from trenches J and L, and the moat. The assemblage of animal bone and shell came from a wide variety of context types including layers, as well as the fills of cut features and dates from the medieval period through to the early modern period.

Methods

All anatomical elements were identified to species where possible, with the exception of ribs and vertebrae, which were assigned to general size categories. Species identifications were made with the aid of modern reference collections held by the author and Wessex Archaeology. Mandibles and limb bones were recorded using the zonal method developed by Serjeantson (1996, 195–200) for mammals and Cohen and Serjeantson (1996, 110–12) for birds.

In addition to the above, all undiagnostic fragments over 2cm were assigned to general size categories and smaller splinters to an unidentifiable category. This information was gathered in order to provide an overall fragment count for the entire assemblage. The nature of most archaeological mammal bone assemblages suggests that the majority of fragments categorised as large mammal are likely to belong to cattle or horse, and those in the medium mammal category to sheep/goat or pig.

Tooth eruption and attrition was recorded following Grant (1982) for cattle and pig, and Payne (1973) for sheep/goat. Mandibular age stages were attributed according to Halstead (1985) for cattle, Payne (1973; 1987) for sheep/goat and Hambleton (1999) for pig.

Epiphyseal fusion categories for the post-cranial bones of the three main livestock species follow O'Conner (1989). Epiphyses are recorded as "fused" when the epiphyseal plate joining epiphysis to metaphysis is closed; "fusing" once spicules of bone have formed across the epiphyseal plate and "unfused" if none of these changes had taken place. Bird bones with "spongy" ends were recorded as "juvenile".

In general, measurements follow the conventions of Von den Driesch (1976), with additional measurements following Davis (1992), Payne and Bull (1988) and Cohen and Serjeantson (1996). The presence of butchery marks on mammal bones was recorded following the coded system devised by Lauwerier (1988) with later additions by Sykes (2007b) and further additions by the present author.

Results

Animal bone and shell

Species represented (Table 7.2) The assemblage includes seventeen different species. Bones from livestock species predominate accounting for 74% of the total number of identified specimens present (NISP). Fragments of shellfish (mostly oyster) and bird bones (mostly chicken) are also quite numerous and account for a further 10% and 9% NISP respectively. The remaining 7% of identified fragments is made up of a range of different animals including fish (cod family) and both domestic (dog, cat and horse) and wild mammals (red deer, fallow deer and rabbit).

Species	Medieval	Post-medieval	Modern	Undated	Total
cattle	58	67	12	8	145
sheep/goat	50	78	15	5	148
pig	36	25	5	1	67
dog	3		2		5
cat	5				5
horse			1		1
red deer	4		1		5
fallow deer	3				3
rabbit	1	3	1		5
chicken	12	17		1	30
goose	1	2			3
duck		8			8
pigeon	1				1
woodcock			1		1
Gadidae sp.	9	3			12
oyster	2	33	6	6	47
whelk		1			1
Total identified	185	237	44	21	487
large mammal	158	186	18	37	399
medium mammal	93	121	6	10	230
small mammal	1				1
mammal	113	159	14	10	296
bird	3	12	2	1	18
fish	8	4			12
Total unidentified	376	482	40	58	956
Overall total	**561**	**719**	**84**	**79**	**1443**

Table 7.2: *Number of identified specimens present (or NISP) by broad chronological period. Gadidae sp. = cod family of fishes.*

The numbers of identifiable bones from each period is quite small and this limits the scope of the analysis. Cattle and sheep bones are present in near equal amounts in all periods, and the amount of pig bones is consistently low. This pattern suggests that there was little change in dietary preferences or the supply/procurement of livestock/meat throughout the site's sequence of occupation and use, however the sample size is extremely small so this statement should be treated with caution.

The medieval assemblage is the most varied in terms of dietary range and includes species such as red deer, fallow deer, rabbit, chicken, goose, pigeon, fish and shellfish. Venison does not feature in the post-medieval assemblage, however the consumption of poultry and shellfish increases and duck appears on the menu for the first time. Sykes (2007b, 28) has noted that there is a conspicuous absence of duck bones from most medieval assemblages and has suggested that this reflects cultural taboos concerning the consumption of duck meat during this period. The modern assemblage is extremely small but includes a few species that are not present in the earlier assemblages; these include horse and woodcock.

Body parts (Table 7.3) The body part information of livestock species indicates that most parts of the beef, mutton and pork carcasses are present in the assemblage, and any absences or under-representations can be accounted for by small sample size. Overall the body part information suggests local slaughter, butchery and consumption of animals brought to the castle on the hoof rather than the procurement of selected joints.

Loose teeth are common and this suggests that the assemblage is quite fragmented. Common cattle post-cranial elements include the radius, pelvis and metatarsal, for sheep/goat the most common post-cranial elements are the radius and tibia and for pig the metacarpal. All of these elements show a good survival and recovery rate in most archaeological animal bone assemblages largely because they are all relatively large, robust skeletal elements that are easily observed during hand-excavation.

The five dog bones identified from the assemblage are all isolated bones scattered between unrelated contexts, it is however possible to suggest based on the presence of two right tibiae that the bones are from at least two separate adult animals of similar stature and conformation. Four of the five cat bones are from dump deposit 1155 in trench AA and represent the partial remains of a juvenile animal. It is not uncommon to find the remains of companion animals in general dumps of waste material on urban sites (Thomas 2005, 101).

Skeletal element	cattle	sheep/goat	pig
skull frag.	1	4	4
mandible	6	2	3
vertebra	2	10	5
loose tooth	24	13	13
scapula	3	10	3
humerus	6	14	4
radius	13	25	3
ulna	7	5	3
metacarpal	7	3	12
pelvis	11	12	2
femur	7	9	5
tibia	6	24	5
metatarsal	11	5	3
astragalus	8		1
calcaneus	7	4	
carpal/tarsal	2	3	
1st phalanx	12	4	1
2nd phalanx	8	1	
3rd phalanx	4		
Total NISP	145	148	67

Table 7.3: *Type and number (based on NISP) of skeletal elements from livestock species. All periods combined.*

cattle	Fused	Unfused	% Fused
early	26		100
intermediate	6	8	43
late	2	10	17
final	4	10	29
Total	38	28	58
sheep/goat	**Fused**	**Unfused**	**% Fused**
early	26		100
intermediate 1	1	1	50
intermediate 2	12	1	92
late	6	7	46
final	8	4	67
Total	53	13	80
pig	**Fused**	**Unfused**	**% Fused**
early		3	0
intermediate 1	2	5	29
intermediate 2		5	0
late		5	0
final	1	7	13
Total	3	25	11

Table 7.4: *Number and percentage of fused and unfused epiphyses for livestock species. Fusion categories after O'Conner (1989).*

The deer remains are all post-cranial bones and include the following: for fallow deer a metacarpal, metatarsal and humerus, and for red deer three phalanges, a loose tooth and a tibia. The majority of the deer bones are from medieval contexts and during this period deer hunting was an elite pursuit that culminated in the ritual butchery and division of deer carcasses according to the *Tretyse off Huntying*. As part of this ritual certain joints were gifted to particular individuals based upon their social status and role in the hunt (Sykes 2006; 2007c; Thomas 2007). The parts of the carcass represented in the Taunton Castle assemblage (ie the left shoulder joint) are precisely those that are generally associated with high status sites.

Very little information can be gleaned from the bones of the other mammalian species, however the bird bone assemblage is a little more informative and suggests the following. The absence of certain chicken bones (ie the extremities of the wing and leg, as well as the skull) from the assemblage indicates that only dressed carcasses are represented in the assemblage.

The fish bone assemblage is almost exclusively made up of skull bones, the majority of which are from medieval dump deposit 1155 in trench AA. The predominance of head elements suggests that the fish bone assemblage includes mostly kitchen waste (ie from initial processing or the remnants of fish stock).

Mortality profiles for livestock (Table 7.4) Information relating to the age at which livestock were slaughtered is quite scarce and of limited interpretative value. In general most of the cattle and sheep/goat bones have fused epiphyses and are therefore from skeletally mature animals, while most of the pig bones have unfused epiphysis and are therefore from immature animals. Tooth wear analysis, which is more accurate than fusion data, confirms this basic pattern but is based on only a few complete mandibles. Three cattle mandibles are from adult animals (mandibular wear stage G, after Halstead 1985), while two pig mandibles are from animals aged between 7–21 months (wear stages C and D, after Hambleton 1999).

Most of the chicken bones are from juvenile birds and this suggests that meat production was more important than egg production. The goose bones are also from juvenile birds or "green geese" and these were usually available in May and June (Serjeantson 2002, 42; Stone 2006, 152).

Butchery Butchery marks were only evident on 37 bones in the entire assemblage. Chop marks were recorded with the greatest frequency (76% of all butchery marks) and the majority were observed on cattle bones. This is unsurprising given that larger carcasses require more division in order to reduce the carcass into manageable joints for the purpose of storage, cooking and consumption.

Cut marks were evident on only a small number of bones and generally relate to filleting meat off the bone. One sheep scapula from the modern assemblage had been sawn through the blade. The use of saws as butchery implements appears to have been a fairly late innovation based on the evidence from other sites. In earlier periods saws were primarily used in craft industries such as horn, antler and bone working.

Size and conformation Biometric data is summarised in the archive. No detailed analysis of this information has been attempted due to the small amount of data for each species and period.

Human bone

Ten fragments of human bone were recovered during the electricity cable excavation (see page 92), from contexts 1043 (edge of moat) and 1054 (Castle Way). The following bones were identified from 1043: femur, scapula, metacarpal, first phalanx, premolar tooth and 2 ribs. From 1054 were two femurs (left and right) and one radius. An additional seven small fragments of human bone were also recovered from these contexts but could not be identified to anatomical element.

Single fragments of human bone were also recovered from contexts 495 in trench L and 1128 in trench J. These were identified as a fragment of skull and a first phalanx.

Summary

A small but well-preserved assemblage of animal bone, human bone and shell was recovered from the recent excavations. Analysis of this material suggests that beef and mutton were the main types of animal-based protein consumed at the site during the medieval, post-medieval and early modern periods, with pork, venison, rabbit, domestic poultry, fish and shellfish providing some variety. There is little apparent change in dietary preferences over time but this is based on limited data. Detailed analysis and interpretation of age, butchery and biometric data is severely hampered by small sample size.

7.6 Finds from Castle Green, 2011–12 *John Allan and Naomi Payne*

Medieval pottery

Five contexts produced a total of 14 (158g) Saxo-Norman coarseware sherds, the principal collection (9 sherds) being from context 2020, which is interpreted as a layer of redeposited early medieval soil, most likely laid down during the construction of the medieval castle moat. There were two further medieval sherds from context 2097, also apparently redeposited during the digging of the moat, and a single rim sherd from an in situ medieval layer 2308. The other medieval sherds were residual, one in the fill (2050) of a post-medieval pit, and the other in layer 2006. The medieval pottery is a mix of conventional Upper Greensand-Derived pottery and its variant, commonly found in Taunton, which has calcareous inclusions. These could be of pre-Conquest date but the group is not diagnostic enough to be certain. The rim sherd from context 2020 is from a handled vessel of late 10th- to early 12th-century date.

Post-medieval pottery

No later medieval pottery was present and only four sherds (111g) of 16th-century material, all residual in later contexts. Just over 90% of the assemblage (169 sherds; 3733g) dates from the late 17th to the early 19th century. A 17th-century Portuguese faience sherd is an exceptional find in Somerset, and probably the first known example from the county, although there is a scatter of similar pieces from the main ports of South West England, especially Bristol, Plymouth and Exeter (Casimiro 2015).

Clay tobacco pipe

108 clay pipe fragments (439g) were recovered. This included 88 stems, 4 mouthpieces and 16 bowl fragments. The diagnostic pieces are dominated by late 17th/early 18th-century pipes from Taunton, including the makers William Hunt of Taunton, George Webb of Chard and EC of Taunton and Chard (see pages 135–136).

Glass

A total of 22 sherds of glass (554g) was recovered. The most interesting item is a small, fine, transparent body fragment of *façon de Venise* glass, probably from a late 16th- to 17th-century wine glass, found in an 18th/19th-century context directly beneath cattle market surface (2278). Most of the remaining material (19 sherds) consists of English green bottle glass; where the forms are discernible they are mainly from broad squat "onion" bottles dating from the later 17th or early 18th century. A small piece of window glass of 17th/18th-century date was also noted.

Other finds

Other finds included small quantities of shell, mortar, slag, charcoal and worked flint/chert. Eight pieces of mortar (2108g) were retrieved from six contexts, including four small fragments in association with skeletons SK2099 (one piece), SK2224 (two) and SK2228 (one). A small piece of charcoal (<1g) associated with SK2224 was also recovered.

The small lithic assemblage comprised six pieces of worked chert and flint (24g) including four chert waste flakes, one chert blade and one broken flint blade.

7.7 Human skeletal remains from Castle Green, 2011–13 *Kate Brayne*

The majority of the assemblage consists of disarticulated bone from redeposited contexts. Only five skeletons could be regarded as articulated. The disarticulated bone and the skeletons are described separately below.

The disarticulated bone

It is not possible to analyse disarticulated human remains in the same way as entire or partial skeletons, because an accurate determination of age at death, sex, stature and most pathological conditions depends on the assessment of multiple elements of a skeleton. For example, most adult skeletons display a combination of male and female characteristics, and determination of sex for an individual is based on which sexual features are in the majority. Equally, in order to accurately age a skeleton, several features need to be studied. However, with an assemblage of disarticulated bone, it is not possible to study multiple elements from one individual. Therefore, the first priority is to determine the minimum number of individuals (MNI) that are present in the assemblage. This is the smallest number of individuals that is required to account for the skeletal elements present in the total skeletal assemblage.

The minimum number of individuals from each age category in the disarticulated human bone assemblage from Taunton Castle is as follows:

1	neonate (aged birth–1 year)
2	infants (aged 1–5 years)
3	children (aged 6–11 years)
2	juveniles (aged 12–17 years)
2	young adults (aged 18–29 years)
1	prime adult (aged 30–45 years)
5	mature adults (aged 45–85 plus years)
14	adults of indeterminate age

When calculating the overall MNI for this site it is necessary to add the number of individuals from each category under the age of 18 because the size of the bones makes it possible to identify without doubt that they come from different individuals. Therefore, it can be stated that there are at least eight babies, children and juveniles in this assemblage. However, it is not possible to establish whether the 14 adults of indeterminate age are distinct from the 8 adults of determined age, because the skeletal elements which were used to determine the minimum number of individuals from these age groups were different.

The skeletal elements from which it was possible to determine adult age all included intact dentition either partial or complete mandibles and maxillae. This is because analysis of wear on the teeth is the standard method of assessing age at death in adults. However, the skeletal elements present in maximum quantities from which the MNI of adults was calculated, were all long bone epiphyses, from which it is not possible to establish adult age at death. Therefore, it is necessary to say that in this assemblage there are a minimum of 14 adults, of which at least two were young adults, at least one was in the prime of life, and at least five were aged 45+. It is interesting to note that a MNI of 14 turned up several times in the number of right distal humeri and whole humeri, in the number of left iliae (part of the pelvis) and left acetabulum (the hip joint); in the number of right iliae, and in the number of left distal tibiae and whole tibiae. This may be coincidental, or it may indicate that this assemblage really does derive from fourteen adult graves.

Dental Pathology

The most common palaeopathological lesions identified in this assemblage were caused by tooth decay, known as dental caries. This is typical of any assemblage of human dentition. Caries are caused by bacteria in the mouth metabolizing sugars, resulting in the production of an acid which causes the demineralization of tooth enamel, and eventual production of cavities in the tooth. The two most significant factors in the presence of caries are consumption of sugars (including honey) combined with inadequate dental hygiene. If there are multiple sites of tooth decay in one dental arcade, this is known as rampant caries (caries present on numerous teeth in both usual and unusual locations). This can be associated with reduced salivary gland function, as well as with significant sugar intake in the diet. It is also possible that those individuals who suffered multiple antemortem tooth loss, but display no evidence for periodontal disease (see below), may also have suffered rampant caries, resulting in exfoliation of affected teeth.

Tooth decay can sometimes progress to create a periapical abscess, which is a focus of bacterial infection at the apex of a tooth root, causing pus to accumulate which may drain out through a hole in the bone cortex. The bacterial infection can invade the tooth apex through the cavity created by a caries, but it can also sometimes derive from bacterial plaque (see below). If the infection spreads from the abscess in the blood stream, meningitis and haematogenous osteomyelitis can develop; both of these conditions can be fatal.

A total of thirteen individual elements (partial or complete mandibles and maxillae) presented with either single or multiple caries, periapical abscess, or significant antemortem tooth loss. It is interesting that in this assemblage the majority of dental arcades did not present with caries. A total of thirteen elements out of a total of 41 dental elements which were present in the assemblage (not including individual teeth) represents roughly 31%. This suggests either that dental hygiene was very good in this population, or that they did not consume much sweetened food.

It is also interesting to note that this population does not appear to have had high levels of periodontal disease. Periodontal disease is a term used to describe inflammatory changes in the alveolar bone of the gums, caused by accumulation of mineralised bacterial plaque ("calculus") on the teeth when oral hygiene is inadequate. Eventually, the alveolar bone begins to recede and the teeth loosen in their sockets and ultimately are lost. Periodontal disease is one of the most common dental diseases in both modern and archaeological populations, and a major cause of tooth loss in individuals aged 40 plus (Roberts and Manchester 1995).

Although most of the mature adult dentition in this assemblage showed some mineralised plaque deposits, as would be expected, there were no individuals with pronounced periodontal disease. Most of the mature adult dentition displayed limited deposits of calculus on the buccal and lingual alveolar margins of the teeth, which would be expected in any population, but no individuals in this assemblage presented with profuse accumulations of calculus. Of the dental arcades which displayed high levels of antemortem tooth loss, there was no clear indication that this tooth loss was caused by periodontal disease rather the tooth loss appears to be equally related to dental caries.

Enamel hypoplasia is a defect in enamel matrix formation caused by severe nutritional deficiency or disease, usually during the first few years of life, when the permanent teeth are forming. If enamel hypoplasia is present in the deciduous teeth this indicates that the stress occurred when the child was in utero, owing, for example, to maternal rubella infection or congenital syphilis. Enamel hypoplasia appears as either one or many grooves on the sides of the crowns of the teeth. It is often associated with childhood diseases which are accompanied by high fevers: measles is a common example. Depending on which teeth are affected by hypoplastic defects, and the location of the defect on the individual tooth, it is sometimes possible to establish at what age the episode which created the hypoplastic defect occurred. Enamel hypoplasia is commonly found in archaeological populations, because without antibiotics there were far more incidences of serious childhood bacterial infections. Additionally, food supplies were less predictable, and episodes of malnutrition would have been more common than in the modern developed world. Within this assemblage only one mandible, of a young adult male, displayed numerous pronounced hypoplastic defects of the tooth enamel. There were occasional examples of minor hypoplastic defects on other dental elements and loose teeth, but this was not a commonly presented pathological condition. This may suggest that the population from which this assemblage derived was not routinely affected by malnutrition or severe diseases of childhood.

In summary, this population appears to have eaten limited amounts of sweetened food, and to have practised good techniques of dental hygiene. They do appear to have eaten coarse bread, in general the extent of natural attrition of the crowns of the teeth was very pronounced.

Trauma

Apart from dental pathologies, the most common pathological lesions identified in this assemblage were caused by trauma. Trauma can be defined as any bodily injury or wound (Roberts and Manchester 1995). Traumatic injuries can include both fractures and dislocations. Fractured bones are one of the most common pathological conditions found in skeletal assemblages. Although it is possible to identify at what stage in the healing process of any fractured bone an individual died, if a bone is fully healed, it is not possible to determine how long ante mortem the fracture was sustained. There are three major causes of fractures: acute injury (in the form of accidental injury or intentional violence), underlying disease (in which case a fracture is termed "pathological"), and repeated stress (Roberts and Manchester 1995).

One of the problems of analysing disarticulated bone is that individual bones which show evidence of trauma cannot be related to other skeletal elements in order to give a clearer picture of the nature of the lesion. Frequently it is only the element of the bone which includes the fracture which survives, so there is not even an entire bone to examine, or the articulating joint. Therefore, it is only possible to describe the lesion, without being able to supply any further information.

A total of four bones showing signs of possible traumatic injury were identified in this assemblage:

- A 12th right rib fused onto the right transverse process of the 12th thoracic vertebra. This may be a congenital abnormality rather than the result of a trauma.
- One remodelled right glenoid cavity of the scapula the bone contour was remodelled and extended with osteophyte growth around the inferior margins. This may reflect a stable joint following a dislocation or fracture to the head of the humerus.
- One right first metacarpal with trauma to the distal epiphysis, which appears to have been flattened and displaced laterally. The distal joint has been remodelled with osteophyte growth around margins. Subsequently both articulations of the bone have been affected by degenerative joint disease, evidenced by eburnation, which is present on both the distal and proximal articular surfaces. This suggests that multiple bones on this hand may have been subject to trauma.
- One left distal radius with a healed fracture, and remodelling of the bone shaft.

With a disarticulated assemblage of this nature it is not possible to draw any conclusions about patterns of traumatic injury in this population from these isolated examples.

Mastoiditis

There is one adult right temporal bone which presents with an erosive lesion which may be caused by osteomyelitis of the mastoid process. In the days before antibiotics osteomyelitis, (which is the result of the introduction of pyrogenic bacteria into bone usually staphylococcus aureus or streptococcus) was a common problem. Mastoiditis is the consequence of an ear infection, following which bacteria have spread from the soft tissue into the adjacent bone of the mastoid process. In this case the osteomyelitis presents as an erosive lesion (a sequestrum) on the mastoid process which has smooth, sclerotic edges and some associated peristeal bone formation on the adjacent auditory meatus. There is no evidence of active periosteal bone formation around the sequestrum, so this may be a healed lesion. It is probable that this individual was affected by severe pain during the active stage of this infection.

There is a second adult male skull which presents with a lesion of the right auditory meatus. The auditory meatus is sealed by new periosteal bone, apart from two erosive lesions, which may represent sequestra from which pus may have drained. This lesion may have been caused by a longstanding bacterial inner ear infection. It is possible that as a consequence of this infection and reactive bone deposition, the individual's hearing in this ear was adversely affected.

Skeletons

Estimation of Sex

The sex of individual skeletons is assigned according to morphological criteria: in particular by assessing features of the pelvis and skull, which display the most sexual dimorphism in humans. However, owing to the poor state of preservation of these inhumations, insufficient sexually dimorphic features were preserved to assign a firm sex to any individual.

Estimation of Age at Death

A variety of criteria are employed to assign age-at-death to individuals. Wherever possible, age is estimated using a combination of factors, in order to minimise inaccuracy. The accuracy of adult age estimation depends largely on the completeness and extent of preservation of the individual skeleton. As a general rule, the younger an individual was at death, the more possible it is to assign a precise age. Senile adults are particularly difficult to age with any precision, and it is probable that, in general, aged individuals are consistently underaged in osteological reports.

It is possible to age juveniles fairly precisely using a combination of dental development, diaphyseal length of long bones and degree of epiphyseal fusion (Sundick 1978). Subadults can be aged using dental development and extent of epiphyseal fusion (Brothwell 1981). Once all the epiphyses have fused (at approximately 28 years) age estimation is possible by assessing the degree of dental attrition (Lovejoy 1985); identifying morphological characteristics of the pubic symphyses (Katz and Suchey 1986) and, to a lesser extent, by examining the degree of fusion of the cranial sutures (Meindl and Lovejoy 1985), although this technique has been criticised as there is variation between individuals.

Estimation of Stature

The living stature of individuals can be estimated by taking measurements of the maximum length of the long bones, then applying these to the formulae calculated by Trotter and Gleser (1952). There are some limitations to this technique. The epiphyses of the long bones must be fused, eliminating the possibility of estimating the stature of subadults. Long bone epiphyses begin to fuse at around 16 years (Brothwell 1981), and after this age stature estimates are feasible. In order to make an accurate estimate of stature as many long bones must be measured as possible. Estimates made from single bones are unreliable and incomplete bones cannot be used.

Results

Skeleton 2099

Skeleton 2099 was orientated NE-SW. The right arm was truncated by a post-medieval pit which cut through the southern edge of the grave. Only the left arm, skull and some ribs, vertebrae, pelvis were recovered from this skeleton. Further bones were left in situ because they were lying below the lower limit of the excavation. The bone is in good condition. Approximately 35% of the skeleton is represented in the excavated remains. Using sexually diamorphic features of the skull and pelvis, it was possible to determine that this individual was female.

It was possible to estimate the age at death by analysis of the pubic symphysis using the Suchey Brookes system. This appeared to be at stage 4, which represents an age at death in the range 27–49. The dentition showed high levels of attrition, representing Lovejoy's Attritional Ageing Scheme Stage H, which is usually in the age range 40–50. However, if the molars were lost early then there would have been additional wear on the anterior teeth, which would affect the apparent age at death. It is therefore probable that this individual was closer to 40 than 50 when she died.

There is evidence for degenerative joint disease in the upper 6 thoracic vertebrae. There is erosive lytic pitting on both right and left superior and inferior articular surfaces and remodelling of the joint contour with marginal osteophyte formation. There is no evidence for degeneration of the surfaces of the vertebral bodies. However, when the six vertebrae are articulated, it is apparent that they are deviated laterally from the normal alignment a condition known as scoliosis. There are also erosive lesions on the transverse articular surfaces of these vertebrae, which articulate with the ribs, and on the articulations on the corresponding ribs. Unfortunately, because this skeleton is incomplete it is not possible to identify the cause of this scoliosis, or the consequent degenerative joint disease. Scoliosis can sometimes be a consequence of trauma to one of the lower vertebrae, which causes the alignment of the whole vertebral column to be affected. It can also be a congenital condition. The degenerative lesions on the joints indicate that this individual still had movement in her torso, but her mobility may have been affected, and she may have been affected by pain and stiffness.

This individual presented with antemortem tooth loss of all three left upper molars, and evidence for a large periapical abscess at the cavity for the right upper 1st molar (the rest of the maxilla was not recovered). The lower 2nd right premolar and 1st and 2nd molars also appear to have been lost antemortem, as was the lower left 1st premolar, and possibly the lower left 1st molar. There is a large caries on the buccal aspect of the crown of the lower right 3rd molar, and on the buccal aspect of the lower left 2nd molar, as well as on the root of the left canine at the level of the alveolar margin. This evidence of rampant caries indicates that this individual may have been affected by reduced levels of saliva, which can guard against caries formation. Reduced saliva is symptomatic of other disease conditions. Alternatively, this individual may just have eaten a diet rich in sweetened foods. The maxillary dentition also presented with profuse deposition of mineral calculus, which may reflect poor dental hygiene or reduced levels of saliva. There are no calculus deposits on the mandibular dentition.

Skeleton 2224

Skeleton 2224 was recovered as a disarticulated collection of bones, which were excavated from a context which was interpreted as a coffin because an iron coffin nail was identified. The bone is in poor condition. About 10% of the skeleton is represented. It was possible to estimate the age at death by the dentition, which indicates an age of about 6 years. Both of the deciduous molars are still present, but there is a cavity in the alveolar bone where the unerupted permanent molar was present. It is not possible to establish the sex of children of this age, because the sexually diamorphic features of the skeleton have not yet developed. It is not possible to determine the stature of this individual, because stature cannot be calculated for unfused bones. No pathological lesions or morphological anomalies were identified on the post cranial skeleton.

Skeleton 2228

Skeleton 2228 was lying in a supine position orientated with the head to the west. The grave was truncated by an in situ Victorian drainage pipe, and most of the skeleton was directly below this pipe, and could not be excavated. Therefore, the only part of the skeleton to be recovered was the left shoulder, arm and hand, the left ribs, the left pelvis and a limited number of vertebrae. The recovered bone is in moderately good condition. About 15% of the skeleton is represented.

Although only a limited number of skeletal elements are present, features of the left pelvis, and the general gracile nature of the bones suggest that this individual was probably female. Examination of the sternal end of the 4th left rib indicates that this individual was approximately 43–58 years old. It was not possible to estimate stature. No pathological lesions or morphological anomalies were identified.

Skeleton 2231

Skeleton 2231 was orientated east-west, lying in a supine position. Only the right upper body was recovered, because the grave was truncated by an in situ Victorian drainage pipe. In addition to the articulated skeleton, a disarticulated adult radius and ulna, and a disarticulated infant radius and 2 ulnae were also recovered. It is possible that these disarticulated bones derived from adjacent graves, which had been disturbed when the Victorian pipe trench was dug, and the bones were re-interred into the grave with skeleton 2231. About 20% of the skeleton is represented, in moderately good condition.

This individual was a child, aged about 7–8. This age estimate is based on dental development the first permanent molar was fully erupted, and the 2nd right permanent premolar and molar were present in the alveolar bone, but not yet erupted. It is not possible to establish the sex of children of this age, because the sexually diamorphic features of the skeleton have not yet developed. It is not possible to determine the stature of this individual, because stature cannot be calculated for unfused bones. No pathological lesions or morphological anomalies were identified on the post cranial skeleton. The 1st right molar displayed profuse deposition of calculus on the lingual margin of the tooth crown.

Skeleton 2234

Skeleton 2234 was orientated east-west, lying in an extended position. Only the left and right lower legs, and the proximal right femur were excavated. This individual was an adult, of undetermined sex and age. It was not possible to estimate stature and no pathological lesions or morphological anomalies were identified.

7.8 Radiocarbon Dates *Chris Webster*

In an attempt provide a more confident date for the cemetery and to check assumptions about it, eight samples of human bone were sent for dating to the Scottish Universities Environmental Research Centre. Three of the samples were recovered during work reported here and the other five were chosen from previous recoveries of human bone, now stored in the Somerset County Museum. Details are given in Table 7.5 which also includes the date published by Clements and three dates obtained from work on Castle Green.

As none of the bones were stratigraphically related, either to other skeletons or to structures, the absolute date of death for each was not important but using Bayesian chronological modelling it is possible to provide probability estimates for the starting and ending dates of burial in the cemetery. This simple model is based on the assumptions that all the dates occur in a single phase of burial and that they are evenly distributed throughout it. While these assumptions cannot be proven, there is no reason to doubt that the death rate was fairly constant and that burial started and ended suddenly, when the cemetery was founded and when burial was transferred to the priory. The modelling was carried out using OxCal 4.2 (Bronk Ramsey 2009) and the results are given in Figure 7.22 on the next page. The modelling produces estimates for the start and end dates:

- Start of burial: *530–760 cal AD (95.4% probability)*
- End of burial: *1050–1290 cal AD (95.4% probability)*

The modelled start date indicates the greatest probability around *650 cal AD* which would fit well with a date for the establishment of the minster in the last decades of the 7th century, following the incorporation of the area into the kingdom of Wessex. The end date is less clearly defined due to a plateau in the calibration curve for a period of *c.*200 years after *c.*1150. This unfortunately is unable to distinguish between potential dates in the 12th century following the conversion of the minster precinct into the castle and the grant for the foundation of the priory (presumably with its own burial ground) in 1158. The cemetery is further discussed on page 240.

Lab. Ref	^{14}C age BP	Cal AD	Notes
SUERC-50297	1135±30	770–990	Probably articulated burial beneath moat wall, see page 92
SUERC-50298	1081±30	890–1020	Probably articulated burial, Castle Way, see page 92
SUERC-50302	1248±30	670–880	Loose phalanx, West Passage, see page 68
SUERC-50303	980±30	990–1160	Longbone fragment, Castle Green, 1998, Somerset HER 16781
SUERC-50304	876±30	1040–1230	Longbone fragment, Castle Green (Leach 2005)
SUERC-50305	1329±28	650–770	Articulated burial, Castle Bow (Burrow, I and Dennison 1988)
SUERC-50306	1346±30	640–770	Longbone fragment, St Paul (Clements 1984, No. 10)
SUERC-50307	1046±26	900–1030	Skull fragment, St Paul (Bradbury and Croft 1989, 178)
Other dates			
HAR-2674	1090±70	720–1150	Mixed burials, Coin Room (Clements 1984, 26–29)
SUERC-30738	945±35	1020–1170	Articulated burial, Castle Green (Passmore 2011)
SUERC-30739	1058±35	890–1030	Articulated burial, Castle Green (Passmore 2011)
SUERC-58643	1006±31	970–1150	Articulated burial (skeleton 2099), Castle Green (Rainbird 2015)

Table 7.5: *Details of radiocarbon dates for human bones obtained by SCC for this report and other dates from Taunton Castle. Calibrated ranges are at 2σ (95.4%) and were calculated with OxCal 4.2 (Bronk Ramsey 2009) using the probability method and the IntCal13 calibration curve (Reimer* et al. *2013) with end points rounded outwards to 10 years. Each date is calibrated independently. Dates 50304 to 50307 were obtained with the support of the Maltwood Fund of the Somerset Archaeological and Natural History Society.*

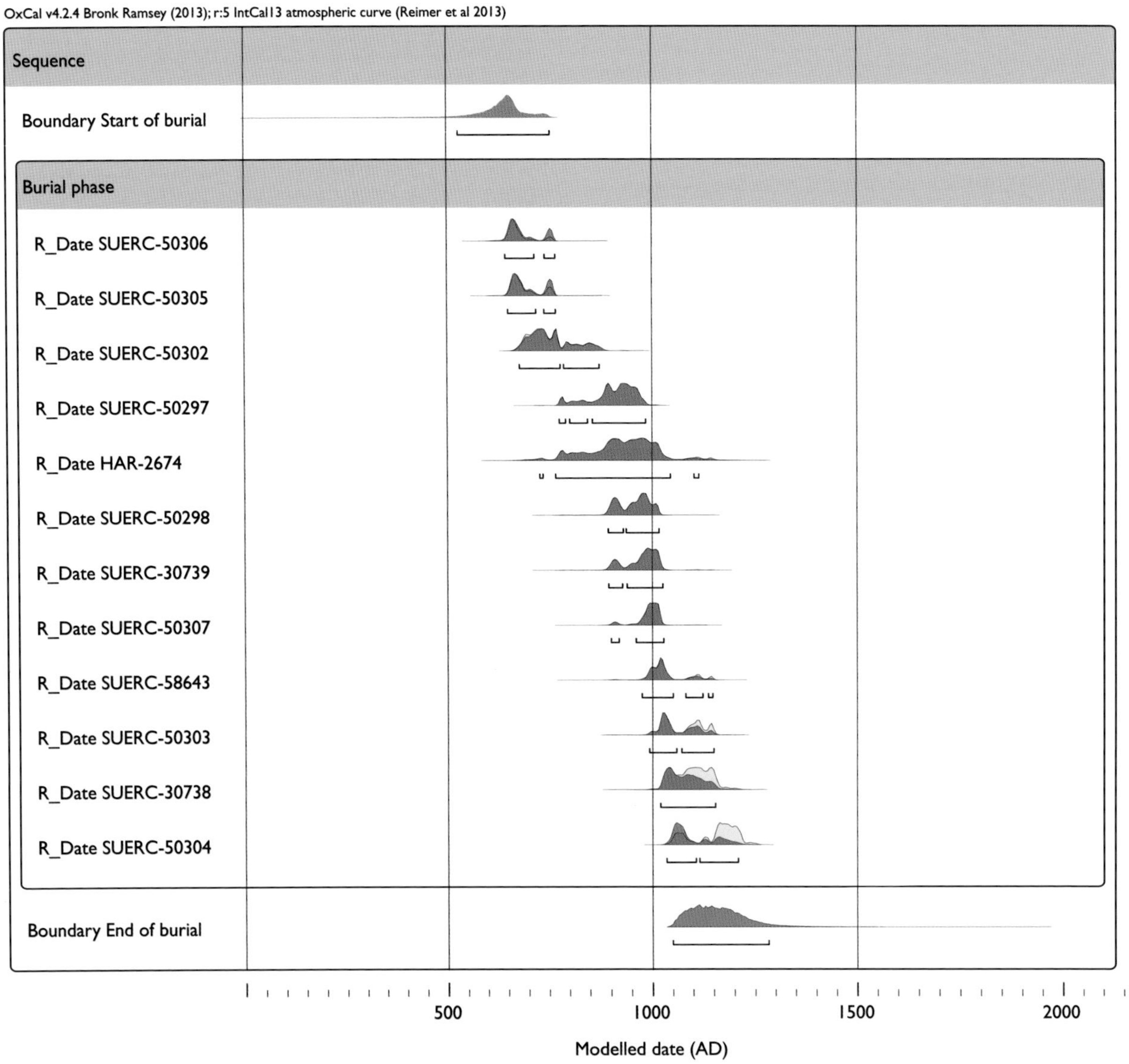

Figure 7.22: *Results of modelling the radiocarbon dates to estimate the start and end dates using OxCAL 4.2 (see Table 7.5 for details.)*

Part II

Description and Interpretation

Chapter 8

The Watergate, the Keep Garden and Ine's Garden

Chris Webster

The area to the east of the castle courtyard has seen the most excavation but unfortunately the standards of recording at the time do not allow a great deal of certainty in interpretation. There are no records of archaeological discoveries during the landscaping of the area and construction of the Wyndham Galleries in 1932/3 but recent excavations along the western edge have clarified some issues.

8.1 Sources of Information

Sloper's work at the north-east corner (see page 35) and Gray's work in the 1920s (page 39) have been discussed. Following Gray's excavations, a plan was completed by AB Botterill in 1930 to aid the design work on the new galleries (SANHS C10-1) and a series of photographs were taken by Humphrey and Vera Joel in the winter of 1932/3 (see page 339). Both of these show walls that Gray did not record and that have subsequently been removed. The area was surveyed and described by Rodwell (1978; 1984a) and limited excavations undertaken by the present author (Trenches B, C and E: see pages 59, 61 and 65).

8.2 The Watergate

To the east of the Great Hall stood a gate, the earliest illustration of which (Figure 1.1 on page 13) shows a simple, round-headed doorway (176) in a wall, closed by a low gate. It is described by Spencer (1910, 41) as similar to Door 59 ("a segmental archway, with a plain chamfer") and to Door 69, and this is how it is shown in Leversedge's drawing (Figure 8.1 on the next page) and photographs. Further information is provided by SANHS 13158 (Figure 8.2 on the following page) which shows the gateway in plan with areas marked "foundations" to the south on either side, seeming to form a gate passage.

On the east side, a wall runs south for a short distance before curving away eastwards from the foundations, which continue southwards and have now been seen to continue south beyond the Great Hall (Wall 411 in Figure 12.1 on page 214). A photograph taken in 1933 (SANHS 13087) shows the curving wall as a substantial block of masonry, becoming lower to the south but with a thinner high wall to the rear. This may be what Leversedge is trying to show on his elevation, the curving wall was certainly there as it is shown on his plan (SRO DD/SAS/c1207/2g). The plan shows the west side foundations as solid masonry with the 1816 privy adjoining to the south.

On the rear (north) of the wall, were two buildings (dilapidated when photographed, Museum PCFILE 1a, probably 1933) that are shown as "Mr Stones premises" in 1833 (SRO Q/AC/3). On the 1888 Ordnance Survey 1:500 plan they are shown as outbuildings to Tone House. This property was bought by SANHS in 1927 using money given by William Wyndham with the intention of housing the society's library. When Gray's excavations uncovered significant walls to the east of the courtyard it was decided to demolish Tone House and use the land for the new gallery (see page 164). The house was demolished in the autumn of 1930 (SANHS minutes: 30/9/1930) but architect's drawings survive from the previous year (SANHS 6027, 6083, 6084).

The Watergate itself must have been demolished with the adjacent wall before the construction of the Wyndham Galleries in 1933. No records appear to have been made but it is just

Figure 8.1: *The Watergate from the south in 1853 by John Leversedge. SANHS 3515.*

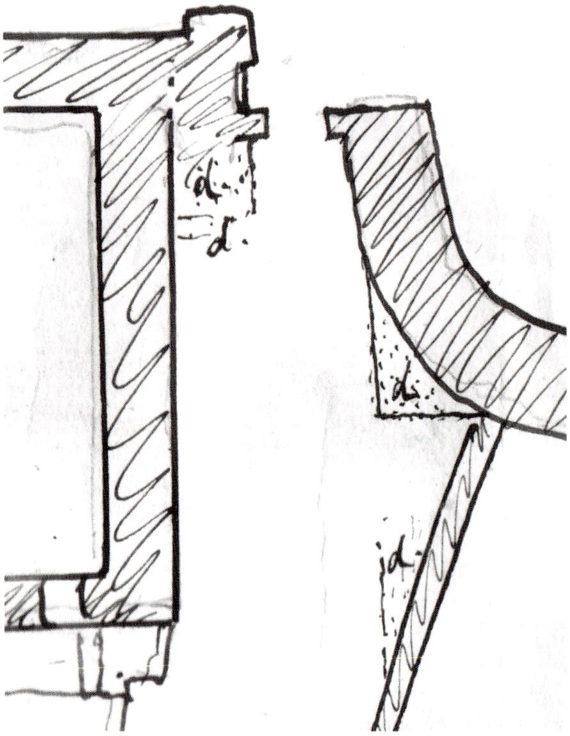

Figure 8.2: *Sketch plan of the Watergate* c.1878. *The key lists d as "foundations". Detail from SANHS 13158.*

possible that some of the stonework of the arch was re-erected to form the gate to Ine's Garden, which is of similar appearance (see Figure 8.13 on page 164). There was already a gateway here (as shown for instance on Botterill's plan, see Figure 8.11 on page 163) but its appearance is unknown.

8.3 The Keep Garden

The area that is now the garden of the Castle Hotel, known since Gray's excavations of the 1920s as the Keep is paradoxically the area most excavated and least understood. Numerous walls were uncovered by Gray but their stratigraphic relationships were not recorded and many are no longer evident. Subsequent to the excavation, the Ministry of Works having declined an offer of guardianship, the area was let to the Castle Hotel and landscaped. While this preserved (most of) the walls, it led to the introduction of features that were not found by Gray and these further complicate interpretation.

Walls C, 23 and related walling

Rodwell (1984a) was unable to record Wall C due to "the presence of luxuriant vegetation" but this was undertaken in 2004 (see page 56) and a small excavation carried out to assess the wall's structure and relationships (see page 59). It was clear from these that Wall C is a single skin of stonework retaining a solid core of packed chert blocks. The rear of this core sloped to the east but its original extent could not be determined due to subsequent disturbance by Gray's excavation. The north end of Wall C (C1–C8, see Figure 8.3 on the facing page for locations) is vertical for 5m (one perch of 16.5 feet), unlike the battered face of most of the wall, and turns eastward for 4.2m (C8–9) forming what Gray interpreted as a corner turret. An inner face is also visible (C10–C12) giving a wall 1.6m thick, which appears to end (C10) at the same place as the north face (C9). Joel 7 and 22 (Figure 8.5 on page 158) show that the wall facing is not carried across this end of the wall and it appears to butt against another wall (23) whose 1933 rebuild was seen in Trench B (page 61) and Trench C (page 63).

It is not clear what Botterill's plan (SANHS C10-1) is trying to show at this point; there appear to be three lines indicating Wall 23, with C9 and C10 apparently bonded to the central one. This may be trying to indicate two phases of Wall 23 with an upper, later part contemporary with Wall C but there is no evidence for this in

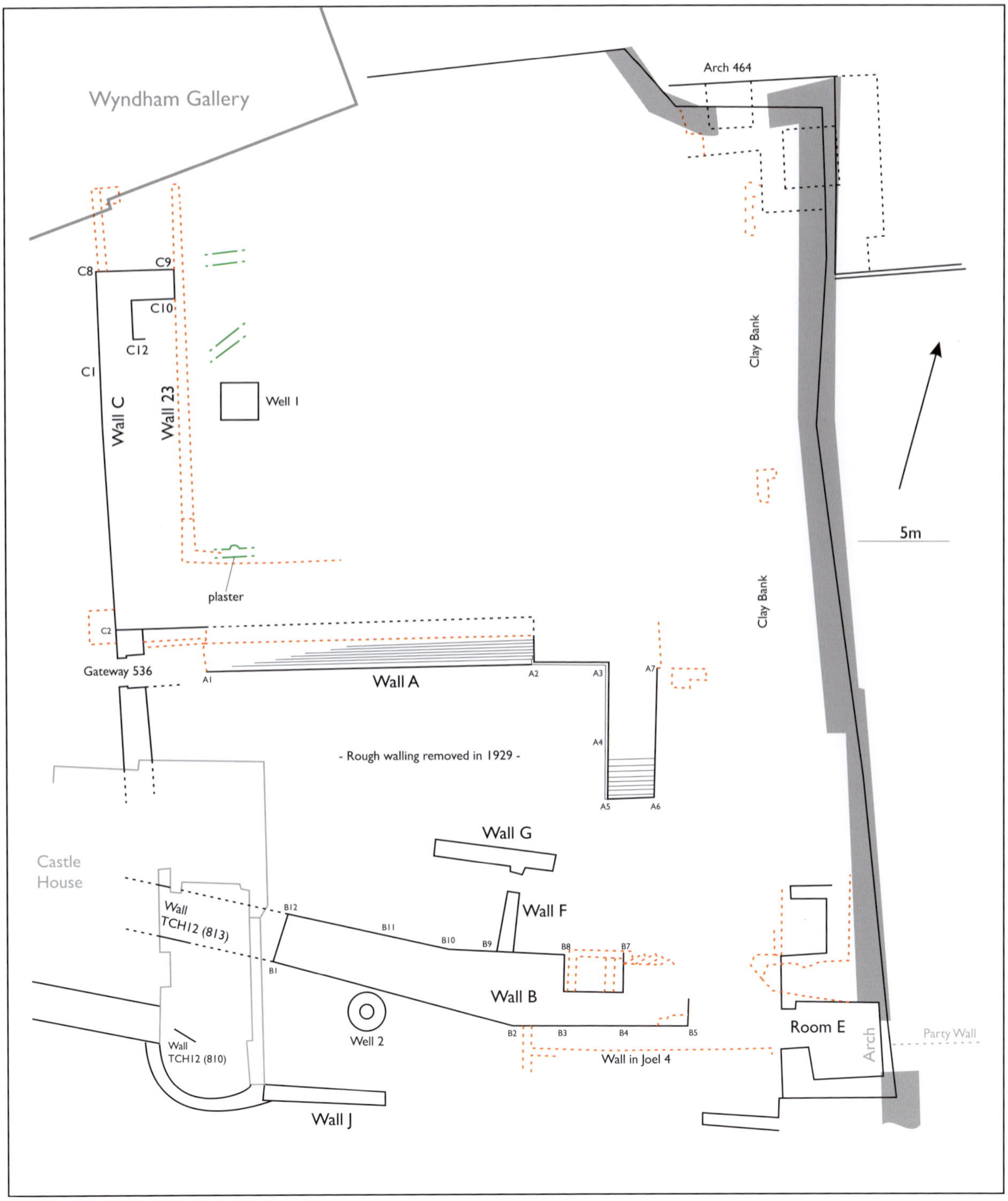

Figure 8.3: *Plan of known features in the Keep Garden based on Rodwell (1984a, Fig. 5) and recent excavations and surveys (this volume and Brigers 2013a). Features shown with a dashed line at the north-east corner have been added from Bidgood's plan (see Figure 3.1 on page 36) and the east curtain wall (grey) from Leversedge's 1852 plan (SANHS 6102). Features in green are from Gray's early trench plan (Figure 3.4 on page 40) and extra details provided on Botterill's plan (SANHS maps C10-1: Figure 8.10, Figure 8.11) are shown in red.*

Figure 8.4: The rear of Wall C looking north after Gray's excavations with Wall 23 in the centre of the picture. Joel 8.

Figure 8.5: The rear of Wall C looking south after Gray's excavations with Wall 23 in the foreground. Point C10 is on the right with point C12 in the centre. Detail of Joel 22.

the photographs (Figure 8.5). The photographs do show that Wall 23 was faced on its west side (Figure 8.4), arguing against Gray's interpretation that Wall 23 formed the inner face of the keep wall.

At the south end of the inner wall face (C12), the Joels' photographs show another return eastwards, this time with very little masonry remaining (Figure 8.5). It cannot be seen at all in Joel 8 (Figure 8.4) which does show that it was not bonded to Wall 23. Nothing is shown at this location on Botterill's plan. Another photograph (Joel 10) shows that Wall 23 continued northwards beyond the excavation and it was seen here in 1992 (see page 56, AC72:7). It was butted by another wall (AC72:4) that ran north-eastwards. The Joel photographs suggest that this wall lay beyond Gray's excavation and it is not shown by Botterill. Both walls were truncated by the construction of the terrace for the Wyndham Galleries without record.

Excavation of Trench E (see pages 65–68) showed that the line of Wall C had been continued to the north in two phases. The earlier (295) was only evidenced by its foundations, which appeared to be contemporary with those of Wall C but were of different character. The nature of the superstructure is unknown, it could have reflected the battered wall to the south or to have been a simple vertical wall. Its later incarnation (286) was certainly coursed to match the battered section of Wall C but was poorly founded and had subsided (see Figure 5.2 on page 67). Joel 2 shows that this section was quite short and became lower to the north; new walling had been added above this, horizontally coursed, and reaching a higher level than the adjacent Wall C. Plans, such as Botterill's, showing this wall are therefore no guide to the original extent of the lower section but both his and Gray's trench plan show a wall returning to the east at the limit of the excavations.

At the southern end, Wall C turns at C2 and runs eastwards (as Wall 78), continuing behind Wall A. This situation is shown on Botterill's plan, which also shows Wall 23 turning east before this point (see Figure 8.3 on the previous page).

From C2 the line of Wall C was continued to C5 where it stopped, forming one side of Gateway 536. All the masonry to the south (C5 to C3)

Figure 8.6: *Looking east along Wall A in 1932/3. Joel 5.*

was 1933 or later. The other side of the gateway was found in Trench H (see pages 71–76), together with evidence for later blocking of the gateway. Wall C then continued southwards underneath Castle House.

Gray's plan shows walls to the east of Wall 23, one of which he describes as plastered on its south face. With the exception of those forming the well, these were not exposed during the landscaping and only the southernmost appears in the Joels' photographs (Joel 23). According to Botterill's plan (see Figure 8.3 on page 157) this is a continuation of Wall 23 having turned eastwards and in the photograph it appears as a narrow wall built of large partly dressed blocks. No plaster is evident on the southern side, the only one visible.

Wall A

It is possible to add a little more to the information recorded by Rodwell (1984a) with the benefit of the Joel photographs and the excavation evidence of Trench C (see pages 61–64). The 1933 facing to the west end was removed in the excavation but revealed little, except that Wall A, like Wall C, was a single skin of masonry retaining a rubble core. The walling appeared to stop (A1, Figure 8.3 on page 157) on the line of Wall 23; this may have been caused by 1933 restoration but Joel 5 (Figure 8.6) does appear to show a vertical face ending the wall at about this location. Botterill's plan seems to show an irregular end and also that Wall 23 did not reach this point having turned east. Only the lower two or three courses survived robbing at this end and the face was no longer present in 2006.

Within Trench C, Wall A appeared to be resting on a line of foundation stones (131) that were on a different alignment (see Figure 4.8 on page 62). This, and the use of different stone, suggests that this is an earlier phase of walling whose foundations were partly reused. It is therefore not evidence for the continuation of Wall A to the west of Wall 23. It was also not possible to confirm the relationship of this foundation with that of the southern extension to Wall C and Gateway 536 but the alignment of Wall A with the gateway indicates that they are not contemporaneous and the construction of Wall A may have necessitated the blocking of the gateway. Wall 131 could have coexisted with the gateway but the foundations suggest that it was earlier.

To the east, section A2 to A3 had been rebuilt in 1933 preventing Rodwell from commenting much but the evidence of Joel 3 (Figure 8.8 on page 161) is that the reconstruction was correctly done. This section was coursed in the same style as Wall C with alternating courses of vertical and chamfered stone in contrast to A1–A2 where all the courses are chamfered. This means that the batter on the wall is less and thus A2–A3 projects. At A2 the chamfered courses of A2–A3 can be seen to turn northwards with those of A1–A2 cut to shape and butting against them. The eastern part of A2-A3 is very eroded but there was evidently vertical walling above the chamfered lower area and both are continued around the corner and along A3–A5. The similarity in style suggests that this is part of the continuation of Wall 78 and that Wall A1–A2 is a later addition to a retaining wall running from A5 to C9.

This style of walling is continued south along the "buttress" from A3 to A4 where the base chamfered course again appears to turn east. This corner is not visible higher up but the whole "buttress" has been extended southwards (A4–A5) from here in a matching style. The other two faces are different. The southern (A5–A6) has large chamfered stones giving a slope of about 45° and the east face (A6–A7) is vertical rubble walling. The area beyond appears to be unexcavated but the Joel photographs show this rubble wall continuing northwards for some distance past a substantial offset shown on Botterill's plan. The northern end appears ragged and Botterill's plan shows an L-shaped piece of masonry to the east of the offset apparently forming part of a wall running east (see Figure 8.3 on page 157). A further L-shaped piece of masonry is shown further north but the nature of these is not clear

Figure 8.7: *Gray's excavations as left in 1930, photographed in the winter of 1932/33. The photographer is standing on the wall of Room E looking west along Wall B. Wall A with "forebuilding" is to the right and Wall G must lie in the unexcavated area between. To the right of the Great Hall, the large section of wall by the Watergate is visible. Joel 18.*

on the Joel photographs.

Comparison between Gray's photograph of Wall A during its discovery in 1927 (Vivian-Neal and Gray 1940, Plate II), the Joel photographs in 1932/3 (Figure 8.8 on the facing page) and its current condition reveal a considerable weathering of the stonework in 90 years. The pristine condition seen in 1927 suggests that the wall cannot have been exposed for long in the medieval period, indicating that the ground to the south of the wall was raised, protecting it, perhaps extending the raised platform as far as Wall B and perhaps contemporary with the blocking of gateway B3–B4 in that wall (below).

Relationships

The evidence suggests that Wall 23 is the earliest and that Wall C was added along its west side, with the area between filled with compacted chert and clay. Wall C continued to the east behind Wall A1–A2, which appears to be a further addition. The section of wall from A2 to A4 appears to be part of Wall C. Both Walls A and C are revetting deposits of compacted material in front of earlier walls but it is not possible to tell if Wall 23 was also a revetting wall or was freestanding.

The Southern Area

To the south of Wall A is a fragment of a substantial wall (B) and two thinner walls (F and G, see Figure 8.3 on page 157).

Wall B was described by Rodwell (1984a) as a curtain wall of three phases. Its south side has a continuous batter; the north side is vertical. Rodwell could see that the earliest part of the wall was from B2–B5, which contained an infilled gateway (B3–B4) that corresponded to an alcove (B7–B8) in the rear of the wall. He also suggested (Rodwell 1978, 3) that, depending on the levels, the gap could have formed the base of a drawbridge counter-balance pit with a gate structure above, but the distance between B3 and B4

Figure 8.8: *Wall A (A2–A3) and the buttress (A3–A5) in 1932/3. Joel 3.*

Figure 8.9: *View along Wall B in 1932/3. Wall F can be seen in the trench to the right of the wall and another, now vanished, wall is visible to the left. Joel 4.*

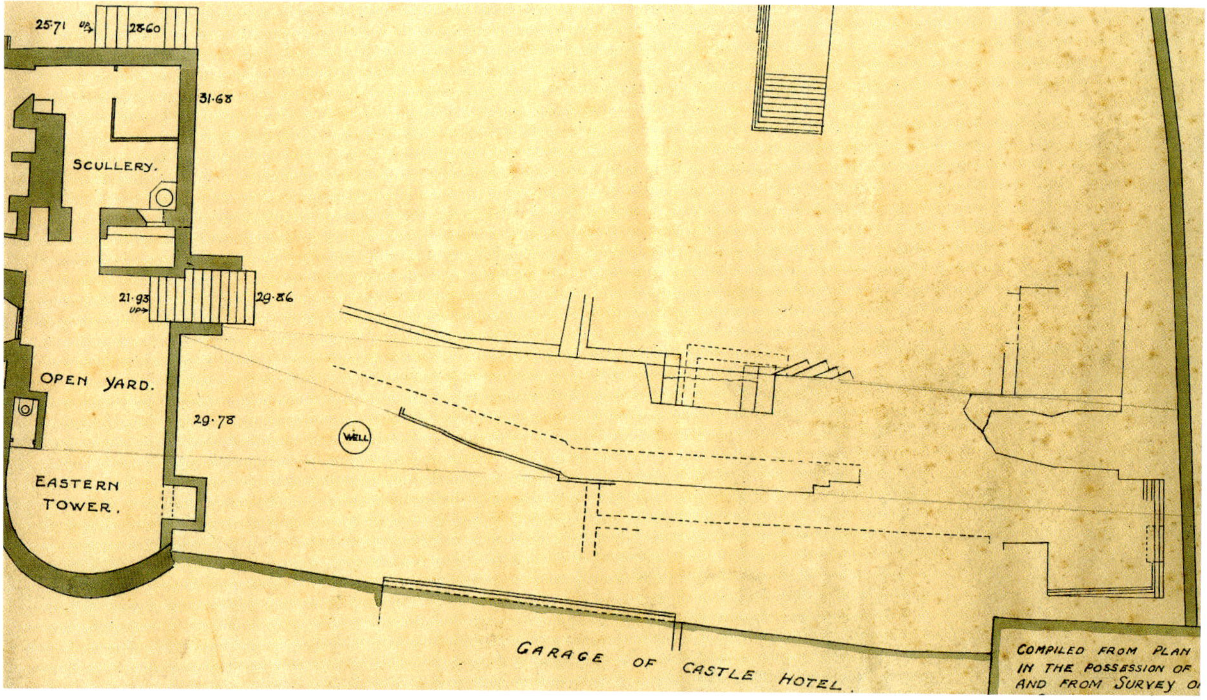

Figure 8.10: *Extract from AB Botterill's plan of 1928–30 showing the area of Wall B and Room E. Detail from SANHS Maps C10-1.*

when compared to the alcove behind (B7–B8), indicates the presence of a rebate for a gate now hidden in the blocking. Botterill's plan shows a more complex arrangement in the alcove with several subsidiary walls that are presumably later (Figure 8.10).

Rodwell could also see that the remainder of the wall (B1–B2) was a replacement on a different alignment of the west end of the wall and suggested that a tower had been removed. Similar joins in the masonry were also visible on the north side at B9, B10 and B11. It was not clear what happened at either end of the wall as these had been rebuilt in 1933 and the Joels' photographs do not help much as neither end appears to have been exposed by then. On Botterill's plan, the south face of the eastern end is shown stepping back northwards before stopping. No end face is shown and the line of the north face has been projected eastwards to join the north wall of Room E. The western end shows no end face and work in 2013 (see page 102) showed that the wall had continued under Castle House.

Wall F can be seen in the Joel photographs (4 and 16), crossing Gray's trench, but its northern end is hidden in an unexcavated area between Walls A and B, as is all of Wall G. This area must have been cleared during the landscaping work of 1933. Rodwell (1984a) could see two phases in Wall F, the southern with a foundation offset apparently bonded to the eastern part of Wall B; the angle of the wall, however, matches better Wall B's western alignment. Wall G is at right angles to Wall F, perhaps with a doorway between them, and these walls appear to represent buildings constructed against the back of Wall B. There were other structures, probably later in date, here as Gray describes (see page 45) contractors removing another wall ("at a high level") to allow access to the site. Gray's measurements suggest that this may have been on the line of the north wall of Castle House.

In addition, Joel 4 shows a wall immediately to the south of Wall B that must also have been removed in the landscaping. It is too far north to have been Wall J and appears to be faced with small stones, perhaps chert. The wall is shown on Botterill's plan (Figure 8.10) running from near Room E (below) to a cross wall, joining Wall B and runing southwards for an unknown distance.

To the east of Wall B is an area that has been heavily rebuilt, Rodwell's (1984a) Room E, of which he thought that the north and east walls were the earliest with the southern wall added. He suggested that this was a medieval or later cellar that had been built out of a corner turret of the castle and his plan (Rodwell 1984a, Fig. 8) suggests that it was connected to Wall B and a wall to the north. Botterill's plan and Joel photographs indicate that much of this is 1933 reconstruction with an empty area between Wall B and Room E. The southern, battered face of Wall B would have coincided with the door to Room E so they are unlikely to be part of the same structure. The east wall of the room appears to be substantial and is shown on Botterill's plan continuing north. It is probably the curtain wall shown on Leversedge's plan (SANHS 6102) and seen below the modern walling by Sloper (see page 35) at the north end. Botterill shows the east and south walls with foundation offsets and also the south side of the "door". The north wall is depicted as irregular with no indication of the north door jamb that is now present. A short length of wall is visible in the Joel photographs forming a west wall to the "alcove" that survives north of Room E. The alcove appears to have a good east wall but nothing much is visible of a north or south wall. Botterill's plan shows a west wall with a doorway at the north end and a short length of the north wall returning eastwards.

Leversedge's plan (SANHS 6102, see Figure 8.3 on page 157) shows an arch through the castle wall in the position of Room E, which it hard to reconcile with Rodwell's description of the east wall being original, unless most of the structure relates to late 19th-century changes. Botterill's plan does seem to show some breaks in the foundation offsets.

The northern and eastern sides

Vivian-Neal and Gray (1940, 66) describe the northern and eastern sides as having "comparatively wide rampart walks", which is curious as they are describing what they considered must have been foundation level. They add that on the eastern side was "an embankment of puddled red marl 90 ft in length, extending along the site of the eastern rampart walk". This can be seen in Gray's section drawing (Figure 3.6 on page 44) and was interpreted on the basis of finds as a "gun emplacement or defensive work" of Civil War date. The section drawing shows that the bank does not reach the east wall but this may have been caused by a robbing trench unrecognised by Gray. Leversedge's plan (SANHS 6102, see Figure 8.3 on page 157) shows the wall thicker than it is now, with various offsets that are not now apparent and which may be represented by the wide foundations shown on Bidgood's plan (Figure 3.1 on page 36). There is a record in the medieval accounts to "wages of masons erecting wall next to the tower on the eastern side, making battlements and arrow slits" in 1265 that may refer to this wall. Bidgood's plan shows a "modern wall" above the foundations and this

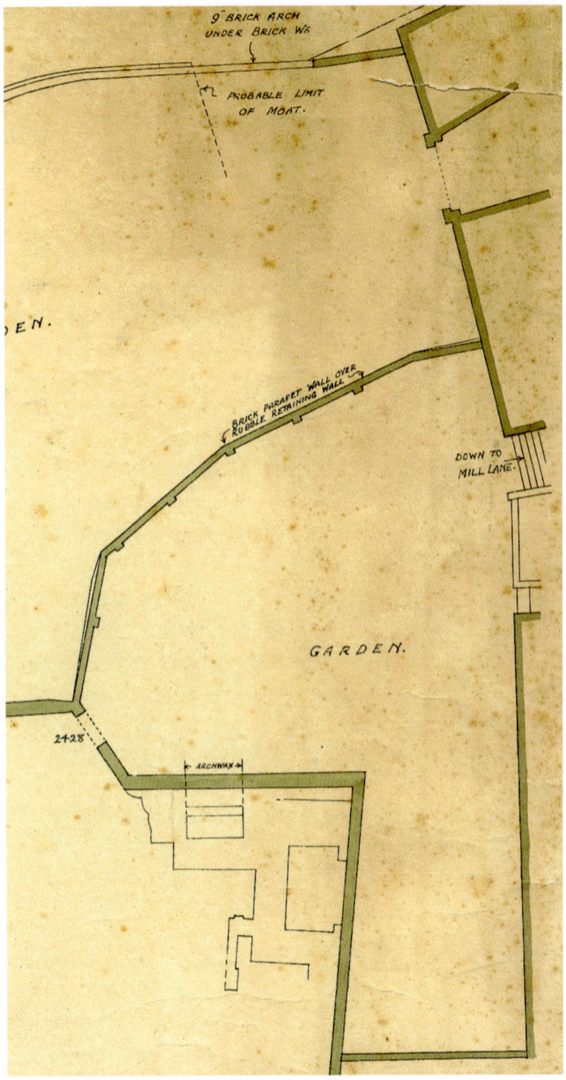

Figure 8.11: *Extract from AB Botterill's plan of 1928–30 showing the north-east area. Detail from SANHS Maps C10-1.*

is recorded as being rebuilt in 1893/4 (SANHS minutes: 13/4/1894).

There is little evidence for the north wall, most of which was destroyed when the Wyndham Galleries were built, but Vivian-Neal and Gray (1940, 65) mention a "trench, a section of which was uncovered during the excavations" that they suggest may have been dug to allow the north wall to be robbed. There is no record of the location of this. Early plans show a large wall curving away from the Watergate (shown on Figure 12.1 on page 214) and running north-east before thinning. The curve may suggest the rear of a round tower – in this location it could be the Kitchen Tower (see page 18). Aerial photographs of 1933 (eg Aerofilms 41094) show this as a high wall, retaining higher ground to the south, as it continues to do where it survives to the east of the Wyndham Galleries.

The wall (782) seen in the lift pit in the Wyndham Galleries appeared to follow the line of the Great Hall and would thus be heading well to the north of the north-east corner.

At the junction of the east and north walls Vivian-Neal and Gray (1940, 66) report the "remains of a tower, with a simple arch of late Norman construction at the base". This was Arch 464, excavated by Sloper (see pages 35–38) and identified by him as the base of a garderobe chute. William Bidgood's records (see Figure 3.2 on page 37) support this interpretation, as the arch is only 2 feet 7 inches (0.8m) high to the springing and is blocked by a wall to the rear. Rodwell (1984a) notes that the arch is pointed and therefore likely to post-date the 12th century. The area inside the walls was exposed again by Gray and photographed by the Joels (Joel 21). Botterill's plan (see Figure 8.11 on the preceding page) shows much the same as Bidgood but has an additional wall running southwards from the tower. The site is marked by Rodwell (1984a, Fig. 5) as a "pit", which appears to be the room shown by Bidgood but the area was covered by gardeners' compost heaps and could not be examined.

Bidgood's plan remains the best evidence for this corner which seems to take the form of a small corner tower containing a room 3.1m square. To the west is a garderobe chute, which does not connect to the tower basement, and must have served a chamber at a higher level, probably in a building running along the wall to the west.

Ine's Cottage and Garden

According to Sloper's notebook (SANHS AR 32), WE Surtees bought a cottage in 1875 and "made some steps to what appeared on exposition of the wall to have been a round tower at the angle and he gave a right of way to the castle property by a path made on purpose through the garden near the Mount". Surtees had "remodelled the cottage and built a castellated tower to it introducing some ridiculous bits of stonework into it so that any person in a hundred years time would wonder why it was built". It became known as Ine's Cottage some time later and the site of the round tower became known as Ine's Garden. Its current appearance, as an irregular polygonal platform, has suggested that it may have been a bastion added in the Civil War.

Sloper originally suggested in his notebook that Arch 464 "probably led from the castle enceinte to this round tower" and that "no doubt an excavation would pay". This he carried out

Figure 8.13: *The gateway into Ine's Garden, possibly reusing masonry from the Water Gate.*

in 1876 (see page 35), showing that the arch was the base of a garderobe chute and disproving the identification of a round tower. The excavation instead suggested that there was an "outwork" composed of red marl. The finds were from the 16th and 17th centuries, which supports a Civil War date but its present appearance may be the result of landscaping after the excavation.

The Wyndham Galleries

As Gray's excavations continued, it became clear that the idea of siting a new museum gallery in the area was not possible and much of the later explorations seem to have been to check where the gallery might be built (Gray 1928a, xvi–xvii). Eventually, the society's architect Sir George Oatley (Whittingham 2011), advised that the walls could not be incorporated into the design (SANHS minutes: 7/8/1928) and that Tone House, which the Society had bought with money from William Wyndham, should be demolished and the new gallery built on its site (SANHS minutes: 27/7/1929). Tone House was demolished in 1931 (Gray 1931, xxx-xxxi) but architectural drawings survive (SANHS 6027, 6083, 6084). These plans were delayed by the discovery of structural problems in the Grand

Figure 8.12: The Wyndham Galleries and link block as built in 1934. Photograph by Harold St George Gray. Note the ragged east end left for completion. SANHS 12572

Jury Room and in Castle House that took priority (Gray 1930a, xix). Work on the new galleries began in September 1933 (SANHS minutes: 4/10/1933) and opened on 3 October 1934 (Gray 1934, xv–xvi).

No archaeological discoveries were reported, perhaps deliberately after the changes of plan caused by Gray's work. The building was designed to be built in stages and at this time only the western two-thirds and two storeys were constructed (Figure 8.12). The final third had to wait until after the running of the museum was handed to Somerset County Council in 1958, when the museum governors, looking for more space, eventually decided to extend the galleries to the east as originally planned. It was decided to save money by not building the new part to sufficient strength for the third floor. CS Williams were given the job with completion intended by end of September (SANHS minutes: 13/5/1959). The Low Ham mosaic was moved from the Great Hall into a vertical position on the specially heightened east wall (SRO A/CNT/4/1: 1/12/1959). The third storey was eventually started in 1973 to house the regimental museum of the Somerset Light Infantry and opened by the Queen Mother the following year.

Discussion

Unfortunately Gray's excavations did not solve the problem of the hotel garden area and have removed much evidence that modern techniques might have been able to use to understand it. It does now seem clear, however, that this was not a simple, one-phase, Norman keep with a forebuilding "that must have resembled closely those at Dover and Newcastle-upon-Tyne" (Vivian-Neal and Gray 1940, 63).

Radford and Hallam (1953, 92) state categorically that the keep replaced a motte "at the NE corner, near the bridge across the Tone" and while they produced no evidence for the existence of a motte, it is not unlikely. Rather than replacing the motte, the mound may have been spread and retained by walls to form a rectangular raised area that was later enlarged, either to provide an increased area or because of structural failure.

Gray believed that the keep stood upon this platform and had such insubstantial foundations that nothing survived for him to find. Few keep foundations have been excavated but that at Wareham (Renn 1960) was found to have walls 4m thick set on foundations 5.2m wide and 1.2m deep; no foundations of this sturdy character were evident in the Keep Garden.

It seems more likely that buildings were constructed around the perimeter of the platform to form what might appear from the outside to have been a "great tower" significantly higher than the rest of the castle. This interpretation may be supported by evidence in the Pipe Rolls. In 1228 is the entry "digging and carrying stone for repairing great tower the motte in part buried by earth [*per terre motte in parte obruta*]" which may suggest that the tower stood on an earth mound and in 1389 "cleaning wards and ramparts of said [high] tower" suggests that there were open spaces within the structure. The idea that the Great Tower might be a collection of structures (including turrets) is further supported by mentions of "buildings within the high tower" in 1373, "divers buildings in the high tower" being reroofed in 1375 and roofing "divers towers in great tower" in 1362.

While stratigraphically Wall C, and therefore the keep-like structure proposed above, appears to be the earliest feature on the site, the presence of re-used stone within it, shows clearly that something preceded it. At Farnham the shell keep is dated to the late 12th century and a similar date at Taunton would fit the style of Arch 464. The first mention of the Great Tower at Taunton in the accounts is in 1234. Gray's Norman dating evidence would be based on the incorporation of earlier material (from the motte?) during the construction of the platform.

The construction of a gun platform along the eastern wall would preclude the presence of a tower keep surviving until after the Civil War but less-substantial buildings may have already been derelict, as described in 1635 (see page 25).

At the southern end, the situation is even less clear. Early plans, such as that used by Warre (1853), show this area higher than the area to the north of Wall A and it is marked as "Site of Norman Keep". Gray showed that this location for the keep was incorrect and uncovered what appeared to be a curtain wall (Wall B) crossing it from east to west with buildings attached to its north side. This wall did not join the south wall of the inner ward and is now known to have continued westwards under Castle House.

Chapter 9

The Great Hall

Chris Webster

The Great Hall is the best known and most studied part of the castle and the recent work for the Museum of Somerset has added much new information. It has, however, shown that previous explanations of the development of the building (principally those of Radford and Hallam 1953) have to be incorrect, without replacing them with new certainties.

9.1 Sources of Information

All pictorial sources before the 19th century are viewed from the south and the Great Hall does not feature greatly in them. The principal early source is therefore SANHS 3506 (Figure 1.1 on page 13) dated to about 1800. This shows the hall from the north-east prior to the re-roofing of 1816, the contract for which also contains a plan, section and elevation (see page 30). Prior to the detailed plans drawn up by Spencer (SRO DD/SAS/c1207/2b,2c) in 1875 there are also plans by Carver (SRO Q/AC/3) in 1833 showing various doorways that were to be blocked in his unimplemented proposals. These doors are also shown in the plan by Leversedge (SRO DD/SAS/c1207/2g, engraved in Warre 1853). Edwin Sloper (1876b) gives the uses of these doors before the SANHS purchase, as well as descriptions of other changes made between the removal of the courts in 1857 and the changes made by SANHS.

9.2 The West Wall

The wall between the hall and the west range was not affected greatly during the Museum of Somerset works, with the exception of the insertion of a services duct through the foundation below Door 236.

Early features

The earliest features of the wall were recorded by Radford and Hallam (1953, 60) when the plaster was removed. They noted that the wall was built of lias rubble and showed the scars of two vaults (see Figure 10.2 on page 191). Excavation revealed the foundation trench for a central wall between the vaults and suggested that these were barrel vaults similar to that in the adjacent undercroft. While possible, this is an assumption and the central wall could have been used to support columns, the interpretation favoured for the similar foundations at Winchester Palace, Southwark (Seeley *et al.* 2006). At the north end is a door (236) leading to the Undercroft, which replaced an earlier door (253) at a lower level. Radford and Hallam (1953, 18, 68) date the earlier door to the 13th century and Radford (1954, 18) suggested that the medieval floor level was 1 foot (0.3m) higher than the present one (on the basis of Fireplace 239, see page 193). The 1953 drawing (SANHS A7 1f; Radford and Hallam 1953, Fig. 6.2) of Door 236, however appears to show the base of the doorframe at the current floor level and the head at 1.52m above this, compared to a more reasonable 2m for the adjacent door (237). Radford and Hallam (1953, 78) state that Door 236 was created by Hammet to access the Crown Court and was converted to a cupboard in 1816. There does not appear to be a great deal of evidence for this. It is certainly shown blocked on Spencer's 1875 plan but may have been affected by the insertion of the privy in 1816 as part of the roofing contract (see page 31).

In the upper part of the wall (Figure 10.2 on page 191) a roofline is visible formed of Hamstone blocks set into the masonry with a square (2 inches) moulding forming the line. The roof was much steeper, and started at a lower level, than

Figure 9.3: Detail of the date carved on Buttress 375 as shown on an undated colour slide. Somerset HER image 30116.

present one; the mouldings continue above the present roof. This roof moulding is contemporary with a line of windows (117–119, 220) in the West Range as shown by the same block of moulded stone being used for both at the base of Window 119. The two lengths of moulding on the north side did not appear to be aligned with each other when measured (as shown on Figure 10.2 on page 191) but this may be a surveying error as no direct measurements were possible.

The early plans show the interior of this wall to be curved (as was the east end) with no indication that this was other than masonry. This cannot have been original as its removal has left no scars. The symmetry with the other end suggests that its construction was part of the changes made by Hammet in *c.*1790 when two courts were formed. It would have obscured Door 237 and must have been removed in or by 1875 when Sloper (1876b) records work to that door.

9.3 The North Wall

The north wall (Figure 9.1 on the facing page; Figure 9.2 on page 170) appears, from its location and thickness to be the curtain wall of the castle. There were few opportunities to examine the wall interior during the recent works, except at the heads of the windows, as little plaster was stripped. The exception was the area between Windows 52 and 53 but this did not produce much new information.

Early features

Externally, the western end of the wall is distinguished by three shallow Hamstone buttresses (437, 438 and 439), joined by a plinth with a chamfered Hamstone moulding (Figure 9.1 on the facing page). This design is also seen on the west side of the West Range and its Norman character led to that building being known as the keep before Gray's discoveries of the 1920s. Radford and Hallam (1953, 60) believed that these buttresses were associated with their first-floor hall as they appeared to stop at the end wall that they believed that they had discovered. In the 2009 excavations, this wall was shown to be nonexistent and it is likely that the series continued, as does the plinth with Hamstone moulding to the east.

The three buttresses are spaced at 6.1m (20ft) centres but with 11.4m (37.4 feet) to the clasping buttress (440) at the western corner. To the east, the next two of any equally-spaced buttresses would have lain in the positions of Windows 53 and 54 and would have been removed. The only evidence is a possible vertical line in the stonework below Window 53 and the spacing of the plinth stones, which would fit around a buttress.

There is a further buttress (436) to the east, not on this spacing and not made of Hamstone, that is probably later and another clasping buttress (375) very similar to the western ones at the north-east corner. It lies 24.4m from Buttress 437, on the same 6.1m spacing, and has a plinth at the same level. Carved into the stone in two places are the initials "HB", one accompanied by a date. Radford and Hallam (1953, 73) read the date as 1659 but a colour slide in the HER collection (Figure 9.3) is titled "Date HB 1650". The slide image is not conclusive and neither, when examined in 2009, was the carving on the wall.

Radford and Hallam (1953, 61) report the discovery of the remains of a window (252) midway between Buttresses 438 and 439 and compare it to one in the West Range (Window 240, see page 189). It is shown on their site drawing (SANHS 6066) within Window 55 and was presumably found while removing the lower blocking of the reveal (see below on page 171).

Internally at the west end is a door (237, Figure 9.2 on page 170) leading, via a short intra mural passage, to a spiral staircase (see page 195). Most of the top and east side of Door 237 has been replaced but the west retains medieval work including a draw bar hole 1.3m deep. The door is shown blocked on Spencer's plan and its repair in 1875 is described by Sloper (1876b): "the head of the circular doorway leading to the turret and roof of the keep had been cut away to make room for a small window. The return of the arch was fortunately in situ and this was easily restored according to the original." Radford and Hallam (1953, 16, 68) date the door to either the mid or first half of the 13th century but this may be on the basis of the documented 1247–48 dates. It does appear likely that the door post-dates the removal of the earlier vaulting which would probably have crossed it.

East of this is a blocked window (208) with an inserted window seat, discovered in 1875 (Sloper

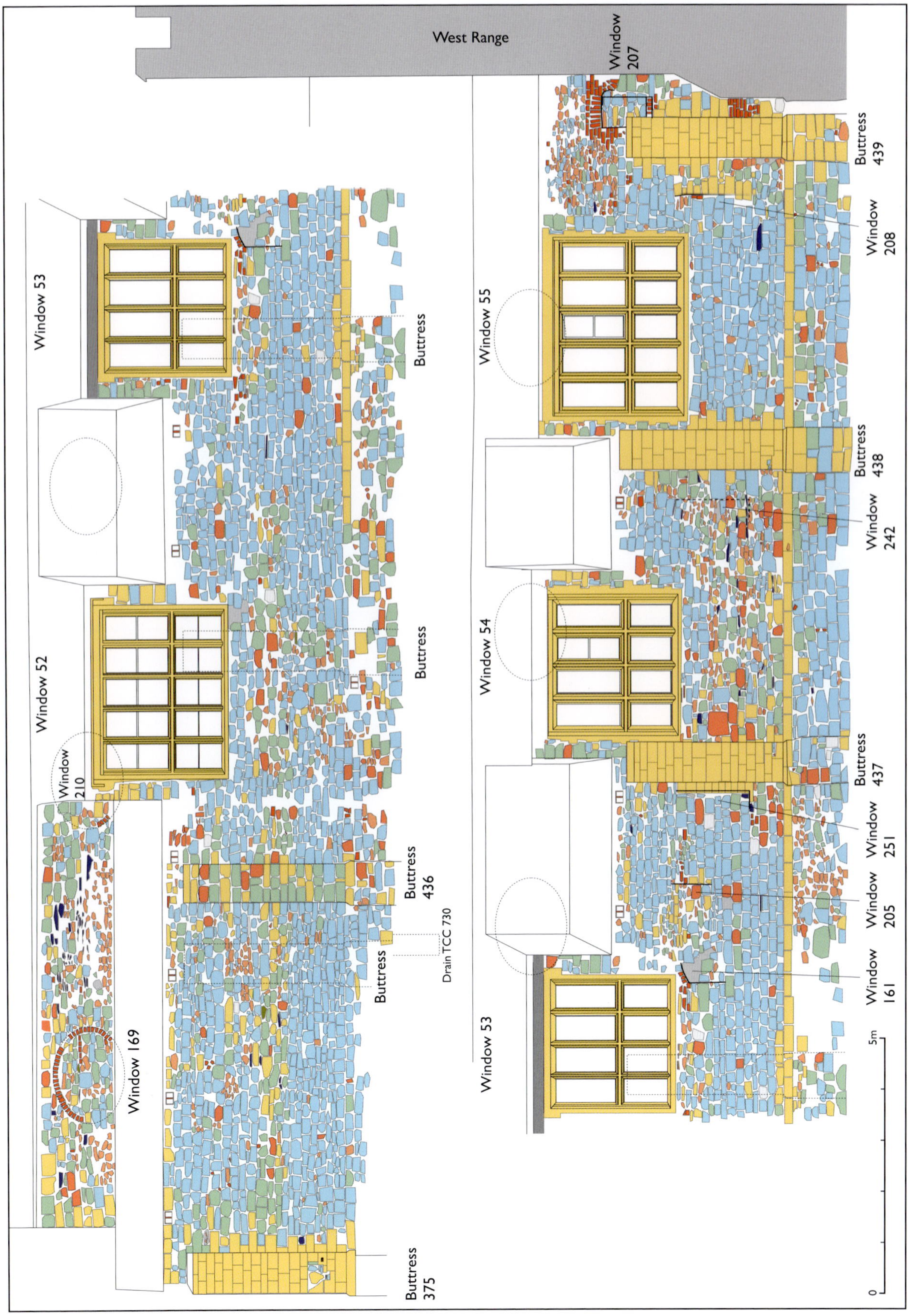

***Figure 9.1:** Elevation of exterior north wall of the Great Hall, showing (dashed) possible positions of other windows and buttresses, based on spacings. See Figure 3 on page 4 for key to colours. Areas of small chert facing have not been recorded in detail.*

__Figure 9.2:__ Elevation of interior north wall of the Great Hall. See Figure 3 on page 4 for key to colours. Areas of small rubble were not drawn in detail.

1876b) and partly removed by Window 55. Faint traces of medieval red-painted false-jointing are visible on the surviving splay. One side of the exterior opening is visible on the outside (Figure 9.1 on page 169), constructed of fine Hamstone ashlar. As with Door 237, it would appear to be later than the removal of the vaulting and its similarity to Window 119 in the west wall may indicate that they (and perhaps Door 237) are contemporary. It seems likely that Window 208 was one of a series; Radford and Hallam (1953, 67) report a blocked window (242), behind a later fireplace (241, below) and their plan (SANHS 6066) indicates "?window jamb" on the exterior. This is not obvious today but might have been suggested by a vertical alignment in the stonework (see Figure 9.1 on page 169). The side of a third window (251) is visible externally and corresponds with two surviving stones of the rear arch left unplastered in 1953 (although they appear to be set lower than those in Window 208).

Later features

The most obvious features of the north wall are the four large windows. Three of these (52, 54, 55) predate the earliest descriptions of the castle and all have been heavily repaired in the 20th century. Windows 54 and 55 were replaced, using Doulting stone in place of Hamstone as the latter could not be obtained, in 1964 (SRO DD/A/CNT/4/2). Previously these appear to have been the earliest, described by Radford and Hallam (1953, 74) as being 16th-century in character but probably reused here. The frame of Window 54 had been inserted upside-down as could be seen from the inversion of the transom. In Window 55 the transom was the correct way up but the rest of the frame had been reconstituted around it to match the style of Window 54. Spencer (1910, 47) states that these were the only two "old" windows in the Great Hall. All four windows sit high in alcoves running the full height of the building but this was not always the case in Window 55 where the alcove is shown infilled at ground level until 1953 when it was partly opened up (the remaining part contains the remains of Window 208, and perhaps follows the line of Window 252).

On the exterior, Window 52 can be seen to replace one of a series of oval windows matching those surviving on the south side (see page 174). Four are shown, all blocked, on SANHS 3506 (Figure 1.1 on page 13) in about 1800 but two have now been removed by the construction of Window 53, in 1863 according to Webb (1874). Part of the brick surrounds of the other two (169, 210) remain in the wall to the east of Window 52. Radford and Hallam (1953, 74–6) citing Sloper (1876b), believed that Windows 54 and 55 were part of the post-Civil War repairs to the castle and that Window 52 was inserted by Hammet to replace the oval windows that were infilled at that time. It is perhaps more likely that there were originally six oval windows, matching those on the south, and that Windows 52, 54 and 55 were all added by Hammet.

The 1816 contract (SRO Q/AC/2) states that "Good and sufficient arches are to be turned over the lintells of the openings of the three windows which are in the said back wall and which give light to the courts of the said assize hall" and these very shallow brick arches were recorded above Windows 52 and 54 in 2009. Above Window 54 the wooden lintels had been replaced with steel in 1950 but timber remained above Window 52, although badly decayed.

As mentioned, medieval Window 242 was discovered by Radford and Hallam (1953, 67) to have been converted into a fireplace (241, SANHS A7-1c), which could be seen to predate Window 54. To the east, Window 251 had undergone more complex changes. Internally these were evidenced by two brick vaults (Figure 9.2 on the preceding page), one narrow and semicircular, the other wider and flatter. The eastern side of the latter had been cut away by Window 53. Externally two pairs of small windows are known, one set replacing the other. SANHS 3506 of *c.*1800 shows two square windows of two lights (205, 206) in this location and the west side of one of them, probably 205, is still visible externally (Figure 9.1 on page 169). Neither the external windows or the vaulted chambers are shown on the 1816 contract drawings (SRO Q/AC/2). These windows were replaced by smaller round-headed windows (160, 161) by 1853 (SANHS 12529, Warre 1853). The east side and three bricks of the arch of one, probably 161, are visible externally at a lower level to that of Window 205. The symmetry of the windows is not matched by the two arches internally and the moving of the window locations suggests some internal change, which is not documented or visible in the structure.

Sloper (1876b) records the previous discovery of the two arches when Window 53 was being built "where the wall had been mutilated to make room for the privies for the prisoners". This part of Sloper's text had been crossed through and replaced by "in making this window Jeboult [the builder, see page 33], after breaking away a portion of the wall, found a doorway on the left hand just large enough for a man to creep through though there was nothing to show that any exit was in existence on the outside of the wall and an arched [?work] on the right-hand side with a square place under the arch. The outside of the hall as it existed before this alteration is shown in [Warre (1853)] with two small windows which Jeboult says were not original but were put in to light the privies [crossed out] cells." Their location, within the wall, might suggest privies and it is not clear why Sloper changed his mind about this identification.

A rectangular brick window (207) surround is visible at a high level on the exterior at the west end (Figure 9.1 on page 169). It is not visible on SANHS 3506 (*c.*1800) but is shown on Leversedge's elevation (1853, SANHS 3515-IV) and so is probably the privy window specified in the 1816 contract (above on page 31). It is probably also the "small window" mentioned by Sloper (1876b) that had damaged Door 237 (above). At the east end of the interior part of a buried wall plate (Figure 9.2 on page 170) was seen when the plaster fell off it but it is not clear to which phase of building this belongs.

9.4 The East Wall

The east wall was not examined inside the hall but the exterior was stripped of hard cement render and recorded (Figure 9.4 on the facing page). Most of the lower part of the wall appeared to be of one build comprising random rubble of predominantly North Curry stone and lias with some Hamstone, chert and brick. Above this the walling was of more evenly mixed stone types with some attempt at coursing. The south-east corner was clasped with Hamstone quoins that are discussed as part of the south wall (below).

The northern end (around Door 393) was brick of two phases, the second relating to the modern doorway. The earlier brickwork, which may relate to the construction of a door to a privy in 1816 (above on page 30), also turned eastwards to form the south face of a block of masonry, whose north-east corner was formed by Buttress 375. The lower part of the brickwork on this south face had been cut away and a brick arch inserted, possibly forming the head of a fireplace. Below this was further brickwork filling the area beneath the arch. In 1875, Spencer's plan shows that this wall lay behind a WC within a small chamber, possibly that constructed in 1816, and by 1910 "furnace chamber no. 2" appears to have been built below it. Plans for this were discussed in 1899 (SANHS minutes: 10/10/1899) but possibly not implemented until after 1908. A fireplace in this location is unlikely and no flue was evident.

The east face of this masonry block is mostly lias with some other stone, including red conglomerate, and appears to form a continuation of the north wall of the hall with a Hamstone capped plinth at the base. It is possible that this plinth returned to the west along the south side of the block of masonry as the plinth appeared to continue but unfortunately the Hamstone coping was damaged during the demolition work and it was not possible to confirm the existence of a deliberate chamfer on this side. High on the east side, next to Buttress 375 is a 1m deep hole (392), presumably to support a substantial (0.23m, 9 inch square) timber. SANHS 3506 of *c.*1800 (Figure 1.1 on page 13) shows the top of this area as broken towards the south above a thin wall which joins it from the east. The privy is just visible through a gate in the wall.

The upper part of the main wall is occupied by two large adjacent timber windows (101/102) which Radford and Hallam (1953, 75) likened to the stone ones at the other end of the hall (54, 55) and regarded similarly as re-use of 16th-century material. They note that a different window is shown in SANHS 3506 (see Figure 1.1 on page 13) and suggest that this "may be a mistake on the part of the artist". SANHS 3506 shows a single, apparently pale stone, window in a coped gable with a string course, or possibly a timber lintel, above. There is evidence from the contract of 1816 (SRO Q/AC/2) that SANHS 3506 is correct. The removal of this gable is described in the contract: "The eastern or pointed end wall of the said assize hall to be taken down to the top of the end window and the wall made good with a lintel at a proper level to receive a wall plate for hipping the new roof". It was noted that the head of the window was "about 16 inches" above the height of the new ceiling and that "part of the ceiling which is contiguous thereto is to be stepped down from the lintel of the said window to the nearest building beam".

There were, therefore, no plans to replace the window at that time but if the measurements in the contract can be relied on, it would seem likely that the current window was inserted as part of these works as its head (and thus the foot of the hipped roof) is 20 inches above the 1816 ceiling level. There is also evidence in the stonework for the removal of a beam, longer than the width of the window, from below it at an unknown date.

The early plans show the interior end of the hall to be curved (as was the west end), with no indication that this was of different construction to the wall itself. This "apse" was removed in 1899 (Bramble 1899, 2–3; SANHS minutes: 13/7/1899).

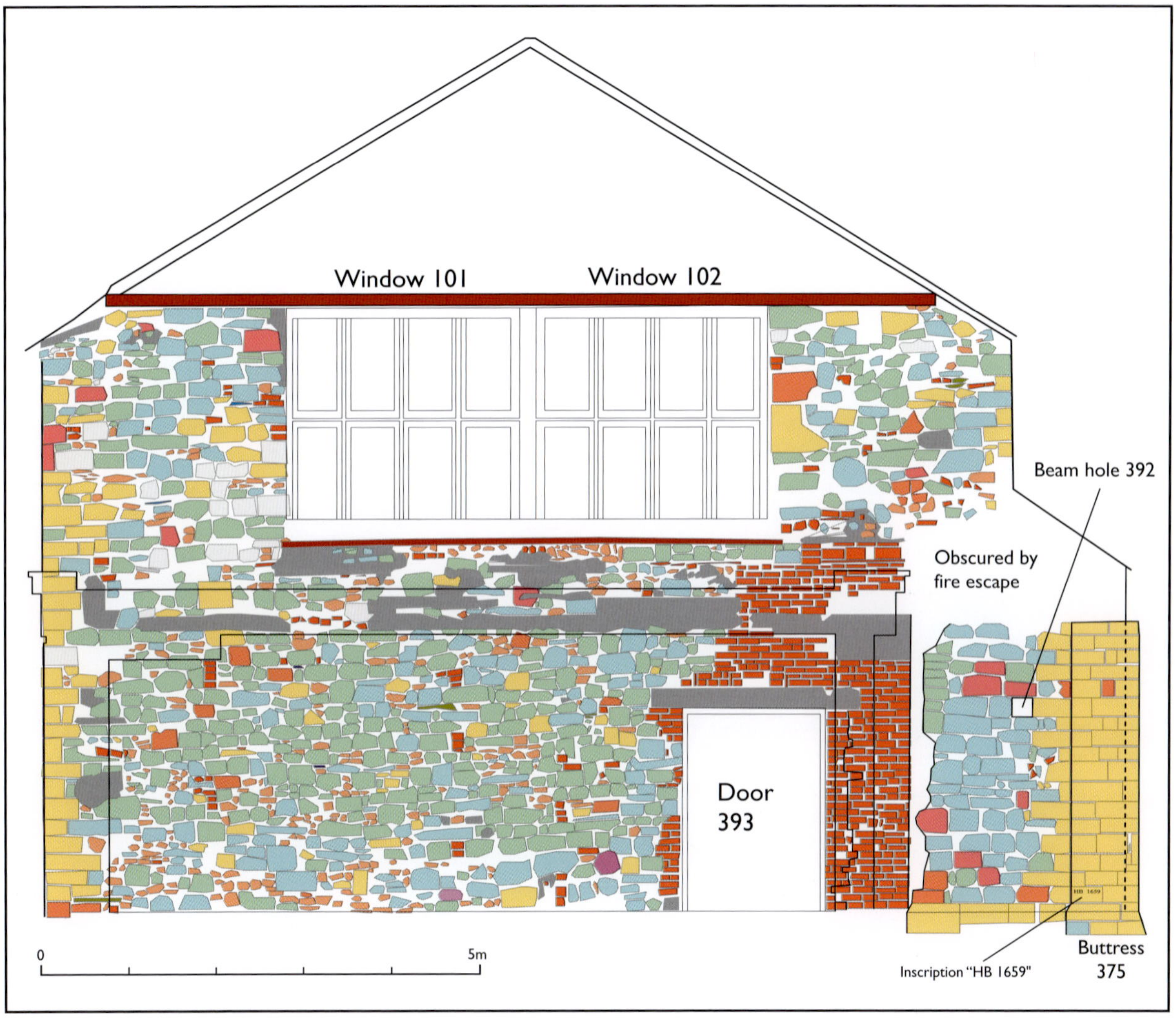

Figure 9.4: *Exterior elevation of the east end of the Great Hall. The position of the 1930s link block, removed in 2009, is outlined. See Figure 3 on page 4 for key to colours.*

No doorways are known until one (Door 393) was cut in 1816 (SRO Q/AC/2) to give access to the privy constructed at that date. This is still present on Spencer's 1875 plan but was, presumably, opened out to the present double doors when the link to the Wyndham Galleries was built in the 1930s.

9.5 The South Wall

The south wall (Figure 9.5 on page 175; Figure 9.6 on page 176) is the most complex and also the best recorded of all the walls of the Great Hall and provides much of the information that can be used to reconstruct the structural history of the hall. Much of the exterior has clearly been refaced since 1875 and the upper part of the interior was plastered in 1952. This was not greatly disturbed in the recent work and so could not be recorded.

Early Features

The earliest features associated with the wall are the buttresses (486, 489) whose foundations were located in excavation in 2008 (above on page 70) but which had also been seen previously. The buttresses appeared to be contemporary with the construction of the wall and the centres of the two foundations lie 18 feet (5.5m) apart. The western buttress (489) was 18 feet from the wall of the West Range suggesting an even spacing along the south wall of the hall.

If, as seems likely, Wall 654 found in the Great Hall excavations (see page 83 and Figure 5.16 on page 84) was the eastern end of this building phase, it lies about 36 feet to the east of Buttress 486 which would make 486 the central buttress; the size of 489 would suggest smaller intermediate buttresses. Buttress 486 appears to be shown as a pencilled addition to Spencer's 1875 plan, labelled "Foundations". This annotation is undated and in a different hand to that showing Wall 411 (see page 68), which is dated 1877. The discovery of the buttress is mentioned by Spencer (1910, 48–9) and it must have been seen again in 1931 when the drainage was changed.

Internally, the location of the South Wall can be seen to fit the roofline evident on the West Range (see page 167) which reaches it at the same height as it reaches the North Wall. There is no certain evidence for windows but it is possible that the jamb of Window 247 (below) does belong to this phase and was reused later. In any event they must have lain between the buttresses and therefore be in the locations of the later windows.

Later features

Large windows

The jamb of a window (247) was discovered in 1875 (Sloper 1876b) and left on view. It appears to be 3.68m (12 feet) high and, assuming it is symmetrically placed between buttress and wall, 3m (just under 10 feet) wide. Radford and Hallam (1953, 72) suggest that these large rectangular windows date to the late 16th century, based on the evidence of Door 163 and the reports by Toulmin (1791, 48) of work by Bishop Horne in 1577. The top of this window is above the eaves of the roofline marked on the West Wall and the wall must have been raised, also blocking Window 119 in the west range. What appears to be the lintel of Window 247 is evident resting on the top of the jamb but the part that would have crossed the window opening has been cut away.

Loose plaster to the east revealed a further length of timber (402), which appeared to have an original E end and to have been cut off at the west. It was set in lias masonry with hard white mortar at a slightly higher level than the lintel of Window 247. Further east again, the western end of another beam (263) was revealed. This was at the same height as the lintel of Window 247 but no jamb could be seen below it. The proposed spacing of the windows would suggest that this would have lain further to the east. Radford and Hallam (1953, 72) believed that these timbers formed a "substantial wall-plate [which] can be traced throughout the length of the [...] wall" but no evidence of this was seen in 2009.

Oval windows

The upper part of the south wall contains five oval windows (142, 143, 144, 154 and 155), the position of a sixth is occupied by door 435 and is now behind the 1931 Entrance Block (Figure 9.5 on the facing page). Each window is 1.4m wide by 0.95m and is currently glazed in a spider's web style, installed between 1931 and 1933 on the evidence of photographs. Prior to this the windows had a simple vertical and horizontal bar that was installed in 1905 (visible in Figure 9.10 on page 181; Anon 1905, 3); their earlier appearance is unknown. Internally the windows have flat based, arched openings (see Figure 9.6 on page 176). It is likely that a similar series of six windows was present in the north wall (see page 171) where evidence for two survives. These windows would appear to have lit a gallery extending around the hall, overlooking an early 18th-century court arrangement.

Pre-Hammet doorways

Door 163 was visible on both sides of the wall. On the outside the moulded jamb and half the head of a flat arch were visible infilled with random rubble. In 1931 photos (SANHS 12550, 12551, Figure 9.10 on page 181) the remains of a relieving arch can be seen above but when plotted (Figure 9.5 on the facing page) this does not seem quite symmetrical with the door. On the inside, one jamb (the west) was visible with large quoins, some chamfered suggesting reused stones. The east side had been cut away by Door 356, and that in turn had been bricked up and cut away by the present door (162). Sloper (1876b), lists Door 356 as the cell door in the Crown Court and says that it was bricked up in December 1877. He also says that the "present centre doorway was in the Crown Court, the partition started a little to the left of its present right edge". This door is seen on Leversedge's plan where it appears to be slightly to the east of the current door (162) but no physical evidence of this could be seen. The location of Door 162 does not appear to have been changed in 1952, although a concrete lintel was inserted, so it is not clear when it was made but it may be part of the 1877 changes. No doors are present at this location on the 1816 plan (SRO Q/AC/2).

To the east, externally, is a large archway (216) with a moulded Hamstone jamb on the west side (Figure 9.10 on page 181). Radford and Hallam (1953, 72) describe it as "10 ft [3.05m] high and 8ft 5 ins [2.56m] wide with a segmental head" and date it to *c.*1500. They also suggest that it replaced an earlier opening but give no evidence for this. Internally the arch could be seen to be filled with brickwork (309), of early 19th-century appearance (Brian Murless, pers. comm.) and, as the gateway is not shown on the 1816 plan (SRO Q/AC/2),

Figure 9.7: *Great Hall roof truss 1 from the east, showing the mortices for the ceiling battens, the iron bands holding the joints and the beam linking to the top of Window 101 to support the hipped roof. The pale timbers are all modern additions.*

but internally this would have been adjacent to the wall corner making it structurally weak.

9.6 The Roof

The roof of the Great Hall appeared to coincide in almost all respects with that laid down in the 1816 contract (see page 30). The only difference was seen in the central truss (Truss 8 in the list below) as this was not required in 1816 because of the partition wall and must have been added when the partition was removed in *c.*1863.

The trusses have carpenters' marks in the form of Roman numerals on the west side and mortices to take the battens of the coffered ceiling. Some of the mortices are only 4–5cm long but others are 30–40cm, perhaps to allow the slotting in of the battens or boards. The former are described as small in the following list, the latter as large. No pattern could be discerned in the number and spacing of the mortices and it was not clear how this related to the construction of the ceiling. The details of the trusses are, from the east:

1. Marked IIII. Supports the hipped end of the roof with an additional beam running to the top of Window 101. Small mortices E and W. See Figure 9.7.
2. Marked VI. Large mortices to E; small to W.
3. Marked VII. Large mortices to E; small to W.
4. Marked IIII. Large mortices to E; small to W.
5. Marked III. Large mortices to E; small to W.
6. Marked VIII. Large mortices to E; small to W.
7. Marked I. Large mortices to E; small to W.
8. No carpenters' marks. No diagonal outer braces and the posts are attached to the beam by large iron screws driven into the soffit. No mortices.
9. Marked II. Small widely-spaced mortices to E; large to W.
10. Marked I. Small widely-spaced mortices to E; large to W.
11. Marked III. The southern inner brace has

been replaced by modern softwood. Irregular (mostly small) mortices to E; mostly large to W.
12. Marked (very roughly) I. Small mortices to E; mostly large to W.
13. Marked I I (letters widely spaced). Very irregular, mostly small, mortices to E; sparse, large to W.
14. Marked II. Sparse (five) small mortices to E; large to W.
15. Marked I. Sparse small mortices at south end of E side but numerous to north end; sparse, small to W.
16. Marked III. Sparse large (with one small) mortices to E; very numerous small to W.

In order to accommodate the new lift at the west end of the Great Hall it was proposed to remove Trusses 15 and 16. After discussion, the latter was removed but Truss 15 was preserved by moving it *c.*30cm to the east. This necessitated cutting the top off the kingpost of Truss 15, as it was inaccessibly nailed to the ridge, and its replacement by the top of the kingpost from Truss 16.

9.7 Buildings on the south wall of the Great Hall

At least four phases of buildings are known to have existed on the south side of the Great Hall facing the Gatehouse. The earliest was a porch covering the entrance to the Great Hall in the 16th century, replaced in the late 18th century by a building to accommodate the Grand Jury Room. Lean-to additions were made to either side of this and later removed. Whilst undertaking repairs to the Grand Jury Room in September 1931, serious structural problems were revealed and it was decided to replace it with a new structure (now the Entrance Block), the gift of William Wyndham on condition that the upper room was used as a school museum. Work was well underway by November (SANHS minutes: 4/11/1931) and the building was ceremonially opened in June the following year (Gray 1932, xxi–xxii).

The excavation for the beam engine pit in 1956 (see page 50) revealed several wall foundations in section but no detailed records were made so that they are undatable. They do not appear to align with any other known walls.

The Porch

Toulmin (1791, 48, see above on page 28) refers to a dated coat of arms on the porch to the Great

Figure 9.8: *Foundations (484) of porch wall looking south with foundations of Buttress 486 in the foreground.*

Hall but otherwise does not describe the porch, nor curiously does he mention that it had been removed to build the Grand Jury Room, while saying that the juries had left the gatehouse two years earlier. The arms were those of Bishop Robert Horne and the date 1577.

Spencer (1910, 48–9) reports "in digging recently to lay a drain some masonry was uncovered which might have been the foundation of the west wall of a porch". The location of "foundations" is marked in pencil on Spencer's 1875 plan in the location of Buttress 486. Both the buttress and the foundations (484/521/530, Figure 9.8) of the porch were discovered in 2008 (see page 70 and Figure 5.3 on page 69). The foundation appears to be sited around Door 163 (see page 174) which Radford and Hallam (1953, 72) date to the late 16th century, although if the east wall is aligned on the next buttress, the door would not be central but be sited in eastern half of the porch (Figure 12.1 on page 214). The foundations and buttress spacing suggest a building extending 4.3m (*c.*14 ft) out from the hall and 6.7m (*c.*22 ft) wide.

The Grand Jury Room

The Grand Jury Room is probably to be dated to 1789 as Toulmin (1791, 48) says that the grand jury was accommodated above the gate "till within these two years" and that Hammet "fit[ed] up a commodious and elegant grand jury room." The need for "due accommodation for the Grand Jury" is the only specific work mentioned in the report of the public meeting in 1786 (*Western Flying Post:* 31/7/1786). As the building

Figure 9.9: *The Grand Jury Room. The gables of Tone House are visible to the right. Undated LEJ Brooke photograph in Somerset Studies Library collections.*

Figure 9.10: *The south side of the Great Hall in October 1931 following the demolition of the Grand Jury Room. The foundations for the Entrance Block are being dug. Door 163 is visible on the left, behind the worker with the wheelbarrow and Door 216 is to the centre by the ladder. An infilled oval window (435) is visible above. SANHS 12250.*

was not demolished until 1931, several plans (the best being Spencer's of 1875, see Figure 12.1 on page 214) and photographs (Figure 9.9 on the previous page) survive. The ground floor was open and the upper floor was supported on wooden columns.

The photographs and 1875 plans show brick walls to east and west with tall round-headed arches but these were not original as Carver's plan of 1832 (SRO Q/AC/2) and Buckler's drawing of 1836 (Figure 12.2 on page 215) show columns here also. The brickwork must have been added sometime before 1865 as it is shown in one of Jeboult's photographs and it may be part of the work that he undertook. The brickwork presumably represents a strengthening of the support for the upper story, the walls of which were constructed of stone rubble. Carver's plan also shows a line of columns along the front of the Great Hall linking to two extensions to the hall at east and west; the whole area is labelled "colonnade" (Figure 12.1 on page 214).

Upstairs, there was a window in the west wall and two towards the east end of the south front. A carved stone coat of arms is visible to the west of the two windows, described by Savage (1822, 261) identically to that described by Toulmin on the porch. Although badly eroded this can be confirmed by close examination of the photographs. A flight of stairs (not shown by Carver or Buckler) ascended in the SW corner to reach the two upstairs rooms, the larger grand jury room with the two windows to the east and the smaller room (for witnesses, according to Sloper 1876b), between the head of the stairs and the wall of the hall. Each room had a door (427, 428) and a fireplace (426, 429) set in the hall wall, the doors communicating with the gallery of the courts (see Figure 9.5 on page 175). The infilling of the doors and fireplaces can be seen in the 1931 photographs (SANHS 12550–12552, Figure 9.10 on the previous page) but this seems to have happened earlier as the plans for renovation in 1931 (SANHS 6043) show them blocked (on the Great Hall side only), with the east door (428) intended for conversion to a window ("opening old door to obtain a view of the interior of the Gt Hall", SANHS minutes: 16/2/1931). The plans show that the proposed renovation primarily comprised the glazing of the openings in the ground floor in a style later adopted for the East and West Passages.

The Court Offices

Nineteenth-century plans (eg Spencer's, see Figure 12.1 on page 214) show a range of buildings along the south front of the Great Hall, which incorporated the ground floor of the Grand Jury Room. Sloper (1876b) describes them as containing the Indictment Room (moved here from the Undercroft) and to have been "composed of timber principally with a few bricks". It is not known what else was housed here but they will be referred to as Court Offices. Spencer's plan shows the buildings in detail but the room names post-date the use by the courts. The structures are drawn with thin walls and supporting columns, shown identically to those of the Grand Jury Room, and were probably based on the colonnade shown by Carver. The stone pads for four columns (one not shown by Spencer) to the west of the Grand Jury Room were excavated in 2008 (see Figure 5.3 on page 69). The westernmost supported a corridor covering access between the two existing doors (60 and 61), which probably survived from Hammet's colonnade together with a wider corridor to the east (within which the colonnade remained) linking the open ground-floor of the Grand Jury Room with a now-infilled door (243). The area of the change in width was occupied by a "boot house" entered only from the courtyard.

The area below the Grand Jury Room is shown with a passage ("entrance lobby") leading to Door 162 with a store room to the east, and then another "entrance passage" leading to Door 358. Beyond the Grand Jury Room is a small "waiting room" and a larger "dressing room" with a fireplace, formed by joining the corner of the Grand Jury Room to an existing wall enclosing a courtyard to the east of the Great Hall (Figure 12.1 on page 214). The original colonnade built by Hammet runs along the wall of the Great Hall, linking these rooms, and with a "WC" at the far east end.

Glimpses of these buildings can be seen through the gatehouse in early postcards (SANHS 12521, 12522, Frith 34885); the waiting room appears to have had a window at high level with two horizontal timbers visible below. It is not clear what infills the wall between these timbers (it appears to be small rubble) but a slate roof is shown clearly sloping up to just above the base of an oval window. The lower part of the Grand Jury Room is filled by wide timber boarding, again with windows at high level and a door at the east end.

The colonnade and later structures at the west end were removed in 1878 when "ruinous buildings" in the courtyard were taken down, the yard "excavated and levelled" and a small window inserted (Anon 1878). Although the location of this window is not stated it was almost certainly

Window 181 (see page 193) replacing Door 60 that had given access to the colonnade. The sketch plan (SANHS 13158, of *c.*1878) shows both east and west buildings ("buildings erected for convenience of assizes and sessions") with the west part additionally indicated as "portion taken down". The eastern part survived at least until 1894 when photographed by Francis Frith and may have been removed in 1900 when the portico beneath the Grand Jury Room was "opened up" (SANHS minutes: AGM 24/7/1900) or earlier "improved by the removal of modern brickwork" (Bramble 1899, 3). There is no mention of clearance of the other buildings however.

The Entrance Block

This building was designed and built in a hurry late in 1931 when the plans to renovate the Grand Jury Room were abandoned due to serious structural problems. William Wyndham had given £200 to fund the renovations in July and a special meeting of SANHS discussed his new offer of £900 for a replacement building with wings to either side. The offer was conditional on the building containing a "school museum". Gray's photographs (SANHS 12551, 12552) record the state of construction, up to the base of the windows, on 15 November, and plans show the proposed structure (SANHS 6040, 6041); stone from the keep garden excavation was used "to a very large extent" (Gray 1932, xxii).

The two wings (which were called loggias on the plans) were single-storey, glass-fronted corridors attached to the south wall of the Great Hall. They reused the wooden columns from the Grand Jury Room and utilised the previous design for the front of that building (SANHS 6043). The western bay of the east corridor was open to provide access to the eastern bay, which was designed to exhibit the State Coach of the High Sheriff of Somerset, which had been used to drive the judge to the assizes (David Walker, pers. comm.).

The upper room of the building was opened as a museum of bygones on 9 January 1933 with a workroom below, Wyndham having given permission for this temporary use, perhaps in view of the new Wyndham Galleries, whose construction began in October (Gray 1933, xxiv). In 1950 the building became the main entrance to the museum and in 1956 a beam engine was emplaced in a large pit (see page 50 for archaeological work). It is likely that the door (173) between the upper floor and the Great Hall was part of the 1952/3 works that built the gallery to which it led.

The east corridor was converted to toilets in 1992 (see page 55) but the west corridor remained in use as gallery space until both corridors were demolished and replaced by new larger structures in 2009–10. The Entrance Block now houses a cafe, extending into the new west corridor, with offices on the first floor. Some of the wooden columns have again been reused to indicate a corridor through the cafe.

9.8 Structural Development

Phase 1: 11th–12th century

The earliest parts of the structure seem, as recognised by Radford and Hallam (1953), to be the north and west walls together with the now-removed, spine wall and south wall (see Figure 5.14 on page 81), which appear to be contemporary with the earliest phase of the West Range. Internally the walls are built of lias blocks and externally they are distinguished by shallow, plain Hamstone buttresses of Norman style. Excavation in 2009 showed that the east wall proposed by Radford and Hallam (1953, 60) did not exist and that the spine wall continued beyond it for an unknown length. The east part of the north wall appears to have been rebuilt but the spacing of the buttresses on the west part suggests that the north-east corner buttress (375) may be of this phase and form the original east end (see page 168), defining a range 49m long and 16m wide. A very similar structure is known at the bishop of Winchester's residence at Southwark where three parallel foundation trenches define a building 88m long (Seeley *et al.* 2006, 36), and, again, 16m wide. Southwark is interpreted as a hall range, intended to form a long, imposing frontage viewed across the Thames from London that was later divided into separate buildings.

The buttresses and small surviving window (240) suggest a Norman date for the building and Radford and Hallam (1953, 60–62) confidently assigned it to the 12th century and the episcopate of Henry of Blois (1129-71). However, the great similarity of the foundation layouts might suggest a similar date to that at Southwark which is dated by dendrochronology to 1190 × 1226 (Seeley *et al.* 2006, 38-9). This however, would be a time when a gothic style, being employed at Wells Cathedral at this date, might be expected. Unfortunately the pipe rolls (see Chapter 1) do not start until 1209 but the absence of any mention of a large building project thereafter would suggest an earlier date, perhaps very early in the episcopate of Peter des Roches (1205–38), shown by the accounts to have been active at Taunton.

Its later use as a hall, the use of the structure at Southwark and a similar range at Bishop's Waltham (Wareham 2000), would suggest that the range held first floor hall, kitchen and services probably with no distinction between them at undercroft level (this seems to have been the case at Southwark and no cross walls were found at Taunton). The high status of the building is indicated by the presence of the decorative buttresses on the curtain wall.

However, an interpretation of this structure as a hall range is complicated by the references in the pipe rolls of the 1240s, which refer to the building of a hall (Hunt 1971) but also to the survival of the "Old Hall" (see page 10) suggesting that the 1246–49 hall did not replace an earlier hall on the site. It is possible that mention in the accounts of a "Great House" in 1218 close to the chapel might refer to this building.

Phase 2: 13th century

The construction of this phase appears to be dated to the well-recorded (Hunt 1971) campaign of building from 1246 to 1249 and to comprise the demolition of the spine and south wall of Phase 1 (at the west end, at least) and the construction of a narrower (31 feet, 9.5m), ground floor hall, with a chamber in the West Range and chapel in the South Range. The accounts only record expenses incurred and there is no mention of costs for demolition or rebuilding which were presumably carried out by estate labour. Structurally the only useful pieces of information are the payments for 25 newels (*noell*) and the ironwork for 10 window shutters. Hunt (1971, 42 n.6) notes that newel appears to be used for "boss" but as the spiral stair does have 25 steps between the Great Hall and the Somerset Room it may well refer to these. The positions of three windows are suggested in the north wall (see page 168) and the presence of the buttresses on the south wall would suggest four more locations. One of these would be occupied by the door leaving three for windows. If these were occupied by two-light windows that required two shutters each and a further small window existed over the door, the total of 10 shutters can be achieved.

Some idea of other aspects of the design of the hall can be gathered by examining other halls of the period; the mid 13th century seeming to be a time when many halls of similar size were constructed. Salzman (1952, 92) also notes that this is a time when a particular type of window, called *stantiva* (which he translates as "upright") is employed in these halls. The earliest he lists is at Feckenham in Worcestershire, which Henry III visited in June 1233 and at which he subsequently ordered significant improvements including making four *estantivas* windows in the hall (Stevenson 1916). Salzman describes the term as puzzling but suggests that it refers to a tall window that rose above the wall top under a transverse gable.

This explanation of the term is used by James and Robinson (1988, 11) when discussing the modernisation in the 1230s of the hall at Clarendon and by Brown and Colvin (1963, 730) at Ludgershall. Henry ordered the construction of a new hall at Ludgershall, 60 feet by 40 with *stantivae* in May 1244 and it appears to have been finished in 1246 (Ellis 2000, 13). Stocker (2000b) suggests that Ludgershall was modelled on the king's hall at Winchester, built 1222–35, which can be seen to have had this style of window. Winchester may have started the fashion but there are also connections with Salisbury, where Stocker (2000b, 95) notes similarities between the tracery recovered at Ludgershall, which enabled the upper parts of the window to be reconstructed (Stocker 2000a), and work at Salisbury Cathedral and in houses in the close, such as the Old Deanery (Drinkwater 1964) where one of the windows survives. This type of hall was still being built towards the end of the century, for example at Stokesay (Munby and Summerson 2002).

Bishop William Raleigh, who ordered the hall at Taunton, had been the king's senior justice from 1234 to 1239 (Crook 2004), would have been familiar with this style of hall, and may well have copied it here. The wall would have been only 3.25m high, which would have not allowed much illumination unless the windows rose above it, and the shadows of other buildings in the courtyard. These windows must have been in the place of the later large rectangular windows but must have been narrower or the dormer of Window 247 would have blocked Window 119 in the West Range. The north side windows were much smaller, as befitted their location in the curtain wall, but probably gave a view over the garden.

These halls are also similar in that many have a width of *c.*30 feet: Taunton 31, The Old Deanery 31, Arthur's Hall, Dover 29 (Brodie 2011) and Stokesay 31, which may have been considered the maximum width for a timber roof span. Winchester (55 feet) had aisles and Stocker (2000b, 92) believes that Ludgershall (39 feet) must also have had arcades, although this could not be proved as any pier bases would have been outside the excavation.

The presence of the West Range containing the chamber indicates the location of the high end of hall but there is not much evidence for arrangements at the low end. The presence of the two pier bases (657 and 895, see page 82) probably indicates a gallery over the screens passage but the arrangement of doorways to kitchens and service rooms to the east is unknown.

Phase 3: 16th century

The next phase that can be documented is associated with bishop Robert Horne in 1577 and this appears to be the next change indicated by the fabric. The dating relies on Toulmin's description of the arms and date on the porch but Radford and Hallam (1953, 72–2) saw problems with this as, although the castle was returned to the bishop by Elizabeth I in 1575 (Williams 1975), there is evidence of continuing royal activity; in May 1578 a warrant was issued to Sir Hugh Paulett (the queen's Chief Steward of the Lordship of Taunton) to collect and spend £300 on repairs to the castle. Horne died on 1 June the following year following an illness (Houlbrooke 2008).

The structural changes comprise the replacement of the 13th-century windows on the south side with large rectangular windows, for which the evidence of one remains (247, see page 174), the raising of the wall to accommodate these and remove the gables, the replacement of the roof required by this and the construction of a porch with a new door into the hall. If it is assumed that the medieval door was in the easternmost bay, then the location of the door was also changed into the next bay west, which may have seen some alterations to the gallery and service arrangements. It is possible that the pier bases (657, 895) relate to this phase but the character of the stonework matches much better the 13th-century work.

Phase 4: 17th century

All the evidence for this phase comes from the east end of the hall, which probably lay outside the hall itself. The fate of the Great Hall area in the civil war sieges is unknown but Radford and Hallam (1953) believed that part of the east end of the north wall, together with the roof, was destroyed and rebuilt in 1659 – the date being conveniently carved on the eastern clasping buttress (375, see page 168). Inside this end of the current hall, several foundations were discovered in 2009, including Drain 730 and Hearth 853 (see page 86) together with associated walls and the well discovered in 1952. Radford and Hallam believed that this area was a courtyard, entered through the gateway or large Door 206, but these remains seem better interpreted as separate kitchen and other service buildings to the east of the hall, although it is possible that they are partitions within it. Drain 730 was filled with demolition rubble as was the well, which in addition contained a piece of armour and two weapon blades. A small group of clay pipes found in the silt in the base of Drain 730 is dated to *c.*1640 × 1670 (see page 133).

The obvious explanation is that this represents clearance after the Civil War but it is not certainly related to the dated initials on Buttress 375. These pose their own questions: why are the initials carved in two places and why would the date of a restoration be carved on the old stonework? The identity of "HB" is also unknown.

Phase 5: Early 18th century

The only datable features are the series of oval windows around the hall, which Radford and Hallam (1953, 75) date to *c.*1700 as do Orbach and Pevsner (2014, 618), though parallels, such as Wren Hall in Salisbury, are believed to be about 15 years later. Concomitant to these windows must be the lengthening of the hall to its present length, the raising of the walls, a new roof, the removal of the 16th-century windows and buttresses from the south side (except those buttresses buried in the porch walls). Apart from the increase in size, the effect would have been to give the building a less medieval, more baroque, appearance. The exact date of these changes is uncertain but they perhaps relate to the formalisation of the use of the hall for courts and may be correlate with substantial changes to Castle House (Chapter 13) around *c.*1700.

Radford and Hallam (1953, 74) believed that Windows 54 and 55 predated, and were incorporated into, this scheme but the evidence appears to be limited to the discovery of a clay tobacco pipe dating to the third quarter of the 17th century in the "masonry of the pier between them". The other two windows in this wall (52, 53) can be seen on SANHS 3506 to post-date the oval windows but no blocked windows are shown in the area around Windows 54 and 55 which occupy their (potential) positions. As the windows themselves employed re-used masonry they could have been placed there at any time and it seems unlikely that they can ever be dated securely.

Phase 6: Late 18th century

Hammet's work in the Great Hall is less clear than in some other locations but, according to

Toulmin (1791, 51), he rearranged the courts and Savage (1822, 264) adds that this involved the division into two rooms. Sloper (1876b) records the removal of this partition in 1863 and notes that it was made of brick. No trace was seen of this wall in the excavations, presumably because of the lowering of the ground to allow for suspended timber flooring but its location is marked by the position of Truss 8 in the roof (see page 179). Radford and Hallam (1953, 75) date the infilling of the northern oval windows and the insertion of Window 52 to these changes. They also include the construction of the "privies" within the wall to this phase.

Sloper (1876b) describes the courts, at the end of their life, with the judges' benches at the east and west ends of the hall, each facing a gallery along the central partition. The prisoners were accommodated in cells beneath the galleries which communicated by a door in the partition. The docks were situated in front of the galleries. Sloper originally thought that the small chambers in the north wall were privies for the prisoners but, for some reason, later crossed this through in his notebook. There was also a gallery along the south side which communicated with the Grand Jury Room.

Certainly belonging to Hammet's work is the replacement of the porch by the Grand Jury Room, and presumably the blocking of Door 163, as by 1816 (SRO DD/Q/AC/2) only the doors at the east and west ends (61, 361) are shown. On the first floor this required the blocking of an oval window (435) and the creation of two doors (427, 429). He also appears to have built a colonnade (see page 182) along the south front of the hall, matching the Grand Jury Room, to provide covered access to the doors.

Phase 7: Early 19th century

Two sources give accounts of work in 1816 but curiously, as Jeffries (1969) noted, neither complements the other. Savage (1822, 263) describes the "hall having again gone considerably into decay, and the town once more in danger of losing the assizes" and says that "a subscription was entered into by the principal inhabitants, amounting to about two hundred pounds, for the purpose of defraying the cost of the necessary repairs. The two courts underwent several judicious alterations, for the better accommodation of the judges, counsel and jurors, and the various officers connected with the proceedings of the assizes and quarter sessions."

Radford and Hallam (1953, 76) assign to these works the construction of the Court Offices (but see below) around the Grand Jury Room and the numerous doors through the south wall described by Sloper (1876b). They note that Savage does not mention the roof and suggest that "it is unlikely that the £200 expended included this item." However, the preamble to the re-roofing contract (see page 30), of which Radford and Hallam were evidently unaware, refers to the sum of £200 raised by subscription and uses it towards the £500 cost of the new roof and closets. Jeffries (1969) discusses these contradictions and shows, from the judicial records, that the hall was certainly re-roofed as agreed in the contract but also that there is remarkably little other evidence from the time. The only mention in the local papers is to the need for a subscription by the townspeople but then no record of the meetings to arrange this or the works themselves.

Carver's plan of 1832 (SRO Q/AC/2), does not show the Court Offices so it is clear that they were constructed after this date. It has not proved possible to identify when they were built.

Phase 8: Later 19th century

The assizes were transferred to the new Shire Hall in 1857 (Sloper 1876b) and the Great Hall used for assemblies and other public meetings. The two rooms were combined into one in 1863 by the removal of the partition and a new window (53) added, as described in a report in the *Somerset County Gazette* of 28/11/1863. Other improvements included the complete reflooring of the hall; this may have been the wooden floor removed in 1952. There is reference to other rooms that may have been in the Court Offices (as suggested by some of Spencer's room names in 1875): "waiting and dressing rooms, ladies' rooms and refreshment rooms and also places for actors musicians, performers &c". The "large gallery" at the western end was retained as well as a "long gallery upwards of 120 feet in length" that must have run the length of the south wall.

After the purchase by SANHS the hall continued to be used as before, until the museum expanded into it in the years around 1900. The galleries had been removed in 1875 (Hunt 1875, 3–4) and the colonnade was taken down in 1878 (Bush and Meek 1984, 16). Major repairs were undertaken in 1899 when the ceiling was removed, the windows reinstated, the floor repaired and the rainwater goods replaced. The "curved apse" at the east end of the hall was removed and decorative brackets placed under the roof beams (Bramble 1899, 2–3; SANHS minutes: 13/7/1899). Building control plans show that the privy at the east end was replaced with a new structure incorpor-

Figure 9.11: The west end of the Great Hall after the completion of the works of 1952/3. Somerset County Museum.

ating a heating system installed in a small basement (SRO D/B/ta/24/1/26/1709).

Phase 9: 20th century

The remaining five oval windows (142, 143, 144, 154, 155) were repaired with oak frames replacing the previous leadwork (Weaver 1904, 3) and in 1930 it was reported that the ceiling in the Grand Jury Room was collapsing (SANHS minutes: 8/1/1930). Later in the year, Stone and Francis architects were appointed to consider its future (SANHS minutes: 6/8/1930). There were no funds to implement their plans until William Wyndham offered to provide these but during the work in 1931 it was decided to demolish and build the Entrance Block with increased funds from Wyndham (SANHS minutes: 4/9/1931). In 1937 money was obtained to refloor the Great Hall but this would have to await the transfer of the exhibits into the Wyndham Galleries (Gray 1937, 13). This never happened as the floor still needed replacement in 1949 (Gray 1948–9, 21). Emergency repairs were undertaken to Window 54 in 1950 (SANHS minutes: 2/5/1950), replacing a wooden beam with steel and the entrance to the museum was moved to the Entrance Block (Seaby 1950, 3).

The major works of 1952/3 can be reconstructed from SANHS records (SANHS Office file C6), together with some photographs and plans. The programme was set out at a meeting on 28 May 1952 with work to start in the Somerset Room a month later. In the Great Hall the works comprised the replacement of the wooden floor with concrete, the construction of a false fireplace (209) to display a medieval overmantel between Windows 53 and 54 and the construction of a gallery and staircase with a new door into the Somerset Room (Figure 9.11). The plans were adjusted to accommodate the staircase that had been acquired from the old vicarage of St Mary Redcliffe in Bristol and in February 1953 the builders (Potters of Taunton) had "exposed an oak beam carrying the wall and roof over the centre bay of the Great Hall." It was agreed to replace both beams with steel joists encased in concrete. This was probably over Window 53, but it could not be confirmed as this area was not exposed in 2009. The works were preceded by the archaeological excavations reported by Radford and Hallam (1953).

The hall was retiled in 1954 × 1955 (Anon 1954/55, 5) and the beam engine installed in a pit in 1956 (see page 50). The Great Hall was fitted with a suspended ceiling below the beams at some time after February 1966, when the idea was suggested to save heating (SRO A/CNT/4/1), and before 1974 (Steve Minnitt, pers. comm.). In 1992 the eastern gallery that had held the coach was converted into toilets (see page 55 for the archaeological work).

Phase 10: 21st century

The works to form The Museum of Somerset were originally designed to have a minimal impact on the structure and buried archaeological deposits. The only contentious issue relating to the changes to the existing building concerned the 18th-century staircase in the Great Hall (Figure 9.11 on the previous page). This had only been added in 1952/3 but there was a great deal of opposition to its removal, both from English Heritage and SANHS. Eventually it was agreed that it could be removed if another building could be found to incorporate it, as long-term storage of the components was not seen as a suitable future for it. A building under repair in Kent was suggested by English Heritage but SANHS insisted that it should not leave the county. By then it had been dismantled, after detailed recording, and SANHS eventually sold it – it is now believed to be in Gloucestershire.

The new works included a steel-framed gallery at first-floor level supported on concrete beams founded on 10 (eventually 12) piles. It was intended that most of the concrete beam and service conduits would sit within the existing concrete floor. Once on site, however, the structural engineer insisted on deeper excavation (leading to the work described in Section 5.4 on page 76) and later that the structure be tied to the medieval walls with over 300 anchors. The 20th-century suspended ceiling was removed and one similar to the 1816 design reinstated. One roof truss (Truss 16) was removed and another (Truss 15) moved about 0.3m eastwards to allow the lift to be installed. On the south side, the 1931 passageways and 1992 toilets were replaced by wider structures, again founded on concrete beams supported by piles.

Chapter 10

The West Range

Chris Webster

The West Range comprises a two-storey block, possibly originally higher, whose northern end is structurally part of the Great Hall, running south from the hall to the Round Tower. Limited excavation in 2009 added little to our knowledge of the building but more was discovered when plaster was stripped. This principally showed the extent of the changes made by Hammet in *c.*1790.

10.1 Sources of Information

The West Range features in several early illustrations, notably the drawing of 1773 (Figure 2.1 on page 28) and Bampfylde's drawing of 1789 (Figure 2.2 on page 31). It appears in several 19th-century plans and photographs and some photographs were taken during the 1952–3 works.

10.2 The Undercroft (Room 23)

The north and west exterior (Figure 10.3 on page 192 and Figure 10.1 on the following page) of the West Range continues the design of the Great Hall north wall with shallow Hamstone buttresses rising from a Hamstone plinth. Buttress 446 is pock-marked with holes presumably from small-arms fire. These were examined by Richard Leese of the University of Huddersfield, who comments:

> After discussing the photos with Glenn [Foard], we [...] think they are impact scars. The fact that there is no obvious sign of radial fractures, or of spalling on the edge of the holes, the scatter and the apparent "cup" shape to them suggests that these are indeed musket impacts (on Buttress 446 at least). The slightly elongated nature of the holes may be due to weathering along the grain of the layers within the sandstone.
>
> The height is peculiar, as at nearly 4m, this is well above the average height that musket impacts tend to appear. The logical conclusion for this I feel is that there is a now vanished earthwork in front of the wall, and what we are seeing is shots that have passed over the fortification.

The impact scars are not visible elsewhere as most of the walls have been refaced with chert, probably by Hammet. Where original stonework survives it is predominantly lias, which appears to have been the usual material for the first phase.

The only opening that does not date to the 18th century is a small loop (240), which has been blocked internally when the wall was thickened (see below). From external examination it appears to have a simple narrow splay behind it extending to the face of the thickening 6 feet (1.8m) behind. Radford and Hallam (1953, 61) liken it to one discovered in the Hall (252, on page 168) but dimensions taken from their plan (SANHS 6066) do not seem to compare well with those of Window 240.

Internally the room is covered by a stone barrel vault 4.66m wide but as mentioned above the evidence of Window 240 shows that originally the room was 6.59m wide. The form of the ceiling previously is not known but may also have been a vault similar to those suggested in the Great Hall. The only early doorway is that to the south (59), with a segmental arch (restored in 1874: Spencer 1910, 40). Spencer's 1875 plan shows that a narrower door opening had been inserted on the south side; the construction of this may have caused the damage to the original arch. There

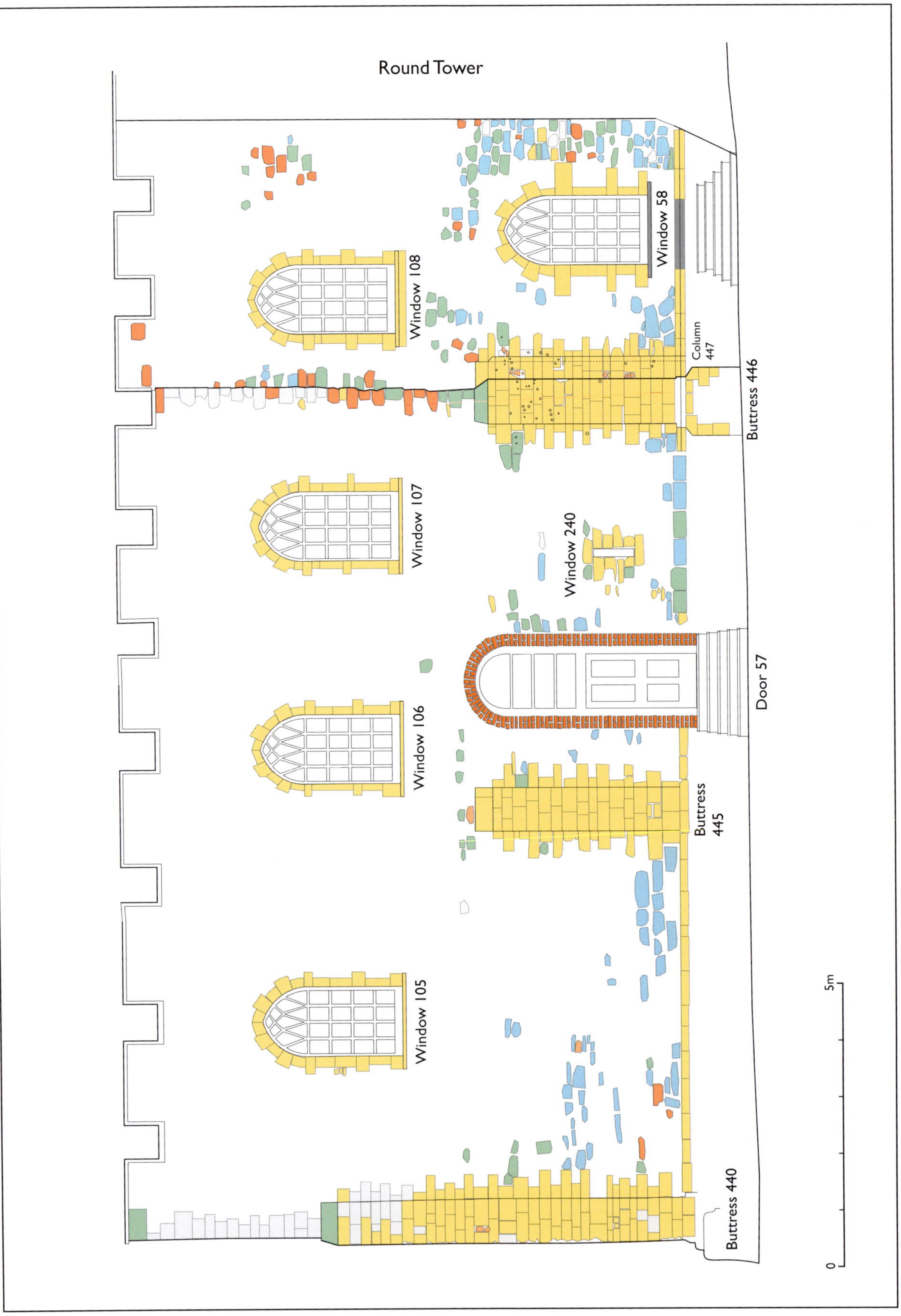

Figure 10.1: *Exterior elevation of the west wall of the West Range. See Figure 3 on page 4 for key to colours. Areas of small chert facing have not been recorded in detail.*

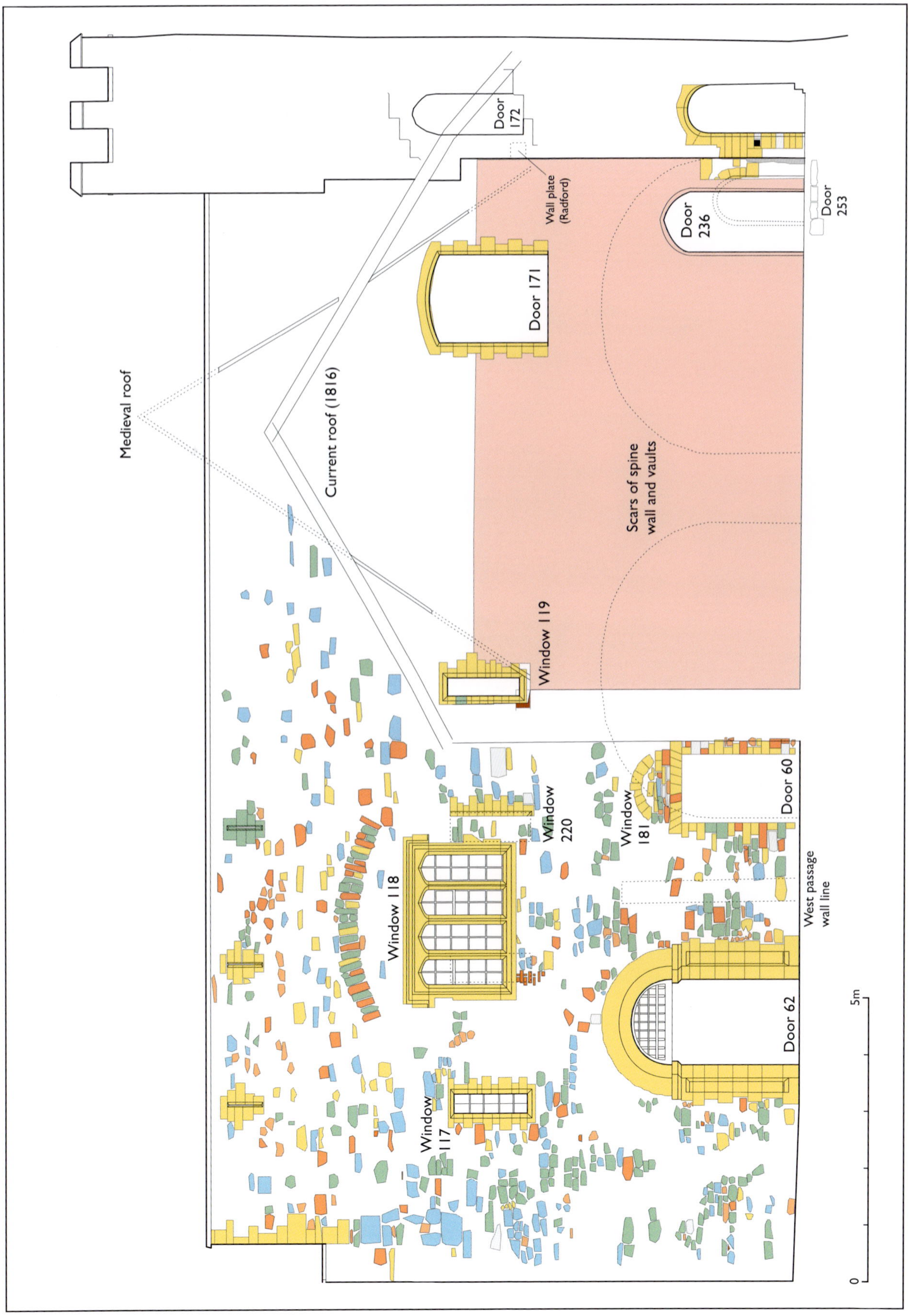

Figure 10.2: *Exterior elevation of the east wall of the West Range. The wall plate in the north wall is taken from SANHS A7-1e. See Figure 3 on page 4 for key to colours. Areas of small chert facing have not been recorded in detail.*

Figure 10.4: The interior west wall of the Undercroft in 1969. Door 57 is to the far left with Fireplace 238 central. Scale 6 feet (1.8m). Somerset HER image 29806.

Figure 10.3: The West Range c.1865–70 showing upper windows before the restorations of 1880. SRO A/BAV/18/5

is diagonal tooling on the original stonework, suggesting a 12th-century date and two drawbar holes, that on the east 1.1m deep and that on the west over 3m. Radford and Hallam (1953, 61) say that the original floor level can be seen in the sides of the opening "some 9 ins [23cm] higher than at present" and note that the door is not in the centre of the wall (see below, page 196).

The door (253) into the Great Hall is discussed on page 167 and brickwork visible in a photograph taken in 1969 before plastering (HER image 29807, Figure 10.5 on the facing page) supports the attribution to Hammet. The corresponding door (60) at the south end of the wall is more complex. It is not clear if there was ever a medieval door here but there was one in 1875, narrowed by a partial blocking on the south side. On the north side there was a wide splay, which survives, and there is evidence that the splay was originally wider, as part of the Great Hall wall is cut away on the diagonal (shown in Figure 5.3 on page 69) and in the Undercroft, the photograph (HER image 29807) shows a large, different area of masonry at this end. If not medieval this door

Figure 10.5: *The interior east wall of the Undercroft in 1969. Door 60 is to the far right and the brick surround to Door 236 is visible to the left. Somerset HER image 29807.*

may be associated with the construction of the Court Offices (see page 182), although brickwork might be expected if that were the case. In 1878 SANHS inserted a window (181) "in Norman style" (Spencer 1910, 44, Figs 6 and 7), later matched by Door 62 (page 197). The window has since been replaced by the door, probably in 1931 when the West Passage was made, but the head survives in the wall and became visible when the passage was demolished in 2009.

There are two features that are probably to be dated to Hammet's work: Window 56 in the north wall and Door 57 in the west wall. The head of the door is shown in 1789 (SANHS 3534, Figure 2.2 on page 31) and probably not in 1773 (SANHS 3504, Figure 2.1 on page 28). The window is shown in the watercolour of *c.*1800 (SANHS 3506, Figure 1.1 on page 13) and features the same brickwork quoins.

The west wall also contains two fireplaces in the thickened wall. The northern (358) has been inserted with brickwork above and to the north (HER image 29806, Figure 10.4 on the preceding page) and probably post-dates Hammet as no chimney is shown on SANHS 3535 (Figure 2.2 on page 31). The extent of the brickwork suggests that it may have replaced an earlier larger fireplace.

The quoins of the other fireplace (239) are of Hamstone, chamfered with roll stops near the floor, which Radford and Hallam (1953, 68) used to determine the medieval floor level. The stones below those with the stops are rough and the chamfer is roughly faded out near the top of the fireplace across a single piece of Hamstone. On both sides the stones below and above this top chamfered one are a different stone. The lintel is a reused piece of timber behind which is solid rubble bedded in cement. In the back of the fireplace is a smaller one formed of a large piece of partly shaped (probably broken) stone resting on two vertical pieces of burnt Hamstone. The wall around this, the back of the large fireplace, is very mixed with areas of slate masonry between large blocks of re-used Hamstone and occasional bricks. It is stepped back at the level of the top of the small fireplace lintel to form a shelf, and the upper part appears to have been roughly repaired with bricks set on edge in concrete. Radford and Hallam dated the fireplace to the 13th century with later replacement of the lintel at a higher level but this date was probably based on their date for the wall thickening. This is now dated to the 17th century; the unusual form may indicate some industrial purpose during the Civil War.

It was not possible to examine the walls in 2009 but photographs in the Somerset HER show them without plaster. The east wall (Figure 10.5 on the previous page) is built of large blocks of lias irregularly coursed, similar to those seen and described by Radford and Hallam (1953, 60) on the other side of the wall in the Great Hall. There is a change in the masonry about 1.5m up where it appears to slope back before the arch of the barrel vault begins. This might indicate the cutting back of the wall to insert the vault but it is also visible in the thickened west wall which is, presumably, the same build as the vault. At the south end and area of different masonry is visible, with smaller stones, browner mortar and without the backward slope. As mentioned above this may represent a wider Door 160 but the join appears to continue vertically up the barrel vault with no sign of an arch over the doorway.

The west wall (Figure 10.4 on page 192) appears identical to the east wall, south of Fireplace 238, but to the north lacks the backward slope and incorporates horizontal timbers to support wooden panelling. Smaller pieces of timber are also incorporated in the brickwork around the fireplace on this side. The incorporation of timbers is seen in Hammet's work in the south range, although there in brick, and may be associated with the insertion of Window 56. Another photograph (HER image 29808) shows timber embedded in brickwork in the adjacent north wall. Spencer's 1875 plan calls this a Dining Room in 1875 so it was probably well-appointed. The floor is shown in the photographs as having a central concrete area with gaps along the edges, presumably where display cases have been removed. This concrete was probably laid in 1952/3 and excavation in 2009 and early photographs indicate a suspended timber floor before this. No signs of medieval floor levels were encountered.

Figure 10.6: *Door 172. The AA carving is on the lowest right quoin. Scale 1m.*

Figure 10.7: *Detail of AA carving next to Door 172. Scale 20cm.*

10.3 The Stair Turret (Room 104)

At the north-east corner of the West Range is a circular stairway in a turret that projects slightly from the north wall. The upper part of this is vertical but at the bottom it is staggered eastwards by means of moulded corbels for no evident reason (see Figure 10.3 on page 192). The area has now been disturbed by the insertion of Window 56 by Hammet. The stair is entered on the ground floor by a short passage from the Great Hall (see page 168) and leads to the Somerset Room and then to the roof of the west range. The top of the tower was rebuilt in 1953 following structural problems (SANHS Office file C6). Five metres above the ground floor level is a blocked doorway (172, Figure 10.6, Figure 10.2 on page 191) which appears to have led onto the north wall of the Great Hall in Phase 2 but the irregular coursing of the masonry conversely suggests that the doorway is an insertion into the stairwell, probably reused from elsewhere. Low on the south jamb is a neat carving comprising the letters AA and a cross within a truncated triangular surround (Figure 10.7). There are traces of paint on the letters and cross and this together with the neatness and position might suggest that the engraving is associated with the masonry work rather than being graffiti, of which there is plenty in the upper parts of the stair.

Figure 10.8: The north end of the Somerset Room in 1884 when the roof was being replaced and the windows altered. The figure is William Bidgood, the curator (1862–1900). SANHS 12556.

10.4 The Somerset Room (Room 103)

The Somerset Room is a large room above the Undercroft and its position suggests that it formed part of the more private areas of the hall complex. The north wall is pierced by two tall windows (103, 104) of which 104 is a restoration, and 103 a rebuild, of 1884. The exterior prior to this can be seen in Figure 10.3 on page 192 where 103 is shown blocked and 104 replaced by a wider, Hammet-style window. The interior stonework appears to show that the openings of the two windows are of one build, together with the staircase door (170), although one window (104) has a flattened head and the other a slight point (Figure 10.8). There are traces, reported by Houghton Spencer (1910, 39) and still visible, that Window 104 had undergone previous changes. Door 170 has a deep drawbar hole like the one at the ground floor door (237) but the coursing of the stonework does not match that of the stairwell.

Apart from the door (171) inserted in 1952, the east side features a row of, originally, four windows (117, 118, 119, 220, Figure 10.2 on page 191). The only one surviving in anything like its original condition is Window 119, the northernmost, but this shows signs of alteration and may have functioned also as a door giving access to the top of the wall in the Phase 2 hall. The fact that the stone moulding for the hall roof is incorporated in one of the jamb stones indicates that this series of windows, and presumably the Somerset Room itself, are contemporary with this phase of the hall (1246–48). Spencer's 1875 plan shows Window 119 blocked and photographs (eg SANHS 12565) show it being restored in 1952.

The next window (220) was discovered and partially unblocked in 1952, although one jamb of the outside was still visible buried in the wall (Figure 10.2 on page 191); the rest was cut away by Window 118. This had also almost completely replaced another early window, a fragment of the south edge is just visible in Figure 10.9.

The replacement window (118) is larger, of four lights, and was probably inserted by Hammet using pieces of several earlier windows (dated to the early 16th century by Radford and Hallam 1953, 71). Examination showed that the cills were of a shelly limestone while the rest is Hamstone and that there are slight differences in the design of the window heads and their degree of wear.

Figure 10.9: Windows 117 and 118 in 1884. The edge of the 13th-century Window 118 is just visible in the centre. SANHS 12557.

Like other rectangular windows inserted at this time it probably had timber lintels; it now has a shallow stone arch. This was inserted in 1884 when the wall above it had to be rebuilt: "W Bigood [sic] told me that a gap wide enough for him to thrust his arm into had been found far extending down the wall of the geological hall on the court side, and that over the Elizabethan window looking into the court it would be necessary to pull down the wall as far as the top of that window" (SRO DD/SF/7/6/142).

Window 117 at the southern end appears to have been restored, probably in 1884 (Figure 10.9); its external coursing does not match that of Window 220, it appears in the photograph as a wallpapered alcove, and is described as "where the old water closet was" in Surtees' letter. Spencer's plan of 1875 shows the WC with some form of window in the alcove.

In the south wall, the modern doorway (156) was inserted by SANHS (Spencer 1910, 38, implies that this was in 1874 but 1884 is more likely) and replaced an earlier door (370) to the east that is shown on Spencer's 1875 plan. Door 370 was cut through the stone wall and had been neatened with bricks. It had a reused timber lintel with a brick relieving arch over, all suggesting Hammet's work.

Four large windows (105, 106, 107 and 108) were inserted in the west wall by Hammet and removal of the plaster above two (105, 106) showed that they were lined with brick, as was the wall above them which incorporated brick relieving arches. On the east wall similar brickwork was visible above stonework reaching 3.4m above the modern floor level. On this side, certainly, the brickwork can only be a lining as on the exterior the medieval roof dripmould rises 0.9m above the top of the internal brickwork. An area where plaster was not removed as it adhered well to the wall above Window 118 may represent the repairs of 1884.

As well as the roof replaced in 1884, which probably replaced one by Hammet, two subsequent roofs have been fitted. In 1957 it was found that the 1884 roof had dry rot and it was decided to replace it with a "steel-decked" one (Anon 1957/8). The SANHS accounts do not record payment for this work and it may have been undertaken by SCC who took over maintenance of the castle in 1958. This roof was itself replaced with sheet metal in 2009 supported on the earlier steel joists. The concrete floor was laid in 1952.

10.5 The Gray Room (Room 43)

The Gray Room (the St George Gray Memorial Library was opened in May 1965) lies to the south of the Undercroft beneath the south end of the Somerset Room (Figure 5.25 on page 93). Its north wall is formed by the hall block and the east and west walls can be seen (internally) to butt against it. The west wall forms the outer wall of the castle and is 6 feet thick, like the adjacent wall of the Undercroft before it was thickened, but it lies at a slight angle to the line of the west side of the Undercroft. Apparently buried by this wall, and visible only in the angle between the wall and Buttress 446, is what appears to be a semi-octagonal column (447) attached to the south wall of the Undercroft. It has the appearance of one side of an arched entrance and Radford and Hallam (1953, 62) suggested that it provided access to the foot of a stair rising to the first floor from the south-west. The coursing of 447 is identical to that of Buttress 446 suggesting that they are contemporary.

A door in the west wall, now Window 58, has brick lining, similar to that inserted by Hammet but it was not visible in 1789 (Figure 2.2 on page 31). It is shown as a door with Hammet-style glazing above in 1895 and steps and hand rails below (SANHS 12504). The change to a window must post-date 1951 when the stairs are recorded as being repaired to allow the use of the door (Seaby 1951, 3).

The interior of the east wall is parallel to the line of the west wall but the exterior continues the alignment of the Undercroft and so is thicker at the north end. During the conversion works to make the library, Hallam (1965) was able to show that this allowed the Somerset Room to be built without an awkward kink in its east wall. The doorway (62) in this wall appears to be an original feature, with diagonally dressed ashlar on its south reveal extending the width of the original wall. The other side has been widened, probably by Hammet, and the equivalent ashlar facing replaced by brick. The doors and surrounds were replaced by SANHS in a Norman style in 1885 (SANHS minutes: 8/5/1885); it is unfortunate that there are no illustrations of what was replaced, although Spencer (1910, 39) describes it as "modern woodwork" and it was presumably contemporary with the widening by Hammet. In the published note of the new work (Anon 1885, 3) it is described as the "east door to the keep of the castle; built of Ham Hill stone, in the simple Norman style of the 12th century", with little or no suggestion that it replaced anything similar.

Hallam discovered the foundations of the south wall (1031), which had been replaced by a large brick-faced arch (66) by Hammet. The wall was seen again in the Round Tower excavation in 1988 (see page 54) and also in 2009 (see page 92).

10.6 Structural Development

Phase 1: 11th–12th century

The Undercroft appears to be contemporary with the first phase of the Great Hall (see page 183) and therefore to have formed the Undercroft to the solar. It does not seem to have communicated with the Great Hall at this date and was presumably used as a store entered from the south. To this was added the Gray Room, possibly part of a stone replacement for a wooden external stair to the solar above (as seen at Stokesay: Munby and Summerson 2002, 7). Radford and Hallam (1953) suggest that the stone phase stairs "must have risen from the S.W., where an oblique angle of ashlar [...] may perhaps be explained as the jamb of an arch at the bottom of the stair" but this seems an unlikely medieval plan – the natural approach would have been from in front of the hall. The buried column or jamb (447) is hard to interpret; it appears to be contemporary with Buttress 446 and, if a jamb, would indicate a large gateway leading westwards immediately adjacent to the hall. It is also not clear why the Gray Room lies at an angle to the hall but it, and the supposed gateway, suggest a boundary presaging the line of the South Range.

Phase 2: 13th century

This phase probably comprises the 1248 entries in the accounts for "Expenses about the chamber" (Hunt 1971). The Somerset Room was extended southwards over the Gray Room and the east wall of the latter was thickened to accommodate this. Four windows were constructed along the east side looking over the roof of the new hall and two in the north wall, perhaps overlooking the garden. The accounts, however, indicate five windows in the chamber, which does not fit with the known six, unless the northern two (103, 104) counted as one and there were no windows in the west wall (no medieval windows were visible in 1773, Figure 2.1 on page 28). Access to the chamber was provided by a spiral staircase and a low door was made from the Hall to the Undercroft. The south end of the chamber presumably communicated with the upper room of the Round Tower, which appears from the accounts to have been the bishop's bedchamber, and to the chapel. The medieval door here has not been located.

It is likely that the building was originally taller, as suggested by the medieval roof line of the hall (Figure 10.2 on page 191), forming a corner tower like that at Bishop's Waltham. The evidence of the 1638 agreement (page 25), however, suggests that there were only two storeys at that date.

Phase 3: 17th–18th centuries

At some date, the west wall of the Undercroft was massively thickened and a substantial barrel vault inserted. Radford and Hallam (1953, 68) date this to the 13th century on the basis of Fireplace 239 but suggest no cause for the changes. A more likely circumstance for the work might be a need to protect the west wall from artillery fire during the Civil War. Toulmin (1791, 47) describes the building as having "a flat roof with parapet walls and embrasures for guns; but part of that roof, within the memory of man, has been taken down, and the present erected in its stead. On viewing the back part of it, there could be, lately, discerned some breaches made by cannon in the old wall." Toulmin was probably viewing the building from the courtyard and so "the back" is likely to have been the west side. He later describes Hammet as "rearing again the decayed walls" (Toulmin 1791, 52) which again may indicate that Hammet's rebuilding was more extensive than just internal conversions.

Toulmin's description is supported by the 1773 drawing (Figure 2.1 on page 28) which appears to show no pitched roof to the west range, if the roof behind it is that of the Great Hall at an incorrect angle. The drawing shows a single large window (probably in the position of Window 107) for which a date of *c.*1700 has been suggested (Thorp and Cox 2010, s3.5). This may indicate an earlier post-Civil War phase of repairs, possibly contemporary with the insertion of the oval windows in the Great Hall and the remodelling of Castle House in *c.*1700.

Hammet's changes were extensive and included the refenestration of all the rooms. Much of the west wall of the Somerset Room may have been rebuilt and the south wall of the Gray Room removed. Externally Hammet used a uniform style of Georgian gothic windows but in the walls facing the courtyard, re-used windows were inserted, as in the South Range. Toulmin reports that Hammet reroofed the Somerset Room, which was presumably the roof removed in 1884, but no pictures of this are known apart from a small area visible in SANHS 3506 (Section 2.2 on page 30). It is presumably the Somerset Room that Toulmin (1791, 49–50) describes as "formerly used as an assembly room, as a theatre, as an armory for the militia and for other purposes", the Undercroft as "a dungeon for prisoners" and the South Range as "rooms that have been occupied as tenements."

Phase 4: 19th century

At some point, the Somerset Room was divided into four bedrooms, each with a fireplace inserted into the wall, and an attic with four rooms inserted into the roof as shown on Spencer's 1875 plan. Savage (1822) reports that it was "occupied as a dwelling-house" and the changes are likely to have happened before 1838 when continuing problems in providing accommodation for visiting judges led to the purchase of the West Range by a company formed for the purpose (see page 32). No structural works are recorded, their expenses being limited to providing a caretaker and gaining income from letting the property with the proviso that the tenant had to vacate during the assizes and quarter sessions.

SANHS bought the castle in 1874 and used the West Range for their museum. Door 62 formed the entrance with displays in the Undercroft, Somerset Room and South Range. The curator was accommodated in the attic until the roof was replaced and new rooms provided for him in the Adam Library in 1884 (Spencer 1910, 38).

Phase 5: 20th century

The Somerset Room was connected to the gallery of the Great Hall in 1952 by the creation of Door 236 and the medieval windows on the east side were conserved and displayed. The roof was replaced *c.*1957. The room was used for museum display until 1996 when a steel mezzanine floor was inserted to hold the school loans collection. On the ground floor, Door 59 was narrowed and a wooden front door for SANHS's offices inserted, probably when SCC took over the running of the museum in 1958; it was later completely blocked for fire safety reasons. The Undercroft was used for visiting exhibitions and decorative steel security screens by the artist James Horrobin were installed behind all the doors and windows.

Phase 6: 21st century

The only structural work during the formation of The Museum of Somerset was the replacement of the roof of the Somerset Room and the opening up of Door 62.

Chapter 11

The South Range

Chris Webster

The South Range is traditionally dated to the 13th century, seemingly on the basis of the standard model of castle development as expounded by Thompson (1912) and others. There is little structural evidence, however, to point to a date before *c.*1500 when the roof was constructed. The range lies along the straight southern curtain wall of the courtyard from the Round Tower to the Gatehouse and then beyond, where it will be described as part of Castle House (Chapter 13).

11.1 Sources of Information

The South Range is well illustrated from the south in historical sources such as the drawings of 1773 (Figure 2.1 on page 28) and 1789 (Figure 2.2 on page 31) as well as numerous photographs.

11.2 The Round Tower (Rooms 46, 121)

The Round Tower is first mentioned in 1271 (see page 18) but may predate the start of the accounts in 1209 as its construction is nowhere recorded. It is not mentioned in the works described in 1246–49, which is curious considering its close relationship with the bishop's chamber and chapel constructed at that time.

Hallam's (1965) work showed that the tower had been built against the wall of the Gray Room (Figure 5.25 on page 93) and this relationship could also be seen on the outside where the Hamstone plinth of the west wall is covered by the wall of the tower. Recording in 1988 (see page 54) showed the foundations of thicker walls internally and although the outside is mostly chert-faced the presence of other stones suggests that the walls were only thinned on the inside. The internal foundations also indicate that the rear wall of the tower was almost straight. Spencer (1910, 39) reported that the other side of the foundation was seen when the staircase was rebuilt in 1910 and was "very wide".

The tower is currently a similar height to the adjacent curtain walls but this may reflect alterations made in the Civil War, when all the walls may have been lowered to better mount cannon. Any evidence will have been removed in the late 18th-century rebuilding but against this suggestion is the 1638 agreement that only refers to two storeys (see page 25). The walls and window openings in the lower room (46) can be seen in the 1988 photographs (Figure 4.3 on page 55) to be brick-lined with embedded timbers to support the panelling, characteristic of Hammet's work, and examination (in 2009) of the upper parts within the roof space of the South Range again showed brickwork. This is consistent with the evidence of the 1773 drawing (Figure 2.1 on page 28) which appears to show the upper part of the tower missing and the rest an ivy-covered ruin with one large window opening. By 1789 (Figure 2.2 on page 31) the tower had been rebuilt with large windows to match those in the Somerset Room (103). The present conical roof is not shown and so it is probably a later addition.

11.3 The Lobby, Landing and Dark Room (Rooms 54, 120, 122)

The Lobby (Room 54)

The only excavation (Trench X, see page 92) did not reach pre 20th-century levels but the removal of asbestos sheeting and some plaster was informative (Figure 11.2 on page 201). The asbestos had been used to dry-line the wall in 1939 (SANHS minutes: 1/2/1939). Brickwork 352 formed the soffit of the arch (66) above the foundations (1031) of the east wall of the Gray Room and incor-

Figure 11.1: *Elevation of the north wall of the South Range. See Figure 3 on page 4 for key to colours. Areas of small chert facing have not been recorded in detail. The stone of the relieving arches shown grey appears to be tufa but was not closely examined.*

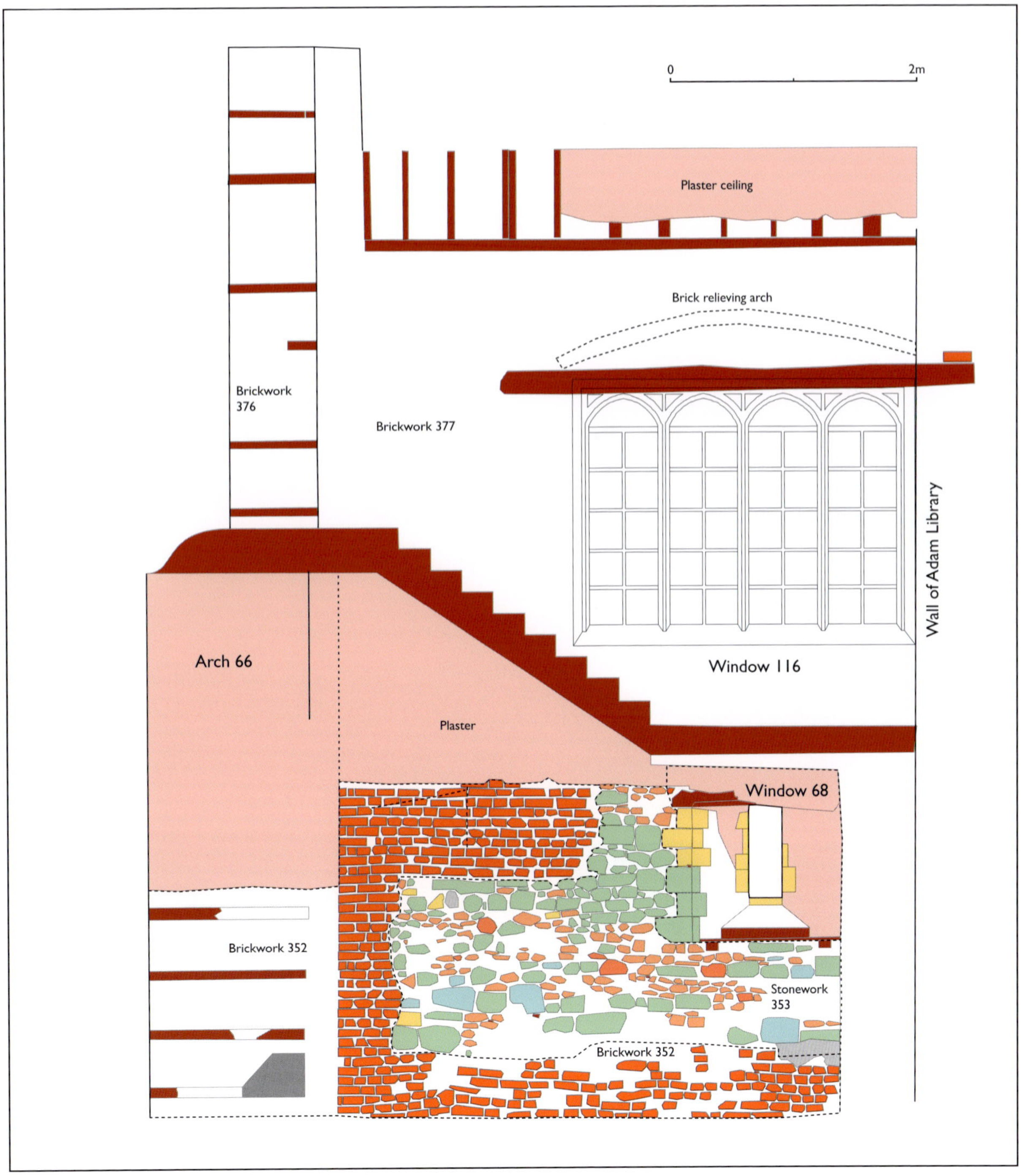

Figure 11.2: *Elevation of interior of north wall of South Range in Rooms 54 and 120. See Figure 3 on page 4 for key to colours.*

porated horizontal timbers (badly rotted) to hold panelling of a style associated with Hammet's work. The brickwork between the timbers was very rough but further eastwards in the adjacent wall it was much neater with one brick extended into the area between each timber to key the work together. The brickwork extended eastwards at the head of the wall towards Window 68 and, at the foot of the wall, to the end of the room.

A similar configuration is seen on the floor above with Brickwork 376 covering an extension of the east wall of the Somerset Room (103) and containing timbers, with continuous brickwork (377) to the east. There is a clear vertical joint at the change of alignment between the two areas but both the bricks and mortar appear identical. The topmost timber has, at its eastern end, a further timber aligned into the wall as if continuing around a corner formed by the vertical edge. This may suggest that Brickwork 377 is slightly later, which would fit with the known progress of Hammet's works (see Adam Library below). Brickwork 377 incorporates Window 116, another early 16-th century window (Radford 1954, 17) inserted by Hammet as shown by the lintel of reused timbers and a brick relieving arch over.

Below, on the ground floor, is an area of rubble stonework (353) incorporating Window 68. The stone is predominantly North Curry sandstone but there has been a great deal of patching, including with chert but no bricks. The window appears to be contemporary with this stonework, with North Curry stone jambs at the base and Hamstone at the top of the inner opening. The reveal is rubble similar to the wall to the west and the exterior formed of moulded Hamstone (Figure 11.1 on page 200). The top of the reveal is formed by a timber lintel, chamfered and stopped at the jambs suggesting that it may be original. It was however set lower than the head of the window externally, probably to accommodate the floor of the room above. The evidence suggests that the window is medieval as it seems to be contemporary with the stone walling and appears to be too high to fit the current first floor level. The lintel may be original and have been lowered.

On the ground floor, the east wall, although of medieval proportions, could be seen to butt against the north wall and was part of the changes to the Coin Room made in 1910 (SANHS minutes: 18/3/1910; Weaver 1910, 4–5). These also saw the construction of a concrete staircase curving round the back of the tower to reach the landing, previously reached by an angled staircase of two flights. This partly cut-off the southern part of the room which was converted into a lavatory (45), reached by a passage under the stair, and a store (44). The dividing wall between these split Window 164/165 to provide light to each. The history of this window is not known but it is probably visible in 1789 (Figure 2.2 on page 31) and may pre-date Hammet.

The landing and stairs (Room 120)

Upstairs, the upper flight of the pre-1875 staircase survived, joining the landings outside the Somerset Room and Adam Library. It was strengthened with steel in 2009. Spencer's 1875 plan shows the previous arrangement of the lower stairs, which reached a small landing and then rose by three steps to reach the landing outside the door (449) to the Adam Library on the north, and also by three steps inside the Dark Room (122) to reach the same level there. The top two of these steps were seen below the floor in the Dark Room in 2009. These steps cross a second doorway (450) into the Adam Library, an awkwardness that suggests that the staircase is not contemporary with Hammet's changes. The upper landing is shown in 1875 with a large circular skylight and pieces of curved moulded plaster were found during repairs in 2008. It is not known when it was removed.

The Dark Room (Room 122)

The Dark Room is set in the thickness of the curtain wall and was probably constructed by Hammet as there is a brick lining to the south wall. The brickwork incorporates a quatrefoil window (174) which appears to have been made from the reused heads of other windows. In the 1789 illustration (Figure 2.2 on page 31) the wall head appears damaged and ivy-covered here, which may provide a reason for rebuilding. Removal of the ceiling in 2009 allowed the recording of the chapel roof (see Section 7.4 on page 140) and also showed brickwork at high levels in the south and east walls, together with large beams inserted to support the medieval roof. It is not clear how the roof was supported while the wall was damaged but some of the beams may have been emergency supports. Spencer shows this as a bedroom in 1875 and it was fitted out for Gray to use as a darkroom following his appointment in 1901 (SANHS minutes: 12/7/1901).

11.4 The Coin Room (Room 40)

So called because it housed the museum collection of coins. It is entered by an apparently medieval doorway (69, Figure 11.1 on page 200) from the courtyard to the north but excavation in

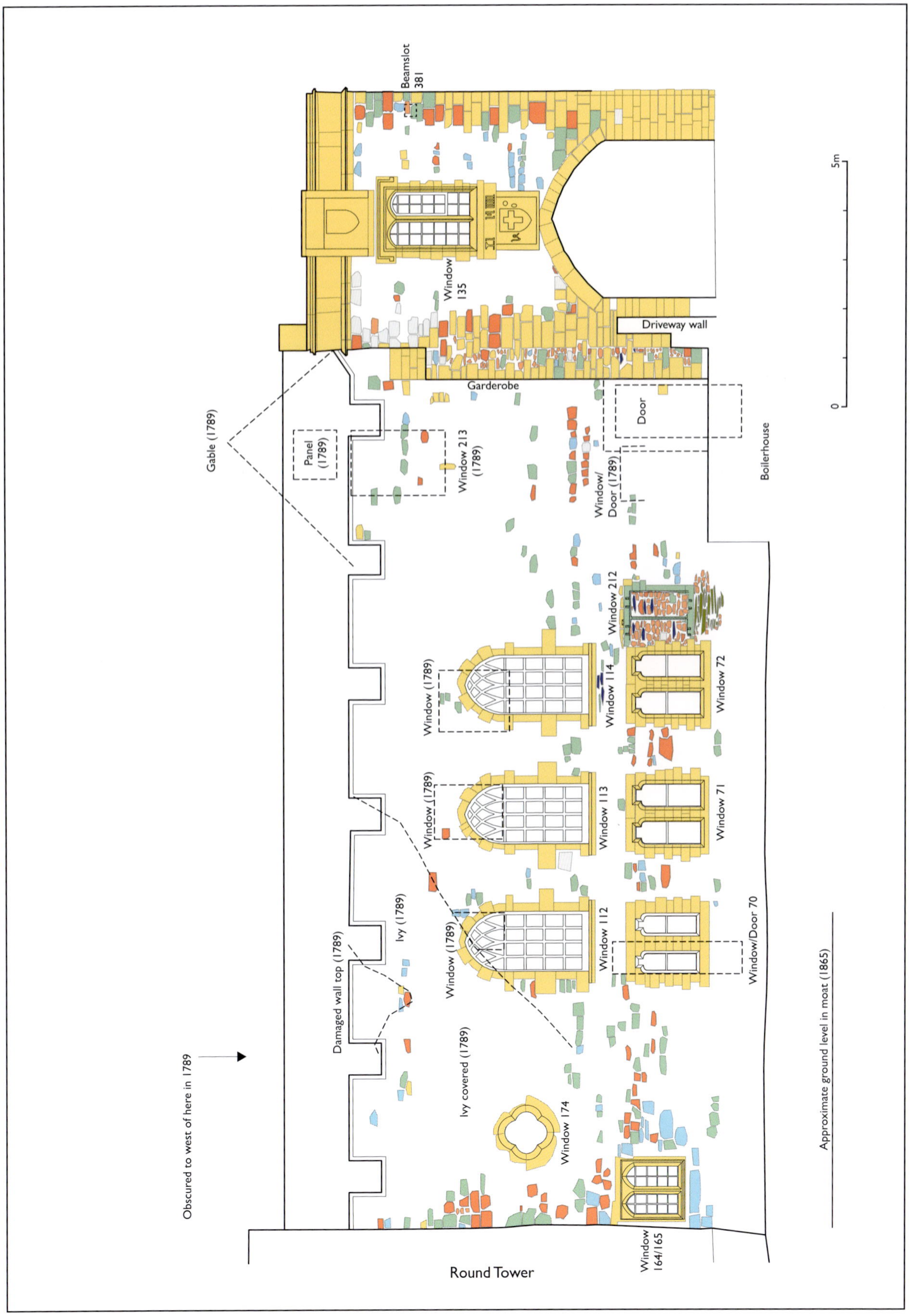

Figure 11.3: *Elevation of the south wall of the South Range. Features dated 1789 have been drawn from a rectification of Bampfylde's drawing (Figure 2.2 on page 31), other features have been added from Sloper's photographs. See Figure 3 on page 4 for key to colours. Areas of small chert facing have not been recorded in detail.*

1972 (Clements 1984) showed, from the foundations that were omitted below the door, that it had originally been wider on the east side and had been infilled with brick. Spencer (1910, 41) likened it in form to Door 59 between the Undercroft and Gray Room, which would suggest an 11th- or 12th-century date but as it has been altered it could have been inserted at any date; the brickwork indicates a post-medieval change, probably by Hammet, to match Window 68. A sketch (SANHS 13158), probably of 1878, shows the door blocked but this may be a mistake as the key simply refers to this as "doorway".

The two windows in the north wall (221, 222) appear to have been inserted by Hammet (like Windows-116 and 118) with brick surrounds and reused-timber lintels. To the west of them is a blocked window (448) with a similar lintel over. The angles of the reveals suggest a single light but they are not equally angled, which may indicate alteration of an earlier opening (Figure 11.1 on page 200). On the outside the entire wall has been refaced with chert but internally, where visible when the plaster was chased for cables, is a mixture of brickwork patches and dressed ashlar.

The south wall, which is over 6 feet (1.8m) thick, has three windows (70, 71, 72) with a further blocked window (212) visible on the exterior. The earliest of the three is Window 72, inserted in 1874 (Spencer 1910, 42–3, Fig. 8, Fig. 9). The window was inserted in an existing reveal, shown on Spencer's 1875 plan, but he does not mention any evidence of the previous window. Nothing is shown in 1789 (Figure 2.2 on page 31) or in Jeboult's photograph of 1865 (Museum 1191/2). The other two windows were inserted in 1910 (Spencer 1910, 39) to match the first. Window 70 replaced a narrow door that had probably been made from a window; the head of one or the other is visible in 1789. Gray recorded the situation before the changes (SANHS 3512), his plan shows the door on the west side of the position of the later window with a fireplace set on the diagonal to the east of it in the thickness of the wall. His plan indicates that the thickness of the wall here (between Windows 70 and 17) was really thinner with the fireplace sitting in an additional piece of masonry. The chimney for this fireplace was found in the parapet in 2009. Window 71 was also inserted into an existing reveal as shown on Spencer's and Gray's plans but again nothing is visible on earlier illustrations of the exterior.

Next to, and partly cut away by, Window 72 are the remains of a stone window frame (212) buried in the wall. The frame is North Curry stone and is badly weathered and damaged. There were two lights, each with a square head. Each light has the remains of two sockets at top and bottom to hold square bars on the diagonal. Above the window is a line of reused Hamstone blocks, one of which appears to be a moulding for the top of an arrow slit. This window does not appear to be shown on the 18th-century illustrations but there could be some confusion with Window 211 (see Section 11.6 on page 206). The provision of bars may identify this area as the bridewell listed in 1638 (see page 25).

The east wall, which is of brick, contains an infilled contemporary fireplace (244) with a door (73) into the strongroom lobby (Room 41) on the north side and a round-headed niche (245) of unknown purpose on the south.

The room was investigated in 1972 when building works to form the Local History Library were monitored following the discovery of human bones. Further burials were discovered under the floor (see page 240) and a well associated with a brick drain was recorded (Clements 1984, 26–8). The north wall was seen to be much rebuilt in brick, the original surviving only up to 0.5m high. A bricked-up window (probably Window 448) was recorded. Archive drawings are mentioned but it has not proved possible to find these amongst the Western Archaeological Trust's papers (SRO DD/WAT/16).

Limited work was undertaken during the Museum of Somerset project, some plaster was chased for electric cables and the ceiling, which was found to be triple boarded, was replaced. The chasing showed only brickwork in the south wall.

11.5 The Adam Library (Room 123)

This room, originally the chapel, was converted into a dining room for the judges and later partitioned into bedrooms. It is entered by a door (449) at the north end of the west wall, which is timber framed with brick infill. There is a similar door (450) at the south end of the wall. Examination of the roof (see Section 7.4 on page 140) showed evidence of an earlier partition slightly to the west of this wall which appeared to predate Hammet's changes as it would have crossed Window 116.

The south wall is the curtain wall of the Inner Ward and is pierced by three Hammet-style windows (112, 113, 114). These windows are not shown in 1789 (Figure 2.2 on page 31), when the similar windows in the Somerset Room and Round Tower are visible and must have been inserted later. They replaced three rectangular windows shown in 1773, the westernmost of which was ivy covered. Only the eastern is

Figure 11.4: *The blind arcading in the Adam Library during repairs, probably in the 1970s. SANHS Hawtin 2.*

Figure 11.5: *Door 248 at the south-east corner of the Adam Library.*

shown glazed, the others appearing to be walled up. Internally, chasing the plaster for electricity cables showed brickwork to about 2m high with stone above.

The east wall can be seen from the outside (Figure 11.1 on page 200) to have formed the end wall of the building and probably contained the east window of the chapel. It is now pierced by a small door (248, Figure 11.5) at the south end leading to a passage (Room 124) partly cut into the curtain wall. Radford (1954, 17) dated the doorway to the 15th-century on stylistic grounds and suggested that it led to the sacristy. Spencer's plan of 1875 shows the passage blocked at the west end forming a "closet" in the next room (Room 125). Limited examination when the plaster was being chased for cables in 2009 showed the ends of laths that would have continued the wall line across the doorway. The laths were supported by battens fixed to a plastered stone wall that aligned with the stone door frame. The lath and plaster aligned with, and is probably contemporary to, the Adam-style fireplace. The moulded frame on the south side of the doorway is buried in the south wall which has been cut back by 20cm to reach the opening suggesting some severe constraint to its location, possibly the chapel east window, to the north. It is not clear, however, where the doorway originally led as it will be suggested below that Room 125 was a late addition after the east window of the chapel had gone out of use.

The north wall is now occupied internally by a blind arcade of three arches with applied, wooden, fluted columns between them. These presumably replaced the chapel windows and on the outside (Figure 11.1 on page 200) can be seen three relieving arches (412, 413, 414) of a white stone (possibly tufa, not seen elsewhere in the castle) mixed with some Hamstone. An area of Hamstone below the west end of 414 may mark the side of the window. To the west a further relieving arch (415) seems to be a smaller span over a predecessor to Window 116. The presence of the relieving arches suggests that the windows themselves had flat tops, and therefore were not those of the 13th-century chapel. The rear wall of the arcade appears to be brick but was only seen at the lowest level when skirting boards were removed. The wall next to Door 120 was seen to be brick from floor to ceiling. A photograph taken during earlier repairs shows that the round arches have chamfered, ashlar quoins behind the wooden mouldings with the soffits pecked for plaster (Figure 11.4). They also show that this wall is lined with lath and plaster in the same way as the east wall.

Analysis of the paint in the room (Hassall 2010) indicated that the present woodwork is not 18th-century; it may be as late as the 1910 library conversion, which also involved fitted bookcases. Originally the room had a dado rail, above which the wall and ceiling was painted with a greyed-white soft distemper. There was no paint below the dado, indicating panelling or papering. The ceiling received a second coat of greyed-white distemper before three later coats that were tinted blue with a pigment invented in 1828. Splashes of paint from the dado rail indicated two phases of stone-coloured oil paint. None of the surviving woodwork was found to have been painted with this colour indicating either an extremely thorough stripping or new wood. In the absence of chemical stripping the latter is far more likely. The doors, windows and skirtings and arches were primed with a buff primer before being painted with a plain grey oil paint based on lead white. The ceiling was painted off-white but there was no paint on the walls; scraps of lining paper suggest that they were wallpapered.

The next scheme used zinc-based oil paints (indicating an early 20th-century date), with a two-tone grey scheme on the joinery and off-white ceiling. The windows (only) were repainted white at some time before the final mid 20th-century pink and white scheme was applied. The original grey schemes were not considered suitable for a colourful new museum and were not recreated.

The roof

The west end of the medieval roof was examined by Stuart Blaylock (Section 7.4 on page 140) who suggests that it dates to the 15th or early 16th centuries. Unfortunately no closer dating was possible as no timbers with enough growth rings for dendrochronology were used in the structure. There is no mention of the construction of the roof in the pipe rolls but there is reference to carpenters erecting the reredos in the chapel in 1494 which may be part of the same work programme. The roof extended over both the Adam Library and the Landing but its junction with the Round Tower was not clear due to damage and later rebuilding. There are also some discrepancies between the plan produced in 1960 (SANHS 6071) and the 2009 study, in the spacing of the moulded rafters. The two rafters seen in 2009 were 1.8m (6ft) apart but the plan shows all the rafters evenly spaced at 1.65m (5ft 6in). The west wall of the Adam Library and the next rafter west are shown in the correct location, so it is possible that the two examined in 2009 (and the possible missing one further west) are the exceptions, expanded to make the roof fit the space. It is also possible that the architect made only a few measurements and then spaced the rafters equally. The east end, beyond a now roofed-over chimney, is more recent and is discussed below.

11.6 The Strong Room and Rooms Above (Rooms 42, 125 and 206)

The strong room was built in 1910 for SANHS and obscures any earlier features of the room. It comprises a brick vaulted chamber built within the earlier walls leaving a corridor to the north and a service duct to the south that communicated with a boiler room built in the moat at the same time. The northern corridor is accessed by a door (75) from the courtyard that matches the main gate arch (409). This door is not shown on Spencer's plan of 1875, the area inside being occupied by a staircase. The door is shown walled up in a photograph of a similar date (SRO A/BAV/18/3, Figure 11.6 on page 208) but it had been opened up by the time of the sketch of 1878 (SANHS 13158) and can be seen in a photograph of *c.*1880 (Figure 11.8 on page 210). The situation in 1836 is less clear, Buckler appearing to show the door walled but not flush with the wall (see Figure 12.2 on page 215). While the door frame may be contemporary with the gate arch, it is not well coursed with the surrounding masonry and may be an insertion. It is not clear from the photographs whether the frame was replaced when the doorway was opened but it is probably visible in the earlier photograph. To the east of the door is a blocked window (403), visible as a cupboard internally and as an area of altered masonry on the outside. Below this is a plinth with a moulded Hamstone top that starts at the junction with the east end of the chapel block and is continued eastwards to Castle House beyond the gateway.

On the south side, Spencer's plan of 1875 shows the room as "scullery" with a window in deep reveals and two fireplaces: one in the east wall and one in the west reveal of the window. The window may be shown in 1789 (Figure 2.2 on page 31) but this may be Window 212. It is certainly visible in 19th-century pictures, such as SANHS 12506 of 1864 × 1874. By the time a photograph was published by Gray (1907) it had been converted to a door, apparently with a brick surround but was infilled when the boilerhouse was built in 1910 and nothing is now visible.

Examination of the stonework above the ground floor on the north side shows that it has been inserted between the gatehouse and the chapel block, unlike the situation on the ground floor which appears contemporary with the gateway. This area may have been left open when the gatehouse was built in order not to block an east window of the chapel.

The infilling appears to pre-date Hammet's time as this area appears with a roof and window visible on the south side in 1773 (Figure 2.1 on page 28). The two north-facing windows (115, 134) are not identical and appear similar to those in the late 15th-century Castle House. Others in this style, however, are attributed to Hammet's changes (such as 116, 221 and 222) and Window 115 does have a timber lintel on the inside, another Hammet characteristic. As this part of the castle was little altered in 2009, no further information could be obtained.

On the first floor, Room 125 is reached by the passageway from the Adam Library and also by a cast iron spiral staircase from the corridor below, inserted as part of the 1910 changes (SANHS 6017). In 1875 the only access was by a staircase of two straight flights from the "scullery" below, the passage being blocked at the west end and used as a cupboard. There was then no access to the floor above from this room but Spencer's plan does show the top of a circular stair within the thickness of the south wall emerging into Room 206. By his 1910 plan (SANHS 6024) the base of the stair is shown in Room 125 but not the upper part. In 1937 Gray reported the discovery of a blocked spiral staircase between the two rooms that he suggested might allow the library to be extended that way (SANHS minutes: 6/1/1937). The rights to use these rooms had been bought from the Manor of Taunton Deane in January the previous year, the records being transferred to the County Record Office. In December 1937 it was reported that space had been cleared to build a new wooden staircase which was completed the following January. (SANHS minutes: 1/12/1937, 5/1/1938).

The lower part of the stair is within the thickness of the wall but the south wall of Room 206 is thinner than that below and it emerges under the rafters of the roof. The north wall is also thinner and contains a probably reused window (134). Early illustrations (such as Figure 2.1 on page 28 and Figure 2.2 on page 31) show that this roof originally had a gable on the south end with a ridge running north to meet the main ridge. It is not clear if this pattern was repeated on the north side as this is not illustrated until 1836 (Figure 12.2 on page 215) when no gable is shown. At this date the south side is shown with a hipped end to the main roof line in this area (SANHS Buckler A) and this is also shown in one of Jeboult's photographs (SRO L/2205). In 1789 the gable is shown with a large window (Figure 11.3 on page 203, Window 213) into which the staircase has probably been built. Above this is shown a coat of arms that Toulmin (1791, 49) says "are the same as those on the porch of the hall, with the addition of the letters R. H. for Robert Horn" and include the same date: 1577. Jeboult says in his scrapbook (SRO L/2205) that this was a sundial and that it was removed to Castle House when the gable was removed by Hammet.

The present roof, which is no longer hipped but ends with a small gable added to the top of the gate tower, is undated but pre-dates 1933 aerial photographs (for example SANHS 13249).

On the exterior of the south wall, next to the gatehouse is what appears to be a buttress that has caused speculation in the past. Sloper (1876a) says that "Mr Spencer considered the buttress to the left of the archway was older than the rest of the building (Exchequer) and had been cut down but I found this buttress hollow and no doubt it had been used for the weight which balanced the portcullis." Vivian-Neal and Gray (1940, 61) also suggested that it might have been a survivor from an earlier gatehouse. Examination shows that the structure is clearly a later addition as it has been tied into cuts into the gatehouse quoins, and stonework repairs in 2009 confirmed Sloper's statement that it was hollow, with a rectangular shaft for most of its height. At the top it was plastered into a circular cross-section and the remains of a timber seat was visible when looking up. This privy appears to have been adjacent to the (now blocked) window within the gable of the room. When it was added and when made redundant are not clear but it is shown, as it is now, with a chamfered capping, on the earliest illustration (Figure 2.1 on page 28) indicating a pre-Hammet date. While it might appear strange to site a garderobe chute immediately adjacent to the entrance to the Inner Ward, discharging sewage into the moat, Johnson (2002, 43) notes that this is not unusual in castles. Indeed, in many cases it is more explicit, with garderobes designed to pour sewage down the walls and moat banks in very clearly visible locations and he suggests that it may be a presentation of the castle as a vast body, a common medieval social metaphor.

11.7 The Inner Gatehouse

The inner side of the Gatehouse appears to be of one build with the ground floor of the south range to the west and also with Castle House (Chapter 13) to the east. All these date to the late 15th century. Toulmin (1791) provides the earliest description concentrating on the coats of arms on the inner and outer faces. The account is a little confusing but seems to say that both sides feature the arms of Thomas Langton (bishop 1493–1501) and that the outer also features an inscription, the

Figure 11.6: *The north side of the gatehouse before the removal of the courtyard buildings in* c.1874. *Door 75 is shown blocked at this date and there appears to be a water tank on the roof. SRO A/BAV/18/3.*

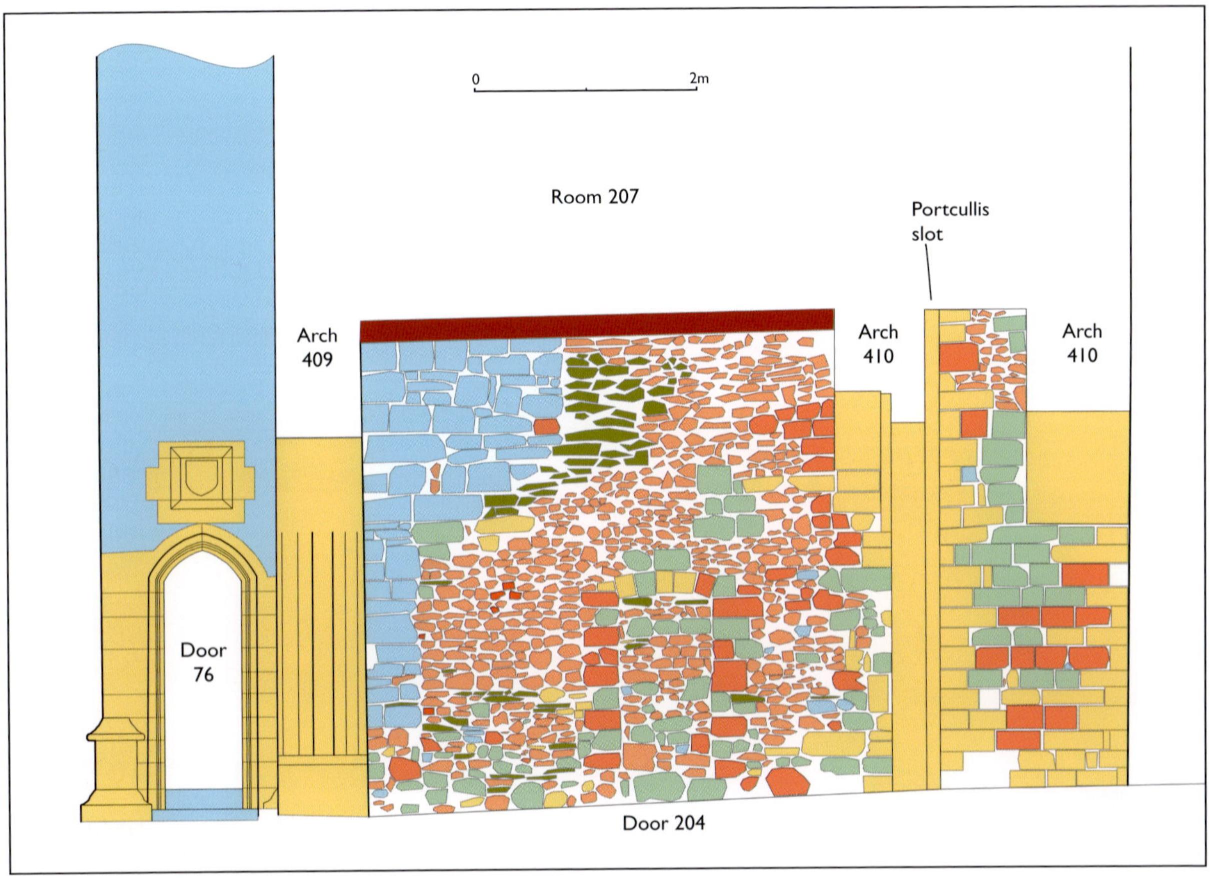

Figure 11.7: *Elevation of the east interior of the Gatehouse. See Figure 3 on page 4 for key to colours.*

bishop's name and the date 1495 (Spencer 1910, 44, read this as 1496, as did Leversedge, SANHS 3515). Above these, on the outer side, were the royal arms of Henry VII (king 1485–1509). Savage (1822) adds that the arms lie above and below the window (213) and also clearly states that the arms on the north side also have the date 1495, though this is contradicted by Leversedge's elevation drawing.

This seems to be the current situation, although the arms on the south front are very eroded. It is also evident that the arms have been moved at some time as Langton's inscription sits uncomfortably on the arms with no border and the royal arms poke above the top of the tower, again lacking the original border. The earliest picture (Figure 2.1 on page 28) shows the panels for the arms, but no detail, with a different window from that currently in place between them and lacking the ornamental Hamstone band around the top of the tower. Bampfylde's drawing of 1789 (Figure 2.2 on page 31) shows the same but with more detail. It is not clear when the window was changed and the ornamental band added but they are both on Leversedge's elevation of 1853 (SANHS 3515). They may be part of Hammet's work on the South Range in *c.*1790. The original window is not mentioned by Toulmin (1791) but was there in 1773 (above), the awkward spacing of the arms, squeezed between arch, window and wall top suggests that it was inserted after the arms, which had to be moved to accommodate it.

The outer arches of the gate are plainer than the inner leading to the suggestion by Spencer (1910, 44) that they remained from an earlier gate. Vivian-Neal and Gray (1940, 61) dated the inner of the two outer arches to the mid 15th century and suggested that the outer arch is a later reconstruction. There is a portcullis slot in front of the gate but no sign of drawbar holes. The passage is not vaulted but has a flat plaster ceiling. The west wall of the gate passage is fairly featureless with roughly coursed lias masonry to the upper parts and more mixed rubble below. There are suggestions of a blocked doorway.

There is certainly a blocked door (204) on the east side, very roughly made with large stone blocks and set into an area of random rubble walling, mostly of chert (Figure 11.7). This contrasts with the neat ashlar (of Ham and red sandstone, some clearly reused) to the passage outside the gate. The inner (north) end of the

Figure 11.8: *The north side of the gatehouse before the replacement of the stair turret in 1883 and after the removal of the courtyard buildings in c.1874. The figure is William Bidgood, curator from 1862–1900, whose pose may suggest that Door 75 is newly unblocked. SANHS 12507.*

passage is neater and mostly constructed of large lias blocks consistent with the rebuilding of the buildings to east and west. The gate passage is asymmetric in plan at the south end, with the inner arch disappearing into the wall on the east but supported on a column to the west. A similar but slighter asymmetry is noticeable as the passage walls meet the arch at the north end; here the west side is more buried. Jeboult in 1867 only recorded foundations for the outer arches (see Figure 2.3 on page 33).

Toulmin (1791, 48) says that the room (207) above the gate was used by the grand jury until two years before he was writing. It is entered by a door from Room 206 and also from the stair turret. The window (213, above) opens to the south and there is a blocked window (404, Figure 11.1 on page 200 and Figure 11.8 on the preceding page) to the north. The window is shown much more clearly by Buckler (Figure 12.2 on page 215 surrounded by a frame, unless he is showing a coat of arms in this position. The room is divided by a low wooden partition with a gate at the east end and a bench along the south side. Until 1936, this and Room 206 were used to store the manorial records of Taunton Deane and were known as the Exchequer but in Toulmin's time this was elsewhere as he says "Besides these appartments, there is in the castle a strong room called the Exchequer in which the records of Taunton-Dean land are reposited". The records may have been moved to accommodate the grand jury as there is evidence (below) that they were here in 1581.

Repointing work in 2009 above the roof of Castle House discovered a large beam slot (381) running north-south within the east wall at the top of the tower. It was not possible to measure with much accuracy due to the limited access afforded by the removal of one stone, but the approximate position where it would have emerged on the south front of the tower is shown on Figure 11.3 on page 203. It appeared too substantial to be a putlog hole both in cross-section and length (over 1m) and was probably to support a timber hoarding across the front of the gate.

The Stair Turret

The stair turret was rebuilt in 1883 (Anon 1883; 1884) but its previous form can be seen in an early photograph (Figure 11.8 on the facing page). It appears to be a later addition to the gatehouse as it breaks the symmetry of the moulded string course near the head of the wall (Figure 11.1 on page 200). This string course is not at the same height as the Hamstone band on the front of the gate (suggested above to have been added by Hammet) and may be contemporary with the inner wall of the gatehouse.

As well as giving access to the room above the gate the stair is also linked by a short passage in the east wall of the gatehouse to Room 118 in Castle House and Spencer's plan of 1875 shows that this was also the arrangement before rebuilding. Above the entrance door (76) is a stone plaque recording the rebuilding with the arms of the Pretor-Pinneys and the inscription "Restituit AD 1883". This seems to have replaced a small pointed window (see Figure 11.8 on the facing page, partly obscured by shadow) above a square headed door. Leversedge's elevation (SANHS 3516 of 1853) suggests that the window has been inserted, possibly with a brick surround. The elevation lacks one of the two windows visible in the photograph as it was hidden by buildings that were omitted from the elevation, but not the plan, by Leversedge (see Figure 12.2 on page 215 which also shows this). Both elevation and photograph show that the top of the tower was composed of different stone (perhaps Morte slate) to the large lias blocks used below.

Julian Orbach (pers. comm.) suggests that the doorway appears to be no earlier than the 17th century and further evidence for a late date for the stair tower is given in a reference of 1581 given by Vivian-Neal and Gray (1940, 75, quoting Whitty 1934) referring to problems of access to the Exchequer caused by decay in the "chapple chamber"; the implication being that this was the only way in at that date. The existence of these problems may have led to the construction of the stair.

11.8 Structural Development

Phase 1: pre-15th century

In the absence of more investigation it is not possible to say a great deal about the early development of the south range. It is clear from the foundations seen in 1988 (Section 4.4 on page 54) that the Round Tower is later than the West Range but nothing is known about the construction of the curtain. It has been linked in the past (by, for example, Radford 1954, 13) to an account entry (for 1209) recording masons "completing new wall" but the accounts do not certainly locate this at the castle. Vivian-Neal and Gray (1940, 59) associate it with Wall B in the keep garden (see Chapter 8) which "may be dated to 1170–1210". This appears less likely now that Wall B has been found continuing under Castle House (see page 160). The first mention of a round tower in the accounts is in 1271 but there is no mention of it during the construction works of 1246–1249 when the chapel and lord's chamber were built. The chapel was recorded next to the Round Tower in 1412, presumably in the Adam Library where it certainly was about a century later when the roof was (re)built. Simon Thurley (pers. comm.) considers that a timber floor would be inappropriate for a medieval chapel, so the vaulted style of the Undercroft and Gray Room probably continued under here. The description of the inner face of the wall seen in the Coin Room in 1972 supports this interpretation as it says that original facing survived only in the lower parts (Clements 1984, 28). The accounts suggest that the room under the chapel was occupied by clerks in 1382 (see page 14).

Phase 2: late 15th century

The buildings along the south range can all be associated with dates in the late 15th century: the style of the roof of the Adam Library and the dated arms on the gatehouse. The pipe rolls record little activity that can be associated with this but do record the visit of bishop Thomas Langton for six days in 1495, which may have initiated the work, and probably again in 1498 (a date also supported by the datestone now on Castle Bow, see page 243). King Henry VII was in Taunton from 4–6 October 1497 suppressing the followers of the pretender Perkin Warbeck (Batten 1876); there is no mention of this in the accounts and he may well have stayed in the Priory. The royal crest and profession of loyalty on the gatehouse will have been ordered by Langton who had supported Richard III at Bosworth but had managed to gain Henry's confidence quickly afterwards (Wright 2009). Langton's death in January 1501, shortly after being elected Archbishop of Canterbury, may have brought the building campaign to an end, leaving the chapel roof unadorned with bosses and unpanelled. The chapel roof does not run over Room 125 and this area was probably open to provide light to an east window.

Phase 3: post-medieval

The most evident changes in the structure are associated with Hammet in the late 18th century but there were clearly some changes before that. The illustration of 1773 (see Figure 2.1 on page 28) shows "domestic" style windows in the Adam Library suggesting that the chapel had gone out of use sometime earlier (it is last mentioned in the accounts in 1539). These windows, and possibly another, are also shown in 1789 (Figure 2.2 on page 31) after the insertion of the Hammet-style windows in the West Range and Round Tower, so the change to the existing matching windows must be later. It is possible that the changes to the South Range post-date Hammet but the style of the Adam Library suggests that, if so, it is not much later and it is more likely to have been part of Hammet's subsequent work mentioned by Toulmin (1791, 52): "he afterwards proceeded to fill up the mote, to lay out the ground round the castle and to fit up a handsome suite of rooms." The changes involved the refenestration of most of the rooms and the insertion of a barrel-vaulted ceiling below the medieval chapel roof. There were also changes to the walls, including the removal of the south wall of the Gray Room and the thinning of the walls of the Round Tower. The upper parts of the tower appear to have been rebuilt, perhaps being unrepaired since damage in the Civil War.

If the suggestion that the ground floor rooms were vaulted is accepted, this would also be the most likely date for the vault to have been replaced by wooden flooring. It must have been removed before the insertion of Windows 221 and 222, which appear coeval with other Hammet changes. It also seems likely that Room 125 was added at this time and the putative chapel east window converted to a fireplace. Door 248 is problematic as it leads to Room 125 but appears to have been plastered over in this phase.

Phase 4: 19th and 20th century

The principal recorded changes were made by SANHS and included the replacement of the lower flight of the staircase, the reinforcement and sound-proofing of the floor of the Adam Library and the insertion of three windows in the south side of the Coin Room. Attempts were made to cure the damp in the Coin Room leading to the construction of a French drain on the north. Other works to attempt to remedy this along the south wall are not dated. Further slight changes were made to convert the Coin Room to a local history library in 1974 but little was changed during the creation of the Museum of Somerset.

Chapter 12

The Courtyard and Driveway

Chris Webster

12.1 The Courtyard

Various structures have been recorded in the courtyard during excavations and building work from 1867 onwards but none have been seen over a sufficient area to produce a coherent plan of early buildings. It is clear, from Jeboult's (1893) statement that when dug for a sewer pipe the ground contained archaeological material for a depth of 4.3m to the north of the inner gate (see page 34), that the area has been greatly disturbed.

Cemetery

Several areas of the western part of the courtyard are known to contain burials from the pre-castle graveyard. These are discussed on page 240.

Medieval buildings

Along the south side of the Great Hall, excavations in 2009 uncovered what appeared to be the clay foundations for a medieval timber building (see page 68) of two phases. Only one corner was seen and it is impossible to interpret.

Parts of two stone walls were seen during the courtyard landscaping (Figure 12.1 on the next page). Wall 1187 was discovered running beneath the wall of Castle House and then turning westwards along the line of the 1988 heating trench (see page 96). It appeared to form the north-east corner of a building that pre-dated Castle House (and possibly the inner curtain wall) and which was aligned with Wall C. The northern side of the building may respect the gateway (TCB 536) discovered in 1988 (Section 5.3 on page 71). Unfortunately Trench H missed the (then unsuspected) corner of Wall 1187 by about 10cm so no stratigraphic relationship between the wall and yard surfaces were determined.

Wall 1175 (see page 96) was similar in character but on a different alignment to Wall 1187. It was seen at the ground surface in the centre of the courtyard and again in 2016 close to the Entrance Block during work to an electricity cable. Here, it survived at more than 0.5m below the modern ground level indicating its substantial nature. It was not recorded inside the Great Hall but its alignment suggests that it probably formed a block at right-angles to the hall, whether they actually joined or not. The facing appeared to indicate that the building lay to the south-west side of the wall, perhaps suggesting that the building was demolished before the inner gate was constructed, in which case the hall may not have extended far enough east to join Wall 1175 at this (unknown) date.

Both Wall 1175 and Wall 1187 contained large amounts of red sandstone, which is uncommon in the surviving buildings and they appear to be the first evidence of an early layout, possibly quadrangular, prior to the establishment of the line of the South Range.

A further wall was probably seen both in 1867 (by Jeboult, see page 34) and 1988 (by Clements, see page 53). This was different in construction to Walls 1175 and 1187 being formed of lias blocks but Jeboult reported it as 5 feet thick (1.5m), so it was clearly substantial. If the walling seen by Jeboult and Clements was the same wall, it is not aligned with any other buildings in the courtyard but does appear to be on the line of Wall B (see page 160) as seen in the Keep Garden and Castle House courtyard. Wall B, however, is of different character, having a battered south face formed of North Curry sandstone.

The courtyard wall (Wall C) and the fragmentary remains of another wall (411), seen in the north-east corner, are discussed in Chapter 8.

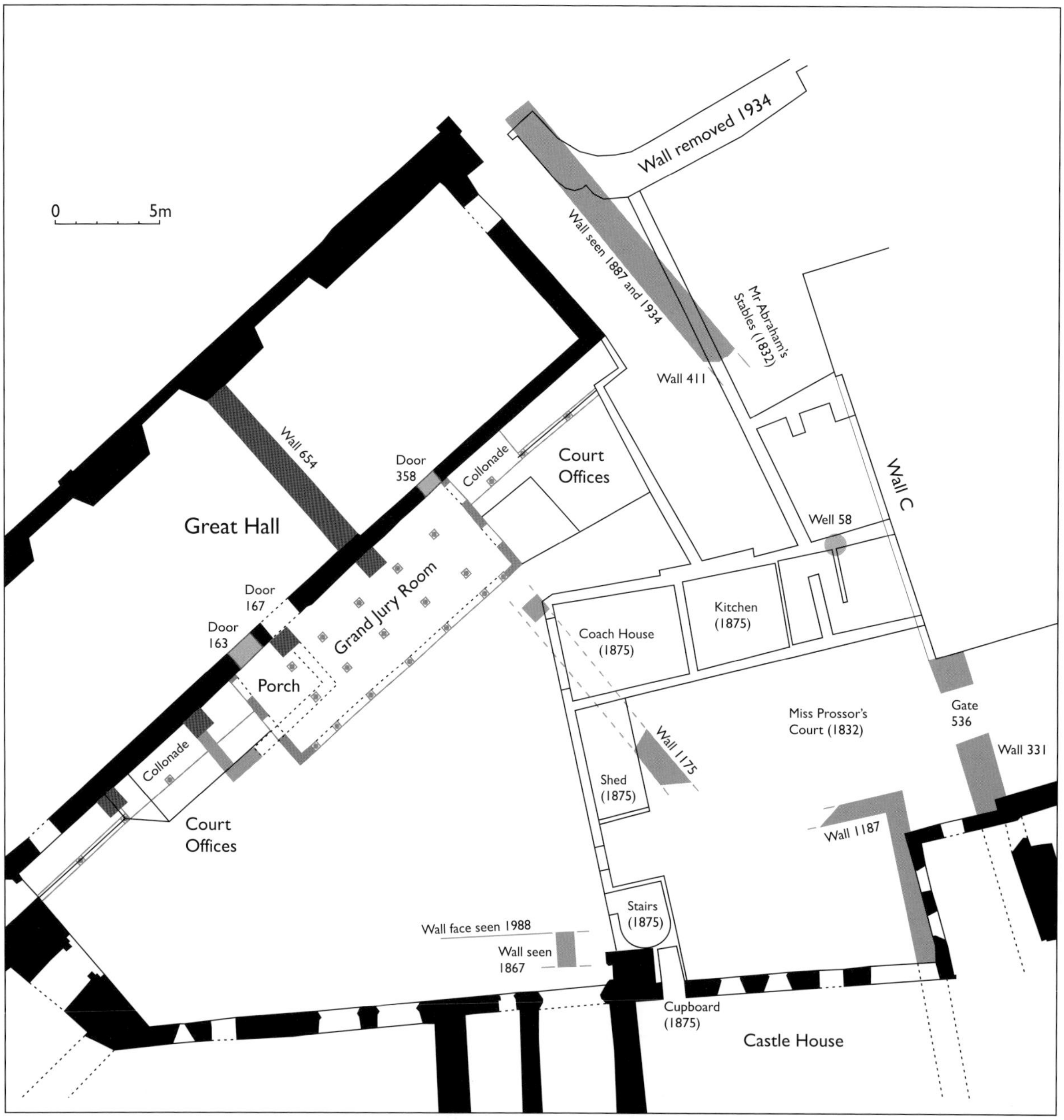

Figure 12.1: *Major structural components in the courtyard, from excavations and historical sources. Grand Jury Room, Court Offices and pre-1870s buildings from Spencer's 1875 plan, Colonnade and some names from Carver's 1833 plan. 1930s buildings omitted for clarity.*

Post-medieval buildings

One of the first actions of SANHS on acquiring the castle was the demolition of buildings in the eastern part of the courtyard. The origins of these buildings are obscure but they are shown on the earliest plans of the courtyard (1832 by Richard Carver, SRO Q/AC/3) and in detail by Spencer in 1875 (SRO DD/SAS/c1207/2b,2c). A building is shown by Carver to the north of and parallel to Castle House; both are shown in the occupation of Miss Prosser. Between is "Miss Prosser's Court", completed by a wall between the two buildings on the west side. Access was by a narrow gateway just to the north of the stair turret. The turret is shown with a projection to the north at its east corner, of unknown function.

To the north of Miss Prosser's buildings, running along the line of Wall C, are stables belonging to Mr Abraham, who occupied the West and South Ranges until bought out by the Lodging Company in 1838 (see page 32). The west wall of Miss Prosser's Court is shown in

Figure 12.2: Buckler's 1836 drawing of the courtyard. On the left is the corner of the Grand Jury Room before the wooden columns were replaced by brickwork. Note that Buckler mistakenly shows the stair turret as octagonal (SANHS Buckler B).

1836 (Figure 12.2) with a pitched roof, evidently covering a building behind. A similar situation is seen in an undated sketch (SANHS Braikenridge Taunton 38) where the roof is clearly seen crossing a window in the stair turret.

By 1875, two entrances are shown: a new one to the court while the earlier one led to a staircase to the first floor, which ran the length of the courtyard wall with another floor above that. The ground floor north of the new entrance is shown as an open "shed" and the upper two floors as "seed store". The east wall of the building extended, on the ground floor only, to reach Castle House where it enclosed a "cupboard" entered through a door on the site of Window 78. The northern building at this date had a coach house at the west end, entered from the west, to the east of which were a kitchen and scullery. The floor above is shown with five bathrooms, presumably remaining from its use as a public baths from 1851 to *c*.1853 (Bush and Meek 1984, 16). Some of these buildings were demolished by SANHS in 1875 but the coach house and a cottage were not removed until three years later (Bush and Meek 1984, 16).

Very few signs of any of these buildings were found in the excavations, suggesting that they were shallow founded and that the ground level has been reduced. Brick walling was found adjacent to the stair turret (see page 96, Figure 5.27), which may represent the northern extension to the turret shown on Carver's plan. Some mortar floors in the north-east corner of the courtyard may also be from this phase.

Recent features

Much of the courtyard was crossed by service trenches and a French drain was discovered (see page 96) along the north side of the Coin Room. It is shown on some of Spencer's later plans and

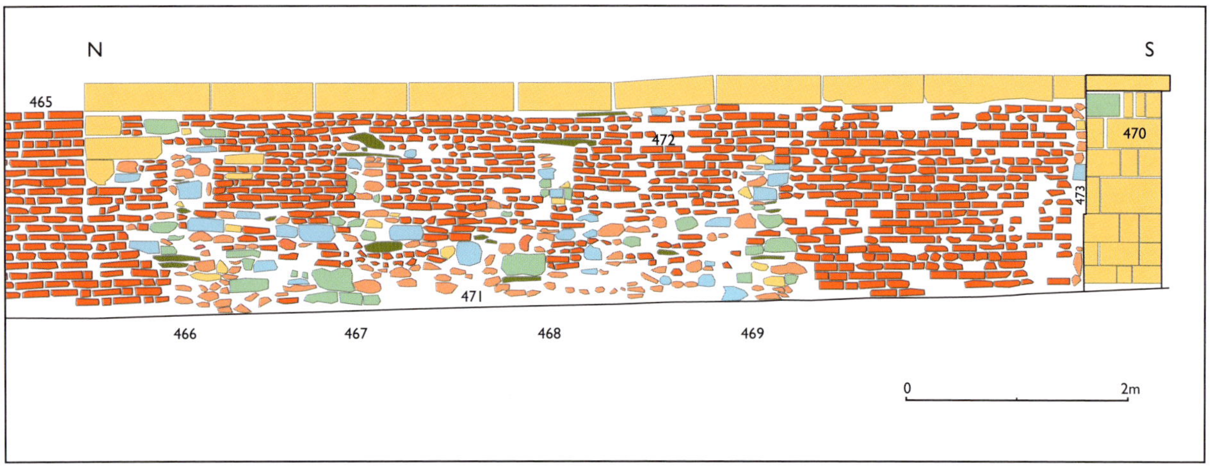

Figure 12.4: *The south end of the east wall along the driveway showing loopholes (466–469). See Figure 3 on page 4 for key to colours.*

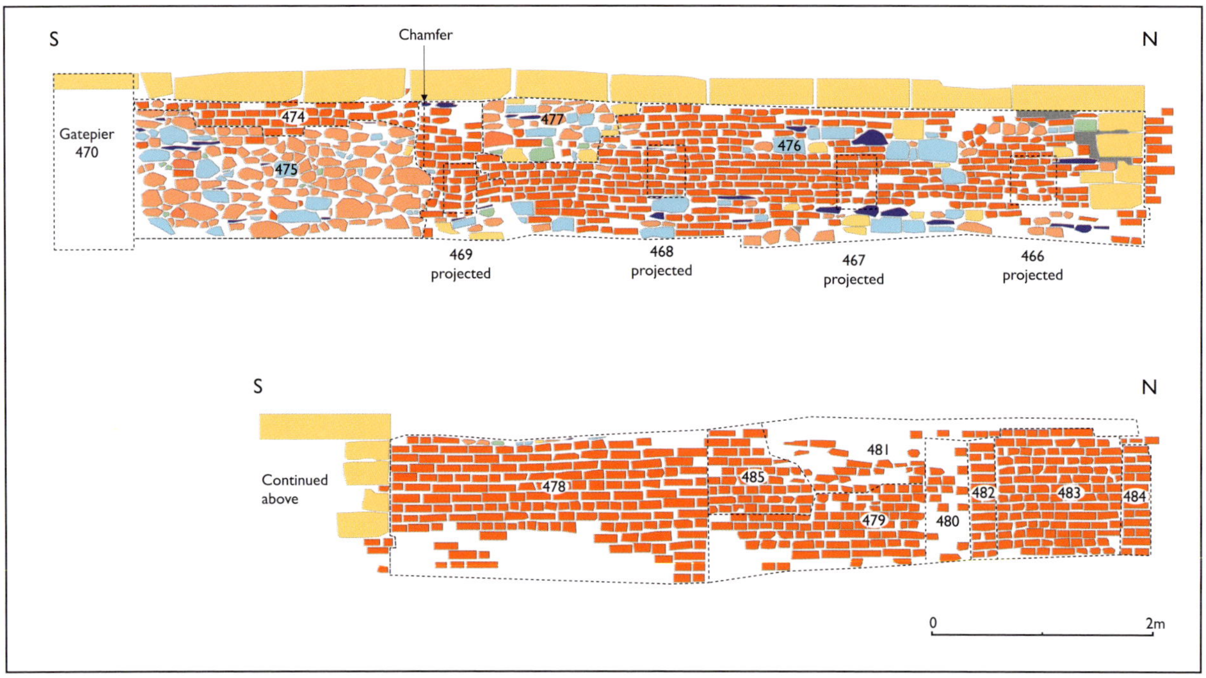

Figure 12.5: *The back (east) of the driveway wall with features on the west side projected. See Figure 3 on page 4 for key to colours.*

is likely to have been constructed in 1910 when the building of a "dry air chamber" is recorded (Weaver 1910, 5).

12.2 The Driveway

The surface deposits of the driveway were examined in 2004 (see page 59) and a trench for electricity and gas dug across them in 2009 and 2013 (Figure 4.6 on page 59) neither of which added to the record made by Jeboult (see page 33). No sign of any of the walls recorded by him was seen, which probably means that they were removed by the trench dug for the sewer in 1867. This was dug to 16 feet (4.9m) deep and may have had to be a considerable width to reach this depth.

The Turnstile

The turnstile was built in 1930 to prevent the public "abusing the society's premises" and it replaced a "modern brick structure (now dilapidated)" (SANHS minutes: 25/3/1930). This earlier structure is shown on Spencer's 1875 plan and

Figure 12.3: Loophole 468 in Driveway Wall after removal of cement pointing. Scale 20cm.

in early photographs. It covered a staircase that gave access into Castle House through a door now replaced by Window 133 and was described on Spencer's plan as "Entrance lobby". Photographs show its brick construction with a single-pitch slate roof. The door into the driveway has a tall round head similar to those of the brickwork supporting the Grand Jury Room (Figure 9.9 on page 181) and of a similar date; it is not shown in Carver's plan of 1832 (SRO Q/AC/3) but is visible in one of Jeboult's photographs (*c.*1865).

Spencer's plan shows the front wall of the building further to the west than the turnstile and its foundations were probably located in 2009 (TCC09, 962) and 2013 (TCH12, 1008).

The 1930 Turnstile building had two doors through which the public had to enter and leave, the drive being blocked by a gate. Marks on the lias slab floor show the location of the turnstile itself. To the north a cupboard was formed from the former stairwell with a trapdoor into Room 118 in Castle House. The materials, for the turnstile building, came from the demolition of Tone House (SANHS minutes: 3/9/1930) but the small window in the south wall was the one removed when Window 70 was replaced in 1910 (Gray 1940, 24).

Driveway wall

Early images (such as Figure 2.1 on page 28) show high walls to both sides of the driveway terminating in piers with large ball finials. The wall on the west side of the drive was replaced by a low chert wall in 1974 and this was removed altogether in 2012, with the exception of a short length at the north, where a new pier was built. On the east side, a brick wall survives reaching south to a Hamstone gatepier, probably one of the original two. This wall is of two phases, the northern (465) is probably contemporary with the pre-Turnstile building (1832 × 1865) as its very northern end is visible in SANHS 12521 with no break in the brickwork between them. This must have replaced an existing wall (with no building) shown by Carver in 1832 (SRO Q/AC/3).

The southern end (471/472, Figure 12.4 on the preceding page) is coped with large, triangular-section, Hamstone blocks and within the wall are three, or possibly four, four blocked openings (466–469), only visible on the west side, each about 0.35m wide and 0.5m high (Figure 12.3). The openings seem too small and low down for windows and would appear to be loopholes. They would not have been useful for defending the inner castle gate and they may be a Civil War addition, providing fire across Castle Green against an attack from the west. The gatepier is not contemporary with the brick wall, so the wall may originally have extended further perhaps forming a barricade across Castle Bow. If this interpretation is correct, it may say something about the state, or possible non-existence of the West Gate (see page 238) at the time. Against this interpretation is the evidence of SANHS 3504 (Figure 2.1 on page 28), which shows the area open in 1773. However, the perspective of the drawing is wrong in several ways and it is likely that wall and moat are foreshortened, their true dimensions being shown on early 19th-century plans, such as Carver's of 1832 (SRO Q/AC/3).

Examination of the east side of the wall in 2013, following the demolition of the hotel garages, showed a more complex picture (Figure 12.5 on the facing page). The northern end contained a bricked-up opening (483) with brick piers (482, 484) flush to either side. The position of the opening was just visible on the west side, where the stone foundations were absent but was not discernible in the brickwork above. The purpose of this entrance is not known but it appears to be shown on Spencer's plan, with the line of a drainage pipe running through it. To the south was what appeared to be another pier (480), beyond which the wall was thinner by about one brick's thickness. Pier 480 had been much damaged, perhaps to cut the wall back to match the area to the south, and because of this it was not possible to be certain that it was a pier rather than a destroyed wall extending eastwards.

The thinner wall comprised several areas of brickwork, one of which (481) appeared to be a recent repair as it showed drips of cement mortar, indicating that it had only been accessible from the west side. The unrepaired area (485) was of similar form to the thicker wall to the south and was bonded into it. Below these was an area (479) of soft, orange bricks, that appeared to be obscured by render. The thicker, southern, part (478) comprised large bricks, of similar character but variable size, 2½ inches deep and up to 10 inches long (most were in the range 8¾ to 9½ inches). This wall butted against the Hamstone quoins of the southern part of the wall.

The southern part (476) was mostly thin, deep red handmade bricks averaging 9 by 4½ by 2 inches but including large pieces of stone. No sign of the rear of the loopholes was evident but some of the pieces of stone may have formed part of them and run the full thickness of the wall. At the extreme southern end, before the pier (470) the lower part of the wall was mostly chert with some lias (475) below a few courses (mostly headers) of brick (474). The upper part of the end of brickwork 476 exhibited a chamfered end of cut bricks that extended into the wall. It was at a higher level than the loopholes and appeared to be one side of a window but no sign of it could be seen on the western face.

Chapter 13

Castle House

Chris Webster

Castle House forms a continuation of the south range to the east of the Gateway and appears to have originated as a late 15th-century lodging block along the curtain wall. It was later converted into a house and extended by a wing to the north. The building was excluded from the Museum of Somerset project but was included in the preliminary survey work by both the architects and the current author. It was subsequently refurbished by the Somerset Building Preservation Trust with exhibition space on the ground floor and holiday accommodation above. This split-use necessitated the provision of a new separate entrance door and the formation of an access route across the moat garden from the turnstile and the carpark to the south.

13.1 Sources of Information

Castle House does not feature clearly in the early sources and antiquarian accounts rarely mention it, presumably because of its domestic character. Early photographs of the north elevation show it much as now, with minor alterations to the fenestration, and few changes are evident from the south, which was in any case obscured by other buildings. A description and interpretation was published by Taylor (1971), which suggested that the building originated as a late 15th-century lodging block with late 17th-century additions. A further examination was made in 2007 by the Somerset Vernacular Building Research Group, whose interpretation closely follows Taylor's (McDermott 2007b).

In 2010 the main roof was successfully dated by dendrochronology, giving a last-ring date for the roof timbers of 1479 but it was evident that there was at least one further decayed ring and probably a further two giving a felling date of 1482 (Bridge 2010). It was not possible to date either the floor beams, which had too few rings, or the north wing roof, which was built entirely of elm.

Prior to the 2012–13 refurbishment work starting, the building was investigated by Keystone Historic Buildings Consultants who also visited during the construction work (Thorp and Cox 2010; 2013). James Brigers undertook excavation work (described in Section 6.2 on page 101) and also recorded elements of the building as work progressed. What follows is based on their reports, the author's examination of the building and on discussions with John Thorp and Jo Cox of Keystone, and James Brigers, as the work progressed.

13.2 The South Block

The south block lies along the north face of the inner curtain wall, which it uses as its rear wall, and adjacent to the Gatehouse, which forms its west wall. It originally comprised four suites, of two rooms each, on two floors either side of a central stair but the east end has been lost in later alterations.

The north elevation (Figure 13.4 on page 223) was originally symmetrically fenestrated around the doorway, with a pair of two-light windows to either side on each floor and a single-light window above the door. Only three remain (122, 123, 124) but there are traces of an earlier frame around Window 80 on the ground floor. Examination of the stonework of the windows suggests it may have been altered to fit into an irregular opening made in the wall and that, therefore, the windows are insertions.

The wall is of large, coursed lias blocks with a two stage plinth, with chamfered Hamstone plinth courses, matching the Gatehouse to the west. Where this has been replaced, below Window 78, the upper plinth course has a hollow

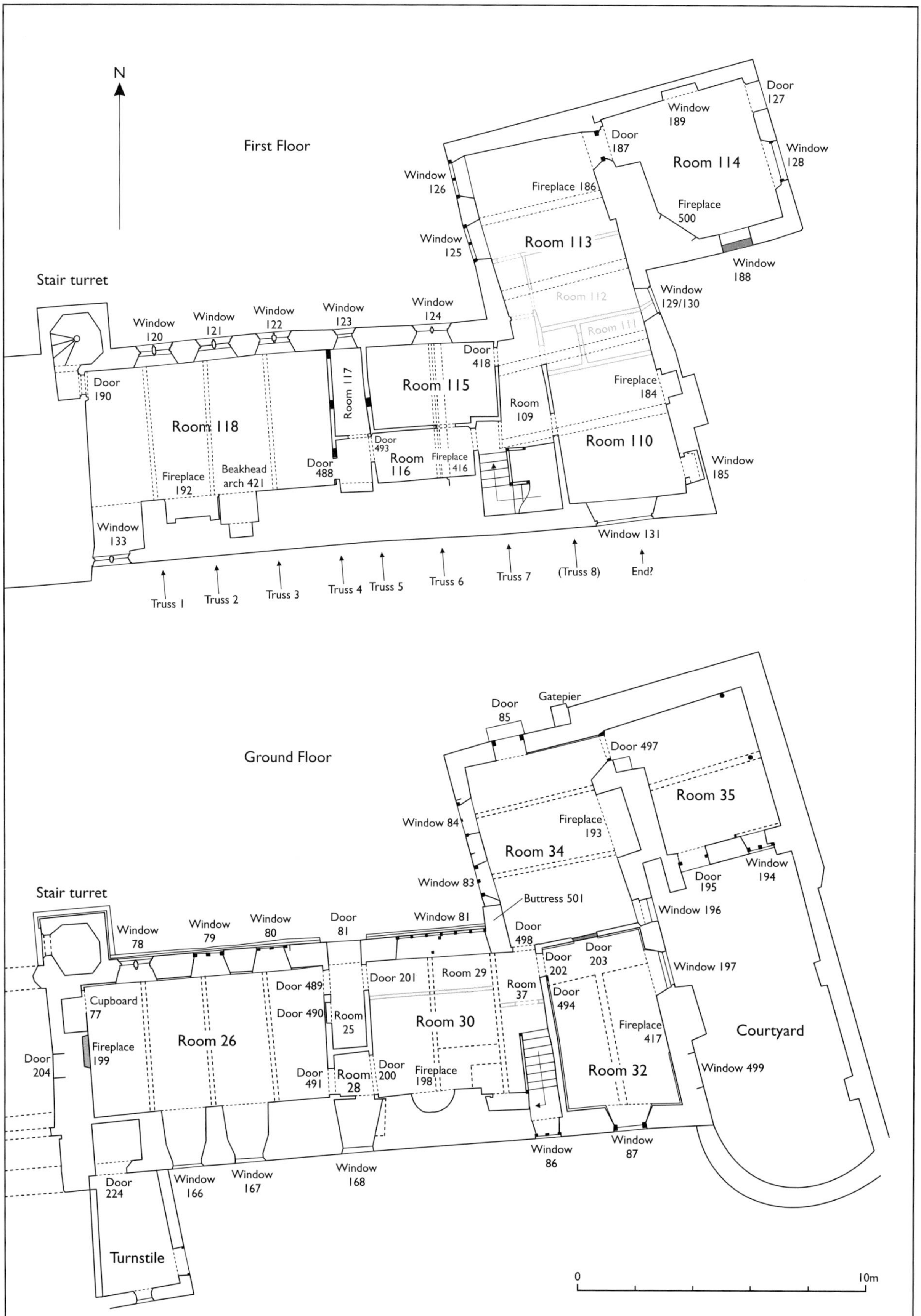

Figure 13.1: Ground and first floor plans of Castle House.

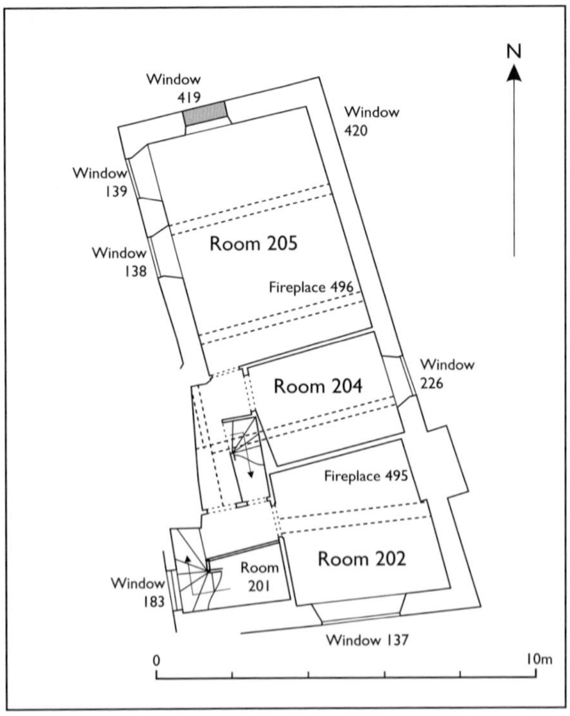

Figure 13.2: *Second floor plan of Castle House.*

chamfer but there is no evidence that this reflects the original style (Thorp and Cox 2013, 4). The scars where two buttresses (502 and 503) have been removed are visible (Figure 13.5 on page 225) and there is a third buttress (501), which was used to form the start of the west wall of the East Wing and survives buried within it. This buttress was recorded by Spencer (1910, 44–45) and left exposed for visitors.

The buttresses appear asymmetrically disposed but the two outer ones (501 and 503) lie halfway between the door and the ends of the building and the central one is as close to the centre as possible without obstructing the door. Buttresses 502 and 503 must have been removed before the shell-porch and Window 79 were added and not before the construction of the East Wing that buried Buttress 501. This would suggest that this was probably one of the *c*.1700 changes described below and possibly contemporary with similar changes seen in the Great Hall (page 185).

The main room on the upper floor and its roof exhibit the best evidence for the early history of the building and for this reason the description will start here. The roof trusses have been numbered from the west and the same number is used for any framing below.

First floor, Room 118

Roof and floor

The roof is currently of four bays with three exposed roof trusses with hollow-moulded arch-braces. The outer trusses have cranked collars but the central truss (Truss 2) has a flat-topped collar and stave holes to support wattle and daub are visible in the rafter above, showing that this was originally a closed truss similar to Truss 4 that forms the east wall of the room. Spencer (1910, 46–7) says that there was a flat ceiling in this room through which the feet of two pairs of arch braces projected "in an imperfect condition [...] adjoining massive horizontal beams forming part of a later reconstruction." It seems likely that this formed part of the same ceiling that survives further east. Curiously Spencer does not mention the arch brace (Truss 6) whose feet are visible in Rooms 115 and 116 today. The version of his plan published with the description (SANHS 6025) shows the location of Trusses 2 and 3, unlike the 1875 version. The western end of the room is shown partitioned off with a bathroom in the northern two-thirds accessed from a passage joining the stairs from the pre-turnstile building to the bedroom. This partition is not on the line of Truss 1, which again might be thought to have been visible below the ceiling. Fireplace 192 (see below) is shown much smaller and this, and the bathroom partition, continue to be shown in 1931 (SANHS 6086) and September 1954 (SANHS 6022), although the bathroom itself and stairs have gone by 1931 and the fireplace appears to have been infilled by 1954.

There was no evidence of joints in the floor beam below Truss 2 and the frame must have been supported on a cill beam at floor level as appeared to be the case further east. The floor joists were supported in pockets in the beams, which were rebated along the edges to the level of the top of the joists. Thorp and Cox (2013, 62) note that this is a style of construction of late medieval floors where no ceiling was intended below; oak boards would have been laid parallel to the joists, fitting into the rebates in the beams, leaving the central part of the beam exposed in the floor. The current boards, however, were laid parallel to the beams, some of which had been hacked down to joist level, and were a mixture of oak and elm, some with short lengths indicating much repair.

The ceiling in Room 118 is likely to have been removed as part of the work that also opened up the fireplace in the south wall and the plans suggest that this might have been between September 1954 (SANHS 6022) and January 1955

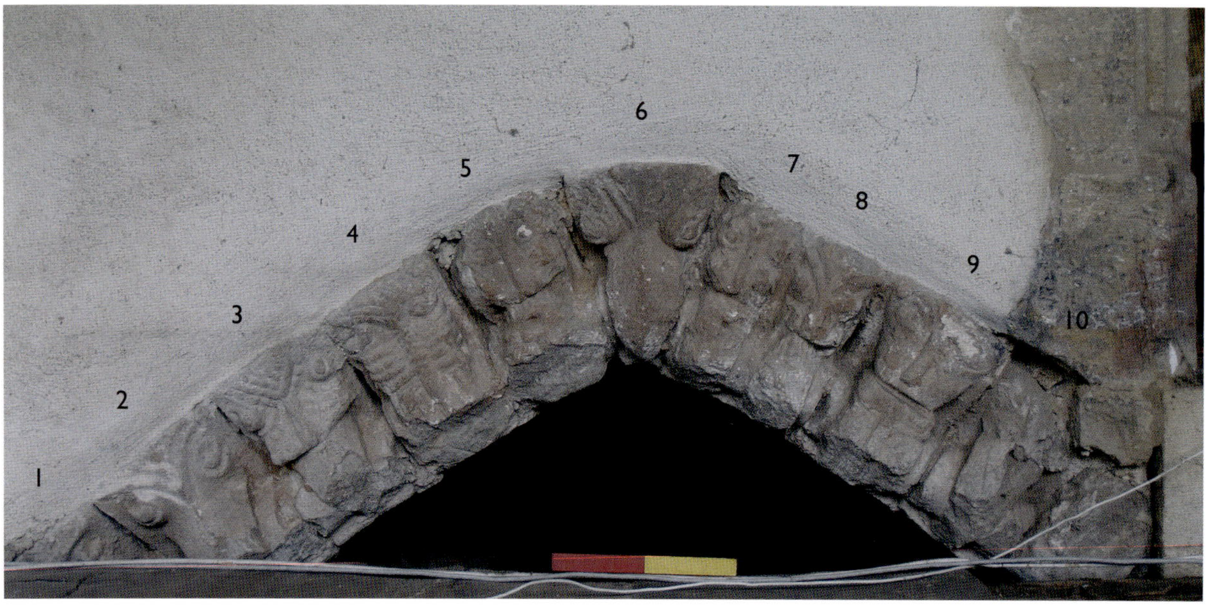

Figure 13.3: *The beakhead arch (421) in Room 118. Scale 20cm. TCB10-64.*

(SANHS 6095, which shows the fireplace at its present size). Considering the discoveries that must have been exposed at the time (the fireplace, roof structure, wall painting and beakhead arch) it seems astonishing that no record of this work has been found. There is a brief mention by Wood (1965, 267), who refers to the fireplace with its paintings, describing them as "recently discovered". Unfortunately she gives no source for the information except to acknowledge the help given by "the late Mr AW Vivian-Neal and Mr RC Sansome and his colleagues at Taunton Castle" for "much kind assistance over the Somerset houses" (Wood 1965, xxx).

South Wall

In the south wall is a large fireplace (192) that Thorp and Cox (2013, 66) date to the mid/late 16th century and which can only have been introduced following the removal of the central partition (Truss 2). To the west of this is a recess (133) with a chamfered Hamstone jamb that Thorp and Cox suggest might have formed a contemporary oriel, although the earliest images (for example, Figure 2.1 on page 28) show no evidence for the survival of this externally. It is also possible that this area formed a garderobe as suggested by the location in the inner room of the lodging and the later openings through the wall on both floors here. In the 19th century a staircase entered the room here from the precursor to the Turnstile (see Section 12.2 on page 216); when this was removed in 1930, a Doulting stone window was inserted (SANHS minutes: 2/7/1930).

Beakhead Arch, 421

Low down to the left of the fireplace is one of the most curious features in the castle, the head of a pointed arch with 12th-century beakhead decoration (421). The opening is partly concealed by the floor but leads to a void that is floored, 16cm below the room floor level, by timberwork forming the soffit of the reveal of Window 167 in Room 26 below. The archway behind the beakheads runs back for 1.03m to where there is a rendered pointed plain arch forming a smaller opening that runs back to 1.5m from the inner wall face. The outer face is estimated to be 0.55m further south.

The lower parts of the beakheads on the outer arch (Figure 13.3) appear to have been deliberately damaged revealing clean North Curry stone. This may have been intended for a rendered chamfer but there is no evidence of mortar and the breaks appear so clean that they may have been done in the 1950s, perhaps before the significance of the arch was seen. The undamaged areas appear to be coloured red. All the beakheads appear to be clasping a roll moulding; the soffits of the voussoirs extend back behind the roll moulding for perhaps 30cm.

The central beakhead (number 6 in Figure 13.3) is the best preserved. It is mostly beak with bulging spiral eyes and chevron "hair" between. Although only *c*.5cm wide, the soffit has been carved to form the point of the arch. To the left (east) is a wider stone (5) with a moustached face. It has slanted oval eyes and a long nose. The beak below the small mouth has been hacked off.

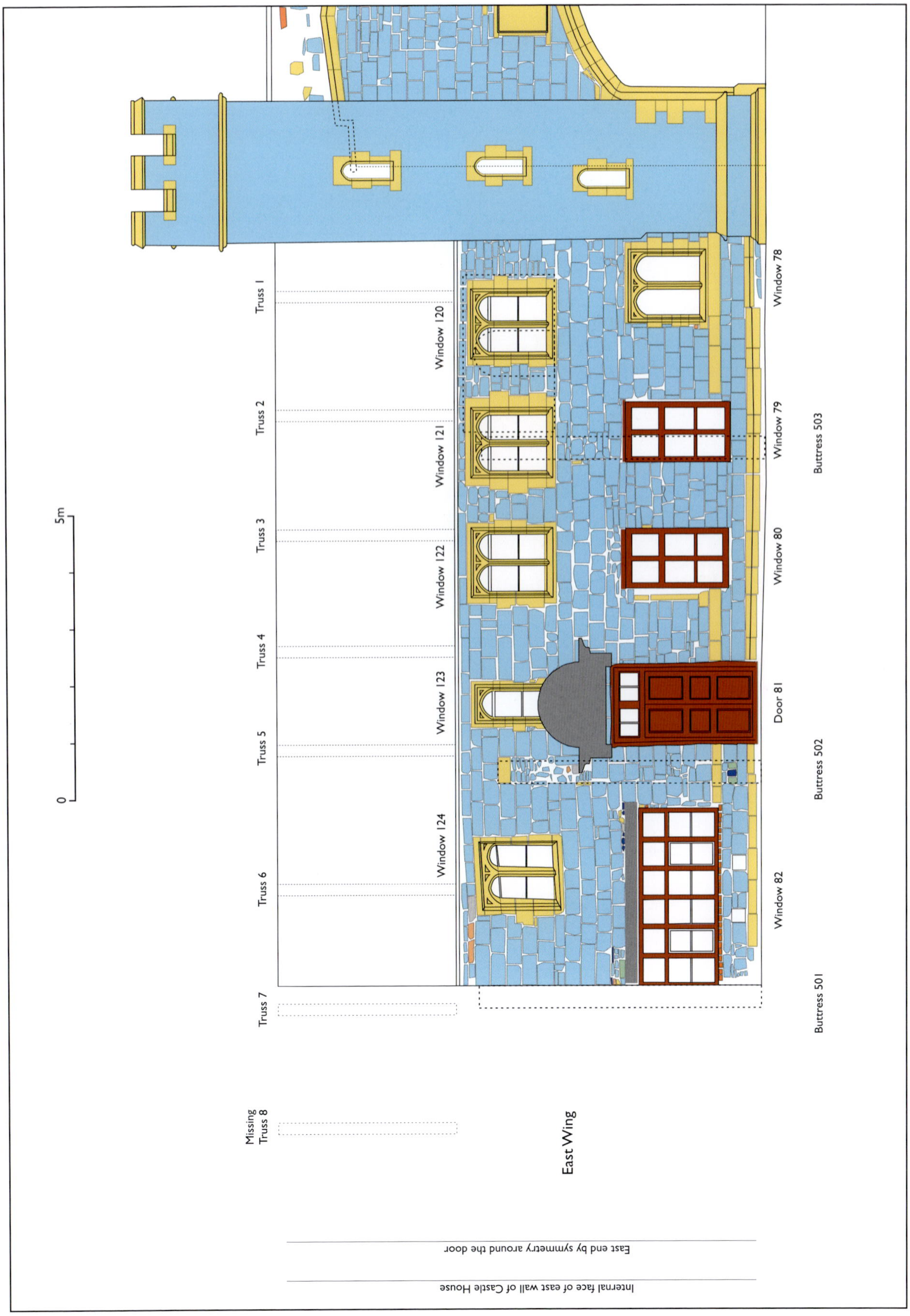

Figure 13.4: *Exterior elevation of the north wall of Castle House. See Figure 3 on page 4 for key to colours.*

The next stone (4) has a flat face with, below the oval eyes, horizontal banding that crosses a raised "nose". The nose continues down through an area of vertical banding before a damaged area. The next (3) has bulging eyes above prominent cross-hatched cheeks, below which is a beak. Above the nose is a chevron infilled with crosshatching. The next (2) is similar to the central one but on broader stone. It has spiral eyes above a beak with curved chevron forehead. The next (1) is mostly hidden by the floor.

To the right of the central head are two thin stones. The first (7) has circular eyes and a long nose leading to a chevron for eyebrows but is otherwise plain. The second (8) has lower-set eyes below a chevroned forehead. The next is a broad stone (9) with oval eyes below curving eyebrows. The nose divides plain cheeks and finishes before a double horizontal line separating the face from the beak. The beak appears to have a central rib. The next (10) is badly damaged but seems to have had a narrow beak on a broad stone with a small facial area above. The final, visible, stone on this side (11) is very badly damaged by the fireplace insertion with only traces of the roll moulding and the location of a thin beak surviving.

The beakheads were examined in 2010 by Ron Baxter of the Corpus of Romanesque Sculpture in Britain and Ireland, who comments that they have clearly been altered from their original position in a round arch, which would almost certainly have been on the outside face of a building. He notes two types of beakhead: "The bird beakhead, with a long, curving beak whose tip rests on a roll (2, 3, 6 and 10) is the archetypal beakhead form, seen at Reading, Sherborne and Old Sarum. Another type has more or less grotesque human heads with beards or tongues resting on the roll and is seen on voussoirs 4, 5, 7, 8 and 9 (voussoirs 1 and 11 are too worn to tell), and also at Lincoln cathedral. A third type where the head is inverted appears at Reading but not here. The beakheads here date from *c.*1125–35 and signify an unusual degree of richness of ornamentation for that date." (Baxter 2010).

The context for this arch is unknown. Although the carvings are 12th-century, they have clearly been reused and cut to fit a pointed arch at some date earlier than the construction of the first floor of Castle House. The arch appears to pierce the curtain wall with a further arch, possibly with a door rebate, but the exterior of this is now invisible behind the chert facing of the south front. Its location, only 8m from the gatehouse, would suggest that it formed an earlier way through and thus that the curtain wall here survived from some earlier plan. The beakheads themselves might have ecclesiastical origins and come from the demolition of the presumed church on Castle Green sometime after the establishment of the priory. Their original date indicates work, probably the rebuilding of the minster church, by Henry of Blois, or possibly William Giffard.

West Wall

The west wall is formed by the east side of the Gatehouse. Stripping of the plaster in 2013 showed that the upper area of the south part of the wall was built of very large blocks of ashlar, the lower four courses of Hamstone, the remainder of Lias. This, Thorp and Cox (2013, 69) note, is likely to have been intended for display and therefore to predate the construction of Castle House. A small area of painted wall plaster survives high on the wall. It appears to show part of the border of an image centred on the wall and Thorp and Cox (2013, 71) suggest that it is of mid/late 16th-century date, although it must predate the ceiling of the room.

The northern part of the wall, beyond a brick-built flue from the fireplace (199) below, is rubble with occasional larger blocks. At the north end is Door 190 with a Hamstone frame that projects awkwardly into the room, exposing undressed parts of the stonework. It has a Tudor-arched head and so could be contemporary with the 1482 lodgings. It gives access to a short passage that leads to the stair turret, although as this appears to be a later addition (see page 211) its original purpose is not clear. Thorp and Cox (2013, 71) suggest that the passage might have originated as a garderobe but would be an unlikely location, discharging into the courtyard. James Brigers (pers. comm.) noted two dressed stones in the wall above the door that gave the appearance of stair treads but this may just be coincidence as there is no other evidence of, or obvious need for, a stair here.

North Wall

The north wall contains three windows, of which only Window 122 is early. Its opening has been altered with dressed Hamstone reveals and the sill has been cut down for a window seat. The other windows (120 and 121) were both inserted in 1955 (SANHS 6095) and one (121) is so dated on the cill. It is possible that the need to replace the windows arose following the removal of the ceiling and partition, if that has been correctly dated to 1954 (above). Thorp and Cox (2013, 63) suggest that the alterations to the opening for the other, original, window (122) were

Figure 13.5: *Castle House in 1895. SANHS 12511.*

carried out at the same time to match the new windows but SANHS 6095 shows the window seat in Window 122 as existing and there are no indications of any other planned changes. Early photographs of the outside (see Figure 13.5) show that the position of Windows 120 and 121 was previously occupied by a single large window glazed in Venetian style.

East Wall

The east wall is formed of a large-panel oak frame (Frame 4, see Figure 13.6 on the next page) with a cill sitting on the cross beam of the floor. Below the tie-beam, the frame is asymmetric with two wide panels to the north and one narrower one to the south forming the doorway (488), enlarged *c.*1700. Most of the panels were filled by wattle and daub but the northernmost had been opened up by the removal of the rail and the cutting back of the northern post. Unless this was necessitated by decay, it would appear to indicate a doorway to an extension of the floored area across the narrow open bay to the east to reach Room 115. The panel was subsequently refilled with smaller panels infilled with brick bonded with lime mortar. The posts to either side each had three shallow mortices suggesting a built-in cupboard here at some date.

Above the tie beam, the northernmost panel had been infilled by modern brick with cement mortar. This brickwork probably dates to the removal of the ceiling; previously this panel is likely to have been open to provide access through the loft as in the other closed frames to the east.

Ground floor, Room 26

This room forms the ground floor west of the entrance, and was probably two rooms in the original lodging, converted to one in the same phase of mid/late 16th-century alterations as Room 118 above. It reached its present form *c.*1700 when the walls were panelled and the ceiling plastered. The chamfered main cross beams were plastered over and the ceiling compartments given a moulded plaster cornice, except for the westernmost where the cornice is missing (Thorp and Cox 2013, 22). From above it could be seen that the ceiling had been laid on water reed, rather than laths.

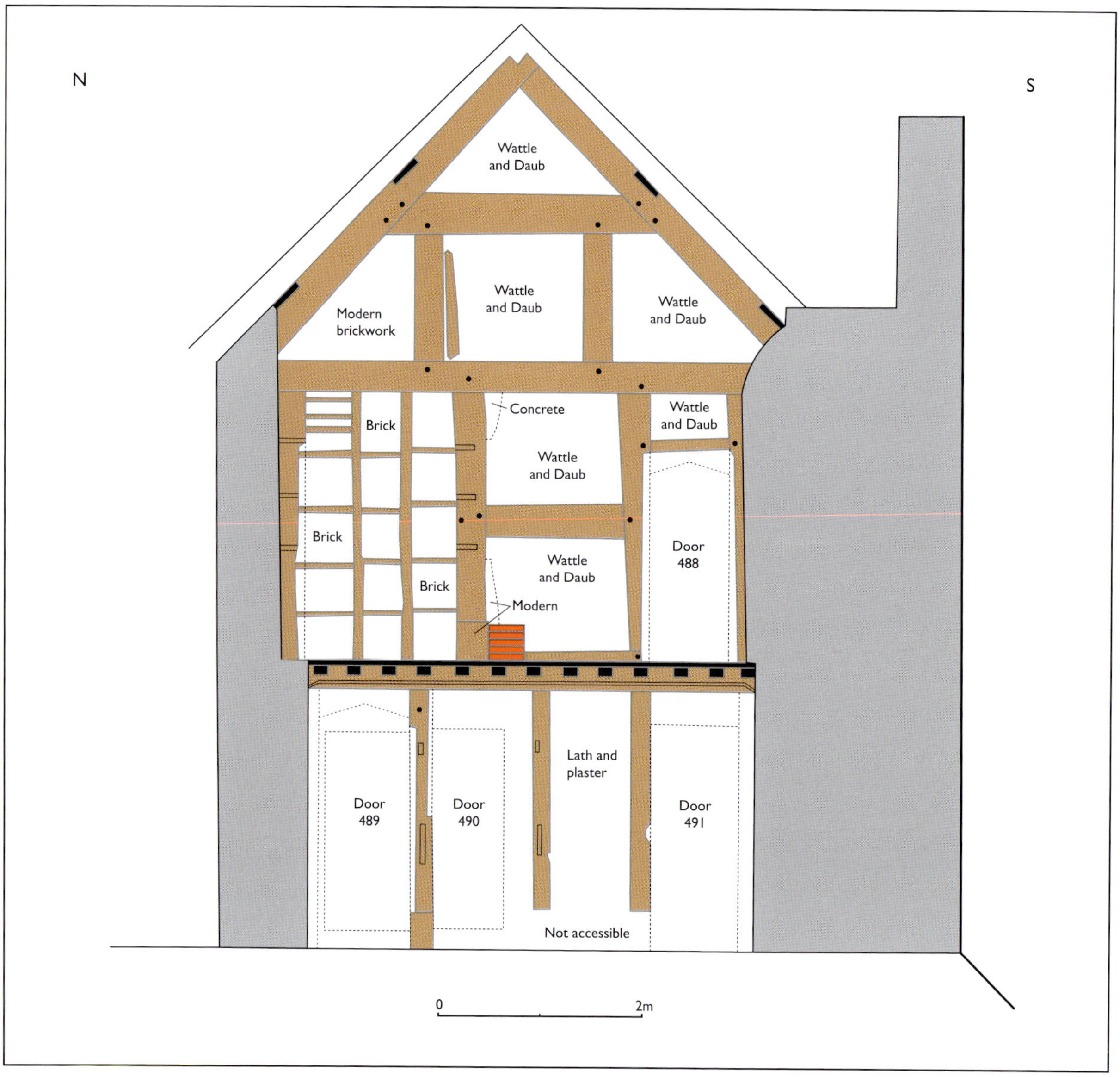

Figure 13.6: *West facing elevation of Truss 4 in rooms 26 and 118 in Castle House. After record drawings by Keystone and James Brigers (Thorp and Cox 2013, Figs 25, 63 and 65).*

South Wall

The south wall of the room is the curtain wall of the inner ward of the castle, which has been pierced by two windows (166, 167). When some of the panelling was removed in 2012 the wall behind, including the window recesses, could be seen to have been faced with brickwork, probably as part of the repairs recorded in 1930 (SANHS minutes). Most of the panelling is *c.*1700 with bolection mouldings, and a moulded dado and box cornice, with areas of repair around the windows and at the west end. The window frames themselves were part of the *c.*1700 scheme, reglazed probably in the late 19th century (Thorp and Cox 2013, 25).

West Wall

The panelling of the west wall was not removed but the fire surround was, revealing a 19th-century brick fireplace (199). The fire surround was superficially of *c.*1700 but Thorp and Cox (2013, 26) believe it is almost certainly a 20th-century replica replacing the 19th-century one visible in early photographs (SANHS glass negatives). This was probably done in 1953 when one of the fireplaces from the second floor (probably 495) was to be removed and used to repair this one (SANHS Office file C6: 6/3/1953). Thorp and Cox (2013, 26) note that there is no evidence for a fireplace here before the 19th century which leaves few other places where one could have been sited, although it seems unlikely that the room was unheated.

To the north of the fireplace was a cupboard formed by carrying the panelling over an alcove. The alcove suggests a door here into the gate passage but it does not align with the visible blocked door (204) on the outside and there is no other sign of it emerging there.

North Wall

The north wall could be seen to have been faced with neat Lias blocks, laid to course like the external face, when some panelling was removed in 2012. The three window openings had been hacked through this. The westernmost (78) was constructed in 1875, to replace a door, when the courtyard buildings were demolished (Spencer 1910, 44). The door opening survives as a cupboard behind replacement panelling below the window. The other two windows (79, 80) appear to be *c.*1700 with 19th-century reglazing (Thorp and Cox 2013, 24). Part of the Hamstone frame of the previous late-medieval window can be seen on the exterior adjacent to Window 80 (Figure 13.4 on page 223).

East Wall

The east wall is formed by the oak frame (Truss 4, see Figure 13.6 on the preceding page) separating the western rooms from the narrow bay containing the stair. Only three internal studs remained, the end ones probably having been removed to widen or insert doorways. None of the studs reached the ground, where they had been replaced by timber supports, probably in the 19th century. On the south face of the northern and central studs were pairs of mortices, the upper with a single peg hole, the longer, lower one with two. The configuration suggests a framed projection, perhaps with angled braces, but no parallels or explanation for such a structure can be offered (Thorp and Cox 2013, 28). The southern stud clearly lacked these mortices but little else could be seen because of plaster.

Three doors pierced the east wall. The northern (489) appears to have been original to the frame, as it retained a mortice with peg hole to support the head of the original doorway, but was later widened. This may have been done as part of the *c.*1700 refurbishments but no door is shown here on Spencer's 1875 plan and much of the work is clearly 20th-century. The space between the central and northern stud had formed a small doorway (490) at some date, with the skirting of the lobby continuing into it. This is shown as an alcove, blocked to the west, on Spencer's plan. At the south end was the third door (491) with a much altered architrave containing *c.*1700 and 19th-century mouldings.

Entrance lobby and stairwell, Rooms 25, 28 and 117

Originally one room, open to the roof, and containing a straight, steep, staircase rising from an entrance lobby behind the entrance door (Door 81) to a first-floor landing. The east and west walls are timber framed (Frames 4 and 5) forming a narrow bay. The east wall is described above (Rooms 40 and 118) but only the upper part of the west frame was exposed, where it could be seen to match the east wall. Details of other features of the west wall are given below (Rooms 30, 115 and 116). The staircase was probably removed as part of the *c.*1700 changes, and a first floor inserted. The ceiling of the upper room is in two parts: the north part is flat and part of the ceiling of the rooms to the east but to the south, the room rises to roof level. There is a 20th-century door in the wall joining the two levels of ceiling, giving access to the roof space.

The southern end of the upper room extends into the curtain wall where a section of the wall plate is missing, probably indicating the former existence of a dormer. The ground floor has been divided into two, probably in the 19th century on the basis of the brick infill to the studwork partition (Thorp and Cox 2013, 31) but before Spencer's plan of 1875. To the south, a closet (Room 28) was created in the curtain wall with a window (168). Brickwork visible in the sides suggests a 19th-century date, possibly contemporary with the partitioning of the room. The closet was lined with re-used oak panelling, mostly of the early or mid 17th century but with some of *c.*1700. Behind the panelling on the east side, the closet could be seen to have cut though a brick-built oven associated with the fireplace (198) in Room 30. The end of the fireplace lintel was also visible.

The main entrance door (81) occupies the north wall and will have been in this location since 1482. Examination of the external masonry suggests that the door has been widened probably by the removal of Hamstone jambs that would have matched the windows. The original may have been similar in style to Door 69 (see page 202) further west. Thorp and Cox (2013, 5) suggest that the door frame may be as early as the *c.*1700 refurbishment but that the door is 19th-century in an 18th-century style. Above the door is an early–mid 18th-century shell-porch on carved brackets that appears too narrow for the doorway. It has been considered that this indicates that it has been reused from elsewhere but the situation may be confused by the door widening and the porch could date to the *c.*1700 remodelling (John Thorp pers. comm.).

Ground floor, Room 30

Originally part of the ground floor lodgings, converted to the entrance hall of the *c.*1700 house by extending it eastwards by half a bay to insert a stair (Room 31). It is crossed by the beam below open Truss 6 and previous removal of plaster showed this to be deeply hollow-chamfered with step stops.

The west wall is formed by Frame 5 with two doors now of *c.*1700 appearance. The northern (201) was presumably the entrance to the 1482 lodging from the front door, matching Door 489 into Room 26. It now has a round-headed boxed arch with simple moulded imposts, keyblock and sunk panelled spandrels. The jambs are panelled with moulded cornices (Thorp and Cox 2013, 32). It matches a door (202) in the opposite wall of Room 30. The southern door (200) is similarly round-arched but plainer.

The south wall is formed by the curtain wall and contains a large fireplace (198) with a rounded back, now clad with late 20th-century plaster and a slim moulded timber frame. It was not further exposed but probably dates to the *c.*1700 changes. A brick oven to its west was seen in Room 28. To the east is a cupboard (422) with a two-panelled door of *c.*1700 under the adjacent stair and in the thickness of the wall. It may possibly have originated as a garderobe or just be a byproduct of the thinning of the wall for the stairwell (Room 31). It is lined with 20th-century concrete blockwork (Thorp and Cox 2013, 38).

The north wall contains a large six-light window (82) of 1938 (SANHS minutes: 4/5/1938) that replaced an earlier one of similar design. It probably originated as part of the *c.*1700 refurbishments (Thorp and Cox 2013, 38).

The east wall was originally the lower part of Frame 7 and was removed when the staircase was inserted in *c.*1700. Evidence for the former framing was found when plaster was stripped from the soffit of the beam at the northern end. Here two mortices were uncovered, one 20cm long to hold the end stud and then a smaller mortice to hold the end stud of the panel infill. Holes for staves to hold the wattle were also evident (Thorp and Cox 2013, 39). The beam was similar to the one within the room, with deep hollow chamfers and long step stops. The line of the beam was used for a partition that had enclosed the stairs, probably in the 1950s as it is shown in situ on plans (SRO D/B/ta/24/1/137/8049) drawn in 1960 when the north part of the room was further partitioned off to form a corridor (Room 29). Both of the partitions were removed in 2011–13 but the eastern was reinstated.

First floor, Rooms 115 and 116

These two were originally a single room, part of the medieval upper lodging suite on the east side of the stairs.

Floor and ceiling

The floor is similar to that in Room 118, to the west, with wide floorboards set parallel to the beams but here the rebates in the beams remain so that the top of the beam is visible. The boards may date to *c.*1700 when the ceiling below was plastered (Thorp and Cox 2013, 78) but it is not clear why the boards were replaced at right angles to the previous direction. The ceiling is plastered with probably 16th-century chamfered crossbeams indicating a usable loft space above (Thorp and Cox 2013, 79).

North wall

The north wall contains one of the three original windows (124) and the foot of the archbrace of Truss 6 can be seen below the ceiling.

West wall

The west wall is formed by Frame 5 with an inserted doorway (492) from Room 117. The door has a crude timber frame and a door of overlapping vertical planks hung on late 19th-/early 20th-century hinges (Thorp and Cox 2013, 77). No opening is shown on Spencer's 1875 plan. At the south end is a square-headed arch (493) clad with late 20th-century joinery that is probably an enlargement of the 1482 doorway.

East wall

The east wall is formed by Frame 7 which originally divided the two lodging rooms. There is a late 20th-century door (418) at the north end onto the landing (Room 109). The southern end of the frame has been removed to construct the stairwell but part of the tie beam extended into that space (see below) and a stud mortice and stave holes were visible in the soffit when plaster was removed. The presence of these suggest that the original door between the two lodging rooms lay at the other end of the wall.

Figure 13.7: Fireplace 416 after discovery and repairs.

South wall

The south wall is the curtain wall and contains a fireplace (416, Figure 13.7) partly uncovered in 2010. The west side and lintel were hollow-chamfered but the east side had been removed by the thinning of the wall for the stairwell. As there is no evidence of fireplaces in the west part of the 1482 lodging block it is assumed that this one must be later, perhaps mid–late 16th century (Thorp and Cox 2013, 85).

Partition

The room is now divided by a partition to form a corridor (Room 116) along the south side. There is a modern window giving light to the corridor but the presence of a black-painted skirting, characteristic of *c.*1680–1740 indicates that the partition is likely to date to the *c.*1700 phase of changes (Thorp and Cox 2013, 80). This dating would fit with that suggested for the removal of the medieval stair and allow access to Room 118 from the new stair.

13.3 The East Wing, Ground Floor

The East Wing has been recognised as an addition since at least the work of Spencer (1910, 44–5), who noted that it partly covered a buttress of the south range. Taylor (1971) believed the East Wing to be one build of the late 17th century and was followed in this by the Vernacular Buildings Group. Keystone's more archaeological approach located several features that suggested to them that only the second storey and attic were that late and that there was an intermediate phase. This they suggest was associated with the mid 16th-century conversion of the lodgings and may have formed a kitchen wing (Thorp and Cox 2010).

The East Wing does not sit at right angles to the South Block but conforms to the alignments of Wall C and other structures in the Keep Garden. It roughly follows Wall 1187 (see page 96) discovered almost beneath its west wall but it is unlikely that Wall 1187 was visible when the East Wing was constructed. At the south end, the curtain wall which forms the south wall of the South Block is missing, replaced by a narrower wall in different masonry which forms the south gable wall of the East Wing. Spencer (Anon 1910) reports that when the floor was relaid in Room 32 the foundations of walls "6 to 7 feet thick like the main portion of the south wall of the castle" were exposed under both the south and east walls of the room. Rodwell (1984a, 22) believed that Wall C had been partly used for the east wall and survived in the thick block of masonry between Rooms 34 and 35 but this seems unlikely to be connected, as the foundations of Wall C as seen in Trench H were not solid. Additionally, if the south wall of the castle turned north here, it would have faced east and Wall C faces west.

Staircase, Rooms 31, 109 and 201

The staircase was inserted into the bay beyond Frame 7 and necessitated the removal of the 1482 roof beyond that point. On the ground floor it was originally open to Room 30, which formed an entrance hall. Its south side is set back behind the interior line of the curtain wall forming the beginning of the thinner section noted above. The style of the joinery indicates a date of *c.*1700 (Thorp and Cox 2013, 41). It rises to a half landing with a window (86), which has joinery and fittings again indicating a date of *c.*1700 (Thorp and Cox 2013, 19), where the stair turns to rise again to the first floor landing (Room 109).

From the landing the stair rises, turning back on itself to reach Room 201 where it currently ends, meeting an east–west balustrade of simpler design. The stair originally continued up into the attic as shown by the secondary joists supporting the attic floor over the stairwell and the presence of laths fixed to the substantial wall plate that supports the roof. These show that the stair-

__Figure 13.8:__ Exterior elevation of the west wall of the East Wing of Castle House. Details of Buttress 501 taken from Spencer (1910, Fig. 12). See Figure 3 on page 4 for key to colours.

well was plastered through the level of the attic floor (Thorp and Cox 2013, 118–19). Problems were evident with the staircase in 1938 when it is described as being "bolted" (SANHS minutes: 9/3/1938), presumably including the metal post joining the different flights.

Room 32

Most of the obvious features of the room date to *c.*1700 but these conceal evidence for the previous phase. This includes the ceiling beams, which have been covered in plaster like other medieval beams. In plan the beams form a T-shape with one running across the building from between Doors 202 and 495 and, to the south, an axial beam dividing the ceiling into two panels with moulded cornices all round. The northern part of the ceiling is lower, at the level of the soffit of the beams.

South wall

The south wall is the thinned curtain wall of the inner ward, built on wide medieval foundations according to Spencer (Anon 1910), although these were not exposed in 2013. Internally the wall had been plastered and this continued into the window (87) reveals. To the west of the window the wall had been lined with probably *c.*1700 brickwork. The wall had then been studded out and covered with lath and plaster above a *c.*1700 style panelled wainscot.

West wall

A studwork partition of *c.*1700 forming one side of the stairwell, with two adjacent doors at the south end, indicated by the use of more neatly squared studs than elsewhere in the partition. The northern door (202) retained its *c.*1700 design on the west, matching Door 201 across Room 30. The east side was plastered revealing only the 19th-century doorframe. Door 494 lay immediately to the south and had been blocked with 20th-century brick (Thorp and Cox 2013, 42, 46). Despite this, no doorway is shown here on any of the early plans and the infill is presumably a replacement of the cob seen on the floor above. The wall is covered by *c.*1700-style panelled wainscot over lath and unplastered daub, which Thorp and Cox (2013, 46) suggest indicates that the wainscoting is part of the original design. Both the wainscoting, and probably the laths and daub, ran over the blocked doorway. As the wainscot appears to date from the *c.*1700 alterations this blocking of the doorway appears to be an early alteration to the plan, perhaps during construction, unless this wall is part of an earlier phase. It is not possible to be more certain about this as the door was reopened in 2012 in the absence of archaeological monitoring (James Brigers pers. comm.).

East wall

The east wall showed a complex history with original walling only evident at the very north end. To the south of this is Window 197, which appears on the outside to be 20th-century in date and to have replaced a doorway. On the inside three phases of window were apparent with a single long timber lintel running over them. The earliest appeared to be coeval with the wall and the opening was later narrowed on the northern side with rough stone blocks and then again with brick. None of these appeared to extend below the 20th-century wainscoting (not removed) indicating windows rather than doorways. The southern side showed only the latest phase, cutting the fireplace structures to the south.

The fireplace (417) originally had a timber lintel, chamfered with small scroll stops, over a hand-made brick opening. This would suggest a 17th-century date but it could be as late as *c.*1700 (Thorp and Cox 2013, 49). The lintel had been cut though by the flue of a smaller 19th-century fireplace that had been bricked-up in the late 20th century. To the south of the fireplace was a large window (499) under an oak lintel almost at ceiling height, reaching to 0.5m above the floor. It was probably of *c.*1700 date and was blocked with brick in a timber frame in the 19th century (Thorp and Cox 2013, 48). The similarities of the lintels of this and Window 197 could indicate contemporaneity and, if so, the height of Window 499 might explain the external appearance of Window 197 as a blocked doorway.

North wall

The north wall is a stud partition, probably of *c.*1700, with a central blocked doorway (203). The doorway is shown on the plans of 1960 (SRO D/B/ta/24/1/137/8049) to be opened up and probably originated at that date.

The plan of the ceiling beams and the presence of two doors (202 and 494) suggests that the room was originally two, with a passageway at the north end, but the evidence of Window 197 argues against this.

Room 34

Thorp and Cox (2013, 50) suggest this is a kitchen added when the lodgings were converted to a self-contained L-shaped house in the mid-16th century. The ceiling is supported on two, probably 16th-century, cross beams coated with *c.*1700 plaster. The eastern end of each is supported on a bolster, presumably because of rotted ends but possibly indicating reused timbers of slightly insufficient length. The room was entered from the south by a door (498), with *c.*1700 ogee-moulded architrave leading from the stairwell.

West wall

The west wall began at the buttress (501) of the lodging block which in 2013 was revealed on the inside as well, together with the stub of the wall that once continued eastward. To the north are two tall, high-transomed, two-light windows replacing *c.*1700 originals. Window 83 had some reused glass and a wrought-iron catch with ornamental backplate, perhaps earlier than *c.*1700 (Thorp and Cox 2013, 11). Externally there was evidence of an earlier, wider window here with a higher cill and that the other window (84) replaced an earlier door, partly infilled with *c.*1700 brickwork; slight traces of this were evident inside but not much plaster was removed.

North wall

The north wall was stripped of plaster, which revealed several areas of concrete including around Door 85. Thorp and Cox (2013, 14) suggest, on the basis of the concrete lintel and style of door and gabled porch, that the door was an insertion of *c.*1930 following the reduction in ground level in the keep area. While this may be true for the current door, early photographs (see Figure 5.2 on page 67) and Spencer's 1875 plan show a doorway here.

East wall

The east wall contained the kitchen fireplace (193) and could be seen to have been built from large lias blocks brought to course, with much modern brickwork. To the south was a small, 20th-century window in a blocked door (196) with a chamfered Hamstone jamb surviving on the exterior south side. Spencer's plan of 1875 shows a passageway formed from the south end of the room leading to the door. The fireplace itself had a chamfered oak lintel with crank-arched head, probably of mid 16th-century date. There was probably an oven concealed behind 19th-century brickwork on the south side (Thorp and Cox 2013, 56). To the north of the fireplace is a door (497) into Room 35.

Figure 13.9: *Timber, probably a principal rafter from Frame 8 of the 1482 roof showing the mortise from an arch brace, reused to form a pad for a ceiling beam in Room 110. TCB10-43.*

13.4 The East Wing, First Floor

This floor originally comprised two rooms (110 and 113) that were converted to three by the time of Spencer's plan of 1875. Between then and the 1910 plan , the central bedroom was further divided into two: Room 111, a lavatory and Room 112, labelled as a dressing room. In 2012, Room 112 was removed.

Room 110

The southern room appeared from the quality of its fireplace (184) to have been the principal chamber in the *c.*1700 house (Thorp and Cox 2013, 91, 94). It had a two-bay ceiling with a chamfered cross-beam stopped only on one side. The beam continued across the stairwell and was supported at its west end by being tenoned into the tie-beam of Frame 7. The next beam northwards is now in Room 111 but originally lay at the north end of the room, a change made between Spencer's plans of 1875 and 1910. This beam retained the *c.*1700 moulded cornice that had been removed in the southern part of the room (Thorp and Cox 2013, 95). The eastern end rested on a substantial pad of two pieces of timber set in the wall. The lower piece contained an axial mortice the full length of the exposed area with peg holes visible (Figure 13.9). It seems likely that this is one of the principal rafters of the 1482 roof, with the mortice being that for the arch brace. Another piece of structural timber was used in a similar position for the next beam to the north (in Room 113).

The south wall had a three-light timber casement window (131) with 18th-century style catches. It is shown in some early illustrations (see Figure 2.2 on page 31) with a Venetian style glazing but this may be artistic invention. The west wall was a lath-and-plaster stud partition of *c.*1700 infilled with cob. The north wall was missing but the east wall contained Fireplace 184, of *c.*1700 with a timber bolection-moulded chimneypiece. To the south of this was a cupboard (185) formed from an earlier window (as could be seen outside). Internally the splays of the window opening were lime plastered North Curry stone but the lower north side was brick suggesting an alteration to the opening before it was plastered. The oak lintel survived just below ceiling height. The window was converted to a cupboard by infilling with brickwork to form a lower, door-sized opening with ogee architrave and a fielded two-panel door. The style of door and its hinges indicated that the conversion was part of the *c.*1700 changes as did the black-painted skirting, which crossed the brickwork.

Room 113

This room was larger than that to the south with a ceiling divided by three cross-beams. The two southernmost were plastered with moulded cornices but the plaster had been removed from the other. Where visible, all were chamfered with step-stops that did not appear to fit the width of the room suggesting reuse. The east end of the middle beam was exposed and could be seen to rest on a timber pad in the wall (Figure 13.10). As this timber had a tenon cut on one end, it too was reused structural timber, probably from the 1482 roof as discussed above (Room 110).

The west wall contained two late 20th-century timber windows (125, 126) replacing *c.*1700 ones. Externally these had flat arches in hand-made brick that matched those in the floor above.

The east wall contained a window (129) at the southern end (later shared with the inserted Room 111). Removal of some plaster showed that the opening was original to the wall although the woodwork was 19th century. To the north of this, was Fireplace 186 with a *c.*1700 bolection moulded chimneypiece. The lintel appeared to be pine, which may suggest a later date (Thorp and Cox 2013, 103). The chamfers of the beam above were stopped behind the wall-line showing that the chimney breast has been extended into the room, which may also explain the difference in date of the lintel and chimneypiece.

To the north of the fireplace was a doorway (187), dated stylistically to *c.*1700, which had been broken through an earlier Hamstone window to communicate with Room 114 in the East Block (Figure 13.11).

Figure 13.10: *Timber, probably from Frame 8 of the 1482 roof with a tenon for an angled joint to the left, reused to form a pad for a ceiling beam in Room 113. TCB10-41.*

Figure 13.11: *Door 187 viewed from Room 114, showing window frame exposed in 1966. The buried corbel lies to its right.*

This earlier window was discovered in 1966 during building work, as was a Hamstone corbel buried in the wall to the north (SRO A/CNT/4/2). It was suggested at the time that this corbel indicated that there had originally been a jettied building on the site (probably by Robert Taylor, the assistant curator, who expanded on the suggestion in his 1971 paper). The remains of this window appear to be in a similar style to the late 15th-century ones surviving in the South Block and earlier commentators (Taylor 1971; McDermott 2007b) have suggested that it was reused from there. Thorp and Cox (2013), however suggest that is a mid 16th-century original feature and reject the suggestion of a jettied building, pointing out that the corbel is probably just reused masonry as it is buried in the wall rather than projecting from it.

13.5 The East Wing, Second Floor

Rooms 202 and 204

Shown as one room on Spencer's 1875 plan and probably partitioned when the attic stairs were altered. The south wall had a modern window (137) in an earlier opening, which like Window 131 below, was shown (probably incorrectly) with Venetian-style glazing in 1789. The west wall was a studwork partition to the stairwell and the east wall contained a blocked fireplace (495). To the north of this, and now in Room 204, was a window (226) with a *c.*1700 frame and an ornamental catchplate.

Room 205

The room is shown subdivided into two bedrooms in 1875. The west wall had two windows (138, 139) matching those of the floor below and there was a blocked window (419) in the north wall visible both externally and as a recess within the room. It was blocked in April 1938 (SANHS minutes: 4/5/1938) and re-opened in 2012. The east wall had a fireplace (496) opened up in 2012, with handmade brick jambs and a chamfered timber lintel with small scroll stops (see Fireplace 417 in Room 32). The painted black skirting of *c.*1700 continued into the fireplace (Thorp and Cox 2013, 111). To the north, removal of plaster to investigate a crack showed one side of a tall window (420) made with squared blocks of North Curry and Hamstone. This was probably infilled when the East Block was constructed.

13.6 The East Wing, Attic

This was reached, as shown by Spencer in 1895, by a flight of stairs running up from the head of the main staircase within a tile-hung dormer (see Figure 13.5 on page 225). The stair may have been added in the 18th century to provide improved access to the roof space for use as school dormitories. The dormer was found to be leaking in 1953 and to have caused substantial water damage to the structure (SANHS Office file C6). It was removed and the stairs turned round. The roof is of five bays between stone gables and is supported by four elm tiebeam trusses with flat collars. Two sets of purlins are notched over shallow trenches in the principal rafters and there is a V-notch for a missing diagonally-set ridge. All the timberwork is rough and clearly not intended for display (Thorp and Cox 2013, 120). The south gable and head of the stairs was extensively rebuilt with brick in 1953.

13.7 The East Block

The ground floor (Room 35) was, until the excavation of the Keep Garden, a semi-basement, probably added as part of the *c.*1700 alterations. It was entered from the kitchen (Room 34) by a door (497) with a ventilation slot above. The style of door and hinges could be early or mid 18th century (Thorp and Cox 2013, 55). The ceiling was supported by an unchamfered cross beam, which was itself supported on a slender turned timber post resting on a concrete pad. A similar post, but without a capital, supported the ceiling in the north-east corner via a bolster. The insertion of these is likely to have been the work reported in 1914 when rotten joists were discovered (SANHS minutes: 11/9/1914).

The south wall contained a modern door (195) and a window (194) of *c.*1700. Originally of three lights, the opening had been reduced so that only two were visible. This seems to have happened between Spencer's plans of 1875 and 1910 (Thorp and Cox 2013, 21). The discovery of a complete wine bottle base of late 18th- or early 19th-century date in the wall core (Brigers 2013a) would appear to give a firm date for the construction of this wall, were it not for the earlier window immediately above.

The upper room (114) is entered via a converted window (187) from Room 113 and had a diagonal fireplace (500) in the south-west corner. The south wall contained a window (188), converted to a cupboard with late 18th-century style doors (Thorp and Cox 2013, 107). The infilled opening was visible on the exterior and the window reinstated in 2013. The east wall contained a large walk-in window (128) with double hung sashes of late 18th- or early 19th-century date. Externally this window could be seen to be an insertion with brick infill around and a rubbed-brick lintel. To the north was a doorway (127) that led into the Keep Garden at ground level before the excavations; subsequently it was provided with a wooden staircase until that became dangerous in 1959 (SRO DD/A/CNT/4/1: 13/2/1959). The north wall contained a large opening (189) rising from the floor almost to the high ceiling. Externally it had been infilled with brickwork and on the inside were roll mouldings extending down to expected cill height suggesting that this was a doorway converted from a window before being blocked.

13.8 Structural Development

Phase 1: pre-1482

Limited evidence from excavation shows that there was at least one earlier layout of buildings in the area of Castle House. The alignment of Wall 1175 (Figure 12.1 on page 214) suggests a phase of building aligned on the Great Hall, perhaps earlier than the south curtain wall. Wall 1187 indicates a large building on a different alignment, one similar to that of Wall C. The wall underlies both ranges of Castle House and again may predate the construction of the curtain. Finally, Wall B was found to continue beneath Castle House (Figure 8.3 on page 157).

It also seems likely that there was a building in the position of the South Block prior to the dendrochronology date of 1482 for the roof of the current building. Assuming that the curtain wall predates it, then it is a suitable location for structures such as the stable next to the inner gate recorded in the pipe rolls in the early 14th century unless that lay on the other side where the "stable below chapel" is recorded in 1345.

The beakhead arch (421) fits into this phase as it must predate the first floor of Castle House but otherwise it remains enigmatic.

Phase 2: the 1482 lodgings

It has been suggested above that the early windows (122, 123, 24) might be insertions; the lack of any sign of earlier windows might support the suggestion that the lodgings were formed from an earlier stable with few openings. The walls, however, appear to be of one build with the walls of the Gatehouse and east end of the South Range, and a late 15th-century date would fit well for that. Thorp and Cox (2010, 3.2) suggest that stylistically the windows might be expected to be a bit later than 1482, which could suggest (slightly) later changes but there is no evidence for these, and the simplest explanation is that the windows are an early example of their type, as might be expected if the design came from Winchester. The bishop at this time was William Waynflete, described as "an active patron of building on an impressive range and scale" so innovation would be likely (Davis 2004; 2007). The plan form is certainly known locally, as noted by Thorp and Cox (2010, quoting unpublished work by Robert Waterhouse) and bears a striking resemblance to lodgings at Haddon Hall in Derbyshire (Emery 1970, 253–44; Faulkner 1963).

Carpenters are recorded in 1482, which may well be a reference to the construction of the lodgings, although this is not explicit and much of the right-hand side of the pipe roll is missing. The account reads "three carpenters raising and repairing the lord's stable next [damage] gate: eight days". As Thorp and Cox (2010) note, this could refer to a completely different building and the roof structure appears to be of higher status than would be expected for a stable. However, there is no other obvious mention of the construction of the lodgings at the appropriate date and there is record of repairs to the walls either side of the inner gate in 1480 that could have been a prelude to the works here and in the West Range.

The original plan of the lodgings seems clear from the roof structure: a central entrance in a narrow bay with two, two-bay rooms to either side on each floor. Each of the rooms probably had a window in the north wall, but evidence only survives in three of the eight rooms, the ones next to the entrance bay.

There are few indications of the interior layouts of the rooms or of their facilities. The only fireplace that could be contemporary is 416 in Room 116 but there is no sign of a corresponding one to the west of the stairs which would have lain in the position of the beakhead arch. The location of the later fireplace (192) in Room 118 is an unlikely position as it would have been on the line of the partition (Frame 2) at that date. There is similarly no evidence for sanitary provision; the most likely explanation is that garderobes were provided in the south wall at either end, the west location being removed by Window 133, the east end having been lost to later changes.

Assuming that the building was originally symmetrical, the east end would have been in a similar position to the current east wall of Castle House (Figure 13.4 on page 223), particularly if this wall was originally thicker as suggested by Spencer's (1910) evidence (Anon 1910). This suggests that the lodgings were built between this wall and the gatehouse and would mean that the east end would not have been at right angles to the rest of the building.

Mid 16th century

There seems to have been a significant change sometime in the middle of the 16th century, which Thorp and Cox (2010) suggest was the conversion of the lodgings block into an independent dwelling that was no longer reliant on the castle kitchens. This involved the conversion of the upper west lodging to a single room (118), the formation of an attic above it and the rooms to the east, and the construction of a kitchen in a range to the south.

Thorp and Cox (2010) show that the single phase proposed by Taylor (1971) for the East Wing is not tenable as there is clearly an earlier window and a door in the ground floor (Figure 13.8 on page 230) that were replaced by *c.*1700 windows. They suggest that this was a two-storey extension with the third floor added later but there is evidence to suggest that, in fact, a single-storey phase subsequently had two storeys added. Although Thorp and Cox (2013) identify many of the ceiling beams on the first floor as of 16th-century date, they also note that the location of the chamfer stops show them to have been reused. Neither a single- nor a two-storey wing would have required changes to the South Block roof but, if the recycled timbers used as pads to support the east end of the ceiling beams in Rooms 110 and 113 came from the demolished Frame 8 of the South Block roof, it would argue that they became available when the addition of a third storey required the changes to the roof and that, therefore the second and third storeys are contemporary. This receives support from the character of the stonework of the west elevation (Figure 13.8 on page 230).

*c.*1700

Most of the surviving interiors show evidence of a substantial refurbishment of the building, which Taylor (1971) dated to the end of the 17th century and Thorp and Cox (2010) to *c.*1700. These changes included plasterwork ceilings, the insertion of windows and fireplaces, and a new staircase. The East Wing was raised to three storeys with a new roof requiring the dismantling of the two eastern bays of the 1482 roof. The southern part of Frame 7 was cut away to insert the stairs but the northern part of the tie beam was retained as a cantilever to support new beams to the east.

18th century

The lower floor of the east block (Room 35) appears, from the evidence of Window 194, to date to the *c.*1700 alterations. The upstairs room (114), however, has early 18th-century features, such as the corner fireplace (500) and a later 18th-century cupboard in a blocked window. The recovery of a late 18th- or early 19th-century glass bottle fragment from the wall core might suggest that the whole block is so dated but Window 128 is of a similar date and is inserted indicating that the wall is earlier. Thorp and Cox (2010) suggest a date between 1720 and 1750 for construction and suggest that some alterations relate to the use of Castle House as a school from before the 1782 dilapidations report (see page 27). These may include the alterations at the top of the staircase which would have given improved access to the roof space, perhaps for dormitories.

19th century

Only minor alterations are evident during the use of the building as a school, which continued until between the 1891 and 1901 censuses. The courtyard buildings were demolished when SANHS purchased the castle in 1874 requiring the insertion of Window 78.

20th century

Several episodes of serious repair are recorded starting in 1907/8 to make the house habitable for the Gray family (SANHS minutes: 6/12/1907). The south wall was causing concern in 1912 (SANHS minutes: 9/2/1912) and the floor of Room 114 in 1914 (SANHS minutes: 11/9/1914). The turnstile was added in 1930 and the access to Room 118 replaced by Window 133; there was other work to address problems in the adjacent south wall. Gray's excavations and the subsequent landscaping necessitated the (re)facing of the exposed exterior of the East Block and the resetting of the gatepier fixed to the north wall, probably early in 1933 (SANHS 13249).

Extensive repairs were undertaken in 1938 that included some new windows and work to the staircase (SRO SANHS minutes: 5/1/1938). Further repairs were needed during the early 1950s, including the removal of the stair dormer, steel supports to some beams and the insertion of Windows 120 and 121. The ceiling in Room 118 was probably removed and the beakhead arch discovered. Room 32 was converted to toilets in 1960 when Room 26 was used as the museum education room. These changes were reverted at an unknown date. In 1959, Room 118 was described: "This room, with a glass partition erected, could house examples from our dress collection ...". The partition was put up in 1962 (SRO A/CNT/4/1) but the room was never used in this way and it was decided in 1973 that access up the spiral stair was unsafe (SRO A/CNT/4/3).

21st century

Major changes were undertaken in 2012/13 when the building was comprehensively refurbished and split into two uses. Several blocked windows and Door 494 were reopened, post-medieval changes to Fireplace 193 were removed as were some late 19th- and 20th-century partition walls.

Chapter 14

Castle Green and the Moats

Chris Webster

There is much less information surviving for the area of the Outer Ward: fewer historical mentions and less archaeological research. The two major surviving structures, Castle Bow and Bishop Fox's school, are discussed in Chapter 15 and Chapter 16; the more limited evidence for other structures is discussed below.

The western side of the outer moat followed the natural line of a stream which flowed into the river Tone. In the medieval period it must have been captured to feed the mill stream which appears to have formed the northern boundary of the castle. To the south it formed the western boundary of the town, forming a wet area that was not developed until the late 17th century (Mason *et al.* 2010). At the south-west corner of the castle, the water was partly diverted eastwards to flow along the southern moat and then northwards along the eastern moat to the mill (Vivian-Neal and Gray 1940, 54).

14.1 The Outer Moat

The eastern and southern sides

Toulmin (1791, 46) says that the moat by the east gate was 25ft wide and 12ft deep but he uses the past tense and the source for his figures is not known. The line of one edge or the other of the moat has been recorded in several places. Moat deposits 5.5m deep were seen when the library was built in 1904 and similar deposits were encountered during building works at Goodman's printers, just east of the Keep Garden, in 1926 (Vivian-Neal and Gray 1940, 58). The construction of an electricity showroom to the south of Castle Bow enabled Gray to record various walls within the moat but most of the material was removed by mechanical excavator (Vivian-Neal and Gray 1940, 55–7). More limited salvage recording was undertaken on the north side of Castle Bow, which recorded only infilling deposits (Exeter Archaeology 1999). To the north, the edge of the moat was seen by Colin Clements behind 6 North Street during building works in 1980 about 12m east of the wall of the Keep Garden (Burrow, I 1984, 53). Similarly to the electricity showroom site, several wells and a substantial cross wall were noted.

Towards the north-east corner of the castle, a section across the moat was excavated in 1980 in Mill Lane (Burrow, I 1984). This showed a complex picture, again with late revetment walls in the moat fill but also a leat of 11th- or 12th-century date. Unfortunately the relationship of the leat and moat had been destroyed by a later wall. Further work was undertaken in 1990 (Webster and Croft 1990, 228) and 1999 (Broomhead 1999) that confirmed these result but provided little new evidence.

The earliest finds recorded from the moat in all these excavations were late 16th or 17th century and related to an extensive episode of infilling that is also seen in the town ditch (for example by Higbee 2001). This may be associated with the presence of gardens in the ditch recorded in the mid 16th century (see page 21) or to clearance or slighting following the Civil War.

The western side

The excavations at Benham's Garage located the western side of the stream valley (Leach and Pearson 1984) but the moat itself was not excavated as it lay under the adjacent cinema. Vivian-Neal and Gray (1940, 55 n.25) report that "a part of the fosse was uncovered" when the cinema foundations were dug but provide no further description, which is curious as Leach and Pearson (1984, 37, 52) report that "two parallel, east–west alignments of squared oak posts were seen within thick deposits of black, waterlogged clay and peat" and the "presence of massive timbers on a direct alignment with the Benham's road, [the 'West Road', see below] discovered during excavations for the Odeon cinema in the 1930s". The source of this information is not given in the published version but an earlier draft preserved in the WAT archives (SRO DD/WAT/16 Fii15) says that "during the construction of the cinema Mr S Webber who worked on the site remembered two rows of timbers running across the moat (shown on fig.1); it will be seen that these are approximately in line with the roadway excavated." The figure referred to is Fig. 10 in Leach (1984c).

Wall fragment

Warre (1853, 26) mentions a "mass of masonry" at the south-west corner of the outer ward and it is shown on his plan running roughly east-west with its west end touching the stream which follows the line of the moat. The key identifies this as "Mass of masonry in Mr Channon's garden." It appears identically on Leversedge's original plan, which formed the basis of the engraving. No further description is given but one of Leversedge's elevation drawings (Figure 14.1) shows it as a much-ruined piece of walling with an irregular hole through which water is flowing. The hole is either barred or has steps within. From the positioning of the number "v" on the plan it is likely that this view is from the south but it is not clear what exactly is being shown. There is no indication of the moat by the end of the wall nor any indication on the plan of the water coming out of the hole.

The angle of the wall shown on the plan might suggest the side of a tower but it could also be interpreted as the remains of part of a weir controlling water flow through the moat. There is no obvious other source for the water shown in the elevation drawing.

Figure 14.1: *Leversedge's 1853 drawing of the masonry at the south-west corner of the outer ward. SANHS 3516.*

14.2 The West Gate

The only known remains of the West Gate are those shown by Leversedge (SRO DD/SAS/c1207/2g) on the north side of Tower Street. Warre (1853, 26) described these as a "small fragment" of masonry and reports the finding of wooden beams during drain digging to the west. He believed these to be part of a barbican but the remains of a bridge seem more likely. If the interpretation of the driveway wall (see page 217) as a Civil War defence is correct, it may imply that the West Gate had been mostly destroyed by that date.

The excavations at Benham's Garage (Leach and Pearson 1984) complicate the picture as they encountered an east–west road running about 30m to the south of Tower Street. The road, referred to as the "West Road" was dated to the later 12th century and was buried by waterlogged silts apparently in the 13th century. Leach and Pearson (1984, 52–3) discuss possible reasons for a realignment of the west exit from the castle with reference to routes out of Taunton to the west but the earlier draft report (SRO DD/WAT/16 Fii15) suggests that the West Road was very short-lived and was "merely a diversion [...] while an original route was being rebuilt or repaired". There may be a historical context for this suggestion as the Pipe Rolls record the completion of the West Gate in 1268 (see page 19); it may be that these construction works required the diversion.

Only limited archaeological works have been undertaken in the area. A watching brief on the digging of foundations within the Winchester Arms did not discover any features that predated the construction of the present building in the early 19th century (Dyer 1998), and service trenching in the road to the south recorded only recently disturbed ground (Passmore 2011).

14.3 The Inner Moat

The upper parts of the inner moat have been examined in several places but it is recorded that the moat was infilled during Hammet's work in *c.*1790 (Toulmin 1791, 52) and later, so few earlier deposits have been observed. Gray dug a hole at the junction of the west and inner moats; this revealed "dark silt and water" at a depth of 2.6m (Vivian-Neal and Gray 1940, 55 n.27). In more recent work in a similar location (Passmore 2010), boreholes recorded the moat deposits to a depth of 5.25m: an initial weathering of the sides followed by natural silting and a final episode of deliberate infilling. It was also clear that the present flat-bottomed, landscaped, ditch is wider (20m) than the medieval moat (less than 8m). This narrower medieval moat was also recorded by Jeboult (see Figure 2.3 on page 33) at the entrance (about 8.7m wide) and this also explains the presence of skeletal remains below the southern wall (see page 92). The change may be associated with Hammet who is described (see page 29) as landscaping the ground around the castle. Material for infilling the moat may have come from widening it to produce a sunken, level garden adjacent to the judges lodgings, although this may be a Civil War remodelling.

To the east of the driveway, the moat appears to have remained at about its medieval width and been filled in more gradually until it was finally obscured in the late 19th century (see page 64).

14.4 Interior Structures

The Mount

A plan reproduced by Robin Bush (1977, 126) shows a sub-oval mound on the south side of the outer ward, in a garden to the west of the School. The plan, produced *c.*1820 by the Charity Commission (1894) to show the property associated with the school, labels it as "Mount". Unless this is landscaped rubble around a collapsed tower or other structure, it would seem likely that it is part of the Civil War defences. An alternative interpretation as a garden earthwork is less probable in this small urban enclosed space. The mound had gone by the time of the Ordnance Survey 1:500 map of Taunton in 1888 and is now under the former Technical Institute, built in 1898 (see Figure 6.1 on page 98). Limited monitoring of highway works adjacent to the site in 1999 (HER 44687) recorded solid red marl immediately below the paving slabs, interpreted then as part of the rampart, but possibly part of the Mount.

Other walls

A wall was found in 1973 (see page 52) in the area of the Castle Hotel carpark (see Figure 6.1 on page 98) which may have formed part of the Constable's Hall complex and Leach (2005) found disturbed wall remains 5m and 8m from eastern end of his trench along S side of Castle Bow but was unable to investigate further. These last two walls were not seen during the monitoring of a larger trench in 2011/12 and may be spurious.

Two walls were located towards the south-east corner of Castle Green in 2011/12 (Figure 6.1 on page 98). One (2262, page 99) ran north-south to the north of the School and is probably that shown on the Charity Commission plan (Figure 16.4 on page 253) dividing two gardens. It had been removed by 1849 (SRO DD/SAS/C212/MAP/152) as the area had been laid out as the Cattle Market. To the north, an east-west wall (2254, page 100) probably formed the south end of a building shown on Wood's map of Taunton in 1840. The building is not shown 20 years earlier on the Charity Commission plan or on the 1888 plan but the wall was abutted on both sides by the market paving scheme which was laid out sometime between 1850 and 1887.

Wall 2256 (see page 99) in the south-west corner formed the western edge of the paved market area and is shown forming a building to the west on the 1888 Ordnance Survey plan. To the north of this, a wall (2414, page 100) running north-west to south-east cannot be correlated with any map evidence but appeared to be of late post-medieval construction. Neither can another substantial wall (2282, page 101) similarly aligned on the east side of the green.

After completion of the paving scheme, nineteen small pits were monitored as they were dug for water mains renewal. Most were within the earlier pipe trenches but two, in Corporation Street, recorded a road surface (presumably late 19th century) and a fragment of wall of probable 17th-century date (Milby 2014).

In 2013, James Brigers monitored work to the west of Castle Bow exposing red clay under the carpark makeup. The clay had been cut by a small pit that appeared to have been used for metalworking but this was not excavated as it was not to be disturbed (Brigers 2013b). It is possible that this was for lead working either during construction or demolition of buildings in the area.

14.5 Cemetery

The presence of human remains in and around Castle Green was first recorded by Toulmin (1791, 45) and they have been disturbed by service trenching ever since. The situation up to the late 1970s was reviewed by Colin Clements (1984), when the first skeleton was radiocarbon dated, showing that the cemetery had originated before the Norman conquest and probably represented the site of the minster church. Some of the bones discovered in the 1970s were reported on (Johnson 1975; Rogers 1984) but the current whereabouts of these bones is unknown.

The first radiocarbon date (860±70, uncalibrated AD) was, as Clements (1984) recognised, likely to be a very rough guide as it came from the mixed bones of several individuals but it allowed him to argue that the cemetery had started earlier than the 11th-century castle and later than the founding of Taunton in the late 7th century. More recent work has extended the extent of both the cemetery and its date of use.

On Castle Green, burials are known from immediately west of Castle Bow (Group 13 in Figure 14.2 on the facing page) and along the road to the west (Groups 2, 14 and 20) as far as Castle Way (Group 19). A few fragments were recorded to the south in Castle Way (Group 16) but little other excavation has occurred in the southern part of Castle Green with the exception of the recent landscaping, which did not penetrate deeply in this area (Rainbird 2015). Burials have been found along the south side of the inner moat (Groups 4, 5, 18 and 21) and presumably cover the area between here and the Castle Bow road to the south.

Clements (1984, appendix 1, appendix 2) records newspaper reports of bones being found in the road "near the cinema in Corporation Street" in 1932 (Group 11) but, as he says, it is not clear whether they were found in Corporation Street itself or just near the cinema. The latter, perhaps in the area of Castle Way, would be more likely as Corporation Street follows the line of the castle outer moat that must have removed any burials. No burials were found in excavations to the south of Corporation Street in 2008 (Mason *et al.* 2010) suggesting that the castle moat followed the line of the southern boundary of the graveyard.

Jeboult (1893) says that he saw human bones from the sewer trench along the drive (Group 6) and Hallam (1965) reported disarticulated human bone from below the Gray Room (Group 8). Clements (1984) records burials from below the north wall of the Coin Room (Group 7) and also in the waterpipe trench across the courtyard (Group 9). Two fragments of bone were found in 2009 close to the north end of the pipe trench (Group 17) but none were seen in Trench Z (this was not excavated archaeologically, see page 94), which was in the location of the burial found by Clements. No human remains were found by Radford and Hallam (1953) below the Great Hall and this absence was confirmed by the work in 2009.

Further afield, burials are known to the west of the castle at St Paul's House (Groups 10 and 15) which perplexed Clements (1984, appendix 2) as the excavations at Benham's Garage (Leach and Pearson 1984), between St Paul and the castle, recorded no burials and indicated that none was ever likely in a waterlogged stream valley. He suggested that this was an extension to the cemetery which was otherwise constrained by the presence of the river and the town. There is no evidence that the medieval chapel of St Paul mentioned in the pipe rolls (see page 23) had burial rights and the burials from a 19th-century convent are reported to have been exhumed when the convent closed. These were reburied in a marked plot in St Mary's cemetery in Wellington Road (David Bromwich, pers. comm.). Two bones were radiocarbon dated to resolve this, and this showed that both sampled burials predated the castle. One was the earliest date so far obtained (640–770 cal AD, see Table 7.5 on page 152), disproving Clement's hypothesis that these burials formed part of a later expansion.

More human remains were found on the site of one of Taunton's gasworks in Tangier (Group 12), which are again a long way from Castle Green. The original report in the *Somerset County Gazette* (2/5/1868, 8) suggested that they were the "remains of soldiers who lost their lives in the sieges of Taunton" but Clements suggested that they might represent re-interments after exhumation during castle building works. Recent work has been targeted on the area (Reed and Whiteaway 2003; McNicol 2010) but no evidence of human bone has been recorded. The gasworks appears to have removed all of the burials and in the absence of evidence of the state of articulation or date of the bones it is not possible to say more about their origin.

While the St Paul date is early, so is the date from the opposite side of the castle, next to the East Gate (650–760 cal AD) and to the north (680–870 cal AD). These indicate a substantial cemetery (or cemeteries) from around the time in the late 7th century that the minster was founded (see page 263) and Bayesian modelling of the dates (see page 151) supports such a start date for

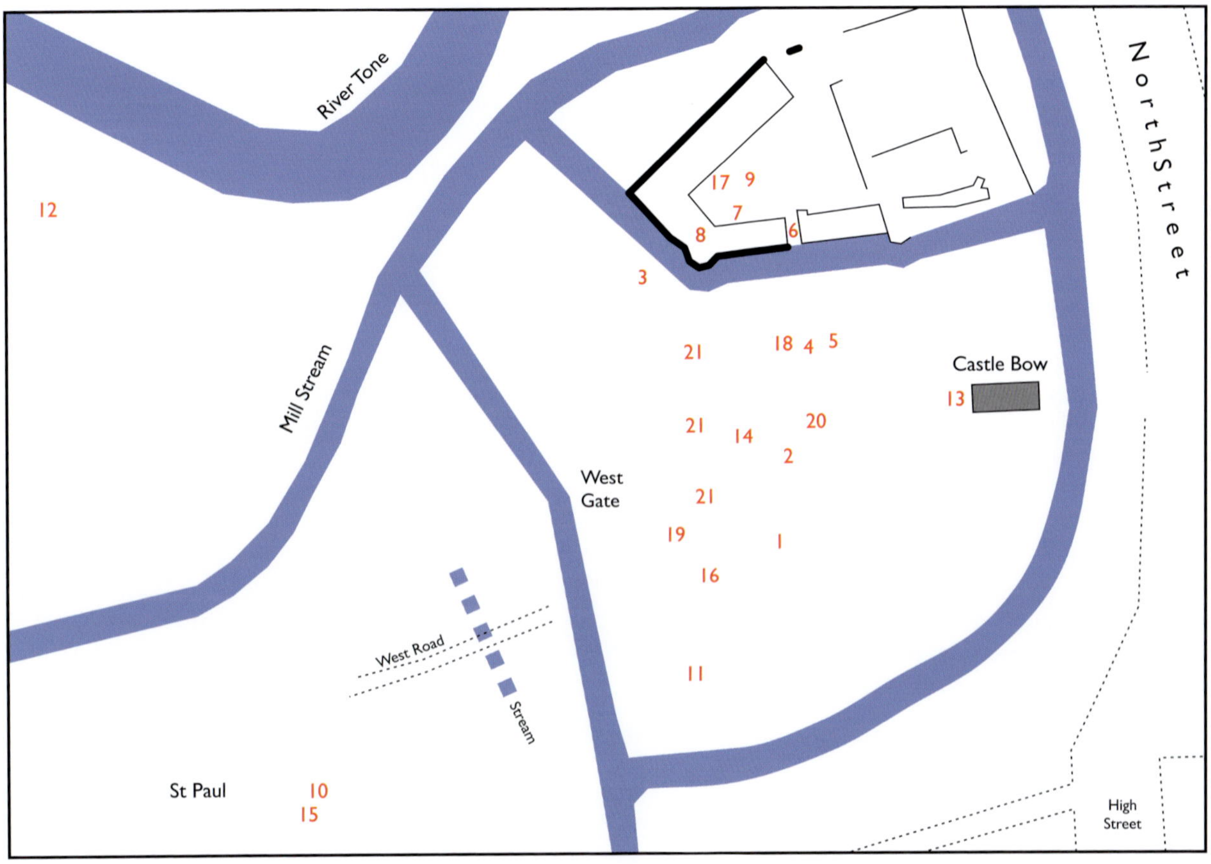

Figure 14.2: *Locations of burial groups. Groups 1–12 are discussed by Clements (1984, 30–31) whose numbering system has been extended for more recent finds. TTNCM accession numbers are given when known. * = radiocarbon dated, see Table 7.5 on page 152.*

1	—	*Cattle Market 1882, not retained*
2	—	*Castle Green 1867–1930, not retained*
3?	56.A.70	*Skull, marked "outer bailey"*
3	56.A.69	*Skull, marked "garden"*
3?	A.3005	*Skull, marked "garden"*
4	72.A.2.1	*Somerset HER 15071. Rogers (1984), note published as 73.A.3.1*
5	72.A.2.1	*Somerset HER 15071. Rogers (1984), note published as73.A.3.2*
6	—	*Inner Gate passage 1867, not retained, see page 33*
7	72.A.2.3	*Somerset HER 32291. Rogers (1984), note published as 73.A.3.3*
8	—	*Gray Room 1964, probably not retained, see page 51, Hallam (1965)*
9	—	*Clements (1984)*
10	70.A.4*	*Somerset HER 44473. Johnson (1975); Rogers (1984)*
11	—	*Cinema area 1932, not retained*
12	—	*Gasworks 1868, not retained, Somerset HER 44493*
13	101/2014*	*Castle Bow 1985, Somerset HER 44602, Burrow, I and Dennison (1988)*
14	37/1988*	*Castle Green gas main 1988, Somerset HER 16781.*
15	102/2014*	*St Pauls House 1989, Somerset HER 44473. Croft (1989)*
16	56/2005*	*Castle Green bus shelters 2005, Somerset HER 18220, Leach (2005)*
17	190/2009*	*Museum West Passage excavation 2009, see page 68*
18	190/2009*	*Edge of inner moat 2009, see page 92*
19	190/2009*	*Castle Green electricity trench 2009, see page 92*
20	24/2010*	*Castle Green gas main 2010, Somerset HER 28338, Passmore (2011)*
21	12/2010*	*Castle Green landscaping 2012–13, see page 97, Rainbird (2015)*

burial. The modelled dates for the end of burial do not confirm that the cemetery continued in use after the castle was built, which is unfortunate as Creighton (2002, 123) notes this is a research question that has not been answered by other sites where a castle was constructed on a Late Saxon cemetery. The date estimate is also unable to indicate if burial is likely to have ceased with the establishment of the priory in the mid-12th century.

The main cemetery appears to cover most of the area of the later castle with the exception of the area of the Great Hall, the eastern part of the Inner Ward and the Keep Garden. One human bone was reported from Gray's excavation (see page 41) but this appears to have been residual and could have been of any date. There are no reports of burials from some other areas, such as the hotel carpark and the southern part of Castle Green but this may reflect an absence of disturbance there. The areas not used for burial presumably reflect other uses: the sites of the Anglo-Saxon church(es) and bishop's hall, for example.

The Castle Hotel

The Castle Hotel is believed to have been built by Josiah Easton in *c.*1816 together with the Winchester Arms that faces it across Castle Green. It cannot have been there in 1814, if the date given for SANHS 12501 and 12527 is correct but there does appear to have been a house (Toulmin's "Porters Lodge") there in 1773 (SANHS 3504), that again cannot have been present in 1814. It is possible that the demolition of this house, provided the impetus to make the sketches of the north side of Castle Bow.

On Carver's plan of 1832 the hotel building is shown as "Mr Easton's House now Mr Mattock's" with the Castle Inn to its east on Fore Street. The outbuildings, including the Billiard Room are in the same ownership, as is the Winchester Arms. Both of the main buildings are shown with semi-circular gardens in front. The bow-fronted extension at the north of the Castle Hotel is first shown on John Leversedge's plan of 1853 (SRO DD/SAS/C1207/2g).

Chapter 15

Castle Bow

Chris Webster

Castle Bow is the name given to the East Gate of Taunton Castle and also to the roadway running through it. The gate formed the main entrance to the castle and faced out onto the market place. It has been incorporated in the Castle Hotel since the early 19th century.

15.1 Sources of Information

Castle Bow is often illustrated, usually as part of the Castle Hotel. There are useful pictures (SANHS 3511, 12476, 12492, 12494, 12501 and 12527; Museum PCFILE 1b) from the years around 1800 that show the structure before this conversion with some details of the upper floor. Toulmin (1791, 45) says that the gate is called the Porter's Lodge and that "although great part is in ruins, yet the arches are very strong and the grooves, in which the port-cullis was let down, are quite perfect. Part of the fourth wall has lately been taken down, to open a passage to the Free School". Sloper has annotated his copy (SANHS AR 21-32): "This was taken down about 1734 as John Mallett of Pitminster, who owned the Fountain Inn contiguous thereto, had a grant from the manor of a little plot of land at the back gate of the Antelope [crossed out] Fountain on condition of his making a passage or doorway through the building called the Bow to be forever used as a gateway or passage to the free school."

Savage (1822) says that the gate has been "lately converted into a dwelling-house" and this may be related to the construction of what is now the Castle Hotel in about 1815. Prior to this there was a house adjacent to the north described by Toulmin (1791, 45) as having the arms of Thomas Langton (bishop 1493–1501) on the front with a mitre above and the date 1498 below. Sloper annotated his copy: "The mitre was removed and inserted on the East side of the Porters Lodge when the building referred to was pulled down and the new erection (Clarkes Hotel) built at the beginning of the 19th century and the date and arms were inserted on the west side of the same." These are shown on Leversedge's elevations (SANHS 3517) and still survive, although both appear to have been moved downwards since Leversedge drew them and the carving of the inner one is very eroded.

15.2 Ground Floor

The present gate passage is 12.8m long with substantial arches at either end. Both are plain, shallow pointed arches with a simple chamfer and both have a substantial flat rib, again chamfered, occupying the central third of the soffit. Behind the eastern arch is the groove for the portcullis noted by Toulmin, and behind that is a further arch, facing east, with a rebate for the gate visible on the rear (west). The jambs of this arch have been removed, although a hinge pintle survives. It is likely that all the archways have been widened in this way. There is then a gap, with a flat ceiling, before another arch of the same type as those at the east and west ends. The arches appear to have undergone few changes since being drawn in SANHS 3511 (Figure 15.2 on page 245), although obviously the upper floors have been added.

The north wall of the gate passage is now pierced by two doors (455 and 457) and two windows (454 and 456, the latter originally a door) all built as part of the hotel as they are not shown in SANHS 3511. That drawing appears to show a single door, containing steps up, with windows to either side that continue into the doorway, reminiscent of a shop front. Above is a tile-covered offset that would have supported a floor or vault. There is no sign of the

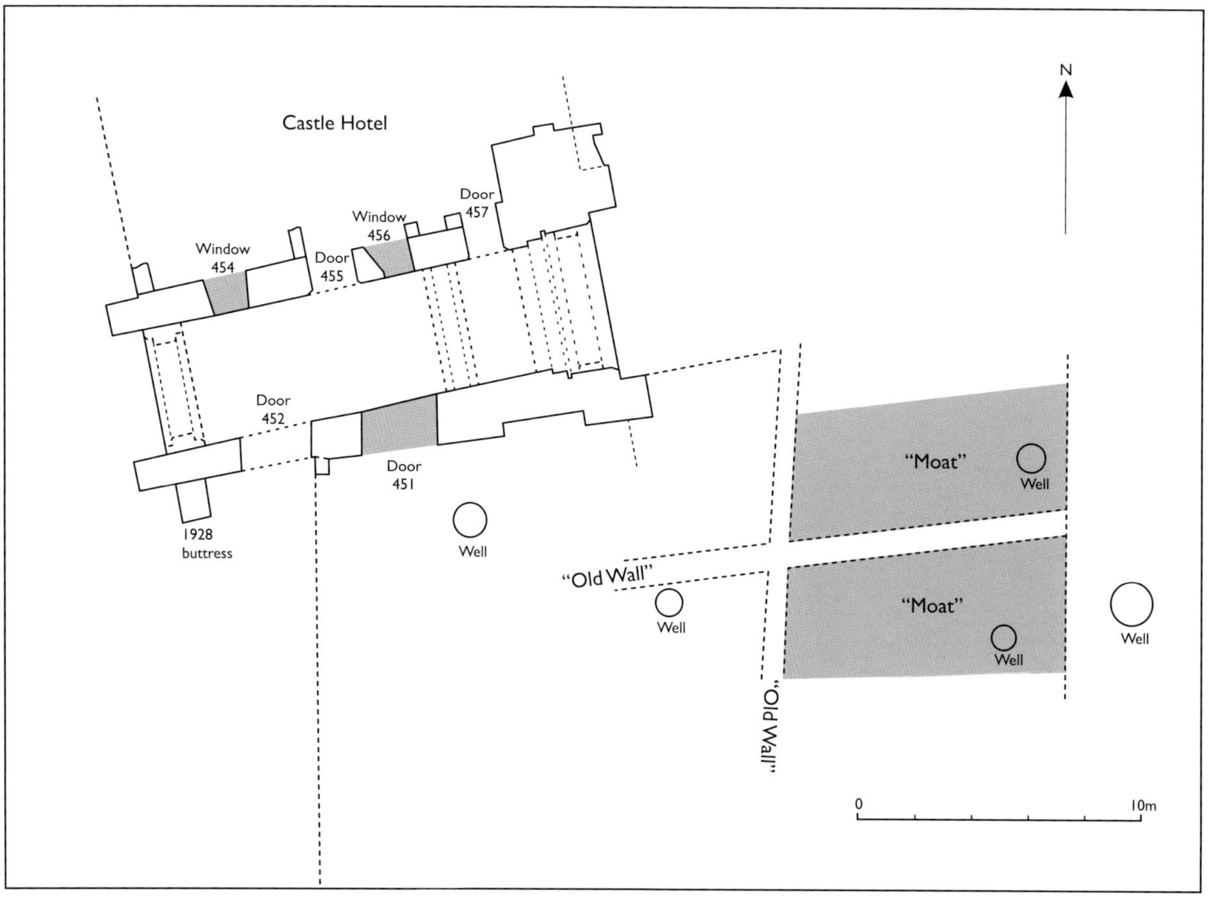

Figure 15.1: Plan of Castle Bow, based on 1928 architects drawings (SRO D/B/ta/24/1/71/1410A), with finds recorded during the construction of the electricity showroom to the south in 1937 (from SANHS 3527)

"shopfront" visible through Door 451 in the 1796 picture (SANHS 12494, Figure 15.3 on page 246) but the rear of the wall is shown in SANHS 12527 of 1814 (Figure 15.4 on page 246). There appears to be a projection from the wall that could accommodate the back of the windows, with a low (possibly half-buried) doorway in the centre. To the left (east) of this is a door (shown more clearly in Museum PCFILE 1b) with walling to the right. The shadow suggests that the wall above these is on about the line of the rear of the projection, and thus that the ground floor wall is thinner.

On the south side, two openings are known. At the west end is large, slightly pointed doorway (452), arched in brickwork and to the east of this is a large area of blocking masonry. SANHS 12494 shows this as a wide, shallow opening (451), again arched in brick. Both are shown in a plan of 1928 (SRO D/B/ta/24/1/71/1410A), where 451 is shown reduced in size with double doors leading into the meat market. SANHS 3511, however, shows only one opening. The drawing appears foreshortened here but it seems most likely that this is Door 451 and, therefore, that Door 452 is later. A board is affixed above Door 451 and this is presumably the entrance to the school mentioned by Toulmin; Door 452 may have been cut to replace it, perhaps when the meat market building was built in 1822 (Bush 1977, 57).

At the west end of the south wall is an external buttress, shown as a proposed work in 1928.

15.3 First Floor

Little survives of the east wall, which is overgrown in SANHS 3511 but can be seen from the east in SANHS 12492 (Figure 15.5 on page 247). There it is shown surviving to perhaps half-storey height with a possible window, off-centre to the north, but this part of the drawing is not clear. A distant view in SANHS 3504 (Figure 15.6 on page 248) of 1773 appears to show a five-light rectangular window.

SANHS 3511 (Figure 15.2 on the next page) shows a small part of the east end of the south wall surviving, which ends with the remains of one side of a window (462) with the springing for the arch. This is also visible from the

Figure 15.2: *Castle Bow from the west in the late 18th or early 19th century. Door 451 is visible on the right with the remains of Window 462 and the suggested piscina (463) above. The head of Door 458 is visible above the arch to the left and Windows 459 and 460, with the suggested aumbry (461) can be seen through the arch. SANHS 3511*

Figure 15.3: *Castle Bow from the south in 1796. The wide opening on the ground floor is Door 451, and those on the rear wall of the upper floor are 458–461. The remains of Window 462 are at the extreme right. Detail of SANHS 12494.*

Figure 15.4: *Castle Bow from the north in about 1814 showing Windows 460 (left) and 459 with the door to the spiral stair to the right. SANHS 12527*

Figure 15.5: *Castle Bow from the east in 1796. SANHS 12492*

outside in SANHS 12494 where the moulding has the appearance of attached columns; this is not shown in SANHS 3511 but this area appears incompletely drawn. Beyond this, within the wall is a smaller opening, with columns forming either side and a trefoil head (463). The interior is shown in shadow, suggesting a niche rather than a window. Unfortunately the area is obscured by another building in SANHS 12494 so this cannot be confirmed but a niche in this position would suggest a piscina, and thus that the room over the gate was a chapel. This would be a not uncommon position for a chapel and there are mentions of a chapel somewhere around the East Gate in the pipe rolls (see page 15).

In the north wall, four openings are visible from the inside, above the missing south wall, in SANHS 12494. The two central ones (459, 460) appear to be a pair of two-light traceried windows, although the western (459) is shown lacking its tracery. They are also shown from the outside (north) in the 1814 engraving (Figure 15.4 on the facing page), both with tracery but Window 459 lacks the central mullion and appears blocked by masonry. The windows appear to have a hood mould above both inside and out. To the east of these is a smaller opening (461) visible on the inside only; it appears to be another niche but no columns are visible and it has a hood mould to match the adjacent windows (459, 460). The presence of what appears to be a shelf (in Figure 15.2) would support the chapel interpretation with this as the remains of an aumbry.

Internally, at the west end, a fourth opening is shown in SANHS 12494, which appears to be a doorway with a pointed arch (458). It is very plain, with no mouldings (although some are shown in SANHS 3511), and seems to have a large rebate for a door. From the north SANHS 12527 shows a round-headed, featureless doorway set in a projecting structure and with a spiral staircase visible within. The view from the west (Figure 15.2 on page 245) supports the identification of a stair turret by showing two small rectangular windows appropriate for such a structure. No stairs are visible in SANHS 12494 and Door 458 may have been at the top of the staircase. The outside door is at a lower level and must have provided access from a now-vanished building to the north. Vivian-Neal and Gray (1940, 60) suggest that this tower is

Figure 15.6: *Castle Bow from the west in 1773. Detail of SANHS 3504 (Figure 2.1 on page 28).*

"late Norman", presumably based on the rounded head of the door shown in SANHS 12527, and note the presence of another tower of the same date at the east end.

Nothing survives of the west wall, unless it is actually that depicted in SANHS 3504.

15.4 Areas to the North and South

The land to the north appears to be open in 1814 (Figure 15.4 on page 246) with a high wall running from the north-east corner of the gatehouse northwards and terminating in a small turret projecting eastwards. The 1928 plan of the Castle Hotel (see Figure 15.1 on page 244) shows a substantial block of masonry surviving within the building at the junction point which may be a survival of this wall. The wall is shown from the east in 1796 (Figure 15.5 on the preceding page) where it appears to lie in front of the face of the gatehouse.

It is not clear if the house described by Toulmin lay in this location; SANHS 3504 (Figure 2.1 on page 28) in 1773 shows buildings further west and this area may have been a garden or yard.

Part of the area to the south was recorded by Gray (see page 47) when cellars were being dug in 1935. Several wells, and walls crossing and lining the moat, were seen but little else. The moat edge was about 4m to the east of the front of the gatehouse and there were no signs of a curtain wall or of towers flanking the gateway.

15.5 Structural Development

As far as can be told from the meagre evidence remaining, the East Gatehouse was of one build of the 13th century, unless Vivian-Neal and Gray's (1940) identification of Norman features is correct, with few visible changes apart from decay until the 18th century. It is likely that its construction is recorded in the pipe rolls in the second half of the 1280s (see page 19). The upper floor appears to have been designed as a chapel but there are few references to it in the documents so it may have been very short-lived and reverted to secular use. The one post-medieval feature is the window shown in 1773 but this may be artistic licence and all the other later features relate to openings cut to give light and access to adjoining properties.

Chapter 16

The Grammar School

Richard Parker and Chris Webster

The school was the last recorded building at Taunton by the Bishops of Winchester, and in some ways marks the demise of the castle as it stands on the southern defences but faces away from the inner ward into the town. Its construction is recorded in the accounts in 1522 when £226 5s 10d was apportioned "towards the fabric of one building called le Scolehouse within the castle" and in the following year when a further £32 13s 4d was spent on the same. This attribution to bishop Richard Fox has been queried in the past, Pevsner (1958, 314) dating the building on architectural grounds to *c.*1480. Vivian-Neal and Gray (1940, 75) noted that there was documentary evidence for a school since the late 13th century and believed that the present building was merely a restoration, as had been previously suggested by Holmes (1911b).

It remained a school until 1885, when increasing success led to a move to larger premises. After this, the building was used by Taunton Borough Council until the opening of The Deane House in 1987. It is currently occupied by SCC's registration service with two of the rooms used for weddings and civil partnership ceremonies.

16.1 Sources of Information

The history of the school is covered by Holmes (1911b), Wicks (1961), Bush (1977; 1983) and Dunning (not dated), summarised by Parker (2014). It is clear that it went through periods of success and failure, the former of which may be evident in alterations to improve the accommodation. There is, however, nothing describing the building until after the Civil War.

The school is mentioned by Toulmin (1791) who describes it as "a large and strong building and adjoining to it is a house for the master". He goes on to say that it was founded by Richard Fox "as appears by an authentic register, kept in Corpus Christi College, Oxford" and that above the entrance are the arms of Fox and of Hugh Oldham, bishop of Exeter. No one else mentions Oldham: Savage (1822, 196n) states that his arms were not there in 1821, there is no reference by the Charity Commissioners (below), and only Fox's arms are shown in Buckler's drawing, but it is not an unlikely association as they were friends, and Oldham had assisted Fox in the foundation of Corpus Christi (Orme 2004). As Oldham died in 1519 the arms, if reported correctly by Toulmin, must have been a form of memorial.

The "authentic register" could not be found when investigated in the early 1820s (Charity Commission 1894). The Commission could find no foundation documents but did discover evidence for the first endowment of the school in 1554, which provided a stipend for the master who should be chosen by the Warden of New College, Oxford (another Winchester foundation). The commissioners' report provides an account of the state of the school at the time and a useful plan (reproduced in Figure 16.4 on page 253).

The school is illustrated by Buckler (see Figure 16.3 on page 251), which appears more accurate in the foreground than to the rear where the building has been shortened and simplified. There are two early photographs by Edward Jeboult (for whom see page 33) both showing the south side in 1865 before the civic conversions. The building is shown in outline on the Ordnance Survey 1:500 plan of Taunton surveyed in 1887 and on subsequent maps.

More recently, the building has been examined by the Somerset Vernacular Building Research Group (McDermott 2007a), who while accepting the 1520s date note similarities in the design of the roof to other local examples that have been dated by dendrochronology to the late 15th century.

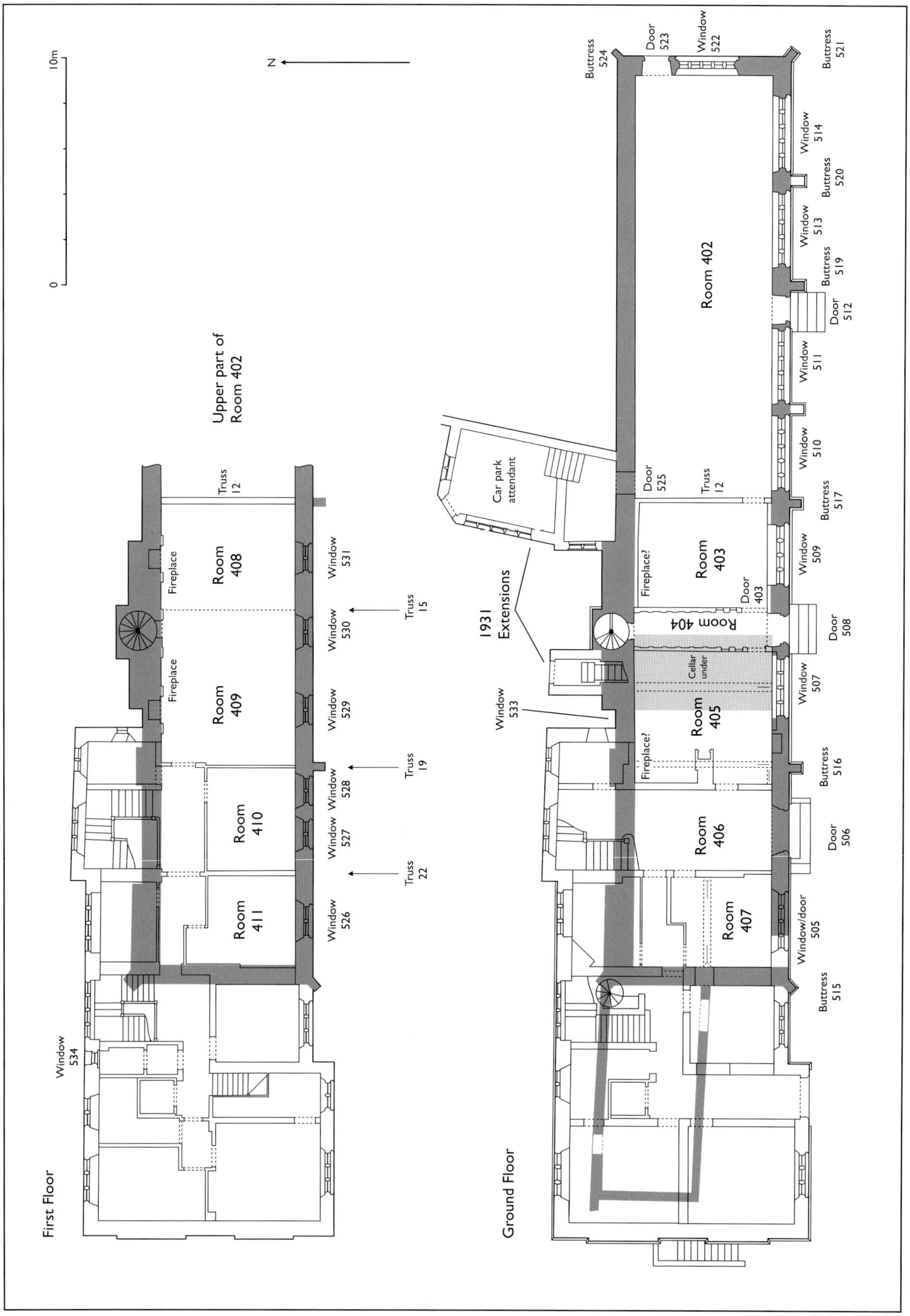

Figure 16.1: *Ground and first floor plans of Bishop Fox's School (The Old Municipal Buildings). The 1522 building and "offices" from the Charity Commissioners' plan are shown in grey. Based on a plan by SCC architects.*

Figure 16.2: *View of the south side of the Grammar School in 2015 with the buttress (515) marking the original west end centre left.*

Figure 16.3: *Buckler's view of the Grammar School dated 1837. The view is idealised at the far end where the two western bays are foreshortened and simplified. SANHS Buckler C.*

To resolve this the school roof was dated, giving a felling date estimated to lie between 1495 and 1527. Close precision was not possible as all the timber had been well trimmed but this does support the documented date (Bridge 2012). No later timbers were found showing that the roof (at least in the area sampled in the attics at the western end of the building) had survived the Civil War. Richard Parker carried out a further detailed examination of the building in 2012/13, with the aims of identifying any possible areas of conflict damage and enhancing the 2007 survey. The report that follows is based on that survey (Parker 2014) and discussions between the present authors.

16.2 The Original Plan

The school was originally *c.*40.8m long by *c.*7.9 wide externally (possibly 8 by 1.5 perches) with diagonal buttresses at the corners. The walls are made of Morte slate rubble with Hamstone details. The building has been extended to the west, destroying the north-west corner, but the original extent is indicated by a buttress (515) half buried in the wall. There are three further buttresses along the south front with two later (post-1863) ones added on the eastern part. The stonework of the buttresses and the cill levels of the doors shows that the ground has been lowered substantially (0.75m at the eastern end), possibly quite recently as the ashlar of the modern buttresses also fails to reach the current ground level (see Figure 16.6 on page 254).

The eastern half of the building is a single open schoolroom, with accommodation on two or three storeys in the western part, all under a single roof structure. Rooms were divided by timber framed partitions, not always on the same alignment on each floor. The original features of the building will be described from east to west, treating the schoolroom and each of the lodgings in turn. Later alterations will be discussed afterwards.

The Schoolroom, Room 402

Roof

In the schoolroom, where it survives best, the roof can be seen to be an exceptionally elaborate arch-braced structure supported on 11 trusses, each consisting of a pair of principal rafters linked by a cambered collar beam, together forming an A-frame. These frames are reinforced by four curved, moulded arch-braces, two upper and two lower, tenoned and pegged into the principals and collars, forming a continuous pointed arch in each truss.

The arch braces all appear to have been slightly truncated at the base as though some decorative element, whether a projecting cusp with a finial or perhaps some form of applied ornament, such as angels, heraldic beasts or carved heads, has been removed. The mouldings of the trusses are also damaged and have been chopped into at intervals by small notches, now infilled, which must formerly have housed joists or battens supporting a post-medieval plaster ceiling. It is likely that the decorative elements of the roof were removed to accommodate this ceiling.

The roof trusses have been reinforced by a complex arrangement of iron straps and also, at intervals, by large iron ties crossing the roof void, linked vertically to the centre of the collar by a tension bar. Some of this work may be contemporary with the buttresses added to the outside, probably in the early 20th century.

In each bay, on both sides of the roof, are three levels of purlins, a moulded and decorated wall plate with a brattished or battlemented cornice and a ridge tree. The purlins and the ridge are linked by three tiers of flat, chamfered wind braces, making an exceptionally rich display (Figure 16.5 on page 254). Details of individual trusses and bays are given in Parker (2014).

The roof, at over 40m long, must be one of the most ambitious of its date – certainly in the West Country.

Walls, doors and windows

The room is lit by four large windows in two pairs in the south wall (510, 511, 513 and 514) and one in the east (522), all of the same design. Each is of five lights, divided into upper and lower halves by a transom, the lights both above and below the transom being provided with uncusped four-centred arched heads with indented spandrels. There are two original doors, one between the pairs of windows in the south wall (512, see Figure 16.6 on page 254) and one at the north end of the east wall (523), each with a monolithic head cut to form a four-centred arch. Above the east door on the outside is a much eroded carved panel, described by the Charity Commission (1894) as "the crest of Fox, Bishop of Winchester ... surmounted by the mitre, with the date of 1522, and the monogram of R. F. under the same, such crest being as at Corpus Christi College, Oxford, (which was also founded by him) a pelican with wings disclosed, feeding her young." At Fox's other school in Grantham, Lincs, there is a statue of a pelican on the apex

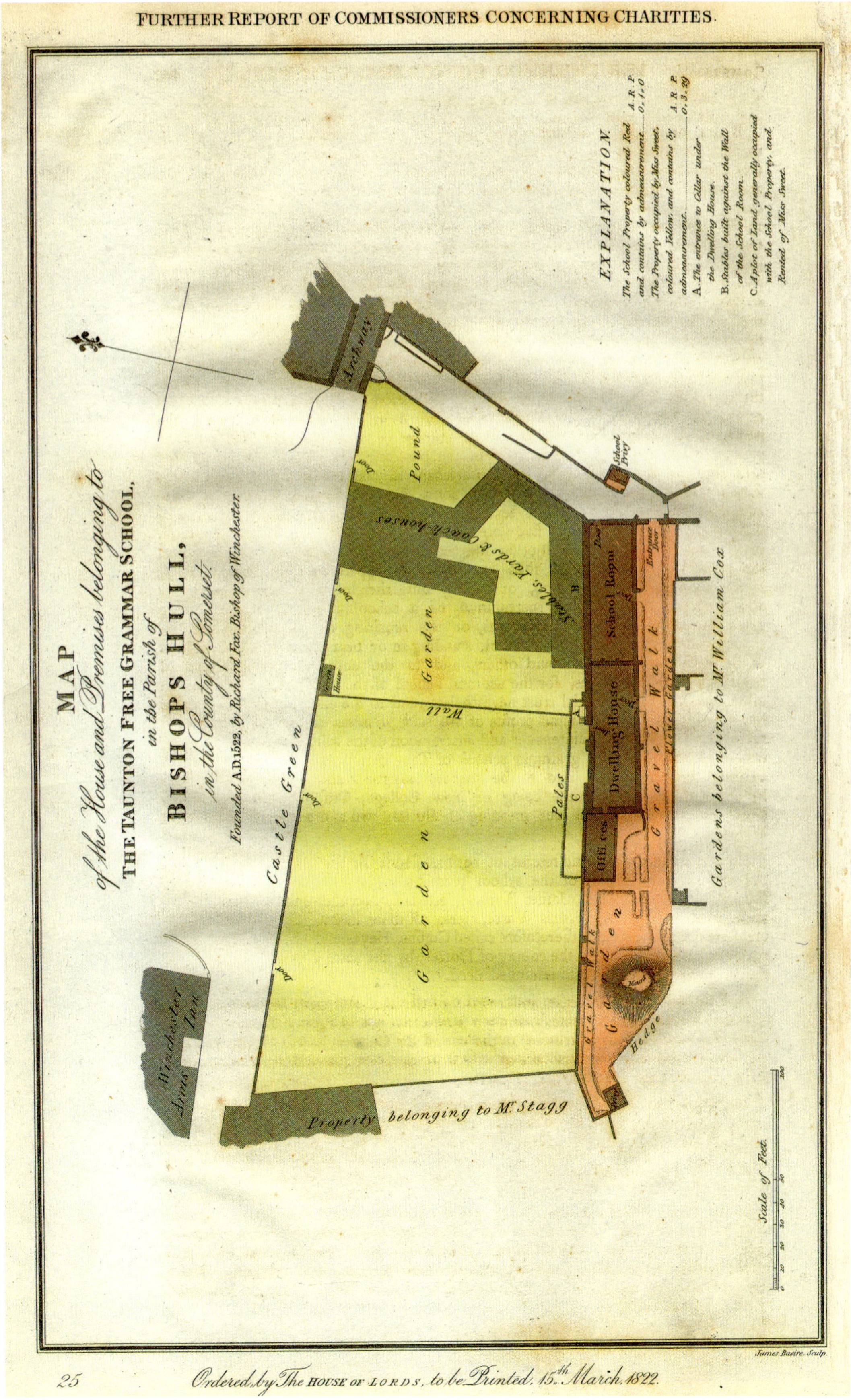

Figure 16.4: *Plan of the School showing the Mount* c.1820, *(Charity Commission 1894).*

Figure 16.5: *Detail of the westernmost bays on the north side of the schoolroom with the facsimile Truss 12 to the left.*

Figure 16.6: *Door 512, the south entrance to the schoolroom, showing the reduced ground level and modern buttress.*

of the gable and Start and Stocker (2011, 229) note that the medieval belief that the bird stabbed itself with its beak to feed its young (vulning) could be seen as applying to feeding the scholars' thirst for knowledge as they passed below.

The north wall is not fenestrated and the only door, at the west end, is an insertion. This door now provides access to a building constructed in 1931 as a carpark attendant's office (SRO D/B/ta/24/1/76/1595). The lack of windows is unusual and must indicate the presence of an earlier building, probably the barn mentioned in the 1525 accounts (see page 22).

The west wall is formed by a timber-framed partition rising the full height of the building (Truss 12). This is entirely obscured by modern cladding, possibly fireproofing, but the original timbers are visible from the adjacent room and these appear to be accurately replicated in facsimile towards the schoolroom. The basic arrangement consists of vertical studs and horizontal rails forming broad square panels. At the top, the triangular panels formed by the converging sides of the roof are braced by curved braces with a vertical stud between the uppermost. It is uncertain to what extent the original infilling of the panels remains, but it is likely that the majority of the medieval work survives, now hidden from view. There is a door at the south end leading to Room 403 but this is unlikely to be part of the medieval plan.

There is no fireplace in the room and no sign of smoke blackening of the roof, although this would have been cleaned off before all the timbers were painted. It is therefore likely that the room was unheated.

Lodging 1, Rooms 403 and 408

Room 403, immediately to the west of the schoolroom is now entirely featureless, having been divided into modern washrooms, but a large, four-light window (509) remains in the south wall. There is a large baulk of masonry in the north wall suggesting the presence of a fireplace and indicating a prestigious part of the accommodation, perhaps occupied by the usher. The room is entered by a doorway (403) with a false four-centred arch forming an almost triangular head, through a plank-and-muntin screen, one of a pair of screens forming a narrow passage (Room 404) across the interior of the building.

Upstairs is now part of the Vivary Room (Room 408/409), formerly the Council Chamber. Evidence that this was originally divided is seen in Truss 15 which has redundant sockets for a collar beam at a lower level, two sockets for curved

Figure 16.7: *The stair and chimney block on the north side of the school. The porch was added over the steps to the cellar in 1931.*

braces above the collar, and small, v-shaped sockets in the soffits of the rafters for housing sprung studs with pointed ends which supported the cob infilling. The closed truss will have resembled that forming the eastern wall of the present room (Truss 12) and must have been a primary feature. See Room 409, below, for details of the surviving principal rafters. The room must originally have been entered through a door in Truss 15 for which no evidence remains.

The Passageway, Room 404

This room is formed by two plank-and-muntin screens running the width of the building that have been much repaired but retain their original character. They do not form a true cross passage as at the north end of the corridor, a doorway with a four-centred ached head leads to a newel stair in the north wall. The details both of screens and the variant four-centred arched doors would be consistent with an early 16th-century date. The external doorway (508) appears to be of early 20th-century date, in Gothic-revival style with a curious four-centred traceried head incorporating glazed spandrels. This replaced an earlier doorway giving access to the passage, shown with a square head by Buckler (Figure 16.3 on page 251).

The stair lies in a substantial projection of the north wall flanked by a pair of chimneys (Figure 16.7). The eastern chimney has two offsets, one below eaves level and the other above, and appears to have served two fireplaces; one on the ground floor in Room 403 and the other on the first floor in Room 408. The western chimney appears to have only one offset, above the eaves line, but it is uncertain whether or not this chimney, which is still a very substantial structure, may not also have served two fireplaces. Both chimneys are now truncated just above roof level, but presumably rose into tall narrow shafts. Between the two chimneys, the stair turret is offset above a high plinth at about 1m above modern ground level, and then broadens at about 2m above ground level to rise in a broad, square bay. At the centre is a small square window lighting the stair within. The turret is roofed below the eaves by two sloping offsets of Hamstone. All the dressings are of Hamstone and the whole composition of chimneys and turret has an elegance which suggests a desire for display.

Lodging 2, Rooms 405 and 409

Room 405 has been much subdivided in recent years, but retains a large four-light window (507), and its ceiling is supported by a pair of very large beams, of different sizes, decorated with very deep, hollow chamfers. The broader beam to the east appears off-centre in the ground floor room, however it lies roughly centrally to a larger room (409) upstairs, now forming part of the former Council Chamber or Vivary Room. It is probably an original feature, and may have formed part of an impressively beamed ceiling to the ground-floor room. There may well have been a fireplace in the north wall, though nothing is now visible, and a small single-light window (533) of probable late-medieval date also survives.

It is conjectured that the western beam, which is narrower than the eastern beam, may have formed part of a further screen or partition defining the original western limit of this room, since it lies more-or-less underneath one of the tall closed trusses dividing the upper floors and roof space. This beam is joined at its southern end by a further beam lying at right angles to it, against the south wall, decorated with the same deep, hollow moulding. It is possible that this formed part of an exceptionally grand ceiling divided into compartments infilled with smaller decorated joists, or perhaps a boarded ceiling. Panelled intersecting-beamed ceilings and boarded ceilings of this type are known from 15th- and early 16th-century contexts in Devon and Somerset (Blaylock 2004, 190; Parker and Collings 2006, 320).

Upstairs is the western part (409) of the current Vivary Room accessed by the newel stair from the passageway (Room 404). The west wall is

Figure 16.8: The south wall of the cellar with the half-blocked window and access to service pipe.

formed by a massively-constructed closed truss (19) similar to Truss 12 (see Rooms 402 and 408 above) but lacking the vertical stud between the uppermost curved braces.

The timbers in this truss are clearly marked with carpenter's assembly marks, including IIV on two of the vertical studs. Other trusses over the Vivary Room are marked X and XI, V, VI and IV on the principal rafters. The numbering does not appear to make sense in terms of the position of the trusses within the roof, regardless of which end they are counted from. All the timbers are marked on the same (eastern) face of each truss, which is perhaps an indication that the confusion of the numbering in this roof is not a consequence of the roof having been dismantled and reassembled in the wrong order, in which case one might expect some of the trusses to have been accidentally reversed. In fact, since several trusses bear two different numbers, it is likely that the numbering relates more to the assembly of each truss rather than to the assembly of the roof as a whole. Had the collars and arch-braces in this section of the roof survived better it might have been possible to make better sense of the numbering system.

There is a cellar below the eastern half of Room 405 that extends part way below the entrance passage (Room 404). The date of this is uncertain but the entrance is shown on the 1821 plan and it may be an early feature. Internally (Figure 16.8) the cellar is brick with a transverse brick vault over, all heavily painted. There is a window in the south wall that is now partly buried by the paved surface outside and adjacent to that on the east is an inserted door that leads to a large diameter ceramic drain holding the electricity supply. The doorway is lined with larger bricks than the walls of the cellar and these

Figure 16.9: The entrance to the cellar within the 1931 porch.

appear to also be evident around the base of the wall indicating that the floor has been lowered. The original entrance to the cellar (Figure 16.9) appears to have been cut through the wall: the brick arch has been flattened to fit beneath the Hamstone plinth course.

Lodging 3, Rooms 406 and 410

The external door (506) to Room 406 was inserted sometime after the Charity Commissioners' plan of 1821 (see Figure 16.4 on page 253) and before Jeboult's photograph of 1865 (SRO T/PH/REA/82). The door shown by Jeboult was replaced by a wider entrance, probably at the same time (*c.*1888) as the staircase was added at the rear giving grand access to the Council Chamber. The two small windows above (527, 528), lighting Room 410, were probably added at the same time replacing two windows, one smaller than the other, shown by Jeboult.

The room retains no visible early features but may have been converted from a third ground-floor chamber, roughly comparable in size to those previously described. This may also have been heated by a fireplace in the rear wall, which was demolished in the 1880s to open the room out into the Victorian staircase hall beyond. The 1821 plan shows a thickening of the wall here that is likely to be a chimney stack. No other features remain visible; however, it is likely that the western wall may preserve some parts of a medieval partition (see Room 407, below).

Upstairs, ceilings have been inserted at about eaves level with attics above and few original features are visible below these. Above, however, the roof is accessible and there is considerable evidence both of the 1522 structure and of alterations to it. The upper part of a large medieval chamber (Room 410) survives, encompassing three bays of the roof. All the arch braces and collar beams have been removed to create headroom for the new attics; the sockets for the collars, and long sockets for the arch braces, can still be identified in the soffits of the principal rafters. The wind braces have either been removed, or are concealed by later plasterwork. It is possible that the survival, or removal, of wind braces might help determine whether or not this attic room was ever lit by dormer windows.

The attic is ceiled at the very apex of the roof and the original timbers survive above this. These are clean, without any trace of smoke blackening, and retain curved wind-braces into the apex of the roof. There is also no trace of any torching, lath or plaster, nor any decorative treatment of the timbers, suggesting that the structure of the roof was originally exposed right to the apex of the roof, and that the rich decorative qualities of the roof structure were displayed. The room is defined by two closed trusses (19 and 22).

The apex of Truss 19 has been infilled with 19th-century brickwork and it is conceivable that lower panels have also been replaced with modern infilling. The western closed truss (Truss 22), however, retains evidence of its original infilling. Part of one of the panels has been removed to create an access hatch into the loft within the apex of the roof and, here, the remains of a cob infill panel survive, supported by small, sprung studs originally housed in V-shaped sockets in the soffit of the principal rafter. Also visible is the top of an angled brace, probably representing one of the curved timbers still visible in the other closed trusses of the roof. The extent of preservation of this truss at lower levels of the building is unknown, but the survival of this panel raises the possibility that much medieval work remains lower down.

The Kitchen, Rooms 407 and 411

Most of the rear and end walls of this part of the building have been lost to early 20th-century additions but the south wall survives with a large late 19th- or 20th-century mullioned window (505), of four lights with arched heads, on the ground floor. Externally, this can be seen to cut through the remains of a tall opening with Hamstone dressings which extend below the level of the plinth, to the presumed ground level. This must represent a former doorway and as the Hamstone dressings are integral to the masonry of the primary walling, it is likely that the doorway represents an original feature.

The Charity Commissioners' plan of 1821 (see Figure 16.4 on page 253) probably shows the original north wall, with a very wide, but shallow projection which, on the analogy of the surviving projections to the east, may have housed a chimney breast. Its size suggests that it accommodated a very large kitchen fireplace. The plan also shows domestic "offices" (now demolished) extending to the west of the buildings and these rooms probably included sculleries, pantries and the other facilities necessary for the running of a large kitchen.

The east wall may be original since a beam, lying at right-angles to those in Room 405, retains a deep hollow chamfer and stepped, run-out stops which respect the line of this wall. It is difficult to account for the different alignment of this beam; it may perhaps have been one of a pair of such beams, one of which has been destroyed, or was perhaps a later insertion into the fabric. Alternatively it might have supported a subdivision within the room above (411), or perhaps a galleried structure within an open void reaching up into the roof. If this was the kitchen of the school, a full height room might well be expected with a gallery or loft over part of the space, perhaps to provide accommodation for servants. Alternatively the kitchen may have been a single storey high, with rooms above. No other features are visible and, as the whole of this corner has been demolished to open the rooms into the extension of 1902, little may survive.

Upstairs, the end two bays of the roof have suffered the most from alterations but can be seen to be wider than all those to the east. New floor levels have been inserted just below the level of the middle purlins and consequently the lower parts of the roof are entirely concealed. The surviving parts of the trusses, on the south side, show evidence of the collars and arch braces, and retain some wind braces (Figure 16.10 on the next page). The trusses also bear scars of whitewash

Figure 16.10: *The upper part of the southern side of Truss 24 at the extreme west end of the school roof. Lath and plaster ceilings can be seen below the purlin, and windbraces with clean timber above.*

which revel that these rooms were formerly ceiled above the level of the upper purlins, like the three bays to the east (Room 410). The remains of a fragment of Gothic tracery in the western gable reveals either that the western wall has been rebuilt or that reused fragments of demolished buildings were employed during the construction of the primary building.

Jeboult's photograph of 1865 (SRO T/PH/REA/82) shows a window (526) in the south wall of Room 411 that appears to be similar to the other surviving late medieval windows. It has now been replaced by a dormer matching the ones in the Vivary Room (Windows 529, 530, 531) and presumably of the same late 19-century date. Changes in the mortar around the window show the presence of the earlier, wider opening.

One other feature may relate to this room. This is a most unusual window (534, Figure 16.11 on the facing page) set in the north wall of the 1902 extension, which consists of a single tall, narrow lancet divided into upper and lower lights by a short transom, recessed deeply into the walling. Both the upper and lower lights have four-centred arched heads like those of the primary windows on the south and east sides of the building. This window, despite its grander architectural features (which do not match those of the other parts of the extension), currently lights only a lavatory on the first floor. It is not easy to account for its presence here but it may be that it has been reused from part of the original north wall. If the original medieval kitchen was open through two storeys, a tall narrow window such as this may well have been provided alongside the large projecting chimney, and it may have been reset here to preserve it.

16.3 Later Alterations

Schoolroom

The eastern part of the building appears to have been barely altered since its construction, although the roof timbers were hidden at some time as the schoolroom ceiling is reported to have been replaced in 1711 (Bush 1977, 124).

Central area

In the central area the major change, apart from subdivision of the ground floor rooms, is the combining of Rooms 408 and 409. The partition is believed to have been removed *c.*1855 (Bush 1983, 71) but there are other changes that are less easy to explain. All but one of the trusses appear to have had their arch-braces removed and only two of the original collar beams now survive, the replacements being clearly distinguished by a vertical break in the centre. By analogy with the western part of the building this might be thought to relate to the insertion of ceilings and attics but a Jeboult drawing, published by Bush (1983, 76), shows the room as the boys' dormitory prior to conversion to the council chamber, complete with arch-braces. It would seem that the roof was restored at some time in the mid 19th century.

Other changes are associated with the conversion to the council chamber after 1886. These include the elaborately shaped and brattished brackets supporting the principal rafters on the south side, and the provision for the ventilation turret in the roof, as well as three large dormer windows on the south elevation. To the north-west, an imposing staircase was added in an extension to the building. This and other modern extensions are not closely dated but all post-date the 1888 Ordnance Survey 1:500 plan (surveyed the previous year). The staircase is likely to have been the earliest as it would be needed to provide better access for the councillors than the newel stair, unless there was an earlier, smaller, stair here as might be suggested by a projection (now demolished) shown on the 1888 plan.

West end

The medieval building was extended by one bay and a three-storey block was built on the western end, both of which extend beyond the medieval building to the north, removing the original north-west corner. These changes are dated to 1902 in the List description (DoE 1975) and are in a style less sympathetic to the medieval work than that of the main staircase. They are cellared throughout so even the foundations of the earlier building will have been removed.

16.4 Structural Development

Sixteenth century

The great school room, though much restored in detail, probably survives intact and unaltered from its foundation. The roof has been repaired and a coved ceiling of post-medieval date has been removed, revealing the elaborate roof structure more or less entirely in its original form. The treatment of the timbers at the opposite end of the roof may show that no part of this roof was originally plastered, but that the whole roof structure, including all the common rafters, was originally exposed; a proud display.

The western part of the building, which was nearly as long as the schoolroom, was divided horizontally into ground and first-floor levels, and appears to have been designed to provide a series of lodgings for the master, usher, and presumably rooms for the boys. There appear to have been three sets of lodgings, each consisting of a heated ground-floor chamber with a first-floor chamber over, each three bays in width. The two eastern lodgings were separated by a passage on the ground floor and perhaps another on the first floor, leading off the newel stair in the north wall, though this passage may have been a later modification and it is possible that the larger chamber, of four bays, was the boys' dormitory, sandwiched between the accommodation for the master and the usher. The third set of lodgings may also have been heated and accessed by a spiral stair, but any evidence for this does not survive due to the early 20th-century alterations to the north wall.

At the western end of the building the character of the roof is different, with wider bays of six common-rafter couples, and possibly without arch bracing to the trusses, though the decorative tiers of wind braces are continued over this part of the building. It is possible that this room was originally open from the floor to the roof, and that it served as a kitchen. The large projecting feature in the north wall, shown on the 1821 plan of the building, might be interpreted as a chimney breast for a large medieval fireplace with one or more tall windows adjacent. The kitchen appears to have had its own entrance, now cut by a later window (505). This room may have been storeyed at a relatively early date by the addition of a first floor structure supported on an axial beam. Presumably the accommodation was then extended into the upper part of the kitchen, and the process of dividing the large chambers into smaller and smaller rooms began.

Figure 16.11: *The possibly reset medieval kitchen window (534) amongst the late 19th- and early 20th-century windows of the extensions.*

The Civil War

Although efforts were made to identify traces of damage in the Civil War, by examining the timbers to show signs of historic repair, no conclusive evidence of damage was observed. The disposition of either adzed or sawn timbers throughout the roof, which might have betrayed different phases of construction, or perhaps crude mid 17th-century reinstatement of a damaged structure, proved less informative than was hoped. The different timber treatments are distributed very evenly throughout the roof, rather than in large coherent areas suggesting damage from bombardment or fire.

One possibility is that the timber roof structures were completely dismantled and reassembled in a different order following the Civil War damage, perhaps with much additional fabric replicating the original; the redrilling of peg holes in some of the trusses and the confusion of the carpenter's marks may suggest this as a possibility, but it could not be established for certain that these are not just eccentricities of the original builders.

The dendrochronological dating also showed that all the sampled timbers were consistent with a date of 1522. The samples were all taken from the roof at the west end, however, which might have been less affected than the east end but the consistency would also argue against the roof having been dismantled and rebuilt. On balance, it suggests that the building suffered relatively little serious damage to its fabric, and that the expenditure noted on repairs after the war was spent digging it out of the earthworks and reinstating its boundaries and facilities (see page 27).

18th and early 19th-century alterations

By the late 19th century the whole western part of the building appears to have been divided into three storeys by the insertion of floor structures within the upper parts of the first-floor chambers, and the conversion of the roof spaces into either lofts for storage, or further accommodation. It is likely that these alterations were made during one of the periods of success of the school, perhaps under James Upton during the early 18th century (Bush 1977, 124), when pressure for accommodation and the funds for alterations may have been available. Few fixtures and fittings of this period survived the reinstatement of the buildings after the mid 19th century.

The Charity Commission (1894) describe the master's house, in the early 1820s, as consisting of "a hall, two parlours and a kitchen on the ground floor, and four large apartments above with attics, which may be, and have lately been used as bed chambers". The plan shows an extension to the west, annotated "Offices" which is likely to have included sculleries, pantries and other facilities associated with the kitchen. Bush (1983, 71) reports that the master's house was enlarged by William Crotch (master 1831–47) and it is likely that this was in the area to the south of the domestic offices. No evidence for either of these structures will have survived the works of 1902 (below) but it is possible that Crotch's extension is visible in a drawing included as a photograph in Jeboult's scrapbook (SRO L/2205 and T/PH/REA/3/83). This shows, in the background, a building projecting slightly forward of, and the roof slightly above, the medieval structure. There are four windows, classically proportioned, and an extremely tall chimney towards the front of the building.

Mid and late 19th century

The restoration of the school buildings to what was then perceived as their medieval form appears to have begun in the mid 19th century, when the partition between the two eastern sets of lodgings at first-floor level, and the inserted second floor, were removed and new collars and arch braces were inserted to restore the roof structure. Unfortunately it was necessary to demolish one of the primary partitions to effect this alteration, though the state of preservation of this partition at the time cannot be known. This room then became the boys' dormitory, if it had not been before.

More drastic alterations in the late 19th century, after 1887, saw the conversion of this room into a Council Chamber and the addition of an impressive stair in a new staircase wing on the north side. New windows were provided to light the new Council Chamber, and many of the other windows may have been repaired at the same time. This is a likely date for the removal of the coved ceiling in the schoolroom and the repair of the roof with ironwork including ties and strapping, which retained much of the historic fabric intact.

20th-century

In a later and more damaging phase of alterations, the western parts of the building were enlarged in 1902 by the addition of new offices and another staircase. The original north wall and half the original roof at the west end were entirely removed. The ceilings in the western room were raised at the same time, to create more spacious rooms at first-floor level, and a new dormer window was added, matching the late 19th-century dormers of the Council Chamber.

Part III

Discussion

Chapter 17

Chronological narrative

Chris Webster

17.1 Pre-Conquest Activity

The suggestion that the castle was the site of an Anglo-Saxon minster appears to have been first made by Vivian-Neal and Gray (1940) but has since been strengthened by further evidence from the site and also by more recent research on minsters. The presence of a minster at Taunton is known from several charters, for example in AD 904 (Sawyer 1968, S1286) and the burials in Castle Green suggested that it lay in that area. The recent dating programme (Section 7.8 on page 151) has confirmed the Late Saxon date for the cemetery and indicated a likely foundation date in the later 7th-century. The cemetery seems to have been extensive and its limits, particularly to the south and west are not clear (see Section 14.5 on page 240). It does appear to have extended right up to Castle Bow in the east and nearly as far as the Great Hall to the north but there no burials from the east side of the castle courtyard or from the Keep Garden area.

TJ Hunt (1958) suggested that the minster site lay at St Mary Magdalene on the other side of medieval Taunton but this was refuted by Clements (1984, 32), who reinterpreted the one document that suggested that St Mary was the mother church of the area. In fact, the mother church was the Priory church of St Peter and St Paul in succession to the minster and St Mary was fulfilling some of its lay functions.

The pattern of a castle succeeding a minster has now been noted in several places, following the parallel at Hereford (Shoesmith 1980) which Clements (1984) was able to quote and which is graphically described in the *Gesta Stephani:* "while everywhere the townsmen were uttering cries of lamentation [...] because the earth of their kinsfolk's graveyard was being heaped up to form a castle-mound and they could see, a cruel sight, the bodies of parents and relations, some half-rotten, some quite lately buried, pitilessly dragged from the depths" (Potter and Davis 1976). Locally, a similar succession where the castle overlies a cemetery is known at Barnstaple (Miles 1986), Sherborne (White and Cook 2015) and has recently been seen at Exeter (Stuart Blaylock pers. comm.). Blair (2005, 365) gives further examples which suggests that this is not a chance phenomenon. It is a sequence also seen on secular sites where castles are placed over Anglo-Saxon high-status sites without regard for their strategic position (Creighton 2002, 70). It is suggested that this emphasised the new owner's legal right to continue to collect rents and services (Liddiard 2005, 30–1), a factor that may also be important for minster replacement.

The location at Taunton also fits that proposed by Hase (1994) for that favoured for minsters in Wessex. He identified a preference for sites by water but often on the first rise above the flood plain, and also often on the ridge formed by a confluence. Although the modern town obscures it, this is the situation at Taunton where the castle stands on a low promontory projecting into the alluvium of the river Tone and defined on the west side by the former course of a stream, possibly formed by the confluence of the Gaol Stream and the Sherford Brook, both of which have subsequently had their courses canalised. The presence of this stream was noted during the Benham's Garage excavation in the 1970s (Leach and Pearson 1984) and it is known from early reports (for example, Warre 1853) of the topography of the castle that it was used to provide water for the moat on the south and east sides of the castle.

The establishment of the minster may be dated to the later 7th century, when the area became part of Wessex and there appears to have been a conscious imposition of a series of minster churches, probably by King Ine and Bishop Aldhelm (Hall 2000; 2004); although Taunton is not in the list of Aldhelm's foundations. Hall suggests that, in places where these replaced British churches, such as at Street or Sherborne, the minster appears to have been founded on a new site a short distance away, though this has been brought into question by the discovery of 5th-century imported pottery at Glastonbury Abbey in Ralegh Radford's excavation archive (Roberta Gilchrist pers. comm., Gilchrist and Green 2015).

Taunton appears to have been a completely new foundation but this may, of course, only reflect our complete lack of knowledge of the British church in the vale of Taunton (the only 7th-century site known in the area is a cemetery at Cothelstone: Webster and Brunning 2004). The only hints for an earlier location is the folklore tradition that Norton Fitzwarren was a town before Taunton (Vivian-Neal and Gray 1940, 48), but that may just have been inspired by the presence of its prehistoric earthworks. Another potential site may be Creechbarrow Hill, one of the few places locally to retain a British name, which may indicate that it had some greater significance than other locations.

It has been argued by Hall (2009) that this preference for virgin sites was influenced by Anglo-Saxon churchmen's perception of the British church as unorthodox – and in some ways heretical (Yorke 2006; Webster *et al.* 2008, 181–82). Charles-Edwards (2013, 396–97) has suggested that this was a fairly short phase led by archbishop Theodore in the aftermath of the Synod of Whitby (AD 664). Hall (2005, 136) suggests that another characteristic of the English church, promoting its perceived superiority as having been founded directly from Rome by St Augustine, was the use of rectangular enclosures for the new minsters, echoing the form of Roman forts and also the square form of the heavenly Jerusalem described in the biblical Book of Revelation (Blair 2005, 196). Hall identified several rectangular minster enclosures during her survey of minsters in Dorset and the morphology of the later castle enclosure may suggest that Taunton was similar (Hall 2000).

Taunton also fits another of the criteria often seen at these early minster foundations: a geographical placename, usually a river, applied to the whole of a later estate. Bruton provides another Somerset example and Hall further notes that the estates of these foundations were usually in the hands of the early West Saxon bishops, which may be the origins of the Winchester connection (Hall 2005, 141–3).

The Anglo-Saxon Chronicle dates the origins of Taunton to the reign of Ine (king of Wessex 688–726) in an obscure entry under the year 722: "Queen Æthelburh threw down Taunton, which Ine built earlier" (Swanton 2000). This has been taken to indicate a fortification, and also linked in date to the aftermath of a battle between Ine and Geraint of Dumnonia recorded under the year 710. There seems to be no real reason to link these two events apart from their adjacency in date, and the dates assigned to early events in the Chronicle are suspect in any case. The Taunton reference seems to be related more to West Saxon dynastic politics as the Chronicle entry continues "and the exile Ealdberht fled into Surrey and the South Saxons, and Ine fought against the South Saxons". Hall (2000, 81) suggests that Ine's minster at Taunton might have been held by Ealdberht to put pressure on Ine during the power struggle that ended when Ine slew "the ætheling Ealdberht whom he had earlier driven out" in 725.

Henry of Huntingdon, writing in the 12th-century gives more details, possibly taken from a lost version of the Chronicle that he is known to have seen. Henry describes Taunton as a "castrum" that Ine had built and which was taken by Ealdberht "before Queen Æthelburh, wife of Ine captured it by arms and destroyed it and compelled him to flee" (Greenway 1996, 226–7). Unfortunately it is not possible to say if the word *castrum* comes from the supposed original Chronicle entry or whether it is an anachronism by Henry, who may well have known of the Bishop of Winchester's castle. While Blair (2005, 268–70) notes that there are very few references to Anglo-Saxon fortifications before the mid-8th century, Taunton and Somerton (in 733) were both recorded as being attacked, which suggests something of a defensive nature at these two strategic sites in Somerset (Michael Costen, pers. comm.).

It seems likely, therefore, that the origins of Taunton lie in a minster co-located with a royal, later episcopal, hall complex, such as that excavated at Cheddar (Rahtz 1979). Blair (2005) has argued convincingly that this, in fact, may be a common form of urban origin, the minster community possessing many characteristics that would be considered urban and encouraging, through the development of markets, further urbanisation. This model might fit well the unusual street pattern of Taunton (Gathercole 1998), with its triangular marketplace to the south-east of the later castle enclosure and development along the streets (East Street and North Street) leading to it. The presence of burials in the roadway at the East Gate of the castle suggests

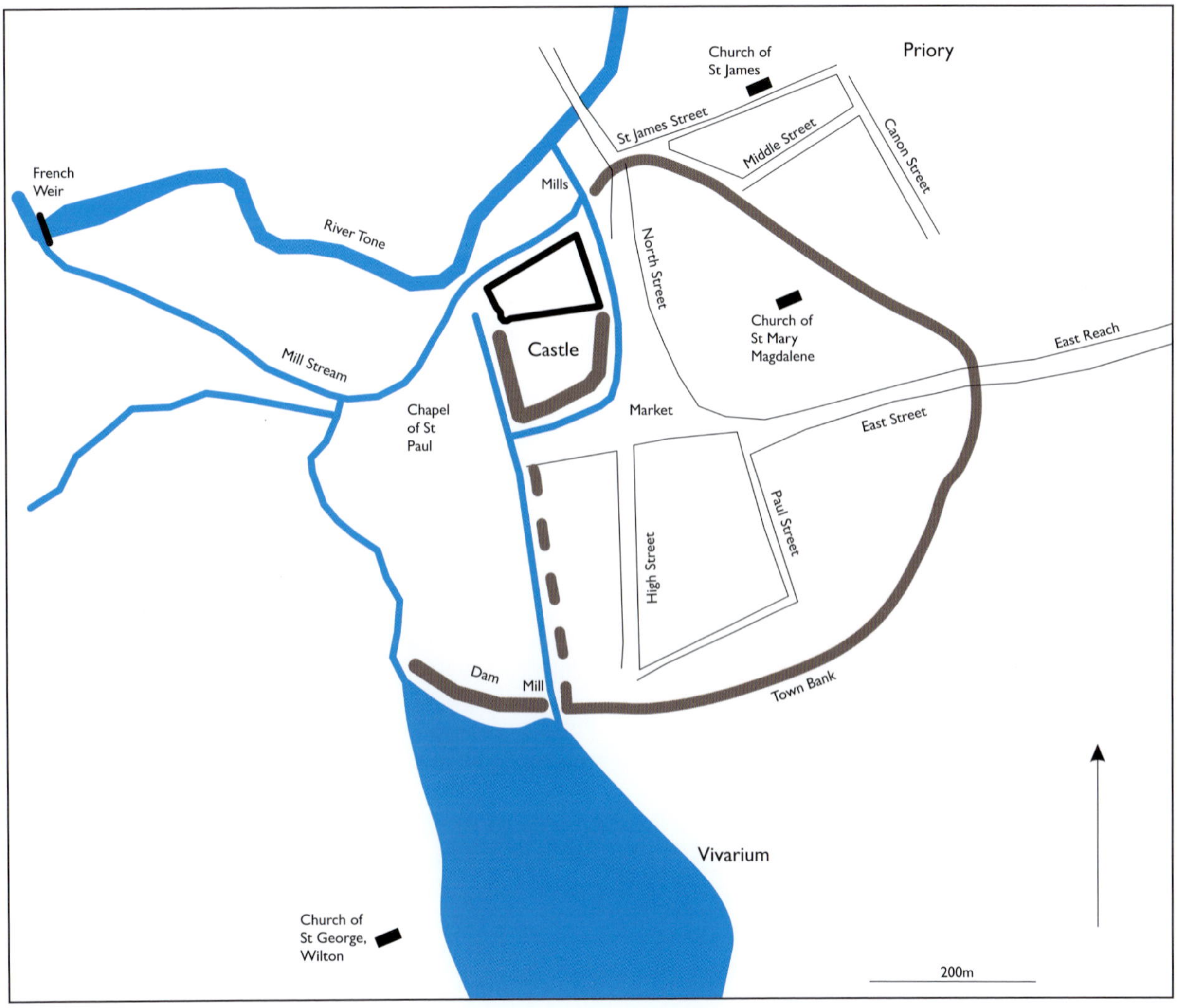

Figure 17.1: *Simplified plan of medieval Taunton after Leach (1984a, Fig. 26).*

that this was not the location of the entrance; it is possible that the alignment of East Street points to an entrance at the south-east corner.

The curiously positioned High Street appears to be a later, planned development as suggested by Bush and Aston (1984, 77), but one that was in place by 1200 (Bennett 1984). The evidence from elsewhere in the town suggests that the present form of the market area is late 12th or early 13th century, although there may have been earlier, less formally laid-out, occupation (Burrow, I 1988). The town was certainly in this area by 1158 when the grant of priory lands was made beyond it (Goodman 1927).

Very few signs of pre-Conquest urban development have been found under the later town with the exception of a few residual early 11th-century sherds from the market place (Weddell 1998). There were also worn sherds (Pearson 1984c, fiche I.A3) found under the town bank at Hawke's Yard (Leach 1984b), which would seem to be best interpreted as residual from manuring fields beyond the settlement. David Dawson (pers. comm.), however, comments that these sherds would appear from the fabric description to be of the 11/12th century. Finds have been made, however, on the west side of the castle site at Benham's Garage (Leach and Pearson 1984) comprising pottery and metalwork.

The minster would have contained several churches, a pattern seen at both British and Anglo-Saxon monastic sites (Blair 1992; Petts and Turner 2009). The castle chapels were dedicated to St Peter (first recorded *c.*1160) and St Nicholas (unlikely to be a pre-Norman dedication, see page 15). A third chapel is recorded, that of St Paul, which appears to lie outside the castle to the west, and the priory takes the names of both Peter and Paul, probably carried forward from the castle site. The minster site probably comprised at least two churches, but whether it would have included the chapel of St Paul is uncertain. The stream bed seen in the Benham's Garage excavation would have divided them but the dates of the burials around St Paul (see page 240) indicate that this area is part of the pre-conquest cemetery and could have had a chapel from that date. There seems no reason for the foundation of a chapel at St Paul later in the medieval period. There was a further church, now St George's, Wilton, about 0.5km south of St Paul (Figure 17.1 on the previous page) that has late Saxon architectural features and is on a similar orientation to the other medieval churches in Taunton (between 15 and 25 degrees north of east), whose origins are obscure but it too may have originated as an outlier to the minster complex.

Unfortunately our knowledge of what buildings, other than a church or churches, might have formed a minster site in Wessex is very limited. Some minsters seem to have been co-located with royal vills but the relationship between the two components is not clear. Cheddar (Rahtz 1979) is one of the few excavated sites with a succession of halls and ancillary buildings in addition to the minster church (assumed to lie beneath the present church of St Andrew) and the chapel of St Columbanus. Rahtz interpreted the site as the centre of a royal estate to which a minster church was attached but Blair (1996) would see the roles reversed with a minster founded with a hall next to it, a relationship that became hidden as the power of the king grew at the expense of the church.

At Taunton we may be seeing a similar phenomenon but here the royal connection was severed by the transfer of the estate to the Bishop of Winchester. Costen (2011, 192) believed that this transfer must have happened by the time of Alfred's will (probably written in the 880s: Keynes and Lapidge 1983, 313) as it is not listed amongst the bequests. Thorn (2012), however, notes that several other royal estates are also omitted and suggests that this was because they were not Alfred's personal property. If the evidence of the 904 charter (Sawyer 1968, S1286) can be believed (it has been considered doubtful in the past but Keynes (1994) expressed more confidence), the town was in the hands of the bishops by then. The charter may record improvements to the landholding shortly after the bishop acquired it as it deals with the removal of onerous duties on Taunton minster and gives control over the market. This was clearly worth doing as a valuable estate was given in exchange. It seems likely that the Anglo-Saxon bishops saw the potential of Taunton and promoted urban development within one of their largest estates.

17.2 The Origins of the Castle

The ownership by the bishops of Winchester survived the Norman conquest although the bishop himself (Stigand) was replaced in 1070 during a wholesale purge of senior Anglo-Saxon figures, possibly a result of the northern revolt of the previous year (Williams 1995, 45–6). The new bishop was Walkelin, William the Conqueror's chaplain, and is possible that a motte and bailey was constructed at Taunton, in these troubled times. Walkelin still held the estate in 1086 as recorded in Domesday. There is no mention of castle or town but the assessment includes several indicators of urban status (64 burgesses, a mint and a market) and Domesday records very few castles, unless their construction had led to the loss of rents.

Walkelin was succeeded in 1100, after a two-year gap, by William Giffard. Vivian-Neal (1954, 2) said that there was a tradition that Taunton Castle was started by Giffard and suggested that the earliest work at the west end of the Great Hall was his. This belief may have come from Warre (1853, 22), who said that he could find "no positive mention" of the castle between 722 and the time of Giffard who "built a strong castle upon the site of the Saxon fortress". Unfortunately he does not state what this first positive mention was and neither Hunt (1964, 3) nor, more recently Prior (2006), gives any source for supporting their attributions to Giffard. In contrast Bush and Meek (1984, 11) say that the evidence for Giffard is "far from contemporary". The earliest mention of Giffard as the founder of Taunton appears to be in Savage's (1822) rewriting of Toulmin (1791). Giffard was certainly active in the reformation of the minster, converting it into a house of Augustinian canons (Hunt 1958, 12–13), and he built at other places, such as Wolvesey (Biddle 1986, 5–6) and Farnham (Riall 2003).

The first historical mention of the presence of a castle at Taunton comes in the oft-repeated statement from the Winchester Annals for 1138 (Luard 1865, 51) that bishop Henry of Blois (Giffard's successor and King Stephen's brother) "built a palatial house in Winchester with a very strong [or forbidding] tower and also the castles at Merdon, Farnham, Waltham, Downton and Taunton" (Riall 2003, 118). The meaning of this statement has been reassessed by Riall in the context of Farnham. He suggests that the text does not necessarily provide evidence for the new-building of Farnham as archaeological work at other castles in the list (Bishop's Waltham and Wolvesey) suggests a start date in the episcopate of William Giffard (1100–29). Riall also notes that the list of Henry's castles comes at the head of a less-often quoted section detailing the numerous castles built by others, including Bishop Roger of Salisbury. Henry's presence at the head of the list seems required in a Winchester annal and it also seems likely that he would have been given the greatest number of castles, even if that meant stretching the meaning of "built". Perhaps most telling is the sentence following the list "And there was no one of any worth or influence in England who did not either build or enforce the defence of their castles" (Riall 2003).

There is, however, circumstantial evidence that the 1138 list may accurately indicate work at the castles. Lidelea, another of the bishop's castles is mentioned in the *Gesta Stephani* (Potter and Davis 1976) as being besieged in 1147 but is otherwise unknown. King and Renn (1971) suggested that Lidelea was a site at Barley Pound, five kilometres west of Farnham, where there were castle earthworks. Close by were two small earthworks that could be identified with the two siege castles in the *Gesta Stephani* account; one has been excavated (Stamper 1984). Barley Pound may have been superseded by Farnham but was still attacked because of its weaker defences (King and Renn 1971). Wherever Lidelea was, it is omitted from the 1138 list suggesting that the list only contains sites that contemporaries would consider as being "built" by Henry of Blois.

Henry of Blois is often credited with the foundation of Taunton Castle but this is on the basis of the 1138 reference. Henry was certainly noted by contemporaries as a great builder, following the lead of Roger of Salisbury and competing with bishops Alexander of Lincoln and Nigel of Ely (Riall 1994). The nature of his work at Wolvesey (Biddle 1986) and Bishop's Waltham (Hare 1987) seems clear but that at Farnham (Riall 2003) and Taunton, less so. In most cases, Henry seems to have been adding to sites where work had been undertaken by his predecessor, William Giffard, and Henry's works seem to comprise the linking of Giffard's structures into ranges and courts (Riall 1994, 11). These works may have become more militarised during the anarchy of King Stephen's reign in which Henry (as Stephen's brother) took an important part. Henry's work at Wolvesey and at Glastonbury Abbey (where he was also abbot) is characterised by a richness of ornamentation (Riall 1994, 17; Gilchrist and Green 2015) with few parallels at Taunton or Farnham. This may suggest that both were more a creation of Giffard.

If a castle had not been developed before the civil war of Stephen's reign, emergency works might have been limited to the construction of fortifications on the line of the minster enclosure, although more extensive plans might have been made (and implemented).

17.3 The 11th- and 12th-century Castle

Urban castles appear to have been part of a Norman tactic to consolidate their hold on England following the conquest. They were usually a royal foundation and tended to occupy one corner of the previous urban settlement, requiring the demolition of property (Pounds 1990, 57). This can sometimes be detected from the Domesday survey when the loss of income from the burgesses is recorded. There is no indication that this happened at Taunton but we do not know where the urban area was in 1086. Domesday records 64 burgesses but as noted above, no archaeological evidence has been found indicating where they lived. The town was certainly in its later medieval location to the east of the castle by 1158 when its boundary was used to define one side of the land granted to the priory by Henry of Blois: "From the east gate to the north gate" (Bush 1984, 104).

The northern area may have been altered to form the castle early in the Norman period, perhaps by cutting the bishop's hall off from the rest of the enclosure and possibly by the construction of a motte in the north-east corner. Various views have been taken on the presence of a motte, initially by Warre (1853, 28) who describes it at the north-east corner above the later arch (464, see page 164). Clark (1872, 72) rejected this but Radford and Hallam (1953, 92) believed that one may have stood somewhere in the area, before being replaced by the keep. This view was firmly opposed by Rodwell (1984a, 20) who noted that "the keep now has the appearance of a stone-encased motte" but that "there is, of course, no evidence for a motte at Taunton and no reason to suppose that one ever existed here." Whilst this is true, the existence of a motte in this area would have provided much of the material that has been used to raise the ground level, and the large feature (766/1065) exposed in the Great Hall in 2009 could have been part of the defences associated with it (see page 80).

Reconsideration of Gray's work in the keep garden has not produced any evidence for a motte but the features that remain do look more like a stone-encased motte than the base of a tower keep. Whilst his methodology and experience was unlikely to identify robbing-trenches it seems unlikely that all traces of a tower keep would have escaped him. Pounds (1990, 20–21) noted that tower keeps required enormous resources of both money and time to build and that only royalty and the very richest barons could afford them. The bishops of Winchester would certainly have had the money but they suffered from another constraint on baronial keeps that Pounds identifies, a fragmentary land holding pattern that encouraged a spread of less expensive castles. If a tower keep was required on the Winchester estates for reasons of prestige, Taunton, far in the west, would probably be the last place where the bishops would have made such an investment.

It is more likely that a composite structure, such as that seen at Farnham occupied the area and was known as the Great Tower. At Farnham, the early motte was later surrounded by a wall and the space between infilled to produce a platform, in that case roughly circular (Thompson 1960b). A drawing by S and N Buck (Figure 17.2 on the facing page) shows Farnham in 1737, before the keep walls were reduced to the height of the motte, which gives a good impression of the appearance of such a structure, which looks very different from the impression obtained today. This raising of ground levels can also be seen at Witney (Allen and Hiller 2002) and Wolvesey (Wareham 2000), where it is interpreted as part of a more widely adopted fashion, perhaps expressing the elevated status of the Bishop.

Unfortunately it seems unlikely that the exact form of the "Great Tower" at Taunton can ever be known as all the upper deposits have been removed by Gray, if they were not destroyed in the Civil War, but the pipe rolls (page 17) contain details of the various structures within it.

The only surviving structures that appear to be securely dated to this period are the north and west walls of the Great Hall and chamber block but the situation here, like much else at Taunton, is actually unclear. If, as seems likely, the present arrangement was constructed during the well-documented building campaign of 1246–49 (Hunt 1971), the pipe rolls indicate that this was not the site of the previous hall (see page 10). The surviving structures bear some resemblance to others of the Bishops of Winchester: Bishop's Waltham, Wolvesey and Witney. These comparisons are discussed by Tim Allen (2002) in relation to Witney who sees in the Winchester residences, a layout of ranges running either side of a corner tower. This is part of a pattern, seen at several 12th-century episcopal residences, of a hall with attached tower. Many of these form part of a quadrangular plan but the residences of Henry of Blois contrast to those (such as Sherborne, Davison 2001; White and Cook 2015) of his contemporary, Roger of Salisbury, by being less regularly laid out and developing into a courtyard plan over time by the accretion of buildings to fill gaps.

The Great Hall area may have originated, therefore, as a range of buildings running along the north side of the castle, perhaps containing the private bishop's hall and chamber, with a more public hall elsewhere on the site, perhaps on the site of the pre-conquest hall. The 1246–49 works saw the building of a ground floor public hall, bishop's great chamber and private chamber in the range leading to the chapel. A similar sequence may be seen at the Bishop of Durham's Norham Castle where a first-floor ceremonial hall was turned into the bishop's accommodation by the addition of further chambers, in this case on upper storeys. The situation at Norham was further complicated by a 15th-century rebuilding to make the structure symmetrical, which gave it the appearance of a 12th-century tower keep – its interpretation until detailed examination (Dixon and Marshall 1993).

This reordering at Norham is a salutary reminder that castle layouts were not static and that, with incomplete evidence, it may not be possible to identify particular structures and certainly not be able to tie them into documentary sources. Without a good knowledge of the early ground plan of Taunton we cannot say where the "Old Hall" might have lain.

Relationship with the priory

The minster underwent significant changes in the 12th century, firstly being regularised as a house of Augustinian canons and then moving from the castle to the priory site. The first was undertaken by Bishop William Giffard in 1120 × 1125 under the first prior, Guy of Merton (Holmes 1911a, 141–44), and was part of a wider reforming movement that peaked later in the century. The Augustinian rule was less clear-cut than others and allowed easier inclusion of irregular communities such as Taunton, one of 80 such collegiate churches in England (Robinson 1980, 13). The reformation of these communities allowed greater control, without the need for the granting of new land, but this control was exercised by the local bishop rather than the central body of other monastic orders. This means that few records survive, particularly from the early years.

In 1158, Henry of Blois did give land to the east of the town to build and support a new priory (Goodman 1927, 198). This seems to be part of a fashion at the court of Henry II as the founding of a monastery (often Augustinian) adjacent to a

Figure 17.2: *S and N Buck's 1737 view of Farnham. (SANHS Collection).*

castle is common at this time (Liddiard 2005). In the case of castles built on earlier church sites, it would have had the additional advantage of freeing space within the castle and at Taunton there may have been another factor: the canons were answerable to the Bishop of Bath and Wells and this jurisdiction may have been seen by Henry of Blois as inappropriate within his castle.

However, the space within the castle may not have become available immediately as, if Robin Bush's (1984) interpretation of the records is correct, the unusual sequence of construction at the priory (leaving the church to last – a reversal of the usual order; Greene 1992, 64) might mean that the minster church (or its Norman replacement) was still used. The retention of an earlier chapel has been suggested at several other castles (Kenyon 1990, 152). A reference to a "church" in the castle in 1282 (Anon 1930-32) may, if not simply a literary device, indicate that it was still present at that date and mentions in the Winchester pipe rolls may continue to the beginning of the 14th century (see page 15). What may have been gained for the castle was the area required for the burial ground.

17.4 The Later Medieval Castle

The existence of the Winchester pipe rolls from 1209 might be thought to increase our knowledge of the layout of the castle but, with the exception of the major campaign of 1246–49, most of this refers to re-building and improvement. This suggests that the overall form of the castle was in place before the beginning of the 13th century but it must be remembered that the pipe rolls are not a complete series and major changes could have been made in the missing years or using funds from another source. This is evident in the well-dated structures of the South Range, which are not recorded in the pipe rolls.

The bishops as builders

The Winchester pipe rolls, were instigated by Peter des Roches (bishop 1205–38) who may have continued the building works of Henry of Blois at Wolvesey and Southwark, in particular remodelling their halls to rival the royal hall at Winchester Castle (Wareham 2000, 9). He was involved in the civil wars of kings John and Henry III and the major work recorded at Taunton was ditching and palisading both the town and castle in 1216.

The largest works recorded in the pipe rolls, the building of the new hall, chapel and chamber (Hunt 1971) were undertaken during the episcopate of William Raleigh (bishop 1242–50) who is not otherwise noted as a builder (Crook 2004).

A century later, one of the greatest of medieval builders, William Wykeham became bishop (1366–1404). He had risen from humble origins to become clerk of the king's works responsible for Edward III's rebuilding of Windsor Castle

(Davis 2007). He continued to be interested in building after becoming bishop of Winchester, using the master craftsmen he had employed in royal service. As well as work at the cathedral and Wolvesey, he founded and built Winchester College and New College, Oxford and carried out work at his residences, most notably Bishop's Waltham (Hare 1988). Little is recorded of work at Taunton apart from major repairs to the structure of the hall roof and £20 spent on a "new" tower whose site is unknown.

Later in the 15th century another great builder occupied the see, William Waynflete (bishop 1447–86). He had been a master at Wykeham's Winchester College before entering royal service and assisting in Henry VI's foundation of Eton College. Shortly after becoming bishop he started to found Magdalen College, Oxford and later grammar schools there and at his birthplace in Lincolnshire. He was pioneering in the use of brick in southern England, perhaps as a result of his connections with Ralph, Lord Cromwell, whose brick castle at Tattershall he would have known. He built a large tower at Farnham (Thompson 1960a) and extended his residence at Esher, again with much use of brick. He spent several months at Taunton at the beginning of 1461, a politically turbulent time, returning to Southwark for the coronation of Edward IV (Davis 2004). It was perhaps a lack of suitable accommodation during this time that prompted the repairs to the lord's chamber in 1467 and the construction of the lodgings (now Castle House) for visitors and retainers later in the century.

Archaeological evidence indicates considerable activity in the south range during the episcopate of Thomas Langton (bishop 1493–1501) and the presence of Langton's arms at several places around the castle led to a belief that he built much of the structure (Toulmin 1791). There is little record of building in the pipe rolls but they do record two visits by the bishop, before and after one by Henry VII (in 1497: not mentioned in the pipe rolls). Having earlier supported King Richard, Langton's alterations may have been primarily cosmetic for the royal visit, such as the addition of the protestation of loyalty to the gatehouse (page 29). Langton's death in 1501 probably provides the explanation for the incomplete roof on the chapel in the South Range (see page 212). His episcopate also features the first record of bricks at Taunton, when in 1499 there is a payment recorded for expenses incurred "in carrying 7 cartloads of brykz from Taunton to Rimpton" (Brian Murless, pers. comm. quoting SRO DD/SP/325/61). Bricks were clearly being made at Taunton, presumably for works to the castle, and it was not worth establishing brickmaking at Rimpton for this small quantity, perhaps for a chimney.

Langton's successor was Richard Fox (bishop 1501–28) who was very active diplomatically for Henry VII and Henry VIII, including negotiations with the Scots whilst bishop of Durham that also included defending Norham Castle during a two-week siege. He became bishop of Exeter and then Bath and Wells but does not appear ever to have visited the sees. After becoming bishop of Winchester, he founded Corpus Christi College, Oxford and is likely to have helped in the foundation of at least two other colleges (Davis 2004). There is no record of him visiting Taunton, so it is not clear why it was chosen as the site to found a school in 1522 – his other school foundation was at his home town of Grantham, Lincs. If Toulmin's report (see page 249) is correct, the connection may be Fox's friend, bishop Hugh Oldham of Exeter, who was to be a major benefactor of Corpus Christi

The layout of the medieval castle

Unlike at Witney (Blair 2002) it has proved difficult to use the information in the pipe rolls to produce a plan of the castle, or in many cases correlate mentions in the pipe rolls with surviving buildings. The pipe rolls do give an overall picture of the buildings in the castle, although it must always be remembered that structures, names and uses will have changed over time. Figure 17.3 on page 273 shows suggested locations for buildings from this evidence.

It is likely that the present courtyard area formed the core of the elite residence but this was not always the case as there was an earlier hall that was replaced by the one here in 1246–49. The location of this earlier hall is not known but if it was later used by the constable, it may have lain to the south of a suggested motte, perhaps in the area now occupied by the Castle Hotel's carpark. The wall seen in 1983 (page 52) may have been part of a building complex in this area, which may have originated as the site of the minster.

The development of the courtyard buildings is not well understood. The hall, chapel and bishop's chamber are recorded being built in the 1240s with the bishop's bedchamber located adjacent to the chapel, which itself lay adjacent to the Round Tower in later accounts. This seems to fit with the surviving layout but the archaeological evidence indicates that there is more than one phase of construction here. The Undercroft, which probably survives from the earliest stone phase of the castle, had the Gray Room added on its south side, covering the curious column next to Buttress 446 that may have formed one side of a gateway. The Somerset Room was extended over the Gray Room, presumably forming the bishop's chamber in 1246.

The relationships of the next building, the Round Tower, to these structures are less clear, The tower is not mentioned before 1271 and could be seen to be later than the Gray Room when the foundations were exposed. No relationship was visible in the room above, where only limited amounts of plaster were removed revealing large areas of brick and rubble stonework. It is therefore not possible to determine whether the tower pre- or post-dates the construction of the Somerset Room in the 1240s. On the east side, it is not known if the tower was built as part of the south curtain of the inner ward or whether this existed before. The construction of the chapel in the 1240s might suggest that this area was constructed at the same time but it could have been built against an existing wall. On balance, it would seem likely that this was a single phase of construction creating the present courtyard running east from the end of the Gray Room and connecting, somehow, with the structures in the Keep Garden, perhaps with a matching round tower. The walls found in excavations within the courtyard would appear to pre-date this phase.

The planning of the hall block itself conforms to underlying concepts that are seen at medieval houses across western Europe (Impey 1999; Meirion-Jones 2012); the building is entered via a porch on the side at one end that leads to a passage between the hall and kitchens. The hall itself is rectangular and is entered from one end forcing a visitor to traverse its length to reach the "high" end and the presence of the lord. Beyond the high end, and inaccessible to many, lie the more private apartments.

The principles behind medieval spatial planning have only recently been considered, it being previously assumed that ideas such as symmetry only became apparent in the renaissance. Most castles do appear to have grown organically but symmetrical planning, for instance, is seen in some (but interestingly, not all) of Edward I's castles in Wales (for example Flint, Harlech and Beaumaris). Even in the more usual, irregular plans, spatial structure is visible, as described by Johnson (2002), who notes, for instance, that the journey into the castle is usually punctuated by a series of right-angled turns where the social status of the space changes. This may show a greater concern for moving through constructed spaces than for formal composition of the building plan in the medieval mind.

This can be seen at Taunton, where a visitor would approach through the town's bustling market place, pass through the East Gate, perhaps being welcomed or having their identity checked, and then cross the outer ward, full of signs of the bishop's wealth, before seeing at right-angles another gate, leading to the inner ward. Through the gate the activity around the bishop's hall could be glimpsed, and if invited, accessed. Turning and passing through the gate, the hall would be visible across the courtyard with its entrance indicated by a porch and the presence of the adjacent kitchen. Entering via the porch and screens passage, another right-angled turn leads to a long walk across the hall to the dais at the far end.

At several points on the journey the visitor would be reminded whose castle was being visited, with heraldic designs displayed above the gatehouses mirroring the badges of the liveried castle servants (Johnson 2002, 74).

Other symbols of elite culture were present around the hall: the dovecot and garden. The former appears to have lain to the west of the hall and to have been joined to it by a palisade (see page 16). The gardens seem to have been between the castle and the River Tone and there may have been two, a smaller formal one (the herbarium next to the lord's hall in 1290) and a larger one, probably partly an orchard between the river and the millstream, reached by a bridge. Again this is a common design feature of castles (Creighton 2002, 73–75).

Roberta Gilchrist (1999, 125–28) discusses the feminine connotations of the garden at elite residences but this would obviously not be the case in a bishop's household and it is not clear what role it played in these circumstances. She does note that gardens were provided for the queen's visits at several bishop's palaces, including Wolvesey, but this Winchester example may be a special case as Edward I paid for works to the chambers and the creation of a garden at the bishop's palace because the royal apartments in Winchester Castle had been destroyed by fire (Brown and Colvin 1963, 863). The gardens at Taunton may have been provided for female guests but, in view of the almost continual absence of the bishop, it is not clear what any of these structures, except the Great Hall, were used for most of the time. They must have been required primarily as symbols of (absent) lordship.

Later, changing social values saw a move to provide less-communal accommodation for visitors than was available in the hall, by the construction of lodgings where guests could sleep and work while still taking part in meals in the hall. The building that is now Castle House was built for this purpose but it was not the earliest, as lodgings are mentioned in the same or similar location in 1375.

In view of the almost total loss of evidence, the Keep Garden area is hard to assess. Apart from turrets, the only structures identified in the pipe rolls are a prison and the knights/soldiers' hall. As mentioned above, the constable's hall lay somewhere on the eastern side of the castle and as it is not mentioned as part of the Great Tower, it is likely that this was to the south of the Keep Garden. From the early 14th century the pipe rolls refer to the constabulary or constable's ward which presumably contained the constable's hall and it is possible that the Keep Garden structures also lay within this ward. No other location can be suggested and it would fit with the suggested change to the layout of the castle in the mid-13th century when the old elite core based around a motte at the north-east corner was replaced by the Great Hall and present inner ward, leaving a suite of structures probably used by the constable.

This may be supported by Bush and Meek's (1984) location of the constable's "quarters" at the East Gate, although they provide no source for their belief. They also suggest that the "building" shown to the left of the gatehouse in SANHS 12527 (Figure 15.4 on page 246) was the constable's hall, whilst admitting that it lay outside the castle. The pipe rolls suggest that the hall lay east–west and it is more likely that it lay within the castle.

This area, now the Castle Hotel's carpark, is also the supposed site of the chapel of St Peter according to Hunt (1964, 4). Again, the source of this location "not far from the inner gate" is not given and Bush and Meek's (1984) location of "in the centre" next to the cowshed may simply be derived from Hunt. Information from the pipe rolls locates a cattleshed between the west gate and the inner gate and also frequently refer to a cattleshed at St Paul. It may be confusion between Peter and Paul that has led to the location of the chapel here.

The outer ward appears to have been devoted to the storage of produce from the estate but it should be remembered that this would also function as a display of the bishop's wealth to those crossing the ward or glimpsing it through the gates. The three *grangia*, bartons, barns and the pound seem to have lain in the southern half; the later location of the pound by the East Gate probably indicates its medieval location. Holway grange stood next to the pound in 1341, and the later Great Barn lay adjacent to the school that was built in 1522. The lack of windows in the north wall of the schoolroom suggests that it lay close enough to block the light. It is not clear which of the earlier granges became the Great Barn but Hull grange appears to have lain close to the West Gate, so the Great Barn must have succeeded Holway or Staplegrove granges, both of which probably lay in the south-east.

The location of the School within the castle also raises the question of its relationship with the southern boundary of the outer ward. The expected form of a building here would be leaning against the castle wall with the entrance to the north. The school, however, is built facing south towards the town and was clearly free-standing as indicated by the buttresses on both sides. This seems to indicate that the southern castle "wall" was not present in the early 16th century and that the school was built on the top of the remnant bank to increase its visibility. The pipe rolls (1545) refer to the loss of rent from two gardens occasioned by the construction of the school, and earlier indications that the wall here was of cob also suggest that this area was no longer enclosed.

There is one indication that there was an entrance to the castle on the south side (see page 19) where a bridge is mentioned but the absence of any other evidence suggests that this is a mistaken identification.

The north-west part of the outer bailey again seems to have been used for storage buildings (cart and cattle sheds), which were divided by walls. These enclosures may also have formed the bartons mentioned in the pipe rolls.

17.5 Post-Medieval

It is unlikely that much building work was undertaken during the troubled years of the Reformation and none is recorded in the final entries in the pipe rolls, which stop in 1545. Following the accession of Elizabeth I, the protestant Robert Horne was appointed bishop in 1560 but the see's property was retained by the crown. The Taunton estate was only returned in 1575 and Toulmin records Horne's arms and the date 1577 on the porch to the Great Hall. As suggested above (page 185) this may be associated with other major changes to the fenestration of the hall. Who exactly was responsible for this work is complicated by a record of payments by the crown to Sir Hugh Poulett for work at the castle in 1578. These were required as "the hall and other buildings are in great decay, both in the walls, timberwork, coverings, windows and roofs" (quoted by Radford and Hallam 1953, 73).

The report that the castle was "much ruinated" in 1635 (page 25) probably indicates continuing

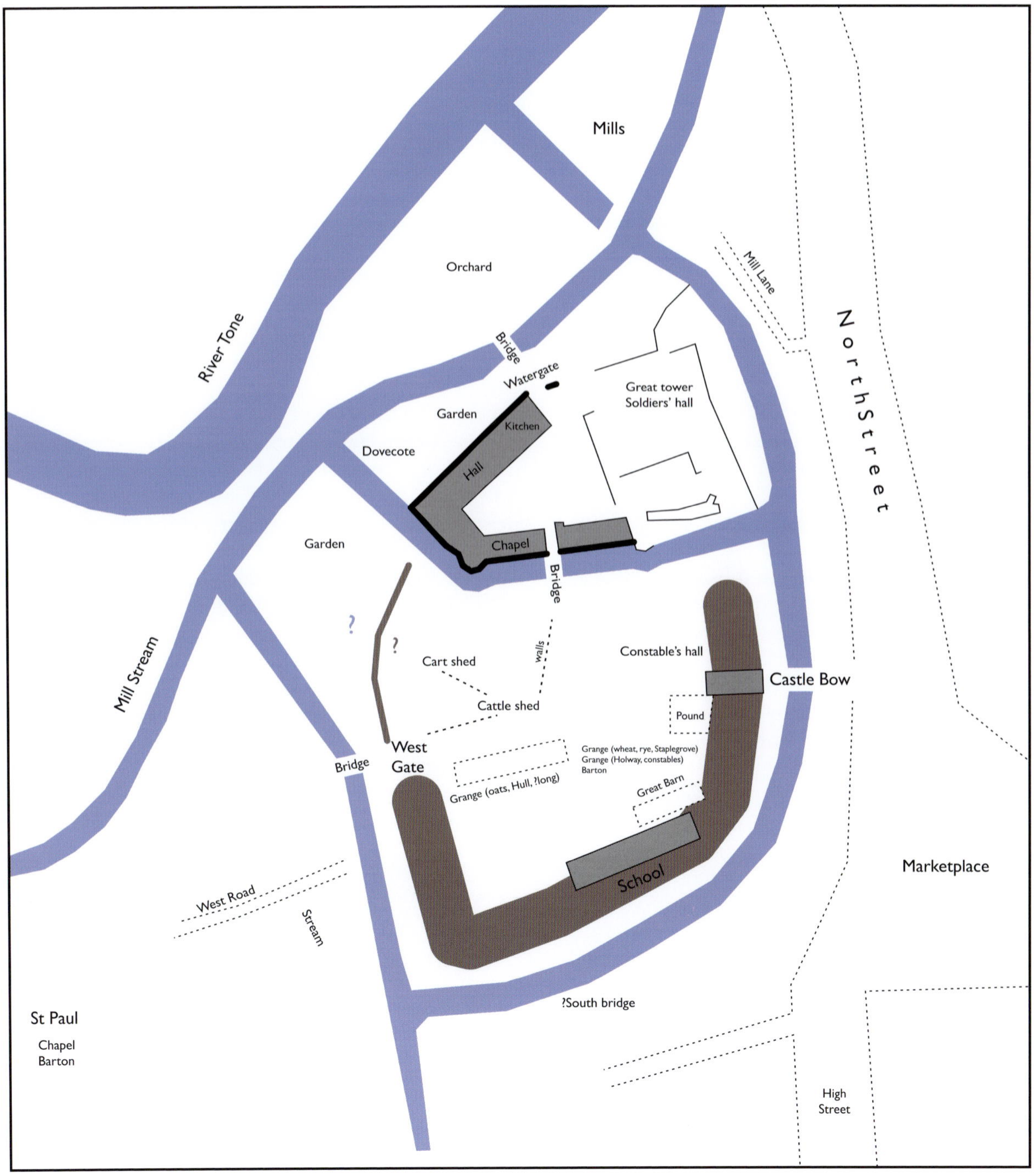

Figure 17.3: *Suggested locations of buildings documented in the Winchester pipe rolls. The position of the moats is after Leversedge (SRO DD/SAS/c1207/2g) and the West Road from Leach and Pearson (1984).*

lack of interest in the castle as does the consolidation of the traditional offices of bailiff and keeper into one, which also included the tenancy of the castle. In 1632 Walter Cliffe and John Palmer took the offices jointly and Cliffe moved into the castle (Bush and Meek 1984, 15).

The Civil War

There appears to be little detailed historical evidence for the castle during the Civil War but the outline of the hostilities is clear (Green 1879; Underdown 1973). Taunton was held initially for parliament until the garrison was forced to withdraw in 1643 by the presence of a large royalist force advancing from Chard. The intended sinking of the garrison's ordnance in the castle moat was prevented by local royalists and captives held in the castle. The castle and town were surrendered on 5 June but royalist control lasted only until July the following year when the garrison of 80 was forced to leave after a week of siege by a parliamentary force under the command of Robert Blake.

Blake was, in turn, besieged by victorious royalist forces returning after the battle of Lostwithiel and despite the reported lack of fortification lines, two attempts to storm the town were repelled. The royalists withdrew to about a mile and attempted to starve the defenders out. This appears to have had the desired effect as Blake offered to surrender the town but not the castle in early November, an offer that was rejected. The garrison was relieved on 14 December and the royalists driven away only to return in April the following year.

The garrison appears to have spent the time building fortifications as these are mentioned for the first time in 1645. The royalists captured one of the outworks (the "vicar's house", presumably on the east side near St Mary Magdalene) on 6 May but were driven back from an attack on the defences of the east gate of the town. The following day, they captured the "gate at the west side and the small sconce by it" but were driven off "by a guard, sheltered behind some entrenchments and barricades cast up purposely to protect it" (Green 1879, 43). Most of the town had fallen by 9 May with only the castle, the church, the "muydens fort" and an entrenchment on the market place still held. The siege was lifted by the arrival of the New Model Army on 10 May, when the town was described as two-thirds destroyed but the castle not mentioned. The royalists returned in June but their unenthusiastic siege was raised on 4 July. In 1646 the garrisons of Taunton and Bridgwater were ordered to be disbanded but they were still there a year later, before Bridgwater was disbanded and Taunton reduced to 100 (Underdown 1973, 137–39).

Post-war legal disputes (see page 26) describe the substantial changes made to the earthwork defences of the castle, including the widening of the inner moat and the construction of earthworks along the southern part of the outer ward. The earth banks described by Allanson could be the remains of a barrier of gabions as there does not seem enough room between the school and the medieval ditch for a conventional dump rampart 6m high. The measurement must, in any event, have been from the base of the ditch.

The evidence gives little suggestion of great damage caused by actual fighting: Hearnshaw (1934) says that one of his students (unnamed) noted in a dissertation that the war appeared to cause little disruption to life in Taunton and the evidence of court sessions (below) is similar. There is no mention of damage or repairs needed to the Great Hall when, in 1656, the owner of the castle, Roger Hill (see page 26), agreed to allow the borough of Taunton to use it for the assizes and other courts in return for a payment of 10s per year (SRO DD/X/WA/5). The burgesses agreed to maintain the hall, including the lead and stone roof, in the same condition as it was at the agreement date, indicating that it was in good condition, and this was clearly more economic as they had been "put to great expense" in preparing other locations (Harbin 1912, xxiv).

Archaeologically, evidence of fortifications has been found outside the eastern side of the medieval town but no clear evidence of the recorded destruction has been recorded within. The pattern of surviving pre-war buildings (Taylor 1974) also does not show clear areas of destruction. There are some features of the castle, however, that may indicate the effects of the war. The first is the brick wall along the driveway, suggested above (page 217) to have contained loopholes. These appear to be forming a rear defence to the West Gate and their presence may fit the historical account of the capture and recapture of the west gate (above).

Other features that may be associated with the war are seen in the west and south ranges and, while not dated, would seem to fit best in this context. The doubling in thickness of the west wall in the Undercroft and insertion of a substantial vault seem to have no structural purpose, other than to resist bombardment at the base of the wall and, perhaps, to provide a platform for heavy guns on the first floor.

Toulmin (see page 29) describes the building as having suffered from "the cannon of its enemies" and as having had a flat roof with gun embrasures in the parapets. He also says that part had been replaced with a new roof "within the memory of man". This would indicate that the earliest image (1773; see Figure 2.1 on page 28) cannot be used to shed much light on the Civil War situation, although the Round Tower still appears ruined. There certainly appears to be some evidence of fighting around the West Range in the form of impact scars on the stonework (see page 189). The height of these may be explained by outworks in front, perhaps the sconce mentioned in the contemporary sources.

There is also archaeological evidence for activity at this time on the east side of the castle where Gray found what he believed to be a clay bank behind the wall acting as a platform for artillery (see page 163). His finds from the area support the dating of this feature, which would have provided the ability to fire over the buildings of the town.

Radford and Hallam (1953) believed that a breach 47 feet (14.3m) long was made in the north wall of the Great Hall and that therefore the roof would have been brought down. There appears to be no definite archaeological evidence for this and the documentary evidence does not record rebuilding of the Great Hall, which would be expected if the assizes were to be held there. The historical evidence suggests that the main attacks on the town were from the south and east and while it would be easy to bombard the castle from the north, an attack across the river would have been much harder. There are also tactical reasons for suggesting a northern bombardment would be unlikely: with the town bridge held by the besieged it would have taken a significant time to move an artillery train round to the north. More significantly, the artillery would not have been available if needed urgently to counter a southern sally by the defenders.

Overall, the castle appears to have faced the fiercest direct assaults from the west; attacks from the south and east required the capture of the town before an assault on the castle could be mounted.

Commonwealth and Restoration

Following the parliamentary victory and reorganisation of the church, the bishops' possessions were seized and Taunton Castle sold to Brampton Gurdon and John Hill on 20 March 1647, in trust for Roger Hill. The sale excluded the Great Barn, which had already been granted away but this was acquired by Gurdon and Hill in the following year (see page 26). The bishops' lands were returned in 1660, after the restoration of the monarchy, but there was continuing instability across the country, and Charles II attempted to control this by ordering the dismantling of castles, including Taunton, as shown by his instruction of 30 June 1662:

> The King to James Earl of Northampton, Lord Lieutenant of Warwickshire. The strength of Coventry is so considerable, by reason of its walls and fortifications, that it is an invitation to mutinous and turbulent spirits [...] these mischiefs must be prevented, either by putting a garrison there [...] or by slighting the walls. Has resolved [...] to cause the gates, walls, and fortifications to be razed and demolished [...] and the materials thereof used for the benefit of the town. He is to be there in person till the walls are totally demolished.
>
> Minute of similar letters to [...] also of a letter to the Lord Lieutenant [and Deputy Lieutenants] of Somersetshire for slighting the walls of Taunton Castle, assigning the materials of the walls to those who will be at the charge and pains of taking them down (Green 1861).

The instruction to the Earl of Northampton to remain on site to ensure that the work was carried out suggests that there had been resistance to earlier demolitions, or possibly reluctance if the costs would not be offset by the value of the rubble. This might be a significant factor at Taunton when the earthen walls are considered, as slighting these would produce little of value. Nothing appears to have happened as a further instruction was issued three months later on 3 October:

> The king to the deputy Lieutenants of Somersetshire. Receives daily accounts that disaffected men are restless in their endeavours to create troubles, and are particularly active in that county; requires them to be very industrious to prevent these designs, by settling the militia and dismantling Taunton Castle, according to late orders and to give an account of their proceedings therein.

This instruction was reinforced on 9 October:

> [Sec. Nicholas to] Lord Poulett. The King hearing that Taunton Castle is not demolished, nor the militia of Somersetshire in the good posture required by seditious practices of factious people in the county sends a letter to the deputy lieutenants to expedite the same. Commissions are issued to Sir John

> Sydenham, and other justices of the peace, to administer to his lordship the oaths required by the Militia Act. Encloses: The King to Lord Poulett, Lord Hawley, and other deputy lieutenants of Somersetshire. For the more effectual dismantling of Taunton Castle, they are to require Mr Ware and the other justices of the peace in that part of the county to assist them.

Bush and Meek (1984, 16) suggested that this demolition must have referred to the keep (to explain its non-survival) but there is no certainty that this is the case. It is only assumption, based on the absence of further commands, that the work was even carried out following the second request and the existence of Gray's gun platform suggests that the keep buildings had been cleared before or during the war. There may also have been earlier parliamentary, or local, slighting based on the destruction of symbols of lordly power. The East Gate, particularly if it displayed heraldic symbols, would be a likely target for this.

Charles II's concerns were different, he was interested in preventing power-bases emerging to rival the newly re-established monarchical state, a concern seen elsewhere in Europe in the 17th century in places that had not undergone the trauma of civil war (Johnson 2002, 173). At Taunton the archaeological evidence shows only the infilling of the castle moat and town ditch as, where examined, these contain large amounts of roof slate accompanied by 17th-century pottery. This need not, of course, be the result of symbolic erasure of these features but a convenient dump for the clearance of building debris resulting from the damage to the town.

Post-medieval layout

Seventeenth- and 18th-century documentation provides some indication of the survival and layout of the castle before the substantial changes to the area in the decades around 1900. These paint a very different picture of the castle to that of the bustling hub of the manor shown by the medieval pipe rolls. Many of the medieval buildings had gone, and those that remained, with the exception of the Great Hall, had been converted to domestic use.

The dilapidations survey of 1782 (page 27) provides the most complete list of the bishop's property but many buildings are not easily identified to modern locations. The main block of structures comprised the inner ward including the "Porter's Lodge, Gateway etc" apparently referring to the Inner Gate. This is confused, as Toulmin (1791, 45) is explicit that the Porter's Lodge was the name given to the East Gate which the dilapidations survey refers to as the "Archway to the Castle Green".

The 17th-century sale and other legal documents (page 26) list even fewer components, principally the mansion house and the stable, together with the green, ditches, pounds, and wards. An added complication is that the parliamentary valuation appears to be based on an earlier one of 1566 so that the form of words used may be traditional and not represent the situation on the ground with any accuracy. Even the location of the mansion house is uncertain; Toulmin indicating that there was a house adjacent to the Castle Bow with the arms of bishop Langton on it, presumably one of those seen in Figure 15.6 on page 248 but this was not mentioned in the dilapidations survey, perhaps as it had passed out of the bishop's ownership. In view of the later ownerships as recorded by Carver (below), this is likely to have been to the north of the gate and to have been succeeded by a house that later became the Castle Hotel.

17.6 The Courts

The first mention of the use of the castle for civil courts, rather than those of the bishop, comes in the pipe rolls for 1536 where 31s 9d was spent "making a place in castle for king's justices to sit by order and virtue of their commission and making les hurdelles and gallows in time of execution". That this was in the Great Hall is supported by other entries: 105s 10½d for "John Sutton and two other tilers 60½ days repairing lord's great hall within castle", "3 men serving tilers 60 days, 24,000 slates, nails from Exeter, 21 bushels tilepins, making 8000 shingles/laths in Newpark and carriage" together with the construction of "a building called le Cage in the middle of Taunton".

This became the castle's main role, with the assizes and quarter sessions held in the Great Hall. They were interrupted to some degree by the Civil War but assizes were held in March 1642 and from August 1647 onwards (Cockburn 1971). Quarter sessions were held from at least 1652, a grand jury in that year considering "the castle hall near Taunton to be the fittest place within the county for the honourable judges and others to meet for the service of the commonwealth at the assizes, being a place time out of mind made use of for that service" (Harbin 1912, xxiv).

Other uses are hinted at by the issuing of a licence for dissenting worship in 1747: "an apartment called the Ball Room in the castle in parish of Bishop's Hull in the occupation of Wm Bailey the elder" for Presbyterians (SRO Q/RRW/1). Presumably this was the Great Hall but William Bailey is otherwise unknown at the castle.

In the later part of the 18th century, concerns were expressed that the castle was not fit for the holding of the courts and this might have a serious effect on the economy of the town. Public subscriptions were raised but appear to have been inadequate requiring the local MP Benjamin Hammet to underwrite the project from about 1786. The works, as described by Toulmin (see page 28), comprised the division of the Great Hall into two courts, a new Grand Jury Room on the south side and the restoration of the south and west ranges for the use of the judges.

Hammet was born in Taunton in 1737, the son of a serge manufacturer, but moved to London becoming a banker, marrying the daughter of Sir James Esdaile, and forming Esdaile and Hammet in Lombard Street. In 1782 he was elected to parliament and in 1786 obtained the office of keeper of the castle from the bishop, in the name of his sons, to enable him to undertake repairs. The senior MP, Alexander Popham, contributed £105, £94 was raised by subscription and Hammet made up to the final cost of £417. Hammet continued to improve Taunton, in 1788 obtaining an act of parliament enabling the demolition of property to construct the street that bears his name (Gray 1942). In 1791 he purchased the Castell Malgwyn tinplate works in west Wales and later constructed a house and pleasure gardens there (Barker 2006). The house, which is now a hotel, has some similar windows to those at Taunton Castle. Hammet died there in 1800.

Examination during the work for the Museum of Somerset showed that the restoration work had been as extensive as described by Toulmin and that most of the historic windows and doors were inserted at this time in addition to contemporary Gothick ones. Tom Mayberry suggests (pers. comm.) that these windows may have come from the courtyard range at Orchard Portman, which was demolished around this time (Mayberry 2011, 247).

Further work was needed early in the following century when the Great Hall was re-roofed but the hall ceased to be used for the assizes when Shire Hall was completed in 1857. Various uses were found for parts of the castle until concern over the preservation of the structure led to its purchase by SANHS in 1874.

17.7 The Museums

Initially the society continued to use the Great Hall for public meetings and housed their museum in the South and West ranges with accommodation for the museum curator on the upper floors. They cleared the buildings from the east part of the courtyard and continued to make changes, some substantial, to the surviving buildings (see for example Figure 10.8 on page 195). Much of this work uncovered features of historic interest, often left exposed, but it also led to the insertion of replica features. Luckily many of these were reported by Spencer (1910) who also produced an excellent set of plans of the buildings in 1875, before most of the changes.

Further significant changes were made in the first decade of the 20th century when the hall was opened as part of the museum and improvements made to the rooms in the South Range. Gray excavated in the orchard to the east of the courtyard throughout the 1920s and in the 1930s three buildings were erected through the generosity of William Wyndham. Gray's lack of interest in his excavation work at the castle continued and there are no records of any archaeological discoveries made during these building works. Following Gray's retirement in 1949, it is noticeable that the 1952 works in the Great Hall were preceded by excavation, although only informal building recording was undertaken. Further excavations preceded changes in the Gray Room but not when the beam engine pit was dug in 1956. The transfer of the museum to Somerset County Council in 1958 made little difference and work was still being undertaken with scant regard for the archaeological importance of the site in the late 1980s.

Minor changes were made in 1992 when improved toilets were constructed in the East Passage, the St James Street almshouse was moved into the courtyard and lift access to the Wyndham gallery was proposed but not built. Continuing concerns about the accessibility of the museum contributed to the development of the Museum of Somerset project, subsequently grant-aided by the Heritage Lottery Fund. The Great Hall had a mezzanine floor inserted, two lifts were provided, the East and West Passages were widened and the West Range re-roofed to form a museum whose visitor numbers have continued to increase. In 2014, Somerset County Council passed control of the museum (and its other heritage functions and staff) to a new South West Heritage Trust.

Chapter 18

Discussion

Chris Webster

18.1 Taunton and the other residences of the Bishops of Winchester

The medieval bishops of Winchester were one of the largest landowners in England (Page 2002) and maintained numerous residences on their estates as well as their main palace at Winchester. In the early middle ages, these are likely to have been visited frequently as part of a peripatetic lifestyle but later bishops concentrated on a Winchester–London axis, with Wolvesey at Winchester, Bishop's Waltham, Farnham and Southwark receiving the majority of attention and expenditure. As has become clear in castle studies over recent years there are no reasons to expect any patterns in the planning of castles belonging to a particular lord, as both the estate and each castle grew organically depending on the needs and fashions at different times and places. Despite this, there are parallels with the other bishopric castles that can provide evidence that can be used at Taunton.

The main residence at Winchester, Wolvesey Palace, is described in the 1138 list (see page 266) as a "palatial house" and was excavated for display by Martin Biddle in the 1960s. The site has only been published as an interim report (Biddle 1969) and site guidebooks (Biddle 1986; Wareham 2000). The first hall is attributed to William Giffard *c.*1110 but most of the first masonry phase is credited to Henry of Blois. This includes an additional hall block, chapel and subsequently a kitchen given the appearance of a small keep. Other parts of the palace appear to have been remodelled to give it a more warlike appearance and the palace is recorded as being attacked in 1141. The extensive ruins that Biddle uncovered are in fine Norman masonry that has no parallels at Taunton. The palace appears to have undergone only fairly small changes after the 13th century until it was replaced by a new palace in a baroque style in the late 17th century.

The residence at Bishop's Waltham shares most similarities with Taunton, though rarely called a castle after its inclusion in the 1138 list. It is the best preserved and probably the most studied (Hare 1987; 1988; Wareham 2000). Much of this has concentrated on the late medieval work of William Wykeham (Davis 2007) and Henry Beaufort but work of the mid/late 12th century survives. This comprises a linear hall range with kitchen along the west side of the enclosure, a tower at the south-west corner containing the bishop's chamber and a range containing the great or audience chamber along the southern side. It is believed that these were built by Henry of Blois or his successor, Richard of Ilchester, over a curving earlier medieval defensive enclosure. To the north was an outer court containing barns, stables and a gatehouse to the town. It appears to have been greatly damaged in the Civil War following its surrender by royalist forces and was subsequently used as a quarry for materials for Wolvesey.

Farnham Castle was one of the favoured residences of the Bishops, as it lay close to the main road between Winchester and London. It appears to have originated as a motte and bailey with a stone tower partly constructed within the motte (Thompson 1960b; 1961; Wareham 2000). Later the motte was encased with a stone wall and towers built around it (see Figure 17.2 on page 269). Residential buildings survive to the south forming a triangle around a courtyard with a substantial brick entrance tower built in the 1470s by William Waynflete (Thompson 1960a).

Winchester, like most dioceses, maintained a house in London for use while the bishop attended parliament or other state duties but Winchester Place, Southwark, was one of the most impressive, built to been seen from the city of London across the Thames. It has mostly been destroyed by later warehousing but excavations in the 1980s and subsequently have uncovered part of the plan (Toy 1944–45; Riall not dated; Phillpotts 1999; Seeley *et al.* 2006). It appears to have been purely residential in character with a long range along the river frontage and subsidiary buildings around courtyards to the rear.

The other two castles in the 1138 list, Downton and Merdon, seem to have had less subsequent use. Downton appears to have been a ringwork with two outer baileys, now landscaped into a garden known as The Moot. There is little evidence for its use after the 12th century. Merdon, was constructed within an iron-age hillfort and has a few stone structures surviving (Webster 1989; Peach 1995). It may be one of the Hampshire castles destroyed in 1155 when Henry of Blois fell out of favour but it continued in use as a hunting lodge throughout the medieval period. The present earthworks appear to form a ringwork to the north and bailey to the south, though the bank dividing them has been removed. At the north end is an unusual stone gatehouse, which had a right-angled entrance passage with the doorways in adjacent walls. Very few other gatehouses of this design are known (Kenyon 1990, 63) and the impracticality led to the rear wall being knocked through to give straight access (Webster 1989).

The bishops also owned other residences, such as Witney (below) and Harwell (Fletcher 1979; Currie 1992, 136–142) in Oxfordshire and East Meon (Roberts 1993c), Hambledon (Roberts 1993b), Bishop's Sutton, Overton (Roberts 1995), Marwell, Highclere, Fareham and Bitterne (Crawford 1944; Macnaghten 1955) in the area around Winchester but most of these were smaller and only equipped to accommodate the bishop and a small retinue. Roberts (2003, 202) indicates the scale of the residences, noting that over £1200 was spent rebuilding Bishop's Waltham in the late 14th century compared to £109 to rebuild the hall and chamber block at East Meon and the complete rebuilding of a bailiff's house for less than £5. The overall cost of the hall, chamber and chapel at Taunton, 150 years earlier, was £173 (Hunt 1971).

Excavations at Witney, (Allen and Hiller 2002) show a manorial centre somewhere in the middle of the size range, although the lack of excavation at the smaller estates may under-emphasise their size as only stone buildings, if anything, survive. Witney comprised a two-storey east range, linked by a tower at the south end to a hall range on the west side of a courtyard entered from the north. This complex lay within a larger curvilinear moated enclosure, containing lodgings and other ancillary structures. To the east was a barton with a dovecot. Despite the defensive character of the structures, Witney is never described as a castle and is not mentioned in the 1138 list.

Taunton Castle is smaller than Wolvesey, and probably Bishop's Waltham, but larger than Witney. Comparison to the major residences is complicated by its location well away from the heartland of the bishopric as shown by the infrequency of episcopal visits. When Bishop Michael Scott-Joynt visited Taunton to celebrate the 1100th anniversary of the 904 charter, he was only the eighth on record and the first since Thomas Langton in 1498 (see Table 1.1 on page 11). Despite this, Taunton was clearly of importance to the bishopric both as an administrative centre and as a castle. It acted as the centre for the manor of Taunton and also as the collection point for agricultural produce from three of the sub-manors: Holway, Hull and Staplegrove (this may be a development of the 1320s, see page 21). The outer ward appears dominated by this activity with numerous references to the agricultural buildings present there but our hazy knowledge of the plan of the castle does not preclude other activities and a neat split between the inner and outer wards may be too easy.

The present inner ward, and probably the area of the Keep Garden, appears to be an elite space, accessed across the inner moat through a gatehouse and it is likely that few of the manor's inhabitants ever saw it, unless required to attend court. What survives contains the bishop's great hall and his private quarters, together with other halls and official residences. Many of these buildings were probably uninhabited for much of the time with flurries of activity preceding the court sessions or the arrival of an important visitor. Visits by the bishop, in particular, are revealed in the accounts by expenditure prior to the stay to bring the buildings up to standard and then again afterwards, the standard having been found wanting.

18.2 Taunton as a Castle

Despite similarities to a manorial centre such as Witney, Taunton was clearly considered to be a castle and was called such throughout its history. It was thought fit to entertain royalty in both the 13th and the 15th centuries and displays many of the characteristic features that appear to define the development of castles throughout the middle ages.

Castle studies underwent a paradigm shift in the 1980s and 90s when the primarily military perception that had continued from the time of GT Clark's *Medieval Military Architecture in England* (1884) began to break down (Liddiard 2005). This was part of a wider academic change caused by the growth of archaeology as a discipline and the investigation of castle sites by generalists rather than military historians and architects. These archaeologists were also of a post-war generation who lacked the military background of most of their predecessors and who saw the past through a more anthropological model – one of symbolism rather than functionalism. More recently, as would be expected, there has been a reaction to this (for example by Platt 2007) and the truth will lie in a combination of both positions. Castles clearly had a military role on the rare occasions that they needed to, and were designed to fulfil that role. Conversely that role was also symbolic, both militarily and socially. A castle that appeared strong and militarily sophisticated was less likely to be attacked and also presented its owner as powerful, a symbolism that some (for example, Windsor Castle) retain to this day. The castle also formed an important symbolic element in medieval story-telling and art (Wheatley 2004) and it is clear that "military" attributes were a normal part of the medieval architectural repertoire, as evidenced by the crenellations of church parapets.

Taunton, because of its very partial survival is unlikely to produce definitive evidence but most of what there is appears to fit a less-military approach to its understanding. It is possible that this is biased in that most of what survives is late medieval in date, a time when the functionalist approach sees castle as in "decline" and the increasing amount of documentary evidence for elite behaviour encourages a more social approach. The early phases at Taunton are particularly poorly represented, with no real evidence for the plan or presence of any particularly class of structure. After the start of the Winchester pipe rolls in 1208 the castle appears to be well-documented, but again there is little detail that can be located. The earliest document that describes the buildings in detail is the 1782 Dilapidations Survey (see page 27) but by then the castle was merely a collection of buildings, used by the courts or rented out as residences.

It is possible to see some similarities between Taunton and Bishop's Waltham in the early phases that may reflect a programme of building activities by Henry of Blois. Both take the form of two ranges of buildings, one containing the hall and kitchens, the other, the bishop's rooms, articulated about a corner tower. The tower at Taunton is less clearly evident than at Bishop's Waltham but the West Range may originally have been more prominent. This form of lordly dwelling, hall and chamber-block, is seen across most of the Norman world, with exceptions in the north of England and south-west France where a tower residence was favoured (Impey 1999; Meirion-Jones 2012).

Both Dixon and Marshall (1993, 430) and Riall (2003, 126) discuss the plan form of Norman bishops' castles noting that they are based around a rectangular courtyard. Taunton appears not to fit this model because of the angle formed by the south range but this may well be a later rearrangement. Wall 1175 (pages 96 and 213) in the courtyard is undated but may belong to this phase and have formed part of the east side of an earlier courtyard.

However, it is also clear that the surviving buildings do not comprise all the elite structures originally at Taunton. The building of a new hall in 1246–49 did not replace the original hall and it is likely that this other hall formed the focus of the elite residential area initially. Most of what is visible now is based around this 1246–48 rebuilding and the earlier structures on this site, assuming that features (the pilaster buttresses often used to demarcate the presence of a hall behind a curtain wall) of the Great Hall and West Range are not anachronistic, may have had different functions. The most likely location for the early hall is probably to the east but evidence for this will be hard to obtain.

The date of the division into two wards is also less clear than once believed (the pipe roll entry for 1208). The inner curtain wall may fossilise an earlier, less substantial division running further north dividing the minster burial ground from the bishop's domestic space but all the buildings currently there appear to date from the decades around 1500. It is even less clear what happens in the area of Castle House, into which at least three earlier walls disappear with no indications of how they could join.

Re-examination of Gray's excavations in the Keep Garden has shown the complexity of the remains there, unfortunately now greatly damaged by Gray's own work. Although it is not clear exactly what stood here, it is certain that it underwent several changes, and that these fit a pattern also seen at Witney and Wolvesey (Allen and Hiller 2002; Biddle 1986). This sees the raising of ground levels by infilling behind retaining walls and is presumably expressing the elevated status of the bishop. Some of this revetment may be simply responses to weakness caused by over-ambitious plans on the platform above but as most of the evidence has been removed it may never be possible to reconstruct this in detail.

The outer ward is, thanks to its economic importance, better reported in the pipe rolls. Its principal role appears to have been as the collecting point for the produce of three of the sub-manors (Holway, Staplegrove and Hull) of the huge manor of Taunton, with three large barns for agricultural produce and bartons to contain animals. It is possible that earlier the produce of the whole manor was collected here as the sub-manors are only mentioned from the mid 14th century. Later, with the decline in rent-collection in kind, the stores went out of use until only one remained to be converted into a stable in the post-medieval period.

The outer ward appears to have been surrounded by cob walling, as described on page 20, with evidence that towers could also be made of this material (page 18). Without the information from the account rolls this would be hard to detect, as presumably the walls stood on raised banks behind the ditches and all trace of the insubstantial foundations required by cob building will have been lost. Gray saw no signs of a curtain wall at the Electricity Showroom in 1937, only what he interpreted as a revetment wall for the moat (see page 47). This use of earth walls does not appear to have been studied much since Mackenzie's (1933–34) work in Scotland apart from brief discussions by Kenyon (1990, 126–30, 141–42) and Higham and Barker (1992, 114). The excavations at Hen Domen in mid Wales (Barker and Higham 1982; Higham and Barker 2000) showed constructional techniques based on vertical posts with clay and wattlework that could have been used at Taunton and they also suggest the possibility of a wall-walk, jettied out over the ditch and enclosed with timber walls and roof. Such a design would explain the references in the accounts to the roofing of the walls, although some of the walls may simply have been thinner and roofed over to keep the cob dry.

Despite the almost continual absence of the lord, or perhaps to remind people of his existence, the castle exhibits all the symbols of medieval elite culture. The castle possessed a dovecot and to the south of the town are a fishpond (*vivarium*, now Vivary Park) and a deer park at Poundisford. Marten-Holden (2001, 52) notes the parallels of these three symbols to the biblical account (Genesis 1:26) of God's gift of dominion over birds, fish and animals.

Little is known of the dovecot but the Winchester episcopal fishponds have been reviewed by Roberts (1986; 1993a) who notes that most, including Taunton's are present before the first account roll in 1209 and that Henry of Blois was noted for their construction by Gerald of Wales in *c.*1198. The fish from these ponds were eaten exclusively by the bishop and his guests, or occasionally were presented as gifts. The fish was usually eaten fresh and so required a pond within one day's journey of episcopal residences but during episcopal vacancies the king assumed the rights to the fish. In February 1241 the king ordered that 100 pike and 200 bream should be taken from the pond at Taunton, the pike to be salted and the bream put in "paste", and half taken to Woodstock quickly, the rest to follow (Chapman 1930, 31).

Live fish were also transported for restocking other ponds as in 1231 when bream were carried from Taunton to Winchester in canvas-lined barrels, the journey taking 15 days and costing £8 3s 9d (Roberts 1986, 130). There are further mentions of the vivarium in the pipe rolls, though these have not been searched comprehensively for this information. Robin Bush (1977, 27) says that there were two ponds, which he probably discovered from the pipe rolls but this may refer to one at the castle (below). A boat is recorded as being repaired in 1219 and a new one was bought in 1283 for 17s 6d. In 1234 repairs are recorded when carters were paid for hauling clay to the pond and in 1285 lime was purchased for a wall around it. Swans were also kept on the ponds, at some estates on artificial islands with nests perhaps to prevent fox predation (Roberts 1986). There were certainly swans at Taunton as their numbers are listed in the pipe rolls.

Fish were also kept in the moat, the pipe rolls record the cost of "a partition called 'gridel' to keep fish in castle ditch" by the postern between the garden and the Meadow of Southam and a hurdle for the same purpose at "la Westgate" in 1347 and 1349. The moat was probably used as a stew pond for storing fish after capture (Roberts 1986). From 1534 it was rented out for fishing. There was also a small fishpond in the garden that was mentioned in 1355 but whether this was primarily ornamental is not known. The use of freshwater fish only for elite feasting is supported by the fishbones found in the excavation as, admittedly from a very small sample, all the fish bones identified were of marine species.

The bishops' park was at Poundisford, four kilometres south of Taunton, where the enclosing bank survives for much of its length. The bishops were rarely recorded hunting in their own parks despite owning the largest number after the crown and the duchy of Lancaster, probably as it was considered unsuitable for churchmen. Professional huntsmen would have been employed to provide venison for feasting and as gifts, and to assist guests if a hunt was organised (Roberts 1988; Sykes 2007a). In contrast to the fishbone evidence (above), the deer bones did indicate the presence of high-status cuts of meat (Higbee, this volume).

Other characteristic features that Taunton shares with many castles are that the most elaborate gatehouse faces into the town, with "weaker" gatehouses facing the open countryside (Pounds 1990, 213; Liddiard 2005, 22), and that this entrance leads off the market place where the greatest number of people will be able to be impressed by it (Creighton 2002, 151–57), although Pounds (1990, 204–5) notes that they were unlikely to have been allowed in. There is also an adjacent monastic establishment, often as at Taunton, served by Augustinian canons who as priests were available to serve the castle chapel (Thompson 1986; Creighton 2002, 127–31). Apart from what appears to have been a fashion for the establishment of these monastic foundations during the 12th century, there may have been an additional impetus in a desire to remove the minster from the castle site.

18.3 Material Culture

The recent excavations at the castle were notable for the paucity of finds, and with one exception, this seems to have been the case from earlier work as well. Comparison with other excavated castles, such as the recently published work at Stafford (Soden 2007), shows that this does seem to represent a significant difference. The excavations at Stafford were far more extensive than at Taunton but it is not just the numbers of finds of all classes that are low, it is also the variety of find-types and their overall quality that is reduced. This pattern is also seen in the bones recovered (Higbee, this volume).

David Dawson (see pages 105–108) notes that there are significant gaps in the pottery sequence, particularly in the late medieval period, and the earliest period is also poorly represented. The exception is the large numbers of 12th-century jar sherds stored in the museum and believed to have come from Gray's work in the Keep Garden area. The context of these sherds is not understood as Gray nowhere mentions them. They are not mentioned in his finds list for the early years of the excavation and it is probable that they were collected by workmen during the later years of clearance work – material that Gray might have discarded if he had been on site.

The pottery is also notable for a lack of more exotic and expensive wares, with only seven sherds of 18th-century finewares from the 2005–13 excavations. This parallels the metalwork finds, which are also characterised by their scarcity. Only four coins were recovered, two of the 18th century and two of the late 20th. This presumably reflects the patterns of activity in and around the Great Hall and patterns of rubbish disposal. The river is a likely location for the latter, which would account for the lack of rubbish pits but it is also likely that the hall was used for activities that did not produce large amounts of rubbish, and if it did, it was carefully cleared. The almost continual absence of the bishops suggests that this was not a domestic area for most of the time with most of the castle's inhabitants living elsewhere, perhaps around the Constable's Hall. The Great Hall is likely to have been cleaned before any occasional use, such as an important visitor, or the holding of a court. The subsequent removal of medieval floor levels will also have contributed to the loss of any discarded material.

One group of features stands out from this picture, the pit complex partly excavated in the West Passage. The clay pipe and glass evidence suggests a date of deposition in the early 18th century. The pit complex seems to have been caused by stone robbing of the Phase 1 building under the Great Hall, perhaps associated with the significant changes identified as Phase 5 (see page 185). What is not clear is where the material used as backfill came from. While it could result from the leisure activities of the judges, it could just as easily have been carted from a tavern in the town.

18.4 Conclusions

The recent work at Taunton, and the re-examination of earlier records have proved both illuminating and frustrating. It is now clear that many of the interpretations put forward by Gray, Radford and others are untenable. They were written in an age of deferment to experts, who in turn felt that they had to express certainty. Lady (Aileen) Fox noted this, particularly in relation to Radford when she said, in a letter to Frances Lynch in 1972 (quoted in Sheridan *et al.* 2008, 2, n5): "the trouble with Radford is that he knows too much, so always finds what he intended." This is seen in the Great Hall where his description of Trench VII (Radford and Hallam 1953, 58) was clearly contradicted by its re-examination in 2009. He simply cannot have seen what he describes as the evidence for the demolished east wall of his earliest hall. Similarly Gray's reconstruction of the keep as having similarities to Dover or Newcastle (Vivian-Neal and Gray 1940, 63) is hard to sustain in the absence of the massive foundations required for a tower keep. Gray himself may have had doubts, which may be one of the reasons that he published so little.

Having demolished previous interpretations it is doubly annoying not to be able to replace them with new certainties. The earliest building in the area of the Great Hall now lacks an east wall, its plan has close parallels to Southwark but that is several hundred years later, and the archaeological evidence for the keep has gone, while there is clear documentary evidence that it existed.

This is partly explained by one thing that is clear, particularly from a study of the Winchester pipe rolls; the castle was undergoing continual change. It is not a single-phase construction like Edward I's castles in Wales, nor does it seem to have neat additions to the structure that can be assigned to phases and dated. The loss of most of the buildings apart from those in the present inner ward makes this harder to assess, but the 1246–49 building of the bishop's new hall, chamber and chapel is the only major building campaign recorded. Most of the castle's overall structure would appear to have been in place before the accounts begin in 1209 but later works comprise repairs and the occasional "new" building. The archaeological evidence reflects this with the walls uncovered in the southern part of the Keep Garden and the courtyard not forming any coherent structures. Indeed it is hard to form any plan by joining them up, particularly if another round tower is included, which suggests that they may all be of different periods.

The finds similarly fail to add to the traditional picture of a castle; there is little military equipment or evidence of elite consumption patterns. Taunton Castle is, in truth, rather odd. Perhaps this is explained by a tension between its status as a castle belonging to one of the richest men in England and its location well away from the axis of power between London and Winchester or perhaps most castles were actually like this, an uneasy compromise between status and expenditure.

Appendix A

Mineralogical Report on Ceramics

Jens Andersen, David Dawson and Gavyn Rollinson

Mineralogical analysis was carried out by QEMSCAN using the methodology described by Andersen *et al.* (in press). Four major mineralogical types were recognised and the key mineralogical characteristics of these types are listed in Table A.1 on the following page. A list of potential minerals included in the QEMSCAN mineral groups is given in Table A.2 on page 287 and a summary of the results in Figure A.22 on page 330.

Results of the Mineralogical Analysis

The most obvious result of the mineralogical analysis is that the sherds from production sites display consistent mineralogical groupings that appear to relate to differences in the local bedrock geology. Although the present dataset does not adequately account for variability within and between sites, these geological correlations to some extent corroborate the existing archaeological groupings. Particularly significant mineralogical differences separate the West Somerset types produced on Triassic bedrock formations from the East and South Somerset types, represented by samples from Donyatt and Wanstrow, that were produced on Jurassic bedrock. The dominance of alkali feldspar over plagioclase and the near absence of kaolinite are the most significant characteristic features of the West Somerset types. Not enough samples from East and South Somerset have been examined to generalise about their particular characteristics.

Many sherds from Taunton Castle are mineralogically similar to the sampled sherds from production sites but they also include additional types that cannot presently be linked to production sites based on the small number of samples studied here.

A further significant observation is that the sherds have significant mineralogical differences between their inclusions and matrix. The abundance of inclusions is very variable, and in some cases in the post-medieval period less than one volume percent. It is particularly worrying that sherds that are visually very similar have significantly different inclusion populations and matrix compositions. This demonstrates, perhaps, how difficult it is to establish the provenance of pottery fabric types based on their inclusion mineralogy using optical microscopy.

Generally (for types A, B, and C) the inclusion populations can be described as simple mixtures of two minerals, and it is likely that they have been derived from distinct sources that are relatively mineralogically pure. While some accidental inclusions are likely, the uniform mineralogy of the inclusions between different types makes it more likely that the pottery was intentionally engineered from components that had been deliberately sourced as appropriate materials for tempering of different wares. Type D in contrast, has a very mixed inclusion population, perhaps reflecting less refinement in the material selection (Figure A.22 on page 330).

Some mineralogical differences undoubtedly have geological explanations, particularly the clay minerals which are always fine grained in geological materials, and therefore distinct matrix components. A more interesting mineral is the plagioclase feldspar, which consistently reports to the matrix. While plagioclase would geologically not always be expected to be fine grained, it appears to be a characteristic component of the clays used for types B, C, and D.

The presence of glauconite is particularly significant in Somerset as it could be used as an indicator of the Upper Greensand derived material identified by Allan *et al.* (2011). It is no surprise,

A	The clay composition of the matrix is dominated by Fe–Al–K silicates with some muscovite/illite. This type has no or little kaolinite. Inclusions are predominantly quartz and K-feldspar. plagioclase feldspar and calcite are absent from both inclusions and matrix. Glauconite is locally significant. Type A appears to be consistent with samples from the West Somerset production sites at Crowcombe (Figure A.14), Langford Budville (Figure A.17), Nether Stowey (Figure A.18) and Wrangway (Figure A.21) and with Taunton Castle fabric types 74, 83 and 89 (Figure A.11 to Figure A.13).
B	The clay composition of the matrix is a mixture of Fe–Al–K silicates and kaolinite (between 1:1 and 2:1) with significant (although less) muscovite/illite. The matrix has significant Fe–Al silicates and plagioclase feldspar. Two subtypes are defined by differences in the inclusions:
B1	Inclusions of quartz and K-feldspar. Glauconite is locally significant but calcite is absent. This subtype includes Donyatt Site 4 (Figure A.15) and the two samples from Wanstrow (Figure A.19 and Figure A.20) as well as two sherds from Taunton Castle fabric types unclassified and type 14 (Figure A.2 and Figure A.7)
B2	Inclusions of quartz and calcite with minor K-feldspar. This subtype includes four medieval sherds from Taunton Castle fabric types 3, 7B, 8 and 15 (Figure A.3, Figure A.5, Figure A.6 and Figure A.8). No examples were studied from potential production sites.
C	The matrix clay composition of type C is closely similar to type B except the content of kaolinite appears to be slightly less. Inclusions are 60–70 percent calcite with the remaining being quartz and minor alkali feldspar. This group includes two medieval sherds from Taunton Castle fabric types 7A and 23 (Figure A.4 and Figure A.9), while no examples were examined from potential production sites.
D	The clay composition of the matrix is predominantly kaolinite and muscovite/illite with only minor Fe–Al–K silicates. Quartz is below 20 percent and plagioclase dominates over alkali feldspar. The inclusion population is much more diverse than in all other types. Around 70 percent is quartz but the remaining 30 percent include alkali feldspar, muscovite/illite, kaolinite, and Fe–Al silicates The group includes Donyatt Site 13 (Figure A.16) and a single sherd from Taunton Castle fabric type 62 (Figure A.10), both of which are post-medieval.

Table A.1: *Mineralogical types*

therefore, that sherds from Donyatt site 4 (type B1) and Langford Budville (type A), which come from sites that are near geological exposures of the Upper Greensand, have significant glauconite. It is more surprising that other samples in close proximity to the Upper Greensand exposures (particularly that from Wrangway) have little if any glauconite.

Of the three medieval sherds that were previously identified to have Upper Greensand components, our results confirm significant glauconite in two (type C) but not the third (type B2). It is particularly striking (on the basis of the occurrence of glauconite), that either the Upper Greensand derived material has been used locally in the production of most of the different mineralogical types (not confined to either the medieval or the post-medieval production), or that glauconite occurs more widely across the county.

The Effect of Firing Earthenwares on their Mineralogy

The very purpose of pottery firing is to introduce mineralogical changes, which as a consequence will alter the physical properties of the pottery fabric. The conditions under which these changes take place fundamentally determine the properties of the final product. However, although the products of the firing are reasonably predictable within the context of individual production sites and periods, the complex mineralogical changes that the materials undergo are only poorly understood.

Most analytical work in relation to pottery firing is either carried out on sherds from archaeological contexts, or from samples prepared from possible clay sources prepared in the laboratory. The essential difference is that it is likely that

Fe sulphides	pyrite, marcasite, pyrrhotite (and possibly jarosite)
Pb glaze	Pb bearing silicates, oxides and sulphides/sulphates
Barite	barite
Chrome spinel	chromite, chrome spinel
Fe Ox/CO_3	siderite, haematite, magnetite, goethite, ochre and limonite
Mn phases	all manganese bearing minerals including pyrolusite, rhodonite, rhodocrosite and umber
Rutile	rutile, anatase, brookite
Ilmenite	ilmenite
Zircon	zircon
REE phases	monazite, xenotime, allanite
Quartz	quartz, opal, chert, flint, chalcedony
Plagioclase feldspar	plagioclase feldspar
K-Feldspar	orthoclase, sanidine, microcline
Muscovite/Illite	muscovite, illite
Fe Al K silicates	iron-bearing clays, biotite mica
Glauconite	any phase with Fe, Al, K, Mg, Si, O
Kaolinite	kaolinite, halloysite, dickite, kyanite, sillimanite, andalusite
Tourmaline	tourmaline
Fe Al silicates	chlorite/clinochlore, nontronite, vermiculite
Mg Al silicates	palygorskite, magnesiochloritoid
Mg silicates	asbestos, talc, serpentine minerals
Ca Fe Al silicates	epidote, zoisite, clinozoisite
Calcite	calcite, chalk, limestone, lime, ankerite, dolomite
Ca phosphates	apatite, tooth and bone material
Others	any other mineral

Table A.2: *Mineral groups used in the QEMSCAN analysis*

the former were fired and exposed to the naked flame in a simple kiln with a regimen of oxidation, reduction and final reoxidation as described by Dawson and Kent (1999, 165–67) following experimental work with Dr Andy Tubb; the latter most often in an oxidising atmosphere in an electric kiln where the firing temperature can be controlled. What has been little explored is what changes occur to the mineralogy of the matrix and inclusions in pottery when fired in the former way. That there are changes can be observed in the finished pottery.

Setting aside the changes to glazes, perhaps the most obvious change is that the matrix changes colour. A typical plain red earthenware clay that will fire orange to red when fully oxidised, will fire grey to black when reduced. When reoxidised however the same ware may change to buff to pale orange in colour. At any event the reoxidised colour will be paler than the fully oxidised colour. A core of reduced clay may be left grey or black while the surface has reoxidised. The principal active constituents here are iron compounds but a similar though less marked change can be seen in other less iron-rich clay bodies. This implies that the firing cycle is changing other constituents as well.

Two observable changes to specific inclusions may be cited. Organic material may, by accident or design, be used to temper the ware such as the grass-tempered ware found at Cadbury-Congresbury (Rahtz 1974, 108). It is not uncommon to find that this material has been burnt out of the fabric leaving voids which may provide a detailed cast of the original. Some types of calcareous material will undergo the conversion to quicklime. This change manifests itself as a problem when the lime rehydrates increasing its volume and causing a spall on the surface of the vessel. It is a fault with certain clays once used in the Bridgwater potteries where the specks of lime were characterised by the clay-diggers in former

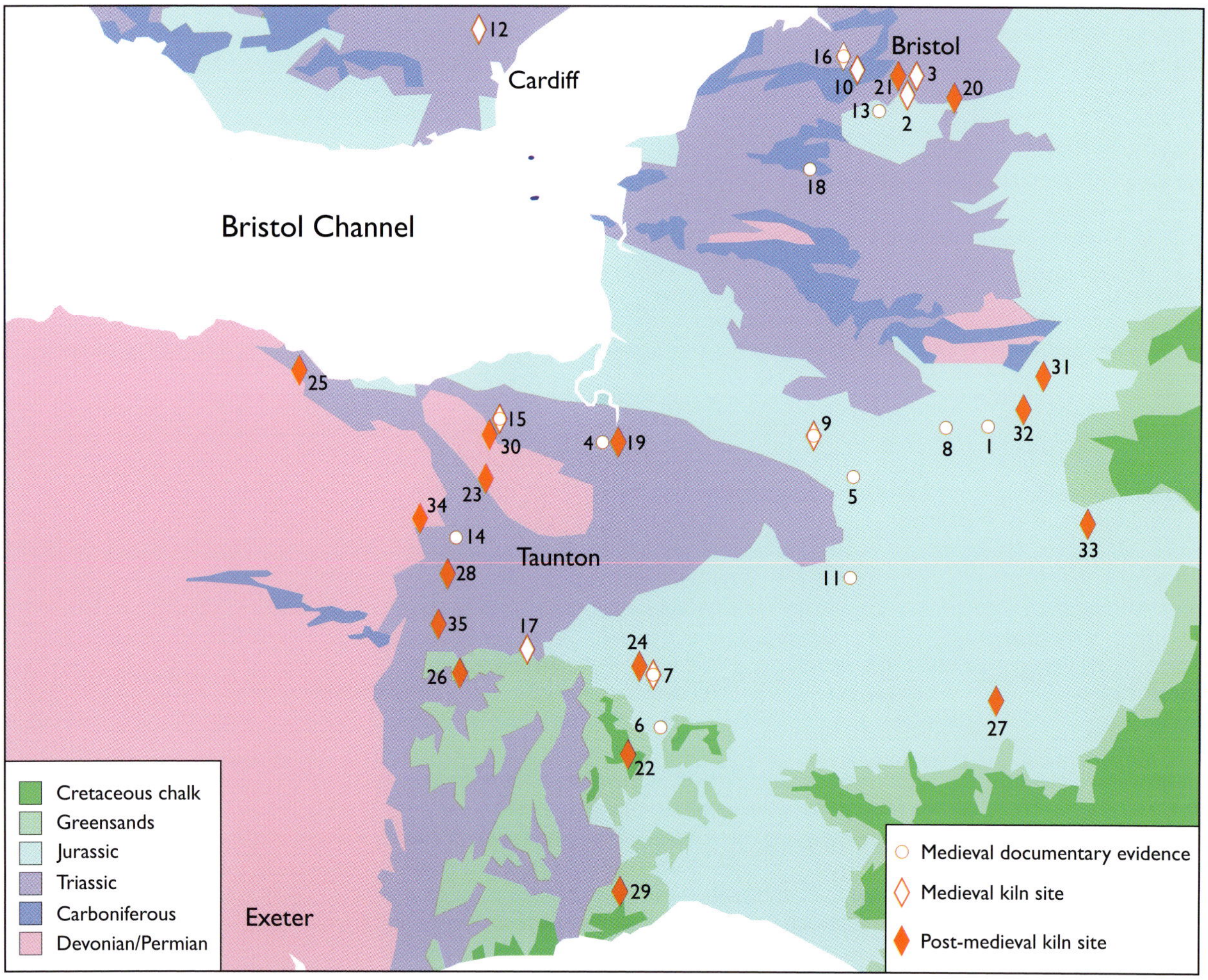

Figure A.1: *Distribution of evidence of post-Roman pottery production sites in Somerset and surrounding area pre 1800. For key to sites see Table A.3 on the next page*

times as "fossilised bird turds." Other calcareous inclusions may leach out during firing and burial leaving a corky surface appearance such as in Pearson's Taunton fabric type 180 (Pearson 1984c, I.47, 11), which is not present at the castle.

A potential explanation for the lack of glauconite identified in our analysis could relate to the thermal stability of the mineral. Geologically, glauconite is an indicator mineral for sediments deposited in marine environments, and it is poorly preserved in rocks that have been subjected to elevated temperatures after their deposition. This causes us to suggest that the thermal stability of glauconite is indeed extremely limited, and it may also break down under certain conditions during firing. A study by Basso *et al.* (2008) documents visual changes to glauconite pellets during the firing process, and we suggest that these changes are not merely changes to the colour but are caused by the thermal decomposition of the glauconite itself. Although we are currently only able to speculate, it may explain the absence of glauconite in some sherds that have previously been linked to Upper Greensand derived materials. We suspect that the red-brown inclusions of Fe-Al silicates and K-feldspar (which are particularly abundant in the sherds from Wanstrow and Donyatt site 13) may represent thermally decomposed glauconite in pottery that had been subjected to somewhat higher firing temperatures than those of the sherd from Donyatt site 4.

To conclude, the process employed in firing most pottery from archaeological contexts will change the chemistry and physical form of the mineralogy of the clay body from its raw state to its fired state in a different way to an oxidising firing under laboratory conditions.

	Medieval potteries
1	Batcombe, documentary evidence of land held by potters 1189 (le Patourel 1968, 123, 125).
2	Bristol Redcliffe (Wilson and Moorhouse 1971, 152).
3	Bristol St Peter, 14th-century pottery waste (Dawson *et al.* 1972).
4	Bridgwater, documentary evidence (le Patourel 1968, 125).
5	Butleigh, documentary evidence of land held by potters 1189 (le Patourel 1968, 123, 125).
6	Chard, documentary evidence of land held by potters 1265 (le Patourel 1968, 123, 125).
7	Donyatt sites 1 and 2, documentary evidence (Coleman-Smith and Pearson 1988; le Patourel 1968, 125).
8	Evercreech, documentary evidence of land held by potters 1272 (le Patourel 1968, 123, 125).
9	Glastonbury, documentary evidence (le Patourel 1968, 125); 14th-century waste pottery from Bove Town (C and N Hollinrake pers. comm.).
10	Ham Green, kiln and mid 12th- to 13th-century pottery waste (Barton 1963; Ponsford 1991).
11	Ilchester, documentary evidence (le Patourel 1968, 125).
12	Llandaff, Cathedral School, 14th-century waste of "Vale ware" pottery and tile (M Redknap and A Forward pers. comm.).
13	Long Ashton, documentary evidence (le Patourel 1968, 125) and possible 13th-century cooking pot waste (Ponsford 1987, 82).
14	Milverton, documentary evidence of land held by potters 1265 (le Patourel 1968, 123, 125).
15	Nether Stowey, documentary reference to right to make pottery *ab antiquo* 1275 and possible kiln site (le Patourel 1968, 104, 125).
16	Pill, documentary evidence of duration from 13th to 18th centuries (le Patourel 1968, 123, 125); 13th-century waste pottery (Ponsford 1987, 81).
17	Blackdown Hills, Upper Greensand derived wares, based on geological examination and ICP analysis (Allan *et al.* 2011).
18	Wrington, documentary evidence of land held by potters 1234 (le Patourel 1968, 125).
	Post-medieval potteries (*waste pottery sampled)
19	Bridgwater (Boore and Pearson 2010).
20	Brislington, St Anne's (Pountney 1920, 23–40).
21	Bristol, pottery production until 1968 including tin-glazed earthenwares and creamware (Pountney 1920; Witt 1979), 18th-century waste of yellow slipwares and stoneware (Barton 1961), 19th-century kilns and waste mocha ware at Crews Hole (Marochan 1962), red earthenwares (Brears 1971, 199–200).
22	Chard and Chardstock, 17th- to 18th-century kiln furniture from field walking (R Carter and P Woods pers. comm.), South Somerset group of wares.
23*	Crowcombe, 16th-century pottery waste (Dawson pers. obsv.), one of the West Somerset group of wares.
24*	Donyatt (sites 4 and 13 sampled), the principal centre of making South Somerset wares (Coleman-Smith and Pearson 1988; Coleman-Smith 2002).
25	Dunster (Dawson and Kent 2008a).
26	Hemyock, 16th-century waste pottery (J. Allen pers. comm.)
27	Holnest, documentary evidence (Brears 1971, 178), late 16th to early 17th-century waste pottery (Dawson and Kent pers. comm.)
28*	Langford Budville, 17th-century waste saggars (Ponsford 1987, 85), 18th-century red earthenware waste (Dawson pers. obsv.), one of the West Somerset group of wares.
29	Lyme Regis, Hole Common, 18th-century waste pottery (Draper 1982).
30*	Nether and Over Stowey (Coleman-Smith and Pearson 1970; Dunning 1985, 195), one of the West Somerset group of wares.
31*	Nunney and Trudoxhill (samples Wanstrow A and Wanstrow B from Nunney Catch) 17th to 18th-century pottery waste identical to and grouped with the Wanstrow or East Somerset wares (Vranch 1988).
32*	Wanstrow, kilns reported (Nunney Catch samples A and B, see 31), a centre making East Somerset wares.
33	Wincanton, Ireson Cottage, 18th-century tin-glazed earthenware kiln and waste (Dawson and Kent 2008b).
34	Wiveliscombe, 17th-century waste pottery (Ponsford 1987, 85).
35*	Wrangway, 17th-century kilns and red earthenware waste (Dawson *et al.* 2001; Pearson *et al.* 2014), one of the West Somerset group of wares.

Table A.3: *Evidence of post-Roman pottery production sites in Somerset and surrounding area pre 1800. For locations see Figure A.1 on the preceding page*

Sample: TC unclassified, context 755	**CSM lab code: C05120010**

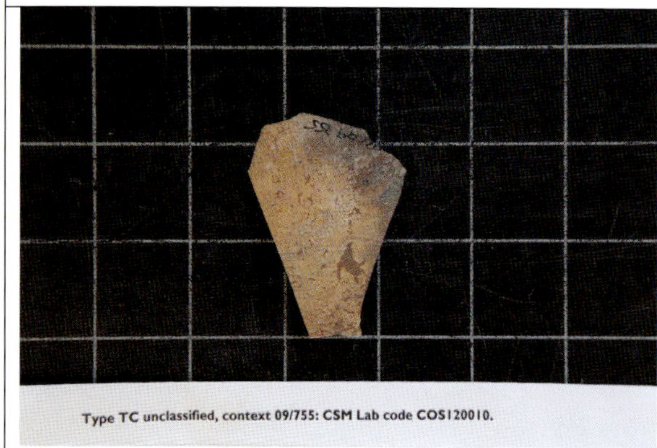

(Grid = 3 x 3 cm)

Fabric description	**Mineralogical description**
Fairly hard-fired reduced and reoxidised red earthenware with light grey zone of reduction below inner surface and reoxidised orange buff, outer surface has eroded leaving patches of hard dark red sandy patches; fine granular structure with specks of white and occasional iron-rich particles; olive green lead-glaze with occasional speckles of reduced iron rusty brown	The sherd has 93 vol% matrix and 3 vol% inclusions. The inclusion population is composed of quartz (~88 vol%) with some K-feldspar (5 vol%). Minor Pb-glaze and matrix components make up the rest. The matrix is composed of kaolinite (29 vol%), Fe-Al-K silicates (26 vol%) and quartz (20 vol%), with minor muscovite/illite (8 vol%), plagioclase (6 vol%), K-feldspar (4 vol%) and Fe-Al silicates (6 vol%).
Form	**Mineralogical type**
Body sherd of a jar, very competently made	B_1
Analogues	
A common post-medieval type from mid and north Somerset	

Visual appearance of thin section (transmitted light)

Mineralogical map

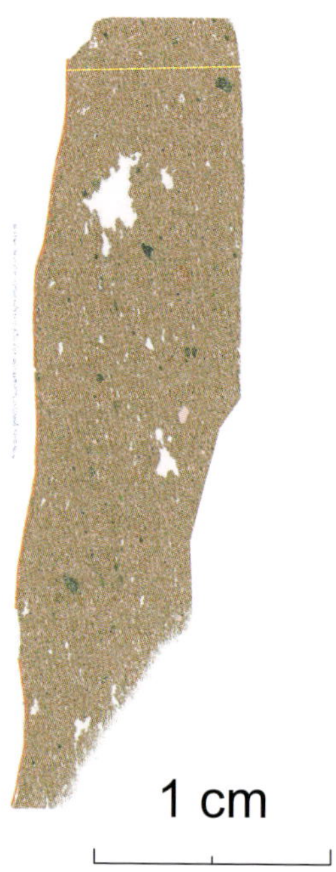

Key to mineral map [1]

- Fe sulphides
- Pb glaze
- Barite
- Chrome spinel
- Fe Ox/CO3
- Mn phases
- Rutile
- Ilmenite
- Zircon
- REE phases
- Quartz
- Plagioclase feldspar
- K-Feldspar
- Muscovite/Illite
- Fe Al K silicates
- Glauconite
- Kaolinite
- Tourmaline
- Fe Al silicates
- Mg Al silicates
- Mg silicates
- Ca Fe Al silicates
- Calcite
- Ca phosphates
- Others

Sample: TC unclassified, context 755	**CSM lab code: C05120010**

Mineralogical composition

	Matrix	Inclusions	Bulk
Fe sulphides	0.012	0.000	0.012
Pb glaze	0.180	4.276	0.971
Barite	0.000	0.000	0.000
Chrome spinel	0.008	0.000	0.007
Fe Ox/CO3	0.019	0.000	0.018
Mn phases	0.004	0.000	0.004
Rutile	0.589	0.062	0.569
Ilmenite	0.076	0.000	0.073
Zircon	0.022	0.000	0.021
REE phases	0.003	0.000	0.003
Quartz	20.019	87.574	21.897
Plagioclase feldspar	5.983	0.629	5.783
K-Feldspar	3.738	4.786	3.744
Muscovite/Illite	7.779	0.109	7.499
Fe Al K silicates	25.563	0.716	24.652
Glauconite	0.181	0.338	0.185
Kaolinite	29.193	0.624	28.146
Tourmaline	0.126	0.000	0.122
Fe Al silicates	6.250	0.758	6.045
Mg Al silicates	0.007	0.000	0.007
Mg silicates	0.008	0.000	0.007
Ca Fe Al silicates	0.009	0.000	0.009
Calcite	0.206	0.019	0.199
Ca phosphates	0.020	0.110	0.022
Others	0.006	0.000	0.006

Particle size distribution

Matrix (< 63 µm) = 97.0 vol%
Inclusions (> 63 µm) = 3.0 vol%

Measurement statistics

Total measurement points = 2344944
Measurement spacing = 10 µm

Visual representation of mineralogy [2]

Matrix	Inclusions	Bulk

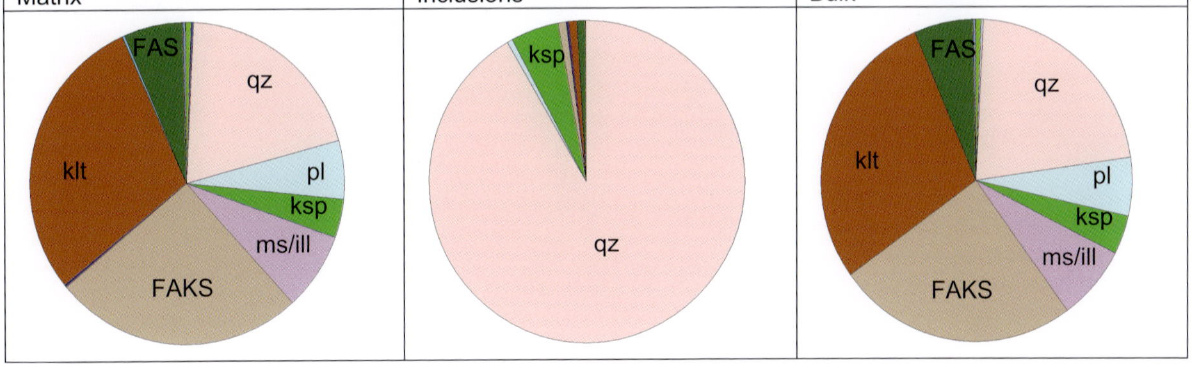

Notes

[1] Mineral groups listed in Table 2.

[2] gz = glaze, qz = quartz, pl = plagioclase, ksp = K-feldspar, ms/ill = muscovite/illite, FAKS = Fe-Al-K silicates, glt = glauconite, kln = kaolinite, FAS = Fe-Al silicates, cc = calcite

Figure A.2: *Mineralogy report on pottery fabric (unclassified) by QEMSCAN analysis. Camborne School of Mines, University of Exeter, Penryn Campus, Penryn, TR10 9EZ*

Sample: TC 003, context 885	CSM lab code: C05120012

	(Grid = 3 x 3 cm)
Fabric description	**Mineralogical description**
Fabric description: a hard-fired ware reduced grey with reoxidised orange blushes; smooth corky surface with water-worn quartz up to 2mm, crushed chert and limestone (microfossils) again up to 2mm in size	The sheet has 76 vol% matrix and 24 vol% inclusions. The inclusion population is almost exclusively made of quartz (92 vol%) and calcite (7 vol%). The matrix is composed of Fe-Al-K silicates (53 vol%) with kaolinite (10 vol%) and plagioclase feldspar (15 vol%) and minor quartz (8 vol%), calcite (5 vol%) and muscovite/illite (4 vol%).
Form	**Mineralogical type**
Rim of hand-built jar [cooking pot] with flared neck	B_2
Analogues	
Mixed Upper Greensand derived materials; 11th-12th centuries	

Visual appearance of thin section (transmitted light)	Mineralogical map	Key to mineral map
	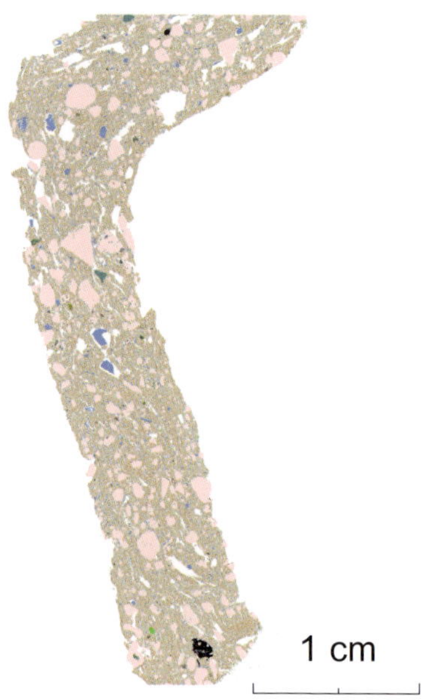	Fe sulphides Pb glaze Barite Chrome spinel Fe Ox/CO3 Mn phases Rutile Ilmenite Zircon REE phases Quartz Plagioclase feldspar K-Feldspar Muscovite/Illite Fe Al K silicates Glauconite Kaolinite Tourmaline Fe Al silicates Mg Al silicates Mg silicates Ca Fe Al silicates Calcite Ca phosphates Others

Sample: TC 003, context 885	CSM lab code: C05120012

Mineralogical composition

	Matrix	Inclusions	Bulk
Fe sulphides	0.019	0.000	0.014
Pb glaze	0.002	0.000	0.001
Barite	0.000	0.000	0.000
Chrome spinel	0.001	0.000	0.001
Fe Ox/CO3	0.507	0.076	0.405
Mn phases	0.018	0.001	0.014
Rutile	0.531	0.014	0.408
Ilmenite	0.009	0.000	0.007
Zircon	0.010	0.000	0.007
REE phases	0.000	0.000	0.000
Quartz	7.617	91.747	27.597
Plagioclase feldspar	15.444	0.066	11.792
K-Feldspar	1.318	0.195	1.052
Muscovite/Illite	4.382	0.025	3.347
Fe Al K silicates	52.811	0.169	40.309
Glauconite	0.091	0.029	0.076
Kaolinite	10.421	0.017	7.950
Tourmaline	0.016	0.121	0.041
Fe Al silicates	1.608	0.083	1.246
Mg Al silicates	0.002	0.000	0.001
Mg silicates	0.040	0.000	0.030
Ca Fe Al silicates	0.240	0.000	0.183
Calcite	4.798	6.755	5.263
Ca phosphates	0.088	0.701	0.234
Others	0.028	0.000	0.021

Particle size distribution

Matrix (< 63 μm) = 76.3 vol%
Inclusions (> 63 μm) = 23.7 vol%

Measurement statistics

Total measurement points = 3271938
Measurement spacing = 10 μm

Visual representation of mineralogy

Matrix

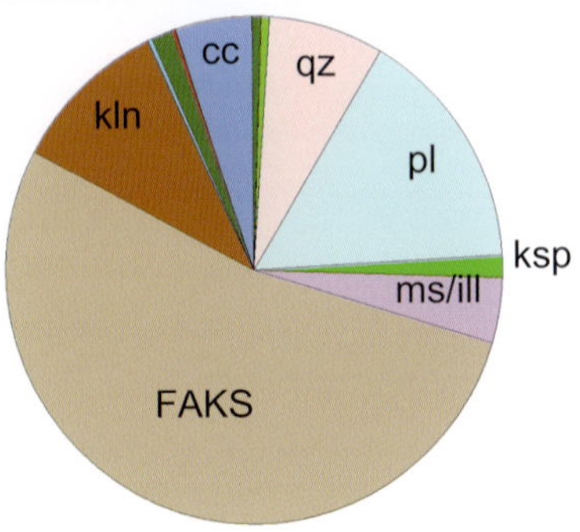

Inclusions

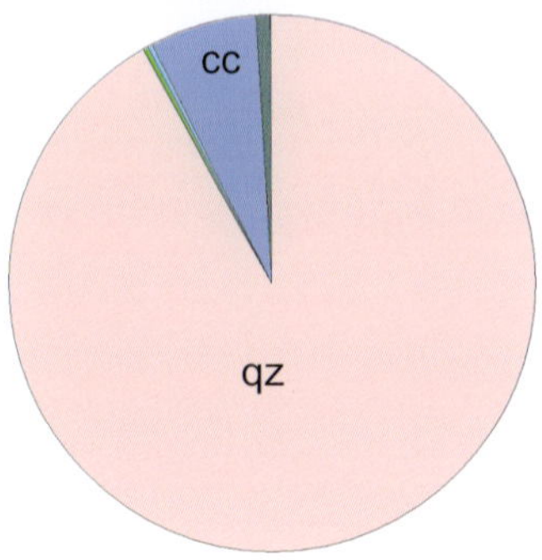

Bulk

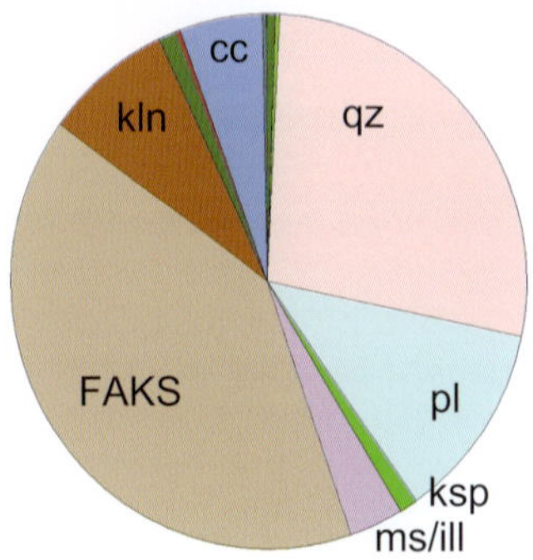

Notes

[1] Mineral groups listed in Table 2.

[2] gz = glaze, qz = quartz, pl = plagioclase, ksp = K-feldspar, ms/ill = muscovite/illite, FAKS = Fe-Al-K silicates, glt = glauconite, kln = kaolinite, FAS = Fe-Al silicates, cc = calcite

Figure A.3: Mineralogy report on pottery fabric 003 by QEMSCAN analysis. Camborne School of Mines, University of Exeter, Penryn Campus, Penryn, TR10 9EZ

Sample: TC 007A, context 45	CSM lab code: C05120003
	 (Grid = 3 x 3 cm)
Fabric description	**Mineralogical description**
Hard-fired coarse earthenware with dark grey reduced core and light grey exterior; with crushed quartz and limestone inclusions <3mm	The sherd has 77 vol% matrix and 23 vol% inclusions. The inclusion population is composed exclusively of calcite (61 vol%) and quartz (39 vol%). The matrix is composed of Fe-Al-K silicates (39 vol%) with kaolinite (14 vol%), calcite (15 vol%), plagioclase feldspar (9 vol%), muscovite/illite (9 vol%) and quartz (7 vol%).
Form	**Mineralogical type**
Body sherd of a hand-built open jar/cooking pot	C
Analogues	
Mixed Upper Greensand derived materials, 11th-12th century	

Visual appearance of thin section (transmitted light)	Mineralogical map	Key to mineral map
	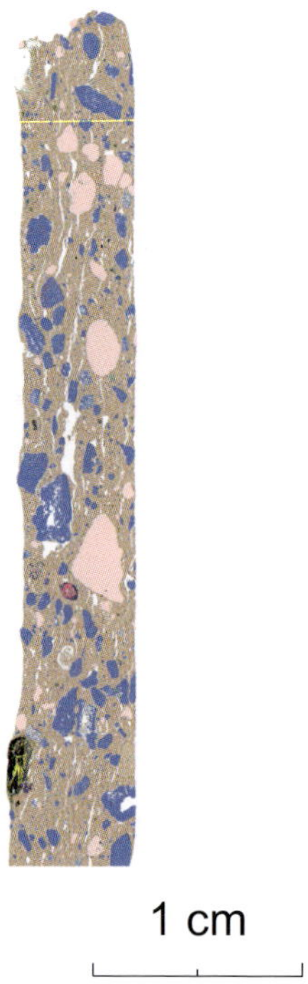	Fe sulphides Pb glaze Barite Chrome spinel Fe Ox/CO3 Mn phases Rutile Ilmenite Zircon REE phases Quartz Plagioclase feldspar K-Feldspar Muscovite/Illite Fe Al K silicates Glauconite Kaolinite Tourmaline Fe Al silicates Mg Al silicates Mg silicates Ca Fe Al silicates Calcite Ca phosphates Others

Sample: TC 007A, context 45 — **CSM lab code: C05120003**

Mineralogical composition

	Matrix	Inclusions	Bulk
Fe sulphides	0.292	0.048	0.235
Pb glaze	0.001	0.000	0.001
Barite	0.001	0.000	0.000
Chrome spinel	0.003	0.000	0.002
Fe Ox/CO3	0.997	0.043	0.775
Mn phases	0.219	0.000	0.168
Rutile	0.460	0.000	0.353
Ilmenite	0.015	0.000	0.011
Zircon	0.008	0.000	0.006
REE phases	0.001	0.000	0.000
Quartz	7.125	38.564	14.423
Plagioclase feldspar	9.409	0.022	7.230
K-Feldspar	2.020	0.052	1.564
Muscovite/Illite	9.142	0.014	7.023
Fe Al K silicates	39.413	0.079	30.282
Glauconite	0.343	0.042	0.273
Kaolinite	13.647	0.023	10.484
Tourmaline	0.020	0.000	0.015
Fe Al silicates	2.179	0.001	1.673
Mg Al silicates	0.007	0.000	0.005
Mg silicates	0.005	0.000	0.004
Ca Fe Al silicates	0.120	0.000	0.092
Calcite	14.500	61.097	25.317
Ca phosphates	0.053	0.015	0.044
Others	0.025	0.000	0.019

Particle size distribution

Matrix (< 63 μm) = 76.8 vol%
Inclusions (> 63 μm) = 23.2 vol%

Measurement statistics

Total measurement points = 2030866
Measurement spacing = 10 μm

Visual representation of mineralogy

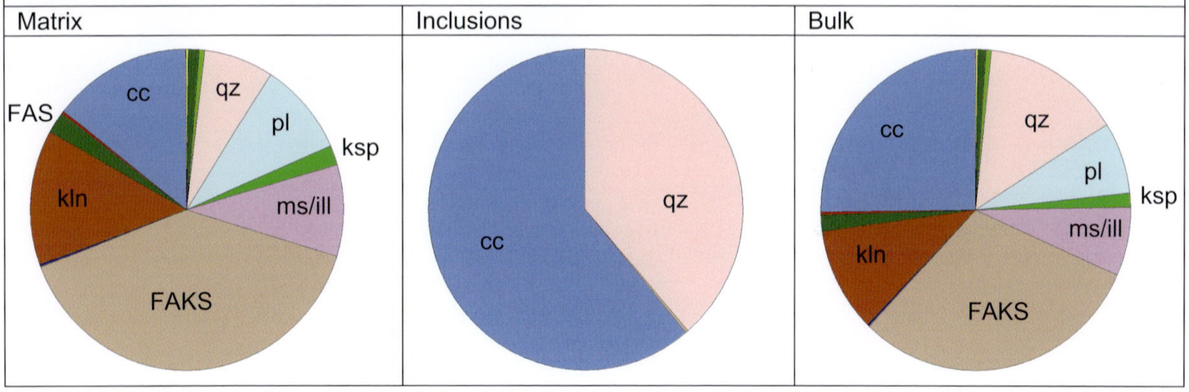

Notes

[1] Mineral groups listed in Table 2.
[2] gz = glaze, qz = quartz, pl = plagioclase, ksp = K-feldspar, ms/ill = muscovite/illite, FAKS = Fe-Al-K silicates, glt = glauconite, kln = kaolinite, FAS = Fe-Al silicates, cc = calcite

Figure A.4: *Mineralogy report on pottery fabric 007A by QEMSCAN analysis. Camborne School of Mines, University of Exeter, Penryn Campus, Penryn, TR10 9EZ*

Sample: TC 007B, context 45	**CSM lab code: C05120004**

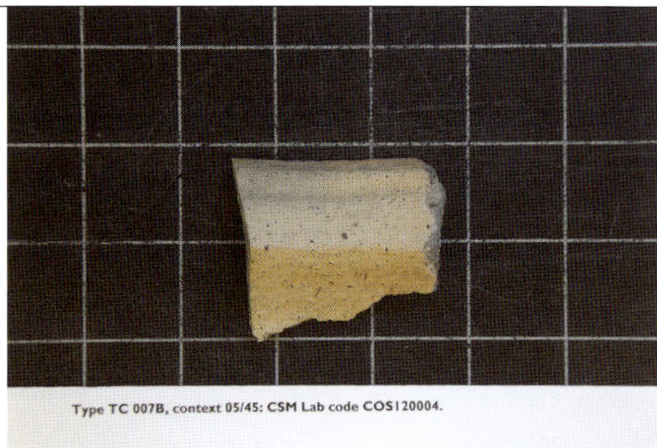

(Grid = 3 x 3 cm)

Fabric description	**Mineralogical description**
Hard-fired course earthenware with reduced grey core and reoxidised orange buff surface with light buff patches; many coloured quartz inclusions <1mm and occasional quartz <3mm.	The sherd has 83 vol% matrix and 17 vol% inclusions. The inclusion population is composed almost exclusively of quartz (~96 vol%) with traces of calcite (2 vol%). The matrix is a mixture of Fe-Al-K silicates (37 vol%), kaolinite (26 vol%) and muscovite/illite (18 vol%) with minor plagioclase (5 vol%), quartz (6 vol%) and Fe-Al silicates (4 vol%).
Form	**Mineralogical type**
Body sherd of a hand-built open jar/cooking pot	B_2
Analogues	
11th-12th century	

Visual appearance of thin section (transmitted light)

Mineralogical map

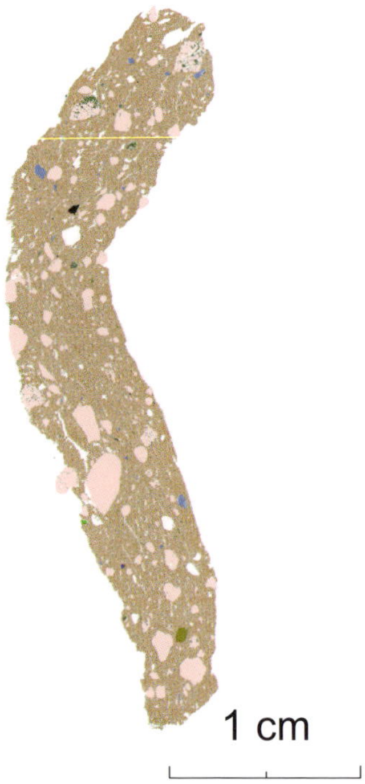

Key to mineral map

- Fe sulphides
- Pb glaze
- Barite
- Chrome spinel
- Fe Ox/CO3
- Mn phases
- Rutile
- Ilmenite
- Zircon
- REE phases
- Quartz
- Plagioclase feldspar
- K-Feldspar
- Muscovite/Illite
- Fe Al K silicates
- Glauconite
- Kaolinite
- Tourmaline
- Fe Al silicates
- Mg Al silicates
- Mg silicates
- Ca Fe Al silicates
- Calcite
- Ca phosphates
- Others

Sample: TC 007B, context 45

CSM lab code: C05120004

Mineralogical composition

	Matrix	Inclusions	Bulk
Fe sulphides	0.001	0.000	0.001
Pb glaze	0.002	0.000	0.002
Barite	0.000	0.000	0.000
Chrome spinel	0.002	0.000	0.002
Fe Ox/CO3	0.153	0.034	0.133
Mn phases	0.011	0.000	0.009
Rutile	0.422	0.000	0.351
Ilmenite	0.008	0.010	0.008
Zircon	0.005	0.042	0.011
REE phases	0.001	0.000	0.001
Quartz	5.954	95.593	21.051
Plagioclase feldspar	5.341	0.030	4.447
K-Feldspar	1.136	0.182	0.975
Muscovite/Illite	17.705	0.093	14.739
Fe Al K silicates	37.298	0.141	31.040
Glauconite	0.069	0.000	0.057
Kaolinite	26.352	0.113	21.933
Tourmaline	0.105	1.066	0.267
Fe Al silicates	3.964	0.369	3.359
Mg Al silicates	0.002	0.000	0.001
Mg silicates	0.047	0.000	0.039
Ca Fe Al silicates	0.064	0.001	0.053
Calcite	1.325	2.183	1.470
Ca phosphates	0.026	0.142	0.046
Others	0.007	0.000	0.006

Particle size distribution

Matrix (< 63 μm) = 83.2 vol%
Inclusions (> 63 μm) = 16.8 vol%

Measurement statistics

Total measurement points = 2057978
Measurement spacing = 10 μm

Visual representation of mineralogy

Matrix | Inclusions | Bulk

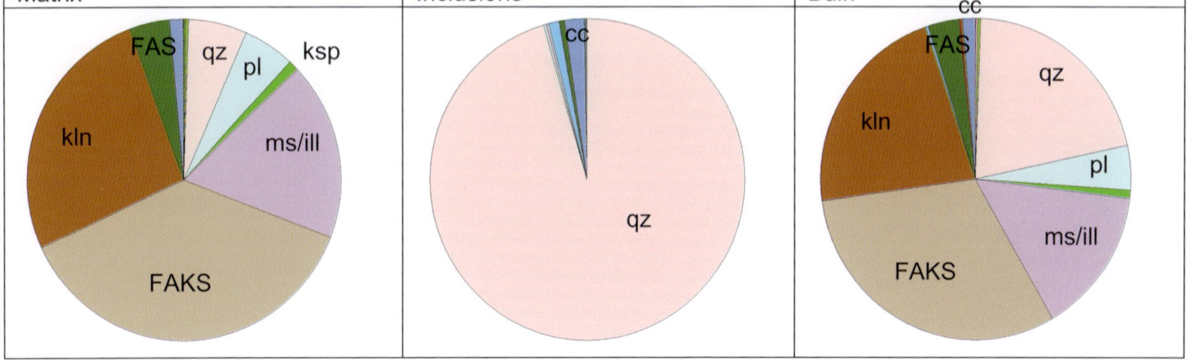

Notes

[1] Mineral groups listed in Table 2.

[2] gz = glaze, qz = quartz, pl = plagioclase, ksp = K-feldspar, ms/ill = muscovite/illite, FAKS = Fe-Al-K silicates, glt = glauconite, kln = kaolinite, FAS = Fe-Al silicates, cc = calcite

Figure A.5: Mineralogy report on pottery fabric 007B by QEMSCAN analysis. Camborne School of Mines, University of Exeter, Penryn Campus, Penryn, TR10 9EZ

Sample: TC 008=026, context 340	CSM lab code: C05120008
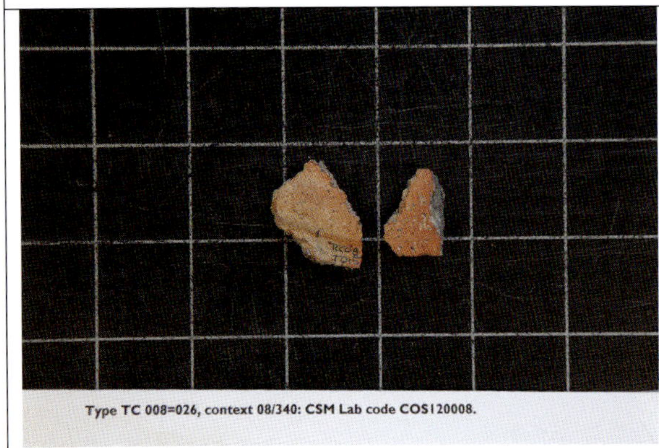	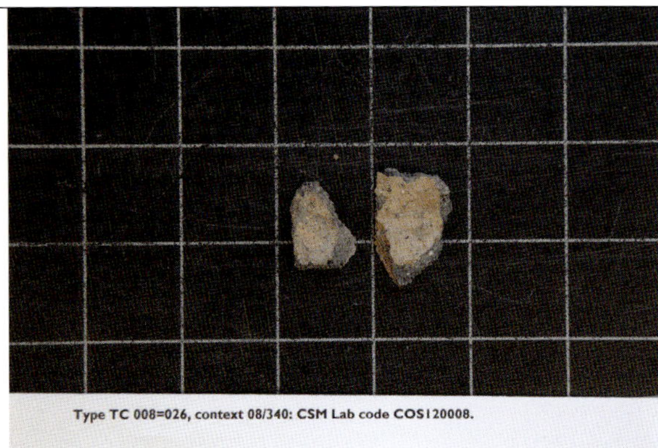

(Grid = 3 x 3 cm)

Fabric description	Mineralogical description
Very coarse reduced grey earthenware with buff oxidised surface with crushed chert, limestone and quartz inclusions <1mm	The sherd has 75 vol% matrix and 25 vol% inclusions. The inclusion population is composed almost exclusively of quartz (~98 vol%) with minor calcite (1 vol%). The matrix is composed of Fe-Al-K silicates (51 vol%) and kaolinite (28 vol%) with minor Fe-Al silicates (4 vol%), quartz (5 vol%), plagioclase (3 vol%), muscovite/illite (4 vol%), Fe-Al silicates (4 vol%) and calcite (2 vol%).
Form	**Mineralogical type**
hand-built cooking pot	B_2
Analogues	
Upper Greensand derived wares 11th-12th century, Taunton 1984 type 52	

Visual appearance of thin section (transmitted light)	Mineralogical map	Key to mineral map [1]
 1 cm	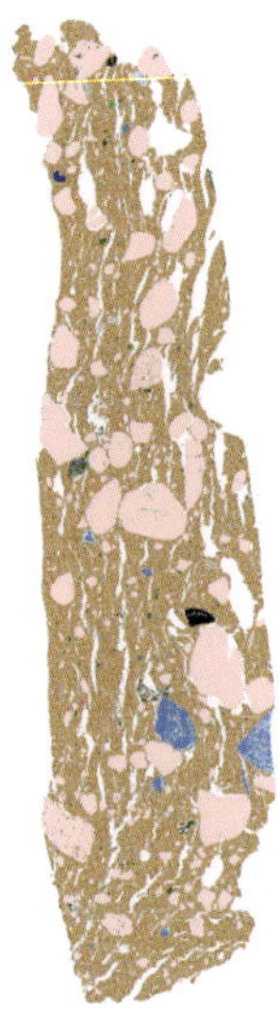 1 cm	Fe sulphides Pb glaze Barite Chrome spinel Fe Ox/CO3 Mn phases Rutile Ilmenite Zircon REE phases Quartz Plagioclase feldspar K-Feldspar Muscovite/Illite Fe Al K silicates Glauconite Kaolinite Tourmaline Fe Al silicates Mg Al silicates Mg silicates Ca Fe Al silicates Calcite Ca phosphates Others

Sample: TC 008=026, context 340 — **CSM lab code: C05120008**

Mineralogical composition

	Matrix	Inclusions	Bulk
Fe sulphides	0.012	0.000	0.009
Pb glaze	0.003	0.000	0.002
Barite	0.000	0.000	0.000
Chrome spinel	0.001	0.000	0.001
Fe Ox/CO3	0.436	0.000	0.325
Mn phases	0.088	0.098	0.090
Rutile	0.281	0.000	0.209
Ilmenite	0.005	0.000	0.004
Zircon	0.001	0.000	0.001
REE phases	0.001	0.000	0.001
Quartz	5.080	98.015	28.715
Plagioclase feldspar	3.112	0.036	2.330
K-Feldspar	0.587	0.080	0.458
Muscovite/Illite	3.824	0.000	2.852
Fe Al K silicates	51.527	0.066	38.440
Glauconite	0.071	0.290	0.127
Kaolinite	28.340	0.080	21.153
Tourmaline	0.035	0.000	0.026
Fe Al silicates	4.251	0.235	3.229
Mg Al silicates	0.001	0.000	0.001
Mg silicates	0.006	0.000	0.004
Ca Fe Al silicates	0.081	0.000	0.060
Calcite	2.223	1.080	1.933
Ca phosphates	0.012	0.021	0.014
Others	0.022	0.000	0.016

Particle size distribution

Matrix (< 63 μm) = 74.6 vol%
Inclusions (> 63 μm) = 25.4 vol%

Measurement statistics

Total measurement points = 987142
Measurement spacing = 10 μm

Visual representation of mineralogy [2]

Matrix

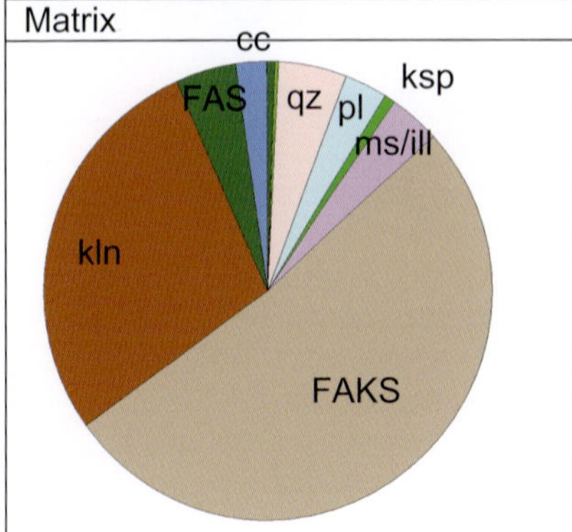

Inclusions

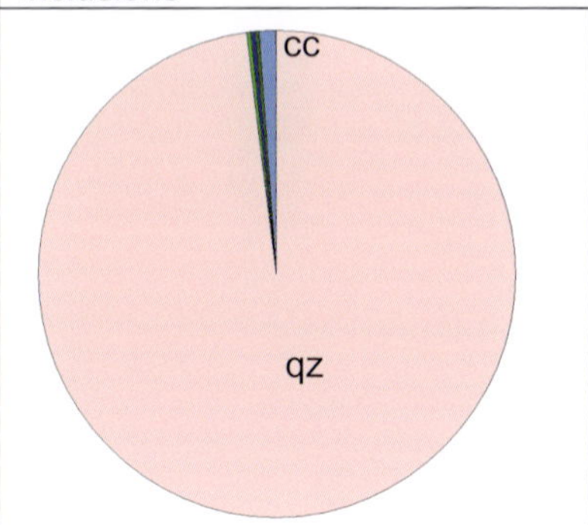

Bulk

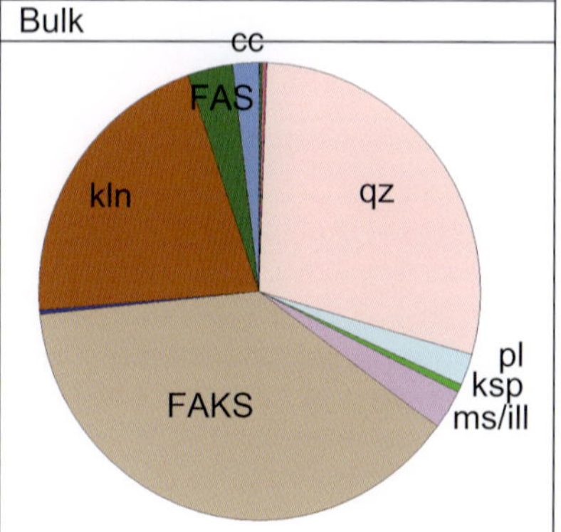

Notes

[1] Mineral groups listed in Table 2.

[2] gz = glaze, qz = quartz, pl = plagioclase, ksp = K-feldspar, ms/ill = muscovite/illite, FAKS = Fe-Al-K silicates, glt = glauconite, kln = kaolinite, FAS = Fe-Al silicates, cc = calcite

Figure A.6: Mineralogy report on pottery fabric 008=026 by QEMSCAN analysis. Camborne School of Mines, University of Exeter, Penryn Campus, Penryn, TR10 9EZ

Sample: TC 014, context 338	**CSM lab code: C05120007**

	(Grid = 3 x 3 cm)
Fabric description	**Mineralogical description**
Fabric description: hard-fired dark grey reduced earthenware with buff oxidised surface and water worn quartz and chert inclusions <1mm	The sherd has 72 vol% matrix and 28 vol% inclusions. The inclusion population is nearly exclusively quartz (99 vol%). The matrix is a mixture of Fe-Al-K silicates (54 vol%) and kaolinite (24 vol%) with minor muscovite/illite (5 vol%), quartz, plagioclase feldspar, Fe-Al silicates, and K-feldspar.
Form	**Mineralogical type**
Flared rim of a hand-built open jar/cooking pot	B_1
Analogues	
Mixed Upper Greensand derived materials, 11th century; Taunton 1984 type 57	

Visual appearance of thin section (transmitted light)	**Mineralogical map**	**Key to mineral map**
	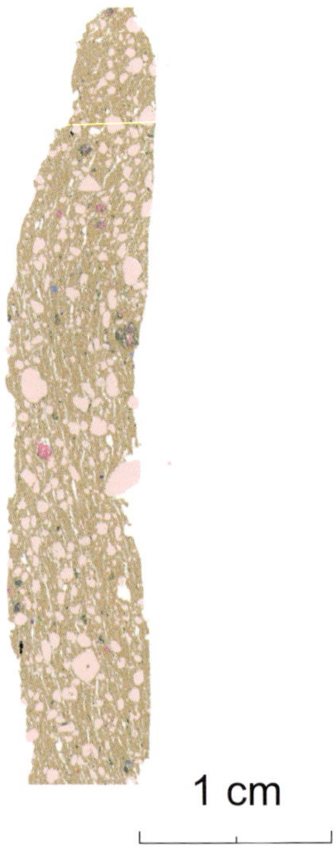	Fe sulphides Pb glaze Barite Chrome spinel Fe Ox/CO3 Mn phases Rutile Ilmenite Zircon REE phases Quartz Plagioclase feldspar K-Feldspar Muscovite/Illite Fe Al K silicates Glauconite Kaolinite Tourmaline Fe Al silicates Mg Al silicates Mg silicates Ca Fe Al silicates Calcite Ca phosphates Others

Sample: TC 014, context 338	CSM lab code: C05120007

Mineralogical composition

	Matrix	Inclusions	Bulk
Fe sulphides	0.001	0.000	0.001
Pb glaze	0.002	0.000	0.001
Barite	0.000	0.000	0.000
Chrome spinel	0.001	0.000	0.001
Fe Ox/CO3	0.066	0.129	0.083
Mn phases	0.795	0.294	0.656
Rutile	0.325	0.000	0.236
Ilmenite	0.017	0.012	0.016
Zircon	0.008	0.018	0.011
REE phases	0.002	0.000	0.002
Quartz	5.449	98.611	31.137
Plagioclase feldspar	2.747	0.000	1.990
K-Feldspar	1.016	0.117	0.768
Muscovite/Illite	5.152	0.022	3.737
Fe Al K silicates	54.122	0.084	39.222
Glauconite	0.298	0.094	0.242
Kaolinite	23.821	0.089	17.277
Tourmaline	0.056	0.000	0.040
Fe Al silicates	5.562	0.255	4.099
Mg Al silicates	0.001	0.000	0.001
Mg silicates	0.022	0.000	0.016
Ca Fe Al silicates	0.030	0.000	0.021
Calcite	0.446	0.275	0.399
Ca phosphates	0.049	0.000	0.036
Others	0.012	0.000	0.009

Particle size distribution

Matrix (< 63 µm) = 72.4 vol%
Inclusions (> 63 µm) = 27.6 vol%

Measurement statistics

Total measurement points = 2319625
Measurement spacing = 10 µm

Visual representation of mineralogy

Matrix | Inclusions | Bulk

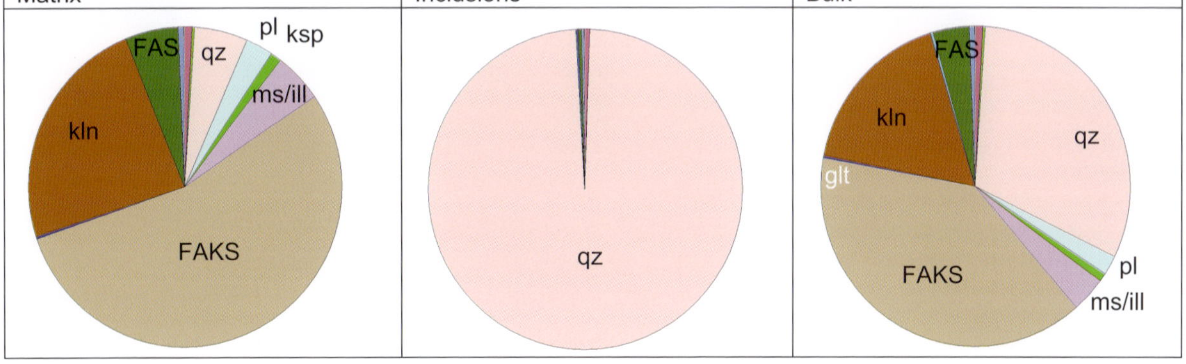

Notes

[1] Mineral groups listed in Table 2.
[2] gz = glaze, qz = quartz, pl = plagioclase, ksp = K-feldspar, ms/ill = muscovite/illite, FAKS = Fe-Al-K silicates, glt = glauconite, kln = kaolinite, FAS = Fe-Al silicates, cc = calcite

Figure A.7: Mineralogy report on pottery fabric 014 by QEMSCAN analysis. Camborne School of Mines, University of Exeter, Penryn Campus, Penryn, TR10 9EZ

Sample: TC 015, context 350	CSM lab code: C05120009

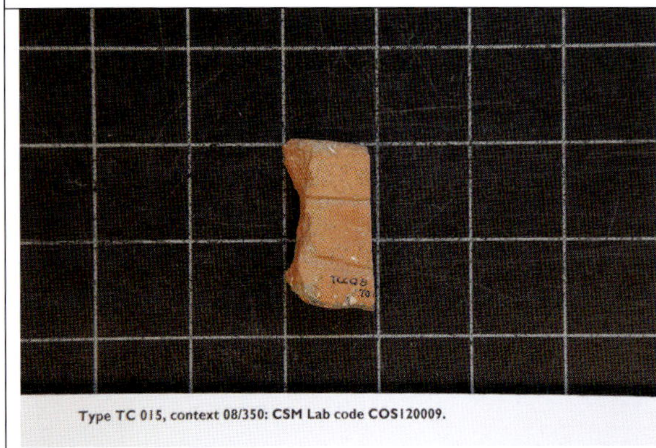

(Grid = 3 x 3 cm)

Fabric description	Mineralogical description
Reduced dark grey earthenware with brick red oxidised surface and quantities of water worn quartz and crushed chert <1mm and occasional limestone	The sherd has 79 vol% matrix and 21 vol% inclusions. The inclusion population is dominated by quartz (89 vol%) with some calcite (10 vol%). The matrix is a mixture of Fe-Al-K silicates (50 vol%) with kaolinite (20 vol%), and muscovite/illite (12 vol%) and minor quartz, plagioclase feldspar, Fe-Al silicates and K-feldspar.
Form	**Mineralogical type**
Hand-built handle with two incised lines, probably from a tripod pitcher	B_2
Analogues	
Mixed Upper Greensand derived materials; 12th-13th century; Castle Neroche	

Visual appearance of thin section (transmitted light)

1 cm

Mineralogical map

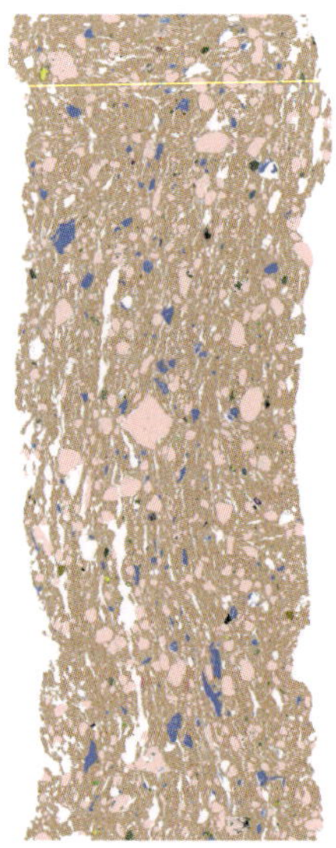

1 cm

Key to mineral map

- Fe sulphides
- Pb glaze
- Barite
- Chrome spinel
- Fe Ox/CO3
- Mn phases
- Rutile
- Ilmenite
- Zircon
- REE phases
- Quartz
- Plagioclase feldspar
- K-Feldspar
- Muscovite/Illite
- Fe Al K silicates
- Glauconite
- Kaolinite
- Tourmaline
- Fe Al silicates
- Mg Al silicates
- Mg silicates
- Ca Fe Al silicates
- Calcite
- Ca phosphates
- Others

Sample: TC 062, context 1105

CSM lab code: C05120014

Mineralogical composition

	Matrix	Inclusions	Bulk
Fe sulphides	0.002	0.000	0.002
Pb glaze	0.043	17.989	0.552
Barite	0.001	0.000	0.001
Chrome spinel	0.007	0.000	0.007
Fe Ox/CO3	0.025	0.209	0.027
Mn phases	0.001	0.000	0.001
Rutile	0.772	0.128	0.764
Ilmenite	0.055	0.000	0.055
Zircon	0.012	0.000	0.012
REE phases	0.002	0.000	0.002
Quartz	17.733	58.153	18.023
Plagioclase feldspar	7.716	1.517	7.635
K-Feldspar	5.641	8.332	5.645
Muscovite/Illite	24.999	3.383	24.723
Fe Al K silicates	9.806	0.358	9.689
Glauconite	0.082	0.000	0.081
Kaolinite	30.189	3.598	29.851
Tourmaline	0.094	0.000	0.093
Fe Al silicates	2.734	5.717	2.750
Mg Al silicates	0.022	0.000	0.021
Mg silicates	0.012	0.000	0.011
Ca Fe Al silicates	0.001	0.000	0.001
Calcite	0.018	0.136	0.019
Ca phosphates	0.015	0.480	0.019
Others	0.016	0.000	0.016

Particle size distribution

Matrix (< 63 μm) = 99.1 vol%
Inclusions (> 63 μm) = 0.9 vol%

Measurement statistics

Total measurement points = 4230938
Measurement spacing = 10 μm

Visual representation of mineralogy [2]

Matrix | Inclusions | Bulk

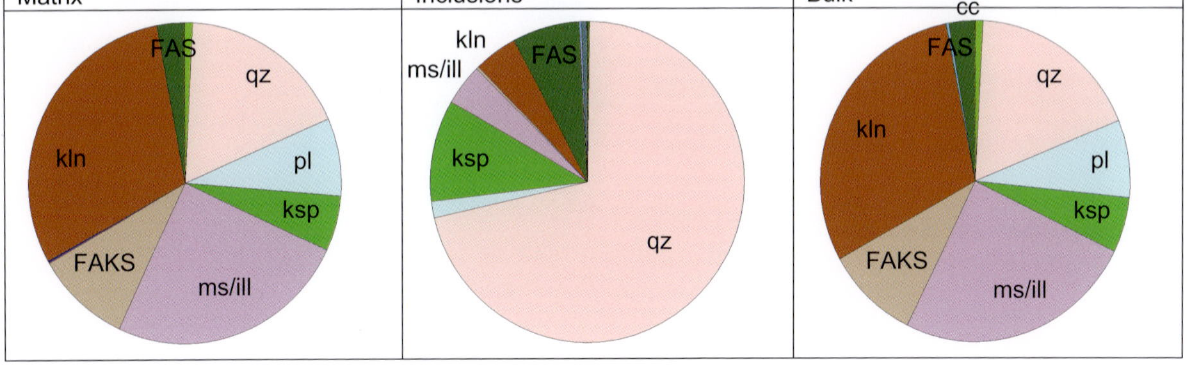

Notes

[1] Mineral groups listed in Table 2.
[2] gz = glaze, qz = quartz, pl = plagioclase, ksp = K-feldspar, ms/ill = muscovite/illite, FAKS = Fe-Al-K silicates, glt = glauconite, kln = kaolinite, FAS = Fe-Al silicates, cc = calcite

Figure A.10: *Mineralogy report on pottery fabric 062 by QEMSCAN analysis. Camborne School of Mines, University of Exeter, Penryn Campus, Penryn, TR10 9EZ*

Sample: TC 074, context 203	CSM lab code: C05120005
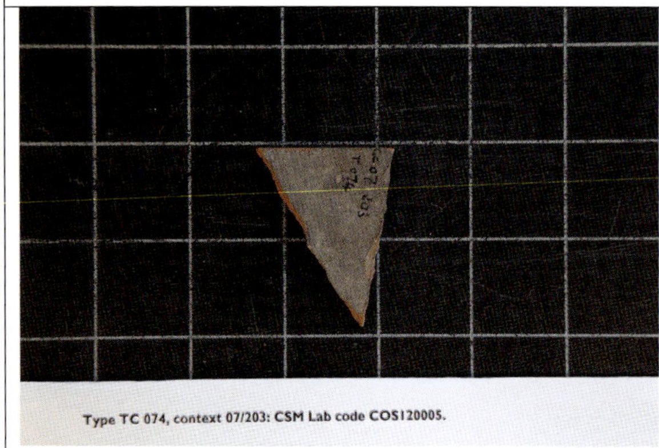 	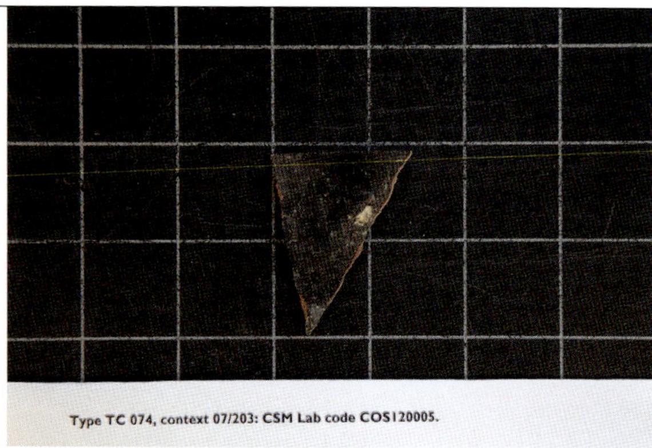 (Grid = 3 x 3 cm)
Fabric description	**Mineralogical description**
Hard-fired reduced and reoxidised red earthenware with brick red core and reduced grey internal fine sandy surface; fine granular structure with lime and ?conglomerate inclusions; lead-glaze has fired to a dark green almost black speckled with white	The sherd has 91 vol% matrix and 9 vol% inclusions. The inclusion population is dominated by quartz (71 vol%) with 23 vol% K-feldspar. The matrix is a dominated by Fe-Al-K silicates (64 vol%) with some muscovite/illite (12 vol%) but no kaolinite. Minor quartz (10 vol%), and K-feldspar (10 vol%) occurs along with traces of Fe-Al-silicates.
Form	**Mineralogical type**
Possibly moulded on a sand-sprinkled former	A
Analogues	
Possibly West Somerset ware 18th century	

Visual appearance of thin section (transmitted light)	Mineralogical map	Key to mineral map
 1 cm	 1 cm	Fe sulphides Pb glaze Barite Chrome spinel Fe Ox/CO3 Mn phases Rutile Ilmenite Zircon REE phases Quartz Plagioclase feldspar K-Feldspar Muscovite/Illite Fe Al K silicates Glauconite Kaolinite Tourmaline Fe Al silicates Mg Al silicates Mg silicates Ca Fe Al silicates Calcite Ca phosphates Others

Sample: TC 074, context 203

CSM lab code: C05120005

Mineralogical composition

	Matrix	Inclusions	Bulk
Fe sulphides	0.004	0.000	0.004
Pb glaze	0.062	5.912	0.842
Barite	0.001	0.000	0.000
Chrome spinel	0.002	0.000	0.002
Fe Ox/CO3	0.098	0.110	0.099
Mn phases	0.032	0.055	0.034
Rutile	0.112	0.002	0.102
Ilmenite	0.036	0.000	0.033
Zircon	0.013	0.000	0.012
REE phases	0.001	0.000	0.001
Quartz	9.655	70.529	15.062
Plagioclase feldspar	0.285	0.000	0.259
K-Feldspar	10.235	22.958	11.344
Muscovite/Illite	11.575	0.050	10.517
Fe Al K silicates	64.482	0.241	58.583
Glauconite	0.360	0.014	0.329
Kaolinite	0.134	0.000	0.122
Tourmaline	0.003	0.000	0.003
Fe Al silicates	2.055	0.079	1.873
Mg Al silicates	0.003	0.000	0.003
Mg silicates	0.013	0.000	0.012
Ca Fe Al silicates	0.005	0.000	0.005
Calcite	0.552	0.017	0.503
Ca phosphates	0.020	0.031	0.021
Others	0.262	0.002	0.238

Particle size distribution

Matrix (< 63 μm) = 91.1 vol%
Inclusions (> 63 μm) = 8.9 vol%

Measurement statistics

Total measurement points = 3178160
Measurement spacing = 10 μm

Visual representation of mineralogy

Matrix

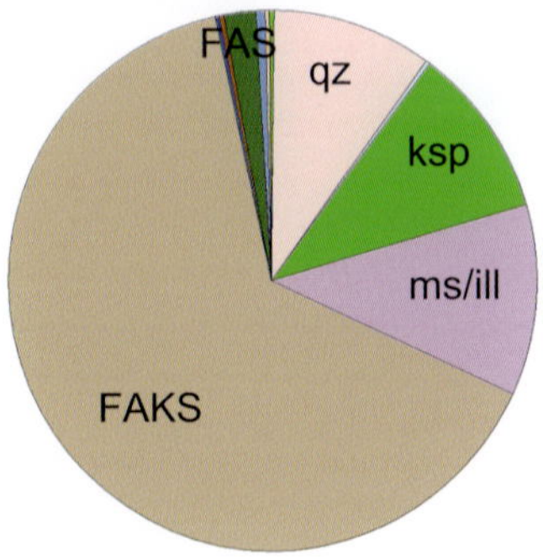

Inclusions

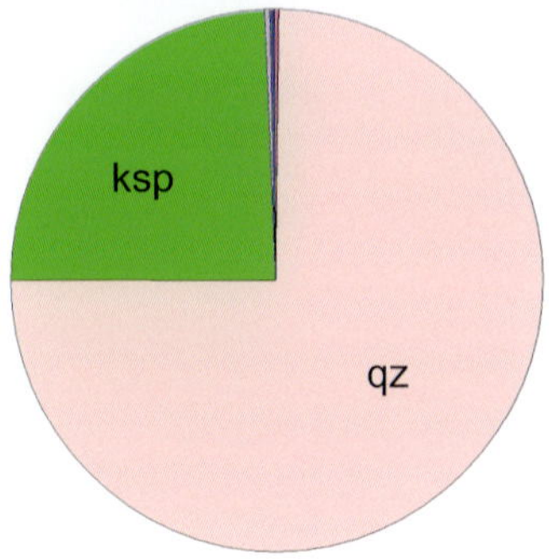

Bulk

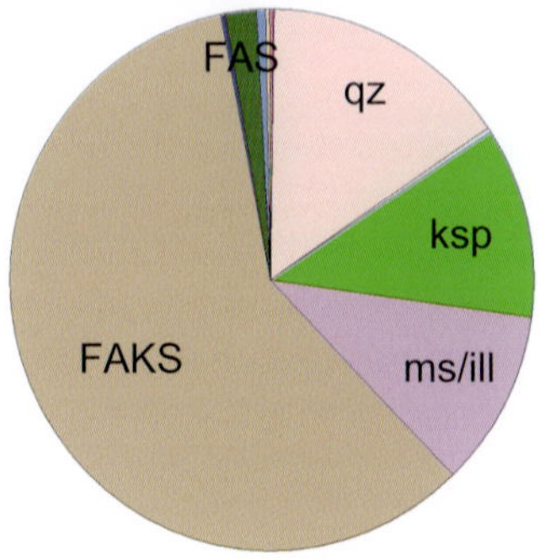

Notes

[1] Mineral groups listed in Table 2.
[2] gz = glaze, qz = quartz, pl = plagioclase, ksp = K-feldspar, ms/ill = muscovite/illite, FAKS = Fe-Al-K silicates, glt = glauconite, kln = kaolinite, FAS = Fe-Al silicates, cc = calcite

Figure A.11: *Mineralogy report on pottery fabric 074 by QEMSCAN analysis. Camborne School of Mines, University of Exeter, Penryn Campus, Penryn, TR10 9EZ*

Sample: TC 083=093, context 231	CSM lab code: C05120006
	 (Grid = 3 x 3 cm)
Fabric description	**Mineralogical description**
Fairly hard-fired oxidised red earthenware with smooth external surface; granular structure to the fabric with few discernible inclusions; glaze appears dull brown speckled all over with dark brown spots from iron-rich particles in the glaze	The sherd has 89 vol% matrix and 11 vol% inclusions. The inclusion population is dominated by quartz (72 vol%) with 23 vol% K-feldspar. The matrix is a dominated by Fe-Al-K silicates (63 vol%) with some muscovite/illite (13 vol%) but no kaolinite. Minor quartz (11 vol%), and K-feldspar (10 vol%) occurs along with traces of Fe-Al-silicates.
Form	**Mineralogical type**
Profile of a shallow wheel-thrown dish with knife trimmed base and internal lead-glaze over rather scribbled white slip-trailed decoration	A
Analogues	
South Somerset ware; 18th -19th century	

Visual appearance of thin section (transmitted light)	Mineralogical map	Key to mineral map
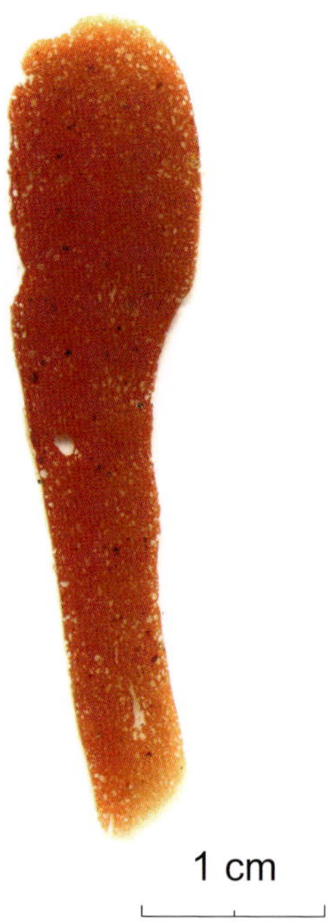	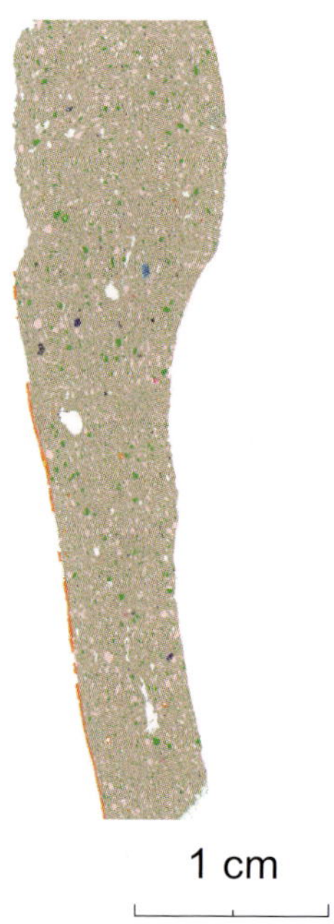	Fe sulphides Pb glaze Barite Chrome spinel Fe Ox/CO3 Mn phases Rutile Ilmenite Zircon REE phases Quartz Plagioclase feldspar K-Feldspar Muscovite/Illite Fe Al K silicates Glauconite Kaolinite Tourmaline Fe Al silicates Mg Al silicates Mg silicates Ca Fe Al silicates Calcite Ca phosphates Others

Sample: Crowcombe 55/1992

CSM lab code: C05120019

Mineralogical composition

	Matrix	Inclusions	Bulk
Fe sulphides	0.003	0.000	0.003
Pb glaze	0.151	0.000	0.141
Barite	0.000	0.000	0.000
Chrome spinel	0.001	0.000	0.001
Fe Ox/CO3	0.030	0.045	0.031
Mn phases	0.226	0.334	0.232
Rutile	0.135	0.093	0.133
Ilmenite	0.034	0.000	0.032
Zircon	0.015	0.101	0.020
REE phases	0.002	0.000	0.002
Quartz	10.748	93.744	16.031
Plagioclase feldspar	0.472	0.000	0.442
K-Feldspar	7.006	5.123	6.886
Muscovite/Illite	6.113	0.135	5.733
Fe Al K silicates	68.351	0.199	64.013
Glauconite	0.211	0.014	0.198
Kaolinite	0.423	0.000	0.396
Tourmaline	0.011	0.000	0.010
Fe Al silicates	4.783	0.170	4.490
Mg Al silicates	0.032	0.000	0.030
Mg silicates	0.059	0.000	0.055
Ca Fe Al silicates	0.001	0.000	0.001
Calcite	0.798	0.040	0.750
Ca phosphates	0.024	0.000	0.023
Others	0.371	0.000	0.347

Particle size distribution

Matrix (< 63 µm) = 93.6 vol%
Inclusions (> 63 µm) = 6.4 vol%

Measurement statistics

Total measurement points = 3911915
Measurement spacing = 10 µm

Visual representation of mineralogy [2]

Matrix | Inclusions | Bulk

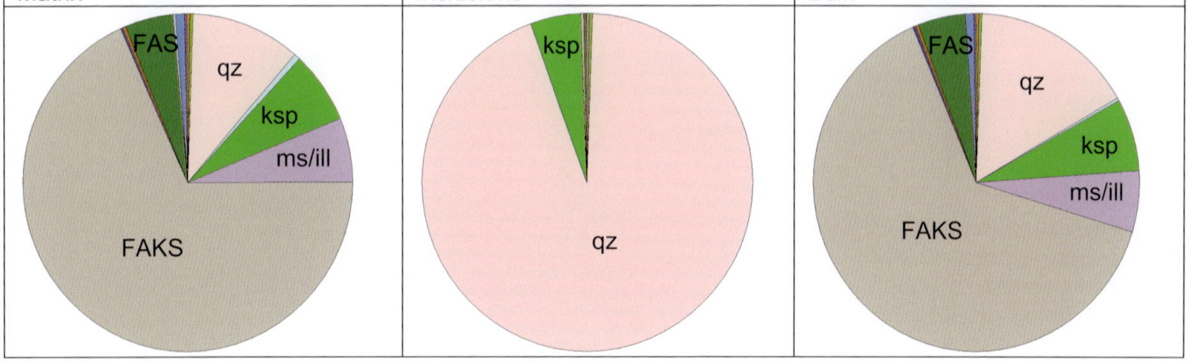

Notes

[1] Mineral groups listed in Table 2.

[2] gz = glaze, qz = quartz, pl = plagioclase, ksp = K-feldspar, ms/ill = muscovite/illite, FAKS = Fe-Al-K silicates, glt = glauconite, kln = kaolinite, FAS = Fe-Al silicates, cc = calcite

Figure A.14: Mineralogy report on pottery fabric 55/1992 by QEMSCAN analysis. Camborne School of Mines, University of Exeter, Penryn Campus, Penryn, TR10 9EZ

Sample: Donyatt Site 4	**CSM lab code: C05120020**
	 (Grid = 3 x 3 cm)
Fabric description	**Mineralogical description**
Fairly hard-fired earthenware reduced grey with a reoxidised orange red sandy interior surface; granular structure with occasional clear quartz <1mm, limestone and dark iron-rich fragments; glaze is a part burnt-off reduced mottled green with darker green specks where iron in the body has bled into the glaze. Some patches of white slip adhere probably shed by another vessel during the firing	The sherd has 86 vol% matrix and 14 vol% inclusions. The inclusion population is predominantly quartz (89 vol%) and glauconite (6 vol%) with minor K-feldspar. The matrix is a mixture of Fe-Al-K silicates (52 vol%) and kaolinite (24 vol%) with some muscovite/illite (10 vol%). The matrix also has minor quartz, plagioclase feldspar, Fe-Al silicates, K-feldspar and glauconite.
Form	**Mineralogical type**
Wheel-thrown neck of a tankard or jug with marks of collaring and external lead glaze	B_1
Analogues	
Donyatt pottery type 8	

Visual appearance of thin section (transmitted light)	**Mineralogical map**	**Key to mineral map**
		Fe sulphides Pb glaze Barite Chrome spinel Fe Ox/CO3 Mn phases Rutile Ilmenite Zircon REE phases Quartz Plagioclase feldspar K-Feldspar Muscovite/Illite Fe Al K silicates Glauconite Kaolinite Tourmaline Fe Al silicates Mg Al silicates Mg silicates Ca Fe Al silicates Calcite Ca phosphates Others

Sample: Donyatt Site 4

CSM lab code: C05120020

Mineralogical composition

	Matrix	Inclusions	Bulk
Fe sulphides	0.005	0.000	0.004
Pb glaze	0.129	1.805	0.369
Barite	0.000	0.000	0.000
Chrome spinel	0.004	0.000	0.003
Fe Ox/CO3	0.020	0.000	0.017
Mn phases	0.056	0.112	0.064
Rutile	0.294	0.015	0.254
Ilmenite	0.021	0.056	0.026
Zircon	0.009	0.112	0.024
REE phases	0.000	0.000	0.000
Quartz	4.589	89.496	16.747
Plagioclase feldspar	2.751	0.000	2.357
K-Feldspar	1.172	0.729	1.109
Muscovite/Illite	9.733	0.038	8.345
Fe Al K silicates	52.231	0.335	44.800
Glauconite	0.822	6.202	1.592
Kaolinite	23.992	0.116	20.573
Tourmaline	0.033	0.000	0.029
Fe Al silicates	3.954	0.970	3.527
Mg Al silicates	0.005	0.000	0.005
Mg silicates	0.009	0.000	0.008
Ca Fe Al silicates	0.052	0.000	0.045
Calcite	0.091	0.000	0.078
Ca phosphates	0.013	0.012	0.013
Others	0.014	0.000	0.012

Particle size distribution

Matrix (< 63 μm) = 85.7 vol%
Inclusions (> 63 μm) = 14.3 vol%

Measurement statistics

Total measurement points = 2377350
Measurement spacing = 10 μm

Visual representation of mineralogy

Matrix

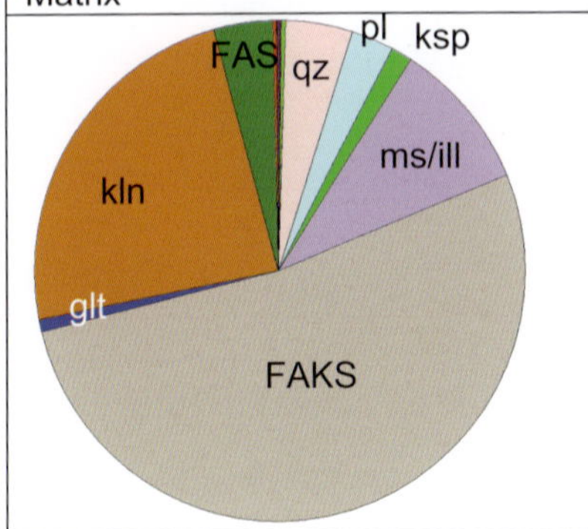

Inclusions

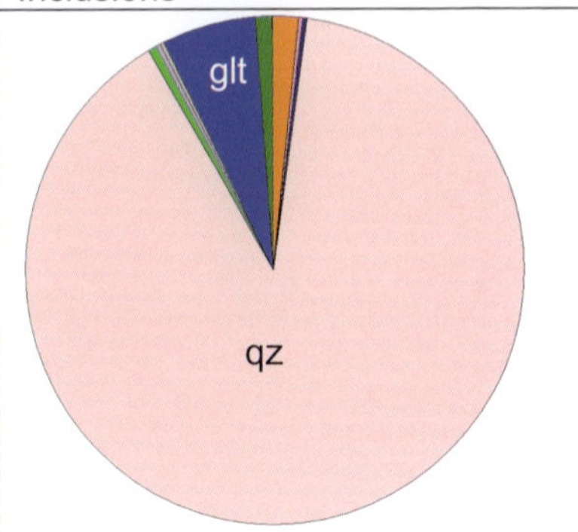

Bulk

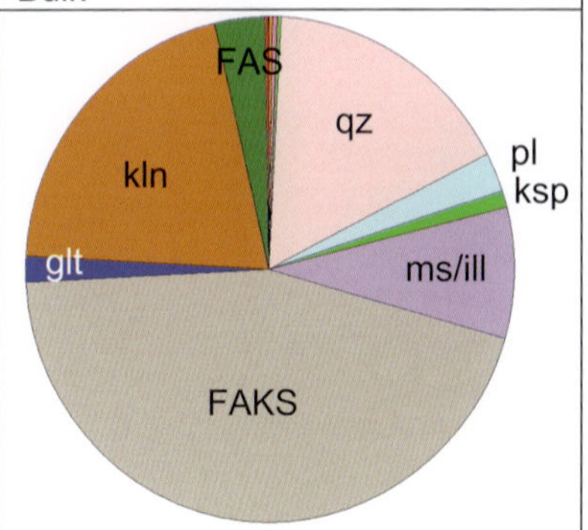

Notes

[1] Mineral groups listed in Table 2.

[2] gz = glaze, qz = quartz, pl = plagioclase, ksp = K-feldspar, ms/ill = muscovite/illite, FAKS = Fe-Al-K silicates, glt = glauconite, kln = kaolinite, FAS = Fe-Al silicates, cc = calcite

Figure A.15: Mineralogy report on pottery fabric Donyatt site 4 by QEMSCAN analysis. Camborne School of Mines, University of Exeter, Penryn Campus, Penryn, TR10 9EZ

Sample: Donyatt Site 13	CSM lab code: C05120021
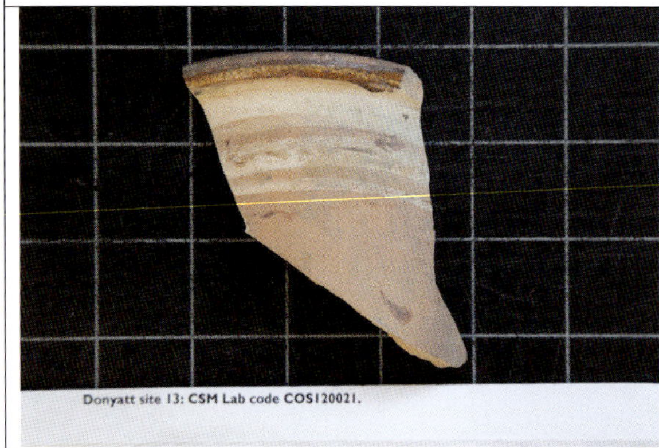	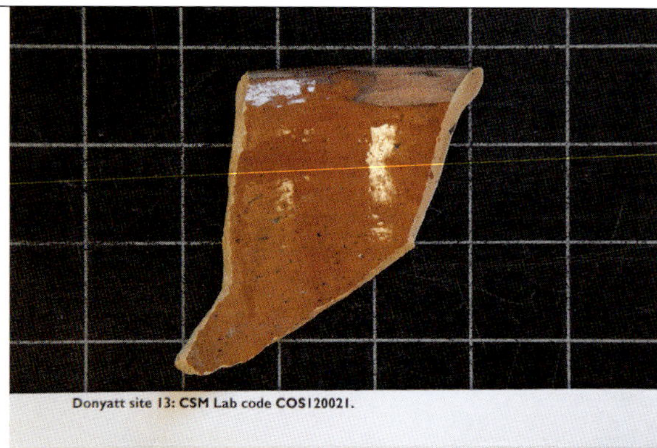
	(Grid = 3 x 3 cm)
Fabric description	**Mineralogical description**
Medium soft fired reduced and reoxidised orange red earthenware with smooth internal surface and fine granular structure with occasional specks of ?quartz; reduced green streaky glaze inside, brown oxidised but mostly burnt off outside	The sherd has 99 vol% matrix and 1 vol% inclusions. The inclusion population is somewhat skewed by a large proportion of lead glaze. Excluding this, quartz dominates over K-feldspar with significant Fe-Al silicates, muscovite/illite and kaolinite. The matrix is a mixture of kaolinite, muscovite/illite and Fe-Al-K silicates with quartz, plagioclase feldspar and K-feldspar. The matrix has minor glauconite.
Form	**Mineralogical type**
Rim of a wheel-thrown bowl with a partly wiped band of white slip below the rim on the outside and an internal lead-glaze	D
Analogues	
Donyatt pottery type 9	

Visual appearance of thin section (transmitted light)

Mineralogical map

Key to mineral map

- Fe sulphides
- Pb glaze
- Barite
- Chrome spinel
- Fe Ox/CO3
- Mn phases
- Rutile
- Ilmenite
- Zircon
- REE phases
- Quartz
- Plagioclase feldspar
- K-Feldspar
- Muscovite/Illite
- Fe Al K silicates
- Glauconite
- Kaolinite
- Tourmaline
- Fe Al silicates
- Mg Al silicates
- Mg silicates
- Ca Fe Al silicates
- Calcite
- Ca phosphates
- Others

Sample: Donyatt Site 13 | **CSM lab code: C05120021**

Mineralogical composition

	Matrix	Inclusions	Bulk
Fe sulphides	0.003	0.000	0.003
Pb glaze	0.099	44.686	0.708
Barite	0.000	0.000	0.000
Chrome spinel	0.009	0.000	0.009
Fe Ox/CO3	0.035	0.154	0.036
Mn phases	0.009	0.000	0.009
Rutile	0.781	0.000	0.772
Ilmenite	0.055	0.000	0.054
Zircon	0.011	0.000	0.011
REE phases	0.001	0.000	0.001
Quartz	15.534	36.701	15.706
Plagioclase feldspar	7.091	0.790	7.018
K-Feldspar	4.530	4.327	4.520
Muscovite/Illite	27.062	3.459	26.788
Fe Al K silicates	10.536	0.364	10.420
Glauconite	0.210	0.018	0.208
Kaolinite	30.381	3.099	30.066
Tourmaline	0.092	0.000	0.091
Fe Al silicates	3.473	6.400	3.494
Mg Al silicates	0.018	0.000	0.018
Mg silicates	0.036	0.000	0.036
Ca Fe Al silicates	0.001	0.000	0.001
Calcite	0.017	0.000	0.017
Ca phosphates	0.005	0.000	0.005
Others	0.011	0.000	0.011

Particle size distribution

Matrix (< 63 µm) = 99.1 vol%
Inclusions (> 63 µm) = 0.9 vol%

Measurement statistics

Total measurement points = 2866664
Measurement spacing = 10 µm

Visual representation of mineralogy

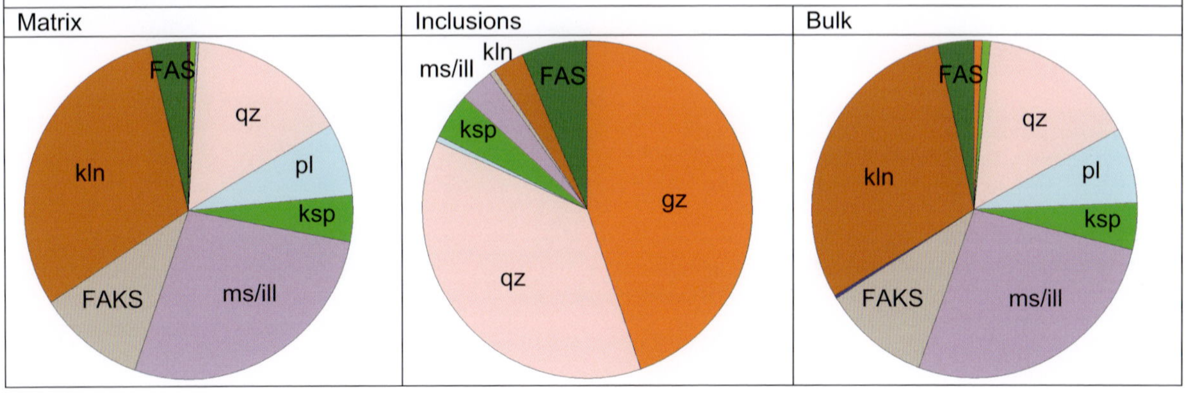

Notes

[1] Mineral groups listed in Table 2.

[2] gz = glaze, qz = quartz, pl = plagioclase, ksp = K-feldspar, ms/ill = muscovite/illite, FAKS = Fe-Al-K silicates, glt = glauconite, kln = kaolinite, FAS = Fe-Al silicates, cc = calcite

Figure A.16: Mineralogy report on pottery fabric Donyatt site 13 by QEMSCAN analysis. Camborne School of Mines, University of Exeter, Penryn Campus, Penryn, TR10 9EZ

Sample: Langford Budville 85/1994	CSM lab code: C05120015
	 (Grid = 3 x 3 cm)
Fabric description	**Mineralogical description**
Medium soft fired reduced and reoxidised orange red earthenware with smooth internal surface and fine granular structure with occasional specks of ?quartz; reduced green streaky glaze inside, brown oxidised but mostly burnt off outside.	The sherd has 93 vol% matrix and 7 vol% inclusions. The inclusion population is composed almost exclusively of quartz (~60 vol%) and K-feldspar (~23 vol%). The matrix is predominantly composed of Fe-Al-K silicates (72 vol%) with some muscovite/illite (11 vol%), K-feldspar (7 vol%) and quartz (6 vol%) and minor Fe-Al silicates and traces of glauconite.
Form	**Mineralogical type**
Rim of a wheel-thrown tankard with internal lead-glaze and collar outside wiped on the rim but which has run and stuck to the pot below during firing	A
Analogues	
West Somerset ware 17th-18th century	

Visual appearance of thin section (transmitted light)	Mineralogical map	Key to mineral map
		Fe sulphides Pb glaze Barite Chrome spinel Fe Ox/CO3 Mn phases Rutile Ilmenite Zircon REE phases Quartz Plagioclase feldspar K-Feldspar Muscovite/Illite Fe Al K silicates Glauconite Kaolinite Tourmaline Fe Al silicates Mg Al silicates Mg silicates Ca Fe Al silicates Calcite Ca phosphates Others

Sample: Langford Budville 85/1994				CSM lab code: C05120015
Mineralogical composition				**Particle size distribution**

	Matrix	Inclusions	Bulk
Fe sulphides	0.025	0.000	0.023
Pb glaze	0.122	15.840	1.189
Barite	0.000	0.000	0.000
Chrome spinel	0.001	0.000	0.001
Fe Ox/CO3	0.052	0.314	0.069
Mn phases	0.028	0.000	0.026
Rutile	0.099	0.015	0.093
Ilmenite	0.025	0.068	0.028
Zircon	0.010	0.021	0.011
REE phases	0.001	0.000	0.001
Quartz	6.410	59.595	10.019
Plagioclase feldspar	0.264	0.000	0.246
K-Feldspar	7.037	23.417	8.149
Muscovite/Illite	10.699	0.154	9.983
Fe Al K silicates	71.772	0.068	66.906
Glauconite	0.843	0.501	0.820
Kaolinite	0.161	0.000	0.150
Tourmaline	0.009	0.000	0.009
Fe Al silicates	2.427	0.006	2.262
Mg Al silicates	0.001	0.000	0.001
Mg silicates	0.005	0.000	0.004
Ca Fe Al silicates	0.000	0.000	0.000
Calcite	0.004	0.000	0.004
Ca phosphates	0.003	0.000	0.003
Others	0.001	0.000	0.001

Particle size distribution

Matrix (< 63 μm) = 93.2 vol%
Inclusions (> 63 μm) = 6.8 vol%

Measurement statistics

Total measurement points = 2484580
Measurement spacing = 10 μm

Visual representation of mineralogy

Matrix

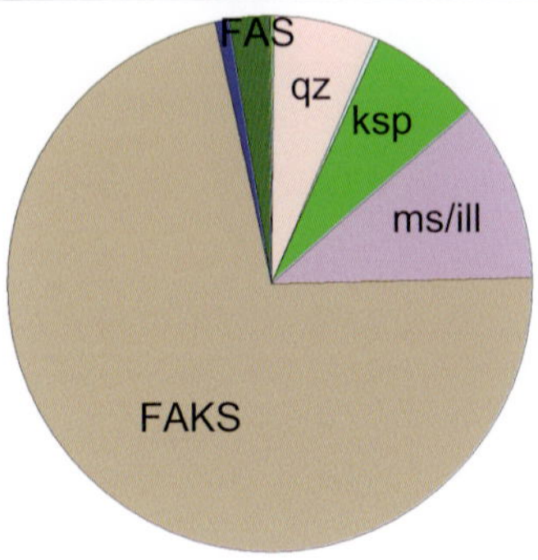

Inclusions

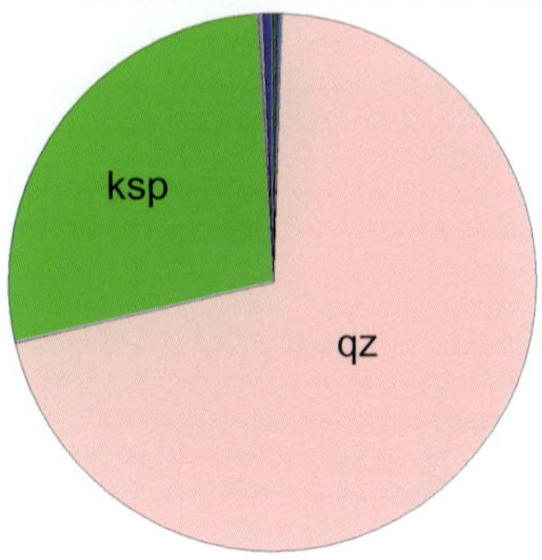

Bulk

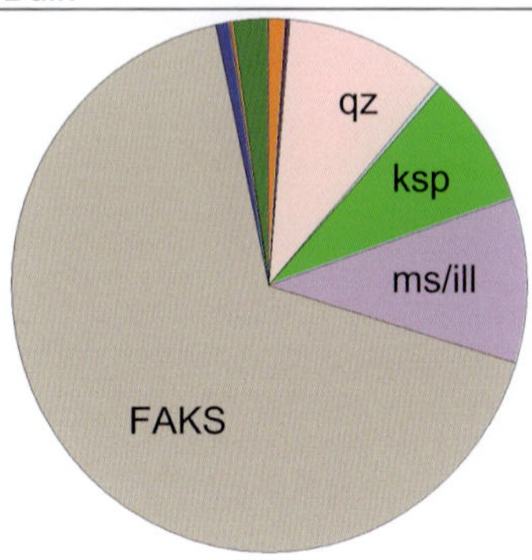

Notes
[1] Mineral groups listed in Table 2.
[2] gz = glaze, qz = quartz, pl = plagioclase, ksp = K-feldspar, ms/ill = muscovite/illite, FAKS = Fe-Al-K silicates, glt = glauconite, kln = kaolinite, FAS = Fe-Al silicates, cc = calcite

Figure A.17: *Mineralogy report on pottery fabric 85/1994 by QEMSCAN analysis. Camborne School of Mines, University of Exeter, Penryn Campus, Penryn, TR10 9EZ*

Sample: Nether Stowey	CSM lab code: C05120022

	(Grid = 3 x 3 cm)
Fabric description	**Mineralogical description**
Fairly hard-fired reduced and reoxidised orange red earthenware with zone of grey reduction below the glaze and flashed darker red smooth surface with patches of orange; irregular granular structure with sparse inclusions mostly specks of lime and scarce lumps <0.5mm of a dark red material (?conglomerate), occasional voids where organic material has burnt out; glaze fired a mottled olive green with pits caused by the lime	The sherd has 98.5 vol% matrix and 1.5 vol% inclusions. The inclusion population is composed almost exclusively of quartz (~59 vol%) and K-feldspar (~30 vol%). with minor Fe-Al-K silicates and Ca phosphates. The matrix is predominantly composed of Fe-Al-K silicates (56 vol%) with some muscovite/illite (14 vol%), K-feldspar (15 vol%) and quartz (11 vol%).
Form	**Mineralogical type**
Part of the base of a wheel-thrown deep bowl with internal lead glaze	A
Analogues	
West Somerset type ware 16th-17th century, Bristol pottery type 230/284	

Visual appearance of thin section (transmitted light)	Mineralogical map	Key to mineral map
		Fe sulphides Pb glaze Barite Chrome spinel Fe Ox/CO3 Mn phases Rutile Ilmenite Zircon REE phases Quartz Plagioclase feldspar K-Feldspar Muscovite/Illite Fe Al K silicates Glauconite Kaolinite Tourmaline Fe Al silicates Mg Al silicates Mg silicates Ca Fe Al silicates Calcite Ca phosphates Others

Sample: Nether Stowey | **CSM lab code: C05120022**

Mineralogical composition

	Matrix	Inclusions	Bulk
Fe sulphides	0.002	0.000	0.002
Pb glaze	0.107	5.981	0.194
Barite	0.000	0.000	0.000
Chrome spinel	0.003	0.000	0.003
Fe Ox/CO3	0.028	0.000	0.028
Mn phases	0.042	0.179	0.044
Rutile	0.130	0.000	0.128
Ilmenite	0.025	0.000	0.025
Zircon	0.024	0.000	0.024
REE phases	0.003	0.000	0.003
Quartz	10.837	59.059	11.558
Plagioclase feldspar	0.562	0.183	0.557
K-Feldspar	15.422	29.962	15.640
Muscovite/Illite	14.427	0.591	14.222
Fe Al K silicates	56.253	2.075	55.441
Glauconite	0.063	0.000	0.062
Kaolinite	0.204	0.000	0.201
Tourmaline	0.016	0.000	0.016
Fe Al silicates	1.318	0.011	1.299
Mg Al silicates	0.002	0.000	0.002
Mg silicates	0.014	0.000	0.014
Ca Fe Al silicates	0.006	0.000	0.005
Calcite	0.181	0.011	0.178
Ca phosphates	0.293	1.948	0.317
Others	0.037	0.000	0.036

Particle size distribution

Matrix (< 63 µm) = 98.5 vol%
Inclusions (> 63 µm) = 1.5 vol%

Measurement statistics

Total measurement points = 3071954
Measurement spacing = 10 µm

Visual representation of mineralogy

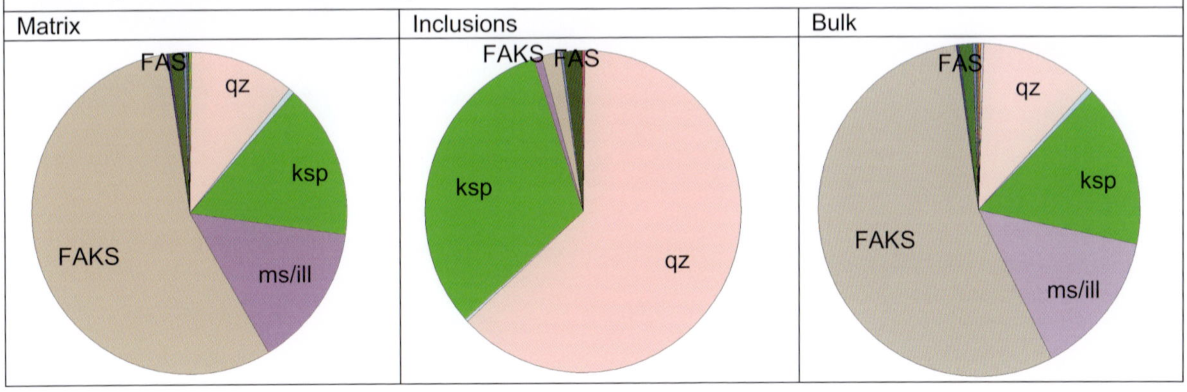

Notes

[1] Mineral groups listed in Table 2.
[2] gz = glaze, qz = quartz, pl = plagioclase, ksp = K-feldspar, ms/ill = muscovite/illite, FAKS = Fe-Al-K silicates, glt = glauconite, kln = kaolinite, FAS = Fe-Al silicates, cc = calcite

Figure A.18: Mineralogy report on pottery fabric Nether Stowey by QEMSCAN analysis. Camborne School of Mines, University of Exeter, Penryn Campus, Penryn, TR10 9EZ

Sample: Wanstrow A	**CSM lab code: C05120017**

(Grid = 3 x 3 cm)

Fabric description	**Mineralogical description**
Hard-fired reduced and reoxidised red earthenware with grey core and outer surface and reoxidised dull red brown zone and inner surface; very fine sandy feel to the surfaces reflecting the fine sandy structure to the fabric; very occasional specks of mica	The sherd has 95 vol% matrix and 5 vol% inclusions. The inclusion population is composed almost exclusively of quartz (~88 vol%) and K-feldspar (~9 vol%) with minor Fe-Al silicates and traces of kaolinite and Fe-Al-K silicates. The matrix is a mixture of Fe-Al-K silicates (42 vol%), kaolinite (21 vol%) and quartz (18 vol%) with some muscovite/illite (6 vol%); minor Fe-Al silicates, K-feldspar and plagioclase feldspar and traces of rutile.
Form	**Mineralogical type**
Body sherd of a wheel-thrown small jar	B_1
Analogues	
East Somerset ware 17th-18th century	

Visual appearance of thin section (transmitted light)

Mineralogical map

Key to mineral map

- Fe sulphides
- Pb glaze
- Barite
- Chrome spinel
- Fe Ox/CO3
- Mn phases
- Rutile
- Ilmenite
- Zircon
- REE phases
- Quartz
- Plagioclase feldspar
- K-Feldspar
- Muscovite/Illite
- Fe Al K silicates
- Glauconite
- Kaolinite
- Tourmaline
- Fe Al silicates
- Mg Al silicates
- Mg silicates
- Ca Fe Al silicates
- Calcite
- Ca phosphates
- Others

Sample: Wanstrow A				**CSM lab code: C05120017**
Mineralogical composition				**Particle size distribution**
	Matrix	Inclusions	Bulk	Matrix (< 63 µm) = 94.7 vol% Inclusions (> 63 µm) = 5.3 vol%
Fe sulphides	0.002	0.000	0.002	
Pb glaze	0.002	0.000	0.002	
Barite	0.000	0.000	0.000	
Chrome spinel	0.006	0.000	0.005	
Fe Ox/CO3	0.040	0.000	0.038	
Mn phases	0.000	0.000	0.000	
Rutile	0.439	0.040	0.418	
Ilmenite	0.076	0.075	0.076	
Zircon	0.022	0.000	0.021	
REE phases	0.002	0.000	0.002	
Quartz	17.733	88.004	21.464	
Plagioclase feldspar	4.309	0.000	4.081	
K-Feldspar	3.171	9.192	3.491	**Measurement statistics**
Muscovite/Illite	6.057	0.023	5.737	
Fe Al K silicates	42.367	0.501	40.144	
Glauconite	0.191	0.000	0.181	Total measurement points = 1699203 Measurement spacing = 10 µm
Kaolinite	20.826	0.293	19.736	
Tourmaline	0.051	0.000	0.048	
Fe Al silicates	4.658	1.872	4.511	
Mg Al silicates	0.004	0.000	0.004	
Mg silicates	0.020	0.000	0.019	
Ca Fe Al silicates	0.003	0.000	0.003	
Calcite	0.009	0.000	0.009	
Ca phosphates	0.002	0.000	0.002	
Others	0.008	0.000	0.007	

Visual representation of mineralogy

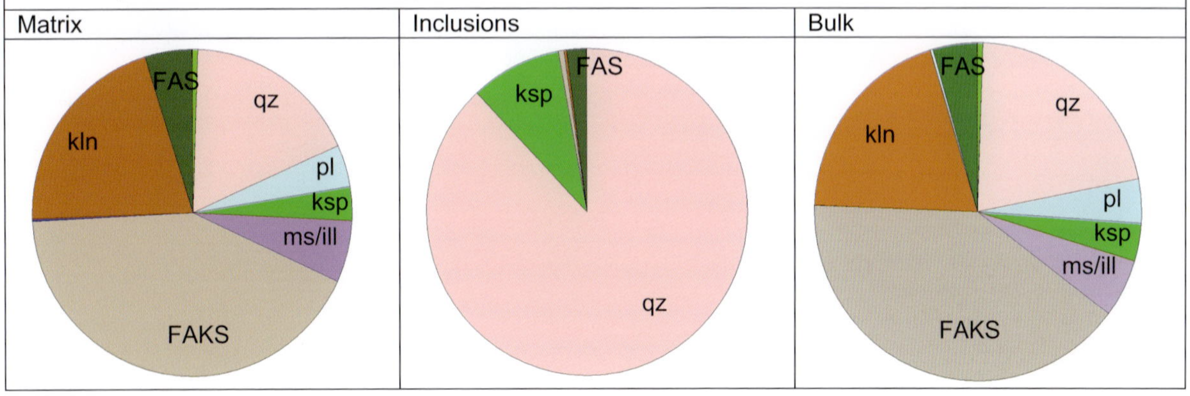

Notes

[1] Mineral groups listed in Table 2.

[2] gz = glaze, qz = quartz, pl = plagioclase, ksp = K-feldspar, ms/ill = muscovite/illite, FAKS = Fe-Al-K silicates, glt = glauconite, kln = kaolinite, FAS = Fe-Al silicates, cc = calcite

***Figure A.19:** Mineralogy report on pottery fabric Wanstrow A by QEMSCAN analysis. Camborne School of Mines, University of Exeter, Penryn Campus, Penryn, TR10 9EZ*

Sample: Wanstrow B	CSM lab code: C05120018
	 (Grid = 3 x 3 cm)
Fabric description	**Mineralogical description**
Fairly hard-fired reduced and reoxidised orange red earthenware with grey reduced core; smooth very fine sandy surface with specks of mica; distinctive laminar structure to the fine sandy fabric and occasional iron-rich inclusions; glaze has fired light olive green with splotches of orange and with black speckles.	The sherd has 90 vol% matrix and 10 vol% inclusions. The inclusion population is composed almost exclusively of quartz (~84 vol%) and K-feldspar (~8 vol%) with small amounts of Fe-Al silicates (2 vol%) and plagioclase feldspar (1.8 vol%). The matrix is a mixture of Fe-Al-K silicates (36 vol%), kaolinite (24 vol%) and quartz (20 vol%) with some muscovite/illite (6 vol%); minor Fe-Al silicates, K-feldspar and plagioclase feldspar and traces of rutile.
Form	**Mineralogical type**
Wheel-throw base of a deep bowl with an internal lead glaze	B_1
Analogues	
East Somerset type ware	

Visual appearance of thin section (transmitted light)	Mineralogical map	Key to mineral map
		Fe sulphides Pb glaze Barite Chrome spinel Fe Ox/CO3 Mn phases Rutile Ilmenite Zircon REE phases Quartz Plagioclase feldspar K-Feldspar Muscovite/Illite Fe Al K silicates Glauconite Kaolinite Tourmaline Fe Al silicates Mg Al silicates Mg silicates Ca Fe Al silicates Calcite Ca phosphates Others

Sample: Wanstrow B

CSM lab code: C05120018

Mineralogical composition

	Matrix	Inclusions	Bulk
Fe sulphides	0.004	0.000	0.003
Pb glaze	0.053	3.995	0.448
Barite	0.000	0.000	0.000
Chrome spinel	0.006	0.000	0.006
Fe Ox/CO3	0.025	0.040	0.027
Mn phases	0.002	0.000	0.002
Rutile	0.542	0.039	0.492
Ilmenite	0.070	0.019	0.065
Zircon	0.021	0.000	0.019
REE phases	0.003	0.000	0.003
Quartz	19.783	83.634	26.185
Plagioclase feldspar	5.208	1.793	4.865
K-Feldspar	3.636	8.118	4.085
Muscovite/Illite	5.970	0.030	5.374
Fe Al K silicates	36.017	0.210	32.427
Glauconite	0.130	0.000	0.117
Kaolinite	23.761	0.157	21.394
Tourmaline	0.083	0.019	0.077
Fe Al silicates	4.655	1.947	4.383
Mg Al silicates	0.001	0.000	0.001
Mg silicates	0.010	0.000	0.009
Ca Fe Al silicates	0.001	0.000	0.001
Calcite	0.011	0.000	0.010
Ca phosphates	0.003	0.000	0.003
Others	0.003	0.000	0.003

Particle size distribution

Matrix (< 63 μm) = 90.0 vol%
Inclusions (> 63 μm) = 10.0 vol%

Measurement statistics

Total measurement points = 1128996
Measurement spacing = 10 μm

Visual representation of mineralogy

Matrix | Inclusions | Bulk

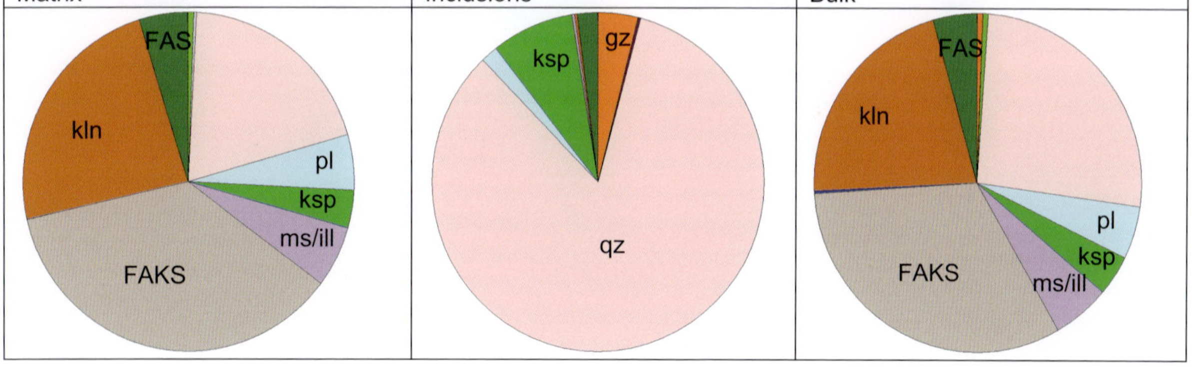

Notes

[1] Mineral groups listed in Table 2.

[2] gz = glaze, qz = quartz, pl = plagioclase, ksp = K-feldspar, ms/ill = muscovite/illite, FAKS = Fe-Al-K silicates, glt = glauconite, kln = kaolinite, FAS = Fe-Al silicates, cc = calcite

Figure A.20: *Mineralogy report on pottery fabric Wanstrow B by QEMSCAN analysis. Camborne School of Mines, University of Exeter, Penryn Campus, Penryn, TR10 9EZ*

Sample: Wrangway 91/1995	CSM lab code: C05120016
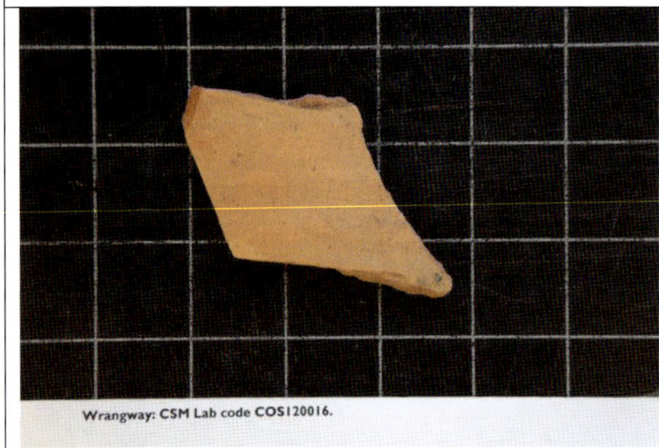	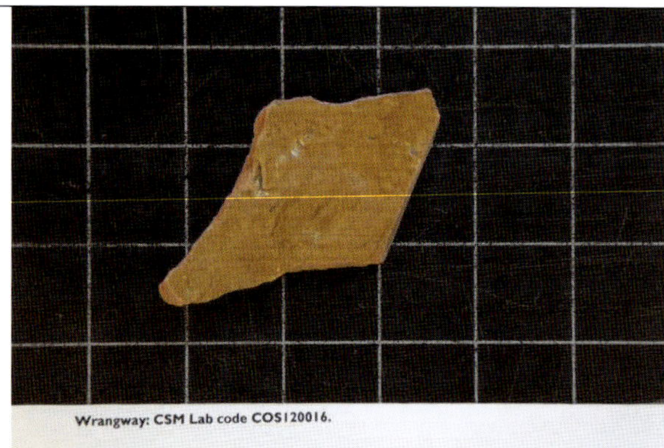 (Grid = 3 x 3 cm)
Fabric description	**Mineralogical description**
Fairly hard-fired reduced and thoroughly reoxidised orange red earthenware with smooth external surface and occasional specks of mica; grainy structure with occasional voids some from burnt-out organic material but others from poorly pugged clay; sparse specks of ?quartz; reduced light olive green lead-glaze streaked where picking up the throwing lines and with tiny pimples where the quartz projects through the surface.	The sherd has 91 vol% matrix and 9 vol% inclusions. The inclusion population is composed almost exclusively of quartz (~75 vol%) and K-feldspar (~25 vol%). The matrix is predominantly composed of Fe-Al-K silicates (65 vol%) with some muscovite/illite (8 vol%), K-feldspar (10 vol%) and quartz (10 vol%).
Form	**Mineralogical type**
Body sherd of a large wheel-thrown jar with internal lead-glaze	A
Analogues	
West Somerset ware 17th-18th century	

Visual appearance of thin section (transmitted light)	Mineralogical map	Key to mineral map
 1 cm	 1 cm	Fe sulphides Pb glaze Barite Chrome spinel Fe Ox/CO3 Mn phases Rutile Ilmenite Zircon REE phases Quartz Plagioclase feldspar K-Feldspar Muscovite/Illite Fe Al K silicates Glauconite Kaolinite Tourmaline Fe Al silicates Mg Al silicates Mg silicates Ca Fe Al silicates Calcite Ca phosphates Others

Sample: Wrangway 91/1995 — **CSM lab code: C05120016**

Mineralogical composition

	Matrix	Inclusions	Bulk
Fe sulphides	0.008	0.000	0.007
Pb glaze	0.222	1.749	0.360
Barite	0.000	0.000	0.000
Chrome spinel	0.003	0.000	0.002
Fe Ox/CO3	0.014	0.019	0.014
Mn phases	0.197	0.000	0.179
Rutile	0.138	0.017	0.127
Ilmenite	0.039	0.041	0.039
Zircon	0.016	0.009	0.016
REE phases	0.002	0.000	0.002
Quartz	10.119	71.305	15.622
Plagioclase feldspar	0.576	0.000	0.524
K-Feldspar	10.293	26.307	11.733
Muscovite/Illite	7.865	0.251	7.180
Fe Al K silicates	65.045	0.134	59.207
Glauconite	0.070	0.000	0.064
Kaolinite	1.665	0.000	1.515
Tourmaline	0.012	0.000	0.011
Fe Al silicates	3.278	0.000	2.984
Mg Al silicates	0.199	0.162	0.195
Mg silicates	0.020	0.000	0.019
Ca Fe Al silicates	0.005	0.000	0.004
Calcite	0.178	0.000	0.162
Ca phosphates	0.032	0.004	0.030
Others	0.004	0.000	0.003

Particle size distribution

Matrix (< 63 μm) = 91.0 vol%
Inclusions (> 63 μm) = 9.0 vol%

Measurement statistics

Total measurement points = 3094633
Measurement spacing = 10 μm

Visual representation of mineralogy

Matrix — Inclusions — Bulk

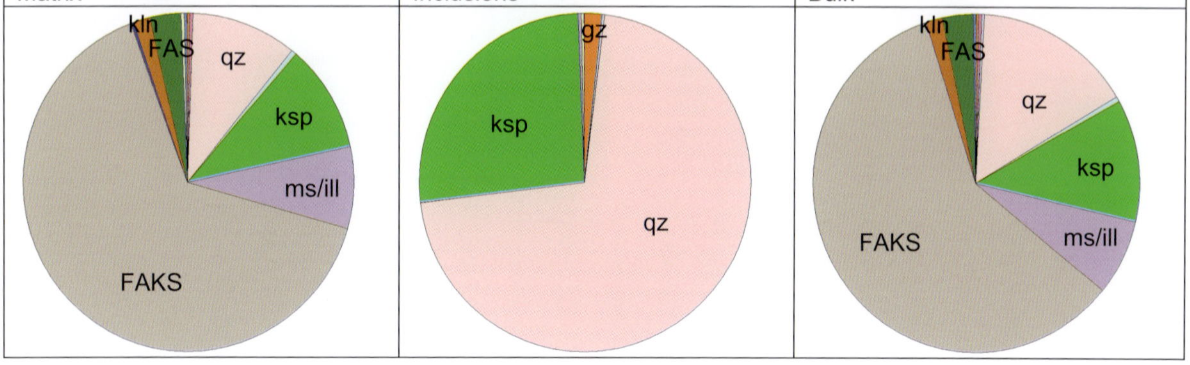

Notes

[1] Mineral groups listed in Table 2.
[2] gz = glaze, qz = quartz, pl = plagioclase, ksp = K-feldspar, ms/ill = muscovite/illite, FAKS = Fe-Al-K silicates, glt = glauconite, kln = kaolinite, FAS = Fe-Al silicates, cc = calcite

Figure A.21: Mineralogy report on pottery fabric 91/1995 by QEMSCAN analysis. Camborne School of Mines, University of Exeter, Penryn Campus, Penryn, TR10 9EZ

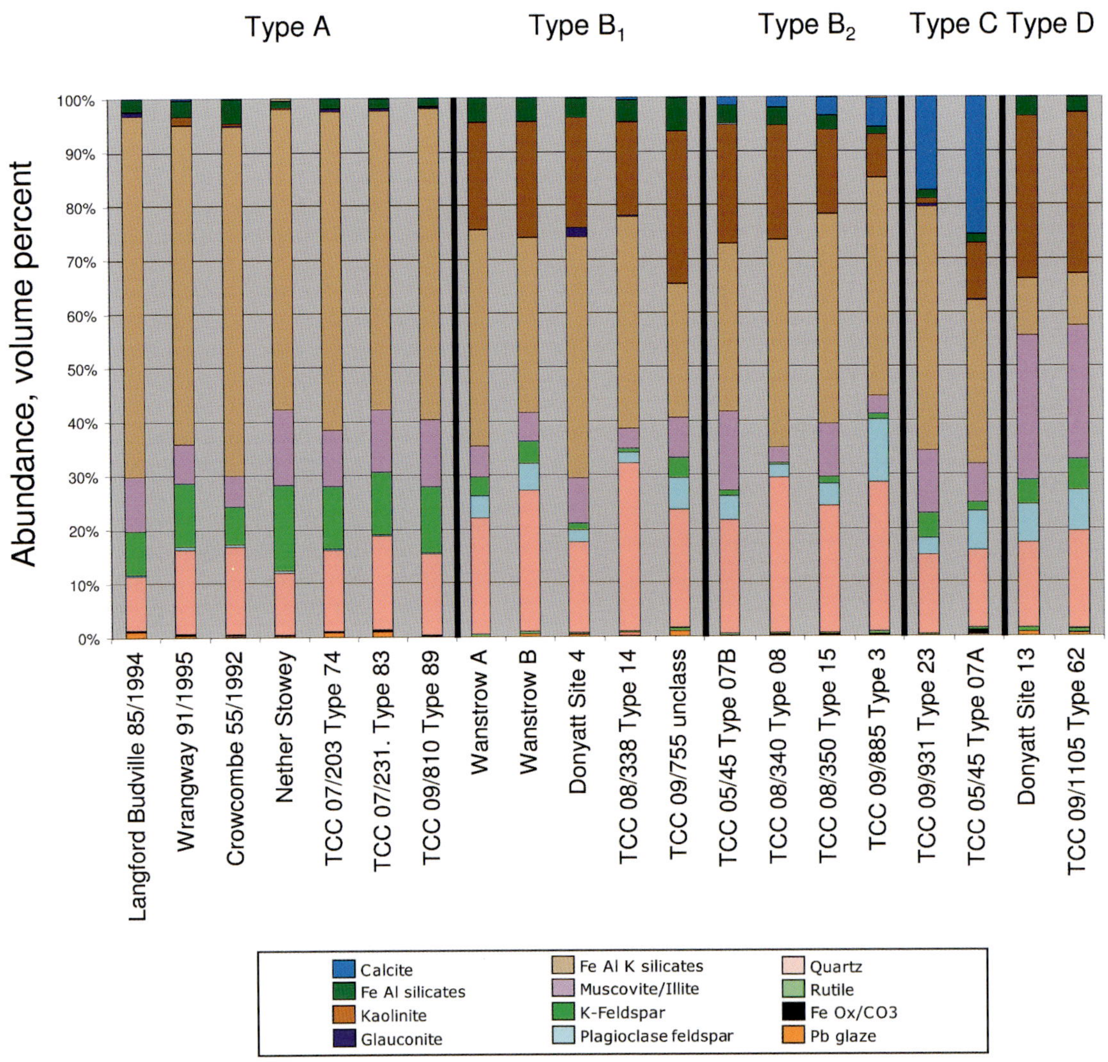

Figure A.22: *Summary of mineral abundances within the studied sherds. The samples have been arranged according to mineralogical similarities leading to the identification of distinct mineralogical types A, B1, B2, C and D. Note how distinctive are the Triassic-derived West Somerset fabrics (type A) from Liassic derived type B and from type C.*

Primary Sources

In the Aerofilms Collection

This commercial collection of aerial photographs has been acquired by the national heritage agencies and made available on the *Britain from Above* website (www.britainfromabove.org.uk/). The original images for England are held in the Historic England archive.

Aerofilms 41094 Aerial view of the castle from the north in May 1933, showing the keep area being landscaped. Walls A and B have been consolidated and the area between them has been recently turfed. Online reference EPW041094. Copy in Somerset Studies Library.

Aerofilms A.5341 Aerial photograph of the castle from the south taken on 13 May 1947. Online reference EAW005341. Copy in Somerset Studies Library. Figure 2 on page 3.

In the Francis Frith Collection

Frith 34885 Postcard showing Gatehouse with pre-turnstile building to right and Grand Jury Room and lean-to through the gate. A girl is flanked by two younger boys in the gateway. Several copies, some tinted are known in the SRO postcard collection. Dated by the Frith Archive to 1884.

In the Hampshire Record Office

HRO 11M59/B1/1–329 Winchester account rolls, 1208–1711.

HRO 11M59/E2/155649 Survey and valuation of the manor of Taunton, part of the Winchester Bishopric Estate, 1566.

HRO 68M74/E/A2 Copy of the Parliamentary Survey made, 1647, of the Bishops of Winchester's Somerset Manors.

HRO W/K1/30 Survey and estimate for restoring dilapidations at Bishopric properties, 1782-1786. Discussed on page 27. A photocopy is held in the SRO (DD/X/BUSH/11).

In the New College Oxford Archives

NCA 1635/7 Correspondence relating to Taunton Free Grammar School and the appointment of masters. Transcribed by AT Wicks, see SRO DD/TBL/45.

In the SANHS Collections

SANHS 3504 Pen and wash drawing of the south front of the inner ward entitled "A View of the Castle and Castle Green in the Parish of Bishops Hull neare Taunton in the County of Somerset" and dated 1773. Figure 2.1 on page 28 and Figure 15.6 on page 248. Discussed on page 29.

SANHS 3506 Watercolour or coloured aquatint print entitled "N.W. View of Taunton Castle. C.C.". Not dated but shows changes made by Hammet in *c*.1790 and predates the re-roofing of 1816. Figure 1.1 on page 13 and discussed on page 30.

SANHS 3511 Ink drawing of Castle Bow gate passage from the west. In pencil on the rear "Taunton Castle gate" and "??1814". Shows in great detail, but at a very oblique view, the features of the gate. Figure 15.2 on page 245.

SANHS 3512 Plan of the Coin Room (Room 40). Written on the rear: "Plan of ground floor of the south wing of Taunton Castle, before the Diamond Jubilee alterations were carried out. Autumn 1908. [signed] H St George Gray mens. et del."

SANHS 3515–3517 A series of 8 elevation drawings on three irregular pieces of card. The locations are numbered and shown on SRO DD/SAS/c1270/2 and on the engraved version in Warre (1853), which dates them to 1853 and identifies the artist as the surveyor John Leversedge. Presumably commissioned by Warre for his paper but not engraved and printed.

I. South elevation of the inner gatehouse (SANHS 3515).

II. North elevation of the inner gatehouse and stair turret (SANHS 3516).
III. The Watergate from the south (SANHS 3515). Figure 8.1 on page 156.
IV. The stair turret at the north-west of the Great Hall and the hall wall with Window 55 (SANHS 3515).
V. A small piece of walling with water flowing through a hole at the base. Located on the plan at the south-west corner of the outer ward (SANHS 3516). Figure 14.1 on page 238.
VI. The arch in Ine's Garden (SANHS 3516).
VII. West elevation of the East Gate (SANHS 3517).
VIII. East elevation of the East Gate (SANHS 3517).

SANHS 3525 Ink drawing on card entitled "Section showing walls &c, of moats &c, Taunton Castle, under roadway from the Castle Green to the Castle Yard, from actual measurement by Ed. Jeboult, Feby 1867". Below is stated "Copied from original in the possession of Mr C Tite, Taunton". Figure 2.3 on page 33 and discussed on page 33.

SANHS 3534 Pen and wash drawing captioned "The South West View of Taunton Castle 1789". Signed by CW Bampfylde. The original for the engraving in Toulmin (1791). Figure 2.2 on page 31 and discussed on page 30.

SANHS 6017 Copy of plan by Houghton Spencer, 1910, with coloured additions showing services across the courtyard. Some additional old drainage discoveries added with a note dated 1923 (Discussed on page 68). This, and SANHS 6024, were prepared at the request of the SANHS committee (SANHS minutes: 17/6/1910).

SANHS 6017a Plan of ground floor of the castle. Signed J Houghton Spencer, August 1910 and used in his published description of the castle (Spencer 1910). Amended, probably by Gray, to rename "Norman Keep" as "Constables Tower" (see Vivian-Neal and Gray 1940, page 55, note 28) and "Store" as "Turnstile" (built 1930).

SANHS 6022 Plan by NHN Darby, architect, of first floor of castle. Dated September 1954 but says based on Spencer 1910.

SANHS 6024 Plan of ground and first floors of the castle with demolished buildings shown in blue. Signed J Houghton Spencer, October 1910.

SANHS 6025 Plan of first floor of the castle. Signed J Houghton Spencer 1910 and used in his published description of the castle (Spencer 1910).

SANHS 6027 Architect's drawing "Taunton Castle: Elevation drawings of Tone House". Surveyed by AB Botterill, September 1929. Oatley and Lawrence, Bristol 26/9/1929. See also SANHS 6083, 6084.

SANHS 6032 Artist's visualisation, from the south-east, of the proposals detailed in SANHS 6043.

SANHS 6040, 6041 Plans, elevations and detail drawings of the "Schools Museum and Workroom" (the Entrance Block). Stone and Francis architects. Not dated but 1931. Discussed on page 183.

SANHS 6043 Plans and elevations of proposed renovation of Grand Jury Room. Stone and Francis, architects, Taunton. Not dated but must be 1931. Discussed on page 182. See also SANHS 6032.

SANHS 6066 Architect's drawing of the castle annotated with the results of the 1952 excavations in the Great Hall (Radford and Hallam 1953). The location of the subsequent excavation (1956) for the beam engine pit is also shown identifying the drawn sections (SANHS 6067–6069).

SANHS 6067 Section drawings of the pit for the beam engine, dug in 1956. Drawn in pencil on graph paper at the scale of 1 inch to one foot (1:12). Sections IV and V are shown but the latter is crossed out and has been redrawn on the reverse. Redrawn in Figure 3.8 on page 49.

SANHS 6068 Section drawing of the excavation for the beam engine, dug in 1956. Drawn in pencil on graph paper at the scale of 1 inch to one foot (1:12). Section III. Redrawn in Figure 3.8 on page 49.

SANHS 6069 Section drawing of the excavation for the beam engine, dug in 1956. Drawn in pencil on graph paper at the scale of 1 inch to one foot (1:12). Inked over with some changes in nomenclature. Sections not numbered but from plan (SANHS 6066) are I and II. Figure 3.8 on page 49.

SANHS 6071 Copy of County Architect's "Taunton Castle Museum: Record Plan of Roof over Adam Library, June 1960". Discussed on page 206.

SANHS 6083 Architect's drawing "Second floor plan (attics) of Tone House" Surveyed by AB Botterill, September 1929. Oatley and Lawrence, Bristol 26/9/1929. See also SANHS 6027, 6084.

SANHS 6084 Architect's drawing "Taunton Castle. Survey of site for proposed extension of museum: Ground floor plan". Surveyed by AB Botterill, September 1929. Oatley and Lawrence, Bristol 26/9/1929. Shows Tone House, grounds, outbuildings and east end of Great Hall. See also SANHS 6027 and 6083.

SANHS 6086 Plan of "Proposed Alterations to Curator's House" with central heating system overdrawn in red. Dated Jan 13 1931 (by heating engineer).

SANHS 6092 Inked drawing on graph paper by Gray titled "Taunton Castle 1924–25" showing two section drawings: "Section on the line A-B of plan. Cutting II" and "Section on the line C-D of plan. Cutting III". Figure 3.6 on page 44.

SANHS 6093 Pen and wash drawing entitled "Plan and sections at excavations at north east corner of Taunton Castle". Signed "Wm Bidgood 187"[6 appended in pencil]. Pencilled annotation "County Gazette 16 May 1876". Note: this should be 13 May. Figure 3.1 on page 36. Discussed on page 35,

SANHS 6094 Untitled plan by Gray showing locations of excavation cuttings I–IV and A–D. Redrawn as Figure 3.4 on page 40.

SANHS 6095 Plan by NHN Darby, architect, entitled "Plan showing new windows in 1st floor room adjoining gatehouse". Dated 26/1/1955.

SANHS 6102 Plan entitled "Plan of a garden in the parish of Taunton St Mary Magdalen [crossed out and replaced by Bishops Hull] proposed to be divided between Mr R Reeves and Mr Stone". Shows east wall of castle, with Ine's Garden and arch. Signed Leversedge 1852.

SANHS 6103 Section drawing of brick gutter and battered wall outside the Drawing Room of Castle House with covering letter dated 7/2/1912 from J Houghton Spencer to SANHS committee describing findings. Redrawn as Figure 3.3 on page 38.

SANHS 12489 Watercolour by Miss LC Hammett. Undated but others by her in the collection are dated around 1921.

SANHS 12490 Watercolour of the north-west corner of the courtyard by Miss LC Hammett. Undated but others by her in the collection are dated around 1921.

SANHS 12492 Watercolour of the approach to Castle Bow. On the rear is pencilled "The outer gateway of Taunton Castle from the East Aug 1796 Jan 1797". Figure 15.5 on page 247.

SANHS 12494 Watercolour of the south side of Castle Bow. On the rear is pencilled "The outer gateway of Taunton castle from the south Aug 1796 - Nov 1796". Figure 15.3 on page 246.

SANHS 12501 Pencil drawing, mounted on card and captioned "Ruins of Taunton Castle as they appeared in 1814 EW" On the rear is a dedication to William Stradling (d. 1859) by E[?] White. It is likely that this is a sketch of SANHS 12527, or its precursor sketch.

SANHS 12506 Engraving titled "Taunton Castle" on loose sheet, showing Round Tower and south front. Signed by Bidgood (curator 1862–1900) and used as the frontispiece to Clark (1872).

SANHS 12507 Photographic print showing William Bidgood, the curator (1862–1900), standing in Doorway 75 by the gatehouse. Not dated but prior to 1883 when the stair turret was rebuilt and possibly taken as a record of the old turret and/or the opening up of Door 75. Figure 11.8 on page 210.

SANHS 12511 Photographic print showing Castle House from the courtyard. Titled on the negative "Courtyard. Taunton Castle. 23655. J.V." indicating it is a product of J Valentine of Dundee, although not a postcard. Possibly the print was given in return for permission to photograph the castle. The firm's records held by the University of St Andrews give a date of 1895.

SANHS 12521 Tinted postcard showing Gatehouse with pre-turnstile building to right and Grand Jury Room and lean-to through the gate. A boy lounges against the east side of the gate and a man is visible in the doorway beyond. Numbered 23658 followed by encircled "JV" indicating it is a product of J Valentine of Dundee. The firm's records held by the University of St Andrews record this number as being of Taunton School and it is likely to have been misnumbered for 23653, which is recorded as "Taunton Castle Gateway" in a batch of photos (23644–23675) taken in Taunton in 1895.

SANHS 12522 Monochrome postcard. Similar view to SANHS 12521 but without figures. Not dated.

SANHS 12527 Loose copy of an engraving used by Warre (1853). Captioned "Taunton Castle. North view of the eastern gate" and "Engraved by WF Elliot, Esq. from a sketch by WP Pinchard Esq. in 1814". At first sight the sketch referred to would appear to be SANHS 12501, both are viewed from an identical location but the name is wrong and there are a few small differences. It is more likely that 12501 is a copy of this engraving. Figure 15.4 on page 246.

SANHS 12529 Engraving titled "Taunton Castle – North Front" published by Warre (1853, 29).

SANHS 12549 Photograph looking along Wall C from the north. It shows the wall to full height with (then recent?) scars left by the demolition of the courtyard buildings in the 1870s; various schoolboys are standing on the masonry. Figure 5.2 on page 67.

SANHS 12550 Photograph, almost certainly by Gray, showing the south front of the Great Hall after the demolition of the Grand Jury Room and before construction had advanced beyond digging foundations for the new Wyndham block. Dated October 1931.

SANHS 12551 Photograph, almost certainly by Gray, showing the construction of the Wyndham entrance building which has reached window cill level. From the south. Dated 15/11/1931.

SANHS 12552 Photograph, almost certainly by Gray, showing the construction of the Wyndham entrance building which has reached window cill level. From the south-east. Dated 15/11/1931.

SANHS 12556 Photograph of the works to the north end of the Somerset Room in 1884. William Bidgood (curator 1862–1900) stands proudly on the wall surveying the destruction. Figure 10.8 on page 195.

SANHS 12565 Photograph of Window 119 in the Somerset Room being repointed. Taken during the 1952 works for The Times (stamp on rear).

SANHS 12566 Photograph of Windows 118, 119 and 220 in Somerset Room. Taken during the 1952 works for The Times (stamp on rear).

SANHS 12567 Posed photograph of Linda Witherill and AD Hallam recording the west wall of the Great Hall. Taken during the 1952 works for The Times (stamp on rear). Participants identified by Linda Witherill (pers. comm. 2014).

SANHS 12568 Posed photograph of Linda Witherill (ladder), Ann Maltby and AD Hallam recording the west wall of the Great Hall. Taken during the 1952 works for The Times (stamp on rear). Participants identified by Linda Witherill (pers. comm. 2014).

SANHS 12569 Posed photograph of excavations at the west end of the Great Hall. Trench I has been excavated and workmen are starting Trench II. Taken during the 1952 works for The Times (stamp on rear). Linda Witherill (pers. comm.) suggests that the figure in the trench is Mrs Hallam. The two men bending over a plan are probably Radford (left) and Hallam. Figure 3.7 on page 48.

SANHS 12570 Posed photograph of Linda Witherill recording the west wall of the Great Hall. Taken during the 1952 works for The Times (stamp on rear). Participant identified by Linda Witherill (pers. comm. 2014).

SANHS 12571 Posed photograph of Mrs Hallam excavating in Trench 1. The woman to the rear is unidentified but may be an "extra" as she is not dressed for the conditions. Taken during the 1952 works for The Times (stamp on rear). Participants identified by Linda Witherill (pers. comm. 2014).

SANHS 13048 Photograph along Wall C from the south. Dated "late August 1933" by Gray on the rear. Probably taken as a record of the area before the construction of the Wyndham Galleries. See also Museum PCFILE 1a.

SANHS 13158 Sketch plan in ink showing alterations, both proposed and already carried out. Not dated but works indicated were carried out in 1878. Figure 8.2 on page 156.

SANHS 13249 Aerial photograph showing landscaping works to keep garden and facing of lower part of Castle House. Aerofilms 41183 dated May 1933 on rear.

SANHS A7-1 Site drawings and pre-publication drawings for Radford and Hallam (1953).

SANHS AR 21-32 Copy of Toulmin (1791) owned by Edwin Sloper (1840–1905) and containing annotations by him.

SANHS AR 32 Notebook belonging to Edwin Sloper (1840–1905) together with numerous press cuttings. The notebook contains, amongst other information gathered about Taunton, a description of the Great Hall before the changes made by SANHS and details of some of the discoveries made during those changes. The bulk of the notes on Taunton Castle appear to have been made in 1876. The notebook is cited by Radford and Hallam (1953) but not all the information they report could be found.

SANHS Braikenridge Taunton 38 Sketch drawing, signed "WFE", of Gatehouse from north and wall of courtyard buildings. Reversed left to right, so presumably drawn from an unlocated incorrectly printed photograph. Catalogued in SRO as A/DAS/1/390/14.

SANHS Buckler A Pen and wash drawing captioned "South View of the Castle at Taunton, Somersetshire" and signed "J Buckler 1836".

SANHS Buckler B Pen and wash drawing captioned "Court Yard of the Castle at Taunton, Somersetshire" and signed "J Buckler 1836". Shows the gatehouse from the north-west with the stair turret and some of the buildings demolished in the 1870s. A corner of the Grand Jury Room appears to the left, supported on a column. The pre-1888 stair tower is shown as polygonal although photographs (see Figure 11.8 on page 210) show that it was rectangular like its replacement. Figure 12.2 on page 215.

SANHS Buckler C Pen and wash drawing captioned "South east view of the grammar school at Taunton, Somersetshire" and signed "JB 1827". Figure 16.3 on page 251.

SANHS C10-1 Plan "compiled from plan prepared by Mr Spencer in the possession of the Somerset Archaeological and Natural History Society and from survey of April and May 1928, April and May 1929, and Sept 1930". Signed Austin B Botterill. Produced as part of the planning for the Wyndham Galleries and showing details of Gray's excavations that are not recorded elsewhere.

SANHS glass negatives: Box 167 Includes two photographs, probably by Gray, showing the drawing room in Castle House (Room 26) from both east and west.

SANHS Gray 1934 Reduced photocopy of a copy of Houghton Spencer's drainage plan (SANHS 6017), the original annotated by Gray in 1933 and 1934. The photocopy has missed part of the original annotation which had been added by typewriter, probably by David Bromwich (SANHS librarian). Neither the original nor the photocopy could be located in 2008. Copy in project archive. Discussed on page 68.

SANHS Hawtin Six monochrome photographic prints in an envelope found in the SANHS office in 2008. The envelope is marked "Photographs during plastering of Adam Library (negatives = F. H.)" and "Photographs from Landing outside Somerset Room (negs = F. H.)" FH is Frank Hawtin and the photographs probably date from repairs in the 1970s. Now in SRO (DD/SAS/2015/1/2).

SANHS Minutes Most of the minutes of SANHS committees survive but there are some important sub-committees that are known to have existed but whose minutes cannot be found.

- Minutes of the council, committees and some sub-committees, 1878–1895 (SRO DD/SAS/G733/1/1).
- Minutes of the council and committees, 1895–1908 (SRO DD/SAS/G733/1/2).
- Minutes of the council, 1909–1922 and committees 1909–1911 (SRO DD/SAS/G733/1/3).
- Minutes of the council, 1923–1936 (SRO DD/SAS/G733/1/4).
- Minutes of the development committee, 1927–1939 (SRO DD/SAS/G733/4/1).
- Minutes of the council, 1937–1974 (SRO DD/SAS/G733/1/5).

SANHS Office file C6 File entitled "Castle reconstruction 1952-4" found in SANHS office during move. To be accessioned to records. Almost entirely letters and reports by FL Hannam of Burrough and Hannam Architects, to SANHS. Now in SRO (DD/SAS/2015/1/10).

SANHS Photos 1934 A strip of monochrome film negatives, some with prints, of the keep garden area discovered in an envelope in the SANHS office in 2008. The envelope indicates that they were printed in 1977 but there is no record of the date they were taken. The landscaping is clearly newly completed with the steel frame of the Wyndham Gallery visible in some shots indicating a date in 1934. One is a photograph of Aerofilms 40913 from the SANHS library and internal evidence suggests that the others may also be rephotographs of original prints that are otherwise unknown. Now in SRO (DD/SAS/2015/1/1).

In Somerset County Council files

SCC CB 35/1/5 Survey of Boundary Wall between Museum and Castle Hotel Gardens. Elevation of east side of Wall C and three profiles across the wall. 6/2/1962. Somerset Property Services files. Discussed on page 61.

In the Somerset Museum Service Collections

M1191 Six monochrome negatives, part of a collection capturing the photographic plates from Edward Jeboult's scrapbook (see SRO L/2205 and T/PH/REA).

PCFILE 1 File of images (prints and negatives), some accessioned. Many are of known originals but the original sources of some have not been located. Among these are:

a A photograph of the area to the east of the Great Hall after the demolition of Tone House (1930) and before the Wyndham Gallery was built (1934). It may well be a companion to SANHS 13087.

b A photograph of a sketch of the north side of Castle Bow. Captioned "Ruins of Taunton Castle, as this appeared 1821". Possibly the original for SANHS 12527, although there are significant differences, particularly the ground level to the right.

TTNCM 48/2004/7a A set of monochrome film negatives in a Kodak envelope with a label on front reading "Negatives", "Taunton Castle" "Great Hall, Somerset Room, Exterior, RF –53". The rear of envelope has *Name* filled in as "Flemming" and *Price* as "4/6". Radford and Hallam (1953) thank Miss Rosamund Fleming for helping with the excavation and she is also credited with their Plate A. This plate does not feature in the collection of negatives. By matching the cut ends of the negatives it has been possible to reassemble 4 strips of film (here lettered A-D) although it is possible that there are missing negatives (such as those used for the plates) that might have allowed them to join. The longest strips thus formed contain 9 negatives and it is possible to suggest the order of them from the evidence of the building works.

Film A (9 frames) shows the excavated trench across the hall with detailed shots of the rubble-filled robber trenches and also details of exposed medieval fabric in the hall.

Film B (5 frames) shows more details of early features in the Great Hall (including breaking into the "privy" that was then converted to display the fireplace overmantel) but can be seen to be later than Film A as the sub-base of the hall floor is in place.

Film C (6 frames) has one exterior shot (of window 240), shots of the overmantel being emplaced and the barrel-vault scars with the concrete floor in place.

Film D (9 frames) comprises outside shots and shots of the windows in the Somerset Room (Room 103).

In the Somerset Historic Environment Record

HER image 29806 Colour slide showing west wall of Undercroft from the north. Dated 1969 and probably taken by Frank Hawtin. Figure 10.4 on page 192.

HER image 29807 Colour slide showing east wall of Undercroft from the north. Dated 1969 and probably taken by Frank Hawtin. Figure 10.5 on page 193.

HER image 29808 Colour slide showing west wall of Undercroft from the south. Dated 1969 and probably taken by Frank Hawtin.

HER image 30116 Colour slide showing detail of date on Buttress 375. Not dated. Figure 9.3 on page 168.

In the Somerset Record Office

A/BAV/18 Album of photographs by William Morley and John Blizzard *c.*1865–70. Mostly of country houses and churches but four are of Taunton Castle.

/3 Photograph by William Morley, before the demolition of the courtyard buildings, showing the inside of the inner gate and stair turret (Figure 11.6 on page 208).

/4 Photograph of an engraving in Taunton Museum. This is SANHS 3511 showing Castle Bow.

/5 Photograph of the West Range from the north west.

/6 Photograph of Castle Bow from the west.

SRO A/CNT/4/1–3 Somerset County Museum Governing Body minutes, reports and accounts. 1958–1974.

SRO A/DWX/19 Pencil drawing signed by William Bidgood giving details of the arch discovered in 1876. Presumably given to George Clark, referred to as "yourself" by reference to his publication (Clark 1872). Found in 2011 with mixed correspondence following the museum move to the Somerset Heritage Centre. Figure 3.2 on page 37.

SRO D/B/ta/24/1/26/1709 Building control plan of minor additions to Taunton Castle: the formation of a new basement heating plant at the east end of the Great Hall, 1899.

SRO D/B/ta/24/1/71/1410A Building control plan of alterations to the Castle Hotel together with a complete set of plans of the then existing building. Submitted in 1929 but some plans dated 1928.

SRO D/B/ta/24/1/76/1595 Building control plan of attendant's office at carpark, Taunton. Dated August 1931 and stamped approved 9/11/1931.

SRO D/B/ta/24/1/137/8049 Building control plan of sanitary accommodation at Taunton Castle Museum, 1960. Children's toilets in Castle House.

SRO DD/SAS/C212/MAP/152 Plan of the Town and Borough of Taunton in the county of Somerset 1849. Published by R Ham and J Leversedge, Surveyors, Taunton.

SRO DD/SAS/c795/TN/147 Minute book titled "Judges' Lodgings Taunton", bequeathed to SANHS by Edwin Sloper 1905 with some loose papers (including printed minutes for 1848, 1851).

SRO DD/SAS/c1193/4 John Cannon's manuscript 1684–1742. Published by Money (2010), the omitted topography of Taunton is on pages 137–8 of the original.

SRO DD/SAS/c1207 Nineteenth-century plans of Taunton Castle.

/2a Block plan of castle signed J Houghton Spencer, 1875. Also shows adjacent landowners and has pencilled drainage runs marked north of Castle Lodge.

/2b Detailed ground-floor plan of Taunton Castle showing buildings, with some later drainage works indicated. Many of the courtyard buildings shown were demolished soon after. Signed J Houghton Spencer, 1875.

/2c Detailed upper floor plans and sections of Taunton Castle. Signed and dated in pencil by J Houghton Spencer 1875. The date suggests that this and DD/SAS/c1270/2b were drawn to help SANHS plan works to the building.

/2d Phase-plan showing periods of Taunton Castle buildings, with overall plan of the castle inset. Not signed or dated but based on 2b and in the style of J Houghton Spencer.

/2e Sketch-plan of "Drain opened at the entrance Nov 1891".

/2f Untitled sketch-plan of drainage investigations. Not dated but one investigation marked "Nov 1893". Location of drains shown on 2a to the west of the castle.

/2g Plan of castle at 1:240 by John Leversedge dated 12 September 1853, the original from which the engraving in Warre (1853) was made. Shows some more detail than the engraving and has eight locations numbered in Roman numerals that correspond to eight elevation drawings (SANHS 3515–3517).

SRO DD/SAS/G733/1/1 SANHS. Minutes of the council, committees and some subcommittees, 1878–1895.

SRO DD/SAS/G733/1/2 SANHS. Minutes of the council and committees, 1895–1908.

SRO DD/SAS/G733/1/3 SANHS. Minutes of the council, 1909–1922 and committees 1909–1911.

SRO DD/SAS/G733/1/4 SANHS. Minutes of the council, 1923–1936.

SRO DD/SAS/G733/1/5 SANHS. Minutes of the council, 1937–1974.

SRO DD/SAS/G733/4/1 SANHS. Minutes of the development committee, 1927–1939.

SRO DD/SAS/2015/1 Papers and photographs found during the SANHS office move in 2008. See SANHS Hawtin, SANHS Office file C6 and SANHS photos 1934.

SRO DD/SF/7/6/142 Letter from W Surtees to WA Sandford about problems encountered during the works in the Somerset Room. 1 May 1884.

SRO DD/SP/18/13 Manor of Taunton Deane, lawday court papers, 1627.

SRO DD/SP/64 Petitions to the Steward of Taunton Castle, *c.*1580–1740.

SRO DD/SP/71 Survey of the Manor of Taunton Deane, 1566.

SRO DD/SP/325 Manor and Liberty of Taunton Deane: compotus rolls, 1418–1745.

SRO DD/SP/356 A poorly catalogued collection of mainly late 17th-century legal papers. Includes a draft brief for an action of ejectment from the castle moat, discussed on page 26 and the agreement to sub-contract the keeping of prisoners in 1638, discussed on page 25.

SRO DD/TBL/45 Notebook titled "History: Taunton Grammar School", donated to Taunton Library. The handwriting suggests that this belonged to AT Wicks and was the basis for his paper on the masters of the school (Wicks 1961). It includes transcripts of 17th-century documents addressed to the Warden of New College, Oxford, which remain in the archives there (see NCA 1635/7). Discussed on page 27.

SRO DD/WAT/16 Records relating to archaeological excavations in Taunton, carried out by Western Archaeological Trust/Committee for Rescue Archaeology in Avon, Gloucestershire and Somerset. The archive was prepared following the standards of the Royal Commission on the Historical Monuments of England but has become muddled in the SRO. The original archive section identifiers are used in this text.

- **Ei3** Contains photocopies of Gray's site notebooks.
- **Fii5** Robin Bush's draft text for Bush and Meek (1984) noting where Marion Meek's text should be inserted.
- **Fii10** One of two draft texts for the discussion of burials in Clements (1984) with pencilled changes that were adopted in the published version. Presumably later than Fii11.
- **Fii11** One of two draft texts for the discussion of burials in Clements (1984). Probably earlier than Fii10.

SRO DD/X/VNL/1 Photocopy of Cartulary of Roger Hill of Poundisford Park, compiled 1653–57 with later additions made *c.*1670. Discussed on page 26.

SRO DD/X/WA/5 Agreement between Roger Hill and burgesses of Taunton for the use of the Great Hall for 10s a year. 25 August 1656. Discussed on page 274.

SRO L/2205 Bound photocopies of Edward Jeboult's scrapbook entitled *The History of the Town of Taunton in the County of Somerset illustrated by 500 photographs*. Dated 1866. Photocopied in the 1980s and the original returned to the owners. The photocopies are poor quality but the plates were photographed – see Museum M1191 and SRO T/PH/REA/3.

SRO M2-801 Uncatalogued microfilm copy of Somerset County Council Architect's Department drawing CB71 E20, Taunton Castle: Extension of Oil Pipe Through Courtyard. October 1963. Discussed on page 51.

SRO Q/AC/2 Contract for the re-roofing of the Great Hall in 1816. Discussed on page 30.

SRO Q/AC/3 Plan of Richard Carver's proposed alterations to Great Hall to improve the assizes court in 1833. They were never carried out and the courts subsequently moved out of the castle. The plan does provide some evidence, in the form of proposed alterations, for the doors in the then existing structure. Also a block plan of Castle Green dated October 1832 showing properties and ownerships, which has pencilled additions showing proposed land purchases for the scheme.

SRO Q/RRW/1 Correspondence, with copies of return of the Clerk of the Peace of places of worship of Protestant Dissenters, stating owner of house, parish and date of registration at the Quarter Sessions (from 1689-1845).

SRO T/PH/REA/3 Copies of photographs of the Taunton area by Edward Jeboult. See SRO L/2205. *c.*1865. The negatives are Museum M1191. Seven show the castle:

- **/12** Castle Bow from the east.
- **/52** South Range from across Castle Green.
- **/53** The South Range and Round Tower before the latest moat infilling.
- **/54** The North end of the West Range.
- **/55** Photograph of a sketch. Titled "Remains of Stephen's castle". Unlocated but possibly the east side behind North Street.
- **/82** The School. Titled "Taunton College" and dated 1865.
- **/83** Photograph of an ink drawing of the school, unusually looking east.
- **/91** The Castle Hotel and Castle Bow from the west.

SRO T/PH/win/1 Manor of Taunton (compotus rolls) – Winchester Accounts, 1209–1545.

In the Somerset Studies Library

LEJ Brooke collection A collection of photographs and notes donated to the library by LEJ Brooke. Several are prints from SANHS negatives but the source of others is unknown.

In the project archive

Joel A set of photographs of the keep garden area taken in the winter (by the leafless trees) of 1932/3 as they show the Wyndham Block which opened on 1 June 1932 (Gray 1932, xxi–xxii) and must have been taken before the landscaping of the area which took place in the spring of 1933 (SANHS minutes: 5/4/1933). They are known from photographs of the original prints, which can be seen to have been in an album, that were found in the Somerset Historic Environment Record in an envelope annotated "Castle Keep Excavations. 20 photographs b/w. Copies of originals in custody of Castle Hotel". The original album could not be found by the hotel in 2009. By coincidence, however, a visitor to the museum in 2007 from Hertfordshire loaned a set of old photographs of Taunton for copying which included copies of those of the garden area. These were marked on the reverse, with glued labels, "Photograph by Humphrey and Vera Joel, Drydon Cottage, Radlett. Tel. Radlett 147" and contained additional photographs of the Castle Hotel and some other places in Taunton. It seems unlikely that the Joels would have been brought specially from Hertfordshire to photograph the ruins but they may have photographed the hotel speculatively with a view to selling the pictures and then been asked to photograph the excavated area.

The Somerset HER photographs comprise 20 prints (including one duplicate) together with two sheets of contact prints. The contact prints show 50 frames whose numbers indicate three strips of film. They show that between one and four shots were taken of each album print and also that two album photos are missing from the printed set. The prints have been assigned arbitrary numbers (1–20) and the two additions from the contact prints numbered 21 and 22. There are 22 photographs in the Hertfordshire set, of which 14 correspond to the HER photos. Of the remaining eight, six are additional photographs of the Castle Hotel and one is of a bathing hut. There is one photograph of the ruins that is not in the HER set (here numbered 23) and all are of a much higher quality than the HER "photos-of-photos".

Bibliography

Alcock, NW. 1968. Devon Farmhouses, Part I. *Report and Transactions of the Devonshire Association*, **100**, 13–28.

Allan, JP. 1984. *Medieval and Post-Medieval Finds from Exeter, 1971–1980*. Exeter: Exeter City Council and University of Exeter.

Allan, J[P], Dawson, D and Kent, O. 2015. Post-Roman pottery. In Gilchrist and Green (2015), 250–78.

Allan, J[P], Horner, B and Langman, G. 2005. Seventeenth- and eighteenth-century pottery waste from the Stella Maris convent school site, Bideford. *Proceedings of the Devon Archaeological Society*, **63**, 167–203.

Allan, J[P], Hughes, MJ and Taylor, RT. 2011. Saxo-Norman pottery in Somerset: some recent research. *Somerset Archaeology and Natural History*, **154**, 165–84.

Allen, T[G]. 2002. Discussion. In Allen and Hiller (2002), 201–26.

Allen, TG and Hiller, J. 2002. *The Excavation of a Medieval Manor House of the Bishops of Winchester at Mount House, Witney, Oxfordshire, 1984-92*. Thames Valley Landscapes Monograph 13. Oxford: Oxford Archaeology.

Andersen, JC, Rollinson, GK and Dawson, DP. in press. Visualisation, quantitative methodology and matrix-inclusion separation of pottery using QEMSCAN: examples of medieval and post-medieval pottery from Somerset. In Sibbesson, E, Jervis, B and Coxon, S (eds) *Insight from Innovation: New Light on Archaeological Ceramics. Papers in honour of Professor David Peacock*. Southampton: Highfield Press.

Anon. 1878. The annual report. *Somerset Archaeology and Natural History*, **24**, 4–5.

Anon. 1883. The annual report. *Somerset Archaeology and Natural History*, **29**, 2–3.

Anon. 1884. The annual report. *Somerset Archaeology and Natural History*, **30**, 1–4.

Anon. 1885. The annual report. *Somerset Archaeology and Natural History*, **31**, 1–3.

Anon. 1905. The annual report. *Somerset Archaeology and Natural History*, **50**, 2–8.

Anon. 1910. Corrigenda and addendum. *Somerset Archaeology and Natural History*, **56**. Addendum to Spencer (1910).

Anon. 1930-32. Amaury de Montfort. *Notes and Queries for Somerset and Dorset*, **20**, 64–65.

Anon. 1952. The annual report. *Somerset Archaeology and Natural History*, **97**, 2–8.

Anon. 1953. Annual general meeting and excursions. *Somerset Archaeology and Natural History*, **98**, 1–3.

Anon (ed). 1954. *Notes on the History of Taunton Castle*. Somerset Archaeological and Natural History Society.

Anon. 1954/55. Abstract of proceedings: report of the council for 1955. *Somerset Archaeology and Natural History*, **99/100**, 5.

Anon. 1957/8. Report of the council for the year 1957. *Somerset Archaeology and Natural History*, **101/102**, 7–8.

Armitage Robinson, J. 1924. A visit to Glastonbury in 1635. *Notes and Queries for Somerset and Dorset*, **19**, 268–274.

Barker, L. 2006. *Castell Malgwyn Tinplate Works*. Unpublished RCAHMW survey report. Aberystwyth: Royal Commission on the Ancient and Historical Monuments of Wales.

Barker, PA and Higham, RA. 1982. *Hen Domen, Montgomery: A Timber Castle on the English-Welsh Border*. London: Royal Archaeological Institute.

Barrowman, RC, Batey, CE and Morris, CD. 2007. *Excavations at Tintagel Castle, Cornwall 1990–1999*. Society of Antiquaries Monograph Series. London: Society of Antiquaries of London.

Barstow, HG. 1998. *1208/9 Pipe Roll of the Bishopric of Winchester: A Translation*. Privately published.

Barton, KJ. 1961. Some evidence of two types of pottery manufactured in Bristol in the early 18th century. *Transactions of the Bristol and Gloucestershire Archaeological Society*, **80**, 160–68.

Barton, KJ. 1963. A medieval pottery kiln at Ham Green, Bristol. *Transactions of the Bristol and Gloucestershire Archaeological Society*, **82**, 92–126.

Barton, KJ. 1966. Medieval pottery from Rouen. *Archaeological Journal*, **122**, 73–85.

Basso, E, Capelli, C, Riccardi, MP and Cabella, R. 2008. A particular temper: mineralogical and petrographic characterisation of ceramic fabrics with glauconitic inclusions. *ArchaeoSciences, Revue de Archaeometrie*, **32**, 93–97.

Bates, EH. 1900. The Particular Description of the County of Somerset. Drawn up by Thomas Gerard of Trent 1633. *Somerset Record Society*, **15**.

Batten, EC. 1876. Henry VII in Somersetshire. *Somerset Archaeology and Natural History*, **25**, 49–79.

Baxter, R. 2010. *Castle House, Taunton: Beakhead Arch in Room TCB 118*. Unpublished report of visit in December 2010. Copy in project archive.

Bennett, J. 1984. No 1 High Street, excavations 1974. In Leach (1984a), 91–98.

Bentley, J. 1987. Robert Anstice: Somerset's first county surveyor. *Somerset Industrial Archaeology Society Bulletin*, **46**, 10–15.

Biddle, M. 1969. Wolvesey: the *domus quasi palatium* of Henry de Blois in Winchester. *Chateau Gaillard*, **3**, 29–38.

Biddle, M. 1986. *Wolvesey: The Old Bishop's Palace, Winchester*. London: Historic Buildings and Monuments Commission for England.

Billingsley, J. 1794. *General View of the Agriculture in the County of Somerset*. London: W Smith.

Bird, WHB (ed). 1907. *Calendar of the Manuscripts of the Dean and Chapter of Wells*, volume 1. London: Historical Manuscripts Commission.

Blair, J. 1992. Anglo-Saxon minsters: a topographical review. In *Pastoral Care before the Parish*, 226–66. Leicester University Press.

Blair, J. 1996. Palaces or minsters? Northampton and Cheddar reconsidered. *Anglo-Saxon England*, **25**, 97–121.

Blair, J. 2002. The evidence of the Winchester pipe rolls, 1208–1398. In Allen and Hiller (2002), 193–97.

Blair, J. 2005. *The Church in Anglo-Saxon England*. Oxford University Press.

Blaylock, SR. 2004. *Bowhill: The Archaeological Study of a Building under Repair in Exeter, Devon, 1977-1995*. English Heritage Archaeological Monograph/Exeter Archaeological Reports 5. Swindon: English Heritage.

Boore, E and Pearson, T. 2010. Red earthenware pottery from the Chandos glass cone, Bridgwater. *Somerset Archaeology and Natural History*, **153**, 131–50.

Boow, J. 1991. *Early Australian Commercial Glass: Manufacturing Processes*. Sydney: Heritage Council of New South Wales.

Bradbury, J and Croft, RA. 1989. Somerset Archaeology 1989. *Somerset Archaeology and Natural History*, **133**, 157–185.

Bramble, JR. 1899. Report of the council. *Somerset Archaeology and Natural History*, **45**, 2–6.

Brears, PCD. 1971. *English Country Pottery: Its History and Techniques*. Newton Abbot: David and Charles.

Bridge, M[C]. 2010. *The Tree-Ring Dating of Timbers from Castle House, Taunton Castle, Somerset*. Unpublished Oxford Dendrochronology Laboratory report. Copy in Somerset HER (PRN 26765).

Bridge, MC. 2012. *The Tree-Ring Dating of the Roof of the Old Municipal Buildings, Taunton*. Unpublished Oxford Dendrochronology Laboratory report. Copy in Somerset HER (PRN 44203).

Brigers, JL. 2013a. *Report on the Results of an Archaeological Watching Brief Conducted during the Restoration and Conversion of Castle House, Castle Green, Taunton, Somerset*. Unpublished report. Copy in Somerset HER (PRN 32040).

Brigers, JL. 2013b. *Report on the Results of an Archaeological Watching Brief to the West of the Castle Hotel. Castle Green, Taunton, Somerset*. Unpublished report. Copy in Somerset HER (PRN 31973).

Brigers, JL. 2016. *Taunton Castle Courtyard, Taunton, Somerset: The Results of an Archaeological Watching Brief*. Unpublished report. Copy in Somerset HER (PRN 34762).

Brodie, A. 2011. *Arthur's Hall, Dover Castle, Kent: Analysis of the Building*. Research Department Report Series 40-11. English Heritage.

Bronk Ramsey, C. 2009. Bayesian analysis of radiocarbon dates. *Radiocarbon*, **51**(1), 337–360.

Broomhead, RA. 1999. *Millers Wine Bar, Mill Lane, Taunton*. Unpublished report in Somerset HER (PRN 44698).

Brothwell, DR. 1981. *Digging up Bones*. Ithaca, New York: Cornell University Press.

Brown, RA and Colvin, HM. 1963. The Royal Castles 1066–1485. In Brown, RA, Colvin, HM and Taylor, AJ (eds) *The History of the King's Works: The Middle Ages*, 553–894. London: HMSO. Two volumes.

Burke, JB. 1853. *A Genealogical and Heraldic Dictionary of the Landed Gentry of Great Britain and Ireland for 1853*. Hurst and Blackett.

Burrow, C. 1988. The Pottery Report. In Burrow, I (1988), 95–164.

Burrow, I. 1984. Excavations at Mill Lane, 1980: the castle moat and associated features. In Leach (1984a), 53–58.

Burrow, I. 1988. Excavations at 5–8 Fore Street, Taunton, 1979. *Somerset Archaeology and Natural History*, **132**, 95–164.

Burrow, I and Dennison, E. 1988. Excavations and recording in Taunton and Wellington, 1982-5. *Somerset Archaeology and Natural History*, **132**, 165–180.

Busch, J. 1987. Second time around: a look at bottle reuse. *Historical Archaeology*, **21**, 67–80.

Bush, R[JE]. 1977. *The Book of Taunton: The Story of a County Town*. Chesham: Barracuda Books.

Bush, RJE. 1983. *Jeboult's Taunton: A Victorian Retrospect*. Buckingham: Barracuda Books.

Bush, RJE. 1984. The priory of St Peter and St Paul. In Leach (1984a), 104–6.

Bush, RJE and Aston, M. 1984. The town; history and topography. In Leach (1984a), 75–79.

Bush, RJE and Meek, M. 1984. The castle: history and documentation. In Leach (1984a), 11–16.

Casimiro, TM. 2015. Portuguese faience in south-west England. In Allan, J, Alcock, N and Dawson, D (eds) *West Country Households*, Society for Post-medieval Archaeology monograph 9, 339–355. Woodbridge: Boydell.

Chapman, JBW (ed). 1930. *Calendar of the Liberate Rolls preserved in the Public Record Office, Henry III, Vol 2, 1240–1245*. London: HMSO.

Charity Commission. 1894. *The Reports of the Commissioners (Commonly known as Lord Brougham's Commission), Appointed in Pursuance of Various Acts of Parliament, to Enquire Concerning Charities in England and Wales, relating to the County of Somersetshire 1819–1837*. London: PS King and Son.

Charles-Edwards, TM. 2013. *Wales and the Britons 350 –1064*. Oxford: Oxford University Press.

Cherry, B and Pevsner, N. 1989. *The Buildings of England: Devon*. Penguin.

Clark, GT. 1872. Taunton Castle: with some remarks upon ancient military earthworks. *Somerset Archaeology and Natural History*, **18**, 60–76.

Clark, GT. 1884. *Mediaeval Military Architecture in England*. London: Wyman and Sons. Two vols.

Clements, CF. 1973. *Castle Green Car Park, Taunton: A Rescue Excavation in January 1973*. Unpublished typescript in Somerset HER (PRN 12283).

Clements, CF. 1984. The inner ward and outer bailey: burials and structures exposed in the 1970s. In Leach (1984a), 26–36.

Clements, C[F]. nd. The Keep: Some features of the west face of the west wall. Unpublished typescript for, but not used in, Leach (1984c). Not dated but c.1975. Copies in Western Archaeological Trust archive Fi2. (SRO DD/WAT/16).

Cockburn, JS. 1971. Somerset Assize Orders, 1640–1659. *Somerset Record Society*, **71**.

Cohen, A and Serjeantson, D. 1996. *A Manual for the Identification of Bird Bones from Archaeological Sites*. London: Archetype Publications.

Coleman-Smith, R. 2002. Excavations in the Donyatt Potteries: Site 13. *Post-Medieval Archaeology*, **36**, 118–72.

Coleman-Smith, R and Pearson, T. 1970. *Excavations at Donyatt and Nether Stowey: Interim Report*. Southampton.

Coleman-Smith, R and Pearson, T. 1988. *Excavations in the Donyatt Potteries*. Chichester: Phillimore.

Costen, M. 2011. *Anglo-Saxon Somerset*. Oxford: Oxbow.

Crawford, OGS. 1944. Bitterne after the Romans. *Proceedings of the Hampshire Field Club*, **16**, 148–55.

Creighton, O[H]. 2002. *Castles and Landscapes: Power, Community and Fortification in Medieval England*. London: Continuum.

Croft, RA. 1988. *Taunton Castle, Western Round Tower: Archaeological Watching Brief*. Unpublished typescript report in Somerset HER (PRN 16778).

Croft, RA. 1989. Taunton, St Paul's House. *Somerset Archaeology and Natural History*, **133**, 178.

Crook, D. 2004. Raleigh , William of (d. 1250). In *Oxford Dictionary of National Biography*. Oxford University Press. Online at http://www.oxforddnb.com/view/article/23042. Accessed 23 March 2014.

Currie, CRJ. 1992. Larger medieval houses in the Vale of the White Horse. *Oxoniensia*, **57**, 81–244.

Davis, SJM. 1992. *A Rapid Method for Recording Information about Mammal Bones from Archaeological Sites*. Ancient Monuments Laboratory Report No. 19/92.

Davis, V. 2004. Waynflete, William (*c*.1400–1486). In *Oxford Dictionary of National Biography*. Oxford: Oxford University Press. Online at http://www.oxforddnb.com/view/article/28907. Accessed 21 April 2014.

Davis, V. 2007. *William Wykeham*. London: Hambledon Continuum.

Davison, BK. 1972. Castle Neroche: an abandoned Norman fortress in south Somerset. *Somerset Archaeology and Natural History*, **116**, 16–58.

Davison, BK. 2001. *Sherborne Old Castle*. London: English Heritage.

Dawson, DP. 1979a. Notes on Bristol yellow slipwares. In Pearson (1979), 204.

Dawson, DP. 1979b. Notes on wasters of mottled wares found in Bristol. In Pearson (1979), 206.

Dawson, DP, Jackson, RG and Ponsford, MW. 1972. Medieval kiln-wasters from St Peter's Church, Bristol. *Transactions of the Bristol and Gloucestershire Archaeological Society*, **91**, 159–67.

Dawson, D[P] and Kent, O. 1999. Reduction fired low-temperature ceramics. *Post-Medieval Archaeology*, **33**, 164–78.

Dawson, D[P] and Kent, O. 2008a. Animated prospect: an 18th-century kiln at the Pottery House in the Old Park, Dunster, Somerset. In Finch, JC and Giles, K (eds) *Post-Medieval Estate Landscapes: Design, Improvement and Power*, Society for Post-Medieval Archaeology monograph 4, 95–112. Woodbridge: Boydell and Brewer.

Dawson, D[P] and Kent, O. 2008b. Wincanton, Ireson Cottage. *Somerset Archaeology and Natural History*, **151**, 243.

Dawson, D[P], Langdon, M, Murless, B, Ponsford, M and Webster, CJ. 2001. Archaeology and the M5 motorway: the gazetteer of sites in Somerset. *Somerset Archaeology and Natural History*, **145**, 39–51.

Dixon, P and Marshall, P. 1993. The great tower in the twelfth century: the case of Norham Castle. *Archaeological Journal*, **150**, 410–432.

DoE. 1975. *Tenth List of Buildings of Special Architectural or Historic Interest: District of Taunton Deane (Somerset)*. London: HMSO for Department of the Environment.

Draper, J. 1982. An 18th-century kiln at Hole Common, Lyme Regis, Dorset. *Proceedings of the Dorset Natural History and Archaeological Society*, **104**, 137–42.

Drinkwater, N. 1964. The Old Deanery, Salisbury. *Antiquaries Journal*, **44**, 41–59.

Dunning, RW. 1985. Nether Stowey. In Dunning, RW (ed) *The Victoria History of Somerset*, volume 5, 190–200. London: Institute of Historical Research.

Dunning, RW. not dated. *A History of the Old Municipal Buildings*.

Dunning, RW and Siraut, MC. 1999. Wincanton. In Dunning, RW (ed) *The Victoria History of England: Somerset*, volume VII, 208–32. Oxford University Press.

Dyer, MJ. 1998. *Archaeological Observations at the Winchester Arms, Taunton*. Unpublished Exeter Archaeology report in Somerset HER (PRN 44681).

Edwards, N (ed). 2009. *The Archaeology of the Early Medieval Celtic Churches*. Leeds: Maney.

Ellis, P (ed). 2000. *Ludgershall Castle: Excavations by Peter Addyman 1964-1972*. Devizes: Wiltshire Archaeological and Natural History Society.

Emery, A. 1970. *Dartington Hall*. Oxford: Oxford University Press.

Exeter Archaeology. 1999. *Archaeological Recording at the Castle Hotel, Taunton*. Unpublished Exeter Archaeology report. Copy in Somerset HER (PRN 44680).

Faulkner, PA. 1963. Haddon Hall and Bolsover Castle. *Archaeological Journal*, **118**, 188–205.

Fletcher, JM. 1979. The Bishop of Winchester's medieval manor house at Harwell, Berkshire, and its relevance in the evolution of timber-framed aisled halls. *Archaeological Journal*, **136**, 173–192.

Fox, CH. 1875. *Memorials, Descriptive and Historical of Taunton Castle*. Taunton: Frederick May.

Gaimster, D. 1997. *German Stoneware 1200–1900: Archaeology and Cultural History*. London: British Museum.

Gathercole, C. 1998. *English Heritage Extensive Urban Survey: Taunton*. Limited circulation Somerset County Council report for English Heritage.

Gilchrist, R. 1999. *Gender and Archaeology: Contesting the Past*. London: Routledge.

Gilchrist, R. 2013. Courtenay Arthur Ralegh Radford. In *Biographical Memoirs of Fellows of the British Academy, XII*, 341–358. British Academy.

Gilchrist, R and Green, C. 2015. *Glastonbury Abbey: Archaeological Excavations 1904–79*. London: Society of Antiquaries of London.

Good, GL. 1987. The excavation of two docks at Narrow Quay, Bristol, 1978–9. *Post-Medieval Archaeology*, **21**, 25–126.

Good, GL and Russett, VEJ. 1987. Common types of earthenware found in the Bristol area. *Bristol and Avon Archaeology*, **6**, 35–43.

Goodman, AW (ed). 1927. *Chartulary of Winchester Cathedral*. Winchester: Warren and Son.

Grant, A. 1982. The use of tooth wear as a guide to the age of domestic animals. In Wilson, B, Grigson, C and Payne, S (eds) *Ageing and Sexing Animal Bones from Archaeological Sites*, BAR British Series 109, 91–108. Oxford: British Archaeological Reports.

Gray, H St G. 1903. Excavations at Castle Neroche, Somerset, June–July 1903. *Somerset Archaeology and Natural History*, **49**, 23–53.

Gray, H St G. 1907. Provincial Museums I: Taunton Castle. *The Expert*, 91–3. 8 July.

Gray, H St G. 1928a. The annual report. *Somerset Archaeology and Natural History*, **74**, xiv–xix.

Gray, H St G. 1928b. Report of the curator of the Somerset County Museum from July 13 1927 to July 17 (annual meeting) 1928. *Somerset Archaeology and Natural History*, **74**, liv–lvi.

Gray, H St G. 1929a. The annual report. *Somerset Archaeology and Natural History*, **75**, xvi–xx.

Gray, H St G. 1929b. Report of the curator of the Somerset County Museum from July 18 1928 to July 19 (annual meeting) 1929. *Somerset Archaeology and Natural History*, **75**, lxiii–lxv.

Gray, H St G. 1930a. The annual report. *Somerset Archaeology and Natural History*, **76**, xviii–xxi.

Gray, H St G. 1930b. A medieval spoon found at Taunton Castle. *Antiquaries Journal*, **10**, 156–58.

Gray, H St G. 1931. The annual report. *Somerset Archaeology and Natural History*, **77**, xxix–xxxiii.

Gray, H St G. 1932. The annual report. *Somerset Archaeology and Natural History*, **78**, xx–xxiv.

Gray, H St G. 1933. The annual report. *Somerset Archaeology and Natural History*, **79**, xxii–xxvii.

Gray, H St G. 1934. The annual report. *Somerset Archaeology and Natural History*, **81**, xiv–xviii.

Gray, H St G. 1937. The annual report. *Somerset Archaeology and Natural History*, **83**, 11–15.

Gray, H St G. 1940. Additions to the museum from 12 July 1939 to 15 July 1940. *Somerset Archaeology and Natural History*, **86**, 18–29.

Gray, H St G. 1941. Corbel, etc, found at Taunton Castle. *Antiquaries Journal*, **21**, 67–68.

Gray, H St G. 1942. Wilton families and worthies. *Somerset Archaeology and Natural History*, **88**, 17–24.

Gray, H St G. 1948–9. The annual report. *Somerset Archaeology and Natural History*, **94**, 19–23.

Green, E. 1879. The siege and defence of Taunton, 1644–5. *Somerset Archaeology and Natural History*, **25**, 33–48.

Green, MAE (ed). 1861. *Calendar of State Papers, Domestic Series, of the Reign of Charles II 1661–1662 preserved in the State Papers Department of Her Majesty's Public Record Office*. London: Longman, Green, Longman and Roberts.

Greene, JP. 1992. *Medieval Monasteries*. London: Continuum.

Greenway, D (ed). 1996. *Henry, Archdeacon of Huntingdon: Historia Anglorum (History of the English People)*. Oxford: Clarendon Press.

Haines, RM (ed). 2010. *The Register of John de Stratford, Bishop of Winchester, 1323–1333*, volume 1. Surrey Record Society.

Hall, H (ed). 1903. *The Pipe Roll of the Bishopric of Winchester 1208–9*. London: London School of Economics and Political Science.

Hall, T. 2000. *Minster Churches in the Dorset Landscape*. BAR British Series 204. Oxford: British Archaeological Reports.

Hall, T. 2004. The reformation of the British church in the West Country in the 7th century. In Ecclestone, M, Gardner, K and Holbrook, N (eds) *Land of the Dobunni*, 49–55. King's Lynn: Heritage Marketing and Publications.

Hall, T. 2005. Sherborne: Saxon Christianity *be Westanwuda*. In Barker, K, Hinton, D and Hunt, A (eds) *Saint Wulfsige and Sherborne: Essays to Celebrate the Millennium of the Benedictine Abbey, 998–1998*, 133–148. Oxford: Oxbow.

Hall, T. 2009. Identifying British Christian sites in western Wessex. In Edwards (2009), 155–171.

Hallam, AD. 1965. Further excavations at Taunton Castle, 1964. *Somerset Archaeology and Natural History*, **109**, 98–103.

Halstead, P. 1985. A study of mandibular teeth from Romano-British contexts at Maxey. In Pryor, F and French, C (eds) *Archaeology and Environment in the Lower Welland Valley, Volume 1*, EAA 27. East Anglian Archaeology.

Hambleton, E. 1999. *Animal Husbandry Regimes in Iron Age Britain: A Comparative Analysis of Faunal Assemblages from British Iron Age Sites*. BAR British Series 282. Oxford: British Archaeological Reports.

Harbin, EHB. 1912. Quarter Sessions Records for the County of Somerset. Vol. 3. Commonwealth 1646–1660. *Somerset Record Society*, **28**.

Hare, JN. 1987. *Bishop's Waltham Palace*. London: Historic Buildings and Monuments Commission for England.

Hare, JN. 1988. Bishop's Waltham Palace, Hampshire: William of Wykeham, Henry Beaufort and the transformation of a medieval episcopal palace. *Archaeological Journal*, **145**, 222–254.

Hase, PH. 1994. The church in the Wessex heartlands. In Aston, M and Lewis, C (eds) *The Medieval Landscape of Wessex*, 47–81. Oxford: Oxbow.

Hassall, C. 2010. *Taunton Castle: Adam Library*. Unpublished report in project archive.

Hawkes, J. 1992. *Taunton Castle Proposed Lift Shaft: Archaeological Evaluation*. Unpublished AC Archaeology report in Somerset HER (PRN 11592).

Hearnshaw, FJC. 1934. Foreword. In Whitty (1934), ix–x.

Higbee, L. 2001. *Archaeological Excavations at CRS Yard, Magdalene Street, Taunton*. Unpublished Exeter Archaeology report. Copy in Somerset HER (PRN 57136).

Higgins, DA and Davey, PJ. 2004. Appendix 4: draft guidelines for using the clay tobacco pipe record sheets. In White (2004).

Higham, R and Barker, P. 1992. *Timber Castles*. London: Batsford.

Higham, R and Barker, P. 2000. *Hen Domen, Montgomery: A Timber Caste on the English-Welsh Border*. Liverpool: Liverpool University Press.

Hinchliffe, J. 1984. Excavations at Canon Street 1977. In Leach (1984a).

Hollinrake, C and Hollinrake, N. 1992a. *The Courtyard, Inner Ward, Taunton Castle. TC92*. Unpublished report. Copy in Somerset HER (PRN 18247).

Hollinrake, C and Hollinrake, N. 1992b. *The Courtyard, Taunton Castle. TCII 92*. Unpublished report. Copy in Somerset HER (PRN 18226).

Holmes, TS. 1911a. Religious houses. In Page, W (ed) *The Victoria History of Somerset*, 68–172. London: Constable.

Holmes, TS. 1911b. Schools. In Page, W (ed) *The Victoria History of Somerset*, 435–66. London: Constable.

Holt, NR (ed). 1964. *The Pipe Roll of the Bishopric of Winchester 1210–11*. Manchester: University of Manchester.

Houlbrooke, R. 2008. Horne, Robert (1513 ×1515–1579). In *Oxford Dictionary of National Biography*. Oxford: Oxford University Press. Online at http://www.oxforddnb.com/view/article/13792. Accessed 19 February 2013.

HPP. 1923. Lionel St George Gray: an appreciation. *The Western Gazette*. 5 October.

Hudson, H. 1993. Wedmore, The Borough. *Somerset Archaeology and Natural History*, **137**, 147.

Hunt, TJ. 1958. *The Ordination of the Vicarage of St Mary Magdalene*. Taunton: Hammett and Co.

Hunt, TJ. 1964. *A Brief History of Taunton Castle*. Somerset County Museum.

Hunt, TJ. 1971. Some 13th-century building accounts for Taunton Castle. *Somerset Archaeology and Natural History*, **115**, 39–44.

Hunt, W. 1875. Report of the council. *Somerset Archaeology and Natural History*, **21**, 2–7.

IGI. 2012. International Genealogical Index. Online at http://www.familysearch.org.

Impey, E. 1999. The seigneurial residence in Normandy 1125–1225: an Anglo-Norman tradition? *Medieval Archaeology*, **43**, 45–73.

James, BLl. 2004. Clark, George Thomas (1809–1898). In *Oxford Dictionary of National Biography*. Oxford: Oxford University Press. Online at http://www.oxforddnb.com/view/article/5461. Accessed 3 June 2013.

James, TB and Robinson, AM. 1988. *Clarendon Palace: The History and Archaeology of a Medieval Palace and Hunting Lodge near Salisbury, Wiltshire*. London: Society of Antiquaries.

Jeboult, E. 1873. *A General Account of West Somerset, Description of the Valley of the Tone and the History of the Town of Taunton. Part 3: The Towns of West Somerset: Taunton*. Taunton: Somerset and Bristol Steam Press.

Jeboult, E. 1893. *A Popular History of West Somerset: with a description of its principal towns, rivers, hills, moors; natural and manufactured productions; past and present habits of the people; area, population and value of parishes; and other interesting information*. Privately printed, 2nd edition.

Jeffries, II. 1969. The assize hall, Taunton Castle, in the early 19th century. In Collis, I P (ed) *Somerset Historical Studies: Essays on Aspects of Somerset History Compiled from Local Records by Members of a University Extra-Mural Course held at the Somerset County Record Office*. Bristol: University of Bristol.

Johnson, GR. 1975. *A Catalogue of Human Skeletal Remains found in and around the Castle Grounds, Taunton*. Unpublished typescript of 1973, updated in 1975. Copy in SRO WAT/16.

Johnson, M. 2002. *Behind the Castle Gate: From Medieval to Renaissance*. Abingdon: Routledge.

Jones, DM (ed). 2011. *Archaeological Evidence for Glassworking: Guidelines for Best Practice*. Swindon: English Heritage.

Jones, J. 2008. *Assessment of a Bulk Sample from Taunton Castle*. Unpublished report in site archive.

Katz, D and Suchey, JM. 1986. Age determination of the male os pubis. *American Journal of Physical Anthropology*, **69**, 427–35.

Kenyon, J R. 1990. *Medieval Fortifications*. London: Continuum.

Keynes, S. 1994. The West Saxon charters of King Æthelwulf and his sons. *English Historical Review*, **109**, 1150–1173.

Keynes, S and Lapidge, M. 1983. *Alfred the Great: Asser's* Life of King Alfred *and Other Contemporary Sources*. London: Penguin.

King, DJC and Renn, DF. 1971. Lidelea Castle: a suggested identification. *Antiquaries Journal*, **51**, 301–3.

Lauwerier, RCGM. 1988. *Animals in Roman Times in the Dutch Eastern River Area*. Nederlanse Oudheden 12. Amersfoort: ROB.

le Patourel, J. 1968. Documentary evidence for the pottery industry. *Medieval Archaeology*, **12**, 101–26.

Leach, P[J] (ed). 1984a. *The Archaeology of Taunton: Excavations and Fieldwork to 1980*. Western Archaeological Trust.

Leach, PJ. 1984b. Hawke's Yard, excavations 1977. In Leach (1984a), 65–73.

Leach, PJ. 1984c. The Priory Barn 1977–78. In Leach (1984a), 111–124.

Leach, P[J]. 2005. *Castle Green, Taunton: An Archaeological Watching Brief 2005*. Unpublished report. Copy in Somerset HER (PRN 18220).

Leach, PJ and Pearson, T. 1984. Benham's Garage, excavations 1973–4 and 1978. In Leach (1984a), 37–53.

Lewcun, M. 1985. The Hunt family identified. *Society for Clay Pipe Research Newsletter*, **8**, 14–21.

Lewcun, M. 1988. *Somerset Pipemakers*. Unpublished manuscript in Somerset County Museum.

Lewcun, M. 2007. Clay pipes and other objects. In Gerrard, C and Aston, M (eds) *The Shapwick Project, Somerset: A Rural Landscape Explored*, Monograph 25. Society for Medieval Archaeology.

Liddiard, R. 2005. *Castles in Context: Power, Symbolism and Landscape, 1066 to 1500*. Bollington: Windgather Press.

Lillford, R. 2011. *A Biographical Dictionary of Architects and Surveyors working in Somerset from 1720–1939*. Unpublished draft.

Lindsey, B. 2012. Historic Glass Bottle Identification and Information Website. Online publication at http://www.sha.org/bottle/index.htm Accessed 22/2/2012.

Locke, R (ed). 1816. *The Customs of the Manor of Taunton and Taunton Deane*. Taunton: James Savage. New edition of 1785 original.

Longworth, C. 2004. Buckley Sgraffito: a study of a 17th-century pottery industry in North Wales – its production techniques and design influences. *Internet Archaeology*, **16**(1). Online at http://intarch.ac.uk/journal/issue16/longworth_toc.html. Accessed 9 January 2014.

Lovejoy, CO. 1985. Dental wear in the Libben population: its functional pattern and role in the determination of adult skeletal age at death. *American Journal of Physical Anthropology*, **68**, 47–56.

Luard, HR (ed). 1865. *Annales Monastici*, volume 2. London: Longman, Green, Longman, Roberts and Green.

Mackenzie, WM. 1933–34. Clay castle-building in Scotland. *Proceedings of the Society of Antiquaries of Scotland*, **68**, 117–127.

Macnaghten, A I. 1955. Bitterne Manor House, Southampton: a new lease of life. *Official Architecture and Planning*, 473–76. September.

Marochan, K. 1962. Crews Hole Pottery, St George, Bristol. *Transactions of the Bristol and Gloucestershire Archaeological Society*, **81**, 189–93.

Marten-Holden, L. 2001. Dominion in the landscape: early Norman castles in Suffolk. *History Today*, **51**(4), 46–52.

Mason, C, Milby, S and Tabor, R. 2010. *Four Alls and Castle Moat Chambers, Corporation Street, Taunton, Somerset: An Archaeological Watching Brief and Limited Excavation Assessment Report*. Unpublished Context One Archaeological Services report. Copy in Somerset HER (PRN 30250).

Mayberry, T. 2011. The Portmans. In James, T (ed) *Along the Wild Edge: A Journey Through the Northern Blackdown Hills*, 241–249. Cullompton: Neroche Landscape Partnership Scheme.

McDermott, M. 2007a. *Report on The Old Municipal Buildings, Corporation Street, Taunton*. Unpublished Somerset Vernacular Building Research Group report.

McDermott, M. 2007b. *Somerset Vernacular Buildings Research Group Survey: Castle House, The Castle, Taunton*. Unpublished report.

McNicol, D. 2010. *Former Gasworks site, Tangiers Road, Taunton, Somerset: Archaeological Watching Brief Report*. Unpublished Oxford Archaeology report. Copy in Somerset HER (PRN 28452).

Meindl, RS and Lovejoy, CO. 1985. Ectocranial suture closure: A revised method for the determination of skeletal age at death based on the lateral-anterior sutures. *American Journal of Physical Anthropology*, **68**, 57–66.

Meirion-Jones, G. 2012. The aristocratic residence in the Plantagenet world: halls, chambers and towers. *Archaeologia*, **161**, 1–49.

Milby, S. 2014. *Castle Green/Castle Bow, Taunton, Somerset: A Programme of Archaeological Monitoring and Recording*. Unpublished Context One Archaeological Services report. Copy in Somerset HER (PRN 31519).

Miles, TJ. 1986. The excavation of a Saxon cemetery and part of the Norman castle at North Walk, Barnstaple. *Proceedings of the Devon Archaeological Society*, **44**, 59–84.

Money, J (ed). 2010. *The Chronicles of John Cannon, Excise Officer and Writing Master*. Oxford University Press for the British Academy. Two vols.

Munby, J and Summerson, H. 2002. *Stokesay Castle*. London: English Heritage.

Noël Hume, I. 1961. The glass wine bottle in colonial Virginia. *Journal of Glass Studies*, **3**, 90–117.

Noël Hume, I. 1970. *A Guide to Artifacts of Colonial America*. New York: Alfred A Knopf.

O'Conner, TP. 1989. *Bones from Anglo-Scandinavian Levels at 16-22 Coppergate*. The Archaeology of York 15/3. London: Council for British Archaeology.

Orbach, J and Pevsner, N. 2014. *The Buildings of England: Somerset, South and West*. London: Yale University Press.

Orme, N. 2004. Oldham, Hugh (*c*.1450–1519). In *Oxford Dictionary of National Biography*. Oxford: Oxford University Press. Online at http://www.oxforddnb.com/view/article/20685. Accessed 18 September 2014.

Oswald, A. 1984. The clay pipes. In Allan (1984), 279–93.

Page, M (ed). 1996. *The Pipe Roll of the Bishopric of Winchester 1301–2*. Hampshire Record Series 14. Winchester: Hampshire County Council.

Page, M (ed). 1999. *The Pipe Roll of the Bishopric of Winchester 1409–10*. Hampshire Record Series 16. Winchester: Hampshire County Council.

Page, M. 2002. *The Medieval Bishops of Winchester: Estate, Archive and Administration*. Hampshire Papers 24. Winchester: Hampshire County Council.

Parker, RW. 2014. *Historic Building Survey of The Old Grammar School or Municipal Buildings, Corporation Street, Taunton*. Unpublished report. Copy in Somerset HER (PRN 44204).

Parker, R[W] and Collings, AG. 2006. The historic buildings and tenurial history of No 2 Broadgate, Exeter. *Proceedings of the Devon Archaeological Society*, **64**, 267–342.

Passmore, AJ. 2010. *Archaeological Monitoring of a Geotechnical Investigation at Taunton Caste, Somerset*. Unpublished Exeter Archaeology report. Copy in Somerset HER (PRN 2933).

Passmore, AJ. 2011. *Archaeological Recording of a Gas Main Replacement at Castle Green, Taunton, Somerset*. Unpublished Exeter Archaeology report. Copy in Somerset HER (PRN 28338).

Payne, S. 1973. Kill-off patterns in sheep and goats: the mandibles from Asvan Kale. *Anatolian Studies*, **23**, 281–303.

Payne, S. 1987. Reference codes for wear states in the mandibular cheek teeth of sheep and goats. *Journal of Archaeological Science*, **14**, 609–14.

Payne, S and Bull, G. 1988. Components of variation in measurements of pig bones and teeth, and the use of measurements to distinguish wild from domestic pig remains. *Archaeozoologia*, **2**, 27–65.

Peach, DL. 1995. *Merdone: The History of Hursley Park*. Hursley Park: IBM United Kingdom Laboratories.

Pearson, T. 1979. The contents of a mid eighteenth-century pit from North Petherton, Somerset. *Post-Medieval Archaeology*, **13**, 183–210.

Pearson, T. 1982. The post-Roman pottery. In Leach, P (ed) *Ilchester Volume 1: Excavations 1974–5*. Western Archaeological Trust.

Pearson, T. 1984a. Clay tobacco pipes. In Leach (1984a), 145–51.

Pearson, T. 1984b. The keep: H St George Gray's excavations, a summary. In Leach (1984a), 17–20.

Pearson, T. 1984c. Medieval and post-medieval ceramics in Taunton. In Leach (1984a), 142–4, microfiche I and II.

Pearson, T, Dawson, D and Ponsford, M. 2014. Evidence for 17th-century pottery production at Wrangway, Somerset. *Somerset Archaeology and Natural History*, 81–103.

Petts, D and Turner, S. 2009. Early medieval church groups in Wales and Western England. In Edwards (2009), 281–99.

Pevsner, N. 1958. *The Buildings of England: South and West Somerset*. Penguin.

Phillpotts, C. 1999. The metropolitan palaces of medieval London. *London Archaeologist*, **9**, 47–53.

Platt, C. 2007. Revisionism in castle studies: a caution. *Medieval Archaeology*, **51**, 83–102.

Platt, C and Coleman-Smith, R (eds). 1975. *Excavations in Medieval Southampton, 1953–1969*, volume 2: the finds. Leicester: Leicester University Press.

Pluskowski, A (ed). 2007. *Breaking and Shaping Beastly Bodies: Animals as Material Culture in the Middle Ages*. Oxford: Oxbow Books.

Ponsford, M. 1974. Appendix: Late Saxon pottery from Bristol. In Rahtz (1974), 120–22.

Ponsford, M. 1987. Evidence for the production of pottery in the West Country *c*.950–*c*.1750. In Vyner, B and Wrathmell, S (eds) *Studies in Medieval and Later Pottery in Wales*, 75–91. Cardiff: University College Department of Extra-Mural Studies.

Ponsford, M. 1991. Dendrochronological dates from Dundas Wharf, Bristol, and the dating of Ham Green Ware and other medieval pottery. In Lewis, E (ed) *Custom and Ceramics*, 81–103. Wickham: APE.

Potter, KR and Davis, RHC (eds). 1976. *Gesta Stephani*. Oxford University Press.

Pounds, NJG. 1990. *The Medieval Castle in England and Wales: A Social and Political History*. Cambridge University Press.

Pountney, WJ. 1920. *Old Bristol Potteries*. Bristol: JW Arrowsmith.

Prior, S. 2006. *A Few Well-Positioned Castles: The Norman Art of War*. Stroud: Tempus.

Radford, CAR. 1954. Taunton Castle: Description. In Anon (1954), 13–19.

Radford, CAR and Hallam, AD. 1953. The history of Taunton Castle in the light of recent excavations. *Somerset Archaeology and Natural History*, **98**, 55–96.

Rahtz, P. 1974. Pottery in Somerset, AD 400–600. In Evison, V, Hodges, H and Hurst, JG (eds) *Medieval Pottery from Excavations: Essays presented to Gerald Clough Dunning*, 95–126. London: John Baker.

Rahtz, P. 1979. *The Saxon and Medieval Palaces at Cheddar*. BAR British Series 56. Oxford: British Archaeological Reports.

Rainbird, P. 2015. *Castle Green Enhancement Scheme, Taunton, Somerset: Results of Archaeological Investigations*. Unpublished AC Archaeology report in Somerset HER (PRN 30398).

Reed, SJ and Whiteaway, TE. 2003. *Archaeological Recording of Geotechnical Investigations on the route of Taunton Inner Relief Road, Taunton, Somerset*. Unpublished Exeter Archaeology report. Copy in Somerset HER (PRN 16096).

Reimer, P, Bard, E, Bayliss, A, Beck, J, Blackwell, P, Bronk Ramsey, C, Buck, C, Cheng, H, Edwards, R, Friedrich, M, Grootes, P, Guilderson, T, Haflidason, H, Hajdas, I, Hatté, C, Heaton, T, Hoffmann, D, Hogg, A, Hughen, K, Kaiser, K, Kromer, B, Manning, S, Niu, M, Reimer, R, Richards, D, Scott, E, Southon, J, Staff, R, Turney, C and van der Plicht, J. 2013. IntCal13 and Marine13 radiocarbon age calibration curves 0–50,000 years cal BP. *Radiocarbon*, **55**(4), 1869–1887.

Renn, DF. 1960. The keep of Wareham Castle. *Medieval Archaeology*, **4**, 56–68.

Riall, N. 1994. *Henry of Blois, Bishop of Winchester: A Patron of the Twelfth-Century Renaissance*. Hampshire Papers 5. Winchester: Hampshire County Council.

Riall, N. 2003. The new castles of Henry de Blois as Bishop of Winchester: The case against Farnham, Surrey. *Medieval Archaeology*, **47**, 115–29.

Riall, N. not dated. *A "lost" palace of the bishops of Winchester*. Online at http://www.medievalarchaeology.co.uk/?page_id=233. Accessed 13/10/2011.

Rippon, S. 2006. *Landscape, Community and Colonisation: The North Somerset Levels during the 1st to 2nd Millennia* AD. CBA Research Report 152. York: Council for British Archaeology.

Roberts, C and Manchester, K. 1995. *The Archaeology of Disease*. Ithaca, New York: Cornell University Press.

Roberts, E. 1986. The bishop of Winchester's fishponds in Hampshire, 1150–1440: their development, function and management. *Proceedings of the Hampshire Field Club and Archaeological Society*, **42**, 125–38.

Roberts, E. 1988. The bishop of Winchester's deer parks in Hampshire, 1200–1400. *Proceedings of the Hampshire Field Club and Archaeological Society*, **44**, 67–86.

Roberts, E. 1993a. The bishop of Winchester's fishponds and deerparks. *Proceedings of the Hampshire Field Club and Archaeological Society*, **49**, 229–231.

Roberts, E. 1993b. Hambledon Manor Farm. *Hampshire Field Club Newsletter*, **19**, 21–22.

Roberts, E. 1993c. William of Wykeham's house at East Meon, Hants. *Archaeological Journal*, **150**, 456–481.

Roberts, E. 1995. Overton Court Farm and the late-medieval farmhouses of demesne lessees in Hampshire. *Proceedings of the Hampshire Field Club*, **51**, 89–106.

Roberts, E. 2003. *Hampshire Houses 1250–1700: Their Dating and Development.* Winchester: Hampshire County Council.

Robinson, DM. 1980. *The Geography of the Augustinian Settlement.* BAR British Series 80. Oxford: British Archaeological Reports. Two vols.

Rodwell, W. 1978. *CRAAGS Report to the SANHS: A Survey of the Keep of Taunton Castle, Somerset.* Unpublished typescript report in project archive.

Rodwell, W. 1984a. The keep and adjacent remains: field survey 1977–78. In Leach (1984a), 20–26.

Rodwell, W. 1984b. A Romanesque stone head from Taunton Castle. In Leach (1984a), 138–140.

Rogers, J. 1984. Human remains from Taunton Castle. In Leach (1984a), 200–201.

Salzman, LF. 1952. *Building in England down to 1540.* Oxford: Oxford University Press. Corrected edition 1967.

Savage, J. 1822. *The History of Taunton in the County of Somerset: Originally written by the late Joshua Toulmin. A new edition greatly enlarged and brought down to the present time.* Taunton: J Poole. Revision of Toulmin (1791).

Sawyer, PH. 1968. *Anglo-Saxon Charters: An Annotated List and Bibliography.* London: Royal Historical Society.

Seaby, WA. 1950. The annual report. *Somerset Archaeology and Natural History*, **95**, 1–7.

Seaby, WA. 1951. The annual report. *Somerset Archaeology and Natural History*, **96**, 1–7.

Seeley, D, Phillpotts, C and Samuel, M. 2006. *Winchester Palace: Excavations at the Southwark Residence of the Bishops of Winchester.* MoLAS monograph 31. London: Museum of London.

Serjeantson, D. 1996. The animal bone. In Needham, S and Spence, T (eds) *Refuse and Disposal at Area 16 East Runnymede: Runnymede Bridge Research Excavations. Volume 2*, 194–224. London: British Museum.

Serjeantson, D. 2002. Goose husbandry in medieval England, and the problem of ageing goose bones. *Actazoologica Cracoviensia*, **45**, 39–54.

Sheridan, A, Schulting, R, Quinnell, H and Taylor, R. 2008. Revisiting a small passage tomb at Broadsands, Devon. *Proceedings of the Devon Archaeological Society*, **66**, 1–26.

Shoesmith, R. 1980. *Excavations at Castle Green, Hereford.* CBA Research Report 36. London: Council for British Archaeology.

Slader, JM. 1968. *The Churches of Devon.* Newton Abbot: David and Charles.

Sloper, E. 1876a. Excavations at Taunton Castle. *Somerset County Gazette.* 13 May.

Sloper, E. 1876b. *Note Book.* Unpublished notebook with cuttings bequeathed to SANHS in 1905. SANHS Library AR 32 (see Primary Sources). Not dated but two parts of castle section are dated 1876.

Soden, I (ed). 2007. *Stafford Castle: Survey, Excavation and Research 1978–1998, Volume 2 – The Excavations.* Stafford: Stafford Borough Council.

Spencer, JH. 1910. Structural notes on Taunton Castle. *Somerset Archaeology and Natural History*, **56**, 38–49. See Anon (1910) for addendum.

Stamper, PA. 1984. Excavations on a mid-twelfth century siege castle at Bentley, Hampshire. *Proceedings of the Hampshire Field Club and Archaeological Society*, **40**, 81–89.

Start, D and Stocker, D (eds). 2011. *The Making of Grantham: The Medieval Town.* Sleaford: The Heritage Trust of Lincolnshire.

Stevenson, WH (ed). 1916. *Calendar of the Liberate Rolls preserved in the Public Record Office, Henry III, Vol 1, 1226–1240.* London: HMSO.

Stocker, D. 2000a. The Architectural Fragments. In Ellis (2000), 200–221.

Stocker, D. 2000b. The Great Tower and Henry III's Great Hall. In Ellis (2000), 83–96.

Stone, DJ. 2006. The consumption and supply of birds in late medieval England. In Woolgar *et al.* (2006), 148–61.

Sundick, RL. 1978. Human skeletal growth and age determination. *Journal of Human Evolution*, **29**, 231–49.

Swanton, M (ed). 2000. *The Anglo-Saxon Chronicles.* London: Phoenix Press, revised edition.

Sykes, N. 2006. The impact of the Normans on hunting practices in England. In Woolgar *et al.* (2006), 162–75.

Sykes, N. 2007a. Animal bones and animal parks. In Liddiard, R (ed) *The Medieval Park: New Perspectives.* Oxford: Windgather Press.

Sykes, N. 2007b. *The Norman Conquest: A Zooarchaeological Perspective*. BAR international series 656. Oxford: British Archaeological Reports.

Sykes, N. 2007c. Taking sides: the social life of venison in medieval England. In Pluskowski (2007), 149–60.

Symonds, H. 1911. Taunton tokens of the seventeenth century. *Somerset Archaeology and Natural History*, **58**, 54–65.

Taylor, R. 1971. Castle House. *Somerset Archaeology and Natural History*, **118**, 25–27.

Taylor, R. 1974. Town houses in Taunton, 1500–1700. *Post Medieval Archaeology*, **3**, 63–79.

Thomas, R. 2005. Perceptions versus reality: changing attitudes towards pets in medieval and post-medieval England. In Pluskowski, A (ed) *Just Skin and Bones? New Perspectives on Human-Animal Relations in the Historical Past*, BAR international series 1410, 95–104. Oxford: British Archaeological Reports.

Thomas, R. 2007. Chasing the ideal? Ritualism, pragmatism and the late medieval hunt. In Pluskowski (2007), 125–48.

Thompson, AH. 1912. *Military Architecture in England during the Middle Ages*. Oxford: Oxford University Press.

Thompson, MW. 1960a. The date of "Fox's Tower" Farnham Castle, Surrey. *Surrey Archaeological Collections*, **57**, 85–92.

Thompson, MW. 1960b. Recent excavations in the keep of Farnham Castle, Surrey. *Medieval Archaeology*, **4**, 81–94.

Thompson, MW. 1961. *Farnham Castle Keep, Surrey*. London: HMSO.

Thompson, MW. 1986. Associated monasteries and castles in the middle Ages. *Archaeological Journal*, **143**, 305–21.

Thorn, FR. 2012. Review of Costen (2011). *Somerset Archaeology and Natural History*, **155**, 225–27.

Thorp, JRL. 1998. Carpentry and framing techniques in Devon buildings up to 1550. In Stenning, DF and Andrews, DD (eds) *Regional Variation in Timber-Framed Building in England and Wales down to 1550: The Proceedings of the 1994 Cressing Conference*. Chelmsford: Essex County Council.

Thorp, JRL. 2013. The wagon roofs at St James's Priory, Bristol. *Vernacular Architecture*, **44**, 31–45.

Thorp, JRL and Cox, J. 2010. *Understanding Castle House*. Unpublished Keystone Historic Buildings Consultants report. Copy in Somerset HER (PRN 26765).

Thorp, JRL and Cox, J. 2013. *Observations During Works at Castle House, Castle Green, Taunton, Somerset*. Unpublished Keystone Historic Buildings Consultants report. Copy in Somerset HER (PRN 32040).

Tite, C. 1901. William Bidgood. *Somerset Archaeology and Natural History*, **47**, 234–36.

Tite, C. 1905. Edwin Sloper, FGS. *Somerset Archaeology and Natural History*, **51**, 182.

Toulmin, J. 1791. *The History of Taunton in the County of Somerset*. Taunton: T Norris.

Toy, S. 1944–45. Winchester House, Southwark. *Surrey Archaeological Collections*, **49**, 75–81.

Trotter, M and Gleser, GC. 1952. Estimation of stature from long bones of American whites and negroes. *American Journal of Physical Anthropology*, 463–514.

Underdown, D. 1973. *Somerset in the Civil War and Interregnum*. Newton Abbot: David and Charles.

Vivian-Neal, AW. 1954. Historical notes. In Anon (1954), 1–8.

Vivian-Neal, AW and Gray, H St G. 1940. Materials for the history of Taunton Castle. *Somerset Archaeology and Natural History*, **86**, 45–78.

Von den Driesch, A. 1976. *A Guide to the Measurement of Animal Bones from Archaeological Sites*. Peabody Museum Bulletin 1. Cambridge, Mass: Harvard University Press.

Vranch, RD. 1988. Fieldwork on eastern Mendip. *Proceedings of the University of Bristol Spelaeological Society*, **18**(2), 321–22.

Wareham, J. 2000. *Three Palaces of the Bishops of Winchester*. London: English Heritage.

Warre, F. 1853. Taunton Castle. *Somerset Archaeology and Natural History*, **4**(2), 18–32.

Weaver, FW. 1904. The annual report. *Somerset Archaeology and Natural History*, **50**, 2–6.

Weaver, FW. 1910. The annual report. *Somerset Archaeology and Natural History*, **56**, 3–13.

Webb, CG. 1874. *The History of Taunton in the County of Somersetshire originally written by the late Joshua Toulmin, DD, greatly enlarged by the late James Savage and further enlarged by Charles George Webb*. Taunton: CG Webb.

Webster, CJ. 1989. Hursley, Merdon Castle. In Hughes, M (ed) *Archaeology in Hampshire: Annual Report for 1989*, 65–69. Winchester: Hampshire County Council.

Webster, CJ. 2007. *Taunton Castle: Archaeological Assessment for the Museum of Somerset Project*. Unpublished Somerset County Council Report.

Webster, C[J], Aston, M, Eagles, B, Evans, D, Gardner, K, Gittos, B, Gittos, M, Hall, T, Horner, B, Pearce, S, Turner, S, Williams, H and Yorke, B. 2008. Early medieval. In Webster, CJ (ed) *The Archaeology of South West England: A Resource Assessment and Research Agenda*, 169–88. Taunton: Somerset County Council.

Webster, CJ and Brunning, RA. 2004. A 7th-century AD cemetery at Stoneage Barton Farm, Bishop's Lydeard, Somerset and square-ditched burials in post-Roman Britain. *Archaeological Journal*, **161**, 54–81.

Webster, CJ and Croft, R A. 1990. Somerset Archaeology 1990. *Somerset Archaeology and Natural History*, **134**, 207–229.

Weddell, PJ. 1998. *Taunton Town Centre Enhancement Scheme 1996: Archaeological Recording and Excavation in Fore Street, The Parade and North Street*. Unpublished Exeter Archaeology report. Copy in Somerset HER (PRN 44678).

Weston, DWV. 2013. *Rose Castle and the Bishops of Carlisle: 1133–2012*. Lancaster: Cumberland and Westmorland Antiquarian and Archaeological Society.

Wheatley, A. 2004. *The Idea of the Castle in Medieval England*. Woodbridge: Boydell and Brewer.

White, H. 2012. The problem of provenancing English post-medieval slipwares: a chemical and petrographic approach. *Post-Medieval Archaeology*, **46**, 56–69.

White, P. 1995. *A Gentleman of Fine Taste: The Watercolours of Coplestone Warre Bampfylde*. Taunton: Hestercombe Gardens Trust.

White, P[R] and Cook, A[M]. 2015. *Sherborne Old Castle, Dorset: Archaeological Investigations 1930–90*. London: Society of Antiquaries.

White, SD. 2004. *The Dynamics of Regionalisation and Trade: Yorkshire Clay Tobacco Pipes c.1600–1800*. BAR British Series 374. Oxford: British Archaeological Reports.

Whittingham, S. 2011. *Sir George Oatley: Architect of Bristol*. Bristol: Redcliffe Press.

Whitty, RGH. 1934. *The Court of Taunton in the 16th and 17th Century*. Taunton: Goodman.

Wickham Legg, LG. 1936. A relation of a short survey of the western counties made by a lieutenant of the military company in Norwich in 1635. *Camden Miscellany*, **26**.

Wicks, AT. 1961. Masters of Taunton Grammar School. *Notes and Queries for Somerset and Dorset*, **27**, 195–96.

Williams, A. 1995. *The English and the Norman Conquest*. Woodbridge: Boydell.

Williams, NJ (ed). 1975. *Calendar of the Patent Rolls: Elizabeth I, Vol 6*. London: HMSO.

Willmott, H. 2002. *Early Post-Medieval Vessel Glass in England* c. *1500–1670*. CBA Research Report 132. York: Council for British Archaeology.

Wilson, D and Moorhouse, S. 1971. Medieval Britain in 1970. *Medieval Archaeology*, **15**, 124–79.

Witt, C. 1979. *Ceramics in Bristol: The Fine Wares*. City of Bristol Museum and Art Gallery.

Wood, M. 1965. *The English Mediaeval House*. London: Phoenix House.

Woolgar, M, Serjeantson, D and Waldron, T (eds). 2006. *Food in Medieval England: Diet and Nutrition*. Oxford: Oxford University Press.

Wright, DP. 2009. Langton, Thomas (c.1430–1501). In *Oxford Dictionary of National Biography*. Oxford: Oxford University Press. Online at http://www.oxforddnb.com/view/article/16045. Accessed 12 March 2013.

Yorke, B. 2006. *The Conversion of Britain*. Harlow: Pearson.

Zupko, RE. 1985. *A Dictionary of Weights and Measures for the British Isles: The Middle Ages to the Twentieth Century*. Philadelphia: The American Philosophical Society.

Index

Italic page numbers indicate illustrations

Y